The Dialectics & Dynamics of

HUMAN RIGHTS in India

(Yesterday, Today and Tomorrow)

Kolkata
Eastern Law House Private Ltd.
54 Ganesh Chunder Avenue
Kolkata 700 013

New Delhi
Eastern Law House Private Ltd.
Govind Bhawan, Room T-2, 3rd Floor
4384/4A, Ansari Road, Daryaganj
New Delhi 110 002

The Dialectics & Dynamics of HUMAN RIGHTS in India

(Yesterday, Today and Tomorrow)

TAGORE LAW LECTURES

by

V.R. Krishna Iyer
Former Judge, Supreme Court of India
Recipient of Padma Vibhushan

Kolkata New Delhi
EASTERN LAW HOUSE

Published and processed by
EASTERN LAW HOUSE PRIVATE LTD.
54 Ganesh Chunder Avenue
Kolkata 700 013
Tel: (033) 4063-2301
Email: mail@elh.co.in
www.elh.co.in

First Edition 1999
First Reprint 2000
Second Reprint 2010
Third Reprint 2018
Fourth Reprint 2025

ISBN 978-81-7177-343-5

Printed at
Sarat Impressions
Kolkata

DE PROFUNDIS

I AM A human being and nothing pertaining to a human is alien to me.

Any person who has drunk deep of the cultural heritage of ancient Indian vintage, justly called 'The Wonder That Was India', gains a vision of the human promise too profound for expression in Western diction and West-bound Eastern thought. The votaries of humanist-rationalist theology and philosophy worship at the church of materialism and science and do produce sublime perceptions and luminous insights; but the Upanishadic visionaries proclaimed the fundamental truth that divinity dwells everywhere, that the presence of the Supreme Power illumines and enlivens the universe and so, the highest manifestation of Creation in the shape of homo sapiens has title to great rights, not by virtue of Covenants, Compacts and Constitutions but because they spring from the Infinite of which each person is a spark. This universal source is the Reality too lofty for our mortal lens to discern if our sights are only materialist-humanist. In Sri Aurobindo's epic lines (*Savitri*) the saint-cum-scientist tells us:

> *"A deathbound littleness is not all we are:*
> *Immortal our forgotten vastnesses*
> *Await discovery in our summit selves;*
> *Unmeasured breadths and depths of being are ours."*

Then, who am I? asks every reflective human and the answer rings back: Thou art that! I am Brahman! TATWAMASI! SOHAM! This profound truth is a fundamental the sages have proclaimed. So I hold, as of universal application to all. I am divine, not servile, puissant, not craven. My personality possesses potential infinity and my human rights are manifestations of this latent majesty.

The pariah and the high-born rise from the same Supreme and are equal in inherent dignity, potential faculty and performance capacity if propitious opportunity were afforded to unfold what lies dormant. If this heavenly perspective were valid on earth, human rights rise to great heights and dive to profound depths, with widest spread, soulfully indefeasible. My conceptual and analytical approach to human rights proceed on this diamond-hard foundation. To put it in plain words, human rights spring from a divine fount and the field of human affairs must accept and respect this categorical imperative. Such is the supremacy of human rights philosophy. How do I relate it to my personal involvement in the battle of the human race in its bleeding spiralling journey towards its higher destiny? The first article of my faith and the last article of my creed explain my basic approach to the larger issue of human rights jurisprudence. I am a human being inhabiting an integral universe of divine Creation; and so, nothing that pertains to dear Mother Earth or affects fellow human beings in their earthly home is alien to me or fails to sensitize me into action or expression. My material, moral and spiritual concern and constituency are therefore co-extensive with humanity and all that sustains the perennial stream of values which promotes the universal well-being and civilisational advance of homo sapiens. No cause is more worthy of a sensitive soul's superlative concern than the cause of human rights which, do remember, are not mere legal titles. They are the quintessence of human justice, the conscience of global jurisprudence. They are holistic and make a person human in his dignity and divinity. Deny them and you diminish human status to that of a brute.

However, we behold chaos in the cosmos; and the inner voice in each of us, the inner driving power, functionally pushes us all—Buddha, Jesus, Gandhi *et al*—on to strive, why struggle, with ceaseless zest and burning conviction, to attenuate suffering, liberate from bondage and enhance happiness world-wide. The divinity that dwells in every person must be afforded opportunity by the State and the Society to manifest this infinite potentiality sans which the right to liberty and equality is but egregious baloney. Such is the ageless progress of the human pilgrim. Such is the source and soul of all human rights. But what do we see around us currently and hear from the whispering gallery of history? *Asuric* (demoniac) forces overpowering *Satvic* (humanist) commandments, and blood and tears drowning the joy of life and developmental prospects. The cornucopia of privations and exploitations is economic and the source of predation is vacuum of spiritual values and dominance of material vulgarity. Human rights, for me, spring from the spiritual nidus nourished, with a sense of balance, by contentment which is sustained by provision *for all* of basic material needs and other conditions which make for joy in life. An exchange between American Economist Higginbothom and Gandhiji may be apt.

Higginbothom said:

> "Spirituality to be meaningful should be three-fourths economics."

Gandhiji replied:

> "Economics too, to be useful, should be three parts spirituality".

"Man's inhumanity to man" is escalating boundlessly before our eyes intra-nationally and internationally; and each passing day brings thoughts too deep for tears and wars too defiant of the United Nations. And "the still sad music of humanity" is unheard by those who wield power and command wealth. Why? Wordsworth comes to mind:

> *The world is too much with us; late and soon,*
> *Getting and spending, we lay waste our powers:*
> *Little we see in Nature that is ours;*
> *We have given our hearts away, a sordid boon!"*

And again—

"What man has made of man".

Man's greed attacks Nature and environment and ecology, and wounded Nature backlashes on the human future.

I am educated by global grief and sensitized by the abhorrence of arrogance and opulence and authoritarian abuse of power. But even when darkness surrounds, great thoughts reveal light. 'There is not enough darkness in all the world to put out the light of one small candle.'

When I speak of commitment to human rights my canvas is universal, my concept indivisible and my fathomless concern exceeds the other values terrestrial. Here again, a Gurudev-Gandhi dialogue drives home my point:

Once Gurudev Rabindranath Tagore asked Gandhiji, "Gandhiji are you so unromantic? When in the early dawn, the morning sun rises, does it not fill your heart with joy to see its reddish glow? When the birds sing does not your heart thrill with its divine music? When the rose opens its petals and blooms in the garden does its sights not bring cheer to your heart?"

The Mahatma replied, "Gurudev, I am not so dumb or insensitive as not to be moved by the beauty of the rose or the morning rays of the sun or the divine music of the birds. But what can I do? My one desire, my one anxiety, my one ambition is when shall I see the red tint of the rose on the cheeks of hungry naked millions of my people? When shall I hear the sweet and melodious song of the birds in place of their agonising sighs? When will such music come out of their soul and when will that day come when the light of the morning sun will illumine the heart of the common man in India? When will I see its lustre and brightness on his face?"

Compassion for all Creation, particularly human fellow-beings, finds its finest hour only when the last and the least person is liberated.

"O Hidden Life! Vibrant in every atom
O Hidden Light! Shining in every creature;
O Hidden Love! embracing all in Oneness;
May each who feels himself as one with Thee,
Know he is also one with every other."

—ANNIE BESANT

These lofty thoughts often inspire me but at the same time when I see around deep sorrow, traumatic suffering and calamities which claim innocent lives I am bewildered and repeat within myself Tennyson's poignant poem:

"But what am I?
An infant crying in the night:
An infant crying for the light:
And with no language but a cry."

Ernakulam, Cochin
1st June 1999

V.R. KRISHNA IYER

A Few Thankful Thoughts and Some Supplemental Reflections–Acknowledgment

Gratitude is a noble response of one's soul to kindness or help generously rendered by another and its acknowledgment is a duty and joyance. So it is that I express briefly my debt to those who have made the delivery and eventual publication of the Tagore Law Lectures possible. My first obligation, irredeemable by verbal expression, is to that once venerable and ancient institution of educational excellence and currently convulsive—the Calcutta University—yet august, vast campus and the Selection Committee whose generous choice has gained for me a humble place in the illustrious procession of Tagore Law Professors. Who am I in the universe of luminous legal scholarship or creative juridical statesmanship but an infant crying for compassionate light, a pilgrim striving to secure human rights and social justice to the larger sector of the global community often dismissed as Unpersons and denied the basic conditions of life sans which the world order suffers from the syndrome of inhumanity? Calcutta University! I shall ever be thankful to you for the fragrant distinction implied in your choice.

Right from the start to the very end, culminating in the Lectures becoming available to the public, Justice A.M. Bhattacharjee, a creative savant, a polemical thinker and a prolific writer, has given me aid in myriad ways, the meed for which is ineffable and mere acknowledgment inadequate. Even so, words are images of feeling and when feeling overflows semantic limits of verbal expression one has to make-do with the imperfect instrumentality of verbalism. The thoughts and ideas embodied in the book are mine and their infirmities, excesses, errors, peccadilloes, even egregious blunders, are mine only. I must confess that the procedures of Universities and the problems between delivering lectures and their incarnation as marketable books are many. I have not had the leisurely patience or canny savvy to tackle these hurdles. The gestation period for University processes is long, and so too the gap between the publishers' acquisition of the right to publish, proof-reading and other issues before the matter manifests as market product. This time lag affects the freshness of the views the author expresses and the flower fades somewhat since thoughts travel along new terrain and the winds of change, as they breathe and blow, affect the author's own opinions even as the old order changeth yielding place to new. 'Ring out the old, ring in the new' is a passion in me. Radical bosoms are restless in an unjust world where human rights are overpowered by inhuman wrongs since Might is Right and even Judges themselves abet, unwittingly of course, and legitimise this perverse process as Anatole France has cynically observed.

I must record my appreciation of Asok De of the Eastern Law House for his devotion, affection and persistent attention in bringing out these Lectures in its present form undeterred by hassles and tediums. The frequent traumas Asok De has undergone, the perennial labours he has invested in the product and the vigilant care he has bestowed from the beginning to the end exacts my admiration. It is easy to buy a book if you are a bibliophile with a purse but the roadblocks, hazards and harrowing experiences of a publisher from winning the manuscript, getting it displayed on the book stalls with a lovely blurb, glossy finish and saleable price and converting his perspiration into profitable returns are vicissitudes difficult to describe. I am thankful to Asok De for his personal concern at every stage and persistent pursuit, overcoming obstacles, to see that the work is completed and the product has a peerless presentability.

Numerous friends had made useful, casual suggestions and meaningful contributions to the preparation of the Lectures as I was struggling to snatch time, amidst a multitude of other commitments, to complete the text and deliver the Lectures. I express profound thanks to these countless friends for their help without which my spasmodic jurisprudential excursions in the compassionate territory of human rights may not have materialised and may be excoriated as random, incoherent assemblage of noetic expressions of a pretentious maverick. All life is a long experiment and these Lectures are but a humble voyage in communication of ideas without credentials and claims except sincerity and humility.

Some Supplementary Cerebrations

Having unburdened myself of the necessary obligation of acknowledging my debt, let me *briefly* tell my readers the later developments in the public law of human rights. Large strides have been made in strengthening the inalienable rights of people, individually and collectively, and, alas, terrible reverses have been suffered by the billions of humans in sustainable development, rights to life and peace and development, to freedom from torture and other fundamental immunities and protective armours without which the boast of human rights vanishes into illusory euphemisms. The United Nations is itself in financial peril and is losing its halo. No longer is this hallowed institution a lustrous hope of humanity, nor are the paradigms galore enshrined in its sacred instruments credible constellation of principles of global justice. Indeed, the world is becoming a jungle with mini-wars and bleeding battles and corporate cannibalism with vast economic empires, exploiting billions of humans and developing nations, with a super-sovereignty and profit-oriented power to grab markets, reducing huge human numbers to *Unpeople* status.

Time never stands still and concepts of human rights and the methodology of their enforcement undergo dynamic change. The human race is far from its final destination or full blossom; nevertheless, its locomotion, despite barbaric breaks, cannot be halted. Africa, massacred, enslaved and colonially exploited, has liberated itself; and South Africa, the sombre State where apartheid suppressed the natives, has become a free nation with a just Constitution. The African Charter on Human and People's Rights is now a tenuous reality. Way back in 1961, African jurists sowed the seed, drafts sprouted, Nairobi Summit fertilised the field and on 21st October 1986 the Charter came into force, duly ratified by an absolute majority of States. "So far as its content and structure are concerned, the Charter contains a list of the prerogatives and obligations which are protected and also of the organs for the protection and defence of those same values.

> "Part I includes not only rights *but also duties,* an approach which, though new in international instruments, accords with the African conception of rights as inseparable from duties. Those rights and duties *apply to individuals and groups alike.* The Charter places special emphasis on the rights and duties of the community (the family, society, the nation, the State), thus giving marked emphasis to the community and non-collectivist approach. Lastly, the Charter accords a place to the so-called *generation rights: the rights to peace, solidarity, a healthy environment and development,* having regard to Africa's place in the concept of nations.
>
> "Two bodies are responsible for ensuring the promotion and protection of *human and peoples' rights:* the African Commission on Human and Peoples' Rights and the Assembly of Heads of State and Government of the OAU".[1]

Importantly, group or community rights are recognised, a factor of great relevance to India whose tribal communities are being robbed of many rights, including the rich resources of bio-diversity. Multinational corporate predators have gained access to economic space and precious natural resources, corruption, intimidation and specious promises of technological transformation being successful strategems, every Party in Power being pathetic victim mindless of illiterate masses mesmerised in many ways.

> "As to the task of protection, this consists, so far as the African Commission on Human and Peoples' Rights is concerned, of examining complaints of human rights violations either by States parties *or by private persons,* whether natural or legal, which are referred to in the Charter by the term "other communications".

This is a creative departure.

This African Charter is a point of achievement as it deals with Human Rights and People's Rights. Those matters here merit our attention. The Preamble stresses them:

1 *The African Charter on Human and Peoples' Rights,* Introduction, page 1, United Nations Publication.

"Recognizing, on the one hand, that fundamental human rights stem from the attributes of human beings, which justifies their international protection and on the other hand, that the reality and respect of peoples' rights should necessarily guarantee human rights;

"Considering that the enjoyment of *rights and freedoms also implies the performance of duties* on the part of everyone;

"Convinced that it is henceforth essential to pay particular attention to the *right to development and that civil and political rights cannot be dissociated from economic, social and cultural rights* in their conception as well as universality and that the satisfaction of economic, social and cultural rights is a guarantee for the enjoyment of civil and political rights".[2]

The right to justice, speedy and impartial, the right to receive information, to express and disseminate opinions, the right to education and cultural life of his community are duties of the State. The aged and the disabled have the right to special measures of protection in keeping with their physical and moral needs. People's rights such as in the wealth of bio-diversity come under State guarantees. A Commission, a Secretary-General, the application of international law etc. represent progressive innovations of a continental instrumentality which Asia needs to heed. Article 60 is pregnant with potential edification for India and Asia:

"The Commission shall draw inspiration from international law on human and peoples' rights, particularly from the provisions of various African instruments on human and peoples' rights, the Charter of the United Nations, the Charter of the Organization of African Unity, the Universal Declaration of Human Rights, other instruments adopted by the United Nations and by African countries in the field of human and peoples' rights as well as from the provisions of various instruments adopted within the Specialised Agencies of the United Nations of which the parties to the present Charter are members".[3]

International law is no longer the vanishing point of jurisprudence. (What about India?).

Asia has, as yet no Charter but, at people's level, one has been drafted and finalised (I have participated in the process) but the States, big and small, must agree if the Charter is to take off. Perhaps, SAARC Law may undertake an institutional exercise in this virgin direction and transnational dimension. Europe has set an example of the impossible being feasible; Africa, with its colonial past and tribal hatreds, has got on the track. The new South Africa, which, till the other day, had the highest rate of judicial executions and extra-judicial torture and thanatos, now constitutionally accords the right to life and other democratic values and has a Constitutional Court with large powers. Canada too has a Charter of Rights and Freedoms. In tomorrow's world the court may well be society's progressive kindly conscience and arbitral authority. The air of free countries may blow

2 *Ibid*, page 5.
3 *Ibid*, pages 18-19.

benignly; and courts may be too pure to breathe the polluted tyranny of the State or violation of the higher law of human rights. Maybes, maybes! The prognostication of human rights protection by the judicial process is a good omen. In Australia, aborigines are recognised as owners of community property in a landmark ruling which has international relevance. From any side of the globe you can sensitively appreciate the wonder of Australian judicial expansion of jurisdiction in favour of fair elections, freedom of industrial tribunals and what not.

The hope for peace and justice in the world springs from the tireless crusade of the common people. The West has put mercantile goods above morality and humanity. This process has to be reversed if the triumph of the human race is to be accomplished.

We are celebrating the Semi-Centennial of two events depicted in the two Quotes given below. Their contradiction can be converted into humane diction only by a crusade which is ceaseless until success.

> "Everyone has the right to work, to just and favourable conditions of work and to protection for himself and his family (and) an existence worthy of human dignity.........everyone has the right to a standard of living adequate for the health and well-being of himself and his family, including food, clothing, housing and medical care."
>
> *Universal Declaration of Human Rights 1948*

> "We have 50 per cent of the world's wealth, but only 6.3 per cent of its population. In this situation, our real job in the coming period is to devise a pattern of relationships which permit us to maintain this position of disparity. To do so, we have to dispense with all sentimentality.........we should cease thinking about human rights, the raising of living standards and democratisation."
>
> GEORGE KENNAN, US Cold War planner 1948

The 21st century agenda of global, liberal human rights and the platform of action and implementation are in our hands. Lawyers and Judges here have a seminal role. If our judicial generation is ossified and retrograde, as they tend to be, the grand Tennysonian image of freedom slowly broadening down in a kind of Fabian long march may ebb and flow and avant-garde *'lawyers for the people'* may have to battle for a new justice age. An eclectic, puissant Bar, bent upon a better world, is the trigger for change, the Bench being but an 'elevated' bracket of the Bar. Judge Power, through Review Jurisdiction over Executive arbitrariness, is earning people's approbation and support from human rights activists a la P I L. The accountability of the Judiciary as a limb of democracy is becoming a basic axiom although in some countries Judges become boneless wonders in robes; and private tyrannies, political and economic, intimidate upright Judges. In that event, human rights regimes will be like billows which break upon the beach and are absorbed by the sands.

The courts in the European Union and the Commonwealth countries are now engaged in building a broad highway of constitutional human rights jurisprudence and internationalisation of public law. The agenda for the twenty-first century summons an adjudicatory power in our courts based on a higher law before which national legislations diminishing or destroying fundamental freedoms must bend or end. True, orthodox Judges and reactionary law-makers may repel these trends. In the words of Justice Stephen Sedley (V.K.) the waters in which we shall be swimming are shark-infested and our human rights armoury at present gives us little protection against the predators. Hopefully, a juridical culture, from constitutions, courts and the United Nations, would be true and effective harbinger of an era of human rights for the humblest, powerless, marginalised masses with the right to a humane society, a just milieu and basic needs overpowering the grabbing greed of Frankenstein's monsters incarnating as Corporate Empires with hidden homicidal agendas driven by consuming passion for maximum profits. If Britain has a Bill of Rights half the battle is won for the world since its influence will be far-flung. Here, read what, in a landmark speech on 1st March 1993 John Smith spoke:

> "I have no hesitation in saying there is an undeniable and pressing need for constitutional reform in this country.........I am arguing for a new constitutional settlement, a new deal between the people and the State that puts the citizen centre stage.........
>
> "Today, Britain is alone amongst major western European nations in not laying down in law the basic rights of its people, and in not giving its people a direct means of asserting those rights through the country's courts...........
>
> "The quickest and simplest way of achieving democratic and legal recognition of a substantial package of human rights would be by incorporating into British law the European Convention of Human Rights.........The Convention is not a vague, untested or uncertain code, but a mature statement of rights which has been interpreted and applied over many years by an expert court in Strasbourg......... Parliament should pass a Human Rights Act that incorporates the rules of the Convention directly into British law, and gives citizens the right to enforce those rules in the courts".[4]

U.N. Human Rights Instruments when ratified, must become the *corpus juris* of that country without fresh incorporation. Such a jural dynamic will be a global glory.

Worldwide, humanity is forcing the ruling class to take human rights seriously. One caveat. Let us not be carried away by political diction and dubious interpretation. George Orwell's words of 1950 vintage are a grave warning:

> "Political language—and with variations this is true of all political parties, from Conservatives to Anarchists—is designed to make lies sound truthful and murder respectable, and to give an appearance of solidity to pure wind".[5]

4 Robert Blackburn and James Busuttil: *Human Rights for the 21st Century* at page 31.

5 *Ibid*, page 81.

Could the best optimist, looking back to the garden path of the last few years, report as historian of human rights that 'it was roses, roses, all the way'? No, never. Why? Because the great enemy of common people's human rights, 'G-7 Multinationals Incorporated', is now globally dominant, to the detriment of the worth of the human person, his/her rights and demand for a broadly egalitarian, non-discriminatory system of social justice; and the United Nations, the nidus and bastion of human rights and peoples' charter, is itself retreating in the face of the furious offensive of the terrible trinity Globalisation, Liberalisation and Privatisation' which has founded a New Establishment with the backing of G-7 (8?) countries and the hegemony of America Inc., the sole Super Power and global gendarmerie. And none to police the police!

Even from the verdicts and victimisation of the vibrant judiciary we get gloomy reports. A Pakistan Chief Justice was eased out of his office by his colleagues' verdict, the latent political leitmotif being the Prime Minister's allergy to the Chief. 'Islamic'-quick public executions and chopping off limbs as punitive justice are being made law in Pakistan although the Opposition opposes. Women's right to appear in public is in danger. But the All Pakistan Trade Union Federation struggles for freedom, dignity and social justice. Some hope! In Jammu and Kashmir, a strong indictment of the Security forces in the killing of 19 innocent civilians at Sailian village chills our bosom. Indeed, custodial deaths in South Asia are becoming cruelly common and Human Rights Commissions are without punitive teeth. Communal riots and homicidal harrying of humans are shockingly frequent and luridly culpable on the part of the State. The Justice Sri Krishna Commission Report (Mumbai) shames the secular escutcheon of India. Bombay was burning in the 1992/93 convulsions but blood and tears did not move the police to staunch the killings, nay, they even stoked the fires, it is alleged. A quote from the Judicial Commission Report is fresh blood:

> "The response of police to appeals from desperate victims, particularly Muslims, was cynical and utterly indifferent. On occasions, the response was that they were unable to leave the appointed post; on others, the attitude was that one Muslim killed was one Muslim less......Police officers and men, particularly at the junior level, appeared to have an in-built bias against the Muslims which was evident in their treatment of the suspected Muslims and Muslim victims of riots. The treatment given was harsh and brutal and, on occasions, bordering on the inhuman......The bias of policemen was seen in the active connivance of police constables with the rioting Hindu mobs, on occasions, with their adopting the role of passive onlookers on occasions, and, finally, their lack of enthusiasm in registering offences against Hindus even when the accused was clearly identified and post-haste classifying the cases in 'A' (True but not detected) summary".[6]

In Sri Lanka, massacres in Jaffna area of innocent civilians and of LTTE—Sri Lankan armies are escalating, the scenario of terror and

6 Report of the Justice B.N. Srikrishna Commission on the Mumbai riots of 1992-1993.

horror being a macabre continuum. Yugoslavia, broken up ethnically, is a scenario of slaughter, refugees, starvation and masses of humans in despair. African States, Ruwanda and Uganda *et al*, for instance, are strewn with corpses, hunger and disease taking a frightening tool, even while tribal wars rage in heartless fury. The saga of human rights is staggeringly gruesome and the United Nations and its Secretary General are impotent onlookers while the whale of a Security Council, led by the U.S., is obsessed with Iraq—the bleeding rest does not visibly exist. Human rights in Asia, with the Asian tigers collapsing, Indonesian protestors for democracy dying, even Malaysian quasi-democracy angrily demanding justice and freedom, evidence the twilight of human rights. Anwar, former Dy. Prime Minister of Malaysia, is in prison. The people, once submissive, are now assertive. They are annoyed with police brutality and are suspicious of judicial integrity. Fear, the foe of human freedoms, is slowly losing ground in Kuala Lumpur.

The story is sad, bad, reminding progressive pessimists with Mathew Arnold's verses: 'Wandering between two worlds, one dead, the other powerless to be born, with nowhere yet to rest my head'. Quo vadis mankind!

The Human Rights Odyssey has many challenging adventures to confront. We have to strip away the layers of deception, dissembling language and other skulduggery to fathom the depth of human rights disaster in the contemporary global habitat. Truth is subversive but is the only liberator. Let us look at the looming catastrophe briefly.

The human universe is shrinking into a global village of intimate fraternity, at the same time there are explosive forces which emasculate the UN and other Institutions which are the haven of hope sustaining human rights.

The crisis facing the United Nations is climaxing functionally, polarisationally and paradigmatically. To humanise the earth was its holistic mission. To barbarize the world is the awesome prospect as a ground reality. Global apartheid survives in different forms, particularly economic, overwhelmingly backed by the Western Powers. The UN, by inaction, abets this process. What is more awesome, the Third World Nuclear Threat is escalating. There are Atomic Ayatollahs, other nuclear suspects and threshold nuclear powers like Pakistan and India jumping to join the nuclear club. Nuclear terrorism is global traumata and the CTBT is more a political weapon for monopoly preservation than the creation of a nuclear-free world. India and Pakistan, with all their people's want and hunger ignored, diverting their scarce resources for dreadful nuclear tests in May 1998, are inconsequential when we remember that there are 36,000 bigger bombs with the great terrorist nations, euphemistically called the Nuclear Club. Any angry moment Globoshima can take place; Our mini-makes are for show and psychic boast when the earth faces annihilation. Let me cite John Pilger:

> "No fuss is made about the Middle East's only genuine nuclear-armed power, whose murderous invasions of a neighbouring country, all of them in violation of at least six UN resolutions and overwhelmingly condemned by the UN General Assembly, have been carried out with impunity. This is Israel, whose

> terrorism, known as 'self-defence', is underwritten by the United States. In 1982, the Israelis invaded Lebanon and killed some 20,000 people. Israeli fighter aircraft bombed refugee camps; death squads of Shin Beth, the Israeli secret police, kidnapped and murdered at will. The unstated reason for this barbarism was, wrote Noam Chomsky, 'to overcome the threat of PLO diplomacy'.[7]

The 'peace process' is, in a sense, a 'war process' as the war on Iraq and Vietnam have proved. Indeed, Anti-Personnel land-mines have been showered from aeroplanes by the U.S. in Vietnam, Cambodia and other countries the U.S. Power hates. They have not the candour to ratify the Ottawa Treaty against land-mines. One blushes to think of Gandhi India, under various pretexts, avoiding signing the Ottawa Treaty. With the end of the cold war, American 'innocence' reincarnated as American imperialism, the G-7 countries being part of the entourage. The Soviet collapse was an opportune time to exploit the Third World. Today, neo-colonialism is back with fury; and economic space, even in Vietnam, is occupied by the West. The U.S. is the UN for practical purposes. The UN's function is until today a process of authorisation and unilateral intervention by powerful member States like the U.S. The expanded NATO does policing of Bosnia, legitimising ethnic cleansing in the Balkans. Russia itself is under the re-invasion by the forces of anti-socialist globalisation. Its economy is shattered, its people desperate, unemployment being at the highest and life expectancy at the lowest. This is the triumph of the U.S. and the tragedy of the UN.

Pol Pot, the dreaded monster of a one-time ruler of Kampuchea was not wiped out by the U.S. It is said that the peace process in that unfortunate land made Khamer Rouge respectable. Thanks to the United Nations, Peace Operation, with its by-products of corruption and yankifying Aids epidemic, has reversed the East Asian march. Cambodia is still in the grip of the worst human suffering. Likewise, in 1992 George Bush made a 'humanitarian intervention' in Somalia where chaos and tribalism and warlords were the rule of life "when the American warlords had completed their adventure in Somalia and taken the media home with them, the story died, as they say. The Marines had left 7,000-10,000 people dead. This was not news".[8]

We thus see that the UN is missing its mission. It is true that there is now a UN Human Rights Commission without power except global glitter. The United States does not pay its dues although it is the largest contributory in principle. The UN is now a pauper and the subsidiary instrumentalities are sick for want of funds. The Bretton Woods Conference of 1945 are instrumentalities formally affiliated to the UN but actually the tools of the U.S. The Fund-Bank duo controls the politics and economics of the world. One earth, many worlds, is the new market geography where the IMF and the World Bank victimise countries for implementing the hidden agenda of capture of markets the world over. The miseries of mankind, particularly of

7 John Pilger: *Hidden Agendas* at page 37.

8 *Ibid*, at page 43.

the weaker nations, are the result of the operation of the Northern Corporate Controllerate with captive consumerism headed by the U.S. The UN, with its prolixity of resolutions, is a pathetic picture with no power except to be a witness of its own founding faiths and fundamental creeds collapsing under the lethal impact of its affiliates—the Fund-Bank duo.

Another adverse force mentally manacling humans, and their rights is the 'infortainment' process, media monopoly and conditioned democracy. How is this mental-moral moronism achieved? By polluting the communication channels with sex, consumerist craze and cultivating crony journalism and media mesmerism through corrupt purchase. Each passing day, these recent years, fills our print and electronic media with materials on a philanderer president of the U.S. or mendicant ministers and messengers to the U.S. from India with no space for the hunger and corruption, rapes and street children in our country. Clinton on Iraq is news; analysis of Indian masses in misery does not qualify for mention. Why? They are Unpeople!

Many reporters in 'soft' States abound in the Third World who are amenable to purchase. The unusual respect, emoluments and other bonanza which journalists gain could turn the head of a saint and small wonder the lesser mortals of the media walk into the trap rendering our democracy vulnerable, reinforcing Big Business through Press monopoly. The Press barons are often tycoons and like in the case of Rupert Murdoch a global media estate may belong to one entity. Diffusion of membership is desirable but it is difficult to achieve. For mooting the idea publicly Justice Sawant, Chairman of the Press Council of India was recently criticised by the Press Proprietariat. Our human right to information is hollow. News corporates condition the presentation of facts and the Third World will hardly get news space or may get distorted depiction.

Freedom of the Press is mirage so long as the media is indentured to the Power Barons in politics who, in turn, do bonded labour to national and international Big Business, using deceptively democratic double-speak and confusing disinformation. The new dimension of macro-victimology is the degradation of the Free Press into pitiful obligees of Global Corporate Controllerate functioning through capture and concentration of media worldwide.

The media diverts our attention on factional trivia, Indo-Pak estrangements and local price spirals but does not furiously focus on the omnipresent, omnipotent, omniscient economic-military-market-grab corporate giantism. The macro-media power of India should have carried on a Grand Inquest of the GATT and Fund-Bank colonialist skullduggery to make Indian sovereign democracy viable. Independent media, engaged in independent investigation, is nearly as important as independent police investigation and independent judicial justice. If powerful M.N.Cs corner influence and interfere with Press freedom, our economic sovereignty will slip into the hands of foreign companies. The cornucopia of big corruption is U.S. Plus Incorporated. Consequence? The Right to Know Truth is on the Cross!

> "Inexorably, over any substantial period of time, economic power translates into political power. The process fattens on itself, increasing its mass as it gains momentum. Once the process is under way, once it builds a private socialism in which ownership of communications media, of banking, and of the means of production is concentrated in a few corporate hands, democratic institutions cannot flourish and, indeed, are undermined".[9]

This now a global malady, an Indian syndrome.

The MacBride Report (*One World Many Voices*)[10] says:

> "An analysis of the cultural flows between countries shows how serious the imbalance is. The media in developing countries take a high percentage of their cultural and entertainment content from a few developed countries, and chiefly from a few large producers in those countries. The flow in the other direction is a mere trickle by comparison. But the problem cannot be stated purely in quantitative terms. The developed countries get the selected best of the culture (chiefly music and dance) from developing countries; the latter get a lot of what on any objective standard is the worst produced by the former. This unequal exchange is inevitably harmful to national culture in developing countries. Their writers, musicians, film-makers and other creative artists find themselves shouldered aside by imported products. Local imitations of imported culture and entertainment do not improve the situation; they too lead to the imposition of external values".[10]

The global media, borderless in its operation and penetrating into every nation, is composed largely of international conglomerates. The Tragedy of the Third World is that the national media and the politicians in power are becoming missionaries of deregulation and advocate open sesame for corporate giants from the West.

> "The most important features of this globalization process are the implantation, consolidation and concentration of advertisement-based commercial media and the parallel weakening of public broadcasting system worldwide, with negative consequences for the 'public sphere'.[11]

Form this angle Indians are in the Intensive Care Ward with no hope of recovery. Newspapers and Viewspapers promote Big Business, mutes the interests of the masses and dooms democratic basics! Indian swaraj is now afflicted by a political epilepsy and even Alzheimer's disease of sorts. Our Public Sector is dismantled; our nationalised banking and now, Insurance business is wounded by foreign companies being given entry. Economic suicide! 'This is not the end. It is not even the beginning of the end. But it is, perhaps, the end of the beginning'. Swaraj, alas, is on the cross'. This is the jejune jurisprudence of human rights, 1998 vintage!

9 Morton Mintz & Jerry S. Cohen: *America, INC* at page 455.
10 Page 163.
11 Edward S. Herman and Robert W. McChesney: *The Global Media* at page 1.

In India, those who rhetorise about Swadeshi are now hospitable hosts of xenophilic media and M.N.C. tunnels of news and views. The global media lords march to the beat of commercialism, autocracy and market-controlled economic authoritarianism. To democratise communications is to prioritise the importance of people's sovereignty.

The covert monopoly drive of the media is symbolised by Murdoch, the global Caesar of the media. Information—communication, concentration in private or Government command paves the way to mind control and spells the end of free societies.

> "What is deeply ironic, wrote David Bowman, is that, having thrown off one yoke, the Press should now be falling under another, in the form of a tiny and ever-contracting band of businessmen-proprietors. Instead of developing as a diverse social institution, serving the needs of democratic society, the Press, and now the media, have become or are becoming the property of a few, governed by whatever social, political and cultural values the few think tolerable.........Looking at the thing historically, you could say that what we are facing now is the second great battle of the freedom of the Press.
>
> "If Marshall McLuhan's 'global village' means anything, it is the power of the global media monopolies and their antipathy to a 'medley of competing voices'. 'It seems grotesque', wrote Bowman, 'that the Press, or rather the media, should be allowed to abuse its social role fatally by rushing on down the road to monopoly ownership. That is a negation of Press freedom'.
>
> "By falling silent, journalists and politicians both negate history; for the struggle for a free Press was always part of the long journey towards universal suffrage and democratic Government. It was a fight for opposing voices to be heard when those in authority considered themselves the custodians of truth: an enduring delusion".[12]

To be silent, when speech is the need, is a slur on the journalist profession and a betrayal of its basic obligation. Publication of half-truths and total lies wrapped in glossy deception is treachery and turpitudinous, exploitation of people's credulity.

We in India have still to struggle for a Freedom of Information Act. The draft bill now prepared by Government has more exceptions than the rule and so the right to know basic to human rights is a casualty. News which concern the Third World are suppressed and we are flooded with news of the North.

> "Ninety per cent of all world news and current affairs now comes to us from fewer and richer and more powerful sources. Three agencies, Associated Press, Reuters and Agence France Presse, supply most of the world's 'wire service' news. One is American, one is British, the other is French. Reuters and A.P. make huge profits selling financial and corporate information; their newsrooms have become centres of the 'free market' crusade. A.P. gets most

12 John Pilger: *Hidden Agendas* at pages 544-545.

of its funding from American clients and devotes most of its coverage to events in the United States.

"Africa accounts for less than 5 per cent of this coverage, most of it concentrated on disasters. The former President of Tanzania, Julius Nyerere, has drily suggested that the people of his country should be allowed to take part in the elections for President of the United States because they are bombarded with as much information about the candidates as Americans are.

"In television there are just two agencies providing foreign news footage to all the world's newsrooms—Reuters Television, formerly Visnews, and World Television Network (WTN), Reuters supplies 400 broadcasters in eighty-five countries, reaching an audience of half a billion people. WTN reaches an estimated three billion people. Another two Western broadcasters, CNN and BBC World, come second. And there is the Internet, which, for all its variety and potential, is essentially an elite operation as most people in the world do not own a telephone, let alone a computer".[13]

Free Press will, unless arrested by a massive movement against Murdochism, become as dead as the dinosaur.

"One of the most eloquent dissenters is the Indian social scientist Vandana Shiva, who has long attacked a Western-imposed 'monoculture of the mind' and called for an 'insurrection of subjugated knowledge' against the 'dominant knowledge' of capitalism. This dominant knowledge leaves out a plurality of paths to knowing nature and the universe', she wrote. 'Ninety per cent of it could be stopped without any risk of human deprivation".[14]

Once the Press becomes the private estate of a few in alliance with the giant global corporations in industry, the mind of Third World middle class can be controlled, conditioned and, eventually, conquered by dissemination of news-views capsules plus plus, masterfully presented using the Circean spell of enchanting misinformation. A kind of coca-cola methodology of doping minds and implementing Hidden Agendas is a fascinating operation but of dangerous potential as Pilger's book has proved, exposing the game of "newsassination" of weaker nations and feeble sectors of the human race. So let me pardonably quote a page from him:

"Regardless of the BBC's enduring facade of impartiality and standards, news is now openly ideological and uniform, as the demands of the market supercult are met. When slow news is included, it is more than likely dressed in a political and social vocabulary that ensures the truth is lost. Thus, in Britain, as in the United States (and Australia), the systematic impoverishment of a quarter of the population is routinely filed under 'underclass', an American term describing a corrupting, anti-social group outside society. The solution to poverty, which is the return of vast wealth taken from the poor by the rich, is seldom given a public airing. The 'new' system of capitalism for the powerless and socialism for the powerful, under which the former are persecuted and the latter are

13 John Pilger: *Hidden Agendas,* pages 531-532.
14 *Ibid,* page 534.

given billions in public subsidies, is rarely identified as such. Terms like 'modernisation' are preferred.

"The Gulf War in 1991 was reported as a technological wonder, an event of bloodless science in which, rejoiced one editorial writer, there were 'miraculously few casualties'. It was one of the most covered wars in history, yet few journalists reported the truth, still widely unknown, that a quarter of a million Iraqis were wantonly slaughtered or died unnecessary deaths.

"Since that bloodfest, the fate of the children of Iraq has been the slowest of news. Who knows that at least half a million children have died as a direct result of the economic sanctions imposed by the Western powers? Who understands that the sanctions are aimed not at bringing down Saddam Hussein, or deterring him from building some mythical nuclear bomb, but at preventing the 'market' competition of Iraqi oil from forcing down the price of oil produced by Saudi Arabia, the West's most important Middle Eastern proxy, next to Israel and biggest arms customer"?[15]

The *Unpeople* of the world are no news. Do you know of half a million children who, according to UNICEF, die out of poverty, one Filipino child dies every hour because the resources are diverted to payment of interest to Fund-Bank Loans? Indian figures are equally ghastly but which Press unearths the hideous secrets beneath our Government budgets? Unpeople in India are adivasis, bonded labour, children under torture and a hundred other disabled people whose right to life, to work, to potable water, fresh air, good health are in jeopardy. Custodial deaths, forced suicides, non-access to food and shelter, of life-sustaining goods, high prices and social injustices galore *are not* news in Bharat while arrivals of glittering cars and shining consumer services are part of publicity-philia.

The have-nots are homeless, hungry and Political Parties have no time for them, being seriously worried over the circuses of Coalitions and Power tournaments and seats in Houses, weakening human solidarity and thereby helping foreign Big Business indirectly. I agree with John Pilger:

"I have become convinced that it is not enough for journalists to see themselves as mere messengers, without understanding the hidden agendas of the message and the myths that surround it. High on the list is the myth that we now live in an 'information age'—when, in fact, we live in a media age, in which the available information is repetitive, 'safe' and limited by invisible boundaries".[16]

There is a news famine in our information age despite the most of the information highway.

Imagine how BBC, the best in the news service world, 'only 3 per cent of peak-time programmes feature anything about the majority of humanity, and almost all of that, is confined to 'minority channels'. 'In the media's global village, other nations do not exist' unless they are

15 *Ibid*, pages 2-3.
16 *Ibid*, page 4.

useful to 'us'—that is the media motto and operation. Indian noises and wranglings and fretting and strutting are not news but local farce and fun. Our media are cybernetically at the mercy of the top media abroad. Our minds and cerebral processes, our noetics and world view are no longer ours but borrowed trappings.

India is glamorised by *mareecha* 'development'. More prestigious hedonism, five-star hotels, golf courses, sky-high buildings, Kentucky chicken, fast foods, fashionable dress and the disease of affluenza are the craze. And hunger, homelessness, right to minimal wants and treatment in hospitals or educational facilities anywhere do not move the pen or print or tele-media. What a contradiction! How mute are even Marxists!

Swadeshi is nearly dead after Sinhanomics has become Government policy like the earlier Manmohanomics and Chidamberomics. The struggle against the neo-imperialists and neo-riches is hard, but must be fought by the Press functionally. We may need guerrilla journalism, naxalite journalism, leftist journalism, people-oriented journalism and anti-GATT journalism. We want soldiers of journalism, sappers and miners, echelons and cadres. This process involves risky investigation, courting Court contempt, provoking wrath, and parliamentary umbrage. There is a big hidden agenda of commodifying humanity in the gold rush of Corporations. The international integration of markets for goods, services and speculative business is pressing societies to alter their traditional practices, so much that, the broad segments of these societies are not able to put up a fight.

The Patents Law is being manipulated to suit the TRIPS trap set by the GATT and is being enforced by the W.T.O. Indian seeds, flowers, crops, fruits, herbs and other invaluable wealth of bio-diversity on which whole people depend for their health are being robbed by the foreign predators. Our rulers have become mendicants and desire only dollar investments. Half of India lives below the poverty line. They are Unpeople and are ignored. Some day they will arise and wipe out the rulers when even onions are beyond their purse. Arms industries flourish today while the right to life has no place in the budget. It needed Amartya Sen, the new Nobel laureate, to tell India of the ethical economics of investment in human beings. Culture and imperialism now are far worse than before. The right to development, to peace, to environment and to fair share in the wealth of the world are a new generation of human rights wholly ignored because of the new market wisdom and dollar democracy. Since the 2nd World War, the arms trade, dominated by the West, has caused the death of an estimated 20 million people—news omitted in our newspapers. What a Peace dividend under the nose of the UN! There are hundred times more investments on weapons to kill than for instruments to nourish humans. With each passing day demonic terror and inhuman horror are on the rise. Vietnam once the symbol of liberation from imperialist to invasion is now the victim of Yanki corruption and CIA manipulation. The world's worst tyrant Pol Pot when driven out into Thailand by the Vietnamis, was welcomed into border camps by American Operation's officials and intelligence agency.

The final battle for freedom and justice remains to be waged in India as elsewhere. Do or die of Gandhian vintage has grim relevance today.

The Asian tiger States are now in deep debt. India is moving down hill whatever the elite media may say. Free speech is unfree and is lost to esoteric big business. However there is hope because the vulnerable and vanquished people are trying to stand up. The latest pronouncement for the future tense of Bharat and the world is best reflected in a quote from John Pilger's *Hidden Agendas*:

> "Beware 'the rumbling out there', says the President of the Federal Reserve Bank. People are dangerously suffering from globophobia, says a senior floor trader in New York. The magnitude of change in the world economy since the end of the Cold War, wrote the eminent American economist, David Hale, has been so dramatic it has given rise to a new political phenomenon......voters now view trade issues in terms of domestic class struggle. In his book, *Has Globalisation Gone Too Far*? another Harvard high priest, Dano Rodrik, wrote 'The international integration of markets for goods, services and capital is pressuring societies to alter their traditional practices so much that in return, broad segments of these societies are putting up a fight.
>
> "The fight has only just begun".[17]

What are the omens like for human rights in the proximate millennium? The delicately woven illusion that globalisation and the Fund-Bank operation will bail out the people of the earth from poverty and privation has now been exposed. It is now clear that the Emperor has no clothes. Never in the course of economic events–not even in the desperate years of the Depression of the 30's has so large a part of the world economy experienced so devastating a fall from grace. For far too long has the myth of global glorious era blinded the under-privileged. Now the time has come for the truth of the lie of trickle down theory being revealed and human rights stand on its own legs.

The last word on history and human rights belongs to T.S. Eliot, although his meaning is a riddle, a mystery and an enigma. "History has many cunning passages, contrived corridors. And issues, deceives with whispering ambitions, guides us by vanities". Is globalisation gory glorification, liberalisation lashing the poor to exploit all resources, and privatisation leeching people to suck profits? What a voodoo?

The last few years have been depressing. The Rao regime sustained by dubious vote, the frequent succession of shaky Governments following the exit of Narasimha, the pot-pourri of parties with BJP and Vajpayee currently in power, have, by their performance, proved that short shrift has been given to Gandhiji's swadeshi and Nehru's self-reliance and the Left, barring ineffectual noises, though luminous but with none to heed, have also all but left the vast *Unpeople* of India in the limbo of desperation and privation. Human Rights have been jettisoned, police lock-up assaults on humans

17 Page 610.

and prison torture of confines cause no surprise. Many States, including Kerala, even now do not have a State Human Rights Commission. What is distressing is that the trend in the Supreme Court and the High Courts is to blink at the left and look at the right, dismissing the Constitution's clearly socialistic ideology. One gathers the impression that in recent years even the gains of the people during the 70's are being whittled down in the Higher Courts. Where are the people (Unpeople) to go when access is formal, dismissal the rule, lawyers highly expensive and Judges impatient and hubristic.

Once I wrote (but I'm slowly getting disillusioned now): the Constitution is our Title Deed of social justice and our task is to create an aware and activist Bench and Bar sensitized by the raw human realities, conceptualised by the Socialist Republic's tryst with destiny.

The human rights prospect for the 21st century is a thing of fancy and fiction because the Executive buckles under GATT pressure and WTO commandments; the legislature is all babel with nothing sharply in favour of the people being fought or achieved, and the Judiciary, with its salaries and perks making a quantum jump and powers grabbed by a sort of *imperium in imperio*, plus prospects of official patronage, including Governorships pathologically persuading them to steer towards the supremacy of the World Finance Capital. Liberties are in twilight and the little Indian is a voiceless vanishing species. This is 1998 update.

The stream of time flows on perennially, and so into the next millennium. Constitutional adjudication, N.G.O. militancy demanding activisation of human rights, people's vote (did not onion price rise do electoral politics in India to throw out Governments which neglected the right to food) and mobilisation of people are hopes in the horizon.

Politicization and commercialization of human rights are a grave signal. A portentous opening by Sir Stephen Sedley[18] is a note of warning for activists. I quote:

> "The end of history seems a good moment to take stock.—Fukuyama's conceit (I mean it in both senses) that the triumph of Western liberalism has stopped the clock of change—has put an end to history—is already waning. We may reflect that human rights themselves have played a sacrificial role in this process, for the demise of the regimes of Eastern Europe was accelerated by a megaphone rhetoric of human rights from States, including our own, with an embarrassing capacity for overlooking human rights abuses among their own allies and clients and even within their own frontiers. The message between the lines has been that human rights are a commodity like any other, capable of being traded for political or economic advantage, and the rhetoric little more than the conduct of politics by other means".

The conquest of human rights by GATTOlogy and WTO authoritaria-nism must be prevented. Future perspectives must be carefully

18 *Human Rights for the 21st Century*, page 1.

considered. Here we may conclude with a note of wisdom culled from the same book:

> "Human rights diplomacy is at a crossroads. During the Cold War human rights issues in international relations were too often used for political purposes which were far from the concern for human rights. On the other hand, often human rights were forgotten for the sake of *raison d'etat*".[19]
>
> "It is difficult to be optimistic regarding the progress in the domain of human rights worldwide if in order to be optimistic it is necessary to believe that in the foreseeable future there will be no humanitarian hells in any part of the world or that there will be paradise for them somewhere on the Earth. But it is possible to be slightly more optimistic regarding the possibility of the gradual progress in a number of countries and regions of the world and believe that at least some of the human rights hells may be healed more or less successfully. Something, certainly can be, and therefore should, be done. Active and skilful human rights diplomacy is needed not only for the sake of international stability, but first of all for the sake of mankind as a whole and every human being".[20]

On planet earth there are no passengers, all are crew; Indians must navigate towards their human rights destiny without respite.

A last thought

Kofi Annan, Secretary General of UN in his message to the world on the 50th Anniversary of Universal Declaration told humanity what is a message for the generations ahead:

> "It is the universality of human rights that gives them their strength. It endows them with the power to cross any border, climb any wall, defy any force.
>
> "The struggle for universal human rights has always and everywhere been the struggle against all forms of tyranny and injustice—against slavery, against colonialism, against apartheid. It is nothing less and nothing different today.
>
> "Young friends all over the world,
>
> "You are the ones who must realize these rights, now and for all time. Their fate and future is in your hands. Human rights are your rights. Seize them. Defend them. Promote them. Understand them and insist on them. Nourish and enrich them.
>
> "They are the best in us. Give them life".[21]

V.R. KRISHNA IYER

19 *Ibid*, page 159.
20 *Ibid*, page 160.
21 UN Newsletter, dt. 13-12-1997.

CONTENTS

TABLE OF CASES

1

Exordium

"I am a man and nothing pertaining to man is alien to me"

—Karl Marx

"Behind the night .... somewhere afar some white tremendous daybreak"

—Rupert Brooke

The Tagore Law Lectures, under the auspices of the Calcutta University, are a luminous series delivered by great scholars and outstanding jurists who, by their deep learning and broad vision, have added to the world's wealth of legal literature. Regarded from this finer perspective, Tagore Law Professorship brings before one's mind a galaxy of juristic celebrities, Indian and foreign, (in the universe of jurisprudence), who have illumined many arcane but important facets of public law lost, until then, in the limbo of legal oblivion and bestowed on justice systems and allied sciences rare creative thinking and radical judicial humanism, often unfolding wider vistas of legal philosophy and noetic-juristic futurism, enriching the mansions of law and administration of justice.

So, when I was informed that the Calcutta University had decided to offer me the Tagore Law Professorship for 1981, with a request to deliver a course of not less than Six Lectures on a subject of (my) own choice relating to outstanding legal or judicial aspects of law, I was, not unexpectedly, but in all humility, pleased with the prospect. Even so, when I glanced at the universally distinguished jurists who professorially decorated the Tagore Law chair in the past, I discovered legendary names like Sir Rashbehari Ghosh, Sir Gooroodas Banerjee, Sir Frederic Pollock, Sir William Holdsworth, Sir Asutosh Mukerjee, Sir Z. Cowen, Justice William O'Douglas, Prof. Rene David, Prof. W. Friedman, Prof. Roscoe Pound, Sir Dinshaw Mulla,

Justice Gajendragadkar, Dr. Nagendra Singh, *et al*, who were earlier Tagore Law Professors. Great by any standard. And I, by chance, began to be a law-person of anti-establishment slant, a juristic maverick, a judicial non-conformist and a suspect 'leftist' (7) who may well be an allergy to vintage jurisprudents and conventional 'brethren'. This subjective streak of scepticism notwithstanding, I accepted the offer but resolved to stick to my own convictions, principles and perspectives in the choice of the subject, the presentation of its facets and the prognosis for humanity which currently is passing through a social pathology that pains me deeply. We live in a world highly sensitive to human rights in their comprehensive connotation. And yet, the menace to human survival and life in dignity and peace has never been so globally grim, even ghastly, that the first concern of contemporary creative jurisprudents must be with the impregnability of human personhood, from the humblest to the highest, under socio-economic conditions and political-cultural structures which make human rights and people's liberation a reality of life.

My social convictions are my verities and values in law and life, and one of my basic commitments is that the dynamic rule of law, as a refined tool of social engineering, must be people-oriented and supportive of human rights and human justice. The dialectics of societal forces, analytically studied, belights the forward march of civilised life and facilitates the radical transformation of the justice system, guided by humanitarian norms and placing the human being as the central figure of progress. Likewise, the integral *yoga* of the divine and the human—a holistic vision of personhood—is for me a philosophical fundamental, with its fall-out on the rule of law and the rule of life and humanity's tryst with destiny. These basics are too profound to be negotiable, too firm to be expediency-friendly. I wonder whether my avant-garde approach to legal issues will blend well with vintage Tagore wisdom or elite judicial tradition.

I am well aware that I am a *quasi*-crimson dissenter and powerless protester against the current unjust world order which is respectably draped in dubious democracy, demonic despotism or sinister shades of both. So too am I sensible of being a futile campaigner for the lowly, the lost and the last, and a vocal critic of grosser injustices against the manacled, the marginalised and the alienated, who often are the voiceless victims of disguised authoritarianism. Procrustean egalitarianism and heartless establishmentarianism permeate, on a global scale, our political structures and pollute, in varying degrees our socio-economic cultures. A just social order demands the evolution and implementation of vibrant values with a mission and passion. The cold neutrality of a judge and the textual dexterity of a lawyer are not enough. The highbrow outlook of robed brethren and gowned professionals often shy away from the poignant problems of the pariahs and the wretched of the earth. Such blue blood jurisprudence is anathema to the outcasts of the world.

Law loses its social purpose when it is lost in juristic jujitsu, logomachic disputes and grammatical constructions. Forensic forays, erudite legalisms and precedential profusion, theoretically away from the sorrows and struggles of life, provoke me to repeat my respectful but sharp criticism of traditional jurisprudents.

> "Their hollow concepts, tea-cup debates, and impotent ideas debase modern jurisprudence. Their obsessions are unworthy and intellectually subversive–especially so in an age when man's annihilation is a possibility, the individual's alienation is a fact, and world political revolution is in process. In a time of Hamlet's choice, of being or not being, can one rationally choose to watch these jurisprudents chalk up the fissures in their logical castles of absurdity, rumble about non-ideological principles of law, acro-arc through logico-linguistic feats of verbomania, distinguish "is" from "ought", just after the "pure law", or dispense sweet allegories about the Light of the Law that failed the Virgin Lady of the Lake? No, for their causes are all shadow causes, fit only for the haunting of some philosophical boneyard. Their grand illusions have nothing to do with life. Such shadow causes, being spiritually dead, can teach nothing about living, a matter of ageless importance. I offer them a return to the basic question of philosophy (and of jurisprudence). That question is Existence, and its subject-matter is the living. Law is for life and judicial judos are socially irrelevant if the human focus is blurred".

Humanism is the soul of justice and of all social sciences. Unfortunately, jurisprudence, when it operates in a milieu of class bias, distorts human justice and inflicts social injustice based on old world orthodoxies. In this context the biting cynicism of Anatole France is revealing.

> "To disarm the strong and arm the weak would be to change the social order which it's my job to preserve. Justice is the means by which established injustices are sanctioned".

Law, in its mock egalitarian pretence, is often unjust in substance. Here again, Anatole France is apt when he tartly tells us:

> "The majestic egalitarianism of the law, which forbids rich and poor alike to sleep under the bridges, to beg in the streets, and to steal bread".

When jurisprudence jettisons human justice the rule of law turns terrorist, when judges with class bias or caste subconscious or insensitive executives and dubious legislators with hidden vested interests are the operators at various stages.

Legal justice often is the novocaine of the uneasy soul and deadens jurists to the tearful realities of the world's traumata. When law blinks at Life, both suffer and the human condition ceases to be the concern of the judicial process. Jurisprudence must, to be relevant to human justice, deal with the burning issues of the world; and compassion, the secret spring and soulful flow, is its noble component.

Close to my conceptual perceptions in this context, is what a Philippine jurist of eminence, Jose W. Diokno, once observed:

> "No cause is more worthy than the cause of human rights. Human rights are more than legal concepts: they are the essence of man. They are what make man human. That is why they are called human rights: deny them and you deny man's humanity ...."

This great idea is the seed which sprouts in my mind as I contemplate a lofty topic for a Six-Lecture Series on Public Law and Social Justice. The true conception of the administration of justice is that "the least concern of the least person is of the highest consideration to the State". In the land of the Buddha and the Mahatma, law without humanism is a hoax and judicial justice sans human rights consciousness is curial abracadabra. This is not to deny that, in our own century, great judges with constitutional erudition transformed by compassion and conscience like Earl Warren and Lord Atkin *et al* have served the cause of humanity in its human rights domain. But one swallow does not make a summer.

The flood of UN instruments notwithstanding, rare are domestic laws which are necessary as the locomotive of a national human rights regimes. The executive launches on rhetoric reversed by reality. The police, with none to police the police, often are guilty of omission and commission, with a violent culture which makes this State infrastructure a close cousin of the *mafia*, the dark underworld and the corrupt political bureaucratic brood for whom human rights are but paper tigers.

And now the judiciary, guilty in some measure but comparatively far less delinquent than the other branches, is fast losing its moral innocence and spiritual source making forensic defence of the human rights of the masses a functional futility or forensic gamble. Who is to guard the guards themselves *(sed quis custodiet ipsos custodes?)* as Juvenal asked.

It is a sombre reflection that the high bench often diminishes, by interpretative dicta and callous disinclinations even minimal human rights legislation, scared, as it were, by the larger freedom and profound worth of the human person some sober legislative chambers may choose to confer on the vast, victimised populace in tune with liberal concepts of personal liberties and fundamental freedoms enshrined in Universal Declaration. Legislatures are far behind UN jurisprudence, and judicial conservatism, at times, is far behind Legislatures and UN Covenants and progressive historic instruments, what with pontific pronouncements appropriate in feudal centuries. Illustratively, I cite an observation of the Privy Council about the Hong Kong Human Rights Bill in 1993. I quote from a seminar publication of the University of Hong Kong where the participants regretted judicial narrowing by limiting the semantic sweep of provisions instead of expanding the sensitive purpose of the statute. Justice Holmes once struck a cautionary note:

> "Judges commonly are elderly men, and are more likely to hate at sight any analysis to which they are not accustomed, and which disturbs repose of mind, than to fall in love with novelties".

Radical human rights jurisprudence is not old legal theology nor familiar jural menu; and senior brethren on the bench view with sclerotic perception and sceptical resistance the higher values of human rights, ecology and environment expressed by progressive law persons and activist social sensitives. We need echelons in all departments of the State who can initiate, interpret, consolidate and metabolize into the *corpus juris* great thoughts about human advance. Mankind's long march towards its high destiny can make headway only if led by far-sighted statesmanship beyond fossil phrases, ossified ideas and narrow horizons.

Great visionaries in public life must rise to look at the worth of the human person from a nobler angle and constructive intent. James Madison's words sound sublime:

> "Human rights are not established by writing words on paper or moving air with one's lips. Human rights are established by building specific types of institutions of quite exact design. Human rights are established further, when such institutions begin to live through organised, articulate, free, law-abiding interests-through free association of every sort among a free people".

Learned Hand, with solemn realism, pleaded for supramental sanity as against savage insanity:

> "Man may be a little lower than angels, but he has not yet shaken off the brute. His passion, his thinking, his body, carry their origins with them. His path is strewn with carnage, the murderer lurks always not far beneath, to break out from time to time, peace resolutions to the contrary notwithstanding. What he has gained has been with immeasurable waste; what he shall gain will be with immeasurably more......... He must grope his way through the murk, as his remote fore -runners groped, in the dark, hot world in which they moved. Look where he will, there are no immutable laws to which he can turn; no, not even that in selfless abnegation he must give up what he craves, for life is self-assertion. Conflict is normal; we reach accommodation as wisdom may teach us that it does not pay to fight........."

Judges must respond, says Michael, J. Parry, to

> "the vital-interests of the poor, especially the non-white poor, and of other persons who exist on the bare margin of society such as prisoners and the mentally disabled. Contemporary non-interpretive review—non-interpretive review in this emergent age of scarcity—must be informed and guided by a developing sensitivity to the moral and political plight of society's marginal persons".

Human rights are writ on a large canvas, as large as the sky. The law makers, lawyers and particularly, the judges, must make the printed text vibrant with human values, not be scared of consequences on the *status quo* order. The militant challenges of today need a mobilisation of revolutionary consciousness sans which civilized systems cease to exist. Remember, we are all active navigators, not idle passengers, on spaceship earth as it ascends to celestial levels of the glorious human future.

It is a false dilemma to separate the political and civil rights and the social and economic rights; and treat, as the US establishment does, the first as of superior priority. The answer is plain:

> "We cannot enjoy civil and political rights unless we enjoy economic, cultural and social rights, any more than we can insure our economic, social and

cultural rights unless we can exercise our civil and political rights. True, a hungry man does not have much freedom of choice. But equally true, when a well-fed man does not have freedom of choice, he cannot protect himself against going hungry".

Peace and Development are also imperative in the Human Rights Agenda. The UN General Assembly adopted a common strategy for the Third United Nations Development Decade as it declared:

> "The stark reality confronting mankind today is that close to 850 million people (now many more millions) in the developing world are living at the margin of existence—enduring hunger, sickness, homelessness and absence of meaningful employment...... The development process must promote human dignity. The ultimate aim of development is the constant improvement of the well-being of the entire population on the basis of its full participation in the process of development and a fair distribution of the benefits therefrom".

Peace too is categoric if a civilized order is to subsist:

> "We must understand and remove the obstacles to peace. When the majority are poor and inequality prevails, conflict arises. When people clash, human rights are oftentimes the first casualties. This situation intensifies the conflict and violence escalates. To enforce the people's right to peace, pressure is required to bring about social justice, to enlarge democratic space, to resolve differences through democratic debate and peaceful avenues".

Indian jurists and statesmen familiar with Art. 38, strive to fashion a Social Order articulated therein:

> "38. *State to secure a social order for the promotion of welfare of the people.*—(1) The State shall strive to promote the welfare of the people by securing and protecting as effectively as it may a social order in which justice, social, economic and political, shall inform all the institutions of the national life.
>
> (2) The State shall, in particular, strive to minimise the inequalities in income, and endeavour to eliminate inequalities in status, facilities and opportunities, not only amongst individuals but also amongst groups of people residing in different areas or engaged in different vocations."

A new world human order which releases the power of the spirit and enriches the human personhood calls for man's return, as KARL MARX said, in "*The Holy Family*", to his "Universal nature in a universal manner, that is, as a total human being".

The growth of human justice in this holistic dimension seems a strange serendipity to traditional judges. But our courts are integral to human rights achievements. So our judicial fraternity must broaden their vision and deepen their compassion. We have miles to go and promises to keep if judges are to be the ultimate custodians of fundamental freedoms. A brief reference to a few summit courts is useful.

Where right and justice are the desiderata, judges have a strategic role to play and a solemn duty to perform. Larger freedoms and deeper regard for the worth of the human person are allergy for those bred in the values of the *status quo ante*.

A "JUDGE" as Lord Denning once observed "must consciously seek to mould the law so as to serve the needs of the time. He must not be a mere mechanic, a mere working mason, laying brick on brick, without thought to the overall design. He must be an architect–thinking of the structure as a whole–building for society a system of law which is strong, durable and just. It is on his work that civilised society itself depends".[1]

It is the task of the court to expound the meaning of meanings revolving round the profundity of personhood. The highest in the scale of Creation is the human being. His rights are in the creative trust of the judiciary. A delectable anecdote by late K.P.S. Menon comes to mind when I consider the function of the judge. The anecdote runs thus: There were three masons working on marble. When asked what he was doing, the first mason replied that he was cutting stones; the next one on being questioned stated that he was making a living; and the last one when interrogated looked up and with passion answered 'I am building a Cathedral'. I would submit that judges or for that matter administrators and legislators must with missionary feeling realise that their job is not the mason's midgetry or disposal of files. The noble task of a public functionary is to expand the horizons of human rights, interpret the depth of human dignity and fortify with all their soul-force those great rights absent which the human being is robbed of his sacred personhood. But alas, 'robed' amnesia is not uncommon since litigative battles where professionals are engaged in hardly focus on the human being but are lost in legalistics and adversarial habitude. At this point, let me quote from a Hong Kong seminar on the Hong Kong Bill of Rights 1991:

> "The judgment of the Privy Council in *Attorney General* v *Lee Kwong-kut; Attorney General* v *Lo Chak-man and another*, delivered on 23rd May 1993 represents in my view a step backwards. While the specific results of the two cases are reasonable, the limitations of the Privy Council's decision lie more in the message that it sends to Hong Kong courts about how one should go about interpreting the Bill of Rights. The central passage in the judgment of Lord Wolf expresses sentiments to which one can hardly object on their face, but which in context are deeply conservative:
>
> "While the Hong Kong Judiciary should be zealous in upholding the individual's rights under the Hong Kong Bill, it is also necessary to ensure that disputes as to the effect of the Bill are not allowed to get out of hand. The issues involving the Hong Kong Bill should be approached with realism and good sense, and kept in proportion. If this is not done the Bill will become a source of injustice rather than justice and it will be debased in the eyes of the public".
>
> "As my colleague Johannes Chan and I wrote:
>
> "No one would object to the need for realism, good sense and avoidance of things being allowed to get out of hand. The question is rather how one ensures this balance, in view of the fact that the Legislature has enacted a Bill of Rights which gives an important emphasis to individual rights. The danger

1 In the Foreword to the book *The Supreme Court of India* by Rajeev Dhavan.

is that such sentiments can easily become an easy justification for adhering to the *status quo* without undertaking the fresh examination of existing law and practice which the enactment of a Bill of Rights should entail. Indeed, this passage has become the almost constant refrain of the Government in the Hong Kong courts in defending Bill of Rights challenges; its subliminal impact is considerable, despite its analytical limitations.

"The Privy Council's approach, propounding an almost intuitive method of determining whether a provision is consistent with the Bill of Rights, is one which encourages the assumption that the *status quo* is consistent with the Bill of Rights, and one which militates against the examination of long-standing and well-accepted laws and arrangements in the light of contemporary human rights standards".[2]

Higher values hallow human rights statutes. UN Covenants and noble instruments, national and international; and jurisprudence, bedrocked on humanism, must summon sublime perceptions, not cribbed constructions. This challenge is a gauntlet which jurists must take up. This is a perennial process and inspirational project which fascinates all lovers of human rights. This is a human culture continually renewing itself amidst contradictions and conflicts, attacks and counter-attacks. Each one of us, whatever his station in society, must fight to uphold the flag of human rights. While the battle rages loud and long, win or lose, the war for human deliverance must go on.

After four score years of sour-sweet terrestrial travel, when, in odd moments, my mind reflects in retrospect over the countless conflicts for human causes fought and lost, I wonder whether I have been nothing but a home of lost causes, however just, forsaken beliefs, however profound, unpopular advocacies, however humane, and impossible loyalties, however sublime. In the sombre sunset of life, in vacant or pensive mood, I realise that one is but an ineffectual militant beating one's tired wings in the void in vain; and the world process itself is but a succedaneum for evils and excesses and succession of corruption and injustice, with dumb sufferers in large numbers insensibly ignored or insultingly injured. And yet, this traumatic whirligig of white-hot conflict is the dramatic crescendo of contemporary times when the New World Economic Order, red in tooth and claw, brutally betrays weary, worn-out mankind; and the grim, global hunger of billions of humans for a happier world order gains militant momentum with a fumy fury, suppressed at times by State gun culture, super-power tantrums and *mafia*-fuelled terror. What a clash of forces in a darkling globe. Borrowing a few passages from Mathew Arnold to project my thoughts, the inconsolate, melancholy scenario, far more miserable than his words convey, is the reality:

"Our unrivalled happiness: what an element of grimness, bareness, and hideousness mixes with it and blurs it; the workhouse, the dismal Mapperly Hills,—how dismal those who have seen them will remember; the gloom, the

2 Hong Kong's Bill of Rights, pp. 2 to 4.

> smoke, the cold, the strangled illegitimate child: ...... And the final touch, short, bleak and inhuman: Wragg is in custody. The sex lost in the confusion of our unrivalled happiness; or (shall I say?) the superfluous Christian name lopped off by the straightforward vigour of old Anglo-Saxon breed:"

This lurid contrast of a divided society of dire distress and dizzy delight is painted with literary power by Charles Dickens in his *A Tale of Two Cities* of his times:

> "It was the best of times, it was the worst of times, it was the age of wisdom, it was the age of foolishness, it was the epoch of belief, it was the epoch of incredulity, it was the season of Light, it was the season of Darkness, it was the spring of hope, it was the winter of despair, we had everything before us, we had nothing before us, we were all going direct to Heaven, we were all going direct the other way."

We witness the tale of two worlds, two or more societies, several sharp contrasts and conflicts and a battle of tenses, classes, genders and what not, and humanity itself in a mood of to be or not to be wandering between two worlds, one dead (or dying?) and the other powerless to be born.

This is the incompatible play of forces which historical materialists and spiritual sensitives behold in global society today; Power versus the people, corporate profit pitted against community good, female gender versus male hubris, bonded labour held by slave-owner—and human rights must struggle for survival in this malignant milieu and confrontational context. Quo vadis humanity?

To win human rights for all mankind is a sublime adventure. The first move begins with awakening the peoples of the earth about the indwelling and inalienable rights which make them worthy of human personhood. This triggering of awareness proceeds from the consciousness that the international community is the largest constituency supporting Project Human Rights. Let me quote Amadou-Mahtar M'Bow, former UNESCO Director-General:

> "To know one's rights is a step towards obtaining their recognition. For the men and women are aware, at this moment, that they still have to struggle, sometimes at the risk of their lives, to try to exercise their basic rights, could not do so with any hope of success unless they could draw comfort and moral and intellectual inspiration from the certainty that the principles underlying these rights are now adopted by the whole international community".[2a]

Among the professions, the legal community and socio-legal activists have a special responsibility in making a success of Operation Awareness. Lawyers, in all theatres of national life, must educate the broad community about human rights. It is the lawyer's high duty to communicate human rights developments to the people and to functionalise the infrastructure,

2a Address to the International Congress on the Teaching of Human Rights in Vienna, Austria, 12th September 1978.

to innovate public interest litigation and to become the locomotive of human rights schemes. The legal profession is fast growing both in terms of the number of lawyers and their areas of specialization. One of the vital areas of growth is in cases involving enforcement of human rights. Many of our lawyers do not appear yet to realise that apart from commercial and corporate legal practice, one upcoming and lucrative area of legal practice is human rights and public interest litigation. In the United Kingdom, Mr. Anthony Lester, QC, is probably one of the most successful and best known British lawyers in practice today. He is the Chairman of Interights, a specialist in human rights cases, and is usually engaged in important human rights cases not only in the United Kingdom but also all over the world. He does not approach these cases with the politician's touch. No. He approaches them purely from the humanist lawyer's angle; and yet he is very successful. We need many Lesters with conviction and compassion. Yes, we have M.C. Mehtas and Shouries, Sheila Barses and others with commitment and spirit of sacrifice. May their tribe increase.

But to be able to play his role properly, a human rights lawyer needs to be properly educated, equipped and exposed. He needs to read widely in the humanities. So, he must have access to a good library. He must master the general principles of law. He must also master national and international human rights norms and principles of their interpretation. He must himself develop a human rights culture. It is important for him to realise that human rights norms are not isolationist in nature; rather they are international in the sense that, subject to express provisions of national Constitutions and laws, the principles and content of international human rights norms are basically the same. The way they have been interpreted in one country can be a useful guide to their approach and interpretation in another. This happens now in South Asia, though inadequately.

A crusading human rights lawyer is a beacon light and surgeon's knife. *People's lawyers*—we need that brood as a public sector in the legal profession—are the vanguard in the battle for human rights. The specialists in human rights jurisprudence, familiar with case-law and growing literature, imbibing the luminous culture and textual texture, is our need. We need competent, kindly cadres.

This task force, properly trained, indoctrinated and battle-scarred, with national networks, international contacts and versatile participations in workshops—such is the daring caring sector of the bar which must be developed and updated if the social mission of law, at the service of victimised categories, is to fulfill itself. Victimology, in the larger dimension and innovative processes, is but burgeoning. Take the law school students to schools and colleges, to women and children and the discriminated and down-trodden, forsaken and forlorn. If that be done with spiritual vision and moral passion we build for the future a professional resource ready for the long march, rich with soulful rewards. Then alone the rule of law and the rule of life will meet and beat the injustices that beset society escalatingly.

Judges too have to learn and be sensitized. The Bangalore Declaration of Commonwealth Judges says:

> "It is essential to redress a situation where, by reason of traditional legal training which has tended to ignore the international dimension, judges and practising lawyers are often unaware of the remarkable and comprehensive developments of statements of international human rights norms. For the practical implementation of these views it is desirable to make provision for appropriate courses in universities and colleges, and for lawyers and law enforcement officials: provision in libraries of relevant materials; promotion of expert advisory bodies knowledgeable about developments in this field; better dissemination of information to judges, lawyers and law enforcement officials; and meetings for exchanges of relevant information and experience.
>
> "These views are expressed in recognition of the fact that judges and lawyers have a special contribution to make in the administration of justice in fostering universal respect for fundamental human rights and freedoms."

Infrastructure, access, aid, enforcement

Human Rights Law has no locomotion on its own unless the necessary infrastructure for receiving information, investigating into events and accusations, providing for prompt adjudication with due process requirements, easy access and legal aid, agencies to prosecute, enforcement of verdicts and delivery of relief—these are the viability aspects which must be vigilantly attended to lest covenants and legislations should slumber in libraries. Each of these items calls for close and creative work if the cornucopia of human rights were to raise the dignity of the humblest, handicapped and humiliated members of society.

The agenda of action begins with education in human rights and ends with their full compliance through law, national and international.

Unpropitious environs for human justice

Walden Bello, in his *Dark Victory,* analyses the spiralling social tension attaining critical mass. The economic south, of which India is a part, is a raging victim of the economic North; and the human rights, especially social and economic, of people under the economic yoke of the G-7 multinationals remain suppressed so long as the structural constrictions and economic python process persist. The southern Sunrise of economic, social and political hope is soon darkened by the dominant hold of Northern cartels and conglomerates. For the masses, their visions of a finer future after decolonisation have vanished and their human rights are ashes and disillusions.

The South Commission (The Challenge to the South) wrote what is Indian truth:

> "For many, there was the hope born of success in their liberation struggles. Everywhere there was talk of equality and progress .... It is important to remember this period of progress and its atmosphere of hope now, when there is deep pessimism in much of the Third World about the prospects of economic development".

The IMF-World Bank's Operation structural Adjustment breaks the spinal cord of Third World economies, pushing increasing numbers of poor people out of survival options. The Bretton Wood's blessings are blighting the prospects of a promising future for the South, and human rights perish where politico-economic independence diminishes. Walden Bello's comment reveals the reason for pessimism.

> "The surrender of leading countries like India to structural adjustment translated in the global arena into a deep erosion of the power and prestige of those institutions that had served as agents of Southern interests: the Non-Aligned Movement, UNCTAD, the Group of 77. The decomposition of the Third World was felt at the United Nations, where the United States was emboldened once again to use that body to front Northern interests, including providing legitimacy for the US-led invasion of Iraq in 1991."

Rollback had succeeded.

> "And as the Third World entered what promised to be an even bleaker decade than the 1980s, the South Commission captured the essence of the contemporary condition of the South: (1) It may not be an exaggeration to suggest that the establishment of a system of international economic relations in which the South's second-class status would be institutionalised is an immediate danger".[3]

It is useful to observe that the common people of the North also suffer and their human rights, economic and social, are truncated. In *Food First* this point has been established:

> "In fact, the majority of the American people are not pitted against the hungry people; these are not the battle lines of the hunger struggle. The struggle is against a system that increasingly concentrates wealth and power. The struggle is against a system profiting on hunger in the Philippines or Brazil just as it is in the United States. The real forces creating hunger pain almost all nations in the world. Once the lines of struggle are clear we can no longer be manipulated by proferrers of guilt and fear".[4]

The dark vision of the 21st century as an era of North-South polarisation between privileged white citizens and coloured backward barbarians is false. Deprived humans, wherever they be, must unite to mount an effective movement for a progressive future based on the reality that, for the most part, the peoples of the North and South share the same condition of being victims of the same counter-revolution that serves the interests of a global minority.

There is trauma and tension within the system and hunger, misery and deprivation, massive and intensive, are a vehicle for a painful awakening and fuelling of a convulsive demand for change. The advocacy of fundamental human rights begins with the bugle of justice summoning people to action. The jurisprudence of human rights removes the need for lawless violence

3 Walden Bello: *Dark Victory*, at page 71.

4 *Food First—Beyond the Myth of Scarcity*, page 502.

in securing a humane systemic transformation. The situation is volcanic. It may seem silent but is pregnant with discontent.

This explosive situation, now quiescent on the surface, may burst with a leonine roar when people awake to the contradiction between insatiable oligo-indulgence and unbearable proletarian pain. They have little to lose save their lives. May be, indignant opposition is muted by police power, but violent agitational movements are active beneath the surface and cannot be totally eclipsed. Boris Pasternak, in *Dr. Zhivago*, says: "History cannot be seen, just as one cannot see grass growing". Long ago, on 27th January 1848, Tocqueville, a Deputy, rose in the Chamber of Deputies. "They tell me that there is no danger because there are no disturbances", he said. "They say that as there is no visible perturbation on the surface of society, there are no revolutions beneath it. Gentlemen, allow me to say that I think you are wrong".

Disturbance is not abroad but it has laid hold of men's minds

As our decade declines, much of the South is relentlessly reaching a state of economic collapse, dashed by rising mass poverty and macro-hunger. By way of aside, one may notice, based on studies, that global hunger itself is, Big Business (vide "*Food First*"). Food dependencia syndrome, the raw slaves—new poor increase, and women and children in bonded labour and sex torture are harsh realities which are the engine of despair and eventual violence. Even the working class in the North, of course not so much as in the South, is vulnerable to the policy of economic rollback unleashed by the capitalism of the North, abusing its domination of the world economy, prising open markets in the South using its huge corporate hegemony. This vampirish process will cleave the new world order as surely as the Berlin Wall once divided East and West. Thus a grave contradiction is emerging as a result of which hot confrontations may shoot up in many countries. US military supremacy adds an aggressive dimension to this clash of forces. Once there was talk everywhere of equality and progress. Now there is a bleeding feeling of dread and despair in much of the Third World. Central to this bitter Southern desperation is the re-subordination of the South to the US dominated global economy on the basis of 'the new economic theology'. The rhetoric of Southern solidarity is losing its reality and we are on the threshold of a GATT-based WTO driven global economic domination escorted by American gendarmerie, as it were. In these circumstances, the old dreams of social justice are like Dead Sea fruit that tempts the eye but turns to ashes on the lips.

What is the relevance of the clashes of economic forces to the jurisprudence of human rights? We will investigate this matter in depth later. Suffice it to say, law is super-structure, economics the basic structure, and both together shape life's culture.

Marx hammered home his thesis that jurisprudence suffers from the dependencia syndrome, being but the janitor of the dominant class mansion. He said: "Your jurisprudence is but the will of your class made into a law for all, a will, whose essential character and direction are determined by the economical conditions of existence of your class .... (Manifesto of the Communist Party)".

I may be permitted to note that this was also adverted to by me, even when speaking judicially, for a Bench of the Supreme Court of India,[5] where I have pointed out that laws of a Country are, by and large, shaped and reshaped, structured and restructured to serve the interest of the ruling or the dominant class as "political philosophy and economic necessity of the dominant class animate legal theory".

It is plain dialectical materialism, applied to the current conditions of clashing opposites, that human rights for most of mankind will fall a casualty since the social, economic and cultural base has been broken. Varnished verbalism, dressed up in bombast, is in contrast to torturous realism, hidden in painted rhetoric. We must take human rights more seriously. Albert Einstein, in an Address in Chicago observed:

> "The existence and validity of human rights are not written in the stars. The ideals concerning the conduct of men toward each other and the desirable structure of the community have been conceived and taught by enlightened individuals in the course of history. Those ideals and convictions which resulted from historical experience, from the craving for beauty and harmony, have been readily accepted in theory by man—and at all times, have been trampled upon by the same people under the pressure of their animal instincts. A large part of history is therefore replete with the struggle for those human rights, a eternal struggle in which a final victory can never be won. But to tire in that struggle would mean the ruin of society".[6]

The South is bankrupt and the human condition is in peril. The dragon's teeth of communal-ethnic discord and savage wars destroy the joy of millions. Inhumanity's fires are stoked by supplies of arms by merchants of weapons and the US trade in military hardware, alongside of talking human rights politics, makes strange reading. Big Powers are brokers of peace and stokers of war and even the United Nations Security Council, on rare occasions though, plays bizarre rules of sanctioning military intervention under pressure and talking pious human rights ideology having buried 'Iraqi civilians' right to life. Former US Attorney General Ramsay Clark exposed this game by industrious investigation.

A world of non-violence and farewell to arms will promote a terror-free human rights-friendly society.

> "The escalation of the arms race and the cutbacks on social programs inevitably lead to a growth in the chronic mass unemployment, to aggravation of social inequality and discrimination, to the emergence of an army of 'new poor' and homeless.

5 *Rohtas Industries* case AIR 1976 SC 425 at 432.

6 Albert Einstein: *Ideas and Opinions*.

> "The real state of affairs as regards the rights and freedoms of citizens in the industrialized capitalist countries runs counter to the international norms that have been laid down in international covenants of human rights.
>
> "Meanwhile, when it comes to human rights issues, the official circles in those countries, above all in the US assume the role of an accuser or a judge in respect to the developing countries although they have no moral right or legal grounds to do so. Their claims to the role of umpire are dictated by their ambitions to interfere in the internal affairs of other countries and nations, to dictate orders to such countries and to use punitive sanctions. At the same time, by inflating the issue of human rights in the socialist countries, the ruling circles in the West are trying to divert world opinion not only from the violations of human rights in the west, but also from such crucial problems as that of ending the arms race and eliminating nuclear weapons.
>
> "The task of ensuring that human rights are observed throughout the world is connected to a very large degree to the task of ending the arms race, reducing excessive military budgets, and reallocating these funds to solve the urgent economic and social problems.
>
> "Today it has become especially clear that only by establishing a comprehensive system of international security and peace will the world be able to eliminate the danger threatening the most essential human right—the right to live without which all other rights are null and void".[7]

When the billion-strong poor have no political freedom to agitate for prime needs, when despair drives chunks of people to turn militant in defence of their right to live in dignity and equal opportunity, the State, controlled by the proprietariat, would seek to suppress the proletariat by arbitrary laws. Another line adopted is to release police terror, regardless of human rights legality. Institutional protection of victims of State violence is often inadequate and repressive organs and violent gangs revel in assaults on people's rights. Civilian morale slumps when the State itself takes sides. And courts look unperturbed at the harsh laws, however undemocratic or despotic they be, and basic freedoms become judicial casualty. The TADA, the MISA, the Emergency Laws *et al,* on which I will dwell later, are cases where lachrymations about breaches of human rights have found poor response and even brutal violations pass judicial scrutiny.

The third line, apart from reactionary statutes and misuse of State machinery, is the misinformation and disinformation methods the state adopts to conceal its crimes, official secrecy being a sanctuary for Government and ignorance of facts or their distortion being a tranquilliser for the public. Even parliaments are kept in the dark or suffer other handicaps. Truth has no chance when it is stifled at birth. Freedom of information is fundamental to fundamental freedoms. Absent the citizen's right to know, State tyranny revels unchecked.

7 *Human Rights in the Capitalist World* at p. 80.

The human essence fails to find expression under legalised repression. Society itself fails to protest or dissent if the right to know is gagged by secrecy of public officials. "A popular Government, without popular information or the means of acquiring it, is but a prologue to a farce or a tragedy; or perhaps both. Knowledge will forever govern ignorance; and a people who mean to be their own governors must arm themselves with the power which knowledge gives".[8]

The ensemble of social relations, which is no abstraction or mysticism but practical life and socialised humanity, is unable to manifest itself because the sources of information are frozen beyond common access and the voices of resistance are terrorised into muteness or corrupted into silence. So much so, human rights violations rarely reach public notice. The State and the laws, dominated by the offending class, are the upas tree under whose shade freedom fails and justice dies.

A brief reflection on the human person

Our vanishing century bears witness to the decadence of the human community. The brighter and darker sides of plan are projected in sharp contrast in *Hamlet* which I quote:

> "What a piece of work is a man! How noble in reason! how infinite in faculty! in form, in moving, how express and admirable! in action how like an angel! in apprehension how like a god! the beauty of the world! the paragon of animals!"

Under decadent conditions, (again quoting from *Hamlet*) "what is this quintessence of dust?". The earth itself, under sinister surroundings loses its lustre. Hamlet soliloquizes: "this goodly frame, the earth, seems to me a sterile promontory; this most excellent canopy, the air, look you, this brave overhanging firmament, this majestical roof fretted with golden fire, why, it appears no other thing to me but a foul and pestilent congregation of vapours". How graphic the glory of the human richness and how vicious the ecological disaster which has been inflicted on mother earth itself. This picture represents in brief the fate of human rights and the saga of progress suffered through history.

Why is law, the law of distributive justice and individual freedom, failing humanity? The answer is money, black money, if you like, the dazzle of sensuous splendour, the surrender to sensuous-sensual consciousness, the pleasure of indulgence and dependence on insatiable wealth, mindless of the many millions whose material and moral requirements count for nothing once the marijuana of money has enslaved the soul. A resurrection of values is needed urgently if humanity's obituary is not to be written right now. To be complacent is to be myopic.

At the bottom of the horrendous mischief which has produced ghastly contradictions in current economic conditions, especially after the

8 James Madison, President of the USA, 1822.

dismantlement of the Soviet Union, is the trinity of recipes propagandised world-wide. They are (*a*) 'market-friendly' visa for MNCs into any country of the South; (*b*) liberalisation of the national economy and liquidation of the public sector which as in India occupies commanding heights as desiderated by a Constitutional mandate to pursue people's policies as paramount items on the agenda of governance, and (*c*) globalisation, by which euphemism is meant global economic conquest by giant corporates without let or hindrance. The object of this powerful change, which the North is imposing on the South through the GATT and the IMF-World Bank Loans, is the predatory operations for which the G-7 countries, particularly the US Incorporated, are notorious. Consumerism of the affluent sector, gratification of the 'gold rush' community and the potential for plunder of native resources, in short, amassing wealth at any cost is the new world acquisitive order. Money-making is the primary goal and moral values became easy victims of insatiable greed. Man becomes poorer *as man*, judged by lasting values of life. Excess and intemperance spoil the moral fibre and a new estrangement of the person from his real being manifests itself through the restless pursuit of profits. Bestial barbarisation and debasing de-humanisation plague civilisation.

A synthesis that transcends the opposites and secures human rights on a firm moral-material basis is the relentless requirement of contemporary times. Human rights flourish only where the material base and cultural consciousness attain a supportive level; and they perish if prime human needs are shockingly neglected and war wears the apparel of peace. Economic justice with an egalitarian ethos is essential if peace and security are to prevail. Nationally and internationally, violence and savagery must surrender to honest peace if humanity were to find on earth a haven of work, wealth and happiness.

Gandhiji, an apostle of non-violence, wrote, long decades back, with passionate sincerity:

> "The contrast between the rich and the poor today is a painful sight......... A non-violent system of Government is clearly an impossibility so long as the wide gulf between the rich and hungry millions persists. The contrast between the palaces of New Delhi and the miserable hovels of the poor labouring class nearby, cannot last one day in a free India in which the poor will enjoy the same power as the richest in the land......... A violent and bloody revolution is a certainty one day, unless there is voluntary abdication of riches and the power that riches give and sharing them for the common good. ....
>
> "According to me, the economic constitution of India, and for the matter of that of the world, should be such that no one under it should suffer from want of food and clothing. In other words, everybody should be able to get sufficient work to enable him to make the two ends meet. And, this ideal can be universally realized only if the means of production of elementary necessaries of life remain under the control of the masses. These should be freely available to all as God's air and water are, or ought to be; they should not be made a

vehicle of traffic for the exploitation of others. Their monopolization by any country, nation or group of persons would be unjust".[9]

Green was Gandhian economics. Gandhi's economic *dharma*, which was basic to his jurisprudence, was, according to E. F. Schumacher, appropriate technology *where man mattered* and draining of the wealth of villages was arrested. Indeed, E. F. Schumacher once called Gandhi the greatest economist of the century. His economics must be transformed into jurisprudence where man and woman matter, fleshing out those principles into appropriate statutes. 'Small is beautiful' is the heart of his economics and of law because the small human has the rights of a human and cannot be drowned in oceanic mass production.

But the *Mahatma* is economic pariah and *goofy* primitive in a world where macro-profiteering and mega-consumerism seduce the soul of the *pro tem* leaders and cadres of the Third World. A battle for human rights Jurisprudence which actualises the richness of personhood is our priority. Development which diminishes the human being and exaggerates dehumanized technology with vast production potential and ghastly deserts of penury is a distortion of authentic human values. The Cocoyoc Declaration strikes the correct note:

> "The multiplication of material wealth has to be dethroned as the purpose of development. 'The goal of development should be not to develop things, but to develop man', says Cocoyoc. 'Development must be aimed at the spiritual, moral and material advancement of the whole human being, both as a member of society and from the point of view of individual fulfilment, says UNESCO.
>
> *** *** ***
>
> "The model of development as material growth gets most of its fuel from the Third World's desire to close the wealth gap with the West, in a possessions race almost as futile as the arms race. The Cocoyoc participants rejected the idea of gaps: The goal is not to catch up, but to ensure the quality of life for all".[10]

More than half a century later, the Delhi Declaration, signed by the then Prime Minister of India, the late Rajiv Gandhi, and the President of the then Soviet Union, Mikhail Gorbachev, proclaimed the need for a non-violent world order with stress on human values, not glittering commodities. Today, the rich revel in luxury, the poor, men, women and children are commoditised.

My submission is that the very right to be human is possible only if the universal basics of existence, material and moral, are preserved. Social justice is at once spiritual and material although it stands negated when a system amorally allows the right to rob or grab and leaves the weak and the meek, with unconcern, to die in neglect or live in starvation or slave

9 *Young India*, dated 15th November 1928.
10 Paul Harrison: *The Third World Tomorrow*, page 41.

condition. Hunger is the trigger of social revolution, and mass servitude is the RDX of creative rebellion. In his great book *The Grapes of Wrath*, John Steinbeck has a passage which expresses what oft was thought but never so well expressed:

> "The fields were fruitful, and starving men moved on the roads. The granaries were full and the children of the poor grew up rachitic, and the pustules of pellagra swelled on their side. The great companies did not know that the line between hunger and anger is a thin line".

All this proves the integral content of human rights, holistically viewed. Sensitive humanists telescope, not view in isolation, all facets of personhood, even if there may be variance in degrees of emphasis. Here springs the difference between socialist compassion and capitalist callousness. India is a Democratic Socialist Republic, not a regimented society or capitalist regime serving the proprietariat.

The human right to distributive justice, the freedom to unfold in full one's faculties and personhood, the assurance that the State will perennially process the socio-economic structures, with egalitarian emphasis, and never depart from the sovereign power of the people to shape their democratic destiny—these are the crimson imperatives of the Constitution. Great goals, hard tasks, but paramount undertaking: Rosa Luxemburg, the German Marxist, asserted that the choice of the West was between socialism and barbarism. Walden Bellow after quoting Rosa Luxemberg writes:

> "The world is confronted with a not dissimilar situation today. Barbarism stares us in the face in many guises—in clean-shaven techno-warriors who manage, from Washington, the death of hundreds of thousands in Middle Eastern battlefields that they experience as sanitized digital images in electronic monitors; in Christian Serbs who rape Muslim women *en masse* and depopulate Muslim villages in the name of ethnic cleansing, in neo-Nazi German Youth who burn down the homes of Turkish guest laborers; in French rightists who advocate mass deportation of undocumented Third World workers to preserve the 'purity' of French culture; in American fundamentalists who have declared moral and cultural war on blacks, Third World immigrants, the women's movement, and liberals in their pursuit of a mythical white Christian America".[11]
>
> "A non-violent world, necessarily requires democracy and socialism with a human soul. We need a system of social relations that checks or restrains the devastating logic of capitalism—at least, capitalism in its Anglo-American, free-market version—to sacrifice individual well-being, community, the environment, and even the long-term viability of the economy itself on the altar of short-term profitability".[12]

The socialist conception of human rights and freedoms radically differs from the ideas of Western liberalism. The former insists that real equality

11 Walden Bellow: *Dark Victory*, page 111.
12 *Ibid* at page 112.

and other freedoms cannot twinkle in the skies or be paper ideals, but must have firm social foundation and material milieu sufficient to confer reality on the exercise of these fundamentals in practice. Valentin Patyulin (USSR) dealing with human rights in socialist society, argues that individuals are free to exercise their fundamental rights only when they are free from exploitation and politico-economic oppression. Only then are the rights and freedoms of citizens not merely proclaimed on paper but are also legally guaranteed and ensured by the laws and moral standards of society, its structure and way of life.

> "Can there be real equality between, say, Henry Ford and his workers? Do the press tycoon Henry Luce and the black unemployed in Harlem have the same rights in the exercise of freedom of speech and the press? Certainly not. In a society where there is no equality in ownership of the means of production the will of one person always encroaches on that of another and the freedom of one means the submission of others."
>
> "As Lenin said, ... the slogan of freedom and equality is merely the lies and humbug of bourgeois society, whose formal recognition of freedom and equality conceals actual economic servitude and inequality for the workers, for all who toil and are exploited by capital, *i.e.* for the overwhelming majority of the population in all capitalist countries".[13]

The right to life, the foremost human right, cannot co-exist with extreme starvation or dreadful destitution. Bread! Bread! perorated Swami Vivekananda. Big business is blind to how the other half of humanity lives or dies; nor do they care or share.

From this perspective, a transformation of the social order is a condition for the enjoyment of human rights. Dr. Patyulin considers:

> "Socialism has proved that genuine, not illusory, individual freedom can be achieved only if society and the State consistently carry out a series of wide-ranging measures. It is not enough to proclaim freedom. What is vital is to provide conditions in which all can exercise it.
>
> *** *** ***
>
> "The right to work, to education, to maintenance in old age, to disability benefits and to free medical service made it possible for everyone really to exercise a whole number of social and political rights and liberties. As for the political freedoms—freedom of speech, of the press, of assembly, processions and demonstrations—the Soviet State not only made them into law, but also guaranteed them by nationalising the mass media such as publishing houses, radio stations, newspapers, magazines, recreation centres, etc. They came to belong to society as a whole and were used in its interest".[14]

It is not merely the Marxian view that human rights are hollow if material bases congenial for their enjoyment are absent for the vast masses.

13 *Human Rights in Socialist Society,* published by Novosti Press Agency Publishing House, Moscow, pages 7-8.

14 *Ibid,* at page 8 & 9.

As said even by Lyndon B. Johnson,

> "Freedom is not enough. You do not wipe away the scars of centuries by saying: Now you are free to go wherever you want, do as you desire ....
>
> "It is not enough just to open the gates of opportunity. All our citizens must have the ability to walk through these gates............We seek not just equality as a right and a theory but equality as a fact and as a result".[15]

Again, here is a quote from McNamara about Lyndon B. Johnson's views in a similar stream:

> "Johnson asked me to join him in a Cabinet Room meeting with business and labour leaders. He wished to obtain their support for the Civil Rights Bill. For an hour he pleaded with his guests to pressure their Congressmen to vote for the bill. He was making little progress. Finally, in total frustration, he said, 'Gentlemen, you all know Zephyr'—I doubt anyone in the room, besides me, knew she was the Johnson's 'long time black cook'. Last summer, as she, Bird, and I drove through Mississippi on our way back to Washington from the ranch, Bird said 'Lyndon, would you please stop at the next gas station? I want to relieve myself'. We did and then returned to the car and drove on for a while when Zephyr said 'Mr. President, would you mind stopping by the side of the road?' Why do you want to stop? I asked. 'I want to relieve myself'. 'Why the hell didn't you do it at that gas station when Bird and I did?' 'Cause they wouldn't let me' she replied. Pounding the table, LBJ in a bitter voice said 'Gentleman is that the kind of a country you want?' Some will say, it was theater. I know it was not."[16]

And now reference may be made to *The Declaration of the Warsaw Treaty Countries* in 1978 as hereunder:

> "The very emergence of the new social system is linked with the striving to translate into reality the principal human right, the right to a dignified existence without exploitation, and to pave the way for the all-round development of the individual. The banner of human rights and freedoms is the banner of socialism".[17]

These radically differing approaches apart, there are flaws in both systems if capitalist privations and socialist regimentations make fundamental freedoms anaemic and frail. A unitive understanding through human rights holism is necessary.

The integrity of the different categories of human rights and peoples' rights is best brought out in the comprehensive Preamble to the *African Charter on Human and Peoples' Rights*. The relevant portion is excerpted here:

> "Recognizing on the one hand, that fundamental human rights stem from the attributes of human beings, which justifies their international protection and

15 Lyndon B. Johnson: *Address to Howard University*, 4th June 1965.

16 McNamara: *In Retrospect*, pages 199-200.

17 The Declaration of the Warsaw Treaty Countries adopted at a meeting of their Political Consultative Committee held in Moscow on 23rd November 1978.

on the other hand, that the reality and respect of peoples' rights should necessarily guarantee human rights;

"Considering that the enjoyment of rights and freedoms also implies the performance of duties on the part of everyone;

"Convinced that it is henceforth essential to pay particular attention to the right to development and that civil and political rights cannot be dissociated from economic, social and cultural rights in their conception as well as universality and that the satisfaction of economic, social and cultural rights is a guarantee for the enjoyment of civil and political rights".

Implementation of these fundamentals including ecological and environmental essentials demands the creation of structures, courts, ombudsman, access to remedial jurisdictions, enquiry commissions, legally recognised social action groups and educative projects.

Food First, a book, reading which is a *must,* argues from the American angle:

"Many people here and in other countries are asking, and, moreover, are actively working to build such social structures. There is no more important work today than explaining this to people in countries like our own. Before they would work for change they have to believe that change is possible, that a culture fixated on individual profit-seeking alone is not 'natural'. The tragedy is that we have had to reach the point where so many people are hungry and malnourished, including millions here at home, before we could begin to see that our system—a system built on the vulnerabilities of the human personality instead of its strengths—can never create a human society.

"Finally, we must not allow our appropriate sense of urgency to lead to frustration and despair. It took centuries to create the structures that cause the worldwide deprivation we now witness. It will take time to construct a human world. That does not belittle our task; that makes it all the more important. Our personal time frames have changed. We must come to understand today's struggle in light of the entire scope of human history. We must not limit our vision by what we see around us today. What we see today may tell us little about what our children and their children are capable of creating".[18]

A New Hunger-free Human Order alone can bring peace, security and freedom.

The composite cultural heritage of humanity, viewed from the socialist or capitalist angle or materialist or spiritual perspective, convinces us that in every individual and group there is an irreducible and non-negotiable presence which we may call human rights. Indeed, considered from the individual or collective approaches, we come to the conclusion that in every civilized society, human rights are an enduring reality. The ideas and ideologies of human rights have engaged mankind from ancient times but have assumed great importance in our times. Social activists and avant-garde

18 *Food First,* page 503.

jurists, spiritual leaders and world statesmen agree that human rights are indivisible even as peace and social justice are integral. A holistic study of this trinity is, to my understanding, of supreme significance to the contemporary world order and global jurisprudence. A broad semantic generosity persuades me to the universal concept of Herbert Spencer:

> *"No one can be perfectly free till all are free;*
> *"no one can be perfectly moral till all are moral;*
> *"no one can be perfectly happy till all are happy".*

A fragmented planet, warring within itself and maddening in an insatiable race for pleasure and more pleasure at the expense of the other, can never be serene, secure or stable. Pathological insensitivity makes for a savage world order where human rights ideology is a stranger. So, let us build a brave new system. Imagine the toll of starvation today: A Hiroshima every three days:

> "We have numbed ourselves so that we do not feel the pain. We have to be asleep in order to protect ourselves from the horror of knowing that twenty-eight people, most of them young children, are dying this very minute—twenty-eight people no different from you or me or our children, except that we had food and they do not".
>
> "We have closed down our consciousness and aliveness to a level where it doesn't bother us. So if you wonder if it costs us anything to allow millions to starve, it does. It costs us our aliveness".[19]

Turn for a moment to the lawless, callous terrorist situation even in India, Gandhi's country: The *Mahatma,* more than three score years ago, painted what is a perennial pathology of Third World countries:

> "If you were to go into the interior, outside the railway track; you will find, as I have found, that the villages are being reduced to dung-heaps, the villagers are not there—vultures are to be seen—because they could not support themselves, and were reduced to carcasses.
>
> "The poor sisters of Orissa have no *saris;* they are in rags yet they have not lost all sense of decency; but I assure you, we have. We are naked in spite of our clothing and they are clothed in spite of their nakedness".[20]

The people's plight is still the same, the numbers who are shelterless, starving, naked and illiterate and victimised being a shame. Yes, there is "growth without justice", five-star mansions and ill-starred millions. India is ranked in the UN Report low in human development. Let me cite a review of the Report for emphasis:

> "The latest Human Development Report, published annually by the United Nations Development Programme, shows that India's social indicators remain a poor comparison with those of South-East Asia and China. The large gap in

19 Morilyn Ferguson: *The Aquarian Conspiracy,* pages 455-456.
20 M.K. Gandhi: *Socialism of My Conception,* pages 108-109.

development indices shows that India has a lot more catching up to do in the social domain compared to its competitors.

"In estimating the human development index, which is a measure of the average achievement of a country in basic human capabilities, the report places India (rank 134) well below China (111) and other countries in South-East Asia. Vietnam (120) is closest to India's ranking, followed by Indonesia (104), Philippines (100), Malaysia (59) and Thailand (58) next in the pecking order.

"When it comes to such basic indicators as the adult literacy level or the infant mortality rate, India is way behind South-East Asia and China.

"India's infant mortality rate (deaths of infants under one year of age per thousand live birth) is a high 82, compared to a low of 13 for Malaysia."

*** *** ***

"Another indicator where India is low down on the list is literacy levels, with half the population unlettered.

"Similarly, when it comes to the percentage of underweight children under age five, India is the worst performer in the group. In fact, at 63 per cent this country has the dubious distinction of having the highest per cent of underweight children in the world, next only to Bangladesh(66 per cent). But when it comes to the percentage of pregnant women aged 15-49 with anaemia, India's figure (88 per cent, which is the worst in the world) makes depressing reading."[1]

The escalating injustice of tragic moment faced by mankind today and the paramount priority of human rights on the universal agenda, are part of the militant manifesto of humanity as a whole. The cultural chronicle of humankind from early days to current times is a saga of blood and tears from age to age.

The commonalty, bleeding with wounds of deprivation, holds aloft the flag of human rights. The moving figure of human fury writes and having writ moves on to defend the finer faith in fundamental human rights, in the dignity and worth of the human person, in the equal rights of men and women in the process of social progress and better standards of rights in larger freedom.

And twenty (or sixty?) million innocent kids are daily forced to labour and robbed of their shining morning phase of life. What a shame and shock!

The World War and after

Global humanity, brutally victimised and stunned by the horror and terror of the World War catastrophe, began to think of defending the billions of humans by ending the bleeding battles and creating the United Nations by an impregnable Charter, inscribing indefeasible freedoms as the fundamental condition for civilised, peaceful and dignified life for every

1 *The Economic Times,* dated 29th August 1996.

member of the human race and every nation on earth, big or small. But—what an illusory but!:—wars, international or internecine, did not die out, nay, even bled the peoples through terrible conflicts, suppressed and massacred innocent civilians and violated viciously every sacred of good life, and made our dear and only planet the ghastly theatre of countless killings and unspeakable cruelties. However, human rights assassinated by Hitler's hordes once, have begun to rise again in search of fresh expression; new instruments are striving for functional revival involving, educating, and sensitizing the vast human brotherhood in a struggle to reassert values. Human history, today, in a graver mood and more macabre measure than H.G. Wells, in his *Outline of History*, meant, becomes more and more a race between education and catastrophe. The future of homo sapiens, what with frequent military threats and gluttonous and corrupt corporate deals and disrupting our biosphere, demands a creative cultural revolution and commands a cosmic systemic commitment to human rights. The MN Cs noxiously operating for profits unlimited must realise that when the deluge comes or vast desertification spreads and massive convulsions consume peace and order there will be no oasis to shelter, no Noah's Ark to survive, no human haven as refuge from annihilation. Bertrand Russell, Albert Einstein, Mahatma Gandhi, great statesmen with vision and finest thinkers with compassion have been worried about the appalling universal drift, from despair to where? Expectations are withering, anxieties are mounting, dreadful prospects are aggravating and disaster is looming.

Politico-economic contradictions, escalating with each passing day, crowd out true harmony and happiness and flowering of human personhood. In the name of Peace, War is waged. In the name of Democracy, Moneyocracy dominates. In the name of plenty, worldwide monopoly multinationals plunder oil and natural resources, create scarcity, shoot down distributive justice, blashpheme socialism, pollute air, water, morality and humanity. In the name of food abundance and green revolution, the spectre of starvation and disease stalk the continents. The global garden of joy, within the grasp of socially sensitized science and humanitarian technology, is turned into a graveyard of privation for the many and profit plus pleasure for Corporate Power. With specific reference to India, gender injustices, juvenile abuse, starvation deaths are a spectre that haunts our land. And what a shame that even in 1996 the right to dignity of Indian women is defiled and there is prevalence of head-load scavenging and carrying night soil—a degrading occupation against which the National Human Rights Commission has remonstrated in a report to the Central Government.

By contrast, look at what the Centre has done to *daridranarayana* India's yuppie counterpart. The latest trends in the consumerist range of our economy, under the new dispensation, is the vulgar proliferation of the pub and disco culture in every city. Wads of notes from bastard nidi are everywhere in the glittering shops and glamoure houses. Says a recent write-up:

"The latest manifestations of the trend are even more dumbfounding. We hear that among the new cars coming into the wide open land of India is Rolls Royce, the mother of all luxury cars. This is priced at the mother of all prices—rupees one crore a car, give or take a few lakhs. What's more impressive is the report that about 50 advance orders have already been booked from Indian customers.

"If that doesn't impress you, be informed that Cartier has just announced plans to open exclusive boutiques in Bombay and Delhi followed no doubt by other metros. The legend is that Cartier sells jewellery. The fact is that Cartier sells snob-value. And its sales manager discovered that India is the country where snob value has the largest appeal. (Remember, India is the only country in the world where car prices are fixed on the basis of what the market will take, that it to say, how much Indian snobs are prepared to pay). That was the secret of Maruti's success. When a plebian thing like Maruti sets the pace, can a patrician attraction like Cartier be far behind? Manmohan Singh allowed what the snob market demands: blanket permission to import watches and solid gold jewellery. The result is that you can now walk into a shop in Delhi and walk out with a watch that costs seventy-seven lakhs of rupees while your girlfriend takes a necklace worth three crores of rupees".[2]

In the name of tourism and reckless industrialisation, our moral order, and eco-environmental system suffer trauma. Wounded nature will avenge the human future. Our natural resources and wealth of bio-diversity are robbed–ask Dr. Vandana Shiva. Our streams are polluted, our air contaminated and our soil is a picture of noxiousness. 'Development' has become a dangerous word because every macro-size project means corruption for the operators and displacement for vast human numbers. The MN Cs have an interest in mega-projects and in consumer business.

The technology of bribery is a sister industry with an intimate ministerial story.

Our girls and their morals are in danger through the vulgarisation of the tourist industry, destitution making prostitution their last refuge.

What prompts me, seeing that everything about human rights is becoming a losing battle, is to respond to the summons of the invisible and enormous human numbers at least by delivering these lectures on the untold story of the ignored Indian. A few lines from *Hamlet* poignantly project my motivation in taking up the theme of the forsaken.

"If thou didst ever hold me in thy heart,
Absent thee from felicity awhile,
And in this harsh world draw thy breath in pain
To tell my story".

Again, another moving spirit has influenced me to take up this cause. Vivekananda's stirring call has a compelling echo from within me and so

2 *Gentleman,* April 1996, pages 12, 13.

I cannot be silent. He exhorts (and I listen) that the wretched of the Indian earth shall be invested with socio-economic rights. His flaming words are volcanic:

> "Do you feel? Do you feel that millions and millions of the descendants of gods and of sages have become next-door neighbours to brutes? Do you feel that millions are starving today, and millions have been starving for ages? Do you feel that ignorance has come over the land as a dark cloud? Does it make you restless? Does it make you sleepless? Has it gone into your blood coursing through your veins, becoming constant with your heart-beats? Has it made you almost mad? Are you seized with that one idea of the misery of ruin, and have you forgotten all about your name, your fame, your wives, your children, your property, even your own bodies? Have you done that? That is the first step to become a patriot, the very first step".

These sombre fears and culpable failures are the *raison d'etre* of the broad rubric on human rights in India as worthy of becoming a proper subject for my Lectures. So it is that I have decided to spread the spectrum of my Tagore Law Lectures.

We belong to the land of *ahimsa*, of non-violence and reverence for each other. The Declaration signed by Prime Minister, Rajiv Gandhi and President Mikhail Gorbachev pledges this:

> "The world we have inherited belongs to present and future generations and this demands that primacy be given to universally accepted human values. The right of every nation and every person to life, freedom, peace and the pursuit of happiness must be recognised. The use or threat of use of force must be abandoned. The right of every people to make their own social, political and ideological choices must be respected. Policies that seek to establish domination by some over other must be renounced. The expansion of nuclear arsenals and the development of space weapons undermine the universally accepted conviction that a nuclear war should never be fought and can never be won.
>
> *** *** ***
>
> "2. Human life must be recognised as supreme:
>
> It is only man's creative genius that makes progress and development of civilisation possible in a peaceful environment.
>
> "3. Non-violence should be the basis of community life:
>
> Philosophies and policies based on violence and intimidation, inequality and oppression and discrimination on the basis of race, religion or colour, are immoral and inadmissible. They spread intolerance, destroy man's noble aspirations and negate all human values.
>
> *** *** ***
>
> "5. The right of every State to political and economic independence must be recognised and respected:
>
> *** *** ***

"6. Resources being spent on armaments must be channelled towards social and economic development.

*** *** ***

"8. Mankind's material and intellectual potential must be used to solve global problems:

> Solutions must be found to global problems such as shortage of food, the growth of population, illiteracy and environmental degradation through the efficient and appropriate uses of the resources of the earth. The world's oceans, the ocean floor as well as outer space are the common heritage of mankind. A termination of the arms race would create better conditions for the purpose.

*** *** ***

> "The danger that threatens mankind is grave. But mankind has the power to prevent a catastrophe, and to pave the way to a nuclear-weapon-free-civilisation. The gathering strength of the Coalition for Peace, embracing the efforts of the Non-Aligned Movement, "the Six-Nation Five-Continent Initiative for Peace and Disarmament", all peace-loving countries, political parties and public organisations give us reason for hope and optimism. The time for decisive and urgent action is now".[3]

And yet brutal violence and sensual excess are exalted or exonerated if duly covered by wealth or political clout. My friend and eminent jurist Soli, J. Sorabjee in Besant Lecture (1992) bemoans the Indian scene:

> "The national scene is no less depressing. Violence seems to stalk the land of *ahimsa*. What has happened in Surat, rape of women after they were dragged onto the streets and video recording of this by the rapists and their accomplices is the bottom line in depravity. Innocent young and old are killed mercilessly by militants supposed to be espousing a noble cause. A religious place is demolished in the name of religion and there is jubilation over this deplorable incident. The mafia rules in Bombay, and rival gang members are killed in broad daylight with impunity. I ask myself and I ask you what is the reason for this outburst of violence, which is becoming a pattern?
>
> "As far as I can see there is more than one reason. In the first place, respect of human life has disappeared. Human life is no longer considered precious; human beings are measured in terms of mass and molecules, forgetting that there is a spiritual spark inherent in every human being and the Divine resides in the heart of everyone. Wrong doing no more seems wrong".

Sorabjee's diagnosis of the malady meets with my concurrence. Compassion is the missing element and corruption is the corroding factor. Human rights die where feeling for life fails. The need for universal fellow-feeling flows from Emily Dickinson's lines:

> *"If I can stop one heart from breaking*
> *I shall not live in vain.*

3 *Delhi Declaration*, dated 27th November 1986.

If I can ease one life the aching or cool one pain
Or help one fainting robin unto its nest again
I shall not live in vain".

Is mankind doomed to privation, destitution and obliteration of human credentials and indwelling divinity? Will the earth be a value enriched garden of human fulfilment for each inhabitant or a horrendous graveyard of human rights with blood and sweat, toil and tears and desertification of that reverence and love and opportunity for development and self-determination, personal and groupwise, which hallows our dear planet as a hospitable home for the whole human family to live in peace and justice? Fifty years after the United Nations sprang to life and nearly half a century since India attained independence have we, the world's heirs, lost the title to universal human rights and the democracy of social justice in its wide sense? Or are we keeping alive and active the fundamental freedoms and dignity and worth of the human person on the luminous agenda of our darkling decadent decade? If we struggle together, the prospect is promising, even with all the ominous signs depressing our hopes and the global power structure operating repressively. Remember, if determined campaigns relentlessly persist, for sure, after the final no, there comes a yes: And on that yes, the future of the world depends.

The earth, our habitat, has resources to create a paradise here. This prospect, with the benevolence of science, would have made life for each a rich heritage. Nature is so gentle, so lovely, so like a crimson flower. But man, greedy man, is a vicious worm. What follows when the worm creeps inside?

That beautiful rose is sicklied and lost.

"O Rose, thou art sick:
The invisible worm
That flies in the night,
In the howling storm,
Has found out thy bed
Of crimson joy:
And his dark secret love
Does thy life destroy".

A glimpse of the past

Ancient days and later ages, with miseries and savageries sprinkled over centuries in many countries, had nevertheless a laudable humanitarian motif. I do not overlook the spells of barbarity but emphasis the ethos of compassion and spirit of justice which enlightened the culture of peoples. The *Rig Veda* is the oldest hymn which speaks of tolerance, unitive perception of divinity and welfare of mankind. One of the texts is illustrative:

"Let noble thoughts come to us from every side".[4]

4 *The Rig Veda*, 1.89.

The grand infusion of noble values and *dharmic* principles as integral to good governance is best exemplified, not merely by the Buddha who renounced the pleasures of a prince's throne and searched for the solution of human sorrows and offered *karuna* (compassion), *samata* (egalite), *prajna* (discernment). On conversion to Buddhism, Emperor Ashoka, gave shape, in indelible rock pillars, the finest juristic principles:

Let me quote Asoka's Rock Edict XII:

> "King Priyadarsi honours men of all faiths, members of religious orders and laymen alike.........Yet he does not value either gifts or honours as much as growth in the qualities essential to religion in men of all faiths.
>
> "This growth may take many forms, but its root is in guarding one's speech to avoid extolling one's own faith and disparaging the faith of others improperly or, when the occasion is appropriate, immoderately.
>
> "The faiths of others all deserve to be honoured for one reason or another; by honouring them, one exalts one's own faith and at the same time performs a service to the faith of others. By acting otherwise, one injures one's faith and also does disservice to the faith of others. If a man extols his own faith and disparages another because of devotion to his own faith, because he wants to glorify it, he seriously injures his own faith.
>
> Therefore concord alone is commendable, for through concord men may learn and respect the concept of *Dharma* accepted by others".

H.G. Wells writes of him:

> "Amidst the tens of thousands of names of monarchs that crowd the columns of history, their majesties and graciousnesses and serenities and royal highnesses and the like, the name of Asoka shines, and shines almost alone, a star. From the Volga to Japan his name is still honoured. China, Tibet, and even India, though it has left his doctrine, preserve the tradition of his greatness. More living men cherish his memory today than have ever heard the names of Constantine or Charlemagne".[5]

Like Emperor Ashoka there was another, Emperor Akbar who also was very liberal in the matter of freedom of faith and religion and importance to education and culture. These are the basics of human rights culture, rare in the medieval times, rarer in our century as the middle east and other parts of the world demonstrate. I may drive home my point about Akbar and his regard for the worth of human person by quoting H.G. Wells whose objectivity is an advantage in assessment. Says Wells:

> "Akbar's distinctive quality was his openness of mind. He set himself to make every sort of able man in India, whatever his race or religion, available for the public work of Indian life. His instinct was the true statesman's instinct for synthesis. His empire was to be neither a Moslem nor a Mongol one, nor was it to be Rajput or Aryan, or Dravidian, or Hindu, or high or low caste; it was to

5 H.G. Wells: *The Outline of History*, 8th Ed., page 402.

be Indian". "During, the years of his training he enjoyed many opportunities of noting the good qualities, the fidelity, the devotion, often the nobility of soul, of those Hindu princes, whom, because they were followers of *Brahma*, his Moslem courtiers devoted mentally to eternal torments. He noted these men, and men who thought like them, constituted the vast majority of his subjects. He noted, further, of many of them, and those the most trustworthy, that though they had apparently much to gain from a worldly point of view by embracing the religion of the court they held fast to their own. His reflective mind, therefore, was unwilling from the outset to accept the theory that because he, the conqueror, the ruler, happened to be born a Muhammadan, therefore, Muhammadanism was true for all mankind. Gradually his thoughts found words in the utterance: 'Why should I claim to guide men before I myself am guided?' And, as he listened to other doctrines and other creeds, his honest doubts became confirmed, and, noting daily the bitter narrowness of sectarianism, no matter of what form of religion, he became more and more wedded to the principle of toleration for all."

"In all seriousness he devoted himself to the work of peace. Moderate in all pleasures, needing but little sleep and accustomed to divide his time with the utmost accuracy, he found leisure to devote himself to science and art after the completion of his State duties".[6]

The current decadence

From that pinnacle of humanist jurisprudence of Ashoka, the glorious Periclean era and Justinian's rule and the reverence for human rights by Imam Ali, *et al*, we have descended, in our own century and decade, to monstrous depths of inequality and debasement. Today, the technological situation which has dehumanised homo sapiens is best brought out from the following quotes:

"The computer 'replaces' man, while automation 'relieves' him of the need to take a direct hand in material production. Where then is the place of man himself? What happens to him? In the age of electronics and informatics, computers and robots, capitalism just makes new millions of people redundant. Redundancy afflicted not only the youth, not only the unskilled labour, it affects those who only recently considered themselves to be irreplaceable, e.g. draftsmen, designers, highly skilled assembly workers, welders, and workers of other trades, which have become unnecessary. A new term has been coined, 'the new poor', meaning those who recently listed themselves among the 'middle class', with roof over their heads and well-paid jobs, but who lost all overnight, joining the ranks of the 'traditionally poor'.

"The rich grow richer, the poor, poorer still—such is one of the inevitable consequences of scientific and technological progress in modern capitalist society.

"The naive notions of scientific and technological progress being an irresistible force pushing society upward the ladder of social progress gave way to more cautious attitudes to the potentialities of science and technology.

6 H.G. Wells: *The Outline of History*, 8th Ed., pages 721 and 722.

More than that, it became clear that they could bring about not only the deliverance of humanity from many maladies of modern civilization, but plunge it into the vortex or calamities and disasters capable of blotting out the entire history of mankind.

"Achievements of biotechnology make it possible to solve the acute food problem, create miraculous medicines, wipe out lethal diseases and tap new sources of energy. But here, too, there is an alternative. Development of biological and chemical weapons from which there will be no escape, manipulation of man's consciousness by means of special psychotropic preparations, and creation of zombies ready to obey the evil genius—all this is not the nightmarish fantasies of the sick mind or images created by monster films. All this is quite feasible if the results of modern biotechnology are put to inhuman uses. Hunger, war, droughts and floods, a direct threat to man's physical and spiritual world—these are also possible implications of the development of science and technology".[7]

Will Durant has described this pernicious portent from a philosopher's angle, and I am sure humane jurists and statesmen must feel like him, as a value debasement and spiritual decline. I quote him to drive home the urgency of the Manifesto of the Human Person:

"Human conduct and belief are now undergoing transformations profounder and more disturbing than any since the appearance of wealth and philosophy put an end to the traditional religion of the Greeks. It is the age of Socrates again: our moral life is threatened, and our intellectual life is quickened and enlarged, by the disintegration of ancient customs and beliefs. Everything is new and experimental in our ideas and our actions; nothing is established or certain any more. The rate, complexity, and variety of change in our time are without precedent, even in Periclean days; all forms about us are altered, from the tools that complicate our toil, and the wheels that whirl us restlessly about the earth, to the innovations in our sexual relationships, and the hard disillusionment of our souls. The passage from agriculture to industry, from the village to the town, and from the town to the city, has elevated science, debased art, liberated thought, ended monarchy and aristocracy, generated democracy and socialism, emancipated woman, disrupted marriage, broken down the old moral code, destroyed asceticism with luxuries, replaced Puritanism with Epicureanism, exalted excitement above content, made war less frequent and more terrible, taken from us many of our most cherished religious beliefs, and given us in exchange a mechanical and fatalistic philosophy of life. All things flow, and we are at a loss to find some mooring and stability in the flux.

"From this confusion the one escape worthy of a mature mind is to rise out of the moment and the part, and contemplate the whole. What we have lost above all is total perspective. Life seems too intricate and mobile for us to grasp its unity and significance; we cease to be citizens and become only individuals; we have no purposes that look beyond our death; we are fragments of men and

7 G. Marinko: *What is the Scientific and Technological Revolution*, pages 29, 30, 31.

> nothing more. Everyone knows his part, but is ignorant of its meaning in the play. Life itself grows meaningless, and become empty just when it seemed most full".[8]

Human deliverance needs a liberative jurisprudence, a dynamic public law with a power to resist evil and promote good. The philosophy of law and legal philosophy must organise Operation Transformation in this dimension.

I have wandered, drifted, divagated and, in melancholy strain unveiled my thoughts. I have done it for a purpose. Not that I am a chronic pessimist. No, I have, like many of my generation, been influenced by Bertrand Russell, that rebellious teller of truth, in my world view. Let me quote from his autobiography to prove his undying optimism and warm humanism:

> "The everyday world presses in upon the philosopher and his ivory tower begins to crumble. The future of mankind more and more absorbs my thoughts. I grew up in the full flood of Victorian Optimism, and although the easy cheerfulness of that time is no longer possible, something remains with me of the hopefulness that then was easy. It is now no longer easy. It demands a certain fortitude and a certain capacity to look beyond the moment to a more distant future. But I remain convinced, whatever dark times may lie before us, that mankind will emerge, that the habit of mutual forbearances, which now seems lost, will be recovered and that the reign of brutal violence will not last forever. Mankind has to learn some new lessons of which the necessity is due to increase of skill without increase of wisdom. Moral and intellectual requirements are inextricably intertwined. Evil passions make men incapable of seeing the truth, and false beliefs afford excuses for evil passions. If the world is to emerge, it requires both clear thinking and kindly feeling. It may be that neither will be learned except through utmost disaster. I hope this is not the case. I hope that something less painful can teach wisdom. But by whatever arduous road, I am convinced that the new wisdom which the new world requires will be learned sooner or later, and that the best part of human history lies in the future, not in the past".[9]

This rationalist sage with prophetic prescience wrote prefatory words to his autobiography which fill my soul with a flood of feelings:

> "It is likely that I shall die before the issue is decided—
>
> I do not know whether my last words should be:
>
> *The bright day is done*
> *And we are for the dark,*
> *Or, as I sometimes allow myself to hope,*
> *The world's great age begins anew,*
> *The golden years return......*
> *Heaven smiles, and faiths and empires gleam,*
> *Like wrecks of a dissolving dream.*

8 Will Durant: *The Pleasures of Philosophy,* pages ix, x.
9 Bertrand Russell: *Adaptation, An Autobiographical Epitome,* page 265.

> "I have done what I could to add my small weight in an attempt to tip the balance on the side of hope, but it has been a puny effort against vast forces.
>
> "May others succeed where my generation failed"

This great man, Bertrand Russell, was a thorough-going humanist and the world's defender against war, particularly Nuclear war. When the Cuban crisis reached frightening fury, alarming the world that a war between America and Russia might break out at any minute, this sage crusader alerted mankind about the grave catastrophe which would inevitably be visited on the human race if the intimidatory atomic war was not somehow inhibited or interdicted. His deep concern is evident from his book '*Unarmed Victory*' where he writes passionately:

> "During the days of 24 and 25 October, those who had knowledge and imagination went through an anxious time. It seemed probable that, at any minute, war between America and Russia would break out and would involve, in all likelihood, the extinction of the human race. If you had private affections, if you had children or grandchildren for whom you loved, you could expect their death in the coming week. Within this brief period of time, there would cease to be any to enjoy the poetry of Shakespeare, the music of Bach or Mozart, the genius of Plato or Newton. All the slow building up of civilization in art and science and beauty would be at an end—forever, so far as this planet is concerned. If you spoke of these things to your friends, they said: But, surely, you can understand the great issues involved. Is the world to be governed by godless Communists (or, alternatively, capacious Capitalists)? Is it not your duty to die for the right, without regard for whatever loss may be entailed? And so the great march towards disaster went on. I asked myself if there were no sane men in the seats of power. At the last possible moment, the answer came: Yes, there was one sane man. It happened that he was on the side of Russia. This was an unimportant accident. His sanity saved the world; and you and I still exist".[10]

The peril to the planet's inhabitant pressured his conscience to intervene, to arrest a nuclear war. There is no doubt, today as in his day, that the destructive power of nuclear weapons could sentence to death the entire global population. The conviction that humanity had a title to a universe of happiness, drove Russell to appeal to the nations of the earth to ban nuclear war and save coming generations.

This passion for human rights burning within the bosom of Bertrand Russell had always inspired me towards a human rights crusade.

My powerful feelings towards human rights, when recollected in tranquillity overflow and seek impassioned expression in the countenance of law and justice.

All that I had said above, like lowing cattle meandering through the meadows at sunset time, is a mental march towards my theme.

10 Bertrand Russell: *Unarmed Victory*, (Penguin Books), page 7.

Here is the noetic nidus of my choice, the reason for the selection of the subject for the Tagore Law Lectures. The Cosmos is in chaos. Independent nations are falling a prey to 'recolonisation' under pressure from various groups with exploitative tactics, using chameleon-like politico-economic colours to suit the country, context and appetite of the ambitious classes and the business community. With Jesus of Nazareth on the Cross and Barabbas, the robber, exonerated, our global system is symbolic of the Barabbasque Order where human rights in their meaningful content, are eclipsed and robbers and traders flourish with the law duly drugged and justice put to slumber.

The broad-brush lines drawn on the global canvas as indicated above induced me to consider the Jurisprudence of human rights as a sensitive subject for my Lectures. It has burning contemporary relevance, embraces justice in all its dimensions but is too vast to be covered by a single lecture series. Moreover, Indian public law, in its human rights vistarama, may be country-specific, if reified and vivified and regarded from its early roots and modern metamorphosis. Human rights have a universal, spiritual base and material superstructure, an absolute minimum and relativist diversities. It struck me that the burgeoning jurisprudence of human rights, viewed from the dialectical angle and dynamic developments may aptly fit my solemn commission for the Lecture series and my conscientious mission of advancing, through the rule of law and system of justice, the dearest cause of humanity—the right to be human, the title to be divine and the defence of peace and harmony in the critical times when a pride of super-power lions, aided by native power-brokers roar 'human rights' but suppress, by overt and covert stratagems, peoples' claims for a just social order enriched by a comprehensive regime of human rights.

So now the subject that falls for consideration is *The Dialectics and Dynamics of Human Rights in India, Yesterday, Today and Tomorrow.*

The concept of human rights is multidimensional but is, equally emphatically, unitive. We murder to dissect, says Wordsworth. Life has an integrity. The right to be human in the global fraternity has a wholeness which suffers if we isolate parts and view pieces. In our time, a magnificent manifesto of the person is being written. The finer focus is on unfoldment of the human being who occupies the centre-stage. Currently, mankind is drifting towards savagery in its dreaded terror and horror. The time has arrived to overcome the crisis by a shift towards a refined, humane paradigm and to convert a destructive into an instructive and luminous world community. The current pathology is our curative opportunity. For sure, this struggle for liberation of the human person will confront political and economic monsters who hold mankind to ransom and say no, in many ways no, to the inauguration of the new age of universal *nirvana* on earth.

My Tagore Law Lectures are part of a perennial chase for that elusive goal where democracy and human rights, in mellifluous confluence, flow all over the globe. For the nonce, my emphasis is on India, against the backdrop of Asia and the international community.

The Indian particularisation in my Lecture notwithstanding, it is indubitable that, transcending geography and history, the international community has vital stakes in human rights everywhere. It is the heritage of humanity and without it, in its quintessence, life left is not fully human life. The progressive march of civilisation is measured by the *quantum* and quality of human rights won through several battles waged over centuries, moving zigzag, and arriving at the present prestigious status which, if actualised as a tremendous achievement of that collective body, in its immensity, described in the dazzling vocabulary of the Charter of the United Nations as "WE THE PEOPLES OF THE UNITED NATIONS". As a starting point of the discussion it may be appropriate to quote the Preamble to the great Charter which expresses the determination:

> "to save succeeding generations from the scourge of war, which twice in our life-time has brought untold sorrow to mankind, and
>
> to reaffirm faith in fundamental human rights, in the dignity and worth of the human person, in the equal rights of men and women and of nations large and small, and
>
> to establish conditions under which justice and respect for the obligations arising from treaties and other sources of international law can be maintained, and
>
> to promote social progress and better standards of life in large freedom.
>
> AND FOR THESE ENDS
>
> to practice tolerance and live together in peace with one another as good neighbours, and
>
> to unite our strength to maintain international peace and security, and
>
> to ensure, by the acceptance of principle and the institution of methods, that armed force shall not be used, save in the common interest, and
>
> to employ international machinery for the promotion of the economic and social advancement of all peoples".

The material and spiritual bases of society, to a large extent, condition the success and failure of human rights. It needs no mention because it is obvious that war is the greatest enemy of human rights, be it at the local or global level. In this context, Art. 1 of the UN Charter, which outlines purposes and principles of this global body has fundamental significance and operational amplitude. Human rights in India or Asia or, for that matter, beyond our Continent will be an edifice built on shifting sands unless, as Art. 1 stresses, international peace and security and removal of threats thereto, are considered a matter of high priority. Breach of the peace, at the international level or internally, can be destructive of human rights. For this reason, it is essential to remember people's rights, as distinguished from individual rights. It is equally necessary to realise not merely civil and political rights but also economic, social, cultural rights and humanitarian justice. The UN is obligated to promote and encourage respect for human rights and for fundamental freedoms for all without distinction as to race, sex, language or religion.

The United Nations Charter is an epic event which marks a new direction in the odyssey of civilised human rights. But glorious instruments with global import may remain ineffectual angels beating their golden wings in vain in the void unless the means of realisation of the great rights inscribed in printed pledges are available for all by shaking up the *status quo* and shaping a New World Human Order nearer to our hearts desire. Great jurisprudence, dealing with the Bill of Human Rights, derives it source and strength from the collective conscience and courage of the sensitive human being. The basic issue is whether those in power do to take human rights seriously.

In my lectures I argue for the manifesto of human personhood not as a placebo nor as a paper promise but as a clear mission to push humanity forward from despair to hope, from alienation to togetherness, from privation to liberation. Environment and ecology, the economic North and the economic South, the universe in its wholeness, must all be governed by the creative jurisprudence which seeks:

> "to see life through all its material disguises; to sense deity, as the earliest men did, in every tree, in every animal, in all love and birth, in all greatness of mind and soul, even in inevitable decay and death; to judge all things in terms of their good for the totality of life; to join a whole will willingly cooperate with growth".[11]

What the world needs is a Universal Human Rights Regime, a code and court with regional centres and jurisdictions worldwide. Decentralisation, local activists with *locus standi* are part of the package. The Global Powers may control the court and make it a weapon of abuse. Mankind is indivisible; so is human justice. But actualisation of remedies is the challenge of the coming millennium. This is the focal point of our global debate.

Tomorrow to fresh woods, and pastures new. Then we will begin, with worldwide, Asia-related and India—specific emphasis, a discussion on the Dialectics and Dynamics of Human Rights in India—Yesterday, Today and Tomorrow.

Human Rights as they unfold through the ages are infinite and universal. But the limits of Lectures force a choice and so I have, without sacrificing the vastness of the subject, limited my particular attention to Indian problems with an Indian depth and prospect. I conclude with the thought that the right to be human has its roots in the *Brahman*. Rabindranath Tagore expresses my feeling in all its profundity:

> "I love India, not because I cultivate the idolatry of geography, not because I have had the chance to be born in her soil, but because she has saved through tumultuous ages the living words that have issued from the illuminated consciousness of her great sons—*Satyam Jnanam Anantam Brahma*: Brahma is Truth, Brahma is Wisdom, Brahma is Infinite; *Santam Sivam Advaitam*: Peace is in Brahma, goodness is in Brahma, and the unity of all beings".

11 Will Durant: *The Pleasures of Philosophy*, page 394.

2

HUMAN RIGHTS CONCEPTUAL AND HISTORICAL REFLECTIONS

WROTE GURUDEV TAGORE from Chicago to C.F. Andrews, a close disciple of Mahatma Gandhi, what is central to the human spirit and human dignity which are the nidi of human rights as India's ancient culture has woven since *Vedic* times:

> "Nothing is of higher value—be it national wealth or independence—than disinterested faith in ideals, in the moral greatness of man.
>
> "The West has its unshakable faith in material strength and prosperity, and therefore, however loud grows the cry for peace and disarmament, its ferocity growls louder, gnashing its teeth and lashing its tail in impatience. It is like a fish, hurt by the pressure of the flood, planning to fly in the air. Certainly the idea is brilliant, but it is not possible for a fish to realise. We, in India, have to show the world what is that truth which not only makes disarmament possible but turns it into strength.
>
> "The truth that moral force is a higher power than brute force will be proved by the people who are unarmed. Life, in its higher development, has thrown off its tremendous burden of armour and a prodigious quantity of flesh, till man has become the conqueror of the brute world. The day is sure to come when the frail man of spirit, completely unhampered by air-fleets and dreadnoughts, will prove that the meek are to inherit the earth.
>
> *** *** ***
>
> "The destiny of India has chosen for its ally the power of soul, and not that of muscle. And she is to raise the history of man from the muddy level of physical conflict to the higher moral altitude.
>
> *** *** ***
>
> "Our fight is a spiritual fight—it is for Man. We are to emancipate Man from the meshes that he himself has woven round him—these organisations of national egoism. The butterfly will have to be persuaded that the freedom of

the sky is of higher value than the shelter of the cocoon. If we can defy the strong, the armed, the wealthy—revealing to the world the power of the immortal spirit—the whole castle of the Giant Flesh will vanish in the void. And then Man will find his *Swaraj*.

*** *** ***

"We, the famished ragged ragamuffins of the East, are to win freedom for all humanity.

*** *** ***

"I have seen the West; I covet not the unholy feast in which she revels every moment, growing more and more bloated and red and dangerously delirious. Not for us is this mad orgy of midnight, with lighted torches, but awakenment in the serene light of the morning."[1]

These lofty words underscore the heart of human rights as more than material arrangements and legal rights. Its basics are deep within the human spirit and beyond the trappings of temporal life.

The sublime blend of the spiritual, moral and material components, as constitutive of the chemistry of human rights, is the profound conceptualisation of *Vedic* Indians often missed in the modern discourse on the subject. It is necessary to grasp the semantic fundamentals of human rights lest their sacred essence be profaned by ignoble misuse and vulgar extensions. As a caveat, one may recall John Press: There are some words a poet fears to write: The purity of language is defiled. The meanings have turned traitor in the night. To guard against such distortions and deviances is the task of the crusader for the worth of the human person. In the sound and fury of verbal battles, we must take care not to corrupt words and confuse goals through use of polluted prose and adulterated ideas. At the same time, the glory and magic of diction, which has divine content and dignity of person, shall not be amputated or debilitated, thereby lessening the lustre and reducing there splendour of the vast expanse of ideas and ideologies implicit in the noble universe of human rights. Indeed, the magnificent concept of human rights, in its human-divine amplitude and altitude, in a fine frenzy rolling, doth glance from heaven to earth, from earth to heaven. Unless you gain insight into the prized potential of the human being you never can get to know the majesty, magnitude and celestial significance of what we loosely call human rights. Read Shakespeare here, over again, to measure the hallowed idea of humanhood:

"I have of late,—but wherefore I know not, lost all my mirth, forgone all custom of exercises; and indeed it goes so heavily with my dispostion that this goodly frame, the earth, seems to me a sterile promontory; this most excellent canopy, the air, look you, this brave overhanging firmament, this majestical roof fretted with golden fire, why it appears no other thing to me but a foul and pestilent congregation of vapours. What a piece of work is a man! How noble

1 From the letter of Rabindranath Tagore to C.F. Andrews dated 2nd March 1921.

in reason! how infinite in faculty! in form, in moving, how express and admirable! in action how like an angel! in apprehension how like a god! the beauty of the world! the paragon of animals! And yet, to me, what is this quintessence of dust? man delights not me; no, nor woman neither, though, by your smiling, you seem to say so".[2]

More than meat which encases the spirit, human creation is infinite and in times of affliction, the appeal to defend the personhood of the lowliest sister is a plea *de profundis*. Human rights are of many dimensions, temporal, moral, cultural and spiritual. This is the broad axiological canvas.

And now, we must accept the founding faith that the true value of a human being and the unlimited, uninhibited scope for manifestation of his/her latent faculties in the body-mind-soul complex, is a broad-spectrum band from the dust to the divine. Human rights that we fight for are not for a happy life, somewhere in etherial space or in heaven but a full soulful life lived in a felicitous social order on earth where group harmony and individual melody will find fulfilment. We envision a World Order of human fellowship, not an incongruous, at times incompatible aggregation of the mighty and the meek, some savage, some simple, the elite of the earth drugged by the opium of criminalised power and the vast populace marred by blood, sweat, toil and tears. These imbalances provoke resistance and, as chain reaction, massacres, mayhems and privations at a time when peace and plenty are of easy access to all, thanks to science and technology if geared to the goodness of humanity. The finest span of homo sapiens in the coming millennium will be a blessing only when, in orderly security and beautiful symphony of social relations, each person, or homogeneous community, rejoices in life; and a global organisation with social sensitivity and corrective capacity sentinels, monitors and corrects with commanding authority and compassionate impartiality, a Just World Human Order.

A worldwide humanscape where all are able to live self-fulfilling lives with creative satisfaction is our destination. But the gap between ideals and realities is widening rapidly and the resolution of contradictions is bafflingly distant. The task of securing human rights is necessarily bound up with the society and State he/she lives in. When we discuss the subject of human rights the integral yoga of *society* and *personality* assumes importance. Einstein has, with telling simplicity, expressed this creative nexus:

"When we survey our lives and endeavours, we soon observe that almost the whole of our actions and desires is bound up with the existence of other human beings. We notice that our whole nature resembles that of the social animals. We eat food that others have produced, wear clothes that others have made, live in houses that others have built. The greater part of our knowledge and beliefs has been communicated to us by other people through the medium of a language which others have created. Without language our mental capacities would be poor indeed, comparable to those of the higher animals; we have, therefore, to admit that we owe our principal advantage over the beasts to the

2 *Hamlet*, Act 2, Sc. 2.

fact of living in human society. The individual, if left alone from birth, would remain primitive and beastlike in his thoughts and feelings to a degree that we can hardly conceive. The individual is what he is and has the significance that he has not so much in virtue of his individuality, but rather as a member of a great human community, which directs his material and spiritual existence from the cradle to the grave".[3]

That exalted humanist and foremost scientist of our century, Albert Einstein, again comments:

"In politics not only are leaders lacking, but the independence of spirit and the sense of justice of the citizen have to a great extent declined. The democratic, parliamentarian regime, which is based on such independence, has in many places been shaken; dictatorships have sprung up and are tolerated, because men's sense of the dignity and the rights of the individual is no longer strong enough. In two weeks the sheeplike masses of any country can be worked up by the newspapers into such a state of excited fury that men are prepared to put on uniforms and kill and be killed, for the sake of the sordid ends of a few interested parties.

*** *** ***

"I believe that better times are coming. Let me briefly state my reasons for such confidence.

"In my opinion, the present manifestations of decadence are explained by the fact that economic and technologic developments have highly intensified the struggle for existence, greatly to the detriment of the free development of the individual. But the development of technology means that less and less work is needed from the individual for the satisfaction of the community's needs. A planned division of labour is becoming more and more of a crying necessity, and this division will lead to the material security of the individual. This security and the spare time and energy which the individual will have at his disposal can be turned to the development of his personality. In this way the community may regain its health, and we will hope that future historians will *explain the morbid symptoms of present day society as the childhood ailments of an aspiring humanity, due entirely to the excessive speed at which civilization was advancing*".[4]

When science remits human toil, the benefit should not be cornered by a few but must be tuned to distributive justice and benefit all denizens of the earth. This consummation is possible in a polity committed to democracy and socialist, secular culture. If human rights are a Supreme value-set, as I hold it is, capitalism red in tooth and claw must be mellowed and softened by social justice and socialistic, decentralised democracy, Only in such a system will individuals and minorities matter and their rights secure legal shelter. And only if society is ordered in such manner that each humble human counts can fundamental freedoms and worth of the human person

3 Albert Einstein: *Ideas and Opinions*, page 130.
4 *Ibid*, pages 14-15.

receive reverential recognition. Sans socialistic texture of society human rights will be mere mirage or tantalising illusion.

Says Einstein, with penetrating perception and without ideological dogmatism, that the crisis of our time needs socialist structuring and humanising of the political economy. I quote his observations:

> "Man can find meaning in life, short and perilous as it is, only through devoting himself to society.
>
> "The economic anarchy of capitalist society as it exists today is, in my opinion, the real source of the evil". "The result of these developments is an oligarchy of private capital, the enormous power of which cannot be effectively checked even by a democratically organized political society. This is true since the members of legislative bodies are selected by political parties, largely financed or otherwise influenced by private capitalists who, for all practical purposes, separate the electorate from the legislature. The consequence is that *the representatives of the people do not in fact sufficiently protect the interests of the underprivileged sections* of the population. Moreover, under existing conditions, *private capitalists inevitably control, directly or indirectly, the main sources of information (press, radio, education)*. It is thus extemely difficult, and indeed in most cases quite impossible, for the individual citizen to come to objective conclusions and to make intelligent use of his political rights".[5]

Acquisitive success becomes a craze at the expense of other people's right to life. The Nobel laureate hits the nail on the head when he concludes:

> "Technological progress frequently results in more unemployment rather than in an easing of the burden of work for all". Prophetic and scientific!

*** *** ***

> "I am convinced there is only one way to eliminate these grave evils, namely through the establishment of a socialist economy, accompanied by an educational system which would be oriented toward social goals. In such an economy, the means of production are owned by society itself and are utilized in a planned fashion. A planned economy, which adjusts production to the needs of the community, distribute the work to be done among all those able to work and would guarantee a livelihood to every man, woman, and child. The education of the individual, in addition to promoting his own innate abilities, would attempt to develop in him a sense of responsibility for his fellow-men in place of the glorification of power and success in our present society".[6]

Harken here to Jawaharlal Nehru, a democrat and socialist in every cell of his soul, who asserted six decades back, in his Lucknow Congress Address:

> "I am convinced that the only key to the solution of the world's problems and of India's problems lies in socialism, and, when I use this word, I do so not in a vague humanitarian way but in the scientific, economic sense. Socialism is, however, something even more than an economic doctrine; it is a philosophy

5 *Ibid,* pages 156-157.
6 *Ibid,* pages 157-158.

of life, and as such also it appeals to me. I see no way of ending the poverty, the vast unemployment, the degradation and the subjection of the Indian people except through socialism. That involves vast and revolutionary changes in our political and social structure, the ending of vested interests in land and industry, as well as the feudal and autocratic Indian states system. That means the ending of private property, except in a restricted sense, and the replacement of the present profit system by a higher ideal of co-operative service. It means ultimately a change in our instincts and habits and desires. In short, it means a new civilization, radically different from the present capitalist order.

*** *** ***

"I am convinced that, if some world catastrophe does not intervene, this new civilization will spread to other lands and put an end to the wars and conflicts which capitalism feeds.

"I do not know how or when this new order will come to India. I imagine that every country will fashion it after its own way and fit it in with its national genius. But the essential basis of that order must remain and be a link in the world order that will emerge out of the present chaos.

"Socialism is thus for me not merely an economic doctrine which I favour; it is a vital creed which I hold with all my head and heart. I work for Indian independence because the nationalist in me cannot tolerate alien domination; I work for it even more because for me it is the inevitable step to social and economic change. I should like the Congress to become a socialist organization and to join hands with the other forces in the world who are working for the new civilization".

More planned economy and State capitalism may create a new slavery if we miss the humanist kinetics of social production and just distribution. Centralisation of political and economic power, with the bureaucracy poised powerfully on top, may be a remedy which aggravates the malady, as the later stages of the Soviet Union dismantlement pathetically established. Human rights can flourish only where social justice, decentralised power and alleviatory ethos, not where degenerate materialism nor formal regimented Kremlinist socialism, with iron in its soul, prevails. A police state, with a privileged elite in power, will not defend human rights; nor can a system of social justice be sustained merely by use of hammer and sickle as symbol or using crimson jargon calling one another comrades. Nor, indeed, can the Statue of Liberty with a torch held aloft nor chanting Abraham Lincoln's profound definition of democracy salvage human rights if the CIA and FBI spy globally and shoot liberally and scotch basic freedoms. Assassination culture practised by Rightist gang-ups of Ku Klux Klan (US) or Skin heads (UK) and suppression of blacks and hispanics and coloureds by using the death row *in terrorem*, cannot promote human rights. The world being kept trepidant about war by the US as on the Bay of Pigs invasion of Cuba, or in the name of containment of communism a la Vietnam, and as alibi for international security, as in the case of Iraq, and waging cold war everywhere subversively are stratagems which make the stars and stripes suspect even when playing human rights diplomacy.

Again, human rights can never co-exist with nuclear arsenals. It is potential genocide to possess Atomic Bombs. Hiroshima is harbinger of Globoshima unless nuclear weapons are totally destroyed to save mankind. Who talks loudest about human rights and who has the largest stockpile of this satanic stuff?

Human rights postulate a spiritual vision and philosophy of divine presence in larger brotherhood as the cornerstone of global democracy. Being holy or unholy is irrelevant; being religious or atheist is immaterial. A revolution in consciousness, a kindly process of active fraternity deeply rooted in the reverence for fellow-beings and the personhood of every other–that is the essence of human rights, and of that fundamental equity which sustains the rhythm of the universe. There is one great society alone on earth and the spirit that unifies it is the source and resource of human justice and humanist jurisprudence. Ecology, environment, nature and cosmic cohesion come alive when we feel the world as one pulsating whole and hear the still, sad music of humanity. When this balance is upset and arrhythmia overtakes social relations, violence and victimisation ensue. Wordsworth versifies the failings and inhumanities he felt: "And much it grieved my heart to think what man has made of man." And Burns did burst in numbers to express his outraged heart:

> *"Man a inhumanity to man*
> *Makes countless thousands mourn!*
> *"O Death, the poor man's dearest friend,*
> *The kindest and the best!"*

From material pleasures as the summum bonum of existence we need to make a radical, ethical paradigm shift.

Does the West accept: "The Kingdom of God is within you" or reject Jesus who said: 'Seek *ye* first the Kingdom of God and all those things shall be added unto you", and adopt instead Nkrumah whose dictum was: 'Seek *ye* first the political Kingdom and all things will be added unto you'. Quest for power and conquest of other's resources cannot lead to a commonwealth of human justice.

The worth of the human person as a non-negotiable value, and the universal spread of *fraternity* which gains reality only if every member has equal title to better standards of life in larger freedom, are ideas which make meaning only in a cultural democracy of social, economic and political dimensions, and a world morally knit together and is committed to peace and security. Otherwise, deadly discrimination and power-greedy injustice will wipe out cosmic comity or make international order merely cosmetic, comic or cunning. The heart of the World Human Process is transcendental. Am I my brother's keeper? Yes: him you can't murder, rings the biblical message through the ages (in the Cain-Abel story). Who am I? Runs the ancient Indian spiritual interrogation; and through the whispering gallery of *Vedic* wisdom comes the answer: Thou art that. Divinity makes us kin in all-embracing skein. No man is an isalnd, entire of itself; every man is a piece of the continent, a part of the main. We are one. If you accept this sublime Enlightenment you stand for human rights. If you negate this unitive perception of universal presence and global family, our civilization is running out and the human race waits for its last lap. Byron's indignant poem tells the truth:

> *"By thy cold breast and serpent smile*
> *By thy unfathom'd gulfs of guile,*
> *By that most seeming virtuous eye,*
> *By thy shut soul's hypocrisy;*
> *By the perfection of thine art*
> *Which pass'd for human thine own heart;*
> *By thy delight in others pain*
> *And by thy brotherhood of cain,*
> *I call upon thee: and compel*
> *Thyself to be thy proper Hell!"*

Hardheaded realists and cold-blooded jurists may dismiss these telling thoughts as glittering or gloomy generalities and blazing or banal ubiquities, may be. But the provenance of profound sentiments is not humdrum legalities. Let us examine briefly the pervasive implications of patrician privileges versus socio-spiritual claims of plebeian humanity. Human rights, to be durable and stable, must, in values and actual use, spring from a revolution of hope and a transformation of consciousness of the world as a whole.

A practical visionary and foremost human rights activist of India, the late Rev. M.A. Thomas, referred to an ideology of human rights which is a contrast to the oligarchic appetite for all that you can grab and corner. In simple narrative form, he brings home the importance of distributive justice in a world of scarcity by stating a North Vietnam episode of distributive deal and the Indian experience where privatisation plays hide and seek with social justice, notwithstanding the Constitution in Art. 39(*b*) and (*c*). M.A. Thomas writes:

> "A friend who used to visit North Vietnam quite frequently in the days when the two Vietnams were still divided told us some time ago how he was struck by the radical values that were being infused into their society. He had observed that if things were available, they were available to all the people; if there was scarcity of any kind, it was for all. If there was no sugar available to the people, it was not available also to the ministers, higher officals and foreign dignitaries who were visiting the country for one reason or another. It was also true that during the American bombing the shelters were common to all. Both upper level officialdom and the ordinary people took shelter in the same place. There were no special facilities for ministers and Government officers.
>
> "In our country it is difficult to imagine this happening. We know from experience that scarcity does not affect all. There is in our midst a group of privileged people who remain unaffected by these shortages. The shortages

> that occur are for the vast majority the poor sections of our society. Every year shortages occur and every year we hear cries of distress going up from the homes of the downtrodden and underprivileged. But during the same time the houses of the affluent and powerful remain well supplied by everything they want. This situation has prevailed so consistently that all the people know about it and it has created much bitterness among them.
>
> "The bitterness is not because there is shortage and they have to do without some things they would like to have, but because of the unfairness of the system which allows some people to have these things while depriving others of these. Those who have are those who have not only the goods but also the money and the power. They know that if they let the situation change they will be the ones to lose. They would like to stay entrenched; they would like to keep their privileges. They would rather use their money and the power they wield to perpetuate the system that is to advantageous to them. The question one asks, then, is whether we can have a just system or a truly human society without putting an end to such inequality. Can we, in other words, bring about an equitable social order while keeping an exploitative system going?[7]

The Asian perspective of human rights, be it Buddhist, Taoist, Maoist, Confucian or Gandhian, also has an ethical fraternal foundation, the emphasis, central to them all, being the harmony of humanity and the end of sorrow. Thus, in brief, the ancient continent of Asia, including Arabia where Islam arose with its message of world brotherhood, peace and welfare of all, has been committed to human rights in a higher altitude.

Western materialism has based human rights sometimes on religious values, sometimes on material considerations, with moral extensions, as in socialist systems, and at other times, during revolutionary spells. Marxian philosophy, using dialectical materialism, accepts the full freedom of every individual as a creative person but holds that economic domination distorts the exercise of such freedom.

No one can deny totally what the materialist conception of history assert, *viz.*,

> "Production of the means to support human life ...... is the basis of every social order; that in every society which has appeared in history the distribution of the products, and with it the division of society into classes and orders, is determined by what is produced and how it is produced, and how the product is exchanged. According to this conception, the changes and political revolutions are to be sought not in the minds of men, in their increasing insight into external truth and justice, but in changes in the mode of production and exchange; they are to be sought not in the philosophy but in the economics of the epoch concerned".[8]

Human civilization, with all its spiritual drives, has been strongly controlled by the forces of production and impulses of sex and wealth even

7 M.A. Thomas: *The Struggle for Human Rights*, pages 94,95.

8 Friedrich Engles.

during the great days of the *Rishis,* although spiritual power has often lifted the human race to summits of success in the moral spiritual sense. Law itself must metabolize public morality but actually obeys economic values and suffers in its credibility in the process.

Says Karl Marx:

> "Law can never be higher than the economic order and the cultural development of society brought to pass by that economic order".

Yet again, the Marxian approach, contained in the Manifesto of the Communist Party, reads:

> "Your jurisprudence is but the will of your class made into a law for all, a will, whose essential character and direction are determined by the economical conditions of existence of your class........."

In this perspective, human rights are conditioned by the class character of the State instrument. When power is controlled by the moneyocracy, a new economic order is a *sine qua non* of human justice. Go at the jugular of monopoly capitalism if you are serious about human rights. Change must begin with the cadres, operators and other functionaries. After all, says Will Durant:

> "When one tries to change institutions without having changed the nature of men, that unchanged nature will soon resurrect those institutions".

Human rights instrumentalities

If human rights are to triumph, executives must be sensitised, legislators ethicalised and judges conscientised. The class to which they belong, the dominant environs which condition them and the values which motorize their thinking are the functional forces which are translated as law in action. Human rights metamorphosis calls for Operation Humanisation with Destination Universal Social Transformation.

Even judges are subtle victims of class prejudice, confusing their partiality with objective verity. Prof. Griffith, in his *The Politics of the Judiciary,* has made the point that, even the judicature, alas, at times, legitimises violations of justice, equity and good conscience, nay, even stultifies progressive jurisprudence. Robes do rob, with learned jargon, the hope of human justice for the wretched of the earth, though in unwitting infrequency and subconscious silence yet. Where, then, is the haven for hapless humanity and manacled majority victimised by the mafiasque social system and arrogant abuse of power? All that we see and hear is the power of property which governs humanity. The familiar lines of Tennyson echo in my mind:

> *"Doesn't thou ear my erse's legs, as they*
> *canters away? Proputty, proputty,*
> *proputty—that's what I ears em say".*

Winston Churchill drove home this point way back in 1911 in the British Parliament:

> "The courts hold justly a high, and I think, unequalled pre-eminence in the respect of the world in criminal cases, and in civil cases between man and man; no doubt, they deserve and command the respect and admiration of all classes of the community, but where class issues are involved, it is impossible to pretend that the courts command the same degree of general confidence. On the contrary, they do not, and a very large number of our population have been led to the opinion that they are, unconsciously, no doubt, biased.[9]

Lord Justice Scrutton, in similar vein, argued:

> "The habits you are trained in, the people with whom you mix, lead to your having a certain class of ideas of such a nature that, when you have to deal with other ideas, you do not give as sound and accurate judgments as you would wish. This is one of the great difficulties at present with Labour. Labour says 'Where are your impartial Judges?' They all move in the same circle as the employers, and they are all educated and nursed in the same ideas as the employers. How can a labour man or a trade unionist get impartial justice? It is very difficult sometimes to be sure that you have put yourself into a thoroughly impartial position between two disputants, one of your own class and one not of your class".[10]

Lord Atkin, in *Liversidge* v *Anderson*,[11] bitterly complained about his colleagues on the bench being more executive-minded than the executive where people's liberties were involved. The inference is that the poor have a dog's chance in court when the establishment is against them. "If the salt hath lost his savour, wherewith shall it be salted".

Lord Atkin's solitary dissent deserves fuller space to demonstrate how he battled in vain against his pro-establishment brethren:

> "...... I view with apprehension the attitude of judges who on a mere question of construction when face to face with claims involving the liberty of the subject show themselves more executive-minded than the executive........... in this country, amid the clash of arms, the laws are not silent. They may be changed, but they speak the same language in war as in peace. It has always been one of the pillars of freedom, one of the principles of liberty for which on recent authority we are fighting, that the judges are no respectors of persons and stand between the subject and any attempted encroachments on his liberty by the executive, alert to see that any coercive action is justified in law. In this case I have listened to arguments which might have been addressed acceptably to the court of King's Bench in the time of Charles I.
>
> "I protest, even if I do it alone, against a strained construction put on words with the effect of giving an uncontrolled power of imprisonment to the minister ....
>
> "I know of only one authority which might justify the suggested method of construction: When I use a word, Humpty Dumpty said in rather a scornful

9 Winston Churchill as Home Secretary in Parliament in 1911.

10 In an Address delivered to the University of Cambridge Law Society on 18th November 1920.

11 1942 AC 206: (1941)3 All ER 338.

tone, it means just what I choose it to mean, neither more nor less. The question is, said Alice, whether you can make words mean so many different things! The question is, said Humpty Dumpty, which is to be the master—that is all."[12]

Similar is the voice of Justice Vivian Bose in favour of the constitutional freedoms of the anti-establishment intellectuals:

"It is perhaps ironical that I should struggle to uphold these freedoms in favour of a class of persons who, if rumour is to be accredited and if the list of their activities furnished to us is a true guide, would be the first to destroy them if they but had the power. But I cannot allow personal predilections to sway my judgment of the Constitution".[13]

Abstract justice as an omnipotence in the sky is no good. Earthly justice and human equity are scarce commodities. Moneyocracy is the macro-controllerate in a world order under Corporate Power geared to the Gold Rush. Even the working class can be tempted to sell their soul and their whole. Corrosive corruption, like a worm, eats up the finest soul.

"O Rose, thou art sick!
The invisible worm
that flies in the night,
In the howling storm,
Has found out thy bed
O crimson joy:
And his dark secret love
Docs thy life destroy".

Beholding this inquietous scenario the world over, the masses find themselves estranged from the conspiracy of *status quo* forces. Individuals and groups, powerless when pitted against the power lite, lose hope. But despair breeds revenge and from outrage and anger emerge militant protest and menacing outbursts. Behind sullen meekness there is smouldering violence. Humanism is not submission but assertion; it is divine dissent, not humiliating genuflexion. Great souls, unbribable leaders organise the battle of justice, for human rights. With dialectical insights, militant movements spring up and captains of revolt courageously interpret history and march with the masses as their forces. That becomes their mission. Marx once defined:

"I am a man, I count nothing human foreign to me"

The human essence is divine and to wipe every tear from every eye–the Gandhian recipe–is where the material values meet the spiritual. To struggle for these values is soulful, even as to resist servility, in its myriad forms and shapes is a duty of humanity. Where a Government is satanic, the cult of resistance becomes a Gandhian religion. This *dharma-karma* coalition is

12 Dissent of Lord Atkin in *Liversidge* v *Anderson* Ibid, p. 361 (All ER).
13 *Krishnan* v *State of Madras* (1951) SCR 621.

the home and hope of human rights, human dignity and personhood. We need tough nobles, committed human stuff for such struggles. How should they be? My poignant anger and pathetic hunger, as I see war, butchery, barbarity, civilian casuality, gender-derogatory carnality and escalating social injustice all-round, appeal for a worldwide transmutation in human consciousness, a sublime global ethos, a retreat from hedonist affluenza and a deep concern for the harrowing segments of humanity. The genome of human rights is a flowering feeling from the heart. Vivekananda's eloquent exhortation is personally inspirational; and I quote:

> "Feel my children, feel, feel for the poor, the ignorant, the down-trodden, feel till the heart stops and the brain reels and you think you will go mad".[14]

Sir Walter Scott wrote in sober prose:

> "We shall never learn to feel and respect our real calling and destiny, unless we have taught ourselves to consider every thing as moonshine, *compared with the education of the heart*".

We need, it seems to me, a holistic vision, a heart culture, a lovely discovery of a seamless web where all life is linked together by a dynamic divinity. My conviction is rooted in the advaitic principles: TAT TVAM ASI (Thou art that). The mystical exclamation of William Blake endorses this intuitive perception when he poetizes:

> ***"Awake! awake! O sleeper of the land of shadows,***
> ***wake! expand!***
> ***I am in you and you in me, mutual in love......***
> ***Fibres of love from man to man......***
> ***Lo! we are One".***

Let us cast a glance at the perversion prevailing in society and State when the administration promotes an unjust economic order. In the Journal of Sri Aurobindo's Ashram a brief reference is made to this perversity:

> "THINK IT OVER.
>
> The Treasuries of the Republic of India are rich enough for champagne, whisky and international drinks in the parties thrown by the ruling class both in the country and abroad, but too poor to provide drinking water to the villagers.
>
> The Treasuries of the Republic of India have sufficient funds to subsidize the setting up of tax-free polluting industries, but are short of funds for depolluting the polluting industries.
>
> The capitals of the States in the Republic of India have free or concessional bungalows and luxurious houses in plenty for the teeming rich politicians and VIPs, including dead ones, but no houses for the slum-dwellers who gave their sweat to build the bungalows and luxurious houses.

14 *The Complete Works of Swami Vivekananda*, vol. IV, page 309.

The Treasuries of the Republic of India are generous enough to provide medical treatment for the VIPs at exorbitant cost abroad, but find themselves short of funds to give medical facilities to the villagers.

The Treasuries of the Republic of India are global enough to provide for airports of international standard, but find themselves unable to provide bus stands of a decent standard for the common man.

Think it over".[15]

Any thinking observer of the global and the Indian scene will exclaim that the world is wheeling towards chaotic inequity.

The world we live in is riddled with fundamental contradictions. These opposing forces spare none, and wear myriad forms, tear down the rights of women and children and shock the conscience of people everywhere. A search for values–from the savage to the civilised–is the drive which propels the history of human rights. Corporate cannibalism, infatuated by escalating super-avarice, versus universal human rights retreating to refugee camps for a while are the forces which clash. Here we must be on the side of the people, the plebeians, the proletarians, the have-not human sector. At a World Symposium on Humanity in 1977 in Vancouver, Roszak pointed out:

> "In our time a secret manifesto is being written. Its language is a longing we read in one another's eyes. It is the longing to know our authentic vocation in the world, to find the work and the way of being that belong to each of us ...... I speak of the Manifesto of the Person, the declaration of our sovereign right to self-discovery".[16]
>
> "My mind goes with Victor Hugo who "prophesied that in the twentieth century war would die, frontier boundaries would die, dogma would die—and man would live. He will possess something higher than these—a great country, the whole earth ...... and a great hope, the whole heaven."[17]

Will he or she inherit a happy universe? The touchstone of a world moral order which can nourish human rights globally must be just and fair and it is here that capitalism and imperialism have failed in the past. The British empire, once so vast that the sun never set over it, was a nation of shopkeepers whose Government was influenced by them. Moral qualms rarely distrubed rich people. In Adam Smith's words:

> "With the greater part of rich people, the chief enjoyment of riches consists in the parade of riches, which in their eyes is never so complete as when they appear to possess those decisive marks of opulence which nobody can possess but themselves".

Corruption is the close cousin of colonial masters. They make no bones about human rights until impeached by history. Edmund Burke's

15 *Sri Aurobindo's Action*, June 1996, page 2.
16 Marilyn Ferguson: *The Aquarian Conspiracy*, pages 37-38.
17 *Ibid*, page 445.

impeachment speech tells how imperial surrogates abroad ride rough shod over people's rights and are acquitted by imperialism, Burke's peroration is here:

> "I impeach him in the name of the people of India, whose rights he has trodden under foot, and whose country he has turned into a desert. Lastly, in the name of human nature itself, in the name of both sexes, in the name of every age, in the name of every rank, I impeach the common enemy and oppressor of all!"

Let me conclude this melancholy critique with a verdict from the great capitalist, economist John Maynard Keynes himself:

> "The decadent international but individualistic capitalism in the hands of which we found ourselves after the (first world) war is not a success. It is not intelligent, it is not just, it is not virtuous and it does not deliver the goods. In short, we dislike it and we are beginning to despise it".[18]

Can the leopard change its spots? No, in an age of technology geared to Power and War. The degeneracy of society is ghastly and homicidal to human rights.

Mr. Soli, J. Sorabji, a noted humanist and convinced human rights activist, in his Besant Lecture 1992, had observed:

> "The moral worth of a society or a community is reflected in its aspirations and the ideals it pursues, the values it cherishes and its sincerity in upholding those values. Throughout history, humanity's chief concern has been the discovery and preservation of values which impart grace and significance to civilization and also to individual human lives. One of the cruelest paradoxes of our times is that an age that has witnessed tremendous scientific progress and technological development has at the same time also witnessed unprecedented decline in moral and spiritual values.
>
> "A brief survey of the general human condition painfully underscores this fact. It was hoped and believed after the overthrow of the Nazi regime and exposure of its ghastly deeds that the concentration camps and other barbarous acts would become things of the past. But horrific scenes of man's inhumanity to man are still daily re-enacted in former Yugoslavia, and the international community regrettably has become a hopeless spectator. Israel, a nation born out of sorrow and suffering, displayed incredible inhumanity by refusing permission to the International Red Cross to supply food and medicines to Palestinian deportees who were starving and freezing. In Somalia, the local warlords engage in loot and plunder, having no compunction in seeing their own people die of hunger and starvation. These scenes are brought to us, thanks to cable-television and I am sure you must have seen those horrifying scenes. I am sometimes reduced to tears when I see young children and old people being starved not because there are no food supplies, but because people playing their own power games have denied supplies to them and allowed them to die".

18 Quoted in Dattopant Thengadi's *Third Way*, page 237.

Soil's thought is sublime. His anguish is deep and from these poignant sources we get the contrast of arrogant affluence resisted by the rebellious human spirit.

There are two extremes which are challenges we face as world citizens while conceptualising the human rights thesis. Unlimited avarice and unquenchable passion, seizing power without scruples, seek to dominate the world's resources. They are the enemies of human rights in widest commonalty spread. What do they gain? They lose their soul and are captives of darker appetites, victims of wealth, not victors of freedom. Gitanjali, in one stanza, poetizes thus:

> "Prisoner, tell me, who is it that bound you? It was my master, said the prisoner. I thought I could outdo everybody in the world in wealth and power, and I amassed in my own treasure-house the money due to my king. When sleep overcame me I lay upon the bed that was for my lord, and on waking up I found I was a prisoner in my own treasure-house".
>
> Prisoner, tell me, who was it that wrought this unbreakable chain?
>
> "It was I, said the prisoner, who forged this chain very carefully. I thought my invincible power would hold the world captive leaving me in a freedom undisturbed. Thus night and day I worked at the chain with huge fires and cruel hard strokes. When at last the work was done and the links were complete and unbreakable, I found that it held me in its grip".[19]

Capitalist craze unjustly battening upon the world's wealth ultimately falls a prey to its own excesses and perishes like a solitary prisoner under death sentence. Out of the ashes of the Old Order springs the Promethean spirit claiming freedom to soar and sing and develop personality in all dimensions. This beautiful thought has been expressed in a magnificent stanza in the *Gitanjali*:

> *"Where the mind is without fear and the head is*
> *held high:*
> *Where knowledge is free:*
> *Where the world has not been broken up into fragments*
> *by narrow domestic walls;*
> *Where words come out from the depth of truth;*
> *Where tireless striving stretches its arms*
> *towards perfection;*
> *Where the clear stream of reason has not lost its*
> *way into the dreary desert sand of dead habit;*
> *Where the mind is led forward by thee into*
> *ever-widening thought and action*
> *Into that heaven of freedom, my Father*
> *Let my country awake".*[20]

19 No. XXXI.
20 No. XXXV.

Such is the blossom festival of global human rights.

I conclude the conceptual part of human rights on this great note.

Some historical reflections on the evolution of human rights

Human rights are those irreducible minima which belong to every member of the human race when pitted against the State or other public authorities or group and gangs and other oppressive communities. Being a member of the human family he has the right to be treated as human once he takes birth or is alive in the womb with a potential title to personhood. When legal ideas were not clear-cut but blurred, ancient *pundits* thought of the doctrine of natural rights founded on natural law, not because it is enacted but because it inalienably belongs to each of us as conceived in civilised political societies. When the priestly order denies this right using religious sanction and authority, the independent mind of man expresses dissatisfaction and defies. When Kings and Queens and other diadems and despotisms sought to suppress the individual's freedom an appeal to natural law was made on the assumption that, beyond religious superirors and crowned heads, there was a system of natural law which embodied reason, justice and universal ethics. Durgadas Basu referes to natural laws and observes:

> "Western scholars date the genesis of this ideal of natural law to Sophocles, more than 400 years before Christ.
>
> "In England, the case for a natural law, superior to man-made law, was argued by Blackstone in the 17th century.
>
> "Once the concept of a higher law binding on human authorities was evolved, if came to be asserted that there were certain rights anterior to society, which too were superior to rights created by the human authorities, were of universal application to men of all ages and in all claims, and were supposed to have existed even before the birth of political society. These rights could not, therefore, be violated by the State".[1]

Obviously, natural law and natural rights have no sovereign sanction for enforcement but remain as an ideal or ideology deriving strength from deeper spiritual sources rather than in the power of the sceptre or the mitre. Sir Edward Coke, nearly five centuries ago, did assert a link between natural rights and common law as a gladsome light of jurisprudence. He has stated with authority:

> *"How long soever it hath continued, if it be against reason, it is of no force in law".*
> *"Reason is the life of the law, nay the common law itself is nothing else but reason ...... The law, which is the perfection of reason".*

The rules of natural justice, sometimes vague and vagarious but rooted in deeper human instincts, survives to this day and has received

1 D.D. Basu: *Human Rights in Constitutional Law*, page 5.

judicial recognition and, therefore, sovereign sanction. The hoary ancestry of natural rights and natural justice has continued and its substance reincarnated in many jurisdictions in many forms and ultimately in the Universal Declaration of Human Rights and subsequent instruments.

With these prefatory observations, one may go straight to the origin of Man and the slow evolution of civilised values, humanitarian justice, and the compelling factors leading to the emergence of Human Rights jurisprudence in the context of violent contradictions and value variations.

Back to the beginning. The odyssey of human rights is of Western vintage; it is useful to go, in some detail into the developments, political, philosophical and legal, from the old Greek days down to the present times of universal human rights and the instruments promulgated by or under the auspices of the United Nations.

3

THE SAGA OF HOMO SAPIENS AND OMEGA OF HUMAN RIGHTS

THE GLOBAL DEBATE on human rights begins with the query: who is a human *being, as distinguished from his simian ancestors, and what endows him* with the attributes of homo sapiens? What is the grand odyssey of man on earth, what the vicissitudes of pluralist society on the march, the evolution of its cultures and the current status of humanity in its radical ascent towards its great destiny? Such a rapid narrative leads us to an autopsy of the corpus of human rights, its strengths and weaknesses in the dynamic present and imminent future. Farewell to the Old World System and greetings to the emergent global picture is an eclectic exercise useful as a prelude to an assessment of the direction and destination of the New World Human Order.

A philosophical perspective, although not of much pragmatic appeal, sets our sights high when dealing with such a sublime subject as the origin and ultimate of human rights. Going by the *Upanishads*, the human-divine pinnacle is *Sat-Chit-Ananda*, is Existence—Consciousness—Beatitude—we are light and joy.

Sri Aurobindo holds that the future is still higher status and that Man

> "is not the last term of the evolution, he is a transitional being. We speak of the evolution of Life in Matter, the evolution of Mind in Matter; but evolution is a word which merely states the phenomenon without explaining it. For there seems to be no reason why Life should evolve out of material elements or Mind out of living form, unless we accept.........that Life is already involved in Matter and Mind in Life because in essence Matter is a form of veiled Life, Life a form of veiled Consciousness. And then there seems to be little objection to a farther step in the series and the admission that mental consciousness may itself be only a form and a veil of higher states which are beyond Mind. In that case, the unconquerable impulse of man towards God, Light, Bliss, Freedom, Immortality presents itself in its right place in the chain as simply the imperative impulse by which Nature is seeking to evolve beyond Mind, and

> appears to be as natural, true and just as the impulse towards Life which she has planted in forms of Matter or the impulse towards Mind which she has planted in certain forms of Life......The animal is a living laboratory in which Nature has, it is said, worked out man. Man himself may well be a thinking and living laboratory in whom and with whose conscious cooperations she wills to work out the superman, the god. Or shall we not say, rather, to manifest God? If evolution manages this difficult passage, the great Equilibrium will be reached, we shall enter 'the vast home' (*Rig Veda,* V. 68.5)".[1]

The human race will rise to a supramental height as inevitably as homo sapiens appeared from among the primates. This quantum jump in evolution is the great spiritual unfolding of man in the evolutionary scale. Matter, with divinity asleep, develops into mind, the thinking instrument; and from there is a new transformation. Herein is the true passage from the animal-man as conceived by the lower evolution to the *human-man* of the new evolution. This is no negation of the human potential on earth, but a realisation of what secretly sleeps within the spirit of Man. In the vibrant diction of Sri Aurobindo referring to this inner realisation 'Heaven's touch fulfils but cancels not our earth'.

The authentic vision of the *seers* of the East thus leads to human fulfilment through human rights in infinite amplitude. Any sensitive thinker with a profound feel will thus view the *vistarama* of human rights from this luminous angle, although pragmatists may look *away* from first things and first principles *towards* the daily events and tremendous trifles. In this essay on human right, its source, stream and final flow into the larger realities of life, one may not perhaps fly to the skies with Aurobindo's thoughts, but still remember the radiant destiny which merges in the divinity that the sages have vividly foretold. Indeed, the universality of human rights is founded on this spiritual fellowship of which Mahatma Gandhi gives a glimpse when he speaks of true patriotism thus:

> "All humanity is one undivided and indivisible family, and each one of us is responsible for the misdeeds of all the others. I cannot detach myself from the wickedest soul".

Let us now revert to the beginning of the saga of Homo Sapiens through its millennial progress.

This we may do, briefly though, from the ancient past and reach out to our dying century by a blitz through the stages of civilization and profusion of faiths in their bearing on human rights. Then we may look at the prospects of the future of Human Rights in India and the world over. The whence and the whither are integral to such a search, set in a historical perspective and making an ethics-sensitive prognosis. The moral-spiritual element becomes relevant if our vision of human rights or *manava dharma* is to possess the sublime factor which belongs to humanism itself. This dimension is stressed by John Kleinig:

1 Satprem: *Sri Aurobindo on the Adventure of Consciousness,* pages 304-305.

> "Unless there is love, care and concern for others as individuals, in addition to the recognition of rights, there remains a moral lack in international relationships. There is something morally inadequate in doing something for another, because it is the other's due. Actions motivated simply by the rights of others remain anonymous or impersonal, whereas if motivated by love, care or concern for the other, their focus is on the other's particularity. Only relations of the latter kind are morally adequate. They are person-specific, whereas rights are species-specific".[2]

The real guarantee of human rights is the activised consciousness of the world community and the people-to-people compassion in universal embrace. No UN instrumentality nor national Constitution, sans people's conscience, can make these basic rights operational. My study of human rights is no mechanical collection of instruments and institutions as a materialist melange or odd olio but a reverence for human dignity and divinity and a militantised fraternity ready to identify with each other in a spirit of mutual belonging. That outlook is the bedrock of any penetrating understanding of the sacredness of man and woman, especially by anyone from the land of Gandhi and Ambedkar. Rabindranath Tagore's haunting humanist profile of Gandhiji compells me to adopt such a fundamentally moral approach. Says Tagore about Gandhi:

> "He (Gandhi) stopped at the threshold of the huts of the thousands of the dispossessed, dressed like one of their own. He spoke to them in their own language; here was living truth at last, and not quotations from books. For this reason the 'Mahatma', the name given to him by the people of India, is his real name. Who else has felt like him that all Indians are his own flesh and blood? In direct contact with truth, the crushed forces of the soul rose again, when love came to the door of India, that door was opened wide.........At Gandhi's call India blossomed forth to new greatness, just as once before in earlier times, when Buddha proclaimed the truth of fellow-feeling and compassion among all living creatures".

What a grandeur! This universal impulse is the hallowed ground for a basic understanding of human rights. This cosmic profundity is at the root of the entire study I undertake. Otherwise there is a hollowness in the erudition, a superficiality in the glossy rhetoric. So it is that Bernard Levind, *The Times of London* columnist, pointed out that:

> "Countries like ours are full of people who have all the material comforts they desire, yet lead lives of quiet (and at times noisy) desperation, understanding nothing but the fact that there is a hole inside them and that however much food and drink they pour into it, however many motorcars and television sets they stuff it with, however many well-balanced children and loyal friends they parade around the edges of it, it aches".[3]

The glory of personhood and the infinite potential latent in that concept is the philosophical foundation of human rights. As a species,

2 Dattopant Thengadi: *Third Way,* page 14.

3 Marilyn Ferguson: *The Aquarian Conspiracy,* page 42.

Homo Sapiens, to which all human beings belong, emerged on earth well over several hundred thousands of years ago and, under hard conditions, wrought his advance through vast stretches in time, evolved from savage state to civilized stage and, by struggles for survival and other compulsive mutations, spiralled up as a cultured, creative, thinking being, with a finer fellowship, higher values and nobler divinity which his animal predecessors did not possess. By way of aside, one must confess, man is fooling about with this treasure and must blush when he recollects how disastrously he has bungled. Mark Twain cynically remarked: "Man is the only animal that blushes" or needs to!

Charles Darwin has expounded, in his *On The Origin of Species by Means of Natural Selection,* that evolution occurs by the fixation of changes (mutation) in the structure of the genetic material and the passing on of these changes from ancestor to descendant. Mankind, despite this great heritage, has so deplorably failed to ascend the sublime spiral of his noble future that George Bernard Shaw, in barbed diction, once remarked that Darwin taught us not that all men were monkeys once but that some monkeys have no tails now!

Gregor Mendel, through studies of plant breeding established his laws governing the nature of inheritance which became the basis of modern genetics. Geographical environment has had its impact on human conditions as on other living organisms; and ecological studies reveal that physical environment also shapes human development. Lysenko, the Soviet scientist, made this point but exaggerated its importance and denied the value of Mendel's discovery. Stalin boosted him for ideological purposes, but oblivion swallowed him and his unveracity). These and other complex factors and myriad mysteries have played a decisive part in the advance of homo sapiens from the first hominid in a process lasting millions of years. Homo habilis, homo erectus, homo sapiens are evolutionary stages ending with all modern races which are members of the subspecies Homo Sapiens Sapiens. Wise, Wise Man, is the meaning of Homo Sapiens Sapiens; and the challenge of contemporary human history is whether modern man is wise at all, eligible for this noble name, or is, in a diabolic fit, drifting ignobly towards global harakiri, greedily trampling, driven by lethal folly and lunatic entropy, over fellow being's rights and reeling towards a denouement of doom at a time when worldwide happiness is in his glorious grasp. Dialectically speaking, currently, mankind is in the menacing grip of a catastrophic contradiction to be or not to be. Plautus long ago noted:

> *"A man is a wolf rather than a man to another man,*
> *When he hasn't yet found out what he's like".*

And, alas, this barbaric mindset holds the earth like a bully. So much so, the satanic factor has clean bowled the sage in man and has forfeited the finer humanism which is the essence of culture. The struggle ahead is to resurrect the lost Jesus in each of us and to sentence Barabbas, the robber, who escaped punishment.

The two extremes, divine and diabolic are brought out in *Hamlet* by Shakespeare which bears excerption:

> "What a piece of work is a man! How noble in reason! how infinite in faculty! in form! in moving, how express and admirable! in action how like an angel! in apprehension how like a god! the beauty of the world! the paragon of animals!"

Be that as it may, today we have, established all over the earth, first in scattered habitations and through jungly conflicts, and later, on a one-world basis conscious of a tryst with destiny, a sensitive humanity, with creative intelligence and higher perceptions, heralding a universal social order of sorts, sustained by a sense of common heritage and progressive goals. But yet, the pity of it, Oh! the pity of it, is that manic appetites and reckless pursuits of pleasure and profit have landed man in a dilemma of greed, violence and gross aggression on nature. What a pathos and bathos that a profound promise of universal dimension stands stultified and a heave of humanitarian hope proves a mirage! Ecology and environment are victimised by tycoon operations and homocentric arrogance so much that neo-progress, as the engine of advance, is now the route to the global graveyard—unless we reverse gear and restore our value-set! Even humanism, where it does not embrace compassion *for all living Creatures*, is cruel. In his "*True Humanism*", Maritain says, "Any form of anthropocentric humanism is in its final analysis an inhuman humanism". Cosmic compassion is the soul of enlightened humanism. Human rights are enriched by such celestial content and expanding hopes from generation to generation. I conclude this strain of thought by an exquisite poem since ideas unalloyed find their finest expression through poetry.

"Look up, my people,
The dawn is breaking,
The world is waking
To a new bright day,
When none defame us,
No restriction tame us,
Nor colour shame us,
Nor sneer dismay

Now brood no more
On the years behind you,
The hope assigned you
Shall the past replace
When a juster justice
Grown wise and stronger
Points the bone no longer
At a darker race

So long we waited
Bound and frustrated,
Till hate be hated

And caste deposed;
Now light shall guide us,
No goal denied us,
And all doors open
That long were closed
See plain the promise
Dark freedom-love!
Night's nearly over,
And though long the climb,
New rights will greet us,
New mateship meet us,
And joy complete us
In our new Dream Time.
To our fathers' fathers
The pain, the sorrow;
To our children's children
The glad tomorrow".

— K. WALKER

Some day the pariah will rise as our equal person and Prometheus will overcome his chained status with the insatiably rich eagle feeding on his liver and overpower unjust Zeus to spread the fire of revolt and power among the proletariat to restore to them the fulness of personhood that belongs to them.

To describe, in a brief space, this long haul of history spread over many millennia, and zigzagged by vicissitudes of violence, struggles for survival and ascent towards a distant *kismet*, which makes up the mighty marathon of humanity, is to compress and capsulate unjustly a wondrous journey of wandering adventures of the human race. The kaleidoscopic chronicle is of varying patterns what with perils and calamities, battles and victories, tragedies and triumphs filling the space of centuries. Our magnificent and, at times, malignant, modern periods are marred by macro-cum-micro wars and, at other times, through inspired by flights to the moon, mars and stars. Man (including woman) has made quantum jumps through scientific discoveries, military conquests and staggering successes in the fields of spiritual, moral and material advance. Such is the thrilling voyage through pre-history and history which has paved the way for a vague international order and woven the warp and woof of the world's plural heritage and composite culture. Science developed and explored nature, with inventions and technologies adding to the arsenal of material accomplishments. History, in its anfractuous course, moved forward; and humanity, generation after generation, came closer to a loosely knit family, overcoming two world wars and other disasters. But even after 50 years of the United Nations, massive massacres of human rights are a potential threat or pathetic fact. World peace and universal order are a gamble or riddle or worse. And the materialist age of *homo-economicus*, wrapped in market-friendly garment and military uniform, has *asuric* dominance. The human contradiction and convulsion is a struggle *within* between the savage and the sapient.

> "In his essay 'Men have Forgotten God', Solzhnitsyn has stated in unequivocal terms that the goal of economics should be "quest for spiritual growth", rather than the pursuit of material growth".[4]

Said Antonio Machado (Campos de Castilla—1917) about hombre:

> "I am living at peace with men and at war with my innards".

That is the human dilemma. A creative coalition of science and spirituality is the desideratum if the rights of man are to be preserved and the wrongs done to him are to be reversed.

As Dorothy Sayers, one of the finest commentators on Dante as well as on modern society, has said:

> "That the Inferno is a picture of human society in a state of sin and corruption, everybody will readily agree. And since we are today fairly well convinced that society is in a bad way and not necessarily evolving in the direction of perfectibility, we find it easy enough to recognise the various stages by which the deep of corruption is reached. Futility, lack of a living faith, the drift into loose morality, greedy consumption, financial irresponsibility, and uncontrolled bad temper; a self-opinionated and obstinate individualism, violence, sterility, and lack of reverence for life and property including one's own; the exploitation of sex, the debasing of language by advertisement and propaganda, the commercialising of religion, the pandering to superstition and the conditioning of people's minds by mass-hysteria and spell-binding of all kinds, venality and string-pulling in public affairs, hypocrisy, dishonesty in material things, intellectual dishonesty, the fomenting of discord (class against class, nation against nation) for what one can get out of it, the falsification and destruction of all the means of communication, the exploitation of the lowest and stupidest mass-emotions, treachery even to the fundamentals of kinship, country, the chosen friend, and the sworn allegiance; these are the all-too-recongisable stages that lead to the cold death of society and the extinguishing of all civilised relations".[5]

Excessively consumerist and horridly hedonist materialism will condemn the planet to annihilation's waste unless we remould the cultural structure of the world nearer to our higher aspirations.

> "What we need, then, is a new paradigm, a new vision of reality, a fundamental change in our thoughts, perceptions and values".[6]

Even John Maynard Keynes, the creative innovator of his slumbering capitalist times, once wrote:

4 Quoted by Dattopant Thengadi in *Third Way*, page 77.

5 *Ibid* at p. 244.

6 *Ibid* at p. 245.

> "The decadent international but individualistic capitalism in the hands of which we found ourselves after the (first world) war is not a success. It is not intelligent, it is not just, it is not virtuous and it does not deliver the goods. In short, we dislike it and we are beginning to despise it".[7]

All these scattered quotations add up to an indictment of crass materialism and skin-deep sensualism as the sordid stuff of human rights. A happier and more holistic perception of the green tree of human rights is necessary if we are to do justice to that great constellation of values, to that noble world heritage which fills us with legitimate pride.

The chaos in the cosmos, the political crisis, economic entropy, moral miasma and spiritual vacuum contribute to the coming collapse of the World Human Order unless we change course and put the human being at the centre stage. The drift towards self-centred pleasures mindless of the misery of others, is the disease of affluenza. The Fifth Act of the coming tragedy is poetised by Tennyson:

> *"Act first, this earth a stage so gloomed with woe*
> *That you all but sicken at the shifting scenes,*
> *And yet be patient, our Playwright may show*
> *In some Fifth Act what this wild drama means".*

It is a disturbing thought that Man is still an animal and human persons share 89% of genes with chimpanzees. The small percentage of residual genes has endowed us with extra-intellect to explore our own body and gain insights into all the creations on earth and the infinite universe. These genes also enable us to think about from where we came; why we are here; where we are going and what status and future belong to us. There is a becoming beauty and glory about authentic human rights beyond the intoxicating delights of champaign and cocaine, and carnal cravings of homo sex and lesbian license. There is a divinity that profoundly shapes the worth of the human person and raises him to the universal stature that belongs to him.

There is a qualitative difference between superficial notions of flesh-bound human rights and those fundamental freedoms rooted in the dignity and worth of the human person. Operation Human Rights is not a pretext for capture of markets and cultural coup to buy up minds or pollute them. Scientists, doctors, philosophers, theologians, politicians, social activists and human rights crusaders must realise the need to fight the brute in man and to convert the human genome into compassionate perfection and finer fellowship. That is the challenge before us all, what with man's inhumanity to man and barbarity to the other gender escalating day after day with hi-tech heartlessness and dangerous depravity, missing the chances of *humanity in harmony and happiness,* which is our true destiny. New material mechanisms are not enough; the human factor must turn celestial. The task is hard, the thought is deep, the consummation of universal happiness is a long way away.

7 *Ibid* at p. 237.

H.G. Wells, one of the visionary thinkers who wrote the *Outline of History*, narrates the story of the early neolithic culture, migrating and spreading, age by age, across land and sea arriving at wonders of achievement. The magnificent prospect for humanity, bloodied by barbarity, has entranced H.G. Wells into a hesitant prophecy:

> "One cannot foretell the suprises or disappointments the future has in store. Before this chapter of the World State can begin fairly in our histories, other chapters as yet unsuspected may still need to be written, as long and as full of conflict as our account of the growth and rivalries of the Great Powers. There may be tragic economic struggles, grim grapplings of race with race and class with class. It may be that 'private enterprise' will refuse to learn the lesson of service without some quite catastrophic revolution. We do not know, we cannot tell. These are unnecessary disasters, but they may be unavoidable disasters. Human history becomes more and more a race between education and catastrophe".[8]

The culture of human rights, unless divinised and humanised in its higher dimensions, may be vulgarised into simian appetites. Humanity, to win its great rights, must unify to intensify the search for knowledge and wisdom and eventually stand upon the earth as upon a footstool, and stretch out towards the stars. Our sages have envisioned our future, as the children of immortality. This distant dream is a fascinating story, but need not cause a pause in this glimpse of the human march. Our focus is on the actualisation of human rights sans which the right to be human becomes a simian illusion!

Although by way of divagation, it may be appropriate briefly to tell the tale of our ancient ancestors. Homo habilis walked upright and appeared some 2.5 million years ago. Homo erectus appeared perhaps 1.75 million years ago. And then came homo sapiens; and our subspecies homo sapiens sapiens occurred between five hundred thousand and fifty thousand years ago. We, of the earth, are all of this subspecies. During the neolithic revolution, agriculture, permanent settlements, domestication of animals, cloth and pottery became our asset. Thus, humanity had a common beginning, although this chance revolution occurred independently in several regions more or less simultaneously.

The cradle of history swung from 4,000 B.C. through several civilizations. Sumerian cities and Kings are remembered for *Hammurabi* who codified laws and thus created rights. Other political and religious developments need not detain us at this stage.

Egypt marked another civilisation which is still admired for its hieroglyphic writing, philosophies and science. The Pharaohs of Egypt are still a wonder of the world.

India produced a great civilisation what with Harappa, and Mohenjodaro and Vedic seers and Upanishadic visionaries. The Indus civilisation, the *Vedas* and the *Upanishads*, the pantheon of gods and the caste system are

8 Page 1158.

part of the Indian heritage. Europe and China have also showered on mankind blessings of culture in many dimensions. The America also developed the first civilisation in the western hemisphere what with temples and sculptures, gods and art forms. Now we enter the classical era of world civilisations and the great empires which sought to unite the world by conquests. Of course, art and literature, religions and discoveries also enriched the world's treasury of values and attainments.

The early empires, the sea peoples and trading peoples, the beginnings of writing and art, the arrival of gods and discovery of stars, the control by priests and kings and so on form a charming cascade in the flow of history. Our concern here, however, is on human rights and turns us on to serfs, slaves, social classes and castes, humanist individuals and inspired leaders demanding a better world and higher human order. We may, therefore, skip this winding travelogue except to notice the common man's (of course, woman's) hapless lot during these dark passages of time and his struggle to be himself, not a commodity. Human rights, our current concern, cannot flourish without basic social conditions, economic advances and moral maturity. H.G. Wells tersely tells us of the fate of the common man through the pages of history.

> "He got rather better tools, better seeds, better methods a slightly sounder shelter, he bartered his produce in a more organised market as civilization progressed. But a certain freedom and a certain equality passed out of human life when men ceased to wander. Men paid in liberty and they paid in toil, for safety, shelter, and regular meals. By imperceptible degrees the common man found the patch he cultivated was not his own; it belonged to the god; and he had to pay a fraction of his produce to the God. Or the god had given it to the king, who exacted his rent and tax. Or the king had given it to an official, who was the lord of the common man. And sometimes the god or the king or the noble had work to be done, and then the common man had to leave his patch and work for his master.
>
> *** *** ***
>
> "There was a process of enslavement as civilization grew; the headmen and leaderly men grew in power and authority, and the common man did not keep pace with them; he fell by imperceptible degrees into a tradition of dependence and subordination.
>
> *** *** ***
>
> "But war brought in a new source of possessions, plunder, and a new social factor, the captive. In the earlier, nomadic times, the captive man was kept only to be tortured or sacrificed to the victorious god; the captive women and children were assimilated into the tribe.
>
> "Parents might sell their children into slavery, and brothers their orphan sisters. Free men who had no means of livelihood would even sell themselves into slavery. And slavery was the fate of the insolvent debtor. Craft apprenticeship again, was a sort of fixed-term slavery.
>
> *** *** ***

> "The least kindly aspect of slavery has always been gang slavery. If it did not figure very largely in the ancient cities, it was very much in evidence elsewhere".[9]

From slavery to freedom, from darkness to light—that is the story of homo spaiens in its meaningful advance.

Alexander the Great and his victories marked an epoch in human affairs. Science, in its widest sense, gave life and light to mankind and the first germination of the earth as a common homoe occurred. H.G. Wells in his *The Outline of History*, at this point, observes:

> "The rest of the history of mankind is very largely the history of those three ideas of science, of a universal righteousness, and of a human commonweal, spreading out from the minds of the rare and exceptional persons and peoples in which they first originated, into the general consciousness of the race, and giving first a new colour, then a new spirit, and then a new direction to human affairs".[10]

Kingdoms and dynasties were founded and other experiments in dictatorships and community rule, coups and revolutions, peaceful and bloody, made history. The locomotion of civilization was fuelled by many motivations but the dominant force, as dialectical materialism discloses, was ultimately the production and seizure of material wealth. Alas, a warm, loving world human order—Creation's final law—has been interrupted by man's baser nature red in tooth and claw, which is capitalism at its carnal, cannibalistic worst.

The view of the socialist brood of politicians was expressed by Eugene V. Debs:

> "The master class has always brought a war and the subject class has always fought the battle. The master class has had all to gain and nothing to lose, and the subject class has had all to lose and nothing to gain".

How long shall this ignoble system last? How shall we ring in the nobler modes of life, with sweeter manners, purer laws?

In Tennyson's oft-quoted lines:

> *"Ring out, wild bells, to the wild sky,*
> *The flying cloud, the frosty light:*
> *The year is dying in the night;*
> *Ring out, wild bells, and let him die.*
> *Ring out the old, ring in the new,*
> *Ring, happy bells, across the snow;*
> *The year is going, let him go;*
> *Ring out the false, ring in the true."*

9 H.G. Wells: *The Outline of History*, 8th Ed., pages 227, 228, 229, 230.

10 *Ibid*, page 373.

The wages of savagery is death of human rights and so a humane order of peace and harmony is an urgent imperative.

We are the heirs of great cultures soaked in of noble values. We have great masters like Leonardo da Vinci whose genius is amazing, Albert Einstein, matchless as humanist and scientist, Mahatma Gandhi, a marvel for all time in the cause of non-violence. Host of other supreme human powerhouses have illumined the highway of progress leading kindly light amidst the encircling gloom. But the brutalities of the world for Hitler to Pol Pot and other butchers of populations have darkened our universe making thoughtful statesmen ask: quo vadis humanity?

The violent world shocks humanity

After many victimisations and victories, spanning long centuries, needless to recount here, the world was plunged in a vast disaster World War I. It was the weariest, bloodiest, most tragic episode up till then. This macro-war tore nations, stunned statesmen and shocked the conscience of mankind into realising the need for a *One world* idea. The darkest hour night ushers in the wee dawn.

> *"Aye on the shores of darkness there is light,*
> *And precipices show untrodden green,*
> *There is a budding morrow in midnight,*
> *There is a triple sight in blindness keen".*
>
> — KEATS

Men felt they had come to a final crisis in the world's affairs and a tragic collapse of the human species, unless sweeping changes in the peaceful relations among nations were better structured. It needed a global gory shock to ram tectonic sense into restructuring international relations to defend peace, justice and human rights. There was chaos in the cosmos and the cherished dream of a better world, frustrated by World War I, was sought to be revived by constructive statesmanship and commitment to humanity. The Great Depression that followed the sorrows of the devastating war inflicted more tensions and traumas which shook the conscience of mankind.

The West, which boasts as if it were the only world, passed through painful pages which may be touched upon to the extent relevant.

Pre-World War I chronicle of human rights—embryonic emergence

The creative happenings of the 19th century which sowed and fertilised ideas of human rights in Europe and elsewhere need to be narrated in some detail to link up the middle ages with the pre-World War I universe, confining our focus to the epic events moulding the development of human rights.

A rapid run-down of the Western World History unfolds political changes propelled by economic and social forces which are the locomotive of radical restructuring of people's consciousness. A sense of pride in the great wonders of the world to which humanity belongs helped a one world feeling promotive of a common belonging, common destiny and common rights in the universe of resources. This awareness, as it slowly awakened, nourished the claim to common human rights. It is this factor of global unity that makes the wonders of the world, as humanity's legacy, relevant to a study of human rights. The Seven Wonders of the ancient world, the Seven Wonders of the Middle Ages and the Seven Natural Wonders of the world make mankind realize the oneness of its marvellous estate. But, alas, the One Creative Wonder which humanity awaits for ages–actualisation of human rights worldwide whereby everyone everywhere will enjoy guaranteed fundamental freedoms–is tantalisingly playing hide and seek, notwithstanding all the deadly wars and massacres and collapse of empires which should have driven home the necessity for the unity of mankind and universality of human rights. Many events which sparked off battles and reforms and revolutions did, through vibrations of popular upheavals and "world storms", advance the cause of humankind although no easy ways to liberate the human personality could be beheld up to the twentieth century. The walk through the wilderness of the world continued and humankind wobbled through time and space.

The pilgrims' progress towards deliverance from oppression and for salvation of human rights, as we approach modern times, takes us to the American Revolution as a giant event with planetary portent. The British Colonies in North America attracted mass immigrations of religious dissenters, the pilgrim fathers fleeing for religious freedom, and poor people from Britain and Europe moving to the new world. But, paradoxical though, the native population suffered deprivation and extermination at the hands of the white immigrants who had escaped from the Slough of Despond. But the Whites, in turn, were in the valley of humiliation, oppressed by the Crown as a colony, provoking rebellion against the British. The American people, after a war, declared Independence and the magnificent document incorporating this overthrow of imperial domination is a foundation of the right to self-determination and the other human rights of people everywhere. For the British Empire, it was the beginning of the end. One leak will sink a ship and one sin will destroy a sinner.[11]

It is appropriate to reproduce the Preamble to the American instrument, what with its international impact pregnant with the people's rights to self-determination and personhood with all its implications. The Declaration of Independence was an Act by which the American Congress, on 4th July 1776, declared the American colonies to be independent of Great Britain. Virginia and other States, which were to join together in the United States, had their own Bill of Rights on the model of the English Bill of Rights. Let us go to the inspirational and evocative alpha of the Declaration of American Independence.

11 John Bunyan: *Pilgrim's Progress.*

> "When in the course of human events, it becomes necessary for one people to dissolve the political bands which have connected them with another, and to assume among the powers of the earth, the separate and equal station to which the Laws of Nature and of Nature's God entitle them, a decent respect to the opinions of mankind requires that they should declare the causes which impel them to the separation.
>
> "We hold these truths to be self-evident, that *all men are created equal*, that they are endowed by their Creator *with certain unalienable Rights*, that among these are *Life, Liberty and the pursuit of Happiness*. That to secure these rights, *Governments* are instituted among Men, *deriving their just powers from the consent of the governed*. That whenever any Form of Government becomes destructive of these ends, it is the Right of the People to alter or to abolish it, and to institute new Government, laying its foundation on such principles and organizing its powers in such form, as to them shall seem most likely to effect their Safety and Happiness. Prudence, indeed, will dictate that Governments long established should not be changed for light and transient causes; and accordingly all experience hath shown, that mankind are more disposed to suffer, while evils are sufferable, than to right themselves by abolishing the forms to which they are accustomed. But *when long train of abuses and usurpations*, pursuing invariably the same object *evinces a design to reduce them under absolute Despotism, it is their right, it is their duty, to throw off such Government*, and to provide new Guards for their future security".[12]

Before leaving the monumental implications of the Declaration of Independence, it may be apt to refer briefly to the American people's upsurge against imperial Britain, asserting the right to self determination. The movement, that destroyed the first British Empire establishing the United States and, indirectly Canada, is historic in the march of humanity towards the creation of a free world although ironically, US neo-imperialism is now holding in economic and military thraldom many parts of the globe. Relations between the American colonies and Britain, primarily over the issue of Parliament's right to tax the colony without their consent, sparked off popular resistance. The Stamp Act crisis, the Boston massacre and the like culminated in the Boston Tea Party (1773). This event was not a delightful Tea Party, but the climax of an anti-imperialist attempt to destroy dutied Tea by American working men. This defiance culminated in the British Parliament's brazen passage of the Intolerable Acts (1774) to punish Massachusetts for the Tea Party. Then came the First Continental Congress (1774) followed by war and victory. After the Declaration of Independence, the Articles of Confederation were prepared. Then came into being the American Constitution of 17th September 1787. One of the world's oldest National Constitutions, this instrument proved to be of seminal significance, especially because a few years later, the first Ten Amendments, the so-called Bill of Rights, were added. Almost every State in the US has a Bill of Rights and so all Americans everywhere in the country enjoy the protection of such Bills of Rights.

12 *Living Document of American History*, page 8.

Abraham Lincoln's Inaugural Address defining Democracy is classic. So too the Emancipation Proclamation (of Slaves). Of course, the Gettysburg Address is immortal and has affected mankind beyond the shores of the United States. The Emancipation Proclamation 1st January 1863 was issued by President Lincoln during the American Civil War, declaring the freedom of all slaves in the Southern States. It read:

> "We even we here, hold the power and bear the responsibility. In giving freedom to the slave, we assure freedom to the free,—honourable alike in what we give and what we preserve. We shall nobly save or meanly lose the last, best hope of earth.
>
> *** *** ***
>
> "And by virtue of the power and for the purpose aforesaid, I do order and declare that all persons held as slaves within said designated states and parts of states are, and henceforward shall be, free; and that the executive Government of the United States, including the military and naval authorities thereof, will recognise and maintain the freedom of said persons".

May be, the words of W. Lloyd Garrison, founding in 1830 the American Anti-Slavery Society, is ideologically apt:

> "Cost what it may, every slave on the American soil must be liberated from his chains. Nothing is to be put in competition, on the score of value, with the price of his liberty; for whatever conflicts with the rights of man must be evil, and therefore intrinsically worthless".
>
> *** *** ***
>
> "If the State cannot survive the anti-slavery agitation, then let the State perish. If the Church must be cast down by the strugglings of Humanity to be free, then let the Church fall, and its fragments be scattered to the four winds of heaven, never more to course the earth. If the American Union cannot be maintained, except by immolating human freedom on the altar of tyranny, then let the American Union be consumed by a living thunderbolt, and no tear shed over its ashes. If the Republic must be blotted out from the roll of nations, by proclaiming liberty to the captives, then let the Republic sink beneath the waves of oblivion.........".

Abraham Lincoln fought slavery and hated it strongly:

> "I hate it because it deprives our republican example of its just influence in the world, enables the enemies of free institutions with plausibility to taunt us as hypocrites, causes the real friends of freedom to doubt our sincerity, and especially because it forces so many good men amongst ourselves into an open war with the very fundamental principles of civil liberty, criticizing the Declaration of Independence, and insisting that there is no right principle of action but self-interest".

From the point of view of human liberties, we may, perhaps make a passing reference to the "Four Freedoms" Speech of President Franklin D. Roosevelt. The second of the Four reads thus:

> "By an impressive expression of the public will and without regard to partisanship, we are committed to full support of all those resolute peoples,

> everywhere, who are resisting aggression and are thereby keeping war away from our Hemisphere. By this support, we express our determination that the democratic cause shall prevail; and we strengthen the defence and the security of our own nation".

A beautiful blend of local and global interest! More importantly, F.D. Roosevelt tried a strategy of creating a Black Cabinet, a lesson India and other countries with depressed classes may well emulate. John Hope Franklin in his book *From Slavery to Freedom* states:

> "One of the most important factors in the achievement of political respectability on the part of the Negroes of the United States was the New Deal Policy of securing the assistance of Negro specialists and advisers in various governmental departments. Seeking the advice of Negroes was not a Roosevelt innovation. Many a President had sought to feel the pulse of the Negro population through one or more Negroes in whom he had confidence.
>
> *** *** ***
>
> "Roosevelt's group of Negro advisers differed from the others in at least four important respects. In the first place, the number of "Black Cabineteers" was fairly large, in contrast to the small number on whom previous Presidents had relied for advice. It is not possible to set an arbitrary number because it was changing constantly and because one cannot always be sure as to whether certain appointees were members of a select circle that may be regarded as a "cabinet". In the second place, they were placed in positions of sufficient importance that both the Government and the Negro population generally regarded the appointment as significant. They were not persons whose relationship with the Government was nebulous and unofficial. They were oath-bound servants of the people of the United States".[13]

They were the Black Brain Trust of the President. This experiment put the slave of yester-years in some top federal roles and filliped the actualisation of Black socio-economic liberation.

The tragic fact remains that Lincoln was assassinated: Kennedy too was martyr more or less for the same cause in Dallas—the great cause of breaking human bondage continues, Constitutional provisions notwithstanding. Even in India of Gandhi, bonded labour is a flourishing business. Tolstoy's words ring poignantly too:

> ***"The abolition of slavery has gone on for a long time. Rome abolished slavery, America abolished it, and we did, but only the words were abolished, not the thing."***

We may solace our souls by a brief sum-up:

> Slavery, in its earlier forms, as in the times of the Romans, in the Feudal Ages, when vassalage and villeinage existed, and in the serfdom of Russia and other northern nations, was attended by many inhumanities and evils; but perhaps in the negro slavery system which prevailed in the British colonies for upwards

13 John Hope Franklin: *From Slavery to Freedom*, pages 530-531.

of 200 years and in certain parts of the United States up to 1865, it attained its highest point of cruelty. Since 1833 no form of slavery has existed within the British Empire.

Perhaps, moving away from the American story of Independence, but involved ideologically in the process, one may indicate by contrast how the Judiciary—the Judges of the US Supreme Court—reacted to the liberation of slaves in America. Chief Justice Roger B. Taney, in the notorious *Dred Scott* case, (1857) made certain obnoxious observations which put to shame the judicial claim as the guardian of human freedoms. A few, out of many judicial dicta in the *Dred Scott*[14] case, reveal how deep was the institution of slavery in the United States of America. Says Justice Taney:

> "He (the slave) was bought and sold and treated as an ordinary article of merchandise whenever a profit could be made by it. This opinion was at that time fixed and universal in the civilized portion of the white race.
>
> "Congress has no power to abolish or prevent slavery in any of its territories.
>
> *** *** ***
>
> "The right of property in a slave is distinctly and expressly affirmed in the Constitution. The right to traffic in it, like an ordinary article of merchandise and property, was guaranteed to the citizens of United States, in every State that might desire it, for twenty years.
>
> "No word can be found in the Constitution which gives Congress a greater power over slave property, or which entitles property of that kind to less protection than property of any other description. The only power conferred is the power coupled with the duty of guarding and protecting the owner in his rights".

Imagine, how even the robed brethren are but the manifestation of terrible prejudices which have sunk in their soul as part of their culture. Human Rights have hoped, not through Judges nor through Presidents (George Washington, the First President of the United States and several other statesmen, who otherwise had glorious role in the framing of the American Constitution owned slaves!) but through the burst of combative conscience of the peoples of the Earth.

Thomas Jefferson once wrote (20th May 1810): "We have long suffered under base prostitution of law to party passions in one Judge, and the imbecility of another. I mention this to emphasise that in the campaign for human rights, the Constitution alone cannot be a liberating force: nor will the Judiciary, on its own, liberally emancipate the slave. Chief Justice Taney, otherwise a capable Judge, struck down the Act of the Congress liberating the enslaved American Negroes."

The French people's demand to freedom

We may next turn to the French Revolution where the people suffered so much that food riots broke out and the absolutism of the Monarch was challenged by people's collective might in assertion of human rights.

14 (1857)19 Howard 393.

Aristocratic resistance to regal absolutism was soon overshadowed by the reformist Third Estate (middle class) which proclaimed itself the National Constituent Assembly, on 17th June, 1789 and took the "Tennis Court Oath" on 20th June to secure a Constitution. The storming of the Bastille by Parisian artisans on 14th July, had great impact throughout France. The reforms contemplated by the Constituent Assembly included abolition of class and regional privileges, a Declaration of Rights, suffrage by taxpayers (75% of males), and the Civil Constitution of the clergy providing for election and loyalty oaths for priests. A republic was declared on 22nd September 1792, in spite of royalist pressure from Austria and Prussia, which had declared war in April (joined by Britain the next year). Louis XVI was beheaded on 21st January 1793, Queen Marie Antoinette was beheaded on 16th October 1795. Radical reforms in the Convention period abolished colonial slavery and passed other pro-poor, secular measures.

This was a people's victory of sorts although division among radicals (Robespierre was executed) spoiled the fulfilment of the people's urges. Nevertheless, it did mark a milestone in the angry march of the world's masses in their hunger for human rights. The Revolution declared France a Republic, executed the royalties but eventually, in a military coup, Napoleon Bonaparte emerged as first consul (Dictator).

The Declaration of Rights, a part of which is reproduced here, is abundant evidence of the human rights militancy of the French Revolution although ultimately the movement failed and Napoleon Bonaparte assumed dictatorial power in the Brumaire coup (1799).

Since this historic FRENCH DECLARATION OF THE RIGHTS OF MAN AND OF THE CITIZEN, 1789, is an invaluable contribution in the global struggle for human rights, it is right to excerpt a part which is luminous:

> "THIS Declaration is an obvious reflection of the ideals which lay behind the French Revolution. It is a fairly complete Code of the principles of constitutional Government and the rule of law, and is the first of its kind. Its inspiration is a liberalism, like that of Locke in England, which leaves a good place for property alongside, liberty. Thus, in spite of the end of revolution in France, the Declaration was to influence many constitutions of the parliamentary type of the nineteenth century and later in Europe and Latin America. The Declaration was affirmed in the Preambles to the French Constitutions of 1948 and 1958.
>
> TEXT
>
> *Article* 1
>
> Men are born and remain free and equal in respect of rights. Social distinctions shall be based solely upon public utility.
>
> *Article* 2
>
> The purpose of all civil associations is the preservation of the natural and imprescriptible rights of man. These rights are liberty, property and resistance to oppression.

Article 3

The nation is essentially the source of all sovereignty, nor shall any body of men or any individual exercise authority which is not expressly derived from it.

Article 4

Liberty consists in the power of doing whatever does not injure another. Accordingly the exercise of the natural rights of every man has not other limits than those which are necessary to secure to every other man the free exercise of the same rights; and these limits are determinable only by the law.

Arttícle 5

The law ought to prohibit only actions hurtful to society. What is not prohibited by the law should not be hindered; nor should any one be compelled to do that which the law does not require.

Article 6

The law is an expression of the common will. All citizens have a right to concur, either personally or by their representation in its formation. It should be the same for all, whether it protects or punishes; and all being equal in its sight, are equally eligible to all honours, places and employments, according to their different abilities, without any other distinction than that of their virtues and talents.

Article 7

No one shall be accused, arrested or imprisoned, save in the cases determined by law, and according to the forms which it has prescribed. All who solicit, promote, execute or cause to be executed, arbitrary orders, ought to be punished, and every citizen summoned or apprehended by virtue of the law, ought immediately to obey, and becomes culpable if he resists.

Article 8

The law should impose only such penalties as are absolutely and evidently necessary: and no one ought to be punished but by virtue of a law promulgated before the offence, and legally applied.

Article 9

Every man being counted innocent until he has been convicted, whenever his arrest becomes indispensable, all vigour more than is necessary to secure his person ought to be provided against by law.

Article 10

No man is to be interfered with because of his opinions, not even because of religious opinions, provided his avowal of them does not disturb public order as established by law.

Article 11

The unrestrained communication of thoughts or opinions being one of the most precious rights of man, every citizen may speak, write and publish freely, provided he be responsible for the abuse of this liberty, in the cases determined by law. "

The revolutionary swell collapsed: but ideas do not die, once they sink in the minds of the people. They burst again when the time is ripe. Every idea is an incitement.

Inspired by the ideals of the French Revolution, new republican regimes sprung into existence–the Batavian Republic (Netherlands) (1795–1806). The Helvetic Republic (Switzerland) (1798 - 1803), and so on. The revolutionary urges were, however, overpowered and the map of Europe was redrawn, as it were, at the Congress of Vienna by monarchs and dictators. The settlement brought a spell of peace. Nevertheless, radical thought spread through the Continent with occasional eruptions. The Vienna Congress could not arrest the advance of liberal ideas in Europe. The 1825 Decembrist uprising in Russia and similar movements elsewhere evidence the undying aspirations of the people.

Progress was stimulated by Science and political thought. Darwin's theory of evolution and Socialist theories in the West generated hopes of a just society. Industrialisation produced a new class of workers, uprooted people from villages who overcrowded towns, generated conditions which together with bad harvests and cholera epidemic created a new proletariat and demand of Republics. The bread of adversity, and the waters of affliction, to put it biblically, nourish uprisings for justice.

You may shoot men dead but ideas continue resurrectionally. The revolutionary contagion spread to Belgium (1830), to Poland and to Germany. Thus though popular upheavals failed to seize power, the people's era had gathered steam; and *that* transformation in the minds of men was a force to be reckoned with in favour of human rights ever thereafter. The *status quo* got a jolt and democratic rights gained space in the agenda of the future.

The materialist interpretation of history enlightens us about the forces which shaped Europe. Friedrich Engels propounded the thesis "that by historical materialism, history for the first time was placed on its real foundation; the obvious fact ... that first of all men must eat, drink and have shelter and clothing and therefore work ...".

Equally importantly, the thinking of people was influenced by scientific and technological advances. Darwin's statement of the theory of evolution (1859) gave a weapon for intellectuals and scientists against theological oppressions and obscurantisms. Reformist ideas led to changes in conditions of women and children, prisoners and mentally ill people. Slavery was barred in many parts of the world.

> History tells us that at one extreme, slaves might be worked to death, as in the Greek mining camps of the 5th-C and 4th-C BC. At the other, slaves were used less as chattels and more as servants, working in households, and to extent even administering them, and acting as tutors to young children.
>
> The scale of the trade built up with the arrival of the Portuguese in Africa and the development of the labour-intensive plantation system in the colonies. The Portuguese dominated the trade in the 16th-C, the Dutch in the early

17th-C, while the late 17th-C was a period of intense competition with the French, British, Danes, and Swedes joining the early practitioners. The British abolished the slave trade in 1807, and the institution of slavery in 1833. There have been various estimates of the number of slaves removed from Africa, the most reliable figure being c. 12.5 million between 1650 and 1850.

It is significant that socialist theories based on ideas of progressive production relations were widely disseminated. Utopian socialists such as Saint-Simon (1760–1825) envisaged an orderly, just society as a feasibility. Again, a model factory town, New Lanark, Scotland, was set up by utopian Robert Owen (1771–1858), and other utopian experiments were tried in the US (Brook Farm, Mass., 1841–47). Bakunin's (1814–76) anarchism represented another extreme of total freedom. Marx (1818–83) posited the inevitable triumph of scientific socialism through a historical process of class conflict. Meanwhile, industrial workers organised trade unions and became a force to be reckoned with. The first International (1864–76) tried to unite workers internationally around a Marxist programme. The Paris commune uprising, though suppressed, produced an indelible impact and social justice became a militant motto to mould the minds of men. May Day, the international symbol of united militant demands of workers rights by demonstrations in Chicago, is proof of the awakening of the world's working class in urging their basic rights. The course of crimson social changes has never been smooth nor ever totally scotched.

The impact of the French Revolution on the Indian Freedom Movement

The French Revolution, with its fundamental demand for liberty, equality and fraternity, has had a special appeal for Indians, in that it affected our own independence movement. And so, I may divagate here to dwell on the influence of the French Revolution on our own Freedom Struggle.

Before that, let us notice a brief criticism about the basic French Charter as deficient, since it spoke about the rights of Man. What about women? Did women participate in the French Revolution? They did. *La tricoteuse*, needles in hand, was an awesome presence during the Terror when Jacobins were on top. Women activists did take part in the uprising. The have-nots among the Parisian women shared revolutionary politics and acted during the bread riots, demanded the right to life, even sat on cannon, chanted the resurgence of the poor and practised the armed politics of subsistence. In spite of their valiant role, women were not given institutionalised participation in political Government. Even so, women's presence, as revolutionary partners, is a lesson of 1789. Women could not be resigned to play the "Helen of Troy, passed passively from male hand to male hand as men pass gold and lead" nor be Sita or Panchali suffering male commands, however, cruel or humiliating. No longer is home the girl prison and the woman's workhouse. The human rights of women are a reality of the New World Human Order. The French Revolution reflected in part.

Ideas sometimes take wings: and as Victor Hugo put it:

> "There is one thing stronger than all the armies in the world: and that is an idea whose time has come".

The Fourth UN Conference at Beijing proves that our sister gender will not suffer subordination, since the idea of egalite incites a perennial process of womanhood's title to her full personality.

The aggressive idea of radical human rights was surging up, the masses were in revolt and authoritarian royalties were facing the wrath of people's challenges.

> *"I sometimes think that never blows so red*
> *The Rose as where some buried Caesar bled:*
> *That every Hyacinth the Garden wears*
> *Dropt in its Lap from some one's lovely Head".*
>
> — OMAR KHAYYAM

The storming of the Bastille and the cynical retort of Queen Marie Antoinette when told of the anger of the starving masses who demanded bread: "If they have no bread, let them eat cake," are straws in the winds of change when people's right to life is imperilled and their right to govern themselves is aflame. Even Vivekananda roared of material needs as integral to human rights.

> "Bread! Bread! I do not believe in God, who cannot give me bread here, giving me eternal bliss in heaven. Pooh! India is to be raised, the poor are to be fed, education is to be spread, and the evil of priestcraft is to be removed ... more bread, more opportunity for everybody ... "Have fire and spread all over. Work, work".[15]

It is interesting, when we trace economic human rights and their roots, to read Nehru on the French Revolution: This is pregnant and portent in thought that human deliverance, once they take wings, go global. Long before Indian liberation, Nehru wrote of the French struggle:

> "In the French Revolution we find a new thing, at any rate on such a big scale—the union of ideas with the economic urge for revolutionary action. Where there is such a union, there is the real revolution, and a real revolution affects the whole fabric of life and society—political, social, economic and religious. We find this happening in France in the last years of the eighteenth century (...).
>
> "It takes a long time to build up the ideology of a people, for new ideas have to filter down gradually to them and few persons are eager to give up their old prejudices and notions. It so happens, often enough, that by the time a new ideology is established and the people have at last succeeded in accepting a new set of ideas, these ideas themselves are somewhat out of date. It is interesting to notice that the ideas of the French philosophers of the eighteenth century were based on the pre-industrial age in Europe: and yet almost at that very time the Industrial Revolution was beginning in England, and this was changing industry and life so much that in reality it was knocking out the bottom from many of the new French theories (...).

15 *The Complete Works of Swami Vivekananda*, vol. IV, page 309.

> "However, that might be, it is clear that these ideas and theories of the French philosophers had a very powerful effect on the Revolution. There had previously been many instances of masses in action in risings and revolts; now there was a remarkable instance of conscious masses in action, or rather consciously guided masses in action. Hence the importance of this great revolution in France".[16]

The blow-up of the Bastille was more than a French fury. It was a banner of humanity's revolt demanding the right to life, dignity and democracy.

Dr. Ambedkar, a dynamic leader with penetrating perception of historical events, recalled the lessons of the French Revolution from an original angle which is pertinent to progressive analysts of pervasive, suppressive social conditions. I quote his views expressed during World War II:

> "There are pessimists who say that there is no guarantee that victory will be followed by a New Order. There is perhaps room for this pessimism. The New Order which is the ideal of labour, has its roots in the French Revolution. *The French Revolution gave rise to two principles, the principle of self-Government and the principle of self-determination.* The principle of self-Government expresses the desire of the people to rule itself rather than be ruled by other whether the rulers be absolute monarchs, dictators or privileged classes. It is called democracy.
>
> "The principle of self-determination expresses the desire of a people united by common ideals and common purposes to decide, without external compulsion, its political status, whether independence, inter-dependence or union with other peoples of the world. This is called nationalism. The hope of humanity was centred on the fructification of these principles. Unfortunately, after a lapse of nearly one hundred and forty years, these principles have failed to take root. The old regime has continued either in all its nakedness or by making sham concessions to these principles. Barring a few countries, there was neither self-Government nor self-determination in the world. All this, of course, is true. But this is no argument against the attitude taken by labour, namely that the preliminary condition for the establishment of the New Order is victory over the forces of Nazism. All that this means is that labour must be more vigilant and that the war must not stop with victory over Nazis, but *there must be no peace unless there is victory over the Old Order wherever it is found*".[17]

The chaos of the French Revolution brought in its wake a coup by Napoleon, not the triumph of the Declaration of Rights!

Indians, as a people, were transformed in their political ideas by the French Declaration of the Rights of Man and Tom Paine's Book. And so, the Indian Constitution reflects in its Preamble the very rights of Man articulated in France in 1789. It is fitting, in this context, to quote excerpts

16 Jawaharlal Nehru: *Glimpses of World History,* (1988 Ed.) pages 361-362.

17 G.S. Lokhande: *B.R. Ambedkar–A Study in Social Democracy,* page 213.

from Nehru's eloquent address in the Constituent Assembly pointedly referring to the French National Assembly in 1789. Harken to his words:

> "My mind goes back to that mighty revolution which took place also over 150 years ago and to that Constituent Assembly that met in that gracious and lovely city of Paris which has fought so many battles for freedom, to the difficulties that Constituent Assembly had and to how the King and other authorities came in its way, and still it continued. The House will remember that when these difficulties came and even the room for a meeting was denied to the then Constituent Assembly, they betook themselves to an open tennis court and met there and took the oath, which is called *the Oath of the Tennis Court*, that they continued meeting in spite of Kings, in spite of the others, and did not disperse till they had finished the task they had undertaken. Well, I trust that it is in the solemn spirit that we too are meeting here and that we too, whether we meet in this chamber or other chambers, or in the fields or in the market-place, will go on meeting and continue our work till we have finished it"[18]

Even as Nehru's India at the moment of Independence recalled the ideas of French Revolution, other parts of the world also responded to the ferment in France. Natural rights gained a new power and emerged on to the grand stage of Western politics associated as it was with revolutions. The idea of a right that belonged to Man gained a new status and assertive vocabulary.

> "Kings claimed divine right in throwing off the shackles of the Pope, and they were led on to claim ever more grandiose powers over the subjects whom they now came to dominate. But the temper of the epoch was such that subjects as well as kings were growing more wilful. In England, king and subjects fell out in 1642, and a long contest took place which was not finally settled until 1688, when James II (son of the Charles I, who had been executed in 1649) fled to France, still babbling about diving right. And in that year it was celar that, so far as England was concerned, natural rights had defeated divine right".[19]

We owe our constitutional freedoms in part to the fighting faith of the French Revolutionists. The French Revolution shook Europe and the insurrectionary liquidation of throned absolutism astonished the world. Radical reforms in the Convention Period (1793-1795) included abolition of slavery, economic measures to aid the poor, support of public education, and a short-lived de-Christianisation. But the balance-sheet turned against democracy because of divisions among radicals, execution of leaders and the rise of the military general Nepoleon Bonaparte. The failure of this remarkable experiment proves Lenin's statement that without a revolutionary theory there can be no revolutionary movement. The absence of a flexible theory, dialectically sound, executed by disciplined cadres and inspired by

18 Quoted in the book, *The Framing of India's Constitution*, Edited by B. Shiva Rao, vol. I, page 123.

19 *Human Right Reader*, Edited by Walter Laqueur & Barry Rubin—Revised Ed., page 5.

charismatic leaders, guided by pragmatic methods and strategic objectives, will spell doom even if the cause be just and the enemy weak. These are lessons of history which those who battle for a just society shall never forget. Likewise, when cannibal violence is used indiscriminately, our sensitivity slowly suffers reverses and human rights cries become a ritual chant, not a burning passion. The ends are defeated by the means. And so, even when millions die of hunger or local wars, as happens currently, we remain unmoved. The toll of starvation today, for instance, is a Hiroshima every three days, twenty-eight people, children included, die every minute: We have a benumbed world which has closed down social consciousness. We have numbed ourselves and claptraps displace compassion. Revolution in human rights needs re-kindling inner feeling and fellowship. And means must be as morally clean as the high ends to be achieved. The Iron Chancellor, Bismarck, like Hitler later, believed in blood and iron. Bismarck told the Prussian House of Deputies in January 1886:

> "Place in the hands of the King of Prussia the strongest possible military power, then he will be able to carry out the policy you wish; this policy cannot succeed through speeches, and shooting-matches, and songs; it can only be carried out through blood and iron".

How ghastly a doctrine which deifies demoniac savagery to the status of statesmanship. Human rights, won by brutality cannot last as indefeasible values when the process and the product are tainted by inhumanity. The gas chamber never leads to the hall of freedom, as the Hitlerite barbarity has demonstrated.

Insurrections of ignorance often defeat themselves and the violent bitterness that follows breeds fanaticism and leads to the fall of revolutions. Brois Pasternak in *Doctor Zivago* stresses a point forgotten by revolutionists:

> "Wars and revolutions, kings and Robespierres, are history's organic agents, its yeast. But revolutions are made by fanatical men of action with one-track minds, geniuses in their ability to confine themselves to a limited field. They overturn the old order in a few hours of days, the whole upheaval takes a few weeks or at most years, but the fanatical spirit that inspired the upheavals is worshipped for decades thereafter, for centuries".

So it is that human rights visionaries sometimes find that "the Government of a revolution is the despotism of liberty against tyranny" (Robespierre). Robespierre himself was killed, so too his companions. The flood of new ideals released by the French revolution could not flow in a creative torrent but ended in scenarios of ghastly sorrow inflicted by *the Terror*. So the hope of a new World Order could not take off for want of finished blue-prints and constructive leaders. Says H.G. Wells:

> "Periods of revolution are periods of action; in them men reap the harvests of ideas that have grown during phases of interlude, and they leave the fields cleared for a new season of growth, but they cannot suddenly produce ripened new ideas to meet an unanticipated riddle".[20]

20 H.G. Wells: *The Outline of History*, 8th Ed., page 912.

After the fall of the revolution, new France rose with a likeness to the old Says Wells:

> "It is more flushed, more vigorous; it wears a cap of liberty instead of a crown; it has a new army—but a damaged fleet; it has new rich people instead of the old rich people, a new peasantry working even harder than the old and yielding more taxes; a new foreign policy curiously like the old foreign policy disrobed; and—there is no Millennium".

The holy war of freedom having failed, there was still a great change in the temper of the Continent. Under the title *The Pause of Reconstruction* and *The Dawn of Modern Socialism*: H.G. Wells points out how failure notwithstanding, the revolutionary effort "swept many obsolescent and evil things away, but many evil and unjust things remained. It solved many problems, and it left the desire for fellowship and order face to face with much vaster problems that it seemed only to have revealed. Privilege of certain types had gone, many tyrannies, much religious persecution. When these things of the ancient regime had vanished, it seemed as if they had never mattered. What did matter was that for all their votes and enfranchisement and in spite of all their passion and effort, common men were still not free and not enjoying an equal happiness; that the immense promise and air of a new world with which the revolution had come remained unfulfilled".[1]

The idea of socialism struck root in Europe and an increasing impulse to revolt against royalties and those of their ilk surfaced more often.

Back to our main thematic discussion. The American Independence and the Bill of Rights, adopted later in 1791, were monumental achievements for mankind, viewed from the human rights angle.

July 14th 1789 was at once a national event and a cosmic portent of more moment than the American Declaration of Independence, although influenced by the latter. Why? The Americans first established modern democracy. The French made it a militant creed. The old order had collapsed symbolically and the commoners had seized power. The new ethos of Liberty, Equality and Fraternity coloured the post-1789 world although Napolean seized power.

The white world expansionism

There was a veneer of stability and Europe spread out to dominate other Continents with imperialism gaining sway worldwide. The vast African interior was conquered by European powers, with slavery gaining currency. The ideology of the "whiteman's burden" and the "civilizing mission" rendered philosophical support to the industrial entry of western Europe into other continents. The westernisation of Asia followed and India became part of the empire, the *Kohinoor* on the crown. Europe dominated Asia, China signed unequal treaties with European Powers and Japan Empires inflict long holidays for human rights and people's voice.

1 *Ibid*, pages 911-912.

An aside

How human rights were crushed by the East India Company and the British Crown is explicated by Karl Marx in an article written by him to *The New York Daily Tribune* in 1853. His remarks run as follows:

> "The profound hypocrisy and inherent barbarism of bourgeois civilization lies unveiled before our eyes, turning from its home, where it assumes respectable forms, to the colonies, where it goes naked. They are the defenders of property, but did any revolutionary party ever originate agrarian revolutions like those in Bengal, in Madras, and in Bombay? Did they not, in India, to borrow an expression of that great robber, Lord Clive himself, resort to atrocious extortion, when simple corruption could not keep pace with their rapacity? While they prated in Europe about the inviolable sanctity of the national debt, did they not confiscate in India the dividends of the rayahs, who had invested their private savings in the Company's own funds? While they combated the French Revolution under the pretext of defending "our holy religion", did they not forbid, at the same time, Christianity to be propagated in India, and did they not, in order to make money out of the pilgrims streaming to the temples of Orissa and Bengal, take up the trade in the murder and prostitution perpetrated in the temple of Juggernaut?
>
> These are the men of "Property, Order, Family and Religion".[2]

The powerful hold of M.N.C. Cs on Delhi proves the supreme rule of foreign capital. Continues Marx:

> "The destructive influence of that centralization upon the markets of the world does not reveal, in the most gigantic dimensions, in inherent organic laws of political economy now at work in every civilised town. The bourgeois period of history has to create the material basis of the new world.
>
> *** *** ***
>
> "When a great social revolution shall have mastered the results of the bourgeois epoch, the market of the world and the modern powers of production, and subjected them to the common control of the most advanced peoples, then only will human progress cease to resemble that hideous pagan idol, who would not drink the nectar but from the skulls of the slain".[3]

To a student of human rights and the fatal blow suffered by India as a colony, there is some vague similarity with a present market-friendly inundation of foreign capital depriving Indians of their natural resources and reducing the poorer strata to destitution.

Imperial rivalries, protectionist trade practices, escalating arms race and economic crisis spread tension and, *pro tanto*, diminished human security. The dialectical understanding of history explains the proximity to war and revolution under those inflammatory conditions.

2 *Selected Works of Karl Marx and Frederick Engels*, vol. I, (Progressive Publishers, Moscow, page 498.

3 *Ibid*, page 498.

The assassination of Austrian Archduke Franz Ferdinand was the pretext for World War I—the matchstick to the magazine. Human slaughter and suffering and German defeat and global disillusionment were the terrible consequences. The Paris Peace Conference (1919), the Russian Revolution (1917) and other European revolutions followed this cosmic carnage. Asia was restive and people were stirred into action. The world was in a swirl and international thinking was boiling. The League of Nations, however, was impotent and symbolic. Even so, humanscape was changing.

Let us look at Europe and its tumults where we left it a little while back. During the nineteenth century the great French ideals and ideas of expansion of empires gathered steam. The world, as a whole, felt the impact. Even literature turned indignant and the arts reflected the revolt of the human spirit. The story of Latin America, United States, China and India come into our ken. The Opium War (1939-42) forced China to its knees even as the East India Company occupied India by a pythonic process. The White world spread and conflicts and contradictions, inevitable in a plural imperialist era, climaxed in the First World War and the *deja vu* of a global graveyard:

> The aftermath of this cosmic cataclysm is interesting, even arresting, but we may confine our focus to the changes wrought in the Human rights map. Of course, the immediate drama, after the cessation of war, has relevance to the development of the New World Order. The rise of totalitarianism, the decadence of democracy, the Soviet revolution and then the greatest of all calamities—World War II which beheld scenes of woe, the like of which no eye had seen, no heart conceived and no human tongue could adequately tell—these world-shaking events, draw our attention. Out of the ashes of this macromassacre, claiming millions dead, rose new forces shaping the formation of the United Nations. Martyrdom has megapower and death is not the end when it embodies an immortal idea. World War I brought our barbaric globe to the peak of casualities with a humbled Germany. The Hitler regime seized power under a democratic Weimar Constitution (1933). The Nuremberg Laws, two racial laws promulgated in Nuremberg in 1935 by the Nazi Party were virtually fatal to Jewish survivals in Germany. The Nazis killed 5-6 million Jews. German bombs wiped out civilians. So did Japanese forces in the East. The Allies, including the Soviets, turned the tide and won the world for freedom's cause. The United Nations Charter was signed in San Francisco on 26th June 1945 by 50 nations.

This capsulated version must now be expanded to give a clearer picture of the terrors and horrors and the treaties and palavers of the post-World War I period. Europe, on the cessation of hostilities, was in a state of armed peace and could burst any time, although people walked around with the hope of business as usual.

Who won or lost is less material than the fact that humanity had invalidated its assumptions of peace, progress and basic values. Two figures stand out at this stage of history. They are the American President Wilson and Lenin of the Soviet Union. Democratic President Wilson came to a table of peace negotiations. The World was dazed, and stunned. Militarist regimes had been defeated. Everywhere there were unwanted privations; everywhere there was mourning. The tale of the dead and mutilated had mounted to many millions. Men felt they had come to a crisis in the world's affairs. There was universal hunger for peace without the power to secure it. People were homeless, without bread and in despair. War economies had a socialist structure to meet basic needs. Hunger can trigger revolutions, especially when there is a contrast between luxury and poverty, side by side:

> "The fields were fruitful, and starving men moved on the roads. The granaries were full and the children of the poor grew up rachitic, and the pustules of pellagra swelled on their side. The great companies did not know that the line between hunger and anger is a thin line."[4]

But a leopard rarely changes its spot, and private capital never its avarice. Private enterprise in Europe was more intent on speculation, cornering and hoarding and continuing luxury production with an eye on maximum profit. The social unrest of the masses, together with the brutalising drill of the war, made the situation in Europe dangerous. The masses were disgusted with the luxury and waste of the rich and the general misery of the poor. Economic injustice and explosive indignation made communist thinking popular. Likewise, the fascist, with totalitarian ideology, became prevalent especially in Italy under Mussolini. Human rights and fascism are incompatible enemies since the former faces ideological death sentence from the latter. Political brigandage and bully rule disdain human rights as bullshit:

Let us get back to the Paris peace process. President Wilson was the moving spirit of the Peace Conference at Paris. To begin with, Wilson unfolded a vision of the World which looked like a blueprint for a better universe where human values would find fertile soil.

> "Secret agreements were to cease, 'nations' were to determine their own destinies, militarist aggression was to cease, the sea-ways were to be free to all mankind". These common places of American thought, these secret desires of every sane man, came like a great light upon the darkness of anger and conflict in Europe. At last, men felt, the ranks of diplomacy were broken, the veils of Great Power 'policy' were rent in twain. Here with authority, with the strength of a powerful new nation behind it, was the desire of the common man throughout the world, plainly said.
>
> Manifestly there was needed some overriding instrument of Government to establish world law and maintain these broad and liberal generalizations upon human intercourse. A number of schemes had floated in men's minds for the attainment of that end. In particular, there was a movement for some sort of world league, a 'League of Nations'. The American President adopted this phrase and sought to realize it. An essential condition of the peace he sought was he declared to be this federal organ. This League of Nations was

4 John Steinbeck: *The Grapes of Wrath.*

> to be the final court of appeal in international affairs. It was to be the substantial realization of the peace. Here, again, he awakened a tremendous echo".[5]

This Professor of Political Science, Wilson, presented himself as a messiah with his Fourteen Points as a definite statement of arrangements for a better world with transparency of Covenants and a General Association of Nations to guarantee the peace of the world. It looked as if a hopeful era in human affairs was dawning; but that was not to be, since the Wilson solution evaporated without making an impact on the World Order. The hopes he had raised vanished as illusions and the edifice of human rights never was built. Europe, when the President touched its shores, was as clay ready for the creative pottery. Never before were the nations so eager to follow a Moses who would take them to the long promised land where wars are prohibited and blockage unknown. The dreamy unreality of the Paris Conference became clear when the grim realities of hard politics came into conflict with Wilson's proposals and a homunculus became the pathetic product as embodied in the Covenant of 28th April 1919. One need not analyse the clauses of the League Covenant which produced a powerless organization although it had an immense reception lit by faith in Wilson. The American President stated about this global creation designed for peace and human advance.

> "At the front of this great treaty is put the Covenant of the League of Nations.........Unless you get the united, concerted purpose and power of the great Governments of the world behind this settlement, it will down like a house of cards. There is only one power to put behind the liberation of mankind, and *that is the power of mankind. It is the power of the united moral forces of the world,* and in the Covenant of the League of Nations the moral forces of the world are mobilized".[6]

The Council of the League was to meet once a year, and according to the Covenant could make only unanimous decisions, save in a few specified instances. This power of Veto proved a disaster since it had no power even to inspect the military preparations of its constituent States. The treaties embodied in the decision of Versailles disarmed Germany and humiliated a proud nation, thus sowing the seeds for the next war. Sir Winston Churchill regarded these humiliating terms as the seed of Hitlerism. Let me quote him:

> "I have always said that if Great Britain were defeated in war I hoped we should find a Hitler to lead us back to our rightful position among the nations".

*** *** ***

> "He (Hitler) embodied the revolt of Germany against the hard fortunes of war.........Adolf Hitler is Fuehrer because he exemplifies and enshrines the will of Germany".

The world paid the global price of the Second World War because myopic European leaders betrayed the hopes of humanity in Paris 1919:

5 H.G. Wells: *The Outline of History*, 8th Ed., pages 1098-1099.

6 Woodrow Wilson: *Address at Pueblo*, 1919.

"The Fourteen Points formulated by the Treaties were like a row of ruined and tattered houses in a bombarded village that the first attempt to produce a World Law thus passed away like a burst of laughter in a tavern". In short, the Wilson phenomenon proved a mirage and Europe drifted towards tension and explosion Hitler, Mussolini.

Franco and Tojo, Generalissimos breed brutal authoritarianism and homicide of human rights.

If Human Rights jurisprudence were jettisoned despite World War I, there was a creative side to the convulsions in the shape of the Russian Revolution of 1917.

> "Military defeats and high casualties caused a contagious lack of confidence in Tsar Nicholas, who was forced to abdicate in March 1917. A liberal provisional Government failed to end the war, and massive desertions, riots and fighting between factions followed. A moderate socialist Government under Kerensky was overthrown in a violent coup by the Bolsheviks in Petrograd under Lenin, who disbanded the elected Constituent Assembly in November 1917".

Weary of War and wary of Czarist oppression, the people, led by the Bolsheviks, sought and secured peace despite the civil war and hostilities of foreign powers. The Red Army defended the revolution and the Communist Party led the Soviet coup. From peace to positive construction of the economy guaranteeing basic rights of the nationalities, Lenin built up an impregnable Soviet Union, although his successor Stalin used terror to generate conformity to the Soviet policy. The 1936 Constitution of the Soviet Union gave guarantee of social and economic rights and inaugurated a rival *system where man mattered* but had to bear political curbs. Party corruption and bureaucratic terrorism can destroy the vitals of the best Constitution as the Soviet collapse seven decades later shatteringly showed.

There were other European revolutions which failed or were suppressed. The Chinese revolution under Sun Yet-Sen produced a republic, later taken over by Chiang Kai-Shek. Long after, a successful Communist revolution under Mao Zedong established the People's Republic of China. In the Middle East, Mustafa Kamal Ataturk produced reforms and secularised the law.

Capitalism was doomed to depression and world-wide financial panic; and economic crisis began with the US Stock Market crash.

By contrast, Russia advanced through planned industrialisation and universal education and collectivisation of agriculture. The Roosevelt administration, in the USA, embarked on social reform and economic amelioration, including protection for Labour Unions.

The economic decline world-wide and the humiliation of Germany with its military mentality were forces which compelled the Axis Powers to start World War II on a scale which spelled massacres of millions and other sufferings. The most massive consequence of this large-scale tragedy was the death of human rights of every shade. The gravamen of this world terrorism, however, was the dropping of two US Atom Bombs on 6th and 9th August 1945 on Hiroshima and Nagasaki, shocking the conscience of humanity and forcing the surrender of Japan within a week. Globoshima, thus perpetrated, deprived the US of its innocence—a criminality which is currently aggravated by the Super Power hunger for nuclear bomb monopoly.

Hiroshima goes down in world victimology as the worst crime on humanity. The atomic bomb dropped there, pressing the button from the military plane with a casualness, on 6th August 1945, claimed a casuality of 150 thousand killed or wounded and most of the buildings of the city destroyed or damaged. Human rights cant and chant are Himalayan hypocracy so long as humanity does not punish the engineers of the Hiroshima tragedy. Nay, more; the potential for Globoshima is currently in the custody of a super-power. Until the last nuclear menace vanishes through collective action, all clap-trap about human rights and peace is but gibberish.

> The war brought 20th century cruelty to its peak. The Nazi regime systematically killed 5-6 million Jews, including some 3 million who died in death camps (e.g. Auschwitz). Gypsies, political opponents, sick and retarded people, and others deemed undesirable were murdered by the Nazis, as were vast numbers of Slavs, especially leaders,
>
> German bombs killed 70,000 British civilians. Some 1,00,000 Chinese civilians were killed by Japanese forces in the capture of Nanking. Severe retaliation by the Soviet army, East European Partisans, Free French, and other took a heavy toll. US and British bombing of Germany killed hundreds of thousands, as did US bombing of Japan (80,000-2,00,000 at Hiroshima alone). Some 45 million people lost their lives in the war.

The right to life lost its reality. Though the civilised world survived the barbaric blitz it was at once both Triumph and Tragedy, as Churchill put it. The overwhelming victory failed to transform the savage past to sage realization of a New World Order. And yet, the hinge of fate did produce a decisive change for the better. For, the United Nations was born (October 1945), the greatest event in the story of humanity which had witnessed countless shifts in its march through millennia, now blood-stained, now beautiful, now human—divine, now sably savage. Now, war is so barbaric, global, technologically heartless and pervasively destructive of life, in human and all other forms that the next World War will be fought with stones (Einstein). Bertrand Russell told us that war, in our scientific age, means, sooner or later, *universal death.* Douglas MacArthur was wise to prescribe the need for an end to war:

> "Military alliances, balances of power, leagues of nations, all in turn failed, leaving the only path to be by way of the crucible of war. The utter destructiveness of war now blocks out this alternative. We have had our last chance. If we will not devise some greater and more equitable system, Armageddon will be at our door".

War in our times of nuclear bombs and chemical weapons means sooner or later universal death. Bertrand Russell (*The Future of Mankind*) predicts:

> "Before the end of the present century, unless something quite unforeseeable occurs, one of the three possibilities will have been realized. These three are:
>
> I. The end of human life, perhaps of all life on our planet.
>
> II. A reversion to barbarism after a catastrophic diminution of the population of the globe.
>
> III. A unification of the world under a single Government, possessing a monopoly of all the major weapons of war".

War starkly means total homicide of entire human rights. Tolstoy's words have a poignant ring as he addressed the Peace Conference on 1909:

> "We have met here to fight against war. The truth is that one may not and should not in any circumstances or under any pretext kill his fellow men".
>
> "We must say what everybody knows but does not venture to say. We must say that by whatever name men may call murder—murder always remains murder and a criminal and shameful thing. And it is only necessary to say that clearly, definitely, and loudly, as we can say it here, and men will cease to see what they thought they saw and will see what is reality before their eyes. They will cease to see the service of their country, the heroism of war, military glory, and patriotism, and will see what exists: the naked, criminal business of murder"!

Anyone who believes in human rights must join the party of compassion and opposition to all wars.

> "If war no longer occupied men's thoughts and energies, we would within a generation, put an end to all serious poverty throughout the world".

4

Epistemological Foundation and Escalating Emergence of Human Rights Jurisprudence

"The conception of human rights is of Central importance in the development of the modern world. Like all such ideas, it is very much theory-laden, implying a general view of man and society, of individuality, politics and the ends of Government. Like all such ideas, it is profoundly historical, expressing the aspirations and seeking to remedy the ills of particular places and times. It is thus an idea with a history, an idea that changes in both content and social function."

—Eugene Kamenka

Jurisprudence is the knowledge of law or, more widely expanded, it is the systematised knowledge of any branch of law. The science of law is what is loosely known as Jurisprudence. It has three facets, namely legal exposition, legal history, and the science of legislation. This is a tentative trinity good enough for practical purposes. The anatomy of the legal system as existing at any given time is the purposes of the first study. 'The purpose of the second is to set forth the historical process whereby any legal system came to be what it is or was. The purpose of the third is to set forth the law, not as it is or has been, but as it ought to be. It deals not with the past or present of any legal system, but with its ideal future, and with the purposes for which it exists. The complete scientific treatment of any body of law involves the adoption of each of these three methods'.[1]

Jurisprudence also covers the theory or philosophy of law. Any student of human rights, in its growth from time to time, will have to dwell upon the philosophical, historical and aspirational aspects of that branch of jurisprudence. Human rights have a global character, although what is

1 Salmond on Jurisprudence.

often studied is the growth of the law from the Greek and Roman and later Western developments. The sociological dimension of human rights jurisprudence deserves special attention even as the humanist emphasis also must be traced from age to age. Any analysis of human rights jurisprudence, in its course through time and space, must be approached through a dialectical method and not merely as a non-committal narration of thoughts and names of thinkers. To make our studies of the evolution of human justice and human rights on a global scale meaningful, we have to locate the epistemological foundation and trace the escalating emergence of human rights jurisprudence.

The sources of human rights may be traced to philosophical thought, spiritual insights and religious revelations in the shape of *dharma* of the Hindus, *dhamma* of the Buddhists, edicts of Asoka inscribed on rock pillars, sermons and teachings of Christianity, concept of *Din*, as distinguished from duniya, of Islam, and Taoism and Confucianism of China and so on. They are streams which flow and fertilise higher values and humanitarian ways of life. These sublime contributions apart, the West has, from early days, developed noetic resources and juristic ideas which have sown the seeds of human rights, broadened and deepened their scope and growth. These 'forefather' ideas and ideologies belong to bygone centuries but their rapid survey is a living link between the past and the present as we take glimpses of the world heritage of human rights. Our civilizational conducted tour of human rights evolution begins, as most Western things do, from the times of the Greeks and Romans, although the East, particularly India, had built glorious mansions of Philosophy and schools of Spirituality long ages ago.

Let us look at the vintage wisdom of the West for our present purpose. The different visions, variegated constructs, theories rooted in religious thought and concepts of humanitarian justice promenade through cultural developments of the Middle Ages and earlier periods, and we behold the red thread of human rights.

The *Encyclopaedia Britannica*, tracing the origin of human rights thoughts, states:

> "But the idea of the inalienable rights of the human being is much older and, in fact, was known to poets, philosophers, and politicians in antiquity and in the Middle Ages. When Sophocles' *Antigone*—the play was composed about 442 BC—says to King Creon:
>
> ***"But all your strength is weakness itself against***
> ***The immortal unrecorded laws of God";***
>
> she invokes the higher law, the law of nature, the natural rights of man. Throughout the centuries there has been a close connection and interdependence between the idea of 'natural law' and the idea of the natural rights of man. These ideas may be found in the works of the Stoics, both Greek and Roman, and in the teaching of early Christianity, St. Thomas Aquinas, and medieval English scholars of the law. They are encountered in the writings of Spanish Theologian-lawyers of the 16th century and in the 17th century in the

> works of the Dutch Hugo Grotius, the founder of modern international law, and of John Milton and John Locke, the ideological architects of the English revolution of that century."

The jurisprudence of human rights, natural law, and materialist interpretation of social forces inevitably adopted various perspectives, conditioned by changing factors. But Greek culture, a distant neighbour of Eastern thought, generally inspired Western scholars for long centuries. And, in that sense, Friedrich Nietzsche is right when he says: 'When we speak of the Greeks, we unwittingly speak of today and yesterday'!

A journey through the Western past is useful since the white man's world of ideas and ideologies still dominates the coloured continents and cultures. In the archaic age of the Greeks, like in ancient Indian scriptures, gods and revelations of the divine will played a part. Ramayana and Mahabharata are heroic Epics which also are revelatory of godist functionalism governing the Ruler's Rule of Law (*Dharma*). A similar chapter in the early development of law is discernible in the West. Homer and Hesiod, in their poetic works, present these trends.

> "Law at that time was regarded as issuing from the gods and known to mankind through revelation of the divine will. Hesiod pointed out that wild animals, fish, and birds devoured each other because law was unknown to them: but Zeus, the chief of the Olympian gods, gave law to mankind as his greatest present. Hesiod thus contrasted the *nomos* (ordering principle) of nonrational nature with that of the rational (or at least potentially rational) world of human beings. Foreign to his thought was the skepticism of some of the Sophists of a later age, who sought to derive a right of the strong to oppress the weak from the fact that in nature the big fish eat the little ones. To him law was an order of peace founded on fairness, obliging men to refrain from violence and to submit their disputes to an arbiter.
>
> Law and religion remained largely undifferentiated in the early period. The famous oracle of Delphi, considered an authoritative voice for the enunciation of the divine will, was frequently consulted in matters of law and legislation. The forms of law making and adjudication were permeated with religious ceremonials, and the priests played an important role in the administration of justice. The king, as the supreme judge, was believed to have been invested with his office and authority by Zeus himself."[2]

Antigone's defiance of King Creon's command (depicted in Sophocles' tragedy) invokes an unwritten law (Superior to the King's Law):

> "Not of today or yesterday they are, but live eternal: (None can date their birth). Not I would fear the wrath of any man (And brave God's vengeance) for defying these."

Divine duty prevailed over legal command in those times. In later periods, temporal winds began to blow.

2 Edgar Bodenheimer: *Jurisprudence* (Indian Reprint 1996), pages 4 and 5.

Greek thought got divorced from religion; and law too became secularised. Justice was thus stripped of mystic attributes and came to be related to social interests.

Thus a 'transvaluation of values' liberating human law from heavenly authority came to prevail. Natural law, which has nexus to human justice, sprouted thus in the West. When the Sophists came, they proclaimed the 'right of the strong' as a basic postulate of 'natural' law. The 'right of might' incarnating as *law* is found in Plato's *Republic* in a famous passage:

> "I declare that justice is nothing else than that which is advantageous to the stronger."
>
> *** *** ***
>
> "Injustice, when great enough, is mightier and freer and more masterly than justice."

This definition of justice had turned the truth upside down, according to Socrates. Plato comes near to caste and caste-based dharma when he exclaims:

> "You in this city are all brothers, but God, as he was fashioning you, put gold in those of you who are capable of ruling; hence, they are deserving of most reverence. He put silver in the auxiliaries, and iron and copper in the farmers and the other craftsmen. For the most part your children are of the same nature as yourselves, but because you are all akin, sometimes from gold will come a silver offspring or from silver a gold, and so on all round. Therefore, the first and weightiest command of God to the rulers is this—that more than aught else they be good guardians of and watch zealously over the offspring, seeing which of those metals is mixed in their souls; if their own offspring has an admixture of copper or iron, they must show no pity, but giving it the place proper to its nature, set it among the artisans or the farmers; and if, on the other hand, in these classes children are born with an admixture of gold and silver, they shall do them honour and appoint the first to be guardians, the second to be auxiliaries. For there is an oracle that the city shall perish when it is guarded by iron or copper..............."Each class, says Plato, must strictly confine its activity to the performance of its own specific functions..........."To mind one's own business and not to be meddlesome is justice."[3]

The Manu concept of fourfold castes and their appropriate *dharma* are proximate ideas.

In his last phase, Plato changed and demanded a 'law state' as against a "non-law" state. He veered to this view in his last work *The Laws*. Justice according to law, not by arbitrary fiat, nor by discrimination among persons, was commended by him. Plato realized that 'no human being.........is capable of having irresponsible control of all human affairs without being filled with pride and injustice'. Aristotle, who stood for 'good life' as the basis of political organization, held the view: "Man, when perfected is the best of animals, but if he be isolated from law and justice

3 Edgar Bodenheimer: *Jurisprudence* (Indian Reprint 1996), pages 7 and 8.

he is the worst of all". The rule of law is an Aristotelian necessity for good governance. The rigidity of law may have to be tempered by equity; and so, Aristotle includes *epieikeia* or equity in his scheme. Equity is "a rectification of law where law is defective because of its generality".

Justice is a basic factor of sound law. Cicero took this view and argued for the play of justice as an imperative of law.

> "'Pestilential' statutes put into effect by nations, he emphasized, no more deserved to be called laws than the rules a band of robbers might pass in their assembly. Cicero thus appeared to favor the position that an utterly unjust law lacks the quality of law."[4]

Jus Naturale is a grand conception of universal significance. Jus Gentium is observed by all mankind, as the Roman jurists claimed. The Stoic philosophers were convinced that discriminations on the score of sex, class, race, or nationality were unjust and contrary to the law of nature. The Stoic influence promoted social equality. Edgar Bodenheimer observes:

> "Since some of the great emperors of that period, like Antoninus Pius and Marcus Aurelius, as well as some of the jurists, like Papinian and Paul, were under the sway of Stoicism, the causal connection between this philosophy and the growth of humanitarian and equalitarian ideas in the Roman Empire should not be underestimated. Various attempts were made to adapt the positive law to the postulates of a Stoic natural law, although the scope of these attempts was limited to certain specific measures and did not affect the main body and institutions of Roman law. The institutions of slavery and the family, especially, were influenced by the spread of the new doctrine."[5]

Slaves had a less harsh deal under later Roman emperors. Humanitarian ideas entered the Roman legal system slowly. Stoic philosophy had an egalitarian impact founded, as it was, by Zeno of Citium who emphasized that all people were equally part of a natural order and should be free from passions and pleasures.

The legal status of women also improved under the Stoic concept of natural law and equality and contributed to her gradual emancipation from the despotic hold of her husband. By the time of Justinian, the Roman woman was independent. The family relations and the rights of children also changed for the better. Stoic natural-law concepts were a benign factor, not the only one. Says Edgar Bodenheimer:

> "All that may be said is that many of the leading men of Roman political and legal life in the late republic and the imperial period stood under the influence of Stoic philosophy, and that it is very likely that this humanitarian philosophy played some part in the legal and social reforms which took place in this period of Roman history. Among the sociological reasons which may perhaps explain why the Stoic philosophy fell on such fertile soil in Rome must be counted the trend toward a universal empire, which was very marked in the last period of

4 Edgar Bodenheimer: *Jurisprudence* (Indian Reprint 1996), page 15.
5 *Ibid* pages 16-17.

antiquity and which led to the creation of the *Imperium Romanum. The Stoic concept of a world-state with a common citizenship and a common law, based on natural reason, acquired a very real and non-utopian meaning under these circumstances.* With the granting of citizenship rights to most of the Roman provincial subjects in 212 A.D., *the idea of a community of civilized mankind (civitas maxima),* as opposed to the parochialism of the small city-states of earlier periods, *had found an approximate realization.* It was no wonder that under these conditions the philosophical concepts of Stoicism, which found additional support in the rise and spreading of Christian ideas, had a significant impact on the political and legal developments of the Roman Empire."[6]

This course of history explains how ideas of human rights dawned in the West. Under Augustus, it has been said, that law was ameliorative. Let me, for general interest, quote a famous passage indicative of humanitarian changes in the law from the time of Augustus:

> "It was the boast of Augustus that he found Rome of brick and left it of marble. But how much nobler will be the sovereign's boast when he shall have it to say that he found law dear and left it cheap; found it a sealed book and left it a living letter; found it the patrimony of the rich and left it the inheritance of the poor; found it the two-edged sword of craft and oppression and left it the staff of honesty and the shield of innocence."

From Emperor Augustus to St. Augustine, natural law bettered human rights. The ideal 'law of nature' conceived men as free and equal; slavery was unknown and people lived as brothers. But gradually mankind deteriorated and injustice overran society, love gave way to greed and passion. The State emerged as an institution. In St. Augustine's opinion "Justice being taken away then, what are Kingdoms but great robberies". The human right to justice oozes through this passage.

St. Thomas Aquinas, the Italian scholastic theologian, was an exponent of cosmic law and natural law. *Lex divina* gained currency through the Old and New Testaments as sources of law. *Thomism* recognised human law (*lex humana*) as the dictate of reason; and insisted that for a State mandate to have the quality of law, it must conform to the postulate of reason. An unjust and unreasonable law, repugnant to the law of nature was *unlaw* and a perversion of law. So, arbitrary and oppressive enactments deserved to be defied. St. Thomas believed in the right of resistance 'which becomes transformed into a genuine duty of disobedience in the case of laws promulgated by tyrants'. Mahatma Gandhi in our century told the British empire that where laws were satanic sedition was his religion. The Thomistic conception of justice obligated also a duty to give each one his due. *Distributive Justice,* which implies equality in a dynamic sense strengthened the claims of social justice and *commutative* justice or corrective principle struck at unjust enrichment at the expense of another and harmful losses suffered at the hands of another were corrected and compensated.

6 Edgar Bodenheimer: *Jurisprudence* (Indian Reprint 1996), pages 19-20.

The Church, as history creatively moved on, was the centre of socio-legal thought and the story of human rights cannot bypass the part of the Church. The Church of Rome had dominance but found its antithesis against the tyrannical theology in the emergent Protestant reinterpretation of the Bible allowing equal value for all souls. Individuals enjoyed a larger degree of autonomy under this view of life. This movement attacked not only the spiritual hierarchical order of Catholicism but also the worldly order of feudalism in its economic and political aspects. The Holy Roman Empire was opposed by the doctrine of national sovereignty. But, later on, human freedom had to struggle against *raison d'etre* which sought to subordinate individuals to absolutist statism. The dialectic of the age then was the battle against despotic monarchy by the law-of-nature philosophy.

> "Three periods may be distinguished in the evolution of the classical law-of-nature philosophy. These periods correspond roughly to three successive stages in the social, economic, and intellectual development of this epoch. The first stage in the process of emancipation from medieval theology and feudalism which took place after the Renaissance and Reformation was marked by the rise of Protestantism in religion, of enlightened absolutism in politics, of mercantilism in economics. To this epoch, which lasted longer in Germany than in the Western countries of Europe, belong the theories of Grotius, Hobbes, Spinoza, Pufendorf, and Wolff. It is a characteristic feature of the theories of these men that the ultimate guaranty for the enforcement of natural law is to be found largely in the wisdom and self-restraint of the ruler.
>
> *** *** ***
>
> "The third epoch was marked by a strong belief in popular sovereignty and democracy. Natural law was entrusted to the "general will" and the majority decision of the people. The most outstanding representative of this stage was the French political thinker Jean-Jacques Rousseau. The third stage in the development of the law-of-nature school had a profound impact on the political and constitutional development of France, while the second form of the law-of-nature school gained the upper hand in the United States of America".[7]

The Thomistic conception of justice was influenced by Cicero and Aristotle. Like the latter, Acquinas held that the equality among humans was part of distributive justice.

As we shall see later, the classical era of natural law was a resistance to the domination of the spiritual life by the Church. The philosophy in which free individual volition had a place of paramount importance could also be traced to the challenge to the Catholic Church. We may well conclude that through the maze of doctrines bearing upon the status of the human individual *vis-a-vis* the Church and royal authority we observe, dialectically examined, the assertion of political, social and economic forces which helped shape the rationalistic and individualistic natural law philosophy. It

7 Edgar Bodenheimer: *Jurisprudence* (Indian Reprint 1996), pages 34-35.

must also be mentioned that, as against the rights of the individual, there emerged another formulation presented by the Italian political philosopher Machiavelli. He glorified the omnipotence of the State and subordinated public life to political necessities of State-craft. Thus, while man was emancipated from the Church, the sovereign State became his master through the doctrine of *raison d'etre*. Every era had to struggle for the rights of man, be it against the Church or the Emperor who subjugated the personhood of the individual.

Hugo Grotius and secularisation of natural law

Grotius, the father of modern humanitarian jurisprudence, secularised the science of law and defined the State as 'an association of free man, joined together for the enjoyment of rights and for their common interest'. A compact of the people is the benign basis of his thesis and if usurpation by the ruler happened, people has a right of overthrow.

The State and the sovereign envisioned by Grotius, enjoyed sovereign power as transferred by the people to be exercised according to the natural law and the law of nations. If the ruler misused his power flagrantly a right of revolt was permissible.

We may skip some great names of jurists and reach down to Hobbes and Spinoza who stood for supremacy of the State. Why? Man is selfish and brutal and aggressive and each man is a wolf to every other man (*homo homini lupus*) contrary to the benign humanism of Grotius. Therefore, savage situations will endanger societal peace and individual liberty. So, Hobbes argued for a compact by which power would be transferred to *one man* or *assembly of men*. This sovereign power was called 'Leviathan' or the 'Mortal God' by Hobbes. Hobbes' pessimism about man led him to the absolutism of the State and the assumption that 'no law can be unjust'. His view of 'enlightened absolutism' could weaken human rights. Spinoza, however, considered liberty to be the highest aim of Government. Government's object is not to change men into beasts or puppets but to develop their minds and bodies freely and in security.

For Spinoza a good Government will grant freedom of speech to its citizens and will not attempt to control their opinions and thoughts. Reason suggests that oppression is an invitation for resistance.

He held that 'no one can long retain a tyrant's sway'. The limits to sovereign power, in Spinoza's view, are set, not by any superior legal rules by which it is restrained, but by the power of the many or by the Government's own well-conceived self-interest. In this sense, Spinoza's sovereign is limited by natural law, and sense of self-preservations.

The story of democracy advanced as a result of the political theory of John Locke and of a French nobleman, Baron Charles Louis de Montesquieu. Both of them agreed about human liberty as the highest goal. When absolutist rulers rose in Europe, a shield of individual liberty against governmental encroachment became necessary. Thus the law of liberty was a response of society to the challenge of despotism.

The law of nature stands as an internal rule to all legislators as well as others, argued Locke. He opposed absolute monarchy and favoured a Government with limited powers. He demanded separation of the legislative from the executive power, but when the rights of people were destroyed what were the people to do? An appeal to heaven, was his answer. Here comes the relevance of Montesquieu who devised a defence of human liberty through the doctrine of separation of powers.

> "Constant experience shows us", he said, "that every man invested with power is apt to abuse it, and to carry his authority as far as it will go". To prevent such abuses it is necessary that power should be checked by power. In Montesquieu's opinion, that form of Government will be safest in which the three powers—legislative, executive, and judicial—are separated; that is, made independent of each other and entrusted to different persons or groups of persons. Furthermore, according to him, they should be so constituted that they hold one another in check."[8]

A combination of Locke's theory of natural law and Montesquieu's doctrine of separation of powers forms the philosophical foundation of the American system and the constitutional division into the trinity of independent branches plus a system of checks and balances. The US Supreme Court was influenced by this political approach. For instance in the case of *Savings and Loan Association* v *Topeka*,[9] it was observed:

> "There are.........rights in every free Government beyond the control of the state. A Government which recognized no such rights, which held the lives, the liberty, and the property of its citizens subject at all times to the absolute disposition and unlimited control of even the most democratic depository of power, is after all but a despotism.........There are limitations on such power which grow out of the essential nature of all free Governments, implied reservations of individual rights, without which the social compact could not exist, and which are respected by all Governments entitled to the name."[10]

It is significant that the Constitution of Virginia of 12th June 1776 declares:

> "That all men are by nature equally free and independent, and have certain inherent rights, of which, when they enter into a state of society, they cannot, by any compact, deprive or divest their posterity; namely, the enjoyment of life and liberty, with the means of acquiring and possessing property, and pursuing and obtaining happiness and safety."[11]

We may safely conclude that law and liberty were becoming comrades in arms at that time in history. In the words of Justice Wilson of the US Supreme Court "without liberty, law loses its nature and its name, and becomes oppression. Without law, liberty also loses its nature and its name and becomes licentiousness". This view was shared by the Founding Fathers of the American Constitution. Edgar Bodenheimer notes:

8 Edgar Bodenheimer: *Jurisprudence* (Indian Reprint 1996), page 49.
9 22 L. Ed. 455 at 461.
10 Edgar Bodenheimer: *Jurisprudence* (Indian Reprint 1996), page 50.
11 Edgar Bodenheimer: *Jurisprudence* (Indian Reprint 1996), page 50.

> "John Adams, Thomas Paine, and Thomas Jefferson were convinced that there existed natural rights which could not be restrained or repealed by human laws. And the view that it was the function of the courts to defend human rights, as recognized and sanctioned by the Constitution, against any violations by the legislature, was held not only by Wilson, but also by Hamilton and Jefferson. Men like James Kent (1763-1847) and Justice Joseph Story (1779-1845) likewise were firm believers in the existence of a natural law. It can safely be stated that there is no country in the world where the idea of a law of nature, understood as a safeguard of liberty and property against governmental encroachments gained a higher significance for the political and social development and the moulding of all political and legal institutions than in the United States of America."[12]

Another great name in the tradition of natural law is Jean Jacques Rousseau. He believed in the theory of social contract and, in his theory, the State expressed the general will and unanimous consent of all citizens. Since the law, in his political scheme, represented the general will it had to be ratified by the people as a whole. In view of this opinion, he held that the English nation, with its representative system, was not a free nation. "It is free only during the election of members of Parliament. As soon as they are elected, slavery overtakes it, and it is nothing". (How true even today, many may say in many democracies).

People's freedoms and pure democracy, as advocated by Rousseau, influenced the French Revolution and invigorated the people.

We may mention two names in English legal history dealing with the 'law of nature'. Sir Edward Coke, as Chief Justice, upheld the doctrine of certain unchangeable principles of natural reason which were above even Parliamentary law. But Sir William Blackstone, in his famous *Commentaries on the Laws of England,* virtually admitted the defeat of Coke's theory, although he did contend that human laws were not valid if contrary to the law of nature. These were only 'ornamental phrases', because, Blackstone admitted what is the law even today in England viz. that Parliament is absolute and without control and commands of reason and justice are but moral restraints on the omnipotence of Parliament. Of course, the present situation in England, as a member of the European community, is somewhat different.

Summing up the gains of the classical law-of-nature school and its various doctrines, Bodenheimer observes what is relevant from the human rights angle:

> "They created the legal instruments by which the liberation of the individual from medieval ties was achieved. The law of nature contributed to the abolishment of villeinage and serfdom. It helped to destroy the medieval guilds and medieval restrictions upon trade and industry. It aided in freeing landed property from feudal burdens. It created freedom of movement and of

12 *Ibid* at page 52.

vocational choice. It inaugurated an era of religious and spiritual freedom. It purged criminal law and procedure of its most serious shortcomings by abolishing torture and humanizing punishment. It did away with witchcraft trials. It sought to achieve legal security for everybody and sponsored the principle of equality before the law. It elaborated the general principles of international law. All these achievements were not due exclusively to the immediate influence and pressure of the natural-law philosophers. Many factors were at work in the process of the liberation of the individual, which started in the sixteenth century, and the vigor and speed of this process were different in the various countries of the Western world. But there can be no doubt that the classical law-of-nature movement was one of the creative and invigorating forces in the rise of liberalism and in the legal reforms which liberalism achieved."[13]

It is necessary to realise that these political thinkers were not writing for entertainment but were moulding militant ideas to shape changes for the better of human lot and rights. For instance, the ferment in the ideas of the Americans against the Island Crown was started by English leaven. John Locke's writings incited modern democratic ideas in America. Thoughts travel; minds respond when conditions torment, Americans could not submit to British oppression and when inflammatory ideas against imperial excesses reached, revolt was fuelled and legitimated by sense of justice. Locke, the son of a Cromwellian soldier, expressed bold republican thinking which spread to America and France. The pen, more than the gun, can shoot over long distance and hit when the time is ripe. H.G. Wells writes on Locke and Montesquieu:

"There was much liberal thought, speech, and sentiment in France at this time. Parallel with and a little later than John Locke in England, Montesquieu (1689-1755) in France, in the earlier half of the eighteenth century, had subjected social, political, and religious institutions to the same searching and fundamental analysis, especially in his *Esprit des Lois*. He had stripped the magical prestige from the absolutist monarchy in France. He shares with Locke the credit for clearing away many of the false ideas that had hitherto prevented deliberate and conscious attempts to reconstruct human society.

*** *** ***

"A group of brilliant writers, the "Encyclopaedists", mostly rebel spirits from the excellent schools of the Jesuits, set themselves under the leadership of Diderot to scheme out, in a group of works, a new world (1766). The glory of the 'Encyclopaedists', says Mallet, lay 'in their hatred of things unjust, in their denunciation of the trade in slaves, of the inequalities of taxation, of the corruption of justice, of the wastefulness of wars, in their dreams of social progress.

*** *** ***

"Side by side with the Encyclopaedists were the Economists or Physiocrats, who were making bold and crude inquiries into the production and distribution

13 Edgar Bodenheimer: *Jurisprudence* (Indian Reprint 1996), page 58.

of food and goods. Morally, the author of the *Code de la Nature* denounced the institution of private property and proposed a communistic organization of society. He was the precursor of that large and various school of collectivist thinkers in the nineteenth century who are lumped together as Socialists.

"Both the Encyclopaedists and the various Economists and Physiocrats demanded a considerable amount of hard thinking in their disciples. An easier and more popular leader to follow was Rousseau (1712-78).[14]

I do indicate, merely sketchily, that the slow gestation of human rights and democracy with socialist content was the product of insemination by radical intellectuals when the womb of history was hospitable to receive and nourish such creative thought, resisting hostile circumstances. Humanist ideas sprout from fertile soil if seeds are sown by progressive thinkers and the season is propitious. The Industrial Revolution in England crushed the economic rights of the common masses. Workers sank, slums rose and exploitation escalated. The explosive process had to be analysed and revolutionary thought, as a locomotive of change, had to shoot out of the brains of sensitive intellectuals. Wide-spread misery, deserted villages, grimy slums, the eclipse of rural and urban people's happiness and human rights found a new Messiah in Karl Marx, a German Jew of scholarly attainments. The proletariat could resist the privation and destitution inflicted by the proprietariat, given 'class consciousness' and readiness to unite and fight for their social and economic rights. These have-nots, with nothing to lose except their lives, were to form a vibrant human solidarity and then, there was a world to conquer and equal human rights to share. Communism, the Marxian social structure, generated an ideological fermentation which haunted Europe. Though popular insurrections failed, the vision did not perish.

It is proper, while tracing the saga of human rights jurisprudence, to notice Karl Marx who shook the world of ideas with revolutionary rupture of the die-hard culture of human bondage. He gave, through the Communist Manifesto, an urgent call to *make* man free, not merely to *talk* philosophy:

"The philosophers have only interpreted the world in various ways; the point is to change it."

A revolutionary quantum jump, having in mind the liberation of people from an extortionate system stormed the world through the Marxian theory of economics. It had its impact on jurisprudence. His theory of law is that jurisprudence is a product of evolving economic forces, that law is a tool used by a ruling class to maintain its power over the lower classes and that under his scheme of communism, law as an instrument of social control will wither away. Karl Marx and Frederick Engels are noted in history for this juridical theory. Law, as a reflection of economic conditions, is an integral part of the doctrine of dialectical materialism and so people will be free under a political, social, religious and cultural order of any given epoch largely as determined by the existing system of production. Law is

14 H.G. Wells: *The Outline of History*, page 885.

only a superstructure erected on top of the economic foundation. Law is not wholly autonomous although conditions of society may also change with powerful legal systems fighting for human freedom. The State influences economic development and law *ultimately* is subordinated by relations of production. Men make their history themselves, only they do so in a given environment which conditions it and on the basis of actual relations already existing. The decisive factor which forms the red thread running through all relations is economic. If law is class-rule, it follows that human freedoms become assured only when a Just World Economic Order is operational. We hark back to the International Covenant on Social, Economic and Cultural Rights of 1966 and hear the echo of Marx's thundering proposition.

Hegel, who preceded Marx, spoke of the process of dialectic. It reveals itself in thesis, anti-thesis and synthesis. The human spirit sets a thesis which becomes the leading idea of a particular epoch. Against this thesis an anti-thesis is set up and from the struggle of both a synthesis develops which absorbs elements of both and reconciles them on a higher plane. This process repeats itself again and again in history. Such is the evolutionary dynamic movement which governs change. When we seek to study the stream of human rights ever moving we must adopt this dialectical approach so that they may be scientific and not stray away by sentimental or chauvinistic passions.

Law cannot be belittled in its importance as a strong factor in safeguarding human liberties. Savigny took the view that law is simply a function of the whole life of a nation. "Law grows with the growth, and strengthens with the strength of the people, and finally dies away as the nation loses its individuality". Lawyers, jurists and judges play an active part, as trustees of the people and representatives of the community spirit, in protecting right and justice.

Herbert Spencer stressed the law of 'equal freedom' adapted to the individualism of the *laissez faire* period. He included, among individual rights, free speech, free belief, the right to light and air and what not. Social rights did not appeal to him, though.

Karl Marx emphasised the material conditions of life as of governing importance. May I remind you, by the way, that thousands of years before Karl Max, the ancient Indian Jurist Kautilya pronounced this thesis and declared that *"Artha Eva Pradhana"*, *i.e.,* the Economic order structures the Society including all its Laws and Rules and Regulations and Norms? According to Marx public law and private law also were determined by economic relations:

"Your jurisprudence is but the will of your class made into a law for all, a will whose essential character and direction is determined by the economic conditions of existence of your class". Engels slightly diluted the rigour by saying that a code of law is not always the blunt, unmitigated expression of the domination of a class. We may conclude that if a society has competing classes laws cannot easily obliterate human rights altogether. Indeed, Marx stood for the full and free exercise of the faculties of every person. Stalin's terrorism cannot destroy Marxian humanism and consequential rights. Socialist legality with a human heart is rich with human justice. Socialist features have influenced or shaped the *corpus juris* of many countries. It is interesting to recall that McCarthy went to the extent of branding Chief Justice Earl Warren a communist because his judgments upheld human freedoms and Jim Crow's egalite. President Eisenhower also shared this view. It was as though, in the deeper layers of Republican psyche, human rights were allergy and anathema.

Anglo-Saxon Jurisprudence—its variations and human rights

Roscoe Pound is the founder of American Sociological Jurisprudence. The quintessence of his philosophy of law is stated thus in his own words:

> "I am content to think of law as a social institution to satisfy social wants—the claims and demands and expectations involved in the existence of civilized society—by giving effect to as much as we may with the least sacrifice, so far as such wants may be satisfied or such claims given effect by an ordering of human conduct through politically organized society. For present purpose I am content to see in legal history the record of a continually wider recognizing and satisfying of human wants or claims or desires through social control; a more embracing and more effective securing of social interests; a continually more complete and effective elimination of waste and precluding of friction in human enjoyment of the goods of existence—in short, a continually more efficacious social engineering."[15]

Here is a positive commitment to meet the social wants and economic needs of the members of the society, through the process of law. One should have expected the great American Judge Oliver Wendell Holmes to blaze the trail in favour of human rights. But Holmes's ethical agnosticism influenced an attitude of pragmatism coupled with recognition of the people's needs. In his own words:

> "The life of the law has not been logic: it has been experience. The felt necessities of the time, the prevalent moral and political theories, intuitions of public policy, avowed or unconscious, even the prejudices which judges share with their fellow-men, have had a good deal more to do than the syllogism in determining the rules by which men should be governed. The law embodies the story of a nation's development through many centuries, and it cannot be dealt with as if it contained only the axioms and corollaries of a book of mathematics."[16]

From the point of view of human rights development the US Supreme Court has supported human freedoms, especially during the Warren era. Liberal values at their finest prevailed during that time, although the same Court in a previous century in the dreadful *Dred Scott* case (1857) had ruled that slaves were bought and sold as ordinary articles of merchandise and so Congress had no power to abolish slavery.

15 *Introduction to the Philosophy of Law*, (Revised Ed.) page 47.

16 Edgar Bodenheimer: *Jurisprudence* (Indian Reprint 1996), page 122.

This dismal jurisprudence has been wiped out, although inequalities of race and gender are prevalent still. What an indelible stain on the Court and American justice! President Abraham Lincoln's Emancipation Proclamation of 1st January 1863, reads:

> "And by virtue of the power and for the purpose aforesaid, I do order and declare that all persons held as slaves within said designated states and parts of states are, and henceforward shall be, free, and that the executive Government of the United States, including the military and naval authorities thereof, will recognize and maintain the freedom of said persons."

Global imperialism operating through Multi-National Corporations is holding human rights of humanity to ransom.

The dynamic rule of law adopted by progressive jurists across the world is a valuable contribution to human right. The International Commission of Jurists, in its Declaration of Delhi, has upheld this radical definition of the "Rule of Law".

> "The Rule of Law is a dynamic concept for the expansion and fulfilment of which jurists are primarily responsible and which should be employed not only to safeguard and advance the civil and political rights of the individual in a free society, but also to establish social, economic, educational and cultural conditions under which his legitimate aspirations and dignity may be realized."

It is fair to close this chapter on legal theories and theorists bearing on the growth of human rights by a reference to Capelletti who spoke of social rights as legal rights important today for the vast masses of humanity who suffer sans dignity, sans basic needs, sans everything. Gandhiji would have called for a *daridra narayana* jurisprudence and I would have described it as Third World/Fourth World Jurisprudence currently being strangled by the lawless process of market-friendly pathology, privatisation robbery and liberal loot on a global scale on the euphemistic philosophy of Might *is* Right. Let me end with a quote from Capelletti explaining this concept:

> "The right of effective access to justice has emerged with the new social rights. Indeed, it is of paramount importance among these new rights since, clearly, the enjoyment of traditional as well as new social rights presupposes mechanisms for their effective protection. Such protection, moreover, is best assured by a workable remedy within the framework of the judicial system. Effective access to justice can thus be seen as the most basic requirement—*the most basic 'human right'*—of a system which purports to guarantee legal rights."[17]

The modern post-World War II dynamics of human rights begins, in a serious sense, with the Nuremburg Trials. A shocked mankind set up a tribunal for trying war criminals. We are concerned not with the preliminaries but with the formulation of the Nuremburg principles.

> "At its second session (5th June–29th July 1950) the Commission formulated a set of seven Principles of International Law recognized in the Charter and in the judgment of the Nuremberg Tribunal. These are:

17 *M. Capelletti,* Rabels Z (1976) 669 at 672.

(1) Any person who commits an act which constitutes a crime under International Law is responsible therefor and liable to punishment.

(2) The fact that internal law does not impose a penalty for an act which constitutes a crime under International Law does not relieve the person who committed the act from responsibility under International Law.

(3) The fact that a person who committed an act which constitutes a crime under International Law acted as Head of State or responsible Government official does not relieve him from responsibility under International Law.

(4) The fact that a person acted pursuant to order of his Government or of a superior does not relieve him from responsibility under International Law provided a moral choice was in fact possible to him.

(5) Any person charged with a crime under International Law has the right to a fair trial on the facts and law.

(6) The crimes hereinafter set out are punishable as crimes under International Law: (*a*) Crimes against peace; (*b*) War crimes; and (*c*) Crimes against humanity.

(7) Complicity in the commission of a crime against peace, a war crime, or a crime against humanity as set forth in Principle (6) is crime under International Law.

The Assembly at its 1950 session sent the Commission's formulation to member-Governments for their comment. The Assembly requested the Commission, in preparing a draft code of offences against the peace and security of mankind, to take account of observations on the Nuremberg Principles made during the session or subsequently received from Governments."

The codification of human rights over the centuries

The procession of philosophies, theories and juristic writings bearing on human rights, from the ancient to the modern times, has transited over thousands of years, even as the ages have been whispering to us through the pages of history. But it is proper to gain glimpses about the codifications and like instruments crystallising, in legal formulations, the rights of the people in the shape of human rights, democratic obligations, social and political claims and immunities. From the obscure mists of the past men have struggled for the right to be treated as humans with dignity, with successes and failures, and codifications have recorded the gains of freedoms. So I conceive it as a complementary part of the study to make a rapid survey of those epic parchments. That is the basis for the recapitulation of the hoary documents which tell us the tale of human rights advancement.

Confining ourselves to the West, the first codifications of something akin to a catalogue of rights–if not yet of all men, then at least of the nobles of the land–began to emerge in compacts between princes and feudal assemblies. One of the earliest of these came in 1188, when the Cortes, the feudal assembly of the Kingdom of Leon (on the Iberian Peninsula), received from King Alfonso IX his confirmation of a series of rights, including the right of the accused to a regular trial and the right to the inviolability of life, honour, home, and property. In the Golden Bull of King Andrew II of Hungary (1222), the King guaranteed, among other things, that no noble would be arrested or ruined without first being convicted in conformity with judicial procedure. The most famous and influential commitment of this kind was in the English Magna Carta, accepted by King John at Runnymede in 1215. Though it was exacted by his feudal barons in their own selfish interest and was by no means intended to assert rights and liberties for all, several of its provisions, among them the famous clause 39 stating that "no free man shall be taken or imprisoned ... or exiled or in any way destroyed ... except by the lawful judgment of his peers or (and) the law of the land", gave expression to the idea of individual freedom and became the symbol of this freedom for centuries to come.

This historic instrument declared the right to justice and equality and Constitutional Government. Royal absolutism surrendered to the browbeating by barons. Its lofty beauty and content is seen from a brief extract:

> "That the English Church shall be free."
>
> "No free man shall be taken or imprisoned or dispossessed, or outlawed or exiled, or in any way destroyed, nor will we go upon him, nor will we send against him except by the lawful judgment of his peers or by the law of the land."
>
> "To no man will we sell, or deny, or delay, right or justice."

When we narrate the English history of the democratic rule of law and the beginnings of human rights, we cannot do justice to the subject without a reasonably adequate reference to Lord Denning's delectably instructive writings on the theme which has flowered today into the rule of law in many countries. He says in *The Family Story*:

> "Alfred was the first of our law-givers. He drew up a code saying: 'Those laws which seemed to be rightest, those I have gathered, and rejected the rest'. That is a point of view which appeals to me."[18]

After the Saxons (Alfred the Great was one) came the Normans. The Norman barons insisted on Magna Carta 1215 A.D. Says Lord Denning:

> "King John oppressed the people. The barons rose against him. The City of London turned the scale. The King assented to the Charter. He did it with his tongue in his cheek. Two months later a Papal Bull declared it void. But after the death of King John, the Charter was re-issued by the young King Henry III. It is that re-issue which is the first in the statutes at large."[19]

Under the heading 'Fount of English Liberty' there is a vivid and enjoyable portrayal of the circumstances in which Magna Carta ripened into the

18 Lord Denning: *The Family Story*, page 7.

19 Lord Denning: *What Next in the Law*, pages 271-272.

great instrument of later international import. Its charming presentation by Lord Denning deserves excerption as it is fine prose and educative:

> "Seven centuries and a half ago, in the month of June 1215, the meadow of Runnymede looked much as it does today. The season was early and the commoners of Egham had cut their hay. To this meadow came the King and the Barons. Their parley culminated in the greatest constitutional document of all time. It is commonly called Magna Carta, or the Great Charter. The proceedings spread over the ten days from 10th June (the Wednesday after Whit Sunday) to 19th June (the Saturday before Trinity Sunday). This year, 750 years later, the occasion is being commemorated over the self-same ten days, 10th June to 19th June and the self-same festivals of the Church.
>
> In 1215 the principal characters were the King, John Lackland, the Archbishop of Canterbury, Stephen Langton, the Barons, led by Robert Fitz-Walter, with the significant backing of William Hardell, the Mayor of London. Their successors in office are coming to the commemoration this year. The Queen is coming to the City of London on the morning of Thursday, 10th June. She will be met at Temple Bar by the Lord Mayor of London. She will go to a service at St. Paul's Cathedral at which will be present all the descendants of the Barons who can be mustered. The address will be given by the Archbishop of Canterbury. The Charter itself will be there, in the form in which it was confirmed by Parliament and became the law of the land.
>
> *The King did not sign*
>
> It is usual to picture King John signing Magna Carta, pen in hand. In point of fact he did not sign it at all. It is doubtful if he could even write. There is no evidence that he could. It is probable that he did not even affix his own seal. That would be done for him by his clerks in Chancery. The rest of the story can, however, be pieced together from the records that have survived.
>
> "On 5th May 1215, many of the Barons openly rebelled against the King. They renounced their fealty to him. When he read their demands, his retort was: 'Why do not the Barons, with these unjust exactions, ask my kingdom?' On 12th May he ordered their estates to be seized. But the Barons marched towards London which, on 17th May, opened its gates to them. This was decisive. The Barons, with the support of London, had the whip-hand. John had to sue for peace. Emissaries went to and fro with safe conduct. At length a truce was arranged from 10th June to 15th June. During those days meetings were to be held at Runnymede. The place suited both sides. It lay next the river between Windsor and Staines. The Barons made their base at Staines, where they were protected by the line of the river. The King had his base at his castle at Windsor. In between was the meadow of Runnymede. It was a good camping ground. There they negotiated, suspicious of each other, in reach of their arms.
>
> *The Great Seal is affixed*
>
> "The first meeting at Runnymede was on 10th June 1215. There were present King John, the Archbishop Stephen Langton, and some baronial envoys. At this meeting the Barons presented their demands and the King submitted to them. According to the historians of today Heads of Agreement were drawn up then

and there on 10th June. The scribe headed them, *'Ista sunt Capitula que Barones petunt et dominus Rex concedit'* (Here are the demands which the Barons seek and the King concedes). The King caused his Great Seal to be affixed."[20]

Things did not run smooth, although John assented, hoping to secure peace:

"The peace did not last long. In a couple of months the parties were again at war. The King looked for aid to Rome. It came. By a Papal Bull dated 24th August 1215, Pope Innocent III purported to annul the Charter. He forbade the King to observe it and he also forbade the Barons to exact its performance. At a Lateran Council he excommunicated the English Barons who had persecuted John, he said, by endeavouring to take from him his kingdom. But John's death on 12th October 1216, at Newark Castle, altered everything. Early in the reign of the young King Henry III the Great Charter was confirmed by his regents. In the year 1225 it was re-issued by the King himself under the Great Seal. Magna Carta then took its final form, word for word, as it stands today as the earliest enactment on the Statute Rolls of England."[1]

Thus the liberties of English men gained status and viability. The guarantee of freedom is in the 39th Clause which has been set out earlier. Equally important is the 40th Clause which guarantees the impartial and prompt delivery of justice. These words have influenced human rights jurisprudence down the centuries. Indeed, law-persons and the laity have given currency to these brave words which are the forerunners of people's rights:

"The greatest of those who gave currency to the words was Sir Edward Coke, Lord Chief Justice of England. Four hundred years after the meeting at Runnymede he forsook his crabbed learning, threw aside his lawyer's commentary and brought out this little gem: 'Upon this chapter, as out of a roote, many fruitful branches of the Law of England have sprung...... As the gold-finer will not out of the dust, threads, or shreds of gold, let passe the least crum, in respect of the excellency of the metall: so ought not the learned reader to let passe any syllable of this law, in respect of the excellency of the matter."

'The reeds at Runnymede'

The constitutional significance of Magna Carta is immense. It was thus measured by Bryce: "The Charter of 1215 was the starting point of the constitutional history of the English race, the first link in a long chain of constitutional instruments which have moulded men's minds and held together free Governments not only in England, but wherever the English race has gone and the English tongue is spoken". When the colonists crossed the seas from England to countries the world over, they took with them the principles set down in the Great Charter. Those who went to

20 Lord Denning: *The Family Story*, pages 229-230.
1 Lord Denning: *The Family Story*, page 230.

Virginia took its very words. When they renounced their allegiance in 1776, they stated in the Declaration of Rights that 'no man be deprived of his liberty, except by the law of the land or the judgment of his peers'. Thence the provisions of the Charter found their place in the Constitution of the United States. There it is revered as much as here.

> "Rudyard Kipling has expressed the feeling we have for the Great Charter as the foundation of our liberties:
>
> *"And still when mob or monarch lays*
> *Too rude a hand on English ways,*
> *A whisper wakes, the shudder plays*
> *Across the reeds at Runnymede."*[2]

The next landmark in the English constitutional history is the Petition of Right of 1628. In enjoyable prose, Lord Denning speaks of the protagonists of this instrument:

> "Coke, while he was Chief Justice of the King's Bench stood up against the pretensions of the King. So he was dismissed from his office. After his dismissal he became a member of Parliament and advocated the liberty of the subject with an energy which was surprising in a man of his age for he was seventy-six when he succeeded in carrying the famous Petition of Right in 1628. He overcame by his arguments and perseverance all the objections and impediments raised against it. I will tell you more of this later."[3]

King Charles I imposed an unjust tax protesting against which Sir Edward Coke, as member of Parliament relied on the Magna Carta and moved the Petition of Right in Parliament. Thus came into existence the Petition of Right which defined unparliamentary taxation, billeting arbitrary imprisonment, and martial law over civilians as illegal. It was conceded by Charles I. The people won the battle.

The Bill of Rights, or Declaration of Rights, came in 1688 (1689), next. King James II was a bad King who dismissed judges and sent Judge Jeffreys on the bloody assize. In this crisis, King James quit the throne in December 1688 and the British throne was offered to William and Mary on condition of their acceptance of the Bill of Rights which became an Act of Parliament. Lord Denning elegantly reproduces these ancient rights and liberties in *What Next in the Law*.

Lord Denning quotes Macaulay:

> "Macaulay describes the importance of the Bill of Rights in these words:
>
> > 'The Declaration of Rights, though it made nothing law which had not been law before, contained the germ of the law which gave religious freedom to the Dissenter, of the law which secured the independence of the Judges, of the law which limited the duration of Parliaments, of the law which

2 Lord Denning: *The Family Story*, page 231-232.
3 Lord Denning: *What Next in the Law*, page 11.

> placed the liberty of the Press under the protection of juries, of the law which prohibited the slave trade, of the law which abolished the sacramental test, of the law which relieved the Roman Catholics from civil disabilities, of the law which reformed the representative system, of every good law which has been passed during more than a century and a half, of every good law which may hereafter, in the course of ages, be found necessary to promote the public weal, and to satisfy the demands of public opinion."[4]

Let us proceed, partly overlappingly. The philosophy of John Locke and the traditions of the Glorious Revolution of 1688, with its Act of Settlement and Bill of Rights paved the way for human rights thinking even in a monarchy. Charles I was tried in 1649 which ended in his execution. These events cumulatively and breathtakingly sowed the seeds of the concept of a new implicit Sovereign, *the people.*

It may be useful to recall a part, at least, of the Bill of Rights, 1688/89.

The Bill of Rights was a part of the major settlement between the Crown and Parliament consequent on the struggles of the Stuart period. Like Magna Carta it is a demarcation of powers primarily, but it also contains general principles of State policy and law. Some of these have come to have universal significance. Thus the prohibition of illegal and cruel punishments was to appear in many other contexts, including the Universal Declaration of Human Rights. The English Bill of Rights as a whole has inspired more sophisticated developments in other countries. In recent years, some British lawyers and public figures have advocated the adoption of a modern Bill of Rights.

The long 'Whereas' portion of the Statute asserts the rights of the "commons assembled at Westminster fully and freely representing all the estates of the people of this realm. The Glorious Revolution (December 1688–February 1689) during which James fled and William and Mary became joint monarchs established a bloodless revolution and the constitutional authority of Parliament.

It is thus seen that the Bill of Rights is an early democratic assertion of peoples' rights. The following quote reinforces the human rights referred to earlier in the text. The King's right to levy money under guise of prerogatives is restricted; the right of subjects to petition the King is validated. The freedom of election, the freedom of speech, the abolition of excessive bail are *inter alia* declared. Yet another part of the Bill of Rights must attract our attention:

> "*And they do claim,* demand and insist upon all and singular the premises as their undoubted rights and liberties and that no declarations, judgments, doings or proceedings to the prejudice of the people in any of the said premises ought in any wise to be drawn hereafter into consequence or example."

4 Lord Denning: *What Next in the Law*, page 274.

England, way back in the 17th century, secured victories in the battle for human rights (the immemorial rights of Englishmen). The English Petition of Right (1628) and the English Bill of Rights (1688) are the product of struggle against tyranny. (The latter, in its full form, is a historic, heroic human rights triumph but is too lengthy to be reproduced.)

Let us recall at this point Tennyson's lines, although Britain still has no Bill of Rights. (Lord Scarman and others of his ilk notwithstanding):

> *"A land of settled Government,*
> *A land of just and old renown,*
> *Where freedom slowly broadens down*
> *From precedent to precedent."*

These great instruments crossed the Atlantic and transplanted the ideas therein in the New World.

> "The American Declaration of Independence (1776), the Virginia Declaration of Rights (1776), and the American Bill of Rights (1791) carried not only the ideas of the earlier English documents but in some cases their very text as well. Nor was it only England that exported its doctrine of rights: the powerful influence of the French philosophers of the Enlightenment is visible among all the American revolutionaries."[5]

Likewise, the American example inspired the French Declaration of the Rights of Man and of the Citizen (1789). The spirit of man has a remarkable power to travel with his suitcase of culture and tradition, spread them wherever he goes and allow them to take root in his new home, nurture them there and reap a value-added harvest of human advance. This progressive process is sometimes reversed because revolution, conditioned by social realities, advances and retreats and, in its long march, zigzags, attacks and withdraws, and, above all with the patience and strategy of historical materialism, changes course; but march it must and it will. History never sleeps; humanity never stands still. Says Emerson:

> "What is a man born for but to be a Reformer, a Remaker of what man has made; a renouncer of lies; a restorer of truth and good, imitating that great Nature which embosoms us all, and which sleeps no moment on an old past, but every hour repairs herself, yielding us every morning a new day and with every pulsation a new life?"

That is why the universal expansion of the British, French and American revolutions spread throughout Europe. Asia, Africa and the Caribbean, why the whole world, have responded to the spiritual summons to struggle for a higher synthesis.

The United States and France, in the matter of fundamental freedoms, influenced the entire continent of Europe and eventually other parts of the world. Curiously, Great Britain does not even now have written constitutional guarantees, although jurists and statesmen are pressing for such a Bill.

5 *Encyclopaedia Britannica,* 15th Ed., vol. 8, page 1183.

An epic event of world-shaking importance is the Russian Revolution of 1917, which wrote into the Constitution basic rights and freedoms with a texture fundamentally different from the other popular convulsions followed by constitutional declarations without provision for concrete enjoyment.

The dynamics of the Russian Revolution is unparalleled because it created a new society founded on Power to the People. The Soviet System, from bottom to top, is a pyramid where peoples' presence is pervasive and multiform. V.I. Lenin, who doubtless had in mind the Declaration of the Rights of Man and of the Citizen adopted by the French National Assembly in 1789, drew up a different Declaration of the rights of labouring and exploited peoples. The Fundamental Law on 10th July 1918 opened with this Declaration vesting all central and local authority in the Soviets. The social and economic resources of the Republic belonged to the people and the Declaration went on to assert that the division of society into classes was abolished and all land was taken over as national property to be transferred to the labouring masses. Workers' control of industry was also proclaimed. Recollecting, as it were, the American Declaration of Independence, the USSR adopted a similar declaration.

> *Article 1* reads: "The Union of Soviet Socialist Republics is a socialist state of the whole people, expressing the will and interests of the workers, peasants, and intelligentsia, the working people of all the nations and nationalities of the country."
>
> *Article 2* begins: "All power in the USSR belongs to the people."

The solidarity of the labouring masses was made basic to the revolutionary State. The right of self-determination to the various nationalities was also granted as a collective right. So much so, the Union was voluntary. Russification was rejected and national minorities, even the smallest, was given cultural autonomy. It is important to remember to-day, when the right of self-determination has become sensitive, controversial and fraught with internascent war, to read the Proclamation promising autonomy in return for support.

The Proclamation grandiloquently reads:

> "Mohammedans of Russia", it began, "Tartars of the Volga and Crimea; Kirghiz and Sartes of Siberia and Turkestan; Turks and Tartars of Transcaucasia, your beliefs and customs, your national institutions and culture, are hereafter free and inviolable. You have the right to them. Know that your rights, as well as those of all the peoples of Russia, are under the powerful protection of the Revolution, and of the organs of the Soviets for workers, soldiers, and peasants. Lend your support to this revolution, and to its Government."[6]

The Constitution does uphold the social and economic rights of the peoples which composed the Union. The Russian Revolution of 1917 aimed at a qualitative transformation, as pointed out in the *Encyclopaedia Britannica*:

6 Sidney and Webb: *Soviet Communism*, 3rd Ed., page 108.

"This basic difference in concepts becomes clear in a comparison of the provisions of the first Soviet Constitution. The First Amendment to the American Constitution provides, among other things, that Congress shall make no law abridging the freedom of speech or of the Press. The Russian Constitution of 1918 'for the purpose of securing freedom of expression to the toiling masses' abolishes all dependence of the Press upon capital and turns over to the working people and the poorest peasantry 'all technical and material means for the publication of newspapers, pamphlets, books,' etc. The US Constitution prohibits abridgment of the right of the people peaceably to assemble, while the Lenin constitution, in order to ensure complete freedom of assembly to the working class and to the poorest peasantry, offers 'all premises convenient for public gatherings together with lighting, heating and furniture'.

"The Soviet Constitution of 1936, while changing the wording, has by and large, maintained this general approach. Western constitutional ideas were designed to prevent interference with fundamental rights mainly, though not exclusively, by the public authorities. The Soviet concept ignores this aspect and promises to make available technical facilities without promising freedom in the choice of the purposes for which they will be used. In trying to draw conclusions from the existence in so many legal systems of catalogues of rights, these differences of basic concept must be kept in mind."[7]

The later Soviet Constitution went further to guarantee Human Rights and make them available in *fact* and not merely in *form*. Articles 39 inscribed the social, economic, political and personal rights while Article 40 guaranteed the right to work (that is, including the right to rest and leisure). Article 41 further provides: The right to health, housing, education and so on. Every such right proceeds to provide facilities ensuring actualisation by citizens, not paper pledges. (The gross infirmities and grave abuses which eventually brought about the liquidation of the Soviet Union does not detract from the vision and embodiment of Human Rights in the 1936 and the later Constitution of 1977). According to Soviet political scientists, democracy without actual economic and social rights is idle talk. There are two meanings and two interpretations of freedom—one formal, in capitalist society, and the other real, in socialist society. A reading of the text of the USSR Constitution reveals this progressive profile of people *enjoying* the right to life in its fullness as a socialist song. But when the notes or tunes go wrong the song jars and ceases to please. Those who have visited and seen and scanned Soviet or Cuban or other socialist country in its better days will appreciate what the Webbs in their classic work call the New Civilization. But when the rhythm was upset and sweet sounds began to turn discordant, the loveliness was lost. It is not the song that is at fault; it is the abuse, the corruption that has polluted the stream. Dr. Ambedkar observed in the Indian Constituent Assembly:

"......... I feel, however good a Constitution may be, it is sure to turn out bad because those who are called to work it, happen to be a bad lot. However bad

7 *Encyclopaedia Britannica,* 15th Ed., vol. 8, pages 1183-1184.

a Constitution may be, it may turn out to be good if those who are called to work it, happen to be a good lot. The working of a Constitution does not depend wholly upon the nature of the Constitution. The Constitution can provide only the organs of State such as the legislature, the executive and the judiciary. The factors on which the working of those organs of State depends are the people and the political parties they will set up as their instruments to carry out their wishes and their politics. Who can say how the people of India and their parties will behave?"[8]

The vices that violated the Soviet system were of the Party bosses and bureaucrats with vested interests. In Stalinist and later years, the regimentation, the crypto-terrorism, the cornering of privileges and corruption of cadres, betrayed the text and tore up the texture of Lenin's revolutionary vision of society and State in a truly free democracy. Glowing rhetoric often lives on lips and tearful reality groans in people's throats.

The truth, as I reflect over the story of human rights, from the definition of democracy by Abraham Lincoln and the first article in the USSR Constitution declaring "a socialist state of the whole people .... all power belongs to the people", is that the perennial process of actualisation of people's power, including a holistic enjoyment of human rights, is a slow flow and a long struggle. Why? The people are alienated from the system. Curran's speech on the right of election is pertinent here:

> "The condition upon which God hath given liberty to man is eternal vigilance; which condition if he break, servitude is at once the consequence of his crime, and the punishment of his guilt."

As for human rights in India, as in most other countries, every activist with trust in ultimate triumph may only repeat, as I often do, the lines from *Gitanjali*:

> ***"The song that I came to sing remains unsung to this day.***
> ***I have spent my days in stringing and in unstringing my instrument.***
> ***The time has not come true, the words have not been rightly set; only there is the agony of wishing in my heart.***
> ***The blossom has not opened; only the wind is sighing by."***

In this unhappy apathy of the people and infantile adventurism of power maniacs, human rights do not rise to the wake-up call of activists. As for the parties and leaders who grab power and pelf at the expense of the common people's right to human resources one may only caution in biblical words:

> "Beware of false prophets, which comes to you in sheep's clothing, but inwardly they are ravening wolves."

8 Speech in the Constituent Assembly on 25.11.1949.

5

Religions, Culture and Human Rights

Legal systems were influenced by religions and faiths. Civilised codes explicitly spelling out human rights, *qua* human rights, did not exist. Even so, theologies and philosophies did fertilise the soil where the rights of man, of groups and denominations could flourish. The history of human rights would be incomplete without tracing their sources in the history of plural religions spreading universal values–and sustaining social systems. Philosopher-kings, rulers who founded religions and emperors who adopted or adapted religions and radiated enlightenment enriched human heritage through the centuries. Rights cannot exist without a legal order. It is, therefore, pertinent to examine the religious roots of human values.

Names of Hummurabi, Justinian, Augustus, Asoka, Manu and Muhammad, *et al*, are some of a host who left behind systems of Justice surviving in the jurisprudential history of mankind. Access to law is basic to human rights and, in that sense, has some relevance to our study. Right and Justice, though largely based on law, *dharma* or *jus*, have their ancient linkage to philosophy and religion which lead communities in shaping value systems and divine ordering.

Plato had warned that law and justice became functional in the social order only if rulers had a righteous outlook:

> "Until philosophers are kings, or the kings and princes of this world have the spirit and power of philosophy, and political greatness and wisdom meet in one, and those commoner natures who pursue either to the exclusion of the other are compelled to stand aside, cities will never have rest from their evils,—no, nor the human race, as I believe,—and then only will this our State have a possibility of life and behold the light of day."

Equal Justice administered by the monarchs in ancient and medieval India are legendary and marvellous instances of impartial remedies are legion; but systematised law and justice, save in the ancient epics and *neeti shastras*, do not mention *human rights*, *qua* human rights, as mandatory obligations. Even Sita, big with child so says Valmiki, left for the forests on the fiat of Rama without fair trial. An advanced justice system was prevalent, as gleaned from texts and chronicles of early periods but Human Rights Charters, as such, are not reported.

Ancient Hindu law and human rights

Scholars who have spent long spans in lucubration on the Hindu *Dharma Sastras* and the *Artha Sastras* and other legal treatises of yore have discovered an amazing system which, *inter alia,* regulates the duties of kings, judges, subjects and judicial as well as regal procedures. The central concept is *dharma* whose functional focus is social order. The profusion of Vedic and other texts and treatises on life and law need not engage us now except to state that social order, patterns of behaviour and regulation of individual conduct were designed to create conditions where man, whatever his office, may develop his true powers and potentialities tuned to a higher moral order. The message is *dharma* as the supreme value which binds kings and citizens, men and women. The cultural heritage of India in the field of jurisprudence has been praised and criticised but its basic principle is harmony and happiness and upholds social stability based on the consensual view of the good and learned in society.

Human rights gain meaning only if there is an independent judiciary to enforce rights. Here the *dharma-sastras* are clear and categoric.

> "The independence of the judiciary was one of the outstanding features of the Hindu judicial system. Even during the days of the Hindu monarchy, the administration of justice always remained separate from the executive. It was as a rule independent both in form and in spirit. It was the Hindu judicial system that first realized and recognized the importance of separation of the judiciary from the executive, and gave this fundamental principle a practical shape and form. The case of *Anathapindika* v *Jeta*, reported in the *Vinaya-Pitaka,* is a shining illustration of this principle. There a prince and a Private citizen submitted their case to the law-court, and the court decided against the prince. The prince accepted such a decision as a matter of course and as binding on him. The evolution of the principle of separation of the judiciary from the executive was largely the result of the Hindu conception of law as binding on the sovereign. Law in Hindu jurisprudence was above the sovereign. It was the *dharma*. The laws were then not regarded so much as a product of supreme Parliaments and legislatures as at present. Certain laws were regarded as above all human authority. Such, for instance, were the natural laws, which no Parliament, however supreme, could abolish. Technically speaking, a supreme Parliament may proclaim a law abolishing the law of gravitation, but it will not, in fact, be abolished by the Parliament's fiat".[1]
>
> "The State was not sacerdotal, nor even paternalistic, the king was subject to the law as any other citizen, and the divine right of kings known to Western political science was unknown in India. On the whole, the aim of the ancient

1 P.B. Mukherji: *The Hindu Judicial System—The Cultural Heritage of India,* vol. II, pages 434-435.

> Indian State may be said to have been less to introduce an improved social order, than to act in conformity with the established moral order."[2]

Human rights and obligations, the powers of the State and their limitations are not only not alien to the dynamic concept of *dharma* but are its very core, assuming the texts to be reflective of the facts of life.

> "*Dharma* as a concept is very wide and comprehensive. It stands for the self-sufficient principle of ordering harmony—the great rationalizer. The term is derived from the root 'dhr' signifying that it 'upholds' and 'sustains' humanity in all its coherence. It is saturated with the notion of truth and righteousness. By reason of its integrating civil, moral and spiritual values, it supplies the basic impetus for human development towards higher and higher possibilities. It is a scheme of regulation which, with its countless norms and precepts and all that it deems sound and serviceable, is sought to be integrated in the values and perspectives of man's total career. Accordingly, *dharma* as a content of the *Dharma-sastras* involves the things of the body, mind, intellect and soul in myriads of interests and values, and there is an inevitable mixing up of secular and empirical matters with those that are purely ethical and spiritual. The writers of the *Dharma-sastras* were alive to this comprehensive character of *dharma,* for they knew that problems of life could not artificially be kept apart. They must meet at a point. This accounts for the wide connotation ascribed to *dharma.*"

*** *** ***

> "Duty is not a tyrant, but a symbol of dignity to be discharged with affirmative joy. The realization of this vast perspective is assured in the *Dharma-sastras* by the wonderful scheme or co-ordination of conduct adapted to different conditions, status and stations of life."[3]

The scope of *dharma* takes, in its vast sweep, human rights as well. Law, in the *dharma* dimension, appears as an ever-present part of a perennial stream of the fundamental philosophy of life and action. One may conclude that the spectrum of legal thought covered by *dharma* did protect human rights. But it is too tall and presumptuous to assert that this cosmic concept articulates the modern specifics of human rights jurisprudence. Indeed, in practice, how far Hindu justice fulfilled the common people's rights, their expectations of egalitarian goodness, economic fair deal and secular non-discrimination in a society of castes and outcastes is notoriously in the negative. Swami Vivekananda accused the ancestors of oppressive culpability and anti-poor insensitivity:

> "Our aristocratic ancestors went on treading the common masses of our country under foot, till they became helpless, till under this torment the poor, poor people nearly forgot that they were human beings. They have been compelled to be merely hewers of wood and drawers of water for centuries, so much so, that they were made to believe that were born as slaves, *born as*

2 P.B. Ganjendra Gadkar: *The Historical Background and Theoretic Basis of Hindu Law – The Cultural Heritage of India,* vol. II, page 421.

3 K.G. Goswami: *Dharma-Sastras: The Cultural Heritage of India,* vol. V, page 72.

> *hewers of wood and drawers of water.* With all our boasted education of modern times, if anybody says a kind word for them, I often find our men shrink at once from the duty of lifting them up, these poor downtrodden people. Not only so, but I also find that all sorts of most demoniacal and brutal arguments, culled from the crude ideas of hereditary transmission, and other such gibberish from the Western world are brought forward in order to brutalise and tyrannise over the poor, all the more."[4]

It is fair, however, to state what has been claimed, by Dr. C.P. Ramaswami Aiyar, for ancient ideas of *dharma* which was, in theory, the King of Kings. Dr. C.P. Ramaswami Aiyar eloquently sums up in proud pages the status of ancient Indian polity:

"The greatest contribution to posterity made by the Hindu tradition was the broad-mindedness, sympathy, and the toleration of different viewpoints exhibited almost alone in India amongst the civilized communities of the earlier days. When Egypt persecuted and hounded out the Jews, when racial and communal conflicts disfigured the history of Babylon and Nineveh, when later on we see that in the States of Greece and Rome slaves formed the basis of those marvellous cultures, and when in the medieval ages the baiting of Jews alternated with the baiting of Roman Catholics by Protestants and *vice versa*, we had the spectacle in India of unfailing hospitality to foreign religions and foreign cultures. It would be unfair and inaccurate not to mention that the Buddhists and Jains suffered some pains and penalties, especially in the South of India. But which country can show anything like the treatment of the Parsees, who, flying from oppression in their own country of Persia, asked for and obtained succour of the wise west-coast king, to whose protection and active encouragement of their faith and tradition they ultimately owe their dominant position in the India of today? Which country can furnish a parallel to what happened in Travancore under the rule of extremely conservative and religious-minded monarchs? From the days when Christian congregations were split into innumerable and warring factions owing to the Arian controversy at the Council of Nicaea and the question of images, the Chera kings of Travancore gave a whole-hearted welcome to the followers of the Eastern Church, whose Patriarch of Antioch even now boasts of a larger following in Malabar than perhaps anywhere else in the world. Which king outside India has surpassed the monarchs of Travancore and Malabar, who conferred sacerdotal honours, presents, lands, and dignities on the ministers, bishops, and archbishops of the Christian Church, with the result that today the largest Christian population in India is found in the State of Travancore? Which ruler in the world's chequered history has enunciated in more moving and powerful language than is found in the Edicts of Asoka the Great, the principles of tolerance and comprehension of differing creeds and ideals co-existing with a spiritual urge towards the consolidation and regeneration of the Ruler's own faith?

4 *The Complete Works of Swami Vivekananda*, vol. III, page 196.

Such have been the marks and the characteristics of Indian civilization not only at its peak points but also through the centuries. Can this instinct of universality, this understanding of all points of view, and the feeling that the realization of the Supreme must connote a sympathy with, and a reconciliation of, many forms of thought and belief, be better expressed than in the words of Tāyumānavar in his *Hymn to Parvati*: 'The light and bliss of supreme knowledge that envelops and absorbs all forms of belief as the ocean absorbs all rivers?' In his Rock Edict Twelve, the Emperor Asoka declares that he does reverence to men of all sects, whether ascetics or householders, and he adds that he who does reverence to his own sect while disparaging the sects of others wholly from attachment to his own, with intent to enhance the splendour of his own sect, in reality by such conduct inflicts the severest injury on his own sect; and he ends the Edict with these ever memorable words: 'Concord is the supreme good (Smavāya eva Sādhuh)'.

This is the idea that underlies the United Nations Organization. It has uniformly characterized the philosophies that have been evolved in India; these have always been based on *ahimsā* and *abhaya* and on the recognition of the conformity and unity of all existence."[5]

Felicity universal in theory, casteist barbarity in praxis, may well be an ironic footnote!

In this background, history holds up the sublime stature of the Buddha as a liberator of humans, humble or high. Siddhartha renounced his princedom and became the Buddha. He taught the Eight-fold Path and his luminous leadership gained many followers including Emperor Asoka. The edicts of Asoka, inscribed in rock Pillars, bear testimony to the noble ruler's recognition of humanism. Compassion for all Creation and reverence for all life—these are the source and strength of human rights. Asoka, for historians of human rights, was a unique beacon light from this angle.

Ahiṃsa¯ or non-violence, tolerance and mercy, humility and concern for living creatures, are the root of human rights. These values were nobly nourished by another contemporary of the Buddha. Vardhamana Mahaveera, the founder of Jainism strengthened the hold of humanitarianism and kindness on its followers, making *ahimsa*¯ the highest liberating principle. True, the Hindu view, at a philosophical level of *dharma,* as mentioned earlier, also glorified humanity and divinity in living beings, with a cosmic vision, thus raising the level of consciousness of people to a higher note of advaita. But in practice, this unitive understanding and universal humanism suffered defeat and setback at the hierarchical rule of the four-fold caste-frame inflexibly operated by the high born with obscurantist obduracy.

Human rights 'sensitives' will agree that the caste system, as a hardened and heartless version of the social classes, is a negation of humanist justice, although, in theory, vertical mobility was conceded.

5 C.P. Ramaswami Aiyar in *Some Aspects of Social and Political Evolution in India—The Cultural Heritage of India,* vol. II, pages 507-508.

The Buddha was the earliest Protestant against casteist injustice. The institution of caste, in its fourfold and multi-fold forms, is a pathological Indian social pattern of life violative of basic human rights. Its origin and manifestations have been controversial throughout Indian history, especially because of the graded inequalities, social, economic and political, which it inflicted on the masses. May be, the social boundaries of functional classification could be found in other communities beyond India. Some historians find elements of patrician and plebeian practices and of colour prejudices even in Europe and America in the bygone centuries. Indeed, it was in Germany that the idea of a natural and necessary conflict, the class war, between the miscellaneous multitudes of the disinherited and exploited, *i.e.* the class conscious proletariat (in Marxist terminology), and the rulers and holders of wealth, whom Bernard Shaw called the proprietariat, found philosophical expression. However, the Indian caste system had a fixity and rigidity unique in the world. Says Wells:

> "This fixity of classes is known to Europeans as the institution of caste (from *casta*, a word of Protuguese origin; the Indian word is *varna*, colour). Its origins are still in complete obscurity, but it was certainly well rooted in the Ganges valley before the days of Alexander the Great. It is a complicated horizontal division of the social structure into classes or castes, the members of which may neither eat nor intermarry with persons of a lower caste under penalty of becoming outcasts, and who may also 'lose caste' for various ceremonial negligences and defilements. By losing caste a man does not sink to a lower caste; he becomes outcast.
>
> *** *** ***
>
> "However caste arose, there can be no doubt of its extraordinary hold upon the Indian mind. In the sixth century B.C. arose Gautama, the great teacher of Buddhism, proclaiming 'As the four streams that flow into the Ganges lose their names as soon as they mingle their waters in the holy river, so all who believe in Buddha cease to be Brahmins, Kshatriyas, Vaisyas, and Sudras'. His teaching prevailed in India for some centuries; it spread over China, Tibet, Japan, Burma, Ceylon, Turkestan, Manchuria; it is today the religion of a large fraction of the human race, but it was finally defeated and driven out of Indian life by the vitality and persistence of the Brahmins and of their caste ideas."[6]

It is tragic but true that caste defies Constitutions and communalism is its cousin. Human rights are a casualty where casteism is the rule of life.

Before parting with the Hindu Chapter it may appropriate to refer to the *Dharma-sastras.* Says Justice Rama Jois:

> "According to Rajadharma, the king was given the power only to enforce the law. *Dharma-sastras* did not confer on or recognise any legislative power in the king. This is the most important distinction between the concept of kingship in India and the concept of kingship in the Western countries. According to

6 H.G. Wells: *Outline of History* pp. 240-241.

> Western concept king was the fountain of all the three important limbs of the State viz., the Legislature, the Executive and the Judiciary. But under the kingship as recognised and established under the *Dharma-sastras* the laws were those laid down by the *Dharma-sastras* themselves. They did not authorise the king to lay down new laws or amend the provisions of *Dharma-sastras*. On the other hand, *Dharma-sastras* also laid down the laws governing the conduct of the king himself (Rajadharma)".[7]

The arbitrary fiat of the ruler is not law, if inconsistent with *dharma*, whose sources are the Vedas, the Smritis and the like. Law and Justice were moulded by Smriti writers according to the changing needs of the society in tune with *sadāchāra* (good custom). Legal literature of the Hindu period owes much to the distinguished law givers of the times as well as to the two epics and the *Artha Sastra* (Kautaliya) and *Sukranitisara*. We are not concerned with the legal history of India of those days which was quite advanced, but with the constellation of rights and duties which constitutes human rights.

Danda neeti or the Law of Crimes obviously regulates the penal dimensions of human rights. The Nyayalaya and Justice administration occupy a high position in the legal system. The *dharma* relating to judges, their qualifications, independence and impartiality receives special emphasis. Indeed the justice system including the rules of equity and provision of *amicus curiae* prove the civilised level of the court process. Going by the text, Rama Jois gives us an account of the excellence of the justice system which protects human rights as well. Fairness and equality are obligations of the king who himself is bound by *Dharma*. Even International Law (*Videsha Neethi*) are covered by the broader amplitude of *dharma*.

We may conclude at this point that human rights are fairly founded in *dharma* which by definition sustains and ensures the progress and welfare of individuals and society.

The quintessence of right and justice, peace and order is best stated by Rama Jois in the following words:

> "*Dharma* protects those who protect it. Those who destroy *Dharma* get destroyed. Therefore *Dharma* should not be destroyed so that we may not be destroyed as a consequence thereof.
>
> The principle laid down in this saying is of utmost importance and significance. In the above shortest saying, the entire concept of Rule of Law is incorporated. The meaning it conveys is that an orderly society would be in existence if everyone acts according to *Dharma* and thereby protect *Dharma*, and such an orderly society which would be an incarnation of *Dharma*, in turn, protects the rights of individuals. Rules of *Dharma* were meant to regulate the individual conduct, in such a way as to restrict the rights, liberty, interest and desires of an individual as regards all matters to the extent necessary in the interest of other individuals, i.e. the society and at the same time making it

7 Justice Rama Jois: *Legal and Constitutional History of India*, Part I, page 13.

obligatory for the society to safeguard and protect the individual in all respects through its social and political institutions. Shortly put, *Dharma* regulated the mutual obligations of individual and the society. Therefore, it was stressed that protection of *Dharma* was in the interest of both the individual and the society. Manu warns, 'Do not destroy *Dharma*, so that you may not be destroyed'. A State of *Dharma* was required to be always maintained for peaceful co-existence and prosperity."[8]

Christianity and humanity

When we think of the evolution of human rights culture in the West, the Greeks appear through the Homeric poems and Hellenic ethos. The Greek State changed its social structure from time to time and the rights of the citizen and slave also varied over time. Democracy prevailed during the 6th, 5th and 4th centuries B.C. But the privileged category dominated the State. As for the concept of people's governance, the Western man owes it to the Greeks. In the history of human freedom, we cannot but remember Socrates, the son of a stone mason. Plato was his younger associate; and together they fought for freedom of thought through the immortal Dialogues. Plato's Academy attracted Aristotle who continued the culture of free thought. Alexander the Great used to consult Aristotle which shows that scientific enquiry was not frowned upon by the Ruler. What historians stress is that Alexander the Great was for mankind the symbol and embodiment of world dominion. When the Romans conquered the Greeks, Caesar became a global figure, as it were. Alexandria was a factory of philosophy and religions and from this ferment new ideas of Human Rights were born.

Sheer comparative interest shows how at about the same period the Buddha transformed the world of thought. He discovered the path–*nirvana* or 'soul serenity' throughout our fevered world. What impresses a student of human rights is the devotion and dedication of Asoka to create a compassionate world order through the Eightfold Path.

"He organised a great digging of wells in India, and the planting of trees for shade. He appointed officers for the supervision of charitable works. He founded hospitals and public gardens. He had gardens made for the growing of medicinal herbs. Had he had an Aristotle to inspire him, he would no doubt have endowed scientific research upon a great scale. He created a ministry for the care of the aborigines and subject races. He made provision for the education of women. He made—he was the first monarch to make—an attempt to educate his people into a common view of the ends and way of life".[9]

In Rome, at about that period, the struggle of the plebeians and slaves for full human rights and fair deal never succeeded in any measure. However, in 509 B.C.:

8 Justice Rama Jois: *Legal and Constitutional History of India,* Part I, page 8.
9 H.G. Wells: *Outline of History,* page 401.

> "Valerius Poplicola (3), the consul, enacted that whenever the life or rights of any citizen were at stake, there should be an appeal from the magistrates to the general assembly. This *Lex Valeria* was "the Habeas Corpus of Rome", and it freed the Roman plebeians from the worst dangers of class vindictiveness in the law courts".[10]

The laws of Rome were written down and in 451-450 B.C. the Twelve Tables became the basis of all Roman Law. Western jurisprudence found Roman Law its well-spring with local variations, native roots, historical reforms and cultural tapestries.

Just compare, for a moment, the human condition in Asoka's India and the Roman empire. Says H.G. Wells:

> "In the third century B.C., when king Asoka was ruling India in light and gentleness, the Romans were reviving an Etruscan sport, the setting on of slaves to fight for their lives. One is reminded of West Africa again in the origin of this amusement: it grew out of the prehistoric custom of a massacre of captives at the burial of a chief. There was a religious touch about this sport; the slaves with hooks, who dragged the dead bodies out of the arena, wore masks to represent the infernal ferryman-god, Charon.
>
> "In 264 B.C., the very year in which Asoka began to reign and the First Punic War began, the first recorded gladiatorial combat took place in the forum at Rome, to celebrate the funeral of a member of the old Roman family of Brutus. This was a modest display of three couples, but soon gladiators were fighting by the hundred. The taste for these combats grew rapidly, and the wars supplied an abundance of captives. The old Roman moralists, who were so severe upon kissing and women's ornaments and Greek philosophy, had nothing but good to say for this new development. So long as pain was inflicted, Roman morality, it would seem, was satisfied.
>
> "Gladiators who objected to fight for any reason were driven on by whips and hot irons. A wounded man would sometimes call for pity by holding up his forefinger. The spectators would then either wave their handkerchiefs in token of mercy, or condemn him to death by holding out their clenched fists with the thumbs held in some fashion that indicated death. Authorities differ here as to the exact signal. Mayor says thumbs up (to the breast) meant death and thumbs down meant 'Lower that sword'. The common persuasion is that thumbs down meant death. The slain and nearly dead were dragged out to a particular place, the spoliarium, where they were stripped of their arms and possessions, and those who had not already expired were killed.
>
> "This organization of murder as a sport and show serves to measure the great gap in moral standards between the Roman community and our own. No doubt cruelties and outrages upon human dignity as monstrous as this still go on in the world, but they do not go on in the name of the law, and without a single dissentient voice."[11]

10 *Ibid*, page 421.
11 *Ibid*, pages 449-450.

These savage pleasures and unconscionable inflictions continued until a new humanist power incarnated in the frail person of a carpenter's son called Jesus of Nazareth. Slavery and savagery were confronted by the non-violent spirit of Christianity, with its message of love, caring and sharing, battling against Roman Pharisaism and imperial Caesarism. Human Rights gained a spiritually militant voice; and the Cross figured as a symbol of sacrifice of regained human dignity and divinity. Universality, higher than territorial possessions, denunciation of unrighteous riches and exploitation of the poor, egalitarianism of all in the eye of God, respect for the despised and the destitute, gentle defiance of harsh authority which Caesar and the priestly hierarchy exercised, a unified vision of the world, with love as its cementing force,–these were implicit in Christ's gospels. He relentlessly opposed the tribal patriotism of the Jews. Just read his selfless rejection of mere family relationship, thus laying foundation for a morally and spiritually-welded *One World.* Here is a biblical anecdote:

> "While he yet talked to the people, behold, his mother and his brethren stood without, desiring to speak with him. Then one said unto him, Behold, thy mother and thy brethren stand without, desiring to speak with thee. But he answered and said unto him that told him, who is my mother? And who are my brethren? And he stretched forth his hand towards his disciples, and said, Behold my mother and my brethren. For whosoever shall do the will of my Father which is in heaven, the same is my brother, and sister, and mother."[1]
>
> Using the Kingdom of God, as distinguished from the empire of Caesar, he 'condemned all the gradations of the economic system, all private wealth and personal advantages.' All men belonged to the kingdom; all their possessions belonged to the kingdom; the righteous life for all men, the only righteous life, was the service of God's will with all that we had, with all that we were, Again and again he denounced private riches and the reservation of any private life".[2]
>
> "And Jesus looked around about, and saith unto his disciples, How hardly shall they that have riches enter into the kingdom of God! And the disciples were astonished at his words. But Jesus answered again, and saith unto them, Children, how hard is it for the them that trust in riches to enter into the kingdom of God! It is easier for a camel to go through the eye of a needle, than for a rich man to enter into the kingdom of God."[3]

It was not merely a moral and social revolution that Jesus urged on the world. His teachings, wrapped in the language of the kingdom of God, had a political bent of the plainest sort. Says H.G. Wells:

> "The directness of his political attack is manifest by such an incident as that of the coin.
>
> "And they send unto him certain of the pharisees and of the Herodians, to catch him in his words. And when they were come, they say unto him, Master,

1 H.G. Wells: *Outline of History,* pages 527-528.
2 H.G. Wells: *Outline of History,* page 528.
3 *Ibid.*

> we know that thou art true, and carest for no man: for thou regardest not the person of men, but teachest the way of God in truth: Is it lawful to give tribute to Caesar, or not? Shall we give, or shall we not give? But he knowing their hypocrisy, said unto them, why tempt ye me? Bring me a penny, that I may see it. And they brought it. And he saith unto them, whose is this image and superscription? And they said unto him, Caesar's. And Jesus answering said unto them, Render to Caesar the things that are Caesar's and to God the things that are God's–which, in view of all else that he had taught, left very little of a man or his possessions for Caesar.
>
> "The whole tenor of the opposition to him and the circumstances of his trial and execution show clearly that to his contemporaries he seemed to propose plainly, and did propose plainly, to change and fuse and enlarge all human life."[4]

The right to dignity, self-expression, and other freedoms even for the destitute and the despised and for those branded as prostitutes were integral to the ideology of Jesus. He, incarnated, as it were, to spread the message of the noblest version of human rights and the divinity of all God's children and opposed exploitation, material and sacerdotal.

He was like some terrible moral huntsmen digging mankind out of the snug burrows in which they had lived hitherto. In Jesus's visionary kingdom there was to be no property, no privilege, no pride and precedence, no motive and indeed no reward but love.

He upheld the dignity of womanhood and argued for a Just World Order, and for that he was executed with extreme cruelty. Imperial law was asserting itself with Roman inhumanity through the crucifixion of this frail figure. In a cosmos of monetary appetite, betrayers of revolutionaries are not hard to get. And Judas betrayed his master. The world today bristles with Judases, compradors and quasi-quislings who are enemies of people's rights from within! Comrade Christ, (Upton Sinclair's phrase) the revolutionary, laid down his life in torturesome pain for the redemption of humanity and Barabbas, a robber, who too was tried and sentenced to death by the same Pontius Pilate, was let off. Roman justice nailed Jesus on the cross and pardoned off Barabbas, the robber! We today, live in a Barabbasque Order with human justice on the cross! Jesus's vain but courageous challenge to overthrow the established (robber) order failed. With crass materialism, thirty pieces of silver could buy betrayers of human justice then–*and now!* and Justice itself, in the cynical words of Anatole France, "is the means by which established injustices are sanctioned". Why? says Anatole France, in this context: "To disarm the strong and arm the weak would be to change the social order which it's my job to preserve". Does it ring a bell in our time, noises of human rights in the United Nations notwithstanding? The zeitgeist, in our vanishing century, is corrupt *vis-a-vis* cherished values of human rights and equal justice.

4 H.G. Wells: *Outline of History,* pages 529-530.

From Christendom and the West the modern State emerged. This historical reality has a bearing on the very structure and texture of human rights. "Politics without history has no root; history without politics has no fruit' (JR Seeley). So let us search through history with our sights set on political developments. The story of human societies tells us of election to offices as a principle, even of monarchs and Caliphs, the Judges of Israel and the Great Khan of the Mongols, until Kublai Khan became the monarch. This elective idea contributed to the right of the people to rule themselves, though indirectly. The Renaissance of Western civilization takes us closer to the worth of the individual and his will to choose the ruler and his religion. Even theology was assailed by democracy, asserting the freedom of faith as well. Wycliff's writings and the Hussite resistance are milestones in the march against religious repression. The fundamental right to equality, following from the concept of human brotherhood, is basic to Christianity.

The great plague: the masses are awake

Then came, in the fourteenth century, the Great Plague, called the Black Death, which wiped out whole populations by a pestilence of unheard-of virulence. Twenty-five million or more died. Shortage of labour and of goods led to compulsion to toil without rise in wages. This provoked a new revolt against the whole system of social inequality fobbed off till then as a divine decree. The Lords and their superior rights were challenged. A spirit, fatal to the fiendish social order of those days, expressed itself in the popular rhyme which condensed the levelling doctrine of John Ball: "When Adam delved and Eve span, who was then the gentleman"? Europe faced peasant revolts and England suffered economic upheavals. The massive upheaval flowing from this colossal misfortune is important. This pestilence unlimited unmasked the enormous inhumanity of the feudal system and infuriated the countless victims.

Towns and villages perished because of the plague. The whole organisation of labour was thrown out of gear. Cultivation collapsed and from these distresses the peasant wars of the 14th century sprang. Shortage of labour and of goods on the one hand and the owners of land, the ignoble nobles and the rich merchants on the other, came into an open conflict. John Ball, a people's priest, preached crimson sermons:

> "Good people", cried the preacher, things will never go well in England so long as goods be not in common, and so long as there be villeins and gentlemen. But what right have they whom we call lords greater folk than we? On what grounds have they deserved it? Why do they hold us in serfage? If we all came of the same father and mother, of Adam and Eve, how can they say or prove that they are better than we, if it be not that they make us gain for them by our toil what they spend in their pride? They are clothed in velvet and warm in their furs and their ermines, while we are covered with rags. They have wine and spices and fair bread; and we oat-cake and straw, and water to drink. They have leisure and fine houses; we have pain and labour, the rain

and the wind in the fields. And yet it is of us and of our toil that these men hold their state."[5]

The Bible became the source of spiritual struggle for material justice. 'Comrade Jesus' incarnated, as it were when black misery stalled Christendom and the proletariat was crushed by the proprietariat. The unfeeling 'haves' were unkind to the harrowing lot of the 'have-nots' who perished in numbers. Christ was a red flag though his high-priests were often with the ex-propriators.

Like the English outbreak, France, Germany and other parts of Europe witnessed insurgency of the labouring classes. H.G. Wells, with a sense of history and of social justice, chronicles:

> "They show a new spirit growing in human affairs, a spirit altogether different from the unquestioning apathy of the serfs and peasants in the original regions of civilization or from the anarchist hopelessness of the serf and slave labour of the Roman capitalists.
>
> "All these early insurrections of the workers that we have mentioned were suppressed with much cruelty, but the movement itself was never completely stamped out. From that time to this there has been a spirit of revolt in the lower levels of the pyramid of civilization. There have been phases of insurrection, phases of repression, phases or compromise and comparative pacification; but from that time until this, the struggle has never wholly ceased. We shall see it flaring out during the French Revolution at the end of the eighteenth century, insurgent again in the middle and at the opening of the last quarter of the nineteenth century, and achieving vast proportions in the world of today. The socialist movement of the nineteenth century was only one version of that continuing revolt."[6]

Human rights rose from the graveyards of mass casualties and macro-injustices, scotched but not killed. In our times, when billions go hungry and face vast infant mortality, human rights activists may turn to the observations of H.G. Wells as he recounts the medieval outbursts:

> "Like its predecessor, our present civilization may be no more than one of those crops farmers sow to improve their land by the fixation of nitrogen from the air; it may have grown only that, accumulating certain traditions, it may be ploughed into the soil again for better things to follow. Such questions as these are the practical realities of history, and in all that follows we shall find them becoming clearer and more important, until in our last chapter we shall end; as our days and years end, with a recapitulation of our hopes and fears—and a note of interrogation."[7]

From pain to power is the dialectic of unjust suffering and supine over lordship. The human spirit fights forward and human rights rise like phoenix. Jesus and his words and deeds kindled in humanity a burning

5 H.G. Wells: *Outline of History,* 8th Ed., page 740.
6 H.G. Wells: *Outline of History,* 8th Ed., pages 741-742.
7 H.G. Wells: *Outline of History,* 8th Ed., pages 742-743.

sense of human values and struggle against the exploiting class. Crucifixion is a continuing operation and the Passion of Christ a cry for human justice.

Islam and human justice: some noble facets

Having dealt with the Hindu, Buddhist and Christian impact on human rights it is fair to dive into Islam and its role in stimulating respect for Human Rights in some parts of the world. It is true that today the fundamentalist sector is a virulent disease among the obscurantists of almost all religions. Functionally they are enemies of human rights, even the right to think freely. Islamic bigotry speaking generally, has a fury and ferocity which has frightened the enlightened world and operated to suppress Human Right and Gender Justice. Nevertheless, much has been done to promote reverence for human rights *by Islam and its Founding Prophet* (Hazrat Muhammad). Unfortunately, Islamic teaching have suffered distortions and deterred fundamental freedoms and the worth of the human person (like other religions, over the ages). A fair appraisal of the Islamic contribution to human progress is appropriate. Muslims came to India centuries ago and are an integral part of the larger Indian community. So Islam deserves attention in any study of Human Rights in India.

Some Islamic countries have scuttled secularism, adopted monarchical despotism and imposed penal sentences too barbaric to be civilized and too incompatible with current progressive ideas of human rights jurisprudence. Even so, the Great Prophet and his followers have made significant chapters to the reform of Arabic life which, in earlier ages, were brutal and absolutist and male chauvinist. A historical perspective helps to do justice to the human rights role of that seemingly aggressive religion.

Professor Akbar S. Ahmed explains the international misunderstanding about Islam in the following words:

> "The images of Islam prevalent in the world are of brutality, fanaticism, hatred and disorder; Libyans killing police women in London, Palestinians hijacking passenger planes, Iranians seizing foreign embassies and Indonesians blowing up the Borobudur temple in Java. The very names of the Muslim leaders of our time—Khomeini, Gaddafi, Arafat—have become symbols of these images. * *
>
> These fears stem partly from a lack of understanding of Islam among non-Muslims and partly from the failure by Muslims to explain themselves. The results are predictable: the hatred on hatred.
>
> * * *
>
> The Muslim leaders, hated and despised, are reduced to Walt Disney villains: 'Kho Maniac, Wacky Kaddafi, Yucky Araft' ('Garbage pail adults', MAD, back cover, September 1986). The repugnance is contagious. * * *".[8]

If Emperor Asoka was marvellous as a Buddhist ruler *vis-a-vis* Human Rights, Emperor Akbar was magnanimous as a Muslim Ruler in a Hindu

8 Akbar S. Ahmed: *Discovering Islam,* (Vanguard Books), page 1.

country. One may rightly conclude that exaggerations have prejudiced the international assessment of Islam, although the splendours and sensual gratifications of the rulers in the seraglios have been responsible for the Great Prophet being more sinned against than sinning.

Islam [the Arabic word for submission to the Will of God (Allah)] (*Aslama* means peace) came to India shortly after the Great Prophet preached his vision and revelation of the Quran from a mountain cave to the Arab tribes and wealthy commercial townsmen. Prof. Akbar S. Ahmed briefly gives the essence of the teaching of Prophet:

> "After Muhammad announced his mission to the world the Quraysh rulers of Makkah were understandably outraged by his preaching. He was claiming Muslims were equal, like the teeth of a comb. There were no lineages nor castes in Islam: *la bedawi fil Islam*—'there is no Bedouinism in Islam'. Muhammad's God demanded justice, the doing of the good and liberality to kith and kin. Worse, his God criticised their wanton ways: He forbids all shameful deeds, injustice and rebellion. Female infanticide, Promiscuity and alcohol were all forbidden.
>
> "Equality, the status of women, the rights of the less privileged (minorities, poorer working groups)—the shibboleths of our age—were reflected in the Prophet's message. It was a revolution the Prophet wished to bring about, to end what came to be known as the Fahiliyya, the dark age. The Quraysh, led by the Umayyads, opposed him resolutely. Hard-headed men, they were also concerned about the effect of his teachings on trade.
>
> *** *** ***
>
> "Shortly before his death the Prophet spoke at Arafat at the Hajjatul-Wida, the farewell pilgrimage. In his address he emphasized the *unity of humanity—the brotherhood between Arab and non-Arab*—and the concept of the ummah: Allah has made you brethren one to another, so be not divided. *An Arab has no preference over a non-Arab,* nor a non-Arab over an Arab; *nor is a white one to be preferred to a dark one,* nor a dark one to a white one."[9]

The holy Quran says: "And *women have rights similar to those against them in a just manner.* Likewise, in matters of divorce Islam is much misunderstood. The Prophet stressed of all things which have been permitted divorce is the most hated by Allah". Islamic jurisprudence sanctions divorce if the marriage has irretrievably broken down. In a Kerala ruling, the Quranic law has been summed up thus:

> "*The Holy Prophet found a dissolute people dealing with women as mere sex-satisfying chattel and he rid Arab society of its decadent value through his doings and the Quranic injunctions*. The sanctity of family life was recognised; so was the stubborn incompatibility between the spouses as a ground for divorce; for it is intolerable to imprison such a couple in quarrelsome wedlock. While there is no rose but has a thorn if what you hold is all thorn

9 Akbar S. Ahmed: *Discovering Islam,* (Vanguard Books), pages 19 and 20.

and no rose, better throw it away. The ground is not conjugal guilt but actual repulsion."[10]

The theory that Islam generously and liberally allows four wives at a time even today for sheer sensual pleasure is a distortion of the sacred Quran. In *Subaida Bevi's* case[11] the Kerala High Court observed:

"Even during the last century the great jurist Ameer Ali said:

'The conviction is gradually forcing itself on all sides, in all Moslem communities, that polygamy is much opposed to Islamic laws as it is to the general progress of civilized society and true culture. In consequence of this conviction a large and growing section of Islamists regard the practice of polygamy as *positively unlawful*'."[12]

The Holy Quran in Chapter IV, Verse 3—frequently relied upon as supporting polygamy— says:

"And if you fear that you cannot do justice to orphans, marry such women as seem good to you, two, or three, or four; but if you fear that you will not do justice, then (marry) only one or that which your right hands possess. This is more proper that you may do justice."

"It is admitted on all hands that this Chapter was revealed to guide the Muslims under the conditions which followed the battle of Unud ...." (*The Holy Quran* by Maulana Muhammad Ali). In another passage the Koran says:

"Ye are never able
To be fair and just
As between women,
Even if it is
Your ardent desire:
...."[13]

It follows from these passages that Koranic injunction has to be understood in the perspective of prevalent unrestricted polygamy and in the context of the battle in which most males perished, leaving many females or orphans and that the Holy Prophet himself recognised the difficulty of treating two or more wives with equal justice and, in such a situation, directed that an individual should have only one wife. In short, the Koran enjoined monogamy upon Muslims and departure therefrom as an exception. That is why, in the true spirit of the Koran, a number of Muslim countries have codified the personal law wherein the practice of polygamy has been either totally prohibited or severely restricted".[14]

10 *A. Yousuf* v *Sowramma* AIR 1971 Ker 261.
11 1970 Ker LT 4.
12 Ameer Ali: *Mohammaden Law.*
13 Chapter IV. Verse 129.
14 1970 Ker LT 4 at page 10 *per* Krishna Iyer, J.

The wife's right to claim divorce and the view that marriage is a contract put the status of woman on an equal footing with man:

Maulana Muhammad Ali in his book *The Holy Quran* has this to say:

> "Divorce is one of the institutions of Islam regarding which much misconception prevails, so much so that even the Islamic law as administered in the courts, is not free from these misconceptions......... . The Islamic law has many points of advantage as compared with both the Jewish and Christian laws as formulated in Deut. and Matt. The Chief feature of improvement is that the wife can claim a divorce according to the Islamic law, neither Moses nor Christ (nor Manu, may I add) conferring that right on the woman........."[15]

* * *

Maulana Muhammad Ali has explained this verse thus:

> "This verse lays down the procedure to be adopted when a case for divorce arises. It is not for the husband to put away his wife. It is the business of the Judge to decide the case. Nor should divorce cases be made too public. The Judge is required to appoint two arbiters, one belonging to the wife's family and the other to the husband's. These two arbiters will find out the facts, but their objective must be to effect a reconciliation between the parties. If all hopes of reconciliation fail, a divorce is allowed, but the final decision for divorce rests with the Judge who is legally entitled to pronounce a divorce. Cases were decided in accordance with the directions contained in this verse in the early days of Islam."

In Mulla's *Principles of Mohammedan Law* (16th Ed.) there is an interesting reference to a Pakistani decision.

> "In an important recent judgment the Pakistan Supreme Court in *Khurshid Bibi* v *Mohd. Amin* PLD 1967 SC 97, has endorsed the Lahore High Court's view in *Mst. Balqis Fatima* v *Najmul Ikram* (1959)2 (WP) p. 321: (1959) Lah 566), that under Muslim Law the wife is entitled to Khula, *as of right,* if she satisfied the conscience of the Court that it will otherwise mean forcing her into a hateful union."[16]

These basics of Islamic matrimonial jurisprudence establish how considerate the law has been to women.

Essentially, Ummah is the community as a whole and social justice is basic to this concept. It is fair to conclude that in the world view of Islam, there is a cosmic brotherhood where all are equal and the welfare of everyone is committed to the care of the world community. In this sense, Islamic principles are not only consistent with but emphasize humanitarian comity. True, the real life Mussalman projects a deviant profile soured by a trace of bigotry. Dr. Sayyid Waheed Aktar, in his paper, at a recent seminar presented the Islamic perspective:

15 Page 96.
16 1970 Ker LT 477 at pp. 482-483.

"History of mankind is a ceaseless quest for freedom. It is a multipronged quest: freedom from want, from fear, from forces of nature, from tyranny of fellow beings, from injustice, from superstitions, from prejudices, from tribal and racial loyalties, and ultimately from his own egocentric existence. Man passed gradually through various stages of realizing all these freedoms, each of which had a material as well as a spiritual aspect. Sheer material freedom means nothing unless it brings in its wake spiritual freedom also. Rather both of them are complementary to each other and are organically inseparable. The quest for freedom suffered setbacks and reverses whenever any one of the two was neglected. The modern civilization suffers from the malady of over-emphasizing the material dimension of freedom, totally or partially neglecting the relevance of spiritual freedom to human existence. Religion has been striving for man's spiritual freedom, while philosophy has been concerned with intellectual freedom. Art and literature have been interested in realizing both of them at a different plane. Science and technology's quest has been always directed towards attaining material freedom. All human activity is a quest for freedom, and all human evolution represents a course of gradual realization of various freedoms. Human evolution is emergent and creative evolution in the sense that at its every stage a higher form of freedom emerged as a result of man's creativity. Human evolution is different and distinguished from biological evolution, for the latter is mechanical and deterministic as compared to the former in which man's aspiration for freedom plays a vital and decisive role. In the course of man's creative evolution Islam emerged as an embodiment of all kinds of freedom at a stage when humanity was in need of a balanced synthesis of material and spiritual freedoms.

*** *** ***

"At that stage human mind was incapable of embracing infinite future possibilities of human creativity, because it had not yet developed the intellectual and empirical tools required for unseen future. The Quran, last of Divine revelations, contained the guiding principles of scientific induction as well as a moral code that could suffice for man's socio-political and economic advancements, ensuring maximum freedom of human action in all the spheres of man's multipronged quest for freedom. The Quran's declaration that God has completed His message (*Din*) and has conferred upon man the best of His rewards points to the fact that *through Islam man* attained the utmost potential to realize his freedom. In order to have a comprehensive view of freedom granted to man by Islam one has to understand the Islamic conception of freedom along with all its implications and practical consequences bearing upon human society, state and economic activity at both the individual and collective levels."

*** *** ***

The social milieu of Arab tribal life and chastening mission of Muhammad have to be integrally grasped to measure his contribution. Says Dr. Aktar:

"Interpretation of the terms like freedom, human right and sovereignty is considered to be a monopoly of technologically advanced powers. Freedom fighters are dubbed as terrorists, while inhuman acts of aggression, suppression,

> subversion, interference against the sovereign nations of the third world by the imperialists are termed as means of safeguarding freedom and human rights of the wronged countries. What is inconvenient to the champions of the open society and human rights is labelled violation of human rights and is condemned in all international forums and mass media. Contrarily the countries openly practising policies of apartheid and racial discrimination such as the South Africa's white minority Government and the Zionist Israel receive all kinds of assistance and support from the civilized West. Military dictatorships and anti-people regimes which serve their Western masters and crush democratic movements of their people are justified in terms of fighting against obscurantism and religious fanaticism. How human rights and freedoms are interpreted is a matter of convenience for the guardians of Western civilization and supremacy. The movements of Islamic resurgence particularly invite the wrath of the standard-bearers of human rights".[17]

This sharp rebuke of the West-tinted human rights propagandists is followed by a positive statement of the Islamic kernel or human freedom steeped in spiritual values. With pardonable pride, Dr. Aktar writes:

> "Harmony in the human collective existence can be maintained and ensured through a balanced and just award of equal rights to all individuals along with freedom to shoulder corresponding obligations with a view that the human rights are accorded to all. Islam brought into existence such a harmonious society for the first time in the annals of human history at a time when the advanced West of toady lived in total darkness devoid of any conception of freedom and human rights. Before the advent of Islam the great Greek civilization had introduced a rudimentary form of democracy in the city states, and later the Romans also put up a semblance of democracy for a short time. But in Greek democracies only free men, not females, had a right to vote, and slaves were not considered of having any rights. The vast Roman empire was virtually a slave state, in which only the free ruling class enjoyed rights. The Byzantine empire that succeeded the Roman empire never practised the teachings of Christ and denied freedom of thought and enquiry to the Christians themselves. The Popes were equally intolerant of free enquiry. In the Christian theocracies and monarchies religious minorities were persecuted and discriminated against. The socio-political structure of the Persian empire was equally oppressive in which only the priests and noblemen enjoyed some rights. In this caste-ridden set-up common men could not even think of freedom. The Indian society and state were also caste-bound, where the lower castes, constituting the vast majority of people, were treated as non-human beings. In such an epoch, Islam emerged with a universal message of human freedom that guaranteed equal rights for all human beings irrespective of their race, colour, nationality, faith and sex. Despite deviating from the path of the Prophet and his true successors Muslim rulers usually observed the Islamic principle of human subjects than any other past or contemporary state. Not only Muslims but also non-Muslims enjoyed full freedom in the states ruled by

17 From a *Paper presented at the International Congress on Nahjul Balagha,* in April 1995.

Muslims. Sayyid Amir Ali, in the *Spirit of Islam,* stating that Islam never interfered with the dogmas of any faith, writes:

"Whist orthodox Christianity persecuted with equal ferocity the Jews and Nestorians, Islam afforded them both shelter and protection. Whilst Christian Europe was burning witches and heretics, and massacring Jews and infidels, the Moslem sovereigns were treating their non-Moslem subjects with consideration and tolerance. They were the trusted subjects of the state, councillors of the empire. Every secular office was open to them along with the Moslems. The Teacher himself had declared it lawful for a Moslem to intermarry with a Christian or Zoroastrian."[18]

"The rights accorded by Islam to non-Muslims, women and slaves were not only unprecedented, in those days, but also distinguished Islam from modern ideologies."

* * *

"Freedom is ensured in the Quran; both inborn and acquired. There is no distinction between a believer and a non-believer in this respect. What is prohibited is evil and what is lawful is good for all men."[19]

Of course, the Hindu dharma and Buddhist dharma preceded Islam with a glorious vision of universal, egalitarian, humanitarian culture where all mankind, why Creation in all its forms, was bound together by a unitive divinity despite religious plurality. Harken to the words of Max Muller who regarded Rig Veda the first word spoken by the Aryan man. These Aryans envisioned Truth without inhibitions and asked deeper questions. Evolving from this vigorous investigation came the Upanishadic monism. Says Nehru:

"The Upanishads are instinct with a spirit of inquiry, of mental adventure, of a passion for finding out the truth about things. The search for this truth is, of course, not by the objective methods of modern science, yet there is an element of the scientific method in the approach. No dogma is allowed to come in the way."[20]

So marvellous has been this philosophical continuity reaching civilization's acme, that Max Muller, more than a century back, paid a rare tribute to it:

"If we were to look over the whole world to find out the country most richly endowed with all the wealth, power, and beauty that nature can bestow—in some parts a very paradise on earth—I should point to India. If I were asked under what sky the human mind has most fully developed some of its choicest gifts, has most deeply pondered over the greatest problems of life, and has found solutions of some of them which well deserve the attention even of those who have studied Plato and Kant—I should point to India.

"And if I were to ask myself from what literature we here in Europe, we who have been nurtured almost exclusively on the thoughts of Greeks and Romans,

18 *Ibid.*
19 *Ibid.*
20 Jawaharlal Nehru: *The Discovery of India,* page 89.

and of one Semitic race, the Jewish, may draw the corrective which is most wanted in order to make our inner life more perfect, more comprehensive, more universal, in fact more truly human a life, not for this life only, but a transfigured and eternal life—again I should point to India."[1]

That apart, we need only note that the major religions, in their finer essence, have cherished higher values beyond goals of materialist pleasures. Material development, without soulful foundation, may be skin-deep, not sublime. A synthesis of values is a necessary process if the reality of human rights becomes a finer fact of life. Pristine Islam reverenced this holistic social-spiritual view of humanity which is the well-spring of human rights, spoiled though by later Muslim rulers to an extent.

Swami Vivekananda, a cyclonic sadhu, matchless, fearless and rationally religious in his forthright eloquence wrote in 1878 to Muslim friend, Sarfaraz Hussain, with astonishing courage and candour:

"Whether we call it Vendantism or any ism, the truth is that Advaitism is the last word of religion and thought and the only position from which one can look upon all religions and sects with love. I believe it is the religion of the future enlightened humanity. The Hindus may get the credit of arriving at it earlier than other races, they being an older race than either the Hebrew or the Arab; *yet practical Advaitism*, which looks upon and behaves to all mankind as one's own soul, *was never developed among the Hindus universally*.

"On the other hand, my experience is that if *ever any religion approached to this equality in an appreciable manner, it is Islam and Islam alone.*

"Therefore I am firmly persuaded that without the help of practical Islam, theories of Vendantism, however fine and wonderful they may be, are entirely valueless to the vast mass of mankind. We want to lead mankind to the place where there is neither the Vedas, nor the Bible, nor the Koran; yet this has to be done by harmonising the Vedas, the Bible and the Koran. Mankind ought to be taught that religions are but the varied expressions of THE RELIGION, which is Oneness, so that each may choose that path that suits him best.

"I see in my mind's eye the future perfect India rising out of this chaos and strife, glorious and invincible with Vedanta brain and Islam body."[2]

Imam Ali, who was second only to the Holy Prophet, expounded a profound fraternity which is the foundation of human rights.

"One must remember that Muslims address each other as brothers and this is the closest relation that exists between two human beings on the basis of mutual respect and equality. In this matter they have been inspired by the Quran that has said, "All Muslims are brethren". No racial, class or family distinction can cause one person to become superior to another."[3]

1 *Ibid*, pages 88-89.

2 *Complete Works of Swami Vivekananda*, vol. VI, pages 416-417.

3 Imam Ali Ibn Abu Talib: *Nahjul Balagha Peak of Eloquence*, page ix.

Ali's injunction include kindness to children and reverence for life. Shi'ism regards the rights of women as a basic principle and gives complete economic independence to women.

His humanitarian aphorism is pregnant with moral excellence.

> "When you gain power over adversary, pardon him by way of thanks for being able to overpower him.
>
> "Such was the largeness of his heart that as he was fatally stabbed during his Ramazan prayers, Hazrat Ali urged his supporters to treat his assassin with humanity."[4]

H.G. Wells, in the *Outline of History* observes objectively: There can be no denying that Islam possesses many fine and noble attributes.

> "A year before his death, at the end of the tenth year of the Hegira, Muhammad made his last pilgrimage from Medina to Mecca. He made then a great sermon to his people * * *.
>
> The reader will note that the first paragraph sweeps away all plunder and blood feuds among the followers of Islam. The last makes the believing Negro the equal of the Caliph * * *.
>
> They created a society more free from widespread cruelty and social oppression than any society had ever been in the world before".
>
> * * *
>
> "Ye people! harken to my speech and comprehend the same.
>
> Know that every Moslem is the brother of every other Moslem.
>
> All of you are on the same equality".[5]

Fairness to Islam as it operated in the Akbar era of India justifies mention of the following provisions during the great ruler's reign, since this has a bearing on human rights:

"(1) He repealed the discriminatory law regarding citizenship and created one common citizenship as also one unanimous system of justice for all.

(2) He prohibited the making of war prisoners as slaves (1562 A.D.).

(3) He abolished Hindu Pilgrims' tax as also Jizya which made invidious discrimination against Hindus (1564 A.D.).

(4) He permitted Hindus and Christians to build temples and churches, respectively.

(5) He permitted Hindus who had been forcibly converted into Islam to revert to the religion of their forefathers (1580 A.D.).

(6) He permitted the buying back from servitude of children who were sold to become slaves by their parents.

4 In a message to the International Congress of Nahajul Balagha, dated 14.4.95.

5 H.G. Wells: *Outline of History*, pages 606-607.

(7) He repealed the law which provided for imposition of death clause for criticising the religion of Islam or the conduct of Prophet Muhammad.

(8) He prohibited Sati unless the concerned Hindu widow wanted to do so voluntarily and without pressure by any one.

(9) He also modified personal law of the Muslims and provided that a Muslim should take only one wife, and could take another only if the first wife was barren.

(10) He prohibited marriage between cousins and other near relations. He also prohibited marriage of a boy below 16 years and girl below 14 years."[6]

Persecution of Rushdie and Tasleema are aberrations from the angle of human rights activists. Religion, when it turns rabid, becomes fatal to human rights. The battle for human rights has to be waged against gory godism everywhere. At the same time, the jurisprudence of human rights must command universal sanction, including from divine authority. Our concern is with the human person and his/her full unfoldment. Everything that fertilises, catalyses and glorifies this central purpose is within our legitimate interest.

Human rights, like other rights, must be enforceable and for this the sanction of a higher secular authority is necessary. Such a view will look for secular law, sanction against violation and a Sovereign who can grant relief to the victim. On this premiss, a modern philosophy of human law, human justice and human rights does not call for a long discussion of the roots of rights lying embedded in different religions. But religion is a powerful source of conduct and obedience and, in India, it is difficult to ignore that source although we are a secular republic. Moreover, religion conditions human reverence for rules of obedience and it is profitable to look at various divinely ordained sets of rules for human action. From the Mosaic law to Maver's Code and Mohammad's Quran, *et al*, we find the sages and seers as law makers. How far can we derive help from such sources for our own universal notions of human rights is therefore a pertinent inquiry in an endeavour to receive reinforcement for the New World Human Order. Such is the justification for the study of emotionally charged areas of divergent religions to the extent of seeking from spiritual, sacerdotal and ancient faiths the validation of the universe of human rights.

Religion, the other side

The great religions of the East and the West have in their creative days contributed human values to the civilised march of mankind. But to balance the assessment, the negative side whereby scriptures, theologies and sectarian denominations have harmed the human cause also deserve mention. An honest man may be the noblest work of God; but an honest God is the noblest work of man. The pity is bad deified coins and counterfeit human piety are many in circulation causing double jeopardy. Human

6 M. Rama Jois: *Legal and Constitutional History of India*, vol. II, page 8.

rights culture includes freedom of religion as against totalitarian trends of ecclesiastical bigotry and intolerant attitudes to other faiths. Indeed, fanatic addictions and inflammatory inhibitions and obscurantist obduracies, blind human reasoning and enslave the minds of the masses. When gods go to war human followers indulge in massacres. So much so, we are constrained to consider the role of religion in the preservation of human rights. The universality of human dignity is the cornerstone of all freedoms and reverence for global fellowship. Religion, in this exalted sense, has been defined by Vivekananda as the divinity in Man—every human being. At the same time, Charles Darwin in the *Descent of Man* has observed:

> "Man with all his noble qualities, with sympathy that feels for the most debased, with benevolence which extends not only to other men but to the humblest living creature, with his god-like intellect which has penetrated into the movements and constitution of the solar system—with all these exalted powers—*still bears in his bodily frame the indelible stamp of his lowly origin.*"

In exquisitely picturesque language, Charles Darwin tells us of the supreme law which explains the cosmic processes:

> "It is interesting to contemplate an entangled bank, clothed with many plants of many kinds, with birds singing on the bushes, with various insects flitting about, and with worms crawling through the damp earth, and to reflect that these elaborately constructed forms, so different from each other, and dependent upon each other in so complex a manner, have all been produced by laws acting around us."

The animal in Man is brought out in the Shavian wit oft quoted: "Darwin taught us not that all men were monkeys once, but that some monkeys have no tail now". Indeed, as Prof. Whitefield pithily put "religion is the last refuge of human savagery".

Similarly, Swift wrote "we have enough religion to make us hate, but not enough to make us love one another". Although Mahatma Gandhi defined religion as Truth, Nehru, his disciple, told Edgar Snow:

> "I want nothing to do with any religion concerned with keeping the masses satisfied to live in hunger, filth and ignorance. I want nothing to do with any order, religious or otherwise, which does not teach people that they are capable of becoming happier and more civilized, on this earth, capable of becoming true man, master of his fate and captain of his soul. To attain this I would put priests to work also, and turn the temples into schools."

Karl Marx who called religion the opium of the people also said: "The imaginary flowers of religion adorn man's chains. Man must throw off the flowers, and also the chains". In short, while freedom of religion is itself a human right, intolerant, expansionist and inflammatory faiths, sects and cults invading temporal affairs in authoritarian fashion, are homicidal to human rights. The world is still in the grip of gory godism. The struggle for human freedom involves the battle for free practice of theism and atheism.

Imperial rulers use religion to their advantage. Says Gibbon, the historian:

"The various modes of worship, which prevailed in the Roman world, were all considered by the people as equally true; by the philosopher, as equally false; and by the magistrate, as equally useful. And thus toleration produced not only mutual indulgence, but even religious concord".

"Religion teaches those who toil in poverty all their lives to be resigned and patient in this world, and consoles them with the hope of reward in heaven. As for those who live upon the labour of others, religion teaches them to be charitable in earthly life, thus providing a cheap justification for their whole exploiting existence and selling them at a reasonable price tickets to heavenly bliss. 'Religion is the opium of the people'—(Marx). Religion is a kind of spiritual intoxicant, in which the slaves of capital drown their humanity and blunt their desires for some sort of decent human existence."

6

The United Nations and its Structure: Whence, Whither and What Hope for Human Rights?

The finest hour of humanity's modern history of human rights dawned when, overpowering Hitler's hordes and Nipponese hounds and their harshest and most horrendous savageries, fifty progressive, peace-seeking leaders of the planet adopted and signed on 26th June 1945 in San Francisco the Charter which founded the United Nations, the hallowed haven of the peoples of the earth. The Charter was drafted on the basis of proposals worked out at Dumbarton Oaks Estate, Washington, in 1944 by the representatives of China, France, the Soviet Union, the United Kingdom and the United States (these five states became the five permanent members of the Security Council and the name 'United Nations' was devised by Franklin D. Roosevelt and was first used in the 'Declaration by United Nations' of 1st January 1942). A declaration of common objectives had been made by Roosevelt and Churchill after a secret meeting off Newfoundland in August 1941 which was later endorsed by the USSR and 14 other States at war with the Axis Powers. Among the 51 original signatories (Poland was the 51st) India figures as one; and so, as a founding member, accepted the Charter obligations. Thus blossomed the world's noblest instrument for peace, security and human rights over the bodies of the totalitarian tyrants, military monsters and blood-thirsty troops who inflicted atrocious casualties of countless millions of humans (around 45 million civilians lost their innocent lives!)

Omar Khayyum's lines grimly come to mind:

> *"I sometimes think that never glows so red*
> *The Rose as where some buried Caesar bled."*

Many Hitlers and Mussolinis had to bleed or suicide before a United Nations could bloom. But how many guiltless lives perished before the rose of peace could flower in crimson hope! And fifty years after, what is the record? Hiroshima (6th August 1945) is blood on American hands still, with 1,50,000 killed or wounded and most buildings of a pretty city destroyed by an atom bomb and Nagasaki, the cruelest criminality of a second atom bomb target, (9th August 1945) which suffered havoc and heaven's justice is yet to descend on the American operators. Nay, the audacity of it, the same Super Power is still coercing the whole world to sign a treaty (CTBT) to get virtual monopoly over global nuclear arsenals. To possess a nuclear bomb is a potential crime against humanity. Humanity's amnesia cannot naively go so far as to forget Hiroshima and the subsequent blood-curdling invasions by the Pentagon a la Vietnam. How can humankind blink at the possible globoshima looming in the distance if a Super Power corners all the sinister weapons capable of wiping out the planet's population and has malignant commercial corporate motives to keep the whole world as its monopoly market?

This 'aside' should not hijack us from the main theme of the United Nations as the harbinger, nurturer and guarantor of human rights worldwide. The creation of this unique institution with universal jurisdiction is an unprecedented event and inconceivably benignant portent born under sombre circumstances of blood, sweat, tears and death sparing no continent, no human category and with a swell of high hope for a glorious future. The futility of the League of Nations,—a beautiful and ineffectual angel—which was founded after World War I but foundered on the rocks of totalitarian realities, sans strong sanctions, effective infrastructure, not even the basic recognition of human beings with inalienable rights as the subject of deep concern and non-negotiable reverence—this poignant feeling persuaded the staggering statesmen of the earth to agree solemnly in the city of San Francisco to the Charter of the United Nations and establish the organization to be known as the United Nations. The dignity and worth of the human person is the first charge on this World Body. For, think of the worth and wonder of this 'paragon of animals' 'infinite in faculty! in form, in moving, how express and admirable! in apprehension how like a god! the beauty of the world!' Such is the profound value of personhood, the repository of human rights to protect, preserve and promote which is a paramount function of the United Nations.

The basic facts about the United Nations must be understood before we proceed further with the inquiry into the development of human rights jurisprudence. The defining moment in world history arrived when, in San Francisco the epic event of cosmic impact occurred and a framework for international cooperation in fostering human rights, self-determination and world peace was forged and fashioned with a phenomenal potential for uniting our human planet to adventure towards a democratic destination and divine destiny. What vistas opened! What distressing memories buried! What a new dawn unfolded!

The UN was formally formed on 24th October 1945 with 51 founder countries. Over the years, the membership has increased in numbers with around 189 countries as members legally committed to cooperate in supporting the objectives of the Charter. This glorious opportunity given to humanity has not fulfilled the great expectations it raised because formidable problems, challenges, dominations and terrorisms, with crushing effect on the human rights of the countries of the South and elsewhere, forced themselves on mankind. Even at this stage, we may hear the Secretary-General Boutros Boutros-Ghali on these problematic developments and ominous forebodings. In his Cyril Foster Lecture at the University of Oxford on 15th January 1996 he observed:

> "As the twenty-first century speeds towards us, a new dialectic has begun. The world is in the grip of two vast and opposing forces: globalization and fragmentation.
>
> "Globalization is generating an array of problems. Financial flows of vast magnitude sweep across the world. Alarming environmental events expose the planet to permanent damage and super massive movements of peoples. Transnational criminal activity grows. Even the powerfully positive global communications revolution generates pressures which our institutions were not designed to address.
>
> "And there are the forces of fragmentation. Rising insecurity and unmet needs on a national scale are leading people everywhere to seek refuge in smaller groups. This can promote the healthy development of civil society—as evidenced by the proliferation of citizens' groups and non-governmental organizations acting in pursuit of public purposes. But fragmentation also can breed fanaticism, isolationism, separatism, and the proliferation of civil conflict.
>
> "The United Nations can help deal with the dialectic of globalization and fragmentation, and help solve the problems it creates, now and in the future.
>
> "But the United Nations cannot fulfil this new role if the present trend continues. The United Nations is trapped by a second dialectic. The problems of globalization and fragmentation have caused vast responsibilities to be given to the United Nations. *But the United Nations has not been given the political, military, material and financial* resources required to accomplish the tasks imposed."

The Chief Executive sounded pathetic with his litany of resourceless languishment. At this time, he must be supported by all activists so that he may not cave in under Big Power pressure. The world's conscience and the nations' consensus are needed to solve these escalating forces and new structures like regional arrangements, non-governmental organizations, parliamentarians, academic and policy research institutions, the media—all are needed to take on greater global roles and strengthen the sinking UN to stay afloat and fulfill its humanitarian tasks. It is a universal instrumentality and inspiration which should never fade or flounder.

Globalization often ends up by weaker nations being gobbled up by economic Gargantuas alias G-7. In moderate diction, the Secretary-General expresses his apprehensions thus:

> "Globalization of the world economy is failing to reach all peoples; too many are excluded or unable to find access to the prosperity it offers. At the same

time, the market economy that is the engine of this vast movement is, by its very logic, driving large numbers of people—in developing, transitional and developed countries alike—into conditions of deepening poverty and despair."

*** *** ***

"In the context of globalization, the need to revitalize international law and to promote its progressive expansion has taken on even greater urgency."

How about the grave issues of fragmentation and helplessness in actualisation of human rights?

"The forces of fragmentation can cause a State—particularly the poorest States—to fail, leaving its people without a Government to protect them from chaos. With many among the international community inclined to turn inward after decades of global ideological confrontation, it is all too easy for Governments, in the virtual absence of public pressure, to consider such conflicts as not in their national interest, and to see no reason for action, direct or indirect.

"Lives lost in one place seem to matter less than lives lost in another. War in one country may get enormous attention, while war in another may be virtually ignored. Violations of the rights of one people arouse far more concern than violations of the rights of another. As a result, some of these conflicts are 'orphans', deprived of international attention and concern."

Refugees flood the world and the disease of civil conflicts and casualties aggravate until the decease of nations. The tidal wave of weapons sales and shooting battles bleed poorer countries financially and physically, so long as the killer industry of armaments manufacture flourishes and profits rise in favour of Big Powers. Listen to the Secretary-General's gloomy plea:

"Macro-disarmament is a vitally important undertaking for the future of international peace and security. But it must not be done at the expense of micro-disarmament—action to control and reduce the massive production, transfer and stockpiling of light weapons around the world.

"Paradoxically, micro-disarmament is resisted by both suppliers and recipients. The richest countries, which possess major weapons, enthusiastically advocate non-proliferation, but lack interest in stopping the spread of light weapons because they are the primary manufacturers and suppliers of such arms. The poorest countries, which lack major weapons systems, are also enthusiastic for macro-disarmament for they have no hope of acquiring such system but lack interest in micro-disarmament because the possession of vast arsenals of small arms is essential to the survival of their regimes.

"The most horrible of these weapons are land-mines. Land-mines are intended to devastate entire populations and destroy the prospects of development for decades. As Secretary-General, I have called urgently for an international convention on land-mines, to totally ban the production, stockpiling, trade and use of all mines and kine components."

The United Nations is caught in a dilemma of realism versus responsibility. American hegemony *vis-a-vis* the aggression on Iraq and the overuse of UN authorisation by the U.S. comes to mind when the Secretary-General argues:

"What are the dangers involved? There is the danger that a multiplicity of actors cannot be coordinated. There is a danger of overreliance upon one State or group of States. There is a danger that authorization could serve to strengthen a particular power's sphere of influence. And there is a danger that overuse of authorization and delegation will damage the image of the United Nations; that the public will fail to understand why the United Nations itself does not act."

The US and lesser nations, be it noted, are enfeebling the UN financially and opposing democratisation of the UN and of the Security Council as well as of international relations in a militarily and economically over-heated human universe. A depressing catalogue of disabilities is reflected in the Secretary-General's speech as he winds up:

"Nothing is more precious to the United Nations than its reputation. That reputation rests on four pillars: impartiality, equity, efficiency and achievement. *A fifth, and indispensable principle, is independence.*

"If one word, above all, is to characterize the role of the Secretary-General it is independence. Article 100 of the Charter is "the one-hundredth Psalm" of the Secretary-General.

"The Secretary-General must be prepared to stand up to any pressure, any criticism, and any opposition in defence of the Charter's call upon all Member States to respect the 'exclusively international character of the responsibilities of the Secretary-General and the Staff and not to seek to influence them in the discharge of their responsibilities'.

"The words of the Charter mean that the Secretary-General's loyalty must be international and nothing but international; that the international civil service must be a real civil service; and that the Organization's integrity must be always sustained. Independence is the key to all these objectives."

Why have I taken up so much space on the Secretary-General and his humiliating lamentations and dialectical presentation? Because the US (and company) is bypassing the UN weakening it and controlling other global Americaphilic institutions a la IMF, World Bank, GATT and WTO. In such rough weather, human rights have to struggle if they are not to be drowned. The Iraqi civilians are now aliens to the very right to life. How betrayed were the non-combatant civilians and how long after the UN/(US) war there was over? Ramsay Clark, a former attorney-general of the US, charged President Bush of war crimes in a people's trial. An enfeebled yet conscientious exercise, doomed to failure though, but sufficient to quicken the soul of humanity against the injustice of Might is Right.

If the UN suffers the attrition syndrome or succumbs to cipherisation, chaos in the cosmos may well be Cassandra's curse. With great eclat the half-century of the United Nations was celebrated with national heads swearing by their commitments to the principles of the UN. At the same time, peoples all over the Earth are scanning and soul-searching, in a demoralised mood, *vis-a-vis* the UN's impotence, quagmired, as it is, in various crises; and a sceptical interrogation mark about its useful survival adds to the global agony. Strengthening the UN and its subsidiaries to serve mankind impartially is an urgency if the whole edifice is not to fall to pieces. The developed world seems hostile even to the UN organisations. Motivated non-cooperation with UN instrumentalities glooms sombrously the world scenario. Let me illustrate:

> "A most recent example is that of the United Nations Industrial Development Organisation (UNIDO). The United States announced its withdrawal from UNIDO last month on several grounds. Though the formal reasons put forth at the organisation's general conference in Vienna were the U.S. administration's budgetary constraints, other factors were cited at a subsequent press conference. These were what the U.S. spokesperson termed as the dubious efficiency record of the organisation as well as the view that only a limited contribution would be made through Government intervention for industrial development.
>
> "What has caused more concern are the indications given at that time of that country's plans to withdraw from several other UN agencies. It appears clear the next targets will be the United Nations Conference on Trade and Development (UNCTAD) or the UN Economic and Social Commission.
>
> "Even as the U.S. is determined, or so it appears, to end its participation in these organisations, there continues to be a chorus of criticism in other developed countries about the performance of the UN agencies. Significantly, however, the withdrawal of the U.S. from UNIDO prompted expressions of support from other major donors such as the European Union (E.U.) and Japan as well as the developing countries like India which are capable of making larger contributions."[1]

The fate of the UNIDO is indicative of the indifference of the developed countries in the matter of funding. There is, as some countries of the South indict,

> "a political bias against providing assistance in the form of public sector intervention to developing economies. This is partly considered to be due to an unwavering faith in the *laissez faire* approach but can also be attributed to apprehensions about the creation of economies like the newly industrialized countries (NICs) of South-East Asia.
>
> * * *
>
> "UNIDO, UNCTAD and the Economic and Social Commission (ECOSOC) are all making efforts for providing assistance to the third world for industrial development and integration with the global economy."[2]

The displeasure of the developed countries hits these benign agencies and depresses prospects of confident help.

The inference is inevitable that the US and its companions frown upon the developmental efforts of the UNIDO. And the like to aid the South. This goes against the spirit of egalitarian globalisation as distinguished from the boloney brand of hegemonic globalisation which is in circulation under

1 *The Hindu*, dated 1st February 1996, page 12.
2 *Ibid.*

high-voltage propaganda by the North. The dismal portent of America and its affluent allies financially strangling the UN and its offspring must be opposed by the American people and by the media and intelligentsia the world over.

This extrapolative essay from known trends is necessitated by the fear of the non-entitisation of the UN, which all mankind must unitedly resist. With this alarming backdrop of a darkling curtain, let us go into the anatomy of the United Nations, its agencies and later developments.

The General Assembly is the plenary body which controls and debates and fulfils the objectives for which "We the Peoples of the United Nations" set it up under the great Charter whose ends are the maintenance of peace and security at the international level and the promotion of the economic and social advancement of all peoples. The purposes of this global marvel include the achievement of 'international co-operation in solving international problems of an economic, social, cultural, or humanitarian character, and in promoting and encouraging respect for human rights and for fundamental freedoms for all without distinction as to race, sex, language, or religion'.

The UN General Assembly stands first. The key weapon, however, is the 15 member Security Council which is dominated by the five permanent members (China, France, UK, Russia, and USA) who each have the power of veto over any resolutions; the remaining 10 are elected for two-year periods. The primary role of the Council is to maintain international peace and security; its decisions, unlike those of the General Assembly, are binding on all other members. The Secretariat, under the Secretary-General employs some 16,000 at the UN's headquarters in New York City and 50,000 world-wide. The Secretary-General is often a significant person in international diplomacy and is able to take independent initiatives. The International Court of Justice consists of 15 Judges appointed by the Council and the Assembly. As only States can bring issues before it, its jurisdiction depends on the consent of the states who are a party to a dispute. The Economic and Social Council is elected by the General Assembly; it supervises the work of various committees, commissions, and expert bodies in the economic and social area, and co-ordinates the work of UN specialized agencies.

Despite the glorious globalism–more verbal than real–of this world body, functionally speaking it is 'a beautiful and ineffectual angel, beating in the void his luminous wings in vain'. It can bark but not bite and its democracy is often a futility and even where disputes are debated the result is but reflective of the Shakespearean lines:

> *"Life's but a walking shadow, a poor player,*
> *That struts and frets his hour upon the stage,*
> *And then is heard no more; it is a tale,*
> *Told by an idiot, full of sound and fury,*
> *Signifying nothing."*

Whatever the voices and noises by the numerous nonentitised nations, the US dominates ultimately. Indeed, one may well be frank in calling a spade a spade and holding that the UN with all its failings, is an international forum for the people and of the people. This includes those people in the world for whom human dignity and freedom are made almost meaningless, except as dreams, because of their poverty, their ignorance and their sufferings under oppression. Tottering diadems and pro-US diluted democracies find comfort in getting aid from the world financial bodies.

The Charter of the UN makes reference to human rights and fundamental freedoms. Of course, in its Preamble, there is noble reaffirmation of "faith in fundamental human rights, in the dignity and worth of the human person, in the equal rights of men and women and of nations large and small". In substance, this haunting idea appears in:

> "Article 1, on the purposes and principles of the United Nations; in Article 13, on the functions and powers of the General Assembly; in Article 62, on the functions and powers of the Economic and Social Council; and in Article 76, on the basic objectives of the International Trusteeship system." * * *.
>
> "In Article 56, all Members of the United Nations pledge to take joint and separate action in co-operation with the Organization for the achievement of purposes enumerated in Article 55, including the promotion of "universal respect for, and observance of, human rights and fundamental freedoms for all without distinction as to race, sex, language, or religion."[3]

UN headquarters is in New York, symbolic of the geographic and functional domination of this institution by the United States. A European Office exists in Geneva; other offices and related organisations are scattered throughout the world.

The UN is the modern nidus of human rights in their rich diversity, whose ancient provenance, though, is immemorial and its paramountcy integral to human personhood. Through the ages human rights have been a high component of human justice with roots deep in divinity, sustained by spirituality and formed the finer layers of great religions. But never has there been a World Body with surrogates from every nation on earth and with focus on the worth of the human person in the secular sense, which makes the UN unique. No more are human rights of vague vintage, of vagarious contours and visionary mintage, in the material source or juridical force or variorum versions. The instruments are clear, the texts are authentic and world opinion and UN authority back this creative collection of living documents. Humanity's Magna Carta, supported by the signature of the largest global institution ever, is now the perennial fountain of humanist international law, jurisprudence of human rights 'in widest commonalty spread' and embracing everything that affects human interests on earth or outer space. It is universal, even celestial. This dynamic wonder and institutional authority does have the power to shape human destiny through its

3 *The United Nations and Human Rights*, pages 2 & 3.

decisions. The United Nations, according to its Charter, is not 'born to blush unseen' but bound to debate all that relates to human betterment and embitterment. And a glimpse of the whole gamut of instruments attributable to the UN convinces us how this cosmic constellation, 'in a fine frenzy rolling, doth glance from heaven to earth, from earth to heaven', reeling off Covenants, Conventions, Declarations, Resolutions and Recommendations which, if implemented, will transmute into 'gold undiscovered' the iron savagery which was the ghastly reality as World War II gassasinated and gorily genocided millions of humans in "patriotic" madness. Between the sublime and the savage 'thin partition do their bounds divide', as the two world wars have diabolically demonstrated. In Shakespearean diction:

> "O God! that men should put an enemy in their mouths to steal away their brains; that we should, with joy, pleasance, revel, and applause, transform ourselves into beasts."

In War men behave like brutish beasts. What Dwight Eisenhower said is tragic truth: "I hate war as only a soldier who has lived it can, only as one who has seen its brutality, its futility, its stupidity".

In similar strain Douglas MacArthur in an Address to Congress in 1951, stated:

> "I know war as few other men now living know it, and nothing to me is more revolting. I have long advocated its complete abolition, as its very destructiveness on both friend and foe has rendered it useless as a method of settling international disputes."

The compulsive necessity for an international institution to interdict human annihilation was stressed by MacArthur as early as 1945:

> "Military alliances, balances of power, leagues of nations, all in turn failed, leaving the only path to be by way of the crucible of war. The utter destructiveness of war now blocks out this alternative. We have had our last chance. If we will not devise some greater and more equitable system, Armageddon will be at our door."

The historic San Franscisco assemblage which agreed to the Charter of the United Nations had, as its goal, the promotion of a world community committed to peace and security and faith in 'fundamental human rights, in the dignity and worth of the human person, in the equal rights of men and women everywhere'.

A bare Charter cannot be kinetic without operational instrumentalities, principles promotive of human well-being, jurisprudence and jurisdiction and capacity to command compliance in case of violation. The United Nations Charter was written in the closing days of the Second World War. Peoples sighed relief. Why?

To refugees from war and persecution in their millions the United Nations has, over the decades, provided shelter and relief. It has acted in the sixties as a major catalyst in the evolution of 100 million people from colonial rule to independence and sovereignty. It has established peace-keeping operations several times to contain hostilities and to help resolve conflicts. It has expanded and codified international law, it has wiped smallpox from the face of the planet. In the nearly five decades of its existence, the Organization has adopted some nearly hundred hard-won legal instruments promoting or obligating respect for human rights in many dimensions, thus facilitating Operation Compassion in the popular imagination about freedom and felicity on earth. The biblical promise seemed to take shape, namely, "Blessed are they which do hunger and thirst after righteousness: for they shall be filled".

The organization and structure of the United Nations and the other instruments and agencies and their efficiency in producing results become all-important if the great expectations of San Francisco are not to evaporate as *vanitas et vanitatem*.

> "The Charter declares that membership of the United Nations is open to all peace-loving nations which accept its obligations and which, in the judgment of the Organization, are willing and able to carry out these obligations.
>
> "States are admitted to membership by the General Assembly on the recommendation of the Security Council. The Charter also provides for the suspension or expulsion of Members for violation of the principles of the Charter, but no such action has even been taken."

For the dreamers of dreams, Humanity Incorporated had come into existence to ensure human rights in October 1945.

In theory, every UN member is obligated to carry out the decisions reached. That is the theology but, in actuality, 'it is a custom more honour'd in the breach than the observance'. Why? Because of the structural weaknesses *writ large* in the Charter which sounds magniloquent but acts with trepidation to such an extent that, on crucial issues and in critical times, the US virtually signs for the UN. Democracy as a desideratum distances away from this finest product of humanity midwifed under conditions of shock and haemorrhage which victimised all the continents.

A few facts about the International Court of Justice and other five organs, which make the UN's presence a source of human happiness and justice, may vivify the scenario. Obviously, the General Assembly is the principal democratic, deliberative instrumentality. Each state has one vote but on important issues a two-thirds majority is needed, including budgetary matters and admission of new members. The simple majority rule does apply only to routine matters, so much so that Big Powers can manipulate decisions using pressure where their interests are involved. Human rights concerns fall within the ambit of the General Assembly.

> "Under the 'Uniting for peace' resolution adopted by the General Assembly in November 1950, the Assembly may take action if the Security Council, because of a lack of unanimity of its permanent members, fails to act in a case where there appears to be a threat to the peace, breach of the peace or act of aggression. The Assembly is empowered to consider the matter immediately with a view to making recommendations to Members for collective measures, including, in the case of a breach of the peace or act of aggression, the use of

armed force when necessary to maintain or restore international peace and security".[4]

"To ensure equitable geographical representation, the presidency of the Assembly rotates each year among five groups of States: African, Asian, Eastern European, Latin American, and Western European and other States.

* * *

"At the beginning of each regular session, the Assembly holds a general debate, in which Member States express their views on a wide range of matters of international concern. Because of the great number of questions which the Assembly is called upon to consider (over 150 agenda items at the 1992 session of the Assembly, for example), the Assembly allocates most questions to its seven Main Committees".[5]

The strongest organ is the Security Council which has responsibility in keeping peace and security worldwide.

"The Council has 15 members: five permanent members—China, France, the Russian Federation, the United Kingdom and the United States—and 10 elected by the General Assembly for two-year terms.

"Each member of the Council has one vote. Decisions on procedural matters are made by an affirmative vote of at least nine of the 15 members. Decisions on substantive matters require nine votes including the concurring votes of all five permanent members. This is the rule of "great Power unanimity", often referred to as the "veto" power. All five permanent members have exercised the right of veto at one time or another. If a permanent member does support a decision but does not wish to block it through a veto, it may abstain.

"Under the Charter, all members of the United Nations agree to accept and carry out the decisions of the Security Council."[6]

The functions and powers of this Council include investigation of international friction, tension, dispute resolution and even to take military action against aggression by economic sanctions and other measures up to use of force to prevent or stop war and foster truce by mediation and despatch of peace-keeping forces. U.S. domination to the point of usurpation has been a widely felt criticism of the Security Council. Now that the Cold War has ended and the Soviet Union liquidated, American might, pressurising the Security Council, plays the gendarmerie role over the globe and the nation's leader in the White House turns into the world's generalissimo. And when the M.N.Cs of the U.S. control the White House the economic domination of U.S. Incorporated bends the police power of the Security Council, using disinformation, misinformation and other brain-washing plus browbeating tactics for furthering commercial interests. Human rights

4 *Basic Facts About the United Nations*, at page 9.
5 *Ibid* at pages 9 & 10.
6 *Ibid* at page 11.

of humbler people become voiceless in such circumstances. Time was when President Woodrow Wilson bluntly stated:

> "The masters of the Government of the United States are the combined capitalists and manufacturers of the United States", he said during his first campaign for the Presidency. "It is written over every intimate page of the record of Congress, it is written all through the history of conferences at the White House, that the suggestions of economic policy have come from one source, not from many sources. .....The Government of the United States at present is a foster child of the special interests".[7]

The present Presidents are pressurised more by the Corporate Heavyweights. Alas, the smaller members are powerless to defend their human rights or collective self-determination. The world today suffers from a dependencia syndrome, the U.S. being a Colossus and the rest underlings.

Economic and Social Council is another body with immense humanitarian potential as the major organ to co-ordinate the economic and social objectives of the UN and the specialised agencies and institutions known as the United Nation's family of organisations. Since economic and social issues have a bearing on the Covenanted human rights, the studies and reports and recommendations by the 'ECOSOC' on international economic, social, cultural, educational, health and related matters are of great importance. The 'ECOSOC' functionally promotes observance of human rights and fundamental freedoms, holds conferences and prepares Conventions for submission to the General Assembly. Many other services are performed by 'ECOSOC' which also consults non-governmental organisations. Thus the Council recognizes N.G. Os as a mediator between the UN and the people in various countries. Over 900 Non-governmental Organisations–informal, unelected but effective mediators and surrogates have consultative status with the Council.

The International Court of Justice is the Judicial organ of the UN, its Statute being an integral part of the UN Charter. Thereby all members of the UN are parties to this Statute.

> "All countries which are parties to the Statute of the Court can be parties to cases before it. Other States can refer cases to it under conditions laid down by the Security Council. In addition, the Security Council may recommend that a legal dispute be referred to the Court.
>
> "Both the General Assembly and the Security Council can ask the Court for an advisory opinion on any legal question; other organs of the United Nations and the specialized agencies, when authorized by the General Assembly, can ask for advisory opinions on legal questions within the scope of their activities."[8]

It is unfortunate that the World Court despite its vast jurisdiction has no binding authority unless States bind themselves in advance to accept

7 In the Prologue to the Book *America Inc.* by Morton Mintz & Jerry S. Cohen.
8 *Basic Facts about the United Nations*, at page 17.

its jurisdiction, in special cases, either by signing a treaty or convention which provides for referral to the Court or by making a special declaration to that effect. Such declarations accepting compulsory jurisdiction may exclude certain classes of cases.

In accordance with Article 38 of its Statute, the Court, in deciding disputes submitted to it, applies–

(*a*) international conventions establishing rules recognized by the contesting States;

(*b*) international custom as evidence of a general practice accepted as law;

(*c*) the general principles of law recognized by nations; and,

(*d*) judicial decisions and the teachings of the most highly qualified publicists of the various nations, as a subsidiary means for determining the rules of law.

15 Judges compose the Court elected by the General Assembly and the Security Council each for a term of 9 years. The Court sits in plenary session at The Hague.

The relevance of the World Court *vis-a-vis* human rights as well as rights of States is significant:

> "Article 1 of the United Nations Charter calls for the adjustment or settlement of international disputes by peaceful means in conformity with the principles of justice and international law. Among the methods of peaceful settlement, the Charter specifies, in Article 33, arbitration and judicial settlement. Under Article 13, one of the General Assembly's functions is "encouraging the progressive development of international law and its codification".
>
> "Since the inauguration of the International Court of Justice in 1946, States have submitted over 65 cases to it, and 20 advisory opinions have been requested by international organizations. Nearly all cases have been dealt with by the full Court, but since 1981 four have been referred to special chambers at the request of the parties. Twelve contentious cases are at present pending. The cases submitted cover a wide range of topics."[9]

A few Supplementary Reflections. The World Court: Does it hold out a human rights future?

Let us begin with a negative assertion by a great scholar:

> "The International Court of Justice is not a human rights Court in the contemporary sense of that term. The Statute of the Court provides, in Article 34, that: "Only States may be parties in cases before the Court". It follows that individuals, corporations, non-governmental organizations, even international governmental organizations, may not be parties to contentious cases before the Court. Moreover, the focus of the large majority of contentious cases between States, and advisory opinions given by the Court in answer to

9 *Basic Facts about the United Nations*, at page 205.

questions of international governmental organizations (the United Nations and its Specialised Agencies) has not been on human rights questions."[10]

Humanity's hopes, however, desiderate that the Court must be enabled to deal with human right issues, not merely disputes among States, although there are pitfalls we must notice. Kindly compare the European Court of Human Rights, the Inter-American Court of Human Rights and some other international judicial bodies which provide for adjudication of human rights. Therefore, the World Court's statute should also be suitably amended to cognize human right questions by modifying Article 34. It is noteworthy that even now it is a fact that questions of human rights have arisen in a number of cases before the World Court and that in some of those cases the Court has rendered judgments or given advisory opinions which have significantly influenced international law bearing on human rights. To deny the World Court's potential to enrich human rights jurisprudence is to abandon an excellent resource on legalitarian grounds of construction of Article 34.

Even the Permanent Court of International Justice, the predecessor of the present World Court, did as far back as 1923 deal with one of the "Minorities Treaties" which were a favoured instrument of the maintenance of human rights in post-World War I years. By a Minorities Treaty which Poland concluded in pursuance of the Treaty of Versailles, Poland undertook "to assure full and complete protection of life and liberty to all inhabitants of Poland without distinction of birth, nationality, language, race or religion". Our endeavour must be to widen the scope of human rights culture, more so when a high authority with institutional potential may be pressed into service. As observed by Schwebel:

> "The Court's opinion in *German Settlers in Poland* today is striking in several respects. The language of Article 55 of the United Nations Charter providing that the United Nations shall promote 'universal respect for, and observance of, human rights and fundamental freedoms for all without distinction as to race, sex, language or religion', mirrors, in its 'without distinction' clause, the terms of the Minorities Treaties. The opinion holds that discrimination in fact is debarred even if discrimination in form is absent. And the Court defines 'civil rights' to include property rights, a holding supportive of the conclusion that human rights in international law include property rights".[11]

Dealing with minority schools in Albania, a dispute arose in 1933 about an Albanian legislation which was challenged as discriminatory. The then Permanent Court ruled on the human right issue implied in the dispute. The Court held:

> "Equality in law precludes discrimination of any kind; whereas equality in fact may involve the necessity of different treatment in order to attain a result which establishes an equilibrium between different situations.

10 Stephen M. Schwebel: '*Human Rights in the World Court*'—Article published in the book *International Law in Transition*, Lancers Books, 1992 at page 267.

11 *Ibid* at page 270.

> "It is easy to imagine cases in which equality of treatment of the majority and of the minority, whose situation and requirements are different, would result in inequality in fact; treatment of this description would run counter to....." Albania's international obligations. It thus concluded that the plea of Albania that, since the abolition of private schools constituted a general measure applicable to the majority as well as the minority, it was in accordance with Albania's international obligations, was unfounded."[12]

Here is a precursor of affirmative action by the Court. Many such instances can be given where the Permanent Court of International Justice and the International Court of Justice have treated questions of human rights and allied questions and the influence of the Court on the evolution of the international law of human rights has been considerable and predominantly constructive. While there may be little prospect in the near terms that the Court will become a Court of human rights, there is ground for the expectation that the court will continue to contribute to the progressive development of the international law of human rights.

The case for broadening the jurisdiction and inclusion of human rights jurisprudence within the scope of the World Court is vital. The Court itself observed in the *Northern Cameroons* case that its judicial function is circumscribed by inherent limitations which are none the less imperative because they may be difficult to catalogue, and may not frequently present themselves as a conclusive bar to adjudication in a concrete case.

Mankind would support the expansion of the World Court's authority to deal with the most legitimate function of ruling on human rights issues. Such an approach seems but an extension and application at International level of the jurisprudence established as far back as 1819 in *McCulloch* v *The State of Maryland* by Chief Justice Marshall. His celebrated observation is good ground for the World Court's justification in adjudication of human rights questions:

> "Let the end be legitimate, let it be within the scope of the constitution, and all means which are appropriate, which are plainly adapted to that end, which are not prohibited, but consist with the letter and the spirit of the constitution, are constitutional."[13]

Prof. Shahabuddeen has argued, based on the above decision of Marshall, C.J. that–

> "It is not easy to see how the very reasonable caveats so thoughtfully built into that wise and generous statement may be justifiably put aside in the case of an international organization such as the International Court of Justice. The Court, as an international organization, is no doubt capable of development. But, in judging the scope and modalities of permissible development, it seems right to bear in mind, not only that the Court is a Court of justice, but that it is

12 *Ibid* at page 272.

13 Shahabuddeen: *The International Court of Justice,* published in the *International Law in Transition, ibid* at page 359.

a court of justice established on an international basis, and that accordingly some circumspection is appropriate both to its intrinsic character and to the basis on which it is organized. More especially is this so for the reason that, if a constitutional amendment is required to facilitate a development, the Court is not helpless: under Article 70 of its Statute the Court can itself take steps to initiate the necessary action, a power which the Court in fact sought to exercise in circumstances of lesser moment in 1969."[14]

The International Court is in transition, but its strength consists in the totality of nations accepting its obligatory jurisdiction. Being one of the six principal wings of the U.N.O. its mandatory jurisdiction is very imperfect, since, until now, only about one-third of the UN Members have opted for its binding jurisdiction. It is true that the 1966 judgment of the Court in South-West Africa cases brought down its esteem when it dismissed Ethiopia's and Liberia's challenge to the racial policies of South Africa. The new Afro-Asian countries regarded the Court as a Whiteman's Tribunal, preserving the politico-legal *status quo* and declining to respond to the basic changes within the world community. However, twenty years later, in 1986 the Court delivered its great judgment in *Military and Para-military activities in and against Nicaragua* (*Nicaragua* v *United States of America*) much to the annoyance of the U.S. which dubbed the Court as anti-West. After the Nicaragua case, the U.S. has debunked the Court, withdrawn from its compulsory jurisdiction and weakened the power and prestige of this noble tribunal. The time has arrived for a global empowerment of the International Court of Justice, if human rights, including abolition of apartheid and like injustices are to find a humanitarian sanctury in The Hague. Judicial conservatism as in the 1966 pronouncement, must be jettisoned. The Third World now looks up to the World Court after the *Nicaragua* Case, where a small State's claim against a super-power was upheld. But who will enforce the verdict of the Court? It is deplorable that the U.S. Government under President Reagan has demonstrated utter contempt for international law, as declared by the Court, and disregarded the United Nations Charter and the Statute of the Court.

"The World Court's resounding condemnation of the Reagan administration's undeclared war against Nicaragua in its unequivocal 1986 decision on the merits in favour of Nicaragua, indeed constitutes an extraordinary document to assert convincingly the relevance of law to an ongoing armed conflict.

"For this reason the very institutional authority of the Court came under enormous hostile criticism and attack from the USA—a country which has been traditionally one of its foremost proponents and strongest supporters."[15]

14 *Ibid* at page 361.

15 R.P. Dhokalia: *International Court in Transition: Challenges to Its Effectiveness*—published in the book *International Court in Transition,* (1994) page 117, Chugh Publications.

The International trumpeter of human rights, the U.S., is a delinquent in its disobedience to the Court's sense of justice and pronouncement of judgment. We need, if human rights are to meet the realities of global life, a Court which none shall defy. Otherwise, The Hague will be a hoax:

> "If some countries demonstrate marked unwillingness to accept the Court's judgments or jurisdiction or accept the Court's jurisdiction subject to reservations on matters falling within their domestic jurisdiction as determined by themselves, or charge the judges of being biased, or prejudiced, it only shows a clear intention to pursue national interests at the price of disregarding international law—an attitude that has been shown by the United States in connection with *Nicaragua*."[16]

Is the world civilised enough to accept the rule of law in matters of human rights and weaker nations' claims? We need to mobilise world opinion and the International Court of Justice must be more explicitly empowered to decide issues which eventually affect minorities and human rights of individuals. No longer can you dismiss 'human rights' as 'nonsense upon stilts'.

The golden jubilee of the UN: what is the prognosis

Will the leaders of the nations vote their confidence in the UN or will the grand institution gradually wither away? If the UN fails, human rights will suffer shock and haemorrhage. The dismantlement of the UN in the near future is the rarest of rare possibilities, but severe criticism of its failings is mounting, especially in the matter of handling of peace-keeping operations and the instrumentation of diplomacy in Bosnia-Herzegovina, its perceived failure in Somalia, which is now back to the anarchic conditions which prevailed when the UN entered the African State four years ago, and the ineptitude in Rwanda where it was unable to prevent genocide that claimed as many as 500,000 Rwandan lives, mostly those belonging to the minority Tutsi clan, are focal points of criticism. Added to this list are perceptions that the UN has grown unwieldy as a result of the creation of too many agencies, some dealing with the same problems. The high cost of peace-keeping and also some reported cases of corruption and maladministration are other charges levelled against the UN. This view has been voiced by competent journalists.[17]

Bosnia was high on the UN agenda in 1995. Massacres of Muslims and Croats, the havoc inflicted and the Serb refugees fleeing and other human rights violations and horrors are reported by the UN peace-keepers. All this the world comes to know because the UN shows concern and discusses issues. A universe of humans without an active UN is a tragedy. A summit meet of UN General Assembly in September-October 1995 brought 150 heads of Governments together to debate issues which bear upon human life everywhere. Dag Hammarskjold's prophetic words in July 1958 ring poignantly true now:

16 *Ibid* at page 157.

17 *The Hindu*, dated 15-10-1995.

> "It is difficult to see how a leap from today's chaotic and disjointed world to something approaching a world federation is to come about....We must serve our apprenticeship and at every stage try to develop forms of international coexistence as far as is possible at the moment.....".

As against the flaws, flounderings, failures, and Security Council biases, there are many plus points. For instance, the decolonisation of the world for which the UN has been instrumental has raised its membership from 51 in 1945 to 185 in 1995. Many serious students of the UN cite the progress made by the Arab States and Israel towards peace as well as the end of apartheid in South Africa and introduction of democracy there as well as in several other countries. It was the strong world opinion created in the UN during many years of debate that paved the way for ending racial discrimination and giving a home state of their own for the Palestinians. The UN's diplomacy in Angola which has been in a state of civil war between the UNITA backed by the United States and the left-oriented Government is offered as another success story. The Angolan rebels have buried their hatchet and agreed to work together to give a development-oriented Government to its war-weary millions. The UN will be launching another peace-keeping operation there deploying several thousand military and civil personnel who will perform the task of preserving peace and conducting democratic elections there for the first time. In Haiti, about 7,000 UN personnel are now policing the state after duly restoring President Aristide back in power after his exile in the U.S. necessitated by a coup staged against him by Haiti's despicable military. If this is not a UN success what else is, defenders ask.

The UN's major success in peacekeeping lies in the role it played in West Asia resulting in the liberation of the tiny but oil-rich nation of Kuwait from the brazen aggression by the Iraqi forces of Saddam Hussain. The U.S. Administration of President George Bush 'no doubt' played a key role, but the counter-invasion of Iraq where terrible civilian casualties occurred, was launched with the help of a coalition of nations under the UN flag. The Iraqi intervention is a controversial issue since many regard it as an American invasion using the UN to serve American interests. A spirit of vendetta, alien to UN ethos, dominated the policy of denying food and medicines to innocent masses inhabiting Iraq. Human rights flag flies half-mast when civilians starve or die because of hostile action, even if the UN is used as proxy or ostensibly.

Spectacular successes in highlighting important issues are notable UN achievements. As a columnist in *The Hindu* points out:

> "The series of population and women's conferences has awakened the world to the dangers of overpopulation and the way the nations of the world could benefit themselves by using the full potential of women. The problem of environment and ecological balance for attaining sustainable development have global implications and the UN has successfully evolved a programme of action.
>
> "In the area of disarmament, the UN may have failed to promote global disarmament despite 40 years of debate but some silver lining is now emerging

in the area of nuclear disarmament. The world's nuclear powers are now agreed to a wrap up of a Comprehensive Test Ban Treaty and bring it before the US at its 51st session. The strong world opinion created by the UN on ending tests and further adding to the stock of fissile material is now paying dividends.

"France faces resistance to its nuclear weapon tests. It is determined to complete the series but has agreed to work for the test ban treaty. China, which conducted a test recently, has promised not to conduct any test after 1996. There is a strong world movement against nuclear testing or building nuclear arsenals. The end of the cold war has given added strength to the global anti-nuclear movement.

"The conclusion of a universal treaty to outlaw the production and use of chemical and biological weapons is another triumph for the United Nations. But the Gulf role of the UN, still being played by it, seems to be receding in the wake of the worst ethnic war in Bosnia-Herzegovina. The UN has deployed the largest peace-keeping force with about 29,000 multinational military personnel. But owing to a variety of reasons like the reluctance of the European powers as well as the United States from joining the fray or giving adequate backup support to the UN troops, the ethnic war has flourished giving the UN a bad name."[18]

The UN, as the guardian of human rights and defender of world peace, needs financial support, but Big Powers have reneged on paying up the peace-keeping bills and also meeting their assessments for the regular UN budget. A rift between the Republicans and President Clinton has been the root cause of this. The Congress, now dominated by Republicans, does not want any US role in Bosnia and they are holding the White House to ransom that either it backs out of its commitment to contribute troops to Bosnia or face non-cooperation from the Republican-controlled Congress. Indeed, the Republicans with leaders like Mr. Newt Gingrich deliberately diminish the dimensions of UN operations. The weaker the UN, the feebler the confidence of people in the sustainability of human rights.

Mr. Gingrich, the powerful Republican Party leader on Capitol Hill, recently downgraded the UN saying,—

"We have to recognise what won the cold war and what kept the peace was US willingness to lead. If my choice is three Secretaries-General or aircraft carrier, I can tell you which one I prefer to keep the peace in a dangerous world.

"There are other UN critics in the United Sates who ask what return does the US get for the payments both in assessed contribution and other forms of financial support extended to the UN by America."

The UN System is in crisis and inevitably a major victim will be fundamental freedoms so integral to human life in dignity, peace and security. Our dear planet has to have a unifying, humane order. Said Mahatma Gandhi: 'I would not want to live in a world that was not *one*

18 *The Hindu*, Magazine Section, dated 15th October 1995, page 7.

world'. 'The world needs a centre, and some confidence that the Centre is holding: the United Nations is the only credible candidate', (External Affairs Committee, House of Commons of Canada). The UN then is a *must* and it must be strong in the interests of every human member. Many a storm has been weathered in the past but our decade is the most dangerous, jeoparding the very survival of the world body and all that it stands for. And strangely, *now* is the UN most needed to secure peace and defend human rights. Why? The answer is the following:

> "There is unprecedented restiveness among the world's huge population. Traditional nation-state structures are weakening, and long-suppressed cultural and ethnic groups are resurgent. There are severe, potentially catastrophic economic inequities between the North and South, and growing income disparities and poverty throughout the world. The international community also faces massive ecological degradation as a result of industry and population increase. Despite the benefits of modern science and technology, mass famine and disease have increased. Wars about vital resources are all too easy to imagine.
>
> "Armed conflict is spreading across a planet strewn with readily usable weapons and stalked by eager arms merchants. In the last four years the UN has had to mount as many peace-keeping operations as in the whole of its previous history. By early 1993, the UN was deploying 4 times the number of troops, 70 times more police and over 100 times the number of civilian personnel as in 1987, at nearly 10 times the annual cost. As of 30th April 1994 the UN had contributions from 66 countries of 65,838 troops, 2,400 military observers, and 1,307 civilian and police personnel, with possible further deployments (and costs) evolving almost weekly relative to situations like those in Haiti, Rwanda, and former Yugoslavia. The projected costs of peace-keeping rose from some $ 600 million in 1991 to an estimated $ 2.3 billion for 1993.
>
> "The causes and the effects of these phenomena often spill across frontiers, and indeed regions, or draw outside forces into areas of crisis. The truism, 'interdependence', is by no means always as benign as use of the term sometimes implies. Moreover, actions and reactions in the North can have draconian consequences for the South."[19]

We need the UN for social and economic justice. Now that the Cold War is allegedly cold and dead, the present is the time for urgent strategies to meet the challenges of aggravated poverty. A global 'all-win' platform of action can be processed by the UN, given the backing to this near-bankrupt institutional glory. Absolute poverty, in its abysmal depths, is distressing. U. Thant, the then Secretary-General, said in 1963: 'The widening gap in economic progress....between the wealthy and the poor nations (is) ultimately more explosive than political or ideological differences'. Thirty-three years after, under the gargantuan Corporate grip of M.N.Cs and the 'iron hand in a

19 *Renewing the United Nations System* by Elskine Childers with Brian Urquhart 1994, page 12.

velvet glove' stranglehold of Fund-Bank operations, the Third World is reeling, staggering, collapsing, marginalising the UN and its noble and creative agencies.

> "Some 1.4 billion people now live in absolute poverty, 40 per cent more than fifteen years ago. Nearly 1 in every 4 human beings alive today is only existing on the margins of survival, too poor to obtain the food they need to work, or adequate shelter, or minimal health care, let alone education for their children.
>
> "Overall, for the poorest among humankind the past thirty years have been like trying to go up the down escalator. In 1960 the richest one-fifth of the world's population enjoyed 30 times the income of the poorest fifth; by 1989 the richest fifth was receiving 60 times the income of the poorest. Within a single country, this situation would be recognized as the classic condition for a massive and probably violent revolution. The disequilibrium in itself reflects a world without long-term strategic policies, a world in a 'no-win' condition".[20]

Food security is falling; economic recolonisation advancing, poverty deepening, human rights violations escalating because the UN itself is fatigued without finance, wilting without powers and ignored by crypto-imperialist Corporate Power abetted by Bretton Woods-bred organisations.

The Bretton Woods Conference held in the USA in 1944 led to the establishment of the International Monetary System, including the International Monetary Fund (IMF) and the International Bank for Reconstruction and Development (World Bank). This Bretton Woods family of financial institutions has become a Frankenstein's monster, in the sense that at the instance of the interests of the powerful M.N.Cs of the US, they serve to break up the integrity of the native economy, denigrate national institutions and close down projects with social justice goals, socialist policies and public sector enterprises, so that, by the euphemism of structural adjustment, the economies of developing nations suffer strangulation until they submit to the newspeak of *market-friendly* policies of *privatisation, liberalisation* and *globalisation* which are the prescriptions of the IMF for giving loans and other aids to countries in distress. Indeed, the United Nations is progressively being marginalised as a talking shop and the Security Council is becoming a handmaid of the United States, with the result that what suits the White House and the Congress later transforms itself into United Nations resolutions and sanctions. The consequence of some of these unfortunate developments is that the United States, with the Seal of the United Nations, interferes in conflicts among weaker nations or even engineers them and promotes what has been called Reganomics. The social, economic and cultural rights of people are in grave peril on this score.

The UN agencies have done a great deal to alert humanity about environmental ruination a la Rio Summit et al. What is the global reality?

20 *Ibid* at pages 13-14.

> "Science and technology have manufactured and let loose on the planet over 70,000 synthetic chemicals. Earth's remaining forest cover continues to decline from consumerism, urban-industrial encroachment and pollution, unsustainable development models in developing countries, and the demands of swelling populations for fuelwood.
>
> "Here again, in a tight vicious circle, external factors drive internal degradation, in turn affecting the international environment. Forest cover provides a vivid illustration of this process. Under pressure of debt repayments to Northern creditors, and protectionism that denies them other export earnings, developing countries respond to high consumer demand for tropical hardwood in the North (where 20 per cent of humankind consumes 85 per cent of all wood in the world). The felling of so many tropical trees is destroying entire segments of the planet's bio-genetic heritage, and very possibly contributing to global climate change as well.
>
> "The final agreements at the 1992 UN Conference on Environment and Development (UNCED) at Rio de Janeiro involved many disappointments and were only achieved under sustained pressure on Governments by non-governmental organizations. But the enormous work-plan of 'Agenda 21' does indicate the magnitude of inter-governmental cooperation needed to avert a catastrophic breakdown of the planet's eco-systems".[1]

What are human rights where human life has no environmental sustainability or ecological harmony?

Another insufficiently appreciated dimension of collective human rights through group identities and cultural community dignity has surfaced in recent times, necessitating the sympathetic attention of the UN. Lenin had realised at the time of 1917 October Revolution the justice of nationalities claiming their identity. The unity of the world is sound only if there be a pluralist perspective. And its suppression has led to explosions even in the Kremlin-controlled Soviet Union and Eastern Europe. The proof of it is the emergence of a large number of UN members from that region. Hitherto quiescent communities have begun to invoke self-determination. Even in the West, minorities legitimately aspire for larger self-determination. This highly sensitive phenomenon may be best handled by delicate United Nations' diplomacy.

Migrant communities and refugees are alarmingly increasing and who will take care of them except an agency under the UN?

> "In 1951 when UNHCR was established there were some 1.5 million legally classified Refugees world-wide; there are now nearly 20 million. Another estimated 24 million people are displaced within their own countries by ecological, economic and political causes. A significant proportion of these are on the edge of being pressed across one or more national frontiers.
>
> "One in about every 125 human beings alive is currently uprooted from homes, fields, or normal employment. In the world of the 1990s and beyond,

1 *Ibid* at page 15.

> these already unprecedented numbers can expand almost overnight in new political upheavals, as in the Gulf and Yugoslav crises".[2]

Humanity owes these desperate, deprived people compassionate sharing of its resources. UN presence and fair deal is a constructive contribution in this area of kindly internationalism. Thus it is evident that the UN system has to face complex issues and can administer specialised remedial measures. I wonder how the world community will manage its affairs without UN democracy in operation.

The North-South chasm is fraught with great disaster, with none to mediate potently. The UN which could have helped is being devitalised by the U.S. and its allies at a time when that world body could have been pressed into service. Such is the dialectic and dilemma of this international institution fifty years old.

The Charter of the UN promises to save succeeding generations from the scourge of war. But between 1945 and 1992, 149 major wars have taken place and 23 million humans have died. This figure, it is said, is twice the death toll in the entire 19th century. Quo vadis humankind?

We may, in parting, mention the die-hard gender imbalance which afflicts half of humanity despite the Charter's Preamble and Article 8. Likewise, another gross injustice is in the denial of the distributive equity of the world's resources. Decolonisation was completed decades ago, but a minority of nations has an unjustly a large slice of the cake.

How shall 'We, The Peoples of the United Nations' confront this crisis which is reaching its fatal crescendo? It has been rightly said that no institution will endure unless there is behind it considered and complete public support. This paramount requirement can be adequately met only if the organisation can accommodate and give standing to non-governmental bodies. The only scanty provision, as a liaison, is contained in Article 71 of the Charter which runs thus:

> "The Economic and Social Council may make suitable arrangements for consultation with non-governmental organizations which are concerned with matters within its competence. Such arrangements may be made with international organizations and, where appropriate, with national organisations after consultation with the Member of the United Nations concerned."

The importance of N.G.Os was realised at the various summit conferences organised by the UN. Within the ILO's fields of endeavour, trade unions constitute an element of citizen representation in its tripartite structure. UNESCO's National Commissions have engaged various professions and their NGO's. UNICEF's National Committees have built strong supportive bridges between citizens and the Fund's work. The bold initiative of FAO in creating within its secretariat a unit to promote the popular global Freedom From Hunger Campaign must also be noted.

2 *Ibid* at pages 20-21.

A number of Governments have long included national NGO representatives (and/or parliamentarians) in their delegations. Parliamentary committees are paying increasing attention to UN matters. In many countries, with varying degrees of dynamism, United Nations Associations have striven to maintain public interest and knowledge of the world organization, and they have their global World Federation (WFUNA), with a lively student and youth accompaniment (ISMUN).

It is noteworthy that the UN has accorded Consultative status to many peoples' organisations as sentinels on the *qui vive vis-a-vis* human rights, such as the Amnesty International (London) and the Brahma Kumaris Iswariya Vidyalaya (Mount Abu).

Luckily new N.G.Os with humanitarian concerns and expertise are springing up democratising and catalysing UN activities. A troubled and fractured planet has to be transformed into a New World Human Order. Way back in 1945 Earnest Bevin asked for a World Assembly elected directly from the people of the world as a whole, to whom the Governments who form the United Nations are responsible. The battle for human rights must be fought and won by the surrogates of humanity world-wide. Of course, the present UN built at San Francisco shall not be weakened and the world peoples assembly must be complementary, not competitive. Half a century's experience gives us wisdom to concretise this idea.

Human rights are the first human concern. All else must strengthen this imperative. To neglect the UN's activities is to invite pathological portance.

There have been proposals to make the UN a stronger instrument of human rights. In 1993 there was a demand for the establishment of a high level United Nations Commission, for human rights, an idea first advanced, by Uruguay in 1951, repeated in 1967 through ECOSOC. Now at the 1993 Vienna Conference, this demand gained greater consideration. Late in 1993 the General Assembly decided to create such a post, with useful human rights supervisory powers and coordinatory functions. An Ombudsman for the UN System has also been suggested in a recent study.[3] Indeed grave charges about the World Bank and the IMF infringing human rights in developing countries through motivated 'development' and monetary practices have been levelled. Likewise there have been criticisms about the UN peace enforcement processes with accusations of human right abuse, a recent example being the alleged misbehaviour by UNOSOM II forces in Mogadishu and Somalia. All these factors argue for the UN Ombudsman proposal.

Our focus is on human rights and the UN is the foremost instrument with over 70 instruments bearing on human rights having been passed. The wide spectrum of human interests covered by these documents must be supplemented by perennial vigilance.

3 *Renewing the United Nations System* by Erskine Childers-Development Dialogue 1994: 1

> "The human rights movement should itself give equal priority to economic, social and cultural rights together with civil and political rights. It should search for ways to play as prominent a role in the future in the monitoring and implementation of economic, social and cultural rights as it has in the past in the monitoring and implementation of civil and political rights."[4]

Our generation as heir to a great estate of human rights must 'wipe every tear from every eye' and raise every human to his/her full personhood. Nelson Mandela's words way back in 1992 is fitting finale to my thoughts on the UN and human rights:

> "Our common humanity transcends the oceans and all national boundaries. It binds us together in a common cause against tyranny, to act together in defence of our very humanity. Let it never be asked of any one of us—what did we do when we knew that another was oppressed?"

4 Ian Martin, Secretary-General, Amnesty International 1986-1992.

7

Human Rights Revisited and United Nations Incarnates

Mankind, with millions of years as homo sapiens, has a more glorious future awaiting him and the emergence of a new grade of supramental ascent. The human spirit will then be a complete supramental being in a supramental body, says Sri Aurobindo—and.......'earth shall be the spirit's manifest home'. It has to be a collective evolution of all humanity. This ecstatic prospect is in store for the human species as an exalted earthly estate provided the very right to be human is not forfeited or pre-empted by a barbaric process of zoological behaviour and pleasure-prone appetite.

This is not phantasy but a realisable Project Human Future. But all humanity must enjoy the right to be human in crimson spring and the title to human rights without invidious inegalite if the higher status outlined above is to be a success story. So we come back, thrilled by the magnificent estate welcoming the human future to consider the basic culture and materialist essentials which are the inalienable imperatives of a Just World Human Order.

Man is now gasping for breath, now gushing forward, now caught in a quagmire of lust for power and pleasure, now lost in a search for self-realisation and identity with the Absolute. Bitter hatreds and bloody feuds, punctuated by angelic visions and beautiful perceptions have been his legacy. Now, our race is ready to blossom as a lovely flower and musicalize as a heavenly symphony, enlarging the bounds of our soul's noble empire. But the other side of the picture is pathetic, poignant and pervasively privative, with withering values, *asuric* (demonic) appetites and violent vulgarities unlimited. Such is our precarious human universe and riddle of international security that, notwithstanding a wondrous *weltanschauung* and science of life, we are wobbling on the globe, with wisdom versus wickedness, zeno versus epicurus, that the very right to be human, with dignity and divinity, is a tantalising prognosis, alternating between our spiritual and material values.

Will Durant writes on the human quandary:

> "Our culture is superficial today, and our knowledge dangerous, because we are rich in mechanisms and poor in purposes. The balance of mind which once came of a warm religious faith is gone; science has taken from us the supernatural bases of our morality, and all the world seems consumed in a disorderly individualism that reflects the chaotic fragmentation of our character. We face again the problem that harassed Socrates: how shall we find a natural ethic to replace the supernatural sanctions that have ceased to influence the behaviour of men? Without philosophy, without the total vision which unifies purposes and establishes the hierarchy of desires, we fritter away our social heritage in cynical corruption on the one hand, and in revolutionary madness on the other; we abandon in a moment our pacific idealism and plunge into the cooperative suicide of war; we have a hundred thousand politicians, and not a single statesman. We move about the earth with unprecedented speed, but we do not know, and have not thought, where we are going, or whether we shall find any happiness there for our harassed souls. We are being destroyed by our knowledge, which has made us drunk with our power. And we shall not be saved without wisdom."[1]

Here comes the relevance of humanity's creativity in constructing a new world order where every human may fully flower and engineer the earth-bound populace towards the stars, standing on the footstool of this planet, with the power of Prometheus Unbound! In this process, the humblest and the highest, the infant and the aged, are participants. Our composite cultural heritage is at stake if the sum of human wretchedness and disablement of the masses were not abolished. Sans human rights for all, 'the world is a vale of tears' and fears. Ecology and environment integral to Nature, must be happy partners of progress, not victims of human profit gluttony.

Sometimes majestic visions, exciting as catalysts, may project the promise of universal happiness and a golden age. At other times, such glorious expectations suffer humiliation and shrink as illusion. So a *sine qua non* for sustaining the status of human rights perennially is the conscientisation of the people worldwide and their constant invigilation by accessible, effective instrumentalities. Such is the people-oriented *perestroika* we need. Everyone is crew in this humanist navigation. If we slumber when people's rights are crushed, totalitarian guillotine will wipe out the last of us and make mother earth a graveyard of human rights. Niemoller's famous lines about the Nazi regime come to mind when considering the imperative nature of ever vigilant protest every time anyone's human rights are breached or butchered.

"In Germany the Nazis came first for
the communists, and
I did not speak up because I was not
a communist.
Then they came for the Jews, and I

1 *The Pleasures of Philosophy* by Will Durant Invitation, pages XII and XIII.

did not speak because I was not a Jew.
Then they came for the trade unions,
and I did not speak up because I was
not a trade unionist.
Then they came for the Catholics,
and I was a Protestant and so I did
not speak-up.
Then they came for me, and by that
time there was no one left to speak for
any one."[2]

At this point, I deem it right to take a global survey of the march of mankind with its upswings and downfalls and evolutionary spirals towards discovery of the worth of the human person and his/her ascent to self-fulfillment in the noblest sense. Such a backdrop gives meaning to the achievement of human rights and obviates the possibility of slipping and falling again.

The story of the human race runs on as a ceaseless stream, now blocked by rocks, now like billows breaking on the beaches soon to be absorbed. Should 'such ebb and flow........ever be'? We look aghast at ourselves like men betrayed! These are the whirligigs of time. But life goes on–'the still sad music of humanity'! How was jettisoned the prospect of 'an ampler ether, a diviner air'? Alas, greed, tantrums and tensions have mounted. And in Wordsworth's words, "......much it grieved my heart to think what man has made of man". Suddenly, yet inevitably, judged by the laws of historical materialism, tense competitiveness hotted up and a military blow-up brought on the most dreaded chaos in the cosmos, as Churchill called World War I. Science had advanced and technology had translated it into violence and torture–into *thanatology*, the science of death! Humanity was *ex parte*! Wordsworth has versified the unveracity of the unsocial uses of science:

"To thee Science appears but, what in truth she is,
Not as our glory and our absolute boast,
But as a succedaneum, and a prop
To our infirmity."

Churchill himself has once orated:

> "The dark ages may return—the stone age may return on the gleaming wings of science; and what might now shower immeasurable material blessings upon mankind may even bring about its total destruction.
>
> Beware I say! Time may be short."

Terrible contradictions brought us back to the Iron Age! World War I dazed peoples everywhere, nearly brought about the downfall of the Western World and inflicted hardships on the rest. But the birth and death

2 Niemoller: *Victim of the Nazis.*

of a civilization may not condemn whole generations to irreversible despair or spell the end of all Creation. There is green hope of resurrection in history. For, a mere 15 years after Waterloo, did not France shake off its defeat and produce geniuses? Our heritage of savagery has been punctuated by spiritual and moral spells of ascent. The two great wars have taught us a lesson that even when the world is in a shambles the creative intelligence, phoenix-like, will rise from the ashes. The tragedy of war is later obliterated by the triumph of the human spirit; the happy bloom and song of human rights is sure to come out of the decay and dirge of the Old Order. We are, therefore, the builders, the gardeners and composers of an enduring cosmic order whose resplendent feature is value-based humanism and peace for succeeding generations.

> *"We are the music makers,*
> *We are the dreamers of dreams,*
> *Wandering by lone sea-breakers*
> *And sitting by desolate streams;*
> *World-losers and world-forsakers,*
> *On whom the pale moon gleams:*
> *We are the movers and shakers*
> *Of the world for ever, it seems."*
> *"For each age is a dream that is dying,*
> *Or one that is coming to birth."*[3]

May be, what we dream as the texture of the future is but Utopia. What if? "A map of the world that does not include Utopia", said Oscar Wilde, "is not worth even glancing at, for it leaves out the one country at which humanity is always landing. And when humanity lands there, it looks out, and seeing a better country, sets sail. Progress is the realisation of Utopia". A universe minus universal human rights is never an advanced habitat but 'a convocation of political worms'.

We cannot give up hope as if the world is drifting towards hell: We cannot go the Dante way:

> "This way for the sorrowful city. This way for eternal suffering. This way to join the lost people....Abandon all hope, you who enter! (hell)."

Could the world ever exclaim exultantly: Eurika *vis-a-vis* actualisation of human rights in its social, economic and cultural dimensions? The current conditions in India are best projected by a sensitive working class leader K. Ashok Rao (K.A.R.). What applies to India applies to the Third World and to the 'have-not' sector in the First World. Symbolic of the global gloom arising from the contradiction between the riches and the wretchedness we come by anywhere in the world. I quote from K.A.R.:

> *"I feel so sad.*
> *I feel so sad, seeing the beggars*

3 By O' Shaughnessy.

as I walk into the temple,
with my diamond earrings.
I feel so sad, seeing young men
hang out of buses
as I overtake them,
in my air-conditioned car.
I feel so sad, seeing the child
sweep the floor
as I talk to my son,
studying in Cambridge.
I feel so sad, seeing the dirty slums
as I stand on my balcony.
Sorry, I shall be late for cocktails
I can't miss the meeting of
the Committee for Social Justice,
Our American donors are coming.
You can choose to die of malnutrition, hunger
or toxic waste.......
AND A "HUMAN RIGHT" TO MAKE A
"DEMOCRATIC CHOICE".

The pathos of it is that out of this sadness springs a burning rage and out of this despair flames forth a hardened hope of higher values in a better world.

"Hope springs eternal in the human breast" —POPE.

Undying hope is the locomotive of human liberation. We must not anaesthetize our souls with despond but must fight and halt and fight again. As we struggle forward to humanity's tomorrows we must continue to battle and break through the Maginot Line built by the moneyocracy and mafiocracy now worldwide. But like this old French fortification, which failed to stop the attack and was bypassed by Hitler's hordes, human 'progress' will, also move on with a banner of human rights held by the 'haves' and the sword of justice so shaped as to decapitate the 'have-nots' with legal jargon. Undaunted, Project Human Rights must push on backed by global conscience. So it seems to me, now that the military might of a single Super-Power, or the profit-crazy corporatocracy which controls the Group of Seven, may win for the nonce, at the expense of the large human sector more than a billion strong, lost in privation and poverty. But not for ever, because Life must win. In the lush, lavish language of Will Durant:

"Light streams across the fields; buds open and stalks confidently lift their heads; the sap mounts in the trees. Here are children. Here are children: What is it that makes them so joyous, running madly over the dew-wet grass, laughing, calling, pursuing, eluding, panting for breath, inexhaustible? What energy, what spirit and happiness! What do they care about death? They will learn and grow and love and struggle and create, and lift life up one little notch, perhaps, before they die. And when they pass they will cheat death with children, with parental care that will make their offspring finer than themselves. There is the garden's twilight overs pass, thinking themselves unseen; their quiet words mingle with the murmur of insects calling to their mates; the ancient hunger speaks through eager and through lowered eyes, and a noble madness courses through clasped hands and touching lips. Life wins."[4]

What are the instrumentalities and operational possibilities to actualize the constellation of human rights in its universal amplitude? Will the United Nations help all the nations sing in chorus about each of them, and every member within each state, what Tennyson sang of his land:

"A land of settled government,
A land of just and old renown,
Where Freedom slowly broadens down
From precedent to precedent."

How happy, in futuristic terms, is humankind, blessed by Nature and spurred by science! And yet we have a long way to go to make this universal home a warm habitation of joy and happiness. I often remember, in this pensive mood, what I first saw in Jawaharlal Nehru's chamber, a quote from Robert Frost:

"The woods are lovely, dark, and deep,
But I have promises to keep,
And miles to go before I sleep,
And miles to go before I sleep".

Currently, alas, with all our boasts and all our hopes and all the noises of the United Nations, human rights, as a collective reality of life, are but a gleam, 'a beautiful and ineffectual angel, beating in the void his luminous wings in vain'! It shall not be 'all words, and no performance'. 'Suit the action to the word, the word to the action'. The real human rights order is hard stuff, beyond brittle, delusive diction. The task is tough. The UN instruments have given us a vision of a Just World Order and *modi operandi* to actualise it. The point is to harvest the crop.

What is the platform of action? Who will sentinel, monitor, implement and render accountable the great rights enshrined in the universal corpus juris?

A sublime beginning, when projecting the mansions of human rights, may appropriately be an exquisite quote, in grand prose, borrowed from Will Durant, about the rise and fall and renewal of civilizations. The great philosopher observes:

4 Will Durant: *The Pleasures of Philosophy,* page 408.

"History, on whose face mortality is writ; history, whose highest law seems to be the school-boy's rule that everything that goes up must come down: this obituary of men and nations, this funeral procession of races and states, is a picture revealed to us in merciless detail by the researches of the nineteenth century. Never before did men delve so thoroughly or so persistently into the past as during the last one hundred years—unearthing dead civilizations, exhuming forgotten geniuses, and playing Hamlet's "Alas, poor Yorick!" to a billion honourable skulls. The century of progress and historians left a taste of disillusionment and an odor of decay as a legacy to the century of airplanes, radios, and poison gas.

"What a panorama of fatality history unveils! Here is proud Egypt, building on shifting sands an empire more lasting than any later realm, raising temples more magnificent than those of Europe, ruling all Mediterranean peoples, lashing the backs of millions of slaves, and embalming its priests and princes in "houses of eternity". Poor phrase!—nothing remains of all that eternity but white hair growing on rotting bones; and even the pyramids convey a sense of death. The sands swirl up out of the desert around those play houses of superstition in stone; government gold must yearly be spent to cart it away. And as the tourist turns back, wiping away the hostile grains that have crept into the pores of his face, he wonders what would happen if government gold should cease to flow there for a century or two; he visions the sands covering stratum after stratum of those monuments, until the topmost stone of the tallest pyramid is hidden, and not one sign remains of the glory and the brutality that were Egypt."[5]

* * *

"Or pass to Greece, and climb the hill that leads to the Parthenon. Recall how for nine years Ictinus and Mnesicles guided the erection of that modest and perfect temple, so self-restrained in proportions and style, every line so subtly modulated into a curve that the stone takes on almost the warmth and pliancy of human flesh. Recall how for nine years Pheidias and his pupils carved hard marble into figures for the frieze-figures of men so fair that no one looking at them could help but grow a little in mind and character; figures of gods so majestic and serene that no one looking at them could believe in the old deities of rape and rapine any more. For many centuries that temple crowned the Acropolis, its colors brilliant in the sun; many generations were lifted up by the sight of it, feeling that here, if only for a moment, men had been like gods."[6]

Where is Parthenon now?

"The Parthenon is gone. Greece is gone. Rome came, and bestrode the earth like a colossus, so great that none thought it could ever be laid low; intangibles like the birth-rate and the exhaustion of the soil destroyed it; nothing remains of it but memories for dictators to imitate. Crete is gone, Judea, Phoenicia, Carthage, Assyria, Babylon, Persia—they are like gods that have lost their worshippers, temples visited by tourists, but never hearing prayer. Death is on them all.

5 Will Durant: *The Pleasures of Philosophy,* at pages 260-261.
6 *Ibid,* page 261.

> Europe came—Italy, Spain, France, England, Germany—and reared a civilization as mighty as any that history had known, making cathedrals to rival the Parthenon, making science greater than the Greeks', making music such an antiquity had never dreamed of, accumulating and transmitting knowledge and power beyond any remembered precedent. But Spengler rises, and announces to war-befouled Europe: "You are dead. I see in you all the typical stigmata of decay. Your institutions, your democracy, your corruption, your gigantic cities, your science, your art, your socialism, your atheism your philosophy, even your mathematics, are precisely those that characterized the dying stages of ancient states. Another century, and civilization will have found her seat far from you. This is your Alexandrian age."
>
> "America comes, and builds a civilization broader-based than any that the world has ever seen before, destined perhaps to reach greater heights than any that the world has ever reached before. But if there is any validity in history, if the past has any light to shed upon the future, then this civilization too, which we raise with such feverish toil and care, will pass away; and where we labor today, thousands of years hence savages will roam once more.
>
> "Such is the picture which the historian sees in the future as in the past. He concludes that there is only one thing certain in history, and that is decadence; just as there is only one thing certain in life, and that is death."[7]

Lucre-lustful commerce and accumulation of wealth are often a farewell to the finer human soul, precious personhood and the splendour of its sublime creations. Human rights end when coarse conscience and bestial propensities hold sway in the social order. Says Durant:

> "Industry gives wealth, gathers vast taxable populations into a little space, finances imperialistic aggression, and makes for political mastery; but does it make for civilization? Industry exalts quantity, and neglects quality, artistry, difference; once every industry was an art, now every art is an industry; once men employed in manufactures were handicraftsmen, artisans, now they are "hands". Will machinery mechanize man, and coarsen the soul beyond all possibility of spiritual delicacy and growth? Industrial England has never equalled the literature of Elizabeth's, or the pure science of Newton's days, or the painting of the bright dynasty that began with Reynolds and ended with Turner. Germany's great age came with Frederick, Kant, Goethe, and Beethoven; it ended with Bismarck and Von Moltke, blood and iron—and coal. France has had less industry than either England or Germany, and more civilization."[8]

Human heights have scope only in a just scheme of things, not, where 'wealth accumulates and men decay'.

Today, the era of super-power competition is no more; the Soviet Power is dead and the U.S. doth bestride the narrow world like a Colossus, and as hegemonist, has taken over as global gendarmerie. Market-mad Corporate Power is now the vampire *vis-a-vis* feebler peoples everywhere. The corrosive cold war is no longer there but hot wars in all the continents,

7 *Ibid*, page 262.
8 *Ibid*, page 264.

with ubiquitous pools of blood and homicide of human rights, distressingly persist. Functionally speaking, the UN and the Security Council behave at the behest of the U.S. In short, America Incorporated holds our human rights to ransom to sustain and inflate profits unlimited! Big Business is Government and human rights may keep on making noises in vain. How shall we hold in leash the blood hounds that harry the right to life of millions of humans. How then can universal human rights currency cease to be counterfeit and be legal tender? Our human rights fortunes depend on institutionalised outfits with impartial enforcement instrumentalities occupying the commanding heights of the United Nations. So the United Nations is our shield and sword when human rights are in jeopardy. It becomes necessary, therefore, to begin with the basic facts about the United Nations. How was it born? What aspirations did it seek to fulfill? What structures and powers does it enjoy? Who are the *de facto* operators of this world body and how can the UN jurisdiction be pressed into service to articulate and defend human rights? What has been its performance balance-sheet and how far has human rights audit been undertaken with success? What does the future hold for us in the actualisation of fundamental freedoms, the dignity and worth of the human person and respect for human rights and reverence for humanitarian justice? Half a century after the creation of the UN, "We the Peoples of the United Nations" wonder whether every individual or group has the right to identity and autonomy and a future in a cosmos were lucre power corners and consumers wealth and happiness, condemning the largest sector of humanity, sunk in poverty, to conditions of inhumanity, its resources robbed and its culture ruptured. For the few rich—the affluent micro-sector—it is the best of times; for the huge multitude—the indigent macro-sector—it is the worst of times. Human rights diction is balderdash for the have-nots but useful political ploy for the haves. To the indigent Third World and the destitute Fourth World, lying invisible in all the worlds, life's fitful fever is their portion.

The preservation of life, and liberty and the pursuit of happiness sounds hollow if pangs of poverty and privation are the lot of the many with none to redeem the tryst with human justice and humane law.

If the Universal Declaration of Human Rights is to ring true it must enliven the mass of men (who) lead lives of quiet desperation! (Walden Economy).

Let us look at the genesis, the anatomy and the operational methodology of the United Nations which has the primary potential to nest and nurture human rights in varying shades and formations. 50 years have passed since this noble living edifice breathed life and, contrary to the disappointments and disillusionments of nations and peoples, there is a note of hope in the words of Boutros Boutros-Ghali, the Secretary General. Problems proliferate and there is no other way save to seek the aid of the UN as the last bastion. Let me quote the Secretary General, as a preliminary to a portentous study of human rights in their field of action.

"Never before has the United Nations been so well poised to achieve the great objectives of its Charter—maintaining international peace and security, securing justice and human rights and promoting social progress and better standards of life in larger freedom. With the demise of the cold war, the world and the United Nations as an institution have been liberated from the shackles of a debilitating competition. In its place has come a climate of hopefulness, a sense among nations large and small that an opportunity has been regained. At long last, there is a possibility that decisive action can be taken to fulfil the purposes for which the United Nations was created—and which the peoples of the planet expect it to accomplish.

"But where one type of peril recedes, others rise swiftly to take its place; such is the nature of momentous change. Millions of people continue to suffer under conditions of war, tyranny, fanaticism and economic injustice. Ethnic, religious, social, cultural or linguistic conflicts jeopardize State cohesion. The proliferation of weapons of mass destruction threatens to increase, conventional arms are still amassed in many parts of the world. The Earth's fragile environment feels the assault of unsustainable practices. Underlying all this is the most fundamental task of our time: development, which is now commonly understood to include social, political, human and environmental dimensions. It is a comprehensive challenge of vast magnitude.

"The present opportunity must not be squandered. At the United Nations, Member States have pledged themselves to a new spirit of international cooperation. The organization itself is entering a new phase in its history and has never been so action-oriented, so actively engaged, and so widely expected to respond. Now more than ever, the Organization can make a crucial difference for the benefit of all humanity—if the Member States provide the requisite support and political will."[9]

A few observations on the United Nations *vis-a-vis* humanity's aspirations have been made by Sri K.R. Narayanan, the then Vice President of India (and now the President) at the United Nations symposium at the United Nations University at Tokyo on 4th December 1995, with different shades of emphasis and futuristic projections. I quote:

"If, as the poet says, "the past is a bucket of ashes" and "the future an ocean of nothingness", there is nothing that we can learn from the past nor anything that we can bequeath to the future. But, in reality we are all inheritors of the past. We have come 'trailing clouds of glory' from the past or with 'the tradition of dear generations weighing like a nightmare on our brains'. Many of the upheavals in history have been inspired by the memories of a glorious past or provoked by the conditions and the mind-set of the past persisting in the changed circumstances of a new epoch.

"Over the ages, human society has evolved from primitive tribes to nation-states, regional groupings and colossal blocs towards a global society and a one world order. During this long period great empires and world-conquerors have appeared trying, through force of arms, to impose their hegemony over

9 In the Foreword to the Book *Basic Facts About the United Nations*, page VII.

mankind. And great religions have arisen and spread like wildfire trying to create uniformity of faith among people. In spite of all these heroic attempts, the world has remained a multi-national and multi-religious place with immense social, cultural and political diversities. This gave birth to another concept of a world order that is pluralistic based on cooperation as embodied in the United Nations Organisation. If there is any lesson to be drawn from history it is that, in spite of the unifying and globalising tendency of technology and economics, the world is more likely to remain pluralistic, culturally, socially, ideologically and politically than monolithic. For, as the unifying and globalising trends become stronger, the forces making for the separate identities of individuals, communities and groups are also gathering strength. In this context any attempt at hegemony is bound to end up in tragic failure."[10]

After all the terrible mistakes of the past, the world today is hovering around friction and outbreaks of war. Asks Sri Narayanan:

"Do we understand that the quest for hegemony and domination is bound to lead to war? Do we recognise that the old balance of power games will promote conflicts among nations? Are the powers still tempted by the illusion of unipolar power in a pluralistic world?

"Mackinder, the geo-political theorist, held that 'the great wars in history....are the outcome, direct or indirect, of the unequal growth of nations."

"Today the world is strikingly unequal. The gulf between the developed and the developing nations has only widened in the post-War and the post-colonial period. The South has lost its bargaining power in relation to the developed North. Though it is recognised that economic growth in the South is essential to create new, vast markets for sustaining the marvellous productive capacity of the North, this region has not received the attention and cooperation it deserves from the advanced nations. If this vast region languishes as a pool of poverty, undevelopment and exploding population it might turn out for the developed nations what quicksands are to elephants. In fact poverty, illiteracy and ill-health have become the major causes of the population explosion and the environmental catastrophe facing the world today. Many years ago, Jawaharlal Nehru, the first Prime Minister of India, had drawn attention to this fact. He said:

'The existence of under-developed and poverty-stricken nations or peoples is in itself an abiding danger to the maintenance of peace. It has, thus, been increasingly recognised that the welfare and the peace of the world require the extermination of poverty, disease and ignorance from every country so as to build up a liberated humanity'.

Today mankind has the means of exterminating poverty; building up a liberated humanity and a one world. But prosperity and affluence are limited to a fortunate circle of countries and a few of them hold in their arsenals the power to destroy the world many times over."[11]

10 *Mainstream* dated 6th January 1996, page 7.

11 *Ibid*, at pages 7-8.

History has taught us, he says:

> "that freedom is the condition for the development of the individual and society and that democracy is the system that promotes such development and facilitates the differences and diversities of life to exist and flourish within a framework of order. The United Nations provides us such a framework. It is imperative that it is strengthened reflecting the aspirations of mankind as well as the realities of our time."[12]

Thus it is a categorical imperative, arising from the dialectics of contemporary forces, that the United Nations should be fortified and democratised to respond to the challenges of the times.

Human rights: a peep into the past

The edifice of the United Nations is founded on the need to preserve global peace and guarantee human rights worldwide. So it is worthwhile inquiring into the vintage ideas and ideologies and genetics of human rights, parenthetically and historically, but briefly, before examining the anatomy of the United Nations.

The conception of human rights is of central importance in the development of the modern world. Like all such ideas, it is very much theory-laden, implying a general view of man and society, of individuality, politics and the ends of Government. Like all such ideas, it is profoundly historical, expressing the aspirations and seeking to remedy the ills of particular places and times. It is thus an idea with a history, an idea that changes in both content and social function.

Human Rights in the modern sense and individualist ideology is largely of Western vintage, as we have already seen.

But tracing it to its roots the idea of human rights as an issue in religious, political and moral philosophies has an ancient illustrious pedigree. The English Bill of Rights, The American Declaration of Independence, and the French Declaration of the Rights of Man and Citizen, sprouted from the concept of the Universal Human Rights. It must be stated that, although not in explicit covenants, the traditional societies of Asia and other continents did reflect ideas of freedom and other rights as part of those civilisations. *Dharma* in its wider connotation and articulation enshrined human rights.

The Western quest for people's rights gave a sharper edge to what we now call human rights.

The eighteenth century, in Europe and America, drew to its close as the century that had clearly and unequivocally proclaimed the inalienable and imprescriptible rights of man. The proclamations were not, to begin with, the creatures of Gallic enthusiasm, of a revolutionary category of reason run riot in human rights. They were the product of sober English philosophies, English puritanism and non-conformism, 'respectable' English

12 *Ibid*, at page 8.

resistance to absolutism and concern for freedom and toleration. 'They drew, above all, on the philosophy of John Locke and the traditions of the Glorious Revolution of 1688, with its Act of Settlement and compromise, non-individual, Bill of Rights, but with its muted undertones of the great trial of Charles I in 1649. (*Vide* Eugene Kamenka's remarks in the book *Ideas and Ideologies Human Rights*, published by Edward Arnold (Publishers) Ltd. 1978.

This English King provoked a civil war, was tried at Westminster and was beheaded at White Hall. The King *as King* was tried and sentenced for treason by the sovereign people (an idea of dynamic portent). Its impact was felt 130 years later across the Atlantic in a Declaration of Rights of 12th June 1776. It begins as an assertion by the people of Virginia assembled in a free Convention:

I. "That all men are by nature equally free and independent, and have certain inherent rights, of which, when they enter into a state of society, they cannot by any compact deprive or divest their posterity; namely, the enjoyment of life and liberty, with the means of acquiring and possessing property, and pursuing and obtaining happiness and safety.

II. That all power is vested in, and consequently derived from, the people; that magistrates are their trustees and servants, and at all times amenable to them.

III. That Government is, or ought to be, instituted for the common benefit, protection, and security of the people, nation or community, of all the various modes and forms of Government, that is best which is capable of producing the greatest degree of happiness and safety, and is most effectually secured against the danger of maladministration; and that, when a Government shall be found inadequate or contrary to these purposes, a majority of the community hath an indubitable, unalienable, and indefeasible right to reform, alter or abolish it, in such manner as shall be judged most conducive to the public weal."

The next Declaration of the 13 United States of America (4th July 1776) re-affirmed human rights in classic diction. The French Declaration of 1789 by the National Assembly pronounced as sacred rights the sovereignty of the Nation and "the preservation of the natural and imprescriptible rights of man" together with other great rights which have been referred to earlier. In a fresh Declaration (24th June 1793) the great plurality of natural rights found expression. Such is the whole philosophy of liberal democracy which included a statement to the effect that "property is the right to enjoy and to dispose of one's goods, one's revenues, the fruits of one's labour and industry". The young Marx scathingly criticised this French concept as promoting "the guarantee of the economic rights of property, and the social inequality which they necessarily produced. Behind the republic of the market lay the despotism of the factory; behind political equality lay social inequality."[13]

13 *Ideas and Ideologies of Human Rights,* Edited by Eugene Kamenka, page 5.

The slogan, Liberty, Equality and Fraternity has political, social, economic and cultural emanations, thus imparting a shift to the doctrine of human rights which in its concrete spectrum projects social rights too. The new development is discernible in the later battles with new implications. Eugene Kamenka puts it thus:

> "The demand for rights in the seventeenth and eighteenth centuries was a demand *against* the existing state and authorities, against despotism, arbitrariness and the political disfranchisement of those who held different opinions. The demand for rights in the nineteenth and twentieth centuries becomes increasingly a *claim upon* the state, a demand that it provide and guarantee the means for achieving the individual's happiness and well-being, his welfare. These two different conceptions of rights, as we shall see, like the opposed conceptions of 'freedom from' and 'freedom to', stand in constant danger of fundamental conflict with each other—a conflict that dominates our contemporary world."[14]

During the nineteenth century only States figured in the International laws relating to people's rights. Even the Covenant of the League of Nations addressed itself to the issue of settlement of disputes among States and the protection of minorities, but a new approach emerged in the Atlantic Charter of 1941, the Declaration of the United Nations the next year and in the political speeches of war time leaders on the side of the Allies. This positive approach was manifest in the United Nations Charter and more specifically in the Universal Declaration of Human Rights, approved without a dissenting voice in December 1948. Dr. H.V. Evatt of Australia, the then President of the General Assembly voiced the view that this was the first occasion when the world community as such had recognised the existence of human rights and fundamental freedoms transcending the laws of Sovereign States, the millions of men, women and children all over the world many miles from Paris and New York will turn for help, guidance and inspiration to this document.

Going deeper into human rights in its hoary ancestry, we have seen how the Hindu, Buddhist, Christian and Islamic faiths have laid stress on aspects of divinity as constitutive of human dignity and equality. A UNESCO symposium holds that the idea is found "in all the great moral documents of mankind, and in all its aspirations since primitive times".

> "The story of the growing belief in natural or human rights as the eighteenth century saw them is the story of the rise of individualism in the theory and practice of society. Marxists link this with the growth of commodity-production, the development of cities and the merchant-burgher and the increasing importance of the bourgeoisie."[15]

Marxian materialism, with its scientific flavour and economic colour, did not occupy the entire human rights space or supply the total fuel in the struggle for human dignity and other integral values which make man and

14 *Ibid*, at page 5.
15 *Ibid*, page 6.

woman truly human. Religions, with their deep hold on the soul, stirred up demands as the forerunners of human rights in their anti-regal, pro-egalitarian and basic needs for survival. So it is that revolutions and human rights imperatives were fertilised by faiths and conscience.

Human rights ideology puts man at the centre of moral and legal life. The Man who hung on the Cross freed the individual from the societal system with its moral superstitions and hierarchical authoritarianism. A higher moral order is fundamental to Christian-Western evolution of humanism.

> "'Jurisprudence', says Title I of Book I of the Institutes of Justinian, 'is the knowledge of things divine and human, the science of the just and the unjust'."[16]

The divine element in the genome of human rights brought in religion to play a role in the development of humanist principles and natural law. In India it was *Dharma,* in Arabia it was *Islam* and in the Roman Empire, it was *Christianity.* The feudal forces also openly entered the arena when their interests were in peril.

Thus the Church fought the King; the barons challenged the absolutism of the throne; the struggle within the Church turned against Papal infallibility.

> "Nevertheless, the seventeenth-century Englishmen who proclaimed their rights against kings and established church, and the social contract theorists, from Hobbes to Locke and Rousseau, were doing something startlingly new, at least at the level of respectable rather than underground ideology. They were claiming 'liberty' and not 'liberties', and beginning to assert general and not specific rights. They were radically reinterpreting and recasting the language of politics and of social and religious theory. They were proclaiming that the constitution of society was not divinely ordained, that society was not a system of separate historic estates, each with their specific and limited interests, and that the affair of state, the *chose publique,* was not the special and particular prerogative of the king and his governors. They were converting men from subjects into citizens. The point of the social contract was to establish this new conception of public power and of the relationship between the individual and society. The individual suddenly, and on a general scale for the first time, became the point of it all, standing as citizen in direct and not indirect relationship to public affairs and Government, insisting that it existed for *his* advantage and that alone. The theory of the social contract could argue, as Hobbes did, that, once men had surrendered their powers, for their own security, to a sovereign, they had virtually no rights left but a very attenuated right to rebel if their continued existence was threatened. Even so, the theory established the principle that the basis and end of Government was the security, the happiness, the rights of the individual. It is with that recasting of political language and ultimately of political reality that the modern individualist, democratic age begins. And while the roots of this development were nourished especially strongly by religious conceptions and religious conflicts

16 *Ibid,* page 7.

and martyrdoms, the eighteenth century with its doctrine of the rights of man represents both a new and more thorough-going aspiration toward democracy and individualism and a new moral self-confidence in Western European man—new because it is based, for the first time, on something like philosophical argument rather than religious convictions. It is thus bolder, more universal and more directly and frankly forward-looking, and linked m ore closely and comfortably with the new enlightenment, with the belief that man's moral powers will be further heightened by the development of education and science, freeing him from bondage and superstition."[17]

The European man of the 18th and 19th centuries found in the human rights doctrine a support for his aspirations, for his democratic stirrings. But there were critics also who felt the French Revolution's slogans to be mere 'metaphysic rights' (Burke) or perpetual vein of nonsense, flowing a perpetual abuse of words (Bentham). His essay Anarchical Fallacies condemned even natural rights:

> "Natural rights is simple nonsense: natural and imprescriptible rights, rhetorical nonsense—nonsense upon stilts."

Vague *moral* rights were not *positive* rights, not found in codes or customs or decisions.

The criticism of 'natural and imprescriptible rights' went further. Eugene Kamenka writes:

> "To preach morality is easy, to give ethics a foundation is difficult. In traditional moral philosophy, as in popular moralism and moral parlance today, the subject-matter of ethics and the nature of moral demands or prescriptions were confused and obscured in the illogical concept of a normative science or set of normative truths, in the attempt to give ethical judgments and moral demands the objectivity of scientific descriptions as well as the imperative, exhortative force sought by proposals, prohibitions, recommendations and commands. Moral philosophy, in short, paralleled the fraudulence of everyday moral language and commands; it presented as impartial what was partial, as desirable what was merely desired. This appeared most patently in those moral philosophers, and those glib speakers of the English language or other languages, who treated the word 'good' as meaning 'that whose nature requires that it be commended and pursued'."[18]

Western materialism dismissed as hocus-pocus the hallowed notions of human rights while the Indian concept of *dharma,* by contrast, was a dynamic synthesis of the secular and the spiritual, of the material, moral and profounder commands springing from the aspirations of a society in search of order and peace and the individual member's inviolable right to recognition as a person with a soul, a spark of the Absolute. Ralph Walds Emerson (*Brahman*) and Walt Whitman (*Leaves of Grass*) echo in Western tongue this higher field of thought. But the West, with its more popular temporality

17 *Ibid,* pages 8-9.
18 *Ibid,* page 10.

rebuffed the misty mystiques of moral, spiritual intangibles and the Indian fundamentals of Reality. This distance between East and West is best expressed by Kamenka from whose book I have quoted profusely. Read on:

> "The doctrine of natural or human rights, then, is not an empirical description of the consequences implied by an actually existing law of nature, essential or common humanity or historical social contract. The attempt, at various stages in the history of the doctrine, to appeal to these was scientifically fraudulent and remains so. The doctrine of human rights is a *proposal* concerning the morally appropriate why of treating men and organizing society. Like all such proposals that gain force and command respect, it is a complex proposal, attempting to present a systematic view of man and society, taking up associated empirical material, relating and ordering moral preferences. It is to be judged by its internal coherence and logical consistency, by the truth of its associated empirical claims and its relation to relevant empirical material that it may or may not take up and, in the last resort, by its relation and that of its consequences and implications to our own moral beliefs."[19]

Karl Marx too differed from the 'natural rights' dogma of the French revolutionists because it left open the potential for exploitation. The French masses in 1789 fought for human emancipation, not merely by an exercise in pious theory but by pursuing a programme of action. Marx thought this approach to be flawed. K.R. Minogue puts it this way:

> "The French revolutionaries conceived the defect of the *ancien regime* as lying in the invasion, by the arbitrary practices of the Bourbon absolute monarchy, of the space in which a man might live his own life. Declarations of rights, therefore, were prohibitions of such invasion. Each man, in exercising his natural rights, could enjoy his own household free from the threat of arbitrary arrest; he could practice his own religion (or none); he could buy and sell property without interference from grasping and despotic state. Marx believed this account of the evils of feudalism to be fundamentally erroneous. The right of property, the liberty to buy and sell freely, he argued, actually involved a situation in which some men (whom he called the bourgeoisie) would enslave the persons and expropriate the work of large numbers of others (whom he called the proletariat). One kind of undesirable invasion was thus being cured only by facilitating a different and in some ways even more intolerable invasion of human autonomy. The question of human emancipation needed to be understood in terms quite other than the individualist idea of natural rights."[20]

Marx and other ideologists were hostile to the whole idea of natural rights. But Thomas Paine and others of his ilk held the view that 'to every Individual in nature, is given an individual property by nature, not to be invaded or usurped by any'. (Overton: *An Arrow Against All Tyrants*). 'Natural rights are those which appertain to man in right of his existence'.[1]

19 *Ibid*, page 12.

20 *Ibid*, pages 13-14.

1 Thomas Paine: *The Rights of Man*.

Rank materialists who dub the moral order and natural law as moony, or even loony, are somewhat superficial when viewed from the *dharma* angle of India or the *dhamma* idea of the Buddha or Confucianism of China or the Sermon on the Mount of Christ (which I may christen as Jesus Jurisprudence). The roots of divinity and the shoots of morality are not sheer rubbish, not moral arrogance nor religionist opium but the human spirit resisting suppressive regimes. H.L.A. Hart, a great jurist conceives of rights where no corresponding duty is cast:

> "Two people walking along both see a ten dollar bill in the road twenty yards away, and there is no clue as to the owner. Neither of the two are (sic) under a 'duty' to allow the other to pick it up; each has in this sense a right to pick it up. Of course there may be many things which each has a "duty" not to do in the course of the race to the spot—neither may kill or wound the other—and corresponding to these 'duties' there are rights to forbearances. The moral propriety of all economic competition implies this minimum sense of 'a right' in which to say that "X has a right to" means merely that X is under no duty not to.' Hart points out that jurists have isolated rights in this sense and have called them 'liberties'.[2]

Rights can be natural. 'My right to life is not a right against anyone'. All the same, it is a foremost human right to deny which is barbaric. There is divine space in the jurisprudence of human rights even if hedonists may accept only the sanction of pleasure and pain. The human spirit has an inalienable autonomy and indestructible, imprescriptible survival value. Karl Marx fought and wrote impelled by this diamond-hard divine discontent driving him to liberate victimised humanity.

The dissection of the anatomy of the idea of human rights need not detain us although the debate is delectable. No one can deny, whatever his human rights predeliction, that 'each person hath a property in his own person' (Locke) and this funds the profound notion of the worth of the human person (vide, the *U.N. Charter*).

Today, the indubitable status of human rights, acknowledged by all the nations of the earth, makes any further essay into its origins rather redundant. Let me pause at this point by a reference to book prepared for World Law Day, International Legal Protections for Human Rights which opens with these words:

> "The idea of the inalienable rights of the human being was often articulated by poets, philosophers, and politicians in antiquity." This grandiose—and vague—statement is followed by a single specific example, which reads:
>
> When Antigone, in Sophocles' play, written 422 B.C., says to King Creon, "all your strength is weakness itself against the immortal, unrecorded laws of God," she invokes the higher law, the natural rights of man."[3]

2 *Ideas and Ideologies of Human Rights*, Edited by Eugene Kamenka, page 18.
3 Essay by Elaine Pagels: *Human Dignity*, page 1.

The divine origin of human rights is historically and geographically widespread. Marxists claim that the social order reflects inviolable natural laws, analogous to the laws of biology and physics. Social entropy shows up in disorder and so, friction and clashes rising from injustice and frustration will aggravate tension and foil human rights. Real value of peace and human dignity resides in the social order (in the place of the divine order):

> "Where, then, do we get the idea on which contemporary human rights theory rests: that ultimate value resides in the individual, independent from and even prior to participation in any social or political collective? The earliest suggestion of this idea occurs in the Hebrew account which describes Adam, whose name means "humanity", as being created in the "image of God". Written in the seventh century B.C. (and probably told centuries earlier), this account implies the essential equality of all human beings, and supports the idea of rights that all enjoy by virtue of their common humanity."[4]

We may conclude that, as a distant offspring of the divinity in each person, emerged the thought of impregnable individual fundamental freedoms:

> "The idea of a natural law that ensures human rights seems to be a much more recent development, emerging in Europe during the Enlightenment. Borrowing the idea of natural law from Greek philosophical tradition, certain political thinkers used it to counter claims of divine right. Not until the 17th and 18th centuries is expression given to the notion that every human being has rights that are to be recognized—not conferred—by society. In the civil war in England, in the tradition that formed the United States Constitution and in the revolution in France, fought in the name of "liberty, equality and fraternity", we find a new theory of "inalienable" human rights as the constitutive principle of political order. Following this declaration of human rights, a new statement of the purpose of Government appears: "to ensure these rights, Governments are instituted among men."[5]

Speaking realistically:

> "Like the ideas of parliamentary democracy or Marxist political theory, like the ideas of science and technology, or of racial equality, the idea of human rights is gaining momentum and is increasingly becoming a matter of political priorities throughout the world. One essential element of a human rights policy will involve constructing its philosophical and religious basis in terms that will speak to people of various cultures."[6]

What is important to note is that, divorced from religious origin and ideological antagonisms, the very concept of liberty has acquired a semantic duality embracing, on the one hand civil and political rights and, on the other, issues of economic, social and cultural rights. Thus we find the US and the USSR becoming party to the two International Covenants. Professor

4 *Ibid*, at page 4.
5 *Ibid*, at page 6.
6 *Ibid*, at page 8.

Lauterpacht has also dwelt on the two concepts of liberty. The ancient world and the ancient religions had posited that individual humans had rights in their own right. Herodotus, Pericles and other Greek scholars have spoken on human rights. It is well known that in the late Renaissance, in the religious struggles of the previous centuries we find from Gerson to Grotius, the right we call 'human rights' became manifest. The American and the French Declarations bear testimony to the ancient origin of basic human rights. True, Karl Marx disagreed with the notion of natural rights but insisted that such rights were meaningless, unless one has an economic and cultural foundation adequate to take advantage of them. Indeed, the present state of impotence of human rights in its implementation lends strength to this criticism. The pragmatic conclusion is that effectiveness in enforcement is the essence of human rights. Remedial jurisprudence is as important as rights jurisprudence and is the cutting edge of law. From this angle, not the Magna Carta, but the Habeas Corpus Act fleshes out the right by creating a legal claim to present to a court for vindication if there is violation of a person's liberty.

Having already dealt with Euro-American developments right down to World War I, we may continue with the League of Nations and after, in tracing the saga of human rights.

The League of Nation: a transitional phase

The League of Nations, the Constitution of which was drafted at the Paris Peace Conference in 1919, aimed at the creation of an International Judicial Body which, unfortunately, proved to be ineffectual like the League itself. Indeed, it was so fruitless that nothing could be done to stop the later German aggression which burst on Europe as World War II. There were great hopes at Paris where a meeting of 32 Allied and Associated Powers met to draw up a Peace Settlement. The Treaty of Versailles imposed on Germany reparation payments and deprived that proud nation of all its Colonies. The humiliation was avenged by the emergence of Hitler and the new culture of savagery under the Nazi regime virtually annihilated all human rights. We are not interested in the advance and retreat of armies during World War I, but must accept the dialectics of the International Forces clashing with each other and eventuating in World War II. The student of human rights must focus on the Nuremberg trials which were held by the Allies at Nuremberg to try Nazi war criminals by an International Military Tribunal (November 1945 until October 1946). The significance of this event is the concentrated attention of the Allies on the prosecution of war criminals. Indeed, the issue of individual responsibility for war crimes, and the most aggravated culpability by macro-scale inhumanity, had claimed universal publicity since the Allied Powers, even in 1942, had announced that war criminals (of the Axis Powers) would be made to answer for their vilest violations, vicarious as well as direct. The basis for the prosecution lay in the London Agreement of August 1945 for the prosecution and punishment of the major war criminals. It was made clear in the London Charter that the official position of the offender would "not be considered as freeing them from responsibility or mitigating punishment." War Crimes are the most savage tearing up of human rights. In 1946, the General Assembly of the United Nations in Resolution 95(I) reaffirmed these principles as reformulated by the International Military Tribunal in its judgment (and therefore usually referred to since as the "Nuremberg Principles") as generally valid principles of international law.

The United Nations Commission for the investigation of war crimes worked on the task of formulation of the principles of International Law relevant to war crimes. Those principles were set down at the Second Session of the Commission in June-July 1950 as a set of Seven Principles of International Law recognized in the Charter and in the judgment of the Nuremberg Tribunal. These are:

> "(1) Any person who commits an act which constitutes a crime under International Law is responsible therefor and liable to punishment.
>
> (2) The fact that *internal* law does not impose a penalty for an act which constitutes a crime under International Law does not relieve the person who committed the act from responsibility under International Law.
>
> (3) The fact that a person who committed an act which constitutes a crime under International Law acted as Head of State or responsible Government official does not relieve him from responsibility under International Law.
>
> (4) The fact that a person acted pursuant to order of his Government or of a superior does not relieve him from responsibility under International Law, provided a moral choice was in fact possible to him.
>
> (5) Any person charged with a crime under International Law has the right to a fair trial on the facts and law.
>
> (6) The crimes hereinafter set out are punishable as crimes under International Law: (*a*) Crimes against peace: (*b*) War crimes; and (*c*) Crimes against humanity.
>
> (7) Complicity in the commission of a crime against peace, a war crime, or a crime against humanity as set forth in Principle (6) is crime under International Law.
>
> The Assembly at its 1950 session sent the Commission's formulation to member-Governments for their comment. The Assembly requested the Commission in preparing a draft code of offences against the peace and security of mankind, to take account of observations on the Nuremberg Principles made during the session or subsequently received from Governments."

The Nuremberg Principles are now part of Human Rights Jurisprudence. The Nuremberg Tribunal's Charter and Judgment were adopted unanimously by the United Nations General Assembly on 11th December 1946. Article 49 of the Geneva Convention has been considered to be a nucleus of the customary law of nations from time immemorial. It may be rightly said that the recognition of human rights as immemorial is first found, as the basis of modern international legal culture, in the Nuremberg jurisprudence.

The source of International Human Rights as well as other universally applicable human rights is the same, namely the acceptance of the worth and dignity of the human person and the right to life in its profounder dimensions that belongs to everyone. The Apostles of non-violence like the Buddha, Jesus or Gandhi find the right to life threatened where the integrity of the individual is violated, be it during armed conflicts between States or in violent breaches within the State. As for the divergent developments in the field of International Law of armed conflicts, we may deal with them, not as a separate genus but as another branch of Human Rights law with special features.

We may have to deal later with the linkage between the international law of armed conflicts and international human rights law. However, "both human rights law and the international law of armed conflicts have grown out of ideas which predated the development of the sovereign State but the form and practical application of each body of law has been transformed by that development."[7]

In principle, humanitarian jurisprudence embraces both these branches which find their source and strength in humanism. In fact, 1968 (Human Rights Year) marked the beginning of a broader blending of the law of armed conflict and human rights.

> "From 22nd April to 13th May of that year an International Conference on Human Rights met in Teheran under its auspices. The Conference adopted a long series of resolutions on many diverse aspects of the international protection of human rights. Among these was Resolution XXIII, adopted without much debate on the one but last day of the Conference, and by which it requested the General Assembly to invite the Secretary-General to study steps "to secure the better application of existing humanitarian international conventions and rules in all armed conflicts". The Resolution also requested an enquiry into the "need for additional humanitarian international conventions or for possible revision of existing Conventions to ensure the better protection of civilians, prisoners of war and combatants in all armed conflicts and the prohibition and limitation of the use of certain methods and means of warfare."

The General Assembly endorsed this initiative and on 19th December 1968, by Resolution 2444 (XXIII), invited the Secretary-General, in consultation with the ICRC, to undertake the studies requested in the Teheran Resolution. The Resolution was entitled "Respect for Human Rights in Armed Conflicts", and many of the activities of the United Nations relating to the law of armed conflict have since been placed under that banner. With this title the United Nations may be said not only to have indicated the historical origin of its sudden active interest in the law of armed conflict, but to have provided a justification for its radical change of course: under the Charter, the international promotion and protection of human rights are among the main functions of the United Nations."[8]

7 *Essays on International Human Rights*, page 3.
8 Frits Kalshoven: *Constraints on the Waging of War* published by International Committee of the Red Cross, pages 19-20.

Indeed, the General Assembly Resolution 2444–(XXIII), brought the International Committee of Red Cross (ICRC) into a closer nexus with human rights law. From the days of Ashoka and the Dharmasasthras of yore, this overlap of compassionate principles during times of war and special protection of civilian populations has become an active feature of International Law. Thus the 'Law of The Hague', which is a spectrum of laws governing humanist principles during armed conflicts, may well be regarded as integral to human rights jurisprudence since they constitute the foundation of respect for the human person in cases of armed conflicts, internecine or international, as they offer a basic protection to the human person.

Human Rights law and Humanitarian law blend as humanist jurisprudence and derive strength from the same cultural-spiritual source. This sublime jurisprudence has a common moral content and soulful vitality. From generation to generation human rights have survived with cultural variations, peripheral, not fundamental. In short, the human person, as a centre of concern, possesses rights and immunities, because of the very fact that it is a person, a divinised whole, a master of itself which consequently is not a commodity, but a sacred entity, not merely a means to the end, but a noble end itself which must be treated as such. Beyond rhetoric and sentimentalism, human rights law has attained a jural locomotion, an ideology and a full-fledged expression.

History has its own power and the dialectic of peace versus war, Fascism, Nazism and other totalitarian cults opposed by the hunger for security and development has compelled mankind into "the enthronement of human rights", to borrow Winston Churchill's phrase. The International Law of Human Rights is no longer the vanishing point of jurisprudence. One may conclude this human rights discussion–its what and why–by Rabindranath Tagore's message to the London Conference on Civil Liberty in India (approvingly referred to by Mahatma Gandhi).

> "Liberty is a privilege which the individual has to defend daily for himself; for even the most democratic Government tends to be oppressive if its tyranny is tempted by the indifference or cowardice of its subjects. Hence the need for a Civil Liberties Union in any system of Government, and hence the need for such unions to realize that they cannot safeguard liberty for the individual if they do not teach him to defend it for himself by his continual readiness to pay for it by sacrifice. The problem is one not of external organization so much as of inducing the appropriate moral qualities in the individual, of creating in him an awareness of his innate worth as an individual. Otherwise, if the individual is made to care for liberty as a means of attaining mere material satisfaction, then the State will easily tempt him to part with it by holding out to him the bait of better satisfactions; which is what is actually happening in party dictatorships—Red, Black or Brown.
>
> "The English people too, though they are traditionally supposed to cherish liberty for its own sake, have allowed other peoples to be robbed of it without any scruple whatsoever, simply because their greed for material satisfactions

> has been effectively appeased thereby. Perhaps, my English friends will not agree with me there, but when the rivalry for colonial exploitation would become still more acute, the British citizens will find it necessary to arm their Government at home with extraordinary powers to defend their possessions abroad. Then they will suddenly wake up to find that, without meaning it, they have forfeited their own liberty and drifted into a Fascist grip, and maybe, then they will realize that liberty has a true foundation only in the moral-worth of the individuals who compose the State."[9]

The right to be human is under threat from many quarters during our decade, what with nuclear menaces, chemical poisons and psychic cauterisation. So the question again arises; what are Human Rights?:

> "Philosophers have tried to define them. Men and women have sacrificed their lives for them. Wars have been fought over them. Leaders and constitutions have promised them to people. Today they have emerged as an issue that can serve to bring the world together—or tear it apart".

We are at the human rights crossroads of history.

9 *Human Rights Reader,* edited by Walter Laqueur & Barry Rubin at page 124.

8

Columbus, Gama and Colonial Domination of Common People's Rights

Global cultural degenerations and social cataclysms have sometimes emanated from unsuspected small beginnings. Columbus, Gama, Cook, Clive and a number of other adventurist navigators, traders and military administrators have, by their voyages and invasions and conquering consolidations, totally changed the direction and dimension of human history. A dialectical analysis of such changes, with the fate of human rights in the background, is a worthwhile pursuit.

Around five centuries ago humanity bore witness to some European navigators crossing the oceans and landing in other continents. The portent of this 'white' event, as history harrowingly unfolded, was the beginning of the world phenomenon and colonialism and annihilation of millions of humans and their human rights. Anyone concerned with universal human values should not miss this blood-stained chapter if he is to grasp the current dialectics of world forces and the dynamics of a new just international human order struggling to be born.

Spain and the Inquisition, Pope Gregory IX and religious oppression were the medieval seeds of the notorious torture by the Christian Church on alleged heretics (institutionalised savagely by the medieval papacy, although the irony of it is that Christianity owed its birth to Jesus, the Prince of Peace and Compassion who struggled against holy hierarchy and Roman imperialism). The anti-semitic persecution by Spanish Christians and the forced conversion of Muslims to Christianity are the early precursors of the mass slaughter of Jews during our ghastly, gory war-wounded century! The 'culture of death', inequity and corruption prevailed in Christendom in the 15th century. 'Death was so daily, brutality so commonplace, destruction of the animate and inanimate so customary' says historian Huizinga. Millions of humans suffered the stakes and other forms of torture in that European era of intolerant violence. Kirpatrick Sale writes: 'To them, deadly violence was nothing less than the daily stuff of politics'. Machiavelli, at about that period, almost justified this barbarity-brewed legality: 'A prince cannot do all the things for which men are esteemed good, for, in order to maintain the State, he is often obliged to act contrary to humanity, contrary to charity, contrary to religion'. Virtually, this is an ideological validation of State violation of human rights, an embryonic stage of the cannibalistic ethos which later horrified the world around five hundred years later.

The cultural picture of those times can be understood better if we read the European 15th century technology, the use of armaments and firing mechanisms and the fire power of gun powder enabling a small army to wipe out large human numbers. This heartless gun powder facility is the forerunner of modern Western mechanised warfare. A mental, moral pachydermy was needed for human beasts to indulge in senseless killing and crass cruelty. This was provided by the growth of gross materialism and callous capitalism, worship of money, seizure of power and morbid capability for perpetrating inhumanity. Frederick Turner has described this degeneracy poignantly as a method by which "a world millions of years in the making vanished into the voracious insatiable maw of an alien civilisation". Nazi savagery, Hiroshima bomb, chemical warfare and other wicked inflictions of horror and terror our century has beheld and beholds have had their genetic code prepared 500 years ago in Europe which sent Christopher Columbus, Vasco da Gama, Robert Clive and Warren Hastings and company in the name of God, gold and capture of empire. Thus the age of conquest, denying to native populations the basic right to be human, was inaugurated by these voyagers in search of trade and colonies. No civilisation has controlled the world so harshly as the West of the 15th century and after slavery on a mass scale, humiliation of Himalayan hugeness and plunder of the wealth with no qualms of justice became a ruthless reality. Military fortresses and gun powder power made the rule of law the rule of life wherever Colon and those of his ilk reached or landed. America's natives were exterminated to make the territory a British Colony. (American Indians, the original inhabitants of the American continent who arrived in waves and settled there tens of thousands of years ago, were driven back and when the 'whites' gained access, were destroyed or retreated into humble settlements, with their lands and lives lost and human rights gunned down. Rudyard Kipling hortatively poetised on this worldwide European terrorism thus:

> *"Take up the White Man's burden;*
> *Send forth the best ye breed,*
> *Go, bind your sons to exile,*
> *To serve your captives' need."*

The Indian Empire was founded through trade and trickery; and the White world became dominant over the globe committing outrages, slaughtering people and establishing a 'Barabbasque' order or robber regime, crucifying Christ and treating with contempt the Sermon on the Mount. The Prince of Peace had no place in the Empire which, for form, wore the Cross. Sale tells us about those days thus:

> "...... It is important to realise that there is not a single European nation which, when the opportunity came, did not engage in practices as vicious and cruel as those of Spain — and in the case of England, worse — with very much the same sort of demographic consequences."

England expanded and the Royal Navy was the symbol of global power. Sir Walter Raleigh was to declare:

> "Whosoever commands the sea commands the trade, whosoever commands the trade of the world commands the riches of the world, consequently the world itself."

'Rule, Britannia, rule the waves' became the conquering hunger of the British Empire. Decimation and dispersal of native populations through brutal campaigns were the processes in vogue used to dehumanise and demonise native 'Indians' in America as in Asia by the Spanish as by the British. Edmund Burke, in his impeachment speech against Warren Hastings, used diction which generally applied to all the European Powers:

> "I impeach him in the name of the people of India, whose rights he has trodden under foot, and whose country he has turned into a desert. Lastly, in the name of human nature itself, in the name of both sexes, in the name of every age, in the name of every rank, I impeach the common enemy and oppressor of all!"

Captain Cook entered the Pacific and later years doomed the innocent people, what with firearms, alcohol, corruption and annihilation having destroyed the natives. Crucifix in one hand and dagger in the other, Europeans occupied Tahiti and other territories. Mitre and Sceptre go together exterminating people, demolishing dissent, resistance and values of human personhood.

Captain Cook himself was eventually to write in his journal:

> "... we debauch their morals already prone to vice and we introduce among them wants and perhaps diseases which they never before knew and which serve only to disturb that happy tranquillity they and their forefathers had enjoyed. If any one denies the truth of this assertion let him tell what the natives of the whole extent of America have gained by the commerce they had had with Europeans." * * *

In Australia, the aborigines fell back steadily before the English invasion.

> "European diseases removed most of them, and violent death in their futile struggle against the settlers carried away a few more. The prostitution of their women to the white men led on inevitably to sterility or what was almost as bad, a race of half-castes who had no place either in the tribal system or the new European society. And when their own tribal laws collapsed the aborigines found they could not understand the new English laws by which they were governed, especially the law of property. They thought that their tribal hunting grounds were their own, and when they found that this was not so, that they owned nothing, that they had virtually no rights of any kind, that they were

aliens in their own country, they were bewildered and resentful; and when all their protests failed they succumbed into listless serfdom."[1]

When we recapitulate those monstrous episodes and aggressive operations we may usefully remember how in the 1940s and 1950s, Britain conducted nuclear tests in Australia which resulted in an increase in level of cancer, particularly among aboriginals. The effect of radiation on the people of the Marshal Islands between 1946 and 1958 was that the Pacific Islanders had to suffer poverty and ill-health. The then US Secretary of State, Henry Kissinger said: 'There are only 90,000 people out there. Who gives a damn? That is human rights for 90,000 people, compliments of the United States of America.' The French nuclear colonialism in the Pacific and the bombing of the Greenpeace's flagship the *Rainbow Warrior*, the nuclear tests on the Bikini Island plus prove Western contempt for human rights of victims from radiation. The continuum of contradiction between compassion and conquest is visible for sensitive scholars of historical materialism.

Asia and Gama

K.M. Panikkar, in his *Asia and Western Dominance*, describes how the cannon made the Portuguese superior to Indian opponents. However, the Portuguese were superseded by the Dutch who too yielded to the superior English. Battles in Europe decided the destiny of Asian colonial people. With the Indian empire as the Crown's jewel, Britain secured a monopoly market for her expanding industrial development. Moreover, the plantations—tea, rubber, coffee and indigo—made the Indian labourer little more than a slave of the European planter. K.M. Panikkar adds a new dimension to British racism:

> "One other aspect of British authority in India at this period was the conviction held by every European in India of a final and enduring racial superiority. Seton Kerr, a Foreign Secretary of the Government, explained it as "the cherished conviction of every Englishman in India, from the highest to the lowest, by the planter's assistant in his lowly bungalow and by the editor in the full light of the Presidency town—from those to the Chief Commissioner in charge of an important province to the Viceroy on his throne—the conviction in every man that he belongs to a race whom God has destined to govern and subdue."[2]

It is this consciousness of European superiority and Indian inferiority that bastardised the native culture of India. Warren Hastings, the Governor General of India, used torture to secure the Empire. Edmund Burke in the British Parliament narrated the gruesome Hastings processes thus:

> "Those who could not raise the money were most cruelly tortured: cords were drawn tight round their fingers, till the flesh of the four on each hand was actually incorporated, and became solid mass; the fingers were then separated again by wedges of iron and wood driven in between them. Others were tied

1 Fan Yew Teng of Malaysia in a paper presented at the International Conference held at Kuala Lumpur in December 1994.

2 Quoted by Fan Yew Teng in the paper noted above.

two and two by feet uppermost; they were then beat on the soles of the feet, till their toe-nails dropped off.

"They were afterwards beat about the head till the blood gushed out at the mouth, nose, and ears; they were also flogged upon the naked body with bamboo canes, and prickly bushes, and above all, with some poisonous weeds, which were of a most caustic nature, and burnt at every touch. The cruelty of the monster who had ordered all this, had contrived how to tear the mind as well as the body; he frequently had a father and a son tied naked to one another by the feet and arms, and then flogged till the skin was torn from the flesh; and he had the devilish satisfaction to know that every blow must hurt; for if one escaped the son, his sensibility was wounded by the knowledge he had that the blow had fallen upon his father: the same torture was felt by the father, when he knew that every blow that missed him had fallen upon his son.

The treatment of the females could not be described: dragged forth from the inmost recesses of their houses, which the religion of the country had made so many sanctuaries, they were exposed naked to public view; the virgins were carried to the Court of Justice, where they might naturally have looked for protection; but now they looked for it in vain; for in the face of the Ministers of Justice, in the face of the spectators, in the face of the sun, those tender and modest virgins were brutally violated. The only difference between their treatment and that of their mothers was, that the former were dishonoured in the face of the day, the latter in the gloomy recesses of their dungeon. Other females had the nipples of the breasts put in a cleft bamboo, and torn off ... the fathers and husbands of the helpless females were the most harmless and industrious set of men. Content with scarcely sufficient for the support of nature, they gave almost the whole produce of their labour to the East India Company: these hands which had been broken by persons under the company's authority, produced to all England the comforts of their morning and evening tea; for it was with the rent produced by their industry, that the investments were made for the trade to China, where the tea which we use was bought. (From James, S. Mill, *The History of British India*)."[3]

Burke notwithstanding, the impeachment of that imperial instrument, Warren Hastings, failed. Likewise, General Dyer of Jallianwala Bagh atrocity was lionized for his massacre of Indians in 1919. Colour war, racist culture and brutality by John Bull prove that hatred of egalite and human dignity was not a Nazi invention.

The Americans were no better than the Europeans in despising the human rights of the natives, using false stories as the opium to soothe the conscience of the Western public. Mark Twain has said in his novel *The Mysterious Stranger*:

"Next the statesmen will invent cheap lies, putting the blame upon the nation that is attacked, and every man will be glad of those conscience-soothing falsities, and will diligently study them, and refuse to examine any refutations of them; and thus he will by and by convince himself that the war is just, and

3 *Ibid.*

will thank God for the better sleep he enjoys after this process of grotesque self-deception."

Uncle Sam and the story of slavery reveal the pro-slavery chromosomes in the Yankee D.N.A. Abraham Lincoln was a beacon light of human rights and bitter opponent of slavery. But the general trend of the slavery issue in the USA is meaningful. Lincoln's words in his message to Congress, 1st December 1862 read:

> "In giving freedom to the slave, we assure freedom to the free,—honourable alike in what we give and what we preserve. We shall nobly save or meanly lose the last, best hope of earth."

A few more words on slavery and American Independence will be educative for human rights activists. I quote John Hope Franklin:

> "By the middle of the eighteenth century, slavery in the United States was an integral part of a maturing economic system. There had been protests against the slave trade, some colonies had imposed almost prohibitive import duties, and some religious groups, notably the Quakers, had questioned the right of one man to hold another in bondage. There had been, however, no frontal attack upon the institution, and even in the northern colonies, where there was no extensive use of slaves, the majority of the articulate colonists paid little attention to slavery. Their preoccupation with economic and political relations with England doubtless accounted for the widespread indifference with which they regarded slavery.
>
> *** *** ***
>
> "It was almost natural for the colonists to link the problem of Negro slavery to their fight against England. The struggle of Negroes to secure their freedom was growing. When James Otis was penning his eloquent protest on the Rights of the British Colonies in which he affirmed the Negro's inalienable right to freedom, Negroes themselves were petitioning the General Court of Massachusetts for their freedom on the grounds that it was their natural right."[4]

Jefferson's formulation of the Declaration of Independence against the British Emperor is illuminating:

> "He has waged cruel war against human nature itself, violating its most sacred rights of life and liberty in the persons of a distant people who never offended him, captivating and carrying them into slavery in another hemisphere, or to incur miserable death in their transportation thither. This piratical warfare, the opprobrium of infidel powers, is the warfare of the Christian king of Great Britain. Determined to keep open a market where MEN should be bought and sold, he has prostituted his negative for suppressing every legislative attempt to prohibit or to restrain this execrable commerce; and that this assemblage of horrors might want no fact of distinguished die, he is now exciting these very people to rise in arms among us, and to purchase that liberty of which he

4 John Hope Franklin: *From Slavery to Freedom—A History of Negro Americans,* pages 126-127.

deprived them, by murdering the people upon whom he also obtruded them; thus paying off former crimes committed against the liberties of one people, with crimes which he urges them to commit against the lives of another."[5]

This vehement philippic against slavery must be read along with the observations of Chief Justice Taney in the *Dred Scott* case (1857) where the Court held:

> "He (slave) was bought and sold and treated as an ordinary article of merchandise whenever a profit could be made by it. This opinion was at that time fixed and universal in the civilized portion of the white race."
>
> *** *** ***
>
> "Congress has no power to abolish or prevent slavery in any of its territories."
>
> *** *** ***
>
> "The right of property in a slave is distinctly and expressly affirmed in the Constitution. The right to traffic in it, like an ordinary article of merchandise and property, was guaranteed to the citizens of the United States, in every State that might desire it, for twenty years ..."
>
> *** *** ***
>
> "No word can be found in the Constitution which gives Congress a greater power over slave property, or which entitles property of that kind to less protection than property of any other description. The only power conferred is the power coupled with the duty of guarding and protecting the owner in his rights."

From the above, it is clear that the shocking view of the highest Court in the US of those days was that manumission of the slave by the Congress was *ultra vires.* Is it not a puzzle that in the subconscious of the American, there is lurking somewhere a paranoid streak that other people can be socially, economically and politically enslaved. A master nation complex?

There are outlying US areas but the people have a voice but no vote (1) for the delegate in the US House Representatives. The United States is the Super Power and South America, Philippines, Mexico *et al* are free only in name when US interests are at stake.

> "In 1866, US General William Tecumsch Sherman had written to General Ulysses S. Grant in this civilized and humanitarian vein: 'we must act with vindictive earnestness against the Sioux, even to the extermination of men, women and children. Nothing else will reach the root of the case'."[6]

In Vietnam and Korea the aerial bombings were barbaric and it was a crime against humanity to have dropped atomic bombs on Hiroshima and Nagasaki.

> "Over 2 million civilians in North Korea and about 1 million in South Korea were estimated to have been killed.

5 *Ibid* pages 129-130.

6 Quoted by Fan Yew Teng in the paper noted above.

"Just as in the Korean War, chemical and biological weapons were used in Vietnam, including dioxin, a highly poisonous chemical in Agent Orange. As Professor Howard Zinn has pointed out, by the end of the Vietnam war, 7 million tons of bombs had been dropped on Vietnam, more than twice the total bombs dropped by Europe and Asia in World War II—almost one 500-pound bomb for every human being in Vietnam. It was estimated that there were 20 million bomb craters in the country. In addition, poisonous sprays were dropped by planes to destroy trees and any kinds of growth—an area the size of the state of Massachusetts was covered with such poison. Vietnamese mothers reported birth defects in their children". (For more details of aerial bombardment of Third World civilians, see *Killing Civilians from the Air*, CenPeace, 1994).[7]

Africa has been the victim of European vivisection and occupation. One instance of a French soldier's observation is sufficient.

"......you asked me what happens to Algerian women we capture; some we keep as hostages and the rest are auctioned to the troops like animals."

In the operations we have carried out during the last four months I have witnessed scenes that would melt the hardest heart if one had time to let them! I witnessed it all with a frightening indifference. Kill all men over the age of fifteen; take all women and children and put them on a ship for the Marquises Islands or some other destination."[8]

The same story can be repeated with regard to other countries including Latin America. In sum, Hitler was not the first monopolist of mass violation of human rights. All Europeans were his ancestors, Compassion and Empires are old enemies, so much so human rights of Afro-Asians and the economic North are distant neighbours, with basic contradictions dividing them.

Rhodesia, Congo, Libya and many other countries of Africa had rich resources and, therefore, their people were subjugated and their resources robbed. The pattern is the same. The oppressors were praised by Western leaders. For instance, President Eisenhower hailed Portugal's contribution to civilisation and Mussolini was praised by Churchill in 1927, as the greatest law-giver and Roosevelt called the Duce 'that admirable Italian gentleman'.

Latin America reminds us of Chile and Neruda, the Chilean Nobel laureate, who wrote thus:

"My country has been betrayed more than any other in our time. Allende was murdered because he nationalised the other of Chile's subsoil: copper. In both cases, the Chilean oligarchy set bloody revolutions in motion. In both cases, the military played the bloodhounds. The English companies in Balmaceda's time, the North Americans in Allende's time, instigated and financed these military actions."[9]

7 Fan Yew Teng of Malaysia in a paper presented at the International Conference on Re-thinking Human Rights, held at Kuala Lumpur in December 1994.

8 Quoted in the paper noted above.

9 *Ibid.*

The military mind-set of the imperial West considered limited nuclear war as an available weapon. Jimmy Carter candidly admitted that US Government's foreign policy has not exemplified any commitment to moral principles.

Asia, like other continents, has had its share of imperial aggression and colonisation. It thus becomes clear that the credentials of the White human rights champions are not writ in their hearts, but spout from their lips. That is why the Pentagon's black budget is trillions high and nuclear monopoly is claimed as a super-power priority. No study of the prospects of human rights in the New World order will be serious and straightforward unless Governments and leaders in the Third World and the peoples everywhere became aware of historical materialism and the dangers of hunting with the Northern hounds and running with the Southern hares. The Indian surrender at the GATT is a bad omen. The Fund-Bank conditionalities being accepted is another evil portent. The pressure to sign the CTBT, apart from the military ploys used by the US, and other global factors lead to the dialectical verdict of history that human rights, as a universal rule of life, is but double-speak and double-deception. We must beware and be aware that the next century may see the world unfree, if mankind does not unitedly rise to battle for its collective right to be human in the civilised sense and spiritual meaning of dignity and divinity. The right to be human shall not be the vanishing point of jurisprudence.

Conclusion

Are we to assume that the Fifth Act of the tragedy of Afro-Asian, South American humanity has arrived? No. We must assert humanity's title for perennial joy of life and not celebrate the events which imprisoned human freedom through colonial thraldom. There is a move in some places to celebrate the 500th anniversary of the arrival of Vasco da Gama of Portugal at Calicut (India) who came via the Cape of Good Hope. Hope for Europe and despair for Asia! Gama's entry eventually led to commercial and political domination of Europeans over almost all of Asia. The Portuguese with their armaments reached the West Coast of India and Gama adopted terrorism and piracy in the Indian waters. One European Power after another occupied India and gun-boat diplomacy, coupled with White supremacy and Church infiltration, completed the colonisation process. To celebrate our conqueror's success is to hug our chains. In a way, even Japan played the role of the West within Asia by invasion and occupation and played the enslaving game in World War II. Let us beware of wolves in sheep's clothing.

The moral obligations of the Christian countries towards non-Christian continents departed from the teachings of Jesus and permitted their conscience to practice outrages and grab colonial control. American politics and business interests and military mentality is best understood from just one quote I give here:

> "If America wills it so, and constructs several systems of overseas bases, the next war can be broken down into localised conflicts locally dealt with before

they spread all over the world... . Where is the American frontier now? There is no frontier. America fights around the globe."[10]

"We are now in a favourable position .... We should get our bases now and plan not for 10 but for 50-100 years ahead."[11]

"To my mind, the question to be decided is not whether we should or should not use atomic weapons ... the question is rather when and how such weapons should be used. Should we, for example, in the event of war, begin by bombing major centres of population in enemy territory or start with smaller centres important for transportation or specific industries? This question should be answered not so much on the basis of humanitarian principles as from a practical weighing of the long-run advantage to this country."[12]

Other countries according to their lesser abilities have the same disposition towards weaker peoples and their human rights. Human Rights had no place in a situation where the right to grab and bomb was treated as paramount by the strong and torture of non-white Christians was not regarded as anti-Christ. The military mind-set of the American top brass and, in a lesser way, of the European powers too, were really barriers in the way of world peace and social justice. There have been instances when the White House had even toyed with the thought of using nuclear bombs where necessary for its own interest. Indeed, Henry Kissinger in 1957 had said: "limited nuclear war represents our most effective strategy against nuclear powers or against a major power which is capable of substituting manpower for technology". President Nixon, in November 1973, had stated "I can go into my office and pick up the telephone and in 25 minutes 70 million people will be dead". The White House, even during the time of President Bush, had thought of pressing the nuclear button. Now we can discern the diabolic intent behind the CTBT. On the whole, the world is heavens away from security, peace and human rights immunity. Ronald Reagan, who initiated star-war development, called the Soviet Union the Evil Empire. The Soviet Union is dead but there is still an Evil Empire alive. One can only conclude this extraordinary contradiction in contemporary history by quoting Nelson Mandela who, as early as 1953, had spoken against the madness of imperialism thus:

"We have been gagged because we emphatically and openly condemned the criminal attacks by the imperialists against the people of Malay, Vietnam, Indonesia, Tunisia and Tanganyika and called upon our people to identify themselves unreservedly with the cause of world peace, and to fight against the war policies of America and her satellites."

10 George Weller, 1944.

11 General Leslie Grovers, head of the Manhattan Project 1945.

12 W. Walton Butterworth, Director of the Office of Far Eastern Affairs, 15th September 1848.

Spiders cast their fine webs not for lovely silk but for lethal traps. The patriotism of freedom needs vigilance, resistance and capacity to see the enemy wrapped in generous costume.

It may be pertinent before winding up to refer to a few other aspects of colonialism and human rights with closer reference to India.

Students of human rights, as they survey the story of progress, see the zigzag struggle towards gradual advance, sometimes through revolutionary upsurge, sometimes through moderate reforms. As we reach the modern era, we find industry and trade assuming proportions of exploitation. The European beginnings of overseas trade and plunder diabolically developed into sovereign occupation of other countries, using gunpowder and the Bible and assertion of racist superiority. All these processes have been traced by me earlier while dealing with the Columbus conquest and Gama exploits leading eventually to the control of vast parts of the globe by imperial reigns. Human rights are the first casualty of such imperial victories. The British East India Company had a trading monopoly as it entered India and established itself in 1600 only to expand all over, defeating Maharajas and subjugating the local people, suppressing their culture and reducing them to near-slavery by and large. The East India Company became involved in the politics of Power with a Board of Control responsible to the British Parliament. The robbery of Indian resources and the deprivation of the human rights of the Indian people by a mere trading Company became so shocking that the British Government took over the Administration of India from the East India Company. Warren Hastings was so notorious for his trampling under foot Indian people's human rights that on his return to England in 1784 he was impeached in the British Parliament. The British interests in making India a colony and depriving Indians of their sovereignty coincided with the East India Company's domination of the Asian sub-continent. Thus, notwithstanding the seven year impeachment proceedings, Warren Hastings was acquitted and Indian colonisation came directly under the British Crown. Rapacious trade and industrial exploitation are the route to political control and neo-colonialism. Looking at the history of international trade from the vintage point of the end of the 20th century, one is able to behold a *deja vu* of the 16th century colonialism with the East India Company substituted by mammoth transnational corporate power, combined with military power, vesting in the First World and victimising the Third World. The dialectical study of contemporary history unfolds an apprehension that human rights worldwide may become a casualty of the mighty trading nations such as the Group of Seven and like economic Groupings (G-10 for instance). The trail of Columbus, who discovered the New World in the sixteenth century while sailing to reach India but voyaging to other parts of the world, led to vast empires and extermination of native peoples.

The stories of Gama's savagery inflicted on the people of Malabar are barbarous. So too the terrible violence let loose by Affonso d' Albuquerque, the Portuguese Viceroy of the Indies who landed on the Malabar Coast in

1502, conquered Goa, Ceylon, Daman and Diu with sword in one hand and the Cross in the other. Inhumanity and forced religious conversions were ruthlessly practised, with callous unconcern for the humanism of Jesus of Nazareth by this Portuguese navigator-cum-tyrant.

This background is sufficient to shock any human rights activist if any suggestion comes from any quarters to celebrate Columbus or Gama who through trade and treachery, were the operators of the embryonic processes of empire-building. The universal human rights were first lost not when Mussolini and Hitler and the Japanese Emperor crushed mankind. The requiem of human rights, wiped out by European imperial terrorism, was sung, perhaps, silently during the imperial era spread over centuries when the West collectively captured and conquered and literally enslaved innocent and unarmed people and tiny rulers and village republics.

The recolonisation of India via GATT and the Fund Bank conduit suggests a repetition of history, according to scholars like Chakravarthi Raghavan. So long as economic domination by a Super Power and associates continues, the human rights of the Indian people will be under eclipse. Lenin long ago wrote, borrowing from J.A. Hobson's book *Imperialism*:

> "But millions of peasants in India are struggling to live on *half an acre*. Their existence is a *constant struggle with starvation*, ending too often in defeat. Their difficulty is not to live *human lives* —lives up to the level of their poor standard of comfort—but to live at all and not die... . We may truly say that in India, except in the irrigated tracts, famine is chronic—endemic."[13]

Lenin also forecast:

> "The morrow of world history will be a day when the awakening peoples oppressed by imperialism are finally aroused and the decisive long and hard struggle for their liberation begins."[14]

It is extremely interesting to read Lenin's expectation that:

> "The bourgeois nationalism of *any* oppressed nation has a general democratic content that is directed *against* oppression, and it is this content that we *unconditionally support*."[15]

Reading the incisive observations of Marx, Engels and Lenin on India under the British, one suspects whether the second war of liberation, if one may put it with a touch bombast, from the stranglehold of the economic North will be as successful as the Gandian struggle to make the British quit India. Today the Indian human, in substantial measure, is voiceless, (don't be misled by parliamentary noises) because of the upper middle class and the tycoon sector of India playing into the hands of the economic North. In politics and economics, India, like some other Third World countries, is being corrupted morally and materially with he result that there are several

13 *Collected Works of Lenin*, vol. XXXIX, page 427.
14 *Ibid*, vol. XXXVI, page 611.
15 *Ibid*, vol. XX, page 412.

Indias within Indian geography. The materialistic conception of history, or historical materialism applied to the Indian human conditions, proves that Power is still retained with the elitocracy partly for their own benefit and largely as *benami* for the corporate controllerate from abroad. Viewing human rights of the masses, one is inclined to remember Lord Acton:

> "History is not a web woven with innocent hands. Among all the causes which degrade and demoralise men, power is the most constant and the most active."

Coming to basics, as I wind up, *swaraj* of the Indian people is the bedrock of their human rights. Therefore, re-colonisation, overt or covert, economic or political, is fatal to the rights of 950 million Indian humans. Dr. Ambedkar's sombre words, in the final address at the Constituent Assembly on 25th November 1949 have poignant pertinence:

> "On 26th January 1950, India will be an independent country (cheers). What would happen to her independence? Will she maintain her independence or will she lose it again? This is the first thought that comes to my mind. It is not that India was never an independent country. The point is that she once lost the independence she had. Will she lose it a second time? It is this thought which makes me most anxious for the future. What perturbs me greatly is the fact that not only India has once before lost her independence, but she lost it by the infidelity and treachery of some of her own people."

9

Human Rights Realities in India–Prospects of an Asian Charter, Other Continental Experiments

The age of democratic revolution, so the Western historians say, began in Great Britain, France, and the United States. As we promenade through the highway of human rights history we come upon the greens of Runnymede where the rebellious English barons browbeat King John in 1215 to wrest some constitutional rights. The Great Charter or Magna Carta granted equality before the law and other valuable rights. After the Glorious Revolution of 1688 came the Declaration of Rights. A century later, the American colonies made the Declaration of Independence. The brief U.S. Constitution was followed by the first ten amendments, generally called the Bill of Rights, and then came additional amendments guaranteeing equal rights for racial minorities and for women.

After the French Revolution, the National Assembly adopted the Declaration of the Rights of Man and Citizen. European democratic revolutions in 1848, the political changes after World War I, and the formation, on liberation and decolonisation of many Third World countries after World War II, produced a series of Constitutions incorporating fundamental rights for their people. A new world human rights era, as it were, was taking shape on parchment. India was ahead in the matter of human rights, as inscribed in the Constitution, with a Court system as a vigilant sentinel and implementational instrument. Mahatma Gandhi, who led the struggle for Independence, battled, not merely for political liberation but for the composite freedoms found in the Universal Declaration of Human Rights, with his heart on the oppressive human condition. Rabindranath Tagore, a cosmic visionary, was a leader in the valiant movement and regarded the 'innate worth of the individual' as of the essence, beyond acquiring the 'means of attaining mere material satisfaction'. On the whole, the national struggle was resistance to fascist trends and colonial exploitation as necessary, since liberty has 'a true foundation only in the moral worth of the individuals who compose the State'. Revolutionaries, martyrs, crimson ideologues, countless women ready to 'do or die' and great souls, each the pride of the nation, held aloft the banner of human liberation and marched to win swaraj, impregnated with wide-spectrum values covering political, social and economic content and belonging as a birthright of everyone. Thus, when India became free, its democracy encompassed human rights in their comprehensive coverage. Jawaharlal Nehru, as the first Prime Minister and national leader articulated this vision in immortal diction:

> "A moment comes, which comes but rarely in history, when we step out from the old to the new, when an age ends, and when the soul of a nation, long suppressed, finds utterance. It is fitting that at this solemn moment we take the pledge of dedication to the service of India and her people and to the still larger cause of humanity.
>
> * * *
>
> "The service of India means the service of the millions who suffer. It means the ending of poverty and ignorance and disease and inequality of opportunity. The ambition of the greatest man of our generation has been to wipe every tear from every eye. That may be beyond us but as long as there are tears and suffering, so long our work will not be over.
>
> "And so we have to labour and to work and work hard to give reality to our dreams. Those dreams are for India, but they are also for the world, for all the nations and peoples are too closely knit together today for any one of them to imagine that it can live apart. Peace has been said to be indivisible; so is freedom, so is prosperity now, and so also is disaster in this One World that can no longer be split into isolated fragments."[1]

Later was enacted a long Constitution enriched by Fundamental Rights and incorporating social, cultural and economic rights (the latter not judicially enforceable, though). We had reservations about the irony of Bentham: Right is the child of law; from real laws come real rights, but from imaginary laws, from 'laws of nature' come imaginary rights ......'Natural rights is simple nonsense upon stilts'. Of course, Bentham adopts a practical approach to a 'right': "Is it actually enjoyed"? or 'is it really enforced'? In this pragmatic sense "Is it a positive right"? Mere abstractions or omnipotence in the sky are illusions and deceits, according to the Benthamite school. He has a point but goals, even if not immediately enforceable, have a catalytic effect and locomotive power. Human Rights are achieving 'enthronement' in many parts of the world, but in large areas of the globe, human rights territories suffer desertification and for the poor billions of humans the positivism and entitlement of these rights are but a mirage. While partially dissenting from Benthamite cynicism and realism, we may examine the Asian, and particularly the Indian, map and track record. Our juristic aim must be constructively critical; Our social audit must be to repair the deplorable human plight, our democratic

1 *Speech at the Constituent Assembly,* on 14th/15th August 1947.

goal must be to conscientise constitutional instrumentalities and convert rhetoric into actual empowerment of the people. Destination actualisation of every human right by every human being.

There are good examples to decimate our diffidence in may continents and countries. Advances have been made in Western Europe, Africa, Philippines, Hong Kong et al. It is a sad fact that the U.S. itself and many other civilised powers have not ratified important Covenants and Conventions and have violated, without challenge, human rights at home and abroad. India is somewhat better in ratifying UN instruments, although it is a shame that neither the Optional Protocol which enables UN invigilation of human rights violations nor the Anti-Torture Convention has been ratified by Gandhi's India or Lincoln's America.[2]

The magnificent progression of UN instruments, as jurisprudential guidelines in defining and defending human rights, is a tribute to that World Body and a quick march through the major documents is a spiritual serendipity and jural education in itself and an awareness instruction in the vast and wondrous coverage already achieved in moving towards a just and humane society.

An oriental flavour to the study of human rights and the luminous and voluminous instruments emanating from the UN can be imparted only if we first touch the spiritual chords deeper than the material manifestations. We must realise that Buddha and Christ were the greatest Protestants against an unjust social order who challenged the oppressive hierarchy of priesthood and inegalitarian elite which had a vested interest in denying to the populace the moral, ethical, spiritual and temporal dimensions and layers of culture and good things of life. It is important to notice, in this context, that Jesus, the Messiah, and Barabbas, the robber, were brought before Pontius Pilate, the Roman Judge; and Jesus was sentenced to crucifixion while Barabbas was let off though guilty. We thus have a Barabbasque order the world over. The dialectics of the contemporary world consists of the burning contradiction between the sublime system of human rights for which Jesus stood and the predatory process symbolised by Barabbas. Here is a conflict between social justice, compassion and sharing as against freedom to grab and rob mindless of the morality or legality of the means. Those who represent the great cause of human rights must have a culture of the heart and a spiritual commitment to the sufferings of the world's fraternity. Vivekananda's words are apt here:

> "Do you feel? Do you feel that millions and millions of the descendants of gods and of sages have become nextdoor neighbours to brutes? Do you feel that millions are starving today, and millions have been starving for ages? Do you feel that ignorance has come over the land as a dark cloud? Does it make you restless? Does it make you sleepless? Has it gone into your blood, coursing through your veins, becoming constant with your heart-beats?"

2 India has now ratified the "Convention Against Torture and other Cruel, Inhuman or Degrading Treatment or Punishment". Amendment VIII of the U.S.A. Constitution also prohibits infliction of "Cruel and Unusual Punishments" and also "Excessive Fines" or "Excessive Bails".

Tagore called the victims as the eternal tenants of an extortionate system. Gandhi called these vast unfortunates as *daridra narayanas* and Ambedkar named these *dalits, antyajas* (the lowliest and the lost). The Indian mind, in its profound depths, even in its ecological universality, regards as its central commitment the worth of the human person, his happiness and freedom from exploitation. Let me cite an exchange between Gurudev Tagore and Mahatma Gandhi to illustrate the imponderable humanist commitment of the Mahatma:

> "Once Gurudev Rabindranath Tagore asked Gandhiji, 'Gandhiji are you so unromantic? When in the early dawn, the morning sun rises, does it not fill your heart with joy to see its reddish glow? When the birds sing does not your heart thrill with its divine music? When the rose opens its petals and blooms in the garden does its sights not bring cheer to your heart?'
>
> "The Mahatma replied 'Gurudev, I am not so dumb or insensitive, as not to be moved by the beauty of the rose or the morning rays of the sun or the divine music of the birds. But what can I do? My one desire, my one anxiety, my one ambition is when shall I see the red tint of the rose on the cheeks of hungry naked millions of my people? When shall I hear the sweet and melodious song of the birds in place of their agonising sighs? When will such music come out of their soul and when will that day come when the light of the morning sun will illumine the heart of the common man in India? When will I see its lustre and brightness on his face?'"

The kernel of human rights is concern for the human condition, however high or humble be the person. The vulgar sector, affluently placed, ask: Why should I, if the going is good for me, bother about my neighbour and his misery? Why should Cain care to sustain Abel and not kill him for gain? Why should robbery be crime and why not grab as much as you may with unconcern for the lacerated lot of the deprived? The answer is humanism: compassion, love, fellowship and identity with the wretched of the earth. Why compassion and sharing when I can enjoy pleasures and corner treasures and fill my lust, avarice and pride in a monopoly of arrogance and suppression of those who challenge my supremacy and surfeit of pleasurable resources? What is justice, social justice, distributive justice, if might is right and I have might on my side? What if I crush you or throw you to the wild beasts and delight in watching your vain struggle against being devoured? Byron's bitter lines are worth quoting:

> *"By thy cold breast and serpent smile,*
> *By thy unfathom'd gulfs of guile,*
> *By that most seeming virtuous eye,*
> *By thy shut soul's hypocrisy;*
> *By the perfection of thine art*
> *Which pass'd for human thine own heart;*
> *By thy delight in others' pain,*
> *And by thy brotherhood of Cain,*
> *I call upon thee! and compel*
> *Thyself to be thy proper Hell!*

The world is but an animal farm, a zoological theatre, an amoral market-friendly profit-aggressive global order where God can be commanded to support gold through priests and scriptures and sacred abracadabra!

The basic principle on which human rights, people's self-determination and abolition of slavery and the very Charter of the United Nations are bedrocked is the divine essence latent in every human person, the truth of our being or the right to be human. The blend of the material and spiritual values, the perspectives and perceptions which are not skin deep but soul-deep and the sacred spark that belights our life and distinguishes humanity from the brute ancestors–these quintessentials humanize our civilization and invest our march through time and space as an endless journey towards a divine destiny. The measure of human rights is not the loudness of political noises you are free to make nor the Boston Brahmin status you enviously enjoy but the acceptance of the equal dignity and reverential divinity that dwells in each individual and gives her/him title, like any other, to the resources and richness available for all together; justly distributed–each according to her/his needs, not according to the acquisitive ability for rapacity under inequitous circumstances.

Humanity is the highest in the evolutionary scale, manifesting the divinity that dwells within and distinguishes homo sapiens from the simian ancestors who lived in arboreal environs sans the spiritual sensitivity, thinking individuality and personal dignity which makes us all the members of a nobler fraternity. The right to be human is a glorious opportunity and the worth of the human person is nobly inalienable and inheres in everyone, man, woman or child, plebeian or patrician, Jew or gentile, prince or pariah. The profound meaning of democracy, in its many dimensions, is realised only in a society where veneration for brothers and sisters springs from the recognition of the principle of 'one person, one value', regardless of all trappings, temporal and material. Such is the manifesto of the human person, the celestial potential which exists in equal measure in every member of the human race, given real opportunity to unfold. Such, in brief, is the immortal core in every mortal, the undying divinity in every human entity, beyond distinctions of caste and creed, race and colour, sex and country. This universal minimum is present in each one, savage or saint, and its full realisation finds its finest state when the human ascent and divine descent meet at a confluence to incarnate as an *avatar,* a Buddha, Jesus, Muhammad or Vivekanand, Gandhi or other radiant figure commissioned, as it were, by a Higher Power to transform the social order so as to offer for every human being spiritual-material space and fragrant faculties to blossom into the perfection of personality. This is the grand perspective of human values and their nexus with the Supreme Spirit. The struggle for human deliverance and the battle for universal brotherhood is the pith and substance of the magna carta of humanity enshrined in the San Francisco Charter (1945), the Universal Declaration of Human Rights (1948) and the two International Covenants (1966) which spell out the material projections of human rights. Never can you do justice to the concept and creed we stand for without rising to the above philosophic heights far above the political debates and judicial rhetoric which fill the pages of human rights literature. A lofty jurisprudence, doing reverence to the spiritual dimensions of human rights, transcending the tyranny of legal texts, rigidity of religious prescriptions and obduracies of theologies and cults and obsessive addictions fobbed off as human rights, is the sublime desideratum. The New World Order, worthy of the spiritual history of mankind, must reflect the radiant message of divinised humanism, without the wrinkles of obscurantisms, rashness of run-away passions and the wrangles of power blocs building new imperialisms and domestic despotisms, even using human rights chauvinism as an additional weapon in the war for capturing and cornering the resources of the earth and the minds of people. The inauguration of this international human order is hard in our money-manic, blood-stained globalism apparelled in newspeak liberalism. We need inspired cadres and inspiring leaders for this ideological campaign! How greatly we miss Mahatma Gandhi whose spiritual anatomy and holy chemistry of total dedication for human liberation is rare, the rarest of the rare.

> "The human rights movement should itself give equal priority to economic, social and cultural rights together with civil and political rights. It should search for ways to play as prominent a role in the future in the monitoring and implementation of economic, social and cultural rights as it has in the past in the monitoring and implementation of civil and political rights."[3]

Such is the holism of humanism, rights and duties being but radiant emanations.

Our generation as heir to a great estate of human rights must 'wipe every tear from every eye' and raise every human to his/her full personhood. Nelson Mandela's words, way back in 1992, is fitting finale to my thoughts on the UN and human rights:

> "Our common humanity transcends the oceans and all national boundaries. It binds us together in a common cause against tyranny, to act together in defence of our very humanity. Let it never be asked of any one of us—what did we do when we knew that another was oppressed?"

We live in a world where man's inhumanity to man makes countless thousands mourn! (Burns). In our good earth, we still find evil forces which create scenes of woe the like of which no eye had seen, no heart conceived, no human tongue can adequately tell. 'O Death, the poor man's dearest friend, the kindest and the best!'—such is the lot of many for whom human rights mean nothing. They have nothing to lose except their life. The dignity and worth of the human person postulates a spiritual dimension to miss which is to carnalise a sublime concept.

It is fair to state, having noted the Western vintage, that the East did contribute the spiritual substance of human rights sans which the concept would be rootless. As Mahmoud Ayoub pointed out at an International Conference, organised by Just World Trust in 1994.

3 Ian Martin, Secretary-General, Amnesty International, 1986-1992.

"Asian religious traditions and cultures have their own spiritual and moral philosophies which include primordial principles of human worth and dignity. These principles, therefore, can, and should, serve as the primary basis for human rights in Asian countries.

"It will be further argued that the very concept of human rights is a recent Western idea not based in the Judeo-Christian-Islamic worldview, but in post-enlightenment secular culture. The concept, moreover, is based on an individualistic view of society, which is diametrically opposed to the Christian idea of the church as a "universal communion of saints" (*ecclesia*) as well as the Islamic concept of an *ummah* (community) enjoining the good, dissuading from evil and having true faith in God. In contrast, the modern secular Western concept of human rights is a morally neutral concept based not on spiritual or religious principles, but on purely materialistic and social considerations."[4]

This Islamic scholar has traced the spiritual element, in the human rights concept from the Quran and the Prophet and refers to a seminar on human rights in Islam in 1980 in Kuwait which concluded that: 'The time has come to refute the idea that initiation and continued development on the concept of human rights must be exclusively attributed to Western cultures. The seminar admitted that while Islam guarantees fundamental human rights, Muslim States have often deviated from Islamic principles. A call was therefore issued to all Muslims to return to the fundamentals of Islam, and not be swayed to the right and left by the West.'[5]

Indeed, 1972 Charter of the Organisation of the Islamic Conference had endorsed fundamental human rights and committed its members to the United Nations Charter. In 1980, an Islamic Declaration of human rights was presented to the UNESCO essentially agreeing, in an Islamic version and ethos, with the UN Declaration of 1948. The paper presented at the Kuala Lumpur by Ayoub considers Hindu Vedanta and Buddhist dharma and winds up:

"It must be concluded from all this that Asian religious traditions—not only the ones discussed here but those of the rest of Asia as well, have their own profound moral principles that could serve as a framework for the realization of human rights in their own societies. It is high time that the West learn from the East the meaning of moral freedom and the true significance of non-material values rather than dictate to the peoples of Asia its own confused and highly selective principles of human rights.

"It must also be argued that no traditional society would define human rights to mean licentiousness, promiscuity and deviation from the eternal norms that have guided humanity for thousands of years in its quest for ultimate fulfilment. It is arrogant and hypocritical of any country, on the basis of its material wealth and military might, to dictate to selective countries how

4 Paper presented by Mahmoud Ayoub titled *'Asian Spirituality and Human Rights* at the International Conference on Rethinking Human Rights, *held* at Kuala Lumpur in December 1994.

5 *Ibid.*

to live and how to develop and preserve their values and fundamental rights."[6]

Asian cultural pluralism profoundly propounds spiritual, moral principles which uphold the soul of Human Rights of 1984. The West and the East shall not be competitive but complimentary in weaving the garment of human rights holism.

As we will presently see the West assumes an arrogance of science and technology and militarist superiority which often vitiates its human right perspective. An undercurrent of Kipling's slobbery of East is East and West is West is evident in the use by the United States of human rights for Trade and Commerce, for military control of the world and for distorting the semantic connotations of human rights.

A rapid global survey of human rights instruments

The world is one and mankind, in its zigzag course, is collectively creating a universal jurisprudence which begins with that unanimously accepted Bill of human rights, adopted and proclaimed by General Assembly resolution 217A(III) of 10 December 1948. The inherent dignity (I call it divinity) and the equal, inalienable rights of all members of the human family is the foundation of freedom, justice and peace in the world. Thus begins the odyssey of humanity adventuring towards a New World Human Order with better standards of life in larger freedom. The two great International Covenants, one on Economic, Social and Cultural Rights and the other on Civil and Political Rights were adopted in 1966. Twenty years after the Universal Declaration came the historic Proclamation of Teheran. The members of the human family gathered at this Conference dispelled the differences about the integrality of Civil and Political Rights as well as Economic, Social and Cultural Rights. Article 13, the manifestation of this synthesis, solemnly emphasizes: "Since human rights and fundamental freedoms are indivisible, the full realization of civil and political rights without the enjoyment of economic, social and cultural rights is impossible". So effective global implementation policies of economic and social development is an indispensable obligation. What an integral yoga which urges provision for *all human beings* a life consonant with freedom and dignity and conducive to physical mental, social and spiritual welfare. Thus we have a picture of the first generation of human rights, not in insularity but in interdependence.

The right of self-determination, delicate, difficult but deeply dwelling in the soul of colonially crushed peoples, has a nexus with human rights. Without rupture of the national unity and territorial integrity of a country, the right to self-determination by virtue of which peoples freely determine their political status and socio-economic development is upheld in the relevant Declaration passed by General Assembly resolution 1514 (XV) of 14th December 1960. Many other Universal Instruments, frowning upon

6 *Ibid.*

discrimination, have been passed by the Assembly. The rights of women and of the child have also been effectively declared, and the girl child has attracted particular emphasis. Similarly, slavery, servitude, forced labour and like institutions and practices have been condemned by the UN. But rights and freedoms, even if proclaimed by the Global Assembly, cannot achieve success, unless the administration of Justice rises to meet the challenges. So the independence of the Judiciary comes within the scope of UN instrumentalities. The basic principles of the Independence of the Judiciary have been the subject of UN consideration. The General Assembly resolutions 40/32 of 29th November 1985 and 40/146 of 13th December 1985 have formulated the basic principles on the independence of the Judiciary with a request to the member States, through national legislation and practice, to give effect to these principles. Of course, protection of persons subject to detention or imprisonment is necessary, lest penal institutions should become walled, dark cells of torture and dehumanisation.

Human rights sound hollow unless people have the freedom of information. Indeed, the Convention on the International right in this behalf has been approved by the General Assembly resolution 603 (VII) of 16th December 1952. Despite this provision the people of various countries are kept in the dark about their own rights or the functions of public officials at the national and international levels. Transparency is basic to democracy and official secrecy is the State's iron curtain.

> "The great violators of human rights are sovereign governments,...when they choose to be a law unto themselves, there is no effective power to stop them.......The task before us is to find the way to diffuse that power. It needs to be dispersed in two directions. Firstly, downwards to the provinces, to the communities and ultimately to the individuals who constitute our nations.......And secondly, upwards to the continents or regions, and ultimately to Tennyson's dream of "the Parliament of Man, the Federation of the World."[7]

In the world where we live, the question of nationality, of statelessness, asylum and refugees assumes dangerously poignant proportions and the United Nations has Conventions on these subjects. World War II notwithstanding, war crimes and crimes against humanity, including genocide, have been condemned with punitive provisions through appropriate instruments.

Humanitarian law, in our world of violence, internecine and international, deserves grave attention, what with millions of civilians being killed or wounded in many countries. Therefore, the World Body has awakened to the humanitarian dimensions of compassionate jurisprudence. The Geneva Convention of 1949 deals with the wounded and the sick, and quite a few other allied instruments relate to the humane treatment of prisoners of war, protection of civilian persons in times of war, protection of victims of international armed conflicts and kindred categories.

7 ICJ, Secretary-General, Niall MacDermot.

Asian charter: a few more reflections

Pausing for a moment at this point one may observe that among the Eastern thinkers there is an allergy to the presentation of the Universal Human Rights as not truly universal, but largely a set of values which appeal to the white, affluent people of Europe, North America or one of the European settler colonies dotted around the globe. This criticism was voiced at the International Conference (where I participated) held at Kuala Lumpur titled 'Rethinking Human Rights'. Dr. Ziauddin Sardar of Pakistan levels this charge and calls it "the imperium universal human rights". The criticism has been levelled that this world view of human rights belongs to one-sixth of the global population. But what about the rest of mankind, asked Dr. Ziauddin Sardar, while pressing for a different perspective which is less Western and more Asian. He resists the White dominance in the conceptualisation of human rights and considers it necessary to press for peoples' right to secure their daily bread and community living aggravated by acute poverty and spiralling homelessness. The thrust of his submission in his own words is: "Without a basic sustainable economic subsistence civic and political rights have no meaning, the very conditions of scratching the earth for existence preclude enjoyment of and exclude people from the imperium of the dominant agenda of human rights."

Ashis Nandy recalls the Bandung spirit where Nehru played a key role and 29 non-aligned countries met in 1955 to act jointly to defend the identity of the Bandung Conference nations against Western exploitation.

There is no gainsaying the fact that the gamut of universal human rights as projected in 1948 is valid; but the Asian emphasis on the coloured communities' felt needs relates to the Covenant on Social, Economic and Cultural Rights which has not even now been ratified by the U.S.

A similar point of view can be gleaned from Tissa Balasuriya's paper dealing with the 'Historical Dimension of Western Global Domination and its Consequences for Human Rights of five-sixths of Humanity'. Ashis Nandy thoughtfully complains of the politics of human rights and the impact of Western hegemonic policies upon the Asian humans. Balasurya argues:

> "The present world order is mainly a result of the territorial and economic expansion of European peoples to other parts of the earth. From the point of view of the West, the past five hundred years was a period of great expansion and growth. For others, they were very much centuries of defeat, pillage, colonization, exploitation, and marginalization, in diverse forms, genocide.
>
> "The expansion of Europe in those centuries resulted in the *European occupation of most of the habitable land of the earth.* West Europeans occupied North, Central, and South America, Australia, New Zealand, and parts of Africa. They made colonies of the whole of Asia except China, Japan and Thailand. The Russians, and East European people, expanded their empire to the Pacific and the borders of China.
>
> "With superior technology, military forces, and economic power in their hands, they built the present world order to their own great advantage. They

> put in place economic, political, social, cultural, and religious structures and values to suit their domination over the rest of the world."[8]

Right through Asian thought on Human Rights runs a criticism of Asian alienation based on intellectual and materialist domination of Western Powers, resulting in five-sixth of humanity forfeiting its claim to survival, let alone rights. Claude Alvares, an Indian militant intellectual, presents his case powerfully:

> "Decades from now—and I expect sooner rather than later—our descendants are bound to wonder how five-sixths of humanity allowed their lives to be so easily run according to the dictates and needs of the other one-sixth. And that too, often against their own survival interests and futures. If force had been used to ensure such compliance—such as what America used in the Iraq War, for instance—one might be able to understand such a situation. Yet even without the use of an arsenal as formidable as that, five-sixths of the world already are, it appears, as badly demolished as the Iraqis after the war, with options increasingly limited, their creativity crippled and deeper forms of economic, political and cultural serfdom looming on the horizon.
>
> "The demolition I am talking about is the demolition of the mind. One may not see signs of it if one sees the city-state of Singapore or the Makati business centre in Manila or the gaggle of five star hotels in Delhi or even the relative prosperity of KL, but these are also expressions of it in a way. If one digs a little deeper than the surface impression, one sees that (except perhaps for the Japanese and the Chinese) the intellectual devastation is more or less complete. The book trade for instance is completely dominated by the publishing houses of London and New York. So is the media, in which the brown and the black must give enormous attention to the activities of the white, including the failed marriage of the Prince of Wales with his Princess. But there are more insidious collapses: the question of law, medical therapy, educational innovation, academic work, economic management, development theory, agricultural research, or human rights; in all these spheres, we are led by the nose by the intellectual class of the West since our eyes were effectively punctured several decades ago. Even the nice critics of the unwanted and undesirable aspects of policies in these areas are located in the West.
>
> "As Ashis Nandy has said, both the game and the game rules are set by the West, so even the opposition must be in the same language and vocabulary of the West, for the West is still the ultimate arbiter of categories. Debate, if it is carried out, must be in terms of these categories or is not legitimate. There is no political space available for non-players."[9]

Gandhiji's resistance was not only against British imperialism but a civilizational revolt and swadeshi militancy. These bear upon the politics and philosophy of human rights. The demand for a new information order

8 Paper presented at the *International Conference on Rethinking Human Rights,* held at Kuala Lumpur in December 1994.

9 Paper presented by Claude Alvares at the International Seminar noted above.

by Asian countries also springs from this sense of subjugation even in so universal an issue as human rights. How forcefully Alvares drives home his view is seen from the following:

> "500 years ago, there was scarcely and intellectual domination of one society by another society's intellectuals. Today, that scenario stands dramatically altered: the intellectual elite of the one-sixth dominates the conditions of life of the rest of humankind, decides what is good for it, what it should do, how it ought to organize its affairs, what kinds of seeds it ought to plant.
>
> "In his seminal book, *Orientalism*, Edward Said argued that one consequence of the domination of the non-Western world was the creation of an entire political discourse which he dubbed 'the corporate institution for dealing with the Orient—dealing with it by making statements about it, authorizing views on it, describing it, by teaching it, settling it ruling over it: in short, Orientalism as a Western style for dominating, restructuring and having authority over the Orient.
>
> "So even if knowledge is power, power is also knowledge. Power decides knowledge. Those without power are not permitted to either decide knowledge or legitimate it. We know from our own culture in India, for instance, that the Brahmin was the source of knowledge, while others could only be recipients, and still others were considered unfit even to receive. Knowledge reflects power, it reflects interests, specifically a culture's interests."[10]

For America, for instance, the human rights ploy is a strategy of foreign policy and more important than hunger in the coloured continents is lesbianism and homo. Listen to Claude Levi Strauss who says:

> "Anthropology is not a dispassionate science like astronomy, which springs from the contemplation of things at a distance. It is the outcome of a historical process which has made the larger part of mankind subservient to the other, and during which millions of innocent human beings have had their resources plundered and their institutions and beliefs destroyed, whilst they themselves were ruthlessly killed, thrown into bondage, and contaminated by diseases they were unable to resist."[11]

Are the coloured humans mere commodities as the war-time comfort girls were or the Negro named Dred Scott was treated long ago by Chief Justice Taney of the U.S. Supreme Court? Says Claude:

> "We have become things; things do not have rights. Take, as an apt illustration, the latest industry that is being glamourized across the planet: tourism. It does little but convert the third world, its people, its nature into things to be handled, abused, consumed and photographed."[12]

The boys and girls sexually tortured in Goa for Western tourist attraction is a horror story pending as a case in the Court. Even tourism from the North is potential violation of human dignity. Claude continues:

10 *Ibid.*
11 *Ibid.*
12 *Ibid.*

> "I hope to demonstrate the Western science and technology and the form of intellectual hegemony they represent are the biggest threats to human rights across the planet, not human rights as narrowly defined by Western liberal regimes, but human rights as we define them. I will argue that the global domination of the West through its science and technology regime in fact provides the West with an innocuous but effective instrument for depriving the five-sixths of their human rights in an absolute sense."[13]

No doubt, the battles for democratisation waged in the West improved the human condition. While the economic North has enslaved the South, the Universal Declaration of 1948 is a big step forward. But don't cipherise other cultures like the village panchayats of India or the concept of Ummah in Islam and bully Asia, using human rights aggressiveness.

Western science and human rights

The scientific revolution marks the watershed of a new imperium, the control of humanity by the imperium of technology virtually annihilating folk knowledge and arts, folk medicine and traditional wisdom, demonetised as obscurantism by the dictatorship of modern science and Western dominance. 'Progress' is thus monopolised and common people's native skills jettisoned so as to impose a new slavery and accusation of inefficiency, based on the omnipotence of modern science and its alleged excellence. Thus the very concept of 'development' has been westernised and native, primitive assets bastardized. Universal Human Rights and democracy have thus written off the native acquisitions of centuries in the name of high technology, throwing out of employment and drowning in indignity millions of humans, mostly Asians with their ancient cultures (of which they were brain-washed to be ashamed). *Technology* versus the *people* is death sentence on the human rights of rural and tribal billions. Claude Alvares contends:

> "Millions of people, hundreds of communities, from fisherfolk in the fishing industry to the tribals in forests, have had their human rights extinguished, precisely because the state has ruled that development must be based on modern science and technology. This is the core of the human rights problem generated by the imposition of Western science and technology.
>
> "The modern state's prime interest in such development is because of its potential for compromising, eroding and often times, severely diminishing personal or group autonomy, and the creativity that goes with it. Once epistemologic rights are denied, the state can proceed to use so-called scientific criteria to supplant such rights by officially defined needs.
>
> Therefore the state's continuing drive for newer and newer technologies, even as the earlier ones create more poverty and unemployment. Both the superchip of the electronic age, and biotechnology's boasts of superproduction, are basically set to further concentrate the production process in fewer hands, to be directed by even fewer minds. If the majority of the population is to be rendered redundant, then God damn them. They have been rendered

13 *Ibid.*

redundant already at the market stage, they need to be rendered redundant now at the planning stage, and later, at the resource use stage. Their resources, or rather, the resources they survive on now, must sooner or later be made available for the superior processing of the supermachines. And who will be there to argue against the need for further efficiency in an age of looming scarcity?"[14]

What is 'efficiency' in a system of economics where the human being matters? For, human rights are for humans, not machines or micro-chips. The enormous energy of draft animals and biogas in India is discarded and poor Gandhi dismissed as primitive and the country bankrupted by imported oil bills! Is this efficient management of resources? Indian pharmacopoeia and even yogic cures are ridiculed and Western medicines at astronomical prices are forced on the East using new patent laws, the Paris Convention and the GATT and W.T.O. Alvares argues:

"The very definition of 'efficiency' has been changed by 'power'. What we normally understand by 'efficiency' is explained in a simple example given by Felix Paturi. He wrote: 'For 50 harvested energy units, the American farmer invests 250 fuel energy units, the Chinese farmer only a single unit of human energy. This means simply that the primitive countryman of the East works at an efficiency rate of 5000 per cent, and the U.S. farmer equipped with the most advanced technical aids, at an efficiency rate of only 20 per cent.' However, it is American agribusiness that is being promoted and expanded all across the globe. Why?"[15]

The deprivation of human rights by the Corporate Power of the North is via technology and corruption, condemning indigenous methods and processes as primitive or inefficient:

"The arrogance of modern science leads it to actively replace alternate descriptions with its own. While both science and technology become the driving force behind the market, they must actively distrust a market place of cosmologies.

"Democracy without intellectual rights, however, is an empty gift. In principle, every one has rights but when science is invoked, all lose their rights except if they are wealthy and powerful. Dams, nuclear reactors, large industries have more secure rights than the millions of unprivileged people who must make way for them."[16]

So far as India is concerned this intellectual dependency was injected by Macaulay who invented an exotic educational system alienating the people from themselves. It was this cultural debasing syndrome that was opposed by Mahatma Gandhi in *Hind Swaraj*.

"In that slim book, Gandhi declared that modern civilization—or bourgeois civil society organized according to the English pattern—was a foul way of going about the business of living even for the English. He ended up declaring

14 *Ibid.*
15 *Ibid.*
16 *Ibid.*

that banishment to Andaman and Nicobar Islands was not enough punishment for anyone who did anything to propagate European civilization elsewhere. Today, this superstructure is more effectively in place than during his time!"[17]

Our Europology (which includes America) is the Asian pathology *vis-a-vis* human rights. The battle for human rights in the East necessitates war against hi-tech. W.T.O. and the distorted demoniac ideology of 'development' and progress. Ask Medha Patkar, the victims of Narmada displacement, Sundarlal Bahuguna and the Tehri Dam victims how the right to life is ransom for Western model development.

Other experiments in regional charters

It may be mentioned as a progressive trend holding out hope for the future that regional instruments like the Organisation of American States, the Council of Europe, Organisation of African Unity and Conference on Security and Co-operation in Europe, the Helsinki Final Act etc. strengthen the universe of human rights region-wise and reinforcement-wise. The world moves on and agitations and campaigns for mafia groups and vested interests clash and never stand still. The right to development, to clean environment, ecological integrity and conditions of life in safety have also been discussed and provisions made under the auspices of the United Nations. In short, today we have a world where humanity has expressed concern over peace, security, justice and pursuit of happiness. It is in this broad perspective that each country or continent has to make viable provisions for the *dharma* of human rights.

A survey of the UN Instruments with its Covenants, Conventions, Declarations, Basic Principles, Guidelines and the like is so impressive, especially when it deals with helpless categories like refugees, migrant workers, persons with mental illness, religious, ethnic and linguistic minorities and persons potentially liable to suffer enforced disappearances and victims of state vengeance and torture. Among the most meaningful regional instruments is that relating to the Council of Europe which is a paradigm for other Continents. Africa and America have organisations relating to human rights, but Asia has none, which is a tragic failure, although some countries have human rights laws. Of course, there are efforts at setting up, through an Asian Charter of human rights, a similar regional body. The destination is distances away, but the desirability argues for urgent action. In this context, it is good to emphasise that Charters of Human Rights should not prove to be printed futility. As Jefferson long ago mentioned: "The execution of laws is more important than the making of them". It follows that the enforceability of human rights in Asia, as elsewhere, must claim our foremost concern, if despair is not to make the masses fatally impotent or dangerously violent.

Asia, an ancient continent without a Human Rights Charter, must recall its great past and cultural heritage. Let us, in the light of developments in Europe, Africa and America, consider the possibility

17 *Ibid.*

of working on the basic principles to be fleshed out in good time as an Asian Bill of Rights, harmonising with world thought at its humanist best. We are a poor continent rich in value legacy, the home of noble religions but with obscurantist obduracy neglecting their spiritual essence. We have natural and human resources but struggle against foreign exploitation, humiliation and many brands of colonisation, even dehumanisation of women, Pol Pot brand of human extermination and Mao extreme of cultural vandalism. Wars have taught us the dangers of national debility and the urgency of an economic regeneration to meet the basic needs of our most populous penurious humanity.

Economic foundations of human rights

Franklin Roosevelt, way back in 1944, urged that:

> "Basic essential to peace is a decent standard of living for all individual men and women and children in all nations. Freedom from fear is eternally linked with freedom from want. ......
>
> We have come to a clear realization of the fact that true individual freedom cannot exist without economic security and independence. 'Necessitous men are not free men'. People who are hungry and out of a job are the stuff of which dictatorships are made."[18]

What Roosevelt then called a second Bill of Rights may well be regarded as an embryonic basis for an Asian Charter. Among the vital items he listed are:

> "The right to a useful and remunerative job in the industries, or shops or farms or mines of the Nation;
>
> The right to earn enough to provide adequate food and clothing and recreation;
>
> The right of every farmer to raise and sell his products at a return which will give him and his family a decent living;
>
> The right of every businessman, large and small, to trade in an atmosphere of freedom from unfair competition and domination by monopolies at home or abroad;
>
> The right of every family to a decent home;
>
> The right to adequate medical care and the opportunity to achieve and enjoy good health;
>
> The right to adequate protection from the economic fears of old age, sickness, accident, and unemployment;
>
> The right to a good education."[19]

Alas, the grinding Asian indigence is so piteous, beneath the creamy glamour of a layer of largesse and beneficence the M.N.Cs have created to win Judases and infiltrate and extract Asian resources, that the pan-

18 *Human Rights Reader*—Edited by Walter Laqueur & Barry Rubin at page 313.
19 *Ibid*, page 313.

Asian flag of human rights, in united strength, must fly defiant of reactionary forces. The living conditions of the masses, the marginalised and invisibly victimised are steadily worsening. The purchasing power of the vast poverty sector has collapsed; but official economists and soulless statistics experts have their own esoteric jargon to hide reality behind acronyms, and those who wield power in the East often are opium eaters of West is Best. Poverty and lack of human dignity, hand in hand with malnutrition, disease and death, stalk the lands of Asia but even the media and the Parties suffer from myopia and so, there are two societies in each country, one hugely harrowing, the other seemingly drunk making fast bucks and happy with self-centered hedonism.

Economic foundations of human rights have always been emphasised as emerging from *faith in the dignity of man* and equality among men and women without which civil and political rights are but balderdash.

Let me divagate to emphasize, on behalf of Asian cultures, that human rights are no heuristic gift of the West as some scholars like Charles E. Wyzauski Jr. claim. They refute, with noetic assertiveness, that the Ancient World, be it Oriental or Egyptian, Babylonian, Greek or Roman, had no notion of human rights and some misty ideas came from Stoics, Cicero, St. Thomas Aquinos and Dante but they were not essentially human rights. Human Rights emerged first and clearly from the religious struggle in the period "from Gerson to Grotius". Locke, they argue, was source of our doctrines of human rights. Another stream which underscored the economic foundation of human rights, according to Western pundits, is Karl Marx, who as early as 1845 attacked the notion of natural rights, but recognised that most of the political and civil rights were meaningless unless the people had economic justice as a springboard for other human rights. All these West-soaked thinkers are blissfully innocent of *dharma* in ancient India and of the precepts of the Buddha, more than 2500 years ago prescribing *Karuna* (Compassion), *Samata* (Equality), and *Pragna* (Enlightened discernment). Other greats who have stood for social justice in the East are aplenty. Political and economic rights, binding even on Kings, were Indian, not borrowed. The West was oblivious of the East and its great advances. Let us, however, not forget the universality of human values which links the past with the present.

In the Asian perspective, any charter of human rights must affirm economic and social development as a necessary condition for the full realisation of human rights. This theme inevitably emerges from the many pronouncements of the UN (*vide* the Universal Declaration of Human Rights Arts. 22-23-25-28 *et al*) relating, as they do, to economic, social and allied requisites. Freedom from hunger is stressed in Art. 11(2) even as an adequate standard of living is emphasised in Art. 11(1) of the International Covenant. The retarded nations of Asia (and Africa) can never develop unless economic rights are actualised. This is a universal obligation where the West should adopt a developmental ethic whereby the deficiencies of Afro-Asian nations are made good. Regrettably, foreign corporations, far from doing fair trade with underdeveloped Asians, fleece them, including their natural resources such as minerals, their agricultural labour turned into cheap commodities like coffee, tea, cocoa, bananas and sugar. The new economic offensive launched by the North under U.S. hegemony has worsened the situation with Asia, including India, losing much in the trade bargain. What with the GATT treaties and the W.T.O., 'free trade' is a false phrase as the game is played on an uneven playing field. The process is unjust.

> "The toil of countless workers at cheap wages is imported to the rich countries in the form of raw materials or primary products, particularly agricultural products. 'Free trade' is allowed between private importers who bargain from the strength of a rich economy, and private exporters who are part of the weakness of a poor economy."

Privatisation, the new *mantra,* obviously stands for private profit.

"Private exporters in poor countries are not responsible for the well-being of their people. Their interest is to have a margin between what they pay to local producers and workers, and the price they get from foreign importers. They continue to do a good business, at any level of prices and wages, unintentionally retarding economic development and social improvement."[20]

We reach a world of paradoxes and perversities where surpluses exist in the rich countries while two-thirds of mankind suffer from scarcities of nearly everything. Deeper studies reveal the pathetic plight of Asian masses. Human rights in their plenary fulfilment require economic and social development.

> India is one of the unfortunate countries which faces—
>
> "Capital flight and its resulting economic, political and social impact. Capital flight may also reflect money laundering activities resulting from criminal activities such as drugs and arms smuggling and white collar crimes.
>
> "There are many techniques used to expedite capital flight and a significant amount of research has resulted in detailed explanations of capital flight techniques and in estimates of its magnitude. One technique that can be used to move significant amounts of capital out of a country is the over-invoicing of imports and the under-invoicing of exports."[1]

The above study based on American data reveals capital flight from India to the United States through abnormal pricing like over-invoicing and under-invoicing. The authors of the study conclude:

> "Our estimates India's capital flight to the United States during 1993 range from a maximum of $ 4,423 Million to our most conservative estimate of $ 870 Million. Our analysis only considers trade-pricing abnormalities in India-United States trade, and the analysis of trade pricing between India and other

20 *Human Rights Reader*—Edited by Walter Laqueur & Barry Rubin at pages 330-331.

1 *Capital Flight from India to the United States Through Abnormal Pricing in International Trade*—A Study by 3 American Professors dated 5-12-'94.

> countries may also reveal similar levels of capital outflows. Based on our estimates of capital flight from India to the United States, the economic benefits of detecting and deterring the abnormal transaction prices, related to these capital outflows, appears to be substantial."[2]

Small wonder, the bankruptcy of the Indian economy and consequential pauperisation of the Indian masses can be attributed in good measure to the dubious, even fraudulent, management of India's exim policy manipulated by a certain brand of business mafia, the State politicos and bureaucracy blinking at and abetting the plot.

There is sound ground for and feasibility of an Asian Human Rights Charter. Perhaps Asia—Pacific may be a region with sufficient similarities and affinities to justify a common human rights code and related institutions. A small group of activists mooted this idea in Osaka, Japan at the end of June 1992. Drafts were prepared and the final version was titled Human Rights in Asia. The struggle for Human Dignity was endorsed by around 230 N.G.Os from 20 countries of the region.

> "This collective voice from Asia proves that at the level of citizens groups there are concerns and commitments pertaining to human dignity and social justice which transcend ethic, cultural, religious and national boundaries. It is this common concern and common commitment which serves as bond uniting the diverse peoples of Asia."[3]

Such is the nucleus of a Charter. Why an Asian Charter? Geographical proximity and similarities, cultural and other argue for such a Charter as exist in other continents. Dr. Chandra Muzaffar (Director, Just World Trust) tells us many reasons:

> "A holistic, integrated approach to human rights within the Asian context would demand urgent and equal attention to the economic and social rights of the people of the continent. For Asia is where the majority of the world's poor live. In spite of the economic and social progress achieved in various countries, a significant segment of Asia's population does not enjoy some of the most basic economic and social rights—including the right to adequate food, clothing and housing, the right to work, to fair wages, to health, to education.
>
> "Indeed, in some parts of Asia, poverty is so severe that the poor have become trapped in contemporary forms of 'slavery' such as bonded labour, child labour and child prostitution. Poverty is also one of the direct causes of the cruel exploitation of female labour in certain sectors of the economy.
>
> "Even when the incidence of absolute poverty has been reduced, the gap between 'haves' and 'have-nots' appears to be getting wider especially in societies where wealth and power are increasingly concentrated in the hands of the elites. Elite-oriented development of this sort marginalises a significant

2 *Ibid.*

3 Preface to the Book *"Human Rights in Asia"*, published by the Just World Trust, Penang 1992.

segment of society. It also leads to environmental degradation which in turn affects adversely the economic and social rights of present and future generations.

"The situation is made worse when emphasis is given to military expenditure in the national budget. There are many societies is Asia where the growth of militarism has deprived the masses of their basic human rights, including their economic and social rights.

"While the denial and deprivation of economic and social rights is a matter of grave concern, Asian N.G.Os are equally distressed by the gross violation of the civil and political rights of people in the region. Most of the time, it is the State that is responsible for this. This is especially true of military dictatorships and States with marked authoritarian characteristics. Extrajudicial executions, involuntary disappearances, torture, detention without trial or charge, and the use of emergency regulations and security laws are not uncommon. There are also cases where activists championing the cause of human dignity and social justice are subjected to harassment and intimidation. In some instances, they are banished from their country or forced into exile or even physically eliminated. All this shows that in various parts of Asia there is very little tolerance of political dissent."[4]

Besides these factors, armed conflicts mar the peace of societies in many Asian nations. Thousands of civilian casualties and explosions of refugees from unfortunate Asian countries suffer untold sorrows, hungry and shelterless. Treated as the Third World, the West is dumping its yuppie life-style, yankee culture and mega-projects on the creamy layers, impoverishing, displacing and marginalizing the humble masses in the bargain and robbing the continent's riches in the name of investing in high technology.

Ethnic conflicts erode cultural integrity of communities; and macro-projects, fobbed off as developmental wonders, endanger indigenous tribes with deep roots and lovely traditions. Land rights of whole communities wither away because of State victimisation to enrich Kulaks, M.N.Cs and corrupt politicos.

"At stake, are not just the cultural but also the economic, social, civil and political rights of whole collectivities. There are also groups within societies—like the Dalits of India and the Buraku of Japan—subjected to long centuries of discrimination and oppression who are struggling to assert their collective dignity. Even in the case of women, often victims of gender discrimination and outmoded cultural and religious practices; their primary quest is to secure their full rights as a community of human beings.

"More specifically, women as a collectivity want to be seen and accepted as people with the capacity to decide and to act on their own behalf. They want equal access to resources and the political, economic and social support to develop their full potential as human beings. To secure their legitimate rights as a collective group, women realise that there are formidable obstacles in

4 *Ibid*, pages 1-2.

almost every sphere of society which have to be overcome in the interest of equality and justice.

"Collective rights in Asia have yet another meaning. Within the international system, the Asian state in often forced to articulate the collective rights of its citizens in the face of glaring global iniquities. Since the international system allows a privileged minority in the North to control and dominate the rest of humanity, it circumscribes the rights of the people of the South, a huge portion of whom are in Asia. The people in most of Asia have very little freedom to determine their own destinies in an international system dominated by institutions directed by the elite of the North such as the United Nations Security Council, the Group of Seven, the International Monetary Fund (I.M.F.), the World Bank and the General Agreement on Tariffs and Trade (GATT)."[5]

Asia, South America and Africa have suffered from Reaganism and rollback. The rollback strategy, the favourite of the Republican Party of the U.S. set out to dismantle socialist tendencies in the world and the Public Sector thus came in for liquidation by American Operation (via) foreign policy and economic devices using the I.M.F. and the World Bank as handy tools.

At the Algiers Non-aligned Summit of 1973, the Group of 77 urged political unity and policy perspective to gain economic self-sufficiency by campaigns in the UN General Assembly and elsewhere for the Declaration on the Establishment of a New International Economic Order. This was red rag for the Reaganites. Malaysian Prime Minister Mahathir Bin Mohamad and other Asian leaders told the General Assembly, that "all the unclaimed wealth is the common heritage of mankind". This claim enraged the Reaganites who considered most Third World Governments objectionably interventionist and protectionist. Countries like India with a socialistic approach to the problems of poverty and unemployment were the focus of M.N.C. fury. Inevitably, the White House used the Bank-Fund instrumentalities towards *structural adjustments* through loaded loans. Asian countries, like other victim nations, resisted these moves.

"But with the eruption of the Third World debt crisis in mid-1982, a grand opportunity was presented to the Reaganite agenda of resubordinating the South via structural adjustment. As more and more Third World countries ran into greater difficulties servicing the huge loans made to them by Northern banks in the 1970s, the U.S. and the Bretton Woods institutions, John Sheahan notes, took advantage of 'the period of financial strain to insist that debtor countries remove the Government from the economy as the price of getting credit."

*** *** ***

"World Bank and IMF funds to assist the indebted countries make their interest payments promised on condition that they adopted 'economic policies along Reaganomic lines—privatization of state enterprises, an end to subsidies, opening the economies to foreign investment'. In the debtors' view, notes

5 *Ibid*, pages, 2-3.

> Lissakers, 'the proposed reforms.........went much further than the standard IMF nostrums on devaluation, reductions in public-sector borrowing requirement and control over the money supply, and decontrol of wages and prices', and were tantamount to putting the national patrimony on the block."
>
> *** *** ***
>
> "Indeed, with over 70 Third World countries submitting to I.M.F. and World Bank programs in the 1980s, stabilization, structural adjustment, and shock therapy managed from distant Washington became the common condition of the South in that decade."[6]

India, a leader of the non-aligned movement and inclined for a fabian socialist model of development was forced to restructure its economy forcing on it the structural adjustment strategy. Most of Asia succumbed to rollback and the new Social Order was a reversal of the Nehru vision, the Indian Constitution and the success of the Dark Victory of Reaganomics. In sum, Asian economies by and large fell to multinationals, thus defeating the economic and social foundation of Human Rights. The dialectic of the contemporary economic contradictions compels search for common action platforms based on regional pacts by lesser nations in a struggle to gain a fair share of the work, wealth and happiness of humanity on terms of distributive justice lest they be vulnerable to M.N.C. Operations supported by Super Power policies. Necessarily, for mutual advantage and in common interest, the sacred regions team up and organise in flexible structures. The challenge of our times is whether Third World countries can finish as vibrant societies or vanquished colonies. Will they end up even more firmly in the grip of M.N.Cs, the free-booting Frankenstein's monsters? To be or not to be, that is the question.

The very survival of Asian peoples is imperilled by military interventions by the North, particularly the United States. Many proxy wars are fought in Asia and the South, wiping out many millions of humans. Vietnam, for instance, was carpet-bombed, its people and resources subjected to terror and horror unknown in this half-century. And ultimately, the super-culprit, Robert McNamara, quietly pleaded guilty before history of this crime against humanity as Washington's mistake.

These salient grounds are good enough for an Asian Charter like in Europe and elsewhere. The Asian Human Rights Commission, based in Hong Kong, has published the draft of an Asian Charter titled 'Our Common Humanity'. It has a comprehensive Preamble and statement of principles but is vague, yet valuable, in the proposed mechanisms and remedial resources. Asia, the largest continent with the oldest cultures and religions and the longest history of spiritual triumphs and human tragedies, cannot be orphaned without a human rights charter.

There are several unhappy features which render the human rights of Asian peoples vulnerable. For instance, freedom of information, a

6 Walden Bello: *Dark Victory* (Pluto Press 1994) pages 28, 29 and 31.

factor which is fundamental to fundamental rights, is denied in most Asian countries. Likewise, in many parts of Asia those who are labelled "subversives" but are battlers for a better social order, are subjected to torture, inhuman treatment, cruel and degrading punishment, women and children victimised to rape, sexual abuses etc., dissenters sent to secret detention cells, inter-rogation chambers and forced camps which still exist in Asia, in measure qualitatively and quantitatively more than in the West. Pol Pot in Kampuchea is proof of Asian harshness.

The decline and fall of fundamental freedoms, the retreat of respect for the dignity and worth of the human person and the *de facto* reversal, with cover-up double-speak, of not only civil and political but also economic, social and cultural rights, make a mirage of the triune international Bill of Human Rights—the Universal Declaration and the two Covenants. The Asia-Pacific region is more vulnerable to Operation Illusion, what with the financially feeble, structurally fragile N.G.Os to oversee and expose violations, the indigent, inhibited have-not humanity without the means to gain access to remedies, and the blockage of international invigilation of human rights based on the xenophobic cult of 'domestic jurisdiction'.

If Asia on the quantum leap, with the locomotive of the rule of law, is to redeem its tryst with human rights destiny, the legal bugle must stridently blow and the battle for Human Rights, Asia-Pacific-specific, must be waged and won with new perspectives, strategies, infrastructures and empowerments within the global parameters enshrined in the United Nations Charter—not a copycat imitation of Western versions. The pharmacopoeia of Asian social justice must cope with poverty-based pandemic pathology, their manifestations being subject to cultural variations. The First World, however, has no pontifical power to lay down prescriptions and proscriptions while itself violating the great Covenants and other instruments and shall not play the global gendarmerie with oblique objectives and market-capture motivations. (President Carter may be a pure soul, but crypto-commercial forces in the U.S. use his human-rights foreign policy to good trade account! Even now they do.) The Asian human person's claim to fundamental freedoms cannot be diminished by the misleading propaganda that I.M.F.—World Bank—M.N.C. troika can make Asia a paradise by their exploitative 'developmental' boasts of material advance and baskets of bankrupting loans, Asian human rights suffer because of U.S. economic infiltration.

If I may repeat myself to make a case for an Asian Charter, let us, in a mood of realism, note a few other poignant factors. Human rights perish where armed conflicts flourish. Today, Asia is a theatre of local wars, internecine strifes and butchery galore of civilians a la Pol Pot. Refugees pour in; homeless innocents and displaced communities mount in numbers as casualties of human rights violations. Ethnic cleansing and religious confrontations break up the cultural integrity of homogeneous people. Mega-development projects, egged on by foreign funding and corrupt intermediaries, disrupt the dignity and displace the community of indigenous groups.

The voice of Asian solidarity, notwithstanding discordance, can be heard, as Prof. Yash Ghai of Hong Kong insists, although China seeks shelter under the "domestic jurisdiction" plea. An encapsulated version of the argument runs thus:

> "The national treatment of human rights is no concern of other states or the international community to intervene in domestic situations to redress violations. In its 'White Paper', Human Rights in China (1991), the Chinese Government stated that 'Despite its international aspect, the issue of human rights falls by and large within the sovereignty of each state'. The Chinese delegation to the UN Commission of Human Rights at its meeting in February 1993 urged that the World Conference in Vienna should "reiterate the principle of state sovereignty contained in the UN Charter and international law which is the basis for the realisation of human rights."

The Chinese White Paper again argues:

> "Another element in the official view is the relativity of rights, determined by the economic and political circumstances of each country,......the evolution of the situation in regard to human rights is circumscribed by the historical, social, economic and cultural conditions of various nations, and involves a process of historical development. Owing to tremendous differences in historical background, social system, cultural tradition and economic development, countries differ in their understanding and practice of human rights."

The universal factor cannot be ignored under guise of 'relativity.'

A controversial assertion which other Asians may not share fully is made by Singapore. Its White Paper reads:

> "Disputing the proposition that values are universal and common to all mankind, it states that there is a major difference between Asian and Western values in the balance each strikes between the individual and the community; Asian societies emphasise the interests of the community, while Western societies stress the rights of the individual. The Singapore society has always weighted group interests more heavily than individual ones. This balance has strengthened social cohesion, and enabled Singaporeans to pull together to surmount difficult challenges collectively, more successfully than other societies. An emphasis on the community has been a key survival value for Singapore.
>
> "The core values of Asian society are identified as placing society above self, upholding the family as the building block of society, and resolving major issues through consensus instead of contention."

Our common human rights enemy in Asia is the GATT and recolonisation by G-7 economic domination. Corporate Power holds the law at bay and corporate crime proves the law powerless. The soft States of Asia may even be bribed. The giant corporations have no body to be burnt, no soul to be damned, no morals to worry, no spiritual sensitivity to lose. M.N.C. methods are unprincipled and there is no code of conduct for them, not even jurisdiction over their home assets when they play havoc with lives in foreign lands. The Union Carbide Corporation escaped substantially because of the Indian law's inability to reach their culpable directors after causing the world's worst industrial disaster. We must provide for statutory control over M.N.Cs before entry into our countries to protect people's rights and environment. But the West will protest and human rights flag will fly low. Asia must fight for human rights of Asians against Western business domination.

For the present, one may conclude by saying that the Universal Declaration of Human Rights will gain in awareness and implementation if an Asian Charter charted by Asian N.G.Os were fashioned. Asian peoples must be mobilised and now is the time for a jurisprudence of human rights consonant with world values and conditioned by cultural complexities without giving in on fundamentals.

10

THE DIMENSIONS OF THE RIGHT TO DEVELOPMENT AS A HUMAN RIGHT

CREATION, IN OUR mysterious universe, has a purpose often beyond our comprehension, but the very glory of the process and presence of homo sapiens on our planet—the story of the 'descent of man' and the 'origin of the species'—argues that, veiled from human eyes, evolution has been unfolding and the human status is but an intermediate chapter and the drama of development towards man's higher destiny, beyond all disguises, is his divine destination. What once was a hairy quadruped, arboreal in its simian habits, is now moving, amidst struggles, towards supramental achievements. The supreme secret of Creation is Development. So it is that through seeming battles for survival, Man, in his search for the sublime future, claims the fundamental Right to Development as the driving force of his very raison d'etre. If we listen to Charles Darwin a materialist version of this thesis will unveil itself. He says:

> "It is interesting to contemplate an entangled bank, clothed with many plants of many kinds, with birds singing on the bushes, with various insects flitting about, and with worms crawling through the damp earth, and to reflect that these elaborately constructed forms, so different from each other, and dependent upon each other in so complex a manner, have all been produced by laws acting around us."

This developmental continuum is perennially progressive and life rises to higher forms and fuller manifestations. This philosophic foundation for the human right to development is the beginning of the *Declaration on the Right to Development* adopted by General Assembly resolution of 4th December 1986. The discovery of the Self and of the infinite human potential dwelling in each is the finest expression of the Right to Development.

Let us begin on a high note. Swami Vivekananda, that cyclonic sadhu with a cosmic vision, defined education as the manifestation of the perfection already in man and religion as the manifestation of the divinity already in man. (By man, of course, he meant every human being). If perfection is the human potential and divinity his immortal essence, human rights, in their fullness and richness, must mean the plenary unfolding of the human personality. Indeed, in society the Robinson Crusoe paradigm is non-existent; and so, the collective personality of a community, with its distinctive culture, ethos and other conditions of collective life, must also be considered while measuring the quantum and quality of human development. The central point is that human rights focus on the human person since the locus is not material wealth but the human being. The purpose of Development, as the Cocoyoc Declaration has emphasised, should not be to develop *things*, but to develop man (every human person).

It is apposite to stress that: "with a few notable exceptions, development has been pragmatic pursuits, aimed, for the most part, at the multiplication of and insatiable chase for material wealth. Basic values such as justice, cooperation, charity, compassion and respect for nature have not only been subordinated to hedonism but are often trampled underfoot in the gold rush."

Values are implicit in the new development models of the West imitated now by the rest. In addition, there are two general statements which explicitly offer a framework of values. The first is the Cocoyoc declaration, adopted in October 1974, by a symposium convened by UNEP and UNCTAD, on patterns of resource use, environment and development strategies. This is one of the most balanced, enlightened and humane statements on the goals of development. The next project is contained in UNESCO's medium-term plan for 1977-82, officially adopted in 1977. "The UNESCO plan puts forward the idea of 'endogenous development', planned and carried out by each nation in line with its own choices and in accordance with the authentic values, aspirations and motives of its people. The values that inspired development in the early years were exogenous—imposed by or copied from outside from the West, whether capitalist or communist. What is needed is a new, authentic style of development emerging from within each culture, inspired by values derived from the people's deepest roots."

* * *

"Development must be designed, even at the humblest level, as a process of ensuring the advancement of man through his own endeavours, 'says UNESCO. The multiplication of material wealth has to be dethroned as the purpose of development. The goal of development should be not to develop things, but to develop man', says Cocoyoc. 'Development must be aimed at the spiritual, moral and material advancement of the whole human being, both as a member of society and from the point of view of individual fulfilment,' says UNESCO. For example, the right to work, Cocoyoc suggest, involves 'not simply having a job but finding self-realisation in work,' and implies the right not to be alienated by production processes that use human beings as tools.

"The model of development as material growth gets most of its fuel from the Third World's desire to close the wealth gap with the West, in a possessions race almost as futile as the arms race. The Cocoyoc participants rejected the idea of gaps: 'The goal is not to catch up, but to ensure the quality of life for all'. A primary aim, naturally, was to meet the basic human needs of the poorest. But once these 'inner limits' had been passed, mankind had to

> beware of overstepping the 'outer limits' set by the worlds resources and ecologic balances. A certain minimum of consumption had to be guaranteed for all—but there was also a maximum, set by the carrying capacity of the biosphere, and by man's own limited ability to absorb material goods without damage to his physical or mental health. This part of the Cocoyoc declaration was addressed primarily to the West, but it also has a lesson for the elites of the Third World."[1]

The West German Constitution of 1949 provides, in Art. 2(1) that everyone shall have the right to the free development of his personality in so far as he does not violate the rights of others or offend against the Constitutional Order or the moral code. We cannot commoditise personhood in its developmental dimension but must humanise, divinise and holistically conceptualize it if we are to do justice to the grand idea of Development as a Human Right. In this context, we can discern the distortion and deception of the materialist view of progress and the loftier perception of self-fulfilment as the true appreciation of the human ascent towards its high destination. More plainly put, not possession of goods and pride of acquisitions but inner contentment and *joy of being* and realisation of life's meaning, that beats the wild excitements and fitful fever of restless cravings, which makes life a noble earthly span of self-fulfilment; so a paradigm shift is the imperative of a good life.

Jigme Singhye Wangchuck, in profound brevity, expressed it thus:

> "We consider the per capita contentment of people the yardstick of development. Gross national happiness is more important than gross national product."

The dangers of overemphasis of 'gourmand'goals at the expense of higher satisfactions was felicitously spelt out by Martin Luther King Jr.:

> "The means by which we live have outdistanced the ends for which we live. Our scientific power has outrun our spiritual power. We have guided missiles and misguided men."

A possible misunderstanding must be cleared, since social and economic conditions of life do matter, balanced pleasures have a place and mortification and stern austerity are denials which cannot be confused with achievement of human rights. A spiritually sensitive, socially satisfying, economically acceptable culture, where justice to all is integral to the World Human Order, is the desideratum, a 'consummation devoutly be wished'. The process of development as a human right has a wider community orientation. This nexus, in its universal amplitude, is the spirit, source and strength of the Universal Declaration of Human Rights passed by the United Nations Assembly without a single dissent. Herbert Spencer's words are a warning:

> "No one can be perfectly free till all are free; no one can be perfectly moral till all are moral; no one can be perfectly happy till all are happy."

1 Paul Harrison: *The Third World Tomorrow*, at pages 40-41.

This sharing and caring dimension, the ancient Indian mission of *Vasudhaiva Kutumvakam* (every one in the world is our kith and kin), the compassion that the Buddha preached, the love and concern for your neighbour (everyone on earth is a neighbour of the other) preached by Jesus Christ, the world brotherhood conceived by Prophet Mohammad and the grand, global humanism which Bertrand Russell and Einstein and other great thinkers advocated, bring out the finer facets of Development as a human advance.

The Right to Development asserts itself through due perspectives inaugurating new historic ages. Mankind had had many dramatic and traumatic revolutions. Each of these revolutionary discoveries has resulted in a paradigm shift. The paradigm shift is a radical originality in our way of thinking about problems that face society. The Newton paradigm governed for a time but then came revolutionary rethinking through Einstein's special theory of relativity. Thus humanity including every member was effected by new paradigm, new perspectives, new ideologies and new quantum leaps towards the final reach. This proposition is working even today by an active principle of change which can be catalyzed only by the Right to Development we invest in every person and every community.

Development of personality and society is greatly distorted by the ultra-modern predilections and sensual pursuits based on the heady technology which drugs our whole generation. What an opium which retards development and promotes addiction.'

Will Durant, the great American philosopher, has pointed out:

> "The rate, complexity, and variety of change in our time are without precedent, even in Periclean days; all forms about us are altered, from the tools that complicate our toil, and the wheels that whirl us restlessly about the earth, to the innovations in our sexual relationships, and the hard disillusionment of our souls."[2]

We can be worthy of ourselves only if we spell out a lofty Manifesto of the Human Person charged with a new feeling, new direction, new value imperatives. Our patented technology, controlled mostly by transnational companies and unguided by higher consciousness and spiritual depth, is dangerous. 'We are rich in mechanism and poor in purposes'. We reel under the pressure of acquisitive appetites and despise the tranquillity and meditative discovery of our inner being. So we are lawless and lunatic and kill millions of fellow persons without any uneasy feeling in our bosom. We are alienating ourselves from the treasures of universal justice and enthrone in our vacant soul space urges. We are witness to the collapse of contemporary values. Law and Justice are no longer bedrocked on foundations worthy of the Science of the Spirit but shakily rest on the quicksands of acquisitiveness.

Our era of contradictions has inflicted mortal injuries on our value system and atrophied our moral development.

2 Will Durant: *The Pleasures of Philosophy*, page ix.

"More is better—more money, more sex, more property. It is a society with too much freedom, too many expectations. Suicide, drug abuse, depression, divorce, incest, rape and venereal diseases—herpes last year, AIDS this year are the indices, signs of insatiable self-indulgence. People appear to live only to enjoy sex and gorge food. In this direction a vital civilization has gone astray, its exuberance dissipated, its social life a parody of its phallus and palate obsession."[3]

Yes, but the humane minds of change are blowing.

An expansion from self-centred to society-centred outlook on the right to Development is gradually gaining jurisprudential consideration in the current human rights discourse. Raju Ramachandran, a sensitive jurist with pervasive advocacy, has argued:

"In October 1986, the African Charter on Human and Peoples Rights came into force. One of its most noteworthy features is the incorporation of the Right to Development as a "peoples" right. It says "all peoples shall have the right to their economic, social and cultural development with due regard to their freedom and identity and in the equal enjoyment of the common heritage of mankind" and that "States shall have the duty, individually and collectively, to ensure the exercise of the right to development."

The African Charter adopted by the African States' members of the Organization of the African Unity, expressly deal with people's rights, qua-people, and goes further to state that people shall have the right to development and the State shall have the duty to ensure the exercise of the right to development (vide Art. 22). Moreover, it is stipulated in Art. 24, that all peoples shall have the right to a general satisfactory environment favourable to their development. The harmonious development of the family is also protected and an African Commission on human and people's rights shall be established, according to the Charter (vide Art. 13). We thus perceive that respect for life and for the dignity of the human person transcends bare legal rights and underscores the right to development under propitious circumstances and dynamic conditions. Otherwise an ecological crisis confronts humanity as a whole and a sense of fraternity which is the foundation for the next developmental march of mankind is imperilled. There is thus a higher thinking taking whole of the statesmen of the world. We live at a time of great hopes and deep despair, of conflicts and contradictions, of liberation struggles and imperial occupations, of frustrations and defeat of human solidarity to win developmental justice. In these circumstances, echoing the Algiers' Declaration of 1976 (Universal Declaration of the Rights of People), human rights merged into people's rights and fought battles for the establishment of a World Order of Development and Self-determination.

"It is no accident that in December 1986. The UN General Assembly adopted the Declaration on the Right to Development almost unanimously, with the sole dissent of the United States of America. The Declaration, as adopted, was

3 Akbar S. Ahamed: *Discovery of Islam*, pages 43-44.

substantially based on Yugoslav draft which itself reflected a consensus among the governmental experts from the non-aligned countries in the UN working Group. The core conception of the Right to Development is the principle of balance between civil and political rights on the one hand and economic, social and cultural rights on the other. The Western block wanted priority to be given to the former category of rights and the Eastern bloc sought priority for the latter.

"The non-aligned bloc struck a balance by making the Declaration record that the two sets of rights are interdependent and indivisible and that equal attention and urgent consideration should be given to both sets of rights.

"The Right to Development has rightly not been defined by the Declaration. A definition at this stage would prevent, to borrow Upendra Baxi's memorable phrase, "the development of the Right to Development". Some idea of what the Right means is furnished by Judge Kaba M'Baye, now a Judge of the International Court of Justice and First President of the Senegalese Supreme Court. While first articulating the concept in 1971 as the right of all men, he said "each has the right to live better". Almost contemporaneously Professor Carillo Salcedo of Spain, in a series of lectures on the international law of development said: "The right to development as a right of States and peoples must unavoidably be founded on the recognition of every man to a free and worthy life in his community. Every human being has the right to live, which implies the right to aspire to an increasingly better existence. The right to a full individual development which has made it possible to consider the right to development as an essential human right serves as a foundation of, and implies also, the right of peoples as underdeveloped nations to development. Their progress is only justified as long as development serves to improve the economic, social and cultural level of every person."[4]

The wide ranging status of this concept is reflected in the UN. 'Declaration on the Right to Development' dated 4th December 1986 which recognises:

"That development is a comprehensive economic, social cultural and political process, which aims at the constant improvement of the well-being of the entire population and of all individuals on the basis of their active, free and meaningful participation in development and in the fair distribution of benefits resulting therefrom."

Human rights are conceptually dynamic and represent the stirrings and urges of homo sapiens to *develop* materially, morally and spiritually and man cannot be mummified or remain stagnant. A synthesis of the material and spiritual is the dynamics of Development. Vivekananda's oration reveals this brew:

"We talk foolishly against material civilization .... Bread! Bread! I do not believe in a God who cannot give me bread here, giving me eternal bliss in heaven. Pooh! .... more bread, more opportunity for everybody ....

4 Raju Ramachandran: *The Right to Development: Paradigm—Shift in Human Rights* (1990)4 SCC (Journal) page 9.

"Aye, let every man and woman and child, without respect of caste or birth, weakness and strength, hear and learn that behind the strong and the weak, behind the high and the low, behind everyone, there is that Infinite Soul, assuring that infinite possibility and the infinite capacity of all to become great and good."

Science and technology, visions of seers and creations of the intellect are part of the common heritage of humanity from which each human member may learn to develop his personality and stature. This position is a fundamental, as necessarily implicit in the individual's or society's right to development. Development how? Not in a vacuum but under the propitious circumstances of the world's accumulated wisdom and wealth and wonders left behind by previous generations and civilizations. The greatest scientist of today owes much to the legacy of the past. New discoveries use the springboard of the world's previous scientific knowledge.

Universality and private monopoly are incompatibles, viewed from the developmental angle. The philosophy of paternilasion runs counter to the universal human right to development and access to the rich estate of cultural heritage. Philosophically speaking, knowledge is free and the right to develop involves free availability of the composite cultural treasures. That is a battle to be fought separately between the haves and have-nots. Secrecy, even in meditational technology or Vedic knowledge or vintage literature, is also indefensible. If elimination of discrimination is a human right, it follows that access to knowledge cannot have a price-tag and be refused since that leads to exploitation, cornering and victimisation of the weak. The full and free development of the faculties and capabilities of every person postulates availability and opportunity on a substantially equal measure. The dialectic of contemporary conflicts over intellectual property rights, currently global in character after the GATT treaties, is the contradiction between the right to dominate markets and rob resources claimed by the North and the demand for a just share in the wealth of the world by the South. The New World Economic Order must be just and fair if the right to development is to be a reality of jurisprudence. The future of the democracy of economic development is at stake.

The Declaration on Social Progress and Development of 1969 reaffirms the dignity and worth of human person and of social justice and holds that 'man can achieve complete fulfilment of his aspirations only within a just social order and emphasizes the interdependence of economic and social development on an integrated basis.' Indeed, in Art. 2 of the Declaration there is recognition of the combined effect of civil and political rights as well as of economic, social and cultural rights as necessary values. Much later, the General Assembly, adopted by resolution 41/128 of 4th December 1986, proclaimed the Declaration on the Right to Development as an emphatic aspect of human rights. Articles 1, 2(1), 6(2), 8 are reproduced here to bring out the grand spread and great depth of the faculties of the human person:

"*Article 1.*—(1) The right to development is an inalienable human right by virtue of which every human person and all peoples are entitled to participate in, contribute to, and enjoy economic, social, cultural and political development, in which all human rights and fundamental freedoms can be fully realized.

(2) The human right to development also implies the full realization of the right to peoples to self-determination, which includes, subject to the relevant provisions of both International Covenants on Human Rights, the exercise of their inalienable right to full sovereignty over all their natural wealth and resources."

"*Article 2(1)*.—The human person is the central subject of development and should be the active participant and beneficiary of the right to development."

"*Article 6(2)*.—All human rights and fundamental freedoms are indivisible and interdependent; equal attention and urgent consideration should be given to the implementation, promotion and protection of civil, political, economic, social and cultural rights."

"*Article 8*.—(1) States should undertake, at the national level, all necessary measures for the realization of the right to development and shall ensure, *inter alia*, equality of opportunity for all in their access to basic resources, education, health services, food, housing employment and the fair distribution of income. Effective measures should be undertaken to ensure that women have an active role in the development process. Appropriate economic and social reforms should be carried out with a view to eradicating all social injustices.

(2) States should encourage popular participation in all spheres as an important factor in development and in the full realization of all human rights."

'Know thyself', as ancient Indian sages said and is also inscribed on the temple of Apollo at Delphi, is the profound process which is the pinnacle of human ascent for which the plural requisites of development set out in the Declaration are a *must*.

The right to development is an inalienable human right by virtue of which every human person and all peoples are entitled to participate in, contribute to, and enjoy economic, social, cultural and political development in which all human rights and fundamental freedoms can be fully realized. It makes the human person the central subject of development and says that the human person "should be" the active participant and beneficiary of the right to development. It enjoins States to take steps to eliminate obstacles to development resulting from denial of civil and political rights as well as economic, social and cultural rights. Such is the mandate of the Declaration on the Right to Development. Development, as a universal fundamental, transcends mere economic growth sans justice. Likewise, it is not so much an escalation of the material standard of living but a betterment of the quality of life. Even in the North, have-nots abound and they too need to be rescued. Above all, there is a Fourth World within the Third World which, in large numbers, are miserable, destitute and is ignored or suppressed. The Right to Development is for them a quantum jump from despair to hope. It must be remembered that the social and cultural decadence of the North makes development imperative for the North as well.

The Declaration shows that for the first time a holistic view is being taken of human rights. Such a view has emerged thirty-eight years after the Universal Declaration of Human Rights and twenty years after the adoption of the International Covenants of Civil and Political Rights and Economic, Social and Cultural Rights, all of which embodied compartmentalised thinking. The emergence of the Right to Development marks the emergence of the "systems" approach in human rights jurisprudence which is itself part of a worldwide paradigm-shift.

The earth belonged to the indigenous peoples although everywhere they are exterminated or are on the retreat, denied basic rights and equal status and treated as human curiosities who have outlived the time. Such an attitude is a blister, not culture and a deprivation of equal human status to those for whom humanity of today owes much. The Draft Universal Declaration on the Rights of Indigenous Peoples as contained in United Nations Document E/CN. 4/Sub. 2/1988, highlights indigenous peoples human rights, both individual and as groups, the Preamble portion of which is excerpt below drives home the point that indigenous peoples have collective rights and identities:

> "Considering that all peoples and human groups have contributed to the progress of civilizations and cultures which constitute the common heritage of humankind,
>
> "Recognizing the need to promote and protect those rights and characteristics which stem from indigenous history, philosophy of life, traditions and social structures, especially as these are tied to the lands which the groups have traditionally occupied,
>
> "Concerned that many indigenous peoples have been unable to enjoy and assert their inalienable human rights and fundamental freedoms, frequently resulting in insufficient lands and resources, poverty and deprivation, which in turn may lead to rebellion against all forms of oppression."

Part II of the above Declaration states:

> "The collective right to maintain and develop their ethnic and cultural characteristics and identity, including the right of peoples and individuals to call themselves by their proper names.
>
> "The collective right to protection against ethnocide. This protection shall include, in particular, prevention of any act which has the aim or effect of depriving them of their ethnic characteristics or identity, of any form of forced assimilation or integration, of imposition of foreign life styles and of any propaganda directed against them.
>
> "The right to preserve their cultural identity and traditions and to pursue their own cultural development. The rights to the manifestations of their cultures, including archeological sites, artifacts, designs, technology and works of art, lie with the indigenous peoples or their members."

In this context it is significant that the Australian High Court at Canberra had upheld the collective right of indigenous peoples to their culture and composition in case of deprivation.

Conclusion

To hammer home my case, let me cite the inspiring thought of Marilyn Ferguson:

> "The Whole Earth is a borderless country, a paradigm of humanity with room enough for outsiders and traditionalists, for all our ways of human knowing, for all mysteries and all cultures. A family therapist says she urges her clients to discover not who is right or wrong but *what they have as a family.* We are beginning to make such an inventory of the Whole Earth. Every time one culture finds and appreciates the discovery of another, every time an individual relishes the talents or unique insights of another, every time we welcome the unexpected knowledge emerging from inside the self, we add to that inventory.
>
> * * *
>
> "In growing numbers we are finding how people can enrich and empower one another, we are more sensitive to our place in nature, we are learning how the brain transforms pain and conflict, and we have more respect for the wholeness of the self as the matrix of health. From science and from the spiritual experience of millions, we are discovering our capacity for endless awakenings in a universe of endless surprises.
>
> "At first glance, it may seem hopelessly utopian to imagine that the world can resolve its desperate problem. Each year fifteen million die in starvation and many more live in unrelenting hunger; every ninety seconds the nations of the world spend one million dollars on armaments; every peace is an uneasy peace; the planet has been plundered of many of its non-renewable resources. Yet there have been remarkable advances as well. Just since the end of World War II, thirty-two countries with 40 per cent of the world's population have overcome their problems of food scarcity.[5]

The situation is worse now, the casualty list is gloomier and the prognosis more pessimistic. But human solidarity and the strength of the sleeping Leviathan are positive signals.

We are on our way to a new heaven *here* on a new *whole* earth. Universal Development is its name. Indian sages, in the *Upanishads,* had sung this Song Celestial.

The right to development, in its spiritual essence, is founded on a vision of the wholeness of the human being, adopting a systemic, rather than a dissenting approach. Man's ultimate goal is the transformation of his *being,* going beyond parts. 'We murder to dissect, enough of science and art', says Wordsworth. The flower is not a mere assemblage of petals and the finest manifestation of human personality thus lies in wholeness, as a human unfoldment of all that he is in his integrality. In *"Aquarian Conspiracy",* this concept has been expanded in its richness. Roszak, at a World Symposium in Vancouver in 1977, makes this point:

> "In our time a *secret manifesto* is being written. Its language is a longing we read in one another's eyes. It is the longing to know our authentic vocation in

5 Marilyn Ferguson: *The Aquarian Conspiracy* (Palladin Books) pages 445-446.

> the world, to find the work and the way of being that belong to each of us.........I speak of the Manifesto of the Person the declaration of our *sovereign right to self-discovery*. I cannot say if those who have answered its summons are indeed millions, but I know that its influence moves significantly among us, a subterranean current of our history, that awakens in all those it touches an intoxicating sense of how deep the roots of the self reach, and what strange sources of energy they embrace.........".[6]

Fritj of Capra says:

> "The systems view looks at the world in terms of relationships and integration. Systems are integrated *wholes* whose properties cannot be reduced to those of smaller units. Instead of concentrating on basic building blocks or basic substances, the systems approach emphasises basic principles of organisation. Examples of systems abound in nature. Every organism—from the smallest bacterium through the wide range of plants and animals to humans—is an integrated whole and thus a living system. Cells are living systems, and so are the various tissues and organs of the body, the human brain being the most complex example. But systems are not confined to individual organisms and their parts. The same aspects of wholeness are exhibited by social systems—such as an anthill, a beehive or a human family—and by ecosystems that consist of a variety of organisms and inanimate matter in mutual interaction. All these natural systems are wholes whose specific structures arise from the interactions and interdependence of their parts. The activity of systems involves a process known as transaction—the simultaneous and mutually interdependent interaction between multiple components. Systemic properties are destroyed when a system is dissected, either physically or theoretically, into isolated elements. Although we can discern individual parts in any system the nature of the whole is always different from the mere sum of its parts."[7]

The integrative, synthetic view of human rights forms part of this approach. The choice is not between bread and liberty: the task is to ensure enjoyment of both. Integral *yoga*, to use Aurobindo's expression, is the next *yuga* of the human triumph.

The Newtonian, Cartesian world-view saw the universe as a machine and the human observer as something distinct from the observed, says Raju Ramachandran. The discoveries of modern physics have, however, affirmed the view of Advaita Vedanta, that there is no dichotomy between mind and matter. Even body and soul can be seen as a whole. Reading Walt Whitman this unity dawns so brightly:

> "I have said that the soul is not more than the body, And I have said that the body is not more than the soul, And nothing, not God, is greater to one than one's self is."

6 Marilyn Ferguson: *The Aquarian Conspiracy* (Palladin Books) pages 37-38.
7 Quoted by Raju Ramachandran in (1990)4 SCC (Journal) page 11.

Raju argues:

> "The distinction which has been sought to be made all these years between civil and political rights and economic, social and cultural rights is ascribable to the artificial mind—matter distinction, with civil and political rights representing the rights of the mind and economic, social and cultural rights representing the rights of the body. (For the purpose of the present discussion it is unnecessary to take a stand on whether mind and matter are one and the same or whether they are in a state of perpetual complementarity). The West has traditionally given primacy to libertarian values seeking to emphasise the rational, cogitative side of the human person while the Communist bloc has sought to emphasise the fulfilment of physical needs. The cataclysmic events in Eastern Europe has underscored the validity of the holistic view embodied in the Declaration. One set of rights cannot be sacrificed for the sake of another, and more important, the denial of civil and political rights does not ensure economic development and well being either for nations or individuals."[8]

The bankruptcy of vision of the Western industrial civilization and Western science is its focus on material acquisitive achievements as marking or measuring *real* social advance. On the contrary, 'man doth not live by bread only'.

> "What is a man profited, if he shall gain the whole world, and lose his own soul?"

'Is not the life more than meat, and the body than raiment?' and, therefore, the rainbow of values, when spread out, brings out the beautiful colours of development of the individual as well as of the group collectively.

Full development of every person's and every people's latent excellence being the destination of humanity's march, it would follow that all human rights begin with the right to life and are geared to the culmination of universal progress by protecting and promoting the right to development as a fundamental human right. Shakespeare's vision of man (including all humans) illumines the recognition of the right to development deserving of a pride of place. Hamlet reflects on Man:

> "What a piece of work is a man! How noble in reason! how infinite in faculty! in form, in moving, how express and admirable! in action how like an angel! in apprehension how like a god! the beauty of the world! the paragon of animals!

Such is the process and product of development as a human right.

An Omega thought

Who am I? This perennial interrogation summons each human to his wholeness, his right to the richness of life, his potential of divine life. A century which falters or fails to respond is an alias for barbarity and

8 Raju Ramachandran: *The Right to Development: Paradigm-Shift in Human Rights* (1990)4 SCC (Journal) page 9.

graveyard glory. The United States, with 6 per cent of the world's population consumes more than 30 per cent of it's energy resources. How happy is the American with broken homes and gun culture, dollar mania and dizzy drugs and fast life? Remember, true development is human resource at its best. 'There are no passengers on Spaceship Earth. Everybody's crew.'

Human rights are not legalistics, economics and politics. It is transformation of the global regime, and incarnation of a New World Human Order. Homo sapiens is the highest yet in evolution. Towards heavens on earth we march. In Emerson's profound diction: 'So nigh is grandeur to our dust, so near is God to man. When Duty whispers lo, *Thou must,* the youth replies, I can.' Human rights are the foundation and condition which enable the human to say 'I can' and win it.

11

Basics of Judicial Independence and Defence of Human Rights

"No man can be just who is not free".

— President Woodrow Wilson
Speech in July 1912

"The Court should stand at the very top of the pyramid of all bodies that administer the law. So what is needed first and foremost to ensure this is that the Courts of law be genuinely independent of anyone, no matter who he be.

No Court decision should be a hostage to the times, prompted by current political, economic or other motives."

— Valdimir Terebliov
Chief Justice
USSR Supreme Court

What human hunger has precedence over the quest for Justice? What forensic instrument can command creditability if it is overawed by Authoritarian Power or is shot down for ruling against Might in favour of Right? What system of Government deserves to be called civilised where justice to the humblest and the highest is not free and fair and dispensed by judges without fear or favour, affection or ill-will? This vulnerable yet indispensable value of Independence of the Judiciary is not the pampered privilege of elite brethren but the peoples' dearest creed in societies where human freedoms still matter. The emphasis is on Justice, not Justices. The former is the common and, the latter but the constitutional tool. The universal fundamental is *fearless and fair Justice,* and independent and humane justices are integral to the fulfilment of this imperative of the world legal order. If the right to justice is non-negotiable, so is the immunity of the judiciary from intimidation by the Executive, the socio-economic mafia, mass hysteria, media, propaganda or terrorist forces. Insidious temptation, incurable vices and deep-rooted subjective prejudices of judges themselves may menace that conscientious impartiality which is the essence of independent justice. Equal justice beyond pressure or purchase is the product; easy access to the humblest and the hated and early finality without expensive appellate procrastination, is the process; public bearing with intelligent application of the law and social sensitivity to facts is the dynamics, and judgments, with reasons recorded and copies thereof given readily, constitute the democracy of justice.

Justice can never be free where the Justices are not free. When Tun Salleh, the former Chief Justice and Lord President of Malaysia, was dismissed unjustly at the instance of the Prime Minister through a secret trial by a packed tribunal, the aggrieved Judge wrote a book *(May Day For Justice)* where he eloquently articulated some basic ideas relevant to the independence of Judges as a *sine qua non* of freedom. Let me quote:

> "Flags and anthems and marching uniforms, let us face it, will not make us free. No Fighter-Bomber squadron or naval patrol fleet, no policeman on the beat or his secret Special Branch Operation leading innocent men to Room 101 in Police Remand Centres...............is enough to preserve our freedoms. No, not even regular "democratic" General Elections and Parliamentary sessions, oath taking ceremonies and all, can guarantee it. The Constitution, cannot make us free. And most certainly not orchestrated propaganda ditties drooled day and night in saccharine voices.
>
> "As the old saying goes, only the truth can make us free, because all those institutions and their fine trappings can be, and often are, grossly abused and distorted. ....
>
> "Unless the truth is known at every turn, all those fine things can become mere Executive weapons for its own preservation and survival, not the armour to protect and preserve the freedom of the citizen which they are supposed to be.
>
> *"And the few institutions which can prevent such abuse and distortions are open Courts of law with independent judges."*[1]

Democracy, where the bells toll for human rights and human justice, degenerates into crushing tyranny unless the political order keeps the flame of free and fearless justice, institutional and individual, burning. Therefore, people the world over, consider a free judiciary a constitutional fundamental, absent which authoritarian forces and executive fiats may frustrate human rights, pollute or politicise Court verdicts and fob off partisan pronouncements as the rule of law. The broad division of powers, as the guarantee of democratic justice, demands for the judicature a measure of functional autonomy. Montesquieu expressed this view in *The Spirit of the Laws* thus:

> "Again, there is no liberty if the judicial power be not separated from the legislative and executive. Were it joined with the legislative, the life and liberty

1 *May Day for Justice*, page 313.

of the subject would be exposed to arbitrary control; for the judge would be then legislator. Were it joined to the executive power, the judge might behave with violence and oppression.

"There would be an end to everything, were the same man, or the same body, whether of the nobles or of the people, to exercise those three powers, that of enacting laws, that of executing the public resolutions, and of trying the causes of individuals."

The Supreme Court of India has explained in emphatic terms, the superlative importance of judicial independence in a dynamic democracy in *S.P. Gupta* v *Union of India*.[2]

"The concept of independence of the judiciary is a noble concept which inspires the constitutional scheme and constitutes the foundation on which rests the edifice of our democratic polity. If there is one principle which runs through the entire fabric of the Constitution, it is the principle of the rule of law and under the Constitution, it is the judiciary which is entrusted with the task of keeping every organ of the State within the limits of the law and thereby making the rule of law meaningful and effective. It is to aid the judiciary in this task that the power of judicial review has been conferred upon the judiciary and it is by exercising this power which constitutes one of the most potent weapons in the armoury of the law, that the judiciary seeks to protect the citizen against violation of his constitutional or legal rights or misuse or abuse of power by the State or its officers. The judiciary stands between the citizen and the State as a bulwark against executive excesses and misuse or abuse of power by the executive and therefore it is absolutely essential that the judiciary must be free from executive pressure or influence and this has been secured by the Constitution makers by making elaborate provisions in the Constitution to which detailed reference has been made in the judgments in *Sankalchand Sheth's* case.[3] But it is necessary to remind ourselves that the concept of independence of the judiciary is not limited only to independence from executive pressure or influence but it is a much wider concept which takes within its sweep independence from many other pressures and prejudices. It has many dimensions, namely fearlessness of other power centres, economic or political, and freedom from prejudices acquired and nourished by the class to which the Judges belong. If we may again quote the eloquent words of Justice Krishna Iyer:

"Independence of judiciary is not genuflexion; nor is it opposition to every proposition of Government. It is neither judiciary made to opposition measure nor Government's pleasure."

Independence of Courts is a *sine qua non* of impartiality of verdicts. All these arguments add up to the universal value of and global concern for a judiciary which enjoys a large measure of insulation from external percussions, persuasions and prizes plus a milieu and culture of non-intimidation and other forms of control or influence, blandishment or

2 AIR 1982 SC 149 at pages 197-198.
3 AIR 1977 SC 2328.

blackmail, whichever the source and whatever the *modus operandi.* In our world polluted by violence, State terrorism and private or political terrorism, judicial independence is on the hit list. A fair trial by a fearless Judge is as essential for a stable equitable social order, even as a free election is for an authentic democratic order. A tribunal tainted by dependencia syndrome, overt or covert, or is panicked by threats or harbours feelings which foul his free judgment is but a robed marionette or deceptive phenomenon. An office which gives to the people the solemn assurance of discharge of judicial duties 'without fear or favour, affection or ill-will' is a promise difficult to keep and a profile impossible to project unless a demilitarized zone of occupational immunity from threats and temptations is assured for forensic instrumentalities. Such is the integral yoga of Justice and Justices and Justicing!

How deep was the judicial subservience, even in the great days of British justice is symptomatically revealed by the anguished words of Lord Atkin in *Linversidge* v *Anderson* which poignantly ring through the decades:

> "I view with apprehension the attitude of judges who on a mere question of construction when face to face with claims involving the liberty of the subject show themselves more executive minded than the executive. Their function is to give words their natural meaning, not, perhaps, in wartime leaning towards liberty, but following the dictum of Pollock C.B. in *Bowditch* v *Balchin* cited with approval by my noble and learned friend Lord Wright in *Barnard* v *Gorman*: 'In a case in which the liberty of the subject is concerned, we cannot go beyond the natural construction of the statute'. In this country, amid the clash of arms, the laws are not silent. They may be changed, but they speak the same language in war as in peace. It has always been one of the pillars of freedom, one of the principles of liberty or which on recent authority we are now fighting, that the judges are no respecters of persons and stand between the subject and any attempted encroachments on his liberty by the executive, alert to see that any coercive action is justified in law. In this case I have listened to arguments which might have been addressed acceptably to the Court of King's Bench in the time of Charles I."[4]

And these unhappy observations, whatever the boast of British Justice, led to a distressing estrangement and aloofness by other judges and hastened the end of that high-minded judicial martyr. What a price to pay for forthright judicial outspokenness.

That prejudices might weaken judicial impartiality is best illustrated by a telling instance, small event but of significant portent. I quote from "*The Brethren*":

> "Later that term, in a sex discrimination case *Philips* v *Martin Marietta*, Burger wanted to rule in favour of a company that refused to hire women with preschool-age children. He strongly supported the company's policy. "I will never hire a woman clerk," Burger told his clerks. A woman would have to

4 1942 AC 206.

leave work at 6 P.M. to go home and cook dinner for her husband. His first clerk back in 1956 at the Court of Appeals had been a woman, he told them. It had not worked out well at all. As far as he was concerned an employer could fire whomever he wanted and for whatever reason. That was the boss's prerogative.

"When it was suggested that his position amounted to a declaration that part of the Civil Rights Act was unconstitutional, Burger angrily shut off the discussion. He didn't want to argue legal niceties. His experience showed him that women with young children just didn't work out as well as men in the same jobs. The employer was within his rights."[5]

Indeed, the very Court System is under furious pressure in many countries and its functional independence is sought to be subverted by stratagems, scuttled by covert or overt tactics and seduced by occupational bonuses. Genetic engineering, in the sense of hand-picking personal favourities or Party nominees, screening and manipulating candidates even at the time of recruitment so as to ensure judicial genuflection or secret loyalty and eliminating persons of probity and wisdom and social conscience, is one method of undermining the Court's institutional independence. Similarly, during the career of Judges, many carrots are held out to deflect judicial performance from the path of rectitude. Judicial afternoons and evenings are sensitive phases, the incumbents being bothered about post-retiral prospects. The Executive plays upon this weakness to bend the integrity or buy the partiality of the elderly brethren. 'Survival after tenurial death' is a spell the Executive, with its vast reservoir of patronage, uses to purpose and the robed brethren, save the very robust, do succumb, being of brittle morals, immoderate ambitions and commercial conscience. Moreover, the judiciary, as an institution, is itself subjected to attack or is hijacked, criticised, misrepresented, debunked, budgetarily humbled and in many innovative ways made to feel that it is in their interests to toe the line. Even basic facilities are denied and the judicial process is suffocated or is the Cinderella of the State budget.

Constitutional guarantees of judicial independence are sometimes vulnerable to parliamentary or executive displeasure. Having neither the purse nor the sword, the Judiciary yields, unless the national Bar and the mobilised expression of popular opinion within and without the country come to its aid. Unless non-governmental organisations rouse international conscience against high-handed aggression on the independence of the judiciary, and the legal fraternity battles for 'unbounded' Judge Power, the war for free justice and liberty would be lost. My plea is not for Judges being above the law.

The principles of impregnable judicial autonomy are relevant today with democratic dictators, mafia-controlled politicians, Bar burbles and even political terrorists menacing free institutions. That is why modern

5 *The Brethren inside the Supreme Court*, page 123.

Constitutions and International Instruments stress this Independent Justice factor to restrain the rise of unbridled power. Indeed, this factor is fundamental to fundamental rights themselves.

Human rights to enjoy remedial effectiveness must have independent institutional justice and so it is that freedom and integrity of the judicature in any country is a categorical imperative for the realisation of the human rights.

Judicial appointments to the higher Courts have raised sensitive issues which adversely affect occupational independence, politicise the office and shift the focus of societal accountability of judges from the constellation of constitutional values and blameless conduct to the pleasure of the Party which, or personality who, played the political patron in the matter of appointment. Graft, nepotism, favouritism, lobbying and politicking, commercialising and communalising criteria, vices once rare but now becoming common currency are gaining popularity among them. To say that if the power of appointment is removed from Chief Ministers and Prime Ministers and deposited with Chief Justices, judicial behavioural pollution will be eliminated is an illusion. For one, the Chief Justice's office itself is fast being politicised and corrupted. For another, they have their own secretive politics, communal perceptions, favouritisms and patronage factors and wheeler-dealer operations with the political rulers (for their own purposes) that undeserved names are not uncommon in the panels of Chief Justices. Some have a hurrah that even the judgments in the well-known *Judges Case* are personal projections of covert politics and sub rosa sentiments, with prejudices and prospects sleeping in judicial bosoms. While judicial choices are less overtly political, so can good Ministers conscientiously resist party or personal partialities and pressures. Let us not put all our eggs in the Chief Justice-Chief Minister basket but evolve a collective process with wider consultative access, with even dissenting sections of Indians having a voice. The finest principle of natural justice, to which vicarious homage must be paid, is that "whatever touches us all should be decided by all".

An excellent starting point for such a national discussion will be the view expressed in 1977 by Sir Garfield Barwick, a high authority in his own right. Let me quote:

> "In my view, the time has arrived in the development of this community and of its institutions when the privilege of the Executive Government in this area should at least be curtailed. One can understand the reluctance of a Government to forgo the element of patronage which may inhere in the appointment of a judge. Yet I think that long-term considerations in the administration of justice call for some binding restraint of the exercise of this privilege. I make bold to suggest that, in all the systems of Australia where appointments to judicial office may be made by Executive Government, there should be what is known in some systems as a judicial commission—but the nomenclature is unimportant—a body saddled with the responsibility of advising the Executive Government of the names of persons who, by reason of their training,

knowledge, experience, character and disposition, are suitable for appointment to a particular office under consideration. Such a body should have amongst its personnel, judges, practising lawyers, academic lawyers and, indeed, laymen likely to be knowledgeable in the achievements of possible appointees. Such a body is more likely to have an adequate knowledge of the qualities of possible appointees than any Minister of State is likely to have. Some may prefer to pass the actual choice of appointee to such a body: others may prefer that recommendations only may be made by it; yet others may prefer to require the submission by that body of a short panel of names, outside of which the Executive Government may not go: or may not go without public explanation of the reason for doing so."[6]

In Canada, a report by the Special Committee of the Canadian Bar Association recommended:

"That for the appointments made by the federal appointing authority, suggestions of candidates from judges, lawyers, politicians and the public should be encouraged and that before appointments were made there should be meaningful consultations with provincial Attorney-General and the Chief Justice of the relevant Court. It proposed an advisory committee on federal judicial appointments in each Province, the committees to consist of the Chief Justice of the Province or nominee, an appointee of the federal Minister for Justice, an appointee of the provincial Attorney-General or Minister for Justice, two lawyers appointed by the organisations of the legal profession within the Province and two lay persons appointed by the other members of the committee. *An advisory committee* would be consulted by the federal Minister of Justice on all vacancies occurring in its Province. It would consider names suggested by the Minister and from other sources and would itself seek out names of candidates, and would submit to the Minister the names of no fewer than three persons qualified to fill a vacancy. The Minister would be expected to make appointments from the list submitted or to request the committee to bring forward further recommendations.

"The Canadian Report dealt also with appointments to the Supreme Court of Canada and to the Federal Court of Canada. In understanding the recommendations in regard to those Courts it is necessary to bear in mind that in Canada a degree of regionalism in appointment is provided for both statutorily and by custom. The Report recommended that advice on appointments to the Supreme Court would be tendered by the advisory committee or committees within the relevant region. A separate advisory committee for appointments to the Federal Court of Canada and other Federal Courts was recommended."

India has its own vices and limitations, rendered acute by the frequent shifts in power at the Centre and divergent parties ruling at the Central and State levels. Monopoly of power to choose judges, if vested in Chief Justices, may still manifest pathological symptoms of judicial politics and lobbies

6 *Australian Justice System—Report of the Advisory Committee to the Constitutional Commission* 1987, page 69.

and prejudices. The dependencia syndrome has been heightened by the precarious position of acting judges, *ad hoc* judges, acting Chief Justices, transfer of judges, and a miscellany of administrative powers of Chief Justices which can be used to pamper or humiliate particular judges. Chief Justices can play the rude boss and factions and hostilities among the 'brethren' are a common phenomenon. All these deleterious trends shake up both independence and performance and victimise the common litigant and the honest lawyer.

Judicial comity can be and often is violated by mutual jealousies, publicity rivalries and power manoeuvrings within the brotherhood. The *enemy within* is often missed in such discussions, although open accusations hurled against each other undermine judicial solidarity and sometimes personal factors result in unwarranted reversal of one judge's judgments by an allergic appellate bench or is ignored by an anathematic single judge. Decorum and discipline even in obeying Supreme Court rulings are becoming endangered aberrations, (vide, my observations in *Fuzlunbi* v *Khader Vali.*[7] Independence is under strain from within the fraternity and justice is the casualty. (e.g. Justice Tulzapurkar indicting Justice Bhagwati at Pune for 'judgment hawking' and the controversies over Justice Bhagwati's 'rising sun' epistle to the then Prime Minister).

A brief global tour

Luckily, the International Commission of Jurists in 1978 created the Centre for the Independence of Judges and Lawyers to spearhead global campaigns on behalf of the victims of the Bench and the Bar. This Commission required the creation of international standards *vis-a-vis* independence of justice. Efforts were commenced in this behalf and in 1985 the Seventh United Nations Congress on Crime Prevention and Control unanimously adopted the Basic Principles on the Independence of the Judiciary. Dr. L.M. Singhvi, by his study on the *Administration of Justice and the Independence and Impartiality of the Judiciary,* laid a scholarly and practical basis for the project. The 20 Basic Principles on the Independence of the Judiciary were welcomed by the UN General Assembly by Resolution No. 40/146 (13th December 1985) which invited Governments to respect them in their national *corpus juris* and legal praxis. They set forth principles concerning judicial independence as well as guidelines regarding conditions of service, tenure, occupational immunity, professional discipline and termination of judgeship. Judges, unless impregnably defended against Executive hubris, cannot function effectively. A guaranteed tenure is a mandatory principle. Suspension or removal only for reasons of incapacity or gross misbehaviour, judged first by their own peers, must be a condition precedent to punitive exit. These and other principles were the first attempts at protecting the independence of the judiciary. The Ninth Session of the UN Committee on Crime Prevention and Control urged N.G.O.'s and I.G.O.'s to become effectively involved in the battle for adoption of the Basic Principles. The

7 AIR 1980 SC 1730.

UN Committee also requested the States to report to the Secretary General on the implementation of the Basic Principles through national legislation. Currently, the UN Sub-Commission on prevention and discrimination and protection of minorities has sought comments from Governments on the comprehensive Draft Declaration on the Independence of Justice, prepared by Dr. L.M. Singhvi aided by experts. They provide for both individual and collective independence of judges, and set forth minimum standards to be followed in the selection, training, promotion, transfer, discipline and removal of judges. If this progressive course of doing justice to the Justices through International Instruments were kept up, the call of humanity for a fearless Bench and equally fearless Bar may bear fruit.

The despotic proclivity of Executive Authority is an appetite which can be controlled only by militant mobilisation of national and international awareness. A conscientisation campaign is, therefore, highest on the International Agenda of Independence of Justice. Perhaps, the United Nations should adopt and proclaim a Universal Declaration on the Independence of Justice. Again, a monitoring agency or world ombudsman watchdogging the Independence of Justice is a useful expedient. The International Court of Justice, currently not too busy, may, perhaps, be entrusted with this task *pro tem.* A World Institute on the Independence of Justice may, perhaps, be helpful to educate and propagate, as a founding creed and fighting faith, the cardinal principle of judicial independence. Courses in Law Schools and as part of ongoing projects for education of lawyers and judges may conscientize the legal fraternity in this behalf. National Bar Councils and lawyers' organisations must, as a pledge, undertake to popularise and publicise the jurisprudence of Independence of Justice. I agree with my friend Dr. Singhvi when he says:

> "A package programme of technical assistance should be launched for the development of legal institutions, training of lawyers and judges and promotion of the concept of independence of justice in some of the countries where facilities are inadequate: The UNESCO and UN University should also address themselves to these tasks. National, regional and international seminars and exchange programmes for lawyers, judges, draftsmen, law officers and members and staff of law reform commission on a sustained basis with a composite approach inclusive of the twin objectives of the technical assistance plan would be highly beneficial in a variety of ways. I would suggest a Five-Year Integrated Plan for the Development of Legal Institutions and Promotion of Human Rights as a part of the development process.
>
> "A world movement should be organized to build up the defences of the independence of justice in the public mind and in the minds of those who operate systems and sub-systems of power in the society, including judges and lawyers."[8]

8 *Independence of Justice: Indian Bar Review 1987,* pages 587-588.

Michael Kirby of the High Court of Australia makes some jurisprudential observations:

> "As a result of numerous attacks on the independence of the judiciary in many lands, international agencies and conferences of jurists have busied themselves in attempts to state the basic principles necessary to ensure judicial independence."
>
> *** *** ***
>
> "Principles 1, 12 and 18 of the Basic Principles are relevant to the Staples case:
>
> *1.* The independence of the judiciary shall be guaranteed by the State and enshrined in the Constitution or the law of the country. It is the duty of all governmental and other institutions to respect and observe the independence of the judiciary.
>
> *** *** ***
>
> *12.* Judges, whether appointed or elected, shall have guaranteed tenure until a mandatory retirement age or the expiry of their term of office, where such exists.
>
> *** *** ***
>
> *18.* Judges shall be subject to suspension or removal only for reasons of incapacity or behaviour that renders them unfit to discharge their duties.

There is no definition of the judges to whom the Basic Principles apply. But in the preamble it is stated that:

> "The Principles have been formulated principally with professional judges in mind, but they apply equally, as appropriate, to lay judges, where they exist."
>
> *** *** ***
>
> "The Basic principles just mentioned represent the briefest international exposition of the fundamental principles of judicial and legal independence. They have been elaborated in a number of other international instruments. Thus the Minimum Standards of Judicial Independence adopted by the International Bar Association in October 1982 include the following clause:
>
> *20.* (*a*) Legislation introducing changes in the terms and conditions of judicial services shall not be applied to judges holding office at the time of passing the legislation unless the changes improve the terms of services.
>
> (*b*) In the case of legislation reorganizing Courts, judges serving in those Courts shall not be affected, except for their transfer to another Court of the same status.
>
> "Similar in effect to clause 20(*b*) is clause 2.39 of the Universal Declaration on the Independence of Justice. This declaration was adopted at the World Conference on the Independence of Justice in Montreal, Canada on 10th June 1983. It provides (relevantly): '2.39. In the event a Court is abolished, judges serving on that Court shall not be affected, except for the transfer to another Court of the same status.'

> "The Basic Principles adopted by the General Assembly also include principles relevant to the assignment of work of judges. Thus, clause 14 provides: 'The assignment of cases of judges within the Court to which they belong is an internal matter of judicial administration.' But a power of 'administration' must obviously be used for administrative purpose and not to negative a lawful commission held by a judge."

A brief historical-teleological survey of the universal jurisprudence of Independent Justice is a luminous alpha in the human rights saga of our century. Social sensitives will scarce disagree with Cappelletti who rightly made access to justice as basic to human rights.

Fine-tuned to the value of the rights of man as 'the foundation of freedom, justice and peace' and realising that human rights should be protected by the rule of law lest men 'should be compelled to have recourse, as a last resort, to rebellion against tyranny and oppression', the Universal Declaration has proclaimed certain inalienable rights which are the quintessence of human justice. The constellation of fundamental freedoms stored in the cornucopia of this Declaration deserves the activist support of lawyers worldwide. Rights, however solemnly proclaimed and entrenched in great instruments, are but printed futility unless a puissant judiciary, armed with legal authority and remedial jurisdiction, operational and pragmatic, transforms the jurisprudence of human rights into the public law of enforceable justice. From this perspective, the Universal Declaration insists in Art. 8:

> "Everyone has the right to *an effective remedy* by the competent national tribunals for acts violating the fundamental rights granted him by the Constitution or by law."

"Due process" rhetoric meets its Waterloo unless an independent judicature, the elan vital of the justice system, is clothed with Constitutional sanctions. So it is that Art. 10 lays down:

> "Everyone is entitled in full equality to a fair and public hearing by an independent and impartial tribunal, in the determination of his rights and obligations and of any criminal charge against him."

The great Covenant on Civil and Political Rights in Art. 14 also stresses that:

> "Everyone shall be entitled to fair and public hearing by a competent, independent and impartial tribunal established by law."

What is the conscience of the Declaration and the Covenant, in its guarantee of human rights, is the free access to justice and an *impartial and independent judicial process* to enforce this promise. 'A competent, independent and impartial tribunal', is the adjudicatory instrumentality sans which the magna carta of human rights becomes a lifeless, though decoratively dressed, cadaver.

The critical importance of the independent judicial mechanism in a meaningful justice system is well brought out in the "WHEREAS" part of the Universal Declaration which underscores how Human Rights should be protected by the *Rule of Law.* The proposition is axiomatic: no independent judiciary, no rule of law. Law, as the instrument of justice, necessarily postulates the interpretation and application of the law and findings of fact as part of dispute resolution, undeterred by political pressure, executive terror and other forms of reprisal.

The ideology of independence of justice as a creed of universal validity is clear. But it is important to remember that history is also replete with instructive instances of fearless judges suffering crucifixion.

Justice and liberty go together and so, a citizen's liberties can be defended only by judges who resist erosion of their own independence. But even post-war history, with all its battles for human freedoms, is blood-stained with judicial casualties.

The Tun Salleh tragedy, where the former Chief Justice of Malaysia was deposed by the political top boss, displeased by the Summit Justice, is an ominous instance of universal import. Let me recount how the events unfolded and I came to be acquainted with the Salleh story. After all, we live in an indivisible world and what happens in one country will affect or infect another even in the judicial cosmos. Let me narrate to you briefly what shook the bar in Malaysia last year as an Executive invasion of Judicial Independence.

Broadly speaking, Malaysia has a King by rotation who is the Constitutional Monarch ordinarily acting on the advice of the Prime Minister and the Council of Ministers. The Constitutional Scheme is as in the Westminster pattern. The Judges exercise judicial power, the Legislature enacts laws and the Cabinet is the top Executive. There is a Party system as in Parliamentary practice. Unfortunately, some political questions, as in other countries, spring up before the Court and require adjudication based on legal principles. For sometimes,—that is what many told me—the Prime Minister was rather unhappy with certain decisions of the Judges which affected his Party and perhaps his position in the Party which governed the country. The Prime Minister was openly criticising the Judges inside and outside Parliament, detracting from the dignity, impartiality and authority of the Judiciary. Thereupon a large number of Judges gathered and authorized the Chief Justice Mr. Tun Salleh of the Supreme Court to address the King complaining about the improper conduct of the Prime Minister in criticising the Judiciary. This letter of complaint against the improper conduct of ministerial criticism of judges was construed to be improper conduct on the part of the Chief Justice (Lord President, as he is called). The Prime Minister advised the King to suspend the Lord President for this bad behaviour of remonstrating to the King against the objectionable behaviour of the Prime Minister in publicly attacking the Judiciary. The King obediently suspended the Chief Justice and ordered an enquiry by a suddenly fabricated, oddly composed Tribunal. The Chief Justice moved a Bench of his Court for a stay of the Tribunal's Report to the King. Five Judges of the Supreme Court heard and granted an *ad interim* stay. Meanwhile, when the Lord President was suspended, the Judge next to him, Tan Sri Abdul Hamid Omar, was appointed Acting Lord President. This was a day of humiliation for the Judiciary, because the next in rank did not hesitate to occupy the high seat of Lord President. His personal ambition got the better of his commitment to the great institution and the larger cause of the Independence of the Judiciary. Not only that, as Acting Lord President, he recommended the suspension of the five Judges who granted stay of the Tribunal's Report. Another Tribunal was appointed to enquire into the misconduct of the five Judges, the misconduct being the alleged conspiracy to sit as a Bench and the gross impropriety of granting a stay. Ultimately, the Lord President was dismissed by the King and three out of the five Judges who heard the stay petition were also dismissed. 'O! What a fall was there, my countrymen! Then I, and you, and all of us fell down.'

U.S. and U.K.: how conditioned is the system?

A longer intercontinental tour of the territory of judicial independence may illumine our understanding of the issue. We may as well begin with the American Court which enjoys a great reputation of impregnability *vis-a-vis* the President and the Congress—President Nixon found himself thrown out as a direct consequence of a ruling of the Highest Court. It may be of interest to look into genetic and tenurial aspects of the judiciary. Be it noted that there are roses and thorns.

The U.S. system also is zealous about independence of judges. The Supreme Court members have life tenure, handsome salaries, inviolable conditions of office, great prestige and power and public opinion which revolts against judges who privately advise Presidents on extra judicial matters or become trustees or take on other duties which bring incomes. The case of Abe Fortas is an instance in point. Even so, the judicial genetic code of the American 'robed brethren' suffers from some pathological factors. The Court is filled by direct appointments or by periodic elections. All federal posts are by appointments made on nakedly political considerations. Many States have a judiciary elected by popular vote on party basis. Either scheme sacrifices the independence of the incumbent in some measure. The President makes appointments to the federal judiciary and the Governors, in those States where judges hold non-elective posts, openly go by politics and their desire to influence the Court's policies and verdicts through installing persons on the high bench with pronounced views palatable to the President and congruous (often conservative) backgrounds—a sort of genetic engineering of the 'ermined' summit. Inevitably, this political bias, planted by anticipation, invalidates independence indirectly. True, many distinguished judges have overcome this inclination and sense of obligation and defeated Presidential expectations. Chief Justice Earl Warren, a Republican Governor of California, was transplanted by President Eisenhover into the highest judicial office, predicting conservative performance tuned to the Macarthy era, but he exploded such expectations through radical, humanist liberalism on the bench and inaugurated a progressive period of creativity and dynamism through forensic pronouncements. Nevertheless, as a system, politicisation of the judiciary with noxious luxuriance, may demoralise the weaker sections of the people and adversely impact on independence and impartiality, especially in a pluralist society polluted by colour-based divisions and prejudice against the poor minorities. Moreover, the exasperating examination of the judges at the senate level keeps independent judges away from the high posts and oftentimes leads to lobbying by the Presidents for their judicial candidates and cover-up devices by the candidates to pass through the Senate Sub-Committee's screening process. (Imagine Indian judges being appointed on publicly announced reactionary policies and political considerations of the Party in power). We will there have Congress judges, B.J.P. judges, as they have Republican and Democrat appointed judges in United States. However, it must be said that on momentous occasions the judges, overcoming the dependencia syndrome, have voted for liberties and against corruption as in the case of Nixon, the flag salutation cases, the school prayer, segregation and Gidon's trumpet instances *et al.* But overall, remote control of the Court by Presidents and Senates is basically unhappy, viewed from the value-based perspective of independence of the judiciary.

If the post is elective, the situation is worse. The campaign at the polls is on party basis; the judicial candidates have to surrender to the popular palate in matters of crime and punishment, conservative economic stances and allergy towards radical views and socialist slants which may not find favour with the electorate. Some Judges have told me, while I was on tour in the States, that they could not accept any theory of lenient punishment or correctional projects because, in that event, they would lose the next election. By way of aside, it may be noted that more blacks often figure in the dock and the white bracket demand blood-thirsty severity of punishment. A soft judge misses his office in the Federal Court system and his seat at the next State election. I have seen some progressive judges nervous as the election dates draw near. On the whole, all the merits of elections notwithstanding, the casualty in such cases is the independence of the judges concerned. Judicial independence is on the cross if Executive politics or populist noises are the boss; more so where radical issues fall for adjudication. The American Court system, though politically conditioned, still has a reputation for independence, thanks to some great judges like Marshall, Holmes, Hughes, Earl Warren, Brandies, Cardozo, Douglas and Thurgood Marshall. In vain may be, we pray, 'may their tribe increase!'.

The text of the U.S. Constitution provides that the President "shall nominate, by and with the advice and consent of the Senate.........Judges of the Supreme Court". Thus the Executive and the Legislature, both political entities, dominate judicial selection and dilute the independence of the judiciary, especially *vis-a-vis* progressive causes, minority interests and unorthodox thinking. While American judges have commanded veneration, when a sensitive study of their judicial chemistry is made from the human rights angle, it is discovered that the conservative Establishment drains the Courts of their concern when pitted against the social, political, economic vested interests. During World War II, the Vietnam War and on other critical occasions, in judicial review of minority claims, the Court's vote has gone to the Establishment since the days of the *Dred Scott* case.

A general grasp of the underlying systemic deficiencies is necessary to appreciate the criticism. When we test the system not from the elitist view point but that of the refugees from majority oppression or the have-nots and humans without *real* rights, the broad picture presented by Schwartz in the *American Constitutional Law* is insightful. I quote liberally:

> "The method of selection in the federal judicial system in the United States is, in a general way, similar to that followed in England. Appointment to the federal bench, under the relevant constitutional provision, is made by the President, subject to confirmation by the Senate."
>
> * * *
>
> "In some ways, indeed, the appointing authority of the President over the federal Courts is greater than that wielded by the Lord Chancellor and Prime Minister in Britain. The latter are restricted in their choice to barristers of at least ten years' standing, for puisne judges, and to barristers of at least fifteen years' standing or High Court judges, for members of the Court of Appeal. In the United States, there are no such limitations upon the presidential appointing authority. It is true that, as a practical matter, only members of the legal profession may be chosen for judicial office. It should, however, be remembered that the bar in the United States is nothing like the relatively restricted group which makes up the English Bar. The lack of the sharp division between barristers and solicitors in the American system means that the presidential choice is not limited to that portion of the legal profession engaged only in the tasks of advocacy. Nor is the President required to appoint only from among those who are actually active at the bar. In fact, a growing number of judicial appointments are being made from among lawyers whose work does not at all resemble that performed by the active English barrister, such as members of the executive, the legislature or of law faculties, who have not engaged in legal practice for many years. Thus, in the 1954 Supreme Court, eight of its members were appointed from among the groups just mentioned, while the ninth was elevated from his seat on a Court of appeals."[9]

Prof. Schwartz reveals the truth of the politics of judicial appointments bluntly:

> "Perhaps the greatest weakness, in practice, of the system of selecting federal judges in the United States arises from the fact that, all too often, the presidential power of appointment has been used for political purposes. 'The President', states one author in discussing appointments to the Supreme Court, 'can hardly be expected to appoint men, however outstanding they may be, whose views on matters of public policy are known to be radically different from his own. He has personal and political obligations, which being human, he will be tempted to fulfill through appointments to the Court. Besides being President, he is the leader of a political party, and partisan considerations will be borne in mind'. It is true that, in Britain also, similar

9 Schwartz Bernard: *American Constitutional Law*, 1955, pages 131-132.

> remarks have been made in the past with regard to the appointment of judges upon a political basis......... ."

*** *** ***

It is fair to mention the sky-high exceptions like Earl Warren, the great Chief Justice who reigned for long 15 years and exasperated the Conservatives who expected him to be a traditionalist in judicial values. And that intrepid, anti-establishment, dissenting soul of vistaramic wisdom like Douglas and that sensitive giant who never forgot the scars of his black and traumatic years and battled on the bench for the lost causes of the desperate sector like Thurgood Marshall—they too are global beacons. Douglas, hated and loved by his brethren, was 'a lone eagle' but a strong and soaring one. And Marshall too was a great fighter for the lowly and the lost—now a Justice emeritus.

Earl Warren was three-term Governor of California, and Republican Vice-Presidential nominee and was chosen for Chief Justiceship by President Eisenhower for his "middle of the road philosophy". Later Eisenhower remarked that Warren's appointment was "the biggest damned-fool mistake I ever made". Macarthy even accused him of being a communist fellow-traveller. It has been rightly said of the great Warren that he was closest to the Left and led a judicial revolution that reshaped many social and political relationships in America. When Nixon came on the scene it was clear that vacancies on the Court would be fool-proof conservative. In the U.S.A. the President's choice is openly political and even the Senate has political allergies. For instance, the Senate rejected Johnson's nominee, Associate Justice Abe Fortas, as a "crony" of the President. Nixon, when he received the resignation of Warren, was sure to choose, according to Chief Justice Warren, "a reliable practicable man who was committed to Nixon's own philosophy". Indeed, Warren Burger, the eventual successor, had impressed upon Nixon that he was a "solid conservative". Curious to read in the 'Brethren' how Burger had wooed the White House for the high office of Chief Justice. "If ever a man was campaigning for elevation in Judiciary, it was Warren Burger. He was perfectly, clearly politically astute, and he was pushing all the right buttons for the President". Lobbying? The pages in that book dealing with Judge Burger's pre-elevation gambits suggest that notions of judicial aloofness from the Executive are not necessarily nor always an American virtue. President Nixon was bent upon "breaking the back of the working Warren majority". Indeed, Justices Fortas and Douglas had even investigations against them to see if they could be eased out of the Court. Politicising the judicial office is a presidential pastime in the United States but it must also be recorded as a fact of history that sometimes summit judges did beat the presidential hunch and the senate judiciary committee's X-ray. The appointees proved their independence of the source of appointment. Even Warren Burger disappointed Nixon at the final movement when the 'Tape Case' judgment extinguished Nixon's Presidency. Watergate proved to be Nixon's Waterloo because the Burger Court held unanimously against the President's plea of privilege.

The British system

If politicisation undermines judicial independence, the American praxis is a poor model, although the rule is relieved by exceptional marvels. But how is the British system, considered by conservative Indian jurists as paradigm? We must look at the structure through the lens of human rights, minorities and have-not groups, an approach adopted by Prof. Griffith in his "*The Politics of the Judiciary*". The Lord Chancellor is at the apex but he is hundred per cent political, being a member of the Cabinet belonging to the party in power and quitting office with the party. Obviously, his independence must necessarily be circumscribed. Even the Lord Chief Justice is chosen by cruissitudes of politics. The instance of Lord Caldecote is not unique and brings out the political dependency even of the highest office of Lord Chief Justice. R.F.V. Heuston in his "Lives of the Lord Chancellors 1885-1940" reveals:

> "The fall of the Chamberlain Government in May 1940 inevitably affected Caldecote's own position (as the Lord Chancellor). In the confusion of the time it was for some days uncertain what his future would be; but one evening Sir Cland Schuter telephoned......to say that.........Caldecote was offered, and thought it right to accept, his old post at the Dominion office, together with the Leadership of the House of Lords.........Five months later to the day he was appointed (12th October) Lord Chief Justice in succession to Lord Hewart."[10]

Lord Halsbury, a legendary name in the legal world, ascended to the office of Lord Chancellor through political manoeuvres. And Halsbury revelled in political nepotism when making judicial appointments. Says Heuston:

> "Halsbury's judicial appointments have been the subject of considerable comment and speculation, mostly of a critical character......The criticisms are known in outline to most lawyers; they are in effect that Halsbury appointed to the High Court......men of little or no legal learning whose previous career in public life had been largely in the service of the Conservative Party or else were relations of his own."
>
> *** *** ***
>
> "Lord Halsbury had no hesitation in appointing to the High Court or country court judges whose claims rested more on their political or family ties than on their standing at the Bar."[11]

It is violative of impartiality of the judiciary and demonstrative of political dependency of the incumbents, if a study in England has disclosed: "that of 139 judges appointed between 1832 and 1906, eighty were MPs at the date of their appointment, and eleven others had been candidates (six of them more than once). Of these eighty, sixty-three had been appointed while their own party was in office, and thirty-three of them had been Law Officers........."[12]

10 *Ibid,* page 88.
11 *Ibid,* pages 91-92.
12 *Ibid,* page 92.

Even barter of judgeships of the highest decks has marred British Judicial history. Prof. Griffith supports this charge:

> "Lord Simon of Glaisdale has written: 'In 1951 Sir Winston (Churchill) particularly wanted (Sir Walter Monckton) in the unenviable post of Minister of Labour, and (presumably by way of compensation) undertook in writing that he should be appointed Lord Chief Justice on the next vacancy.
>
> "Such an undertaking must have been of very little value. Lord Goddard was then in only his sixth year as Lord Chief Justice, never looked like someone about to retire, and indeed continued in office for three years after Sir Winston gave way as Prime Minister in 1955. But the story shows that Sir Winston had no doubt that the office was solely in his gift."[13]

We are not so much concerned about the packing of the Courts with party men, which is bad in itself, but with the selection process slanting strongly towards conservative ideology. Exceptions only prove the rule and independence as well as impartiality are illusory when class interests creep in. Griffith cites Lord Haldane who, while a practicing barrister, had recorded:

> "I fought my hardest for the Dutch prisoners before the Privy Council this morning, but the tribunal was hopelessly divided, and the anti-Boers prevailed over the pro-Boers. It is bad that so much bias should be shewn, but it is, I suppose, inevitable."[14]

When we speak of independence, it is not merely freedom from crude threats, but presence of open-mindedness where the judicial mind is not foreclosed by prefabricated working from within like unwitting alchemy. Here again, Prof. Griffith illustrates his point:

> "D.N. Pritt in his autobiography told of his many political cases and of one which 'came before a judge of great experience and knowledge, so bitterly opposed to anything left-wing that he could scarcely have given a fair trial if he had tried.
>
> Are such phrases applicable today? Every practising barrister knows before which judges he would prefer not to appear in a political case because he believes, and his colleagues at the Bar believe, that certain judges are much more likely than others to be biased against certain groups, like demonstrators or students, or certain kinds of action, like occupations of property by trade unionists or the homeless."[15]

If the detached perceptions of a judge are polluted by prepossessions and impartiality becomes then a casualty, the British judiciary suffers from some fatal blemishes, as Prof. Griffith, by two quotations, has demonstrated. Let me repeat that page from his book.[16]

13 J.A.G. Griffith: *The Politics of the Judiciary,* page 18.
14 *Ibid,* page 30.
15 *Ibid,* pages 30-31.
16 *Ibid,* page 173.

Winston Churchill once praised and exposed British Justice. I quote him:

> "The Courts hold justly a high, and I think, unequalled pre-eminence in the respect of the world in criminal cases, and in civil cases between man and man, no doubt, they deserve and command the respect and admiration of all classes of the community, but where class issues are involved, it is impossible to pretend that the Courts command the same degree of general confidence. On the contrary, they do not, and a very large number of our population have been led to the opinion that they are, unconsciously, no doubt, biased.
>
> [Hon. Members: 'No, No', 'Withdraw' and interruption.]
>
> [The Secretary of State for the Home Department (Mr. W.S. Churchill) on the second reading of the Trade Unions (No. 2) Bill, 1911 (26 H.C. Deb. Col. 1022).]

Nor is Churchill alone in his criticism. Listen to Lord Justice Scrutton:

> "The habits you are trained in, the people with whom you mix, lead to your having a certain class of ideas of such a nature that, when you have to deal with other ideas, you do not give as sound and accurate judgments as you would wish. This is one of the great difficulties at present with Labour. Labour says 'where are your impartial judges? They all move in the same circle as the employers, and they are all educated and nursed in the same ideas as the employers. How can a labour man or a trade unionist get impartial justice?' it is very difficult sometimes to be sure that you have put yourself into a thoroughly impartial position between two disputants, one of your own class and one not of your class."

[Lord Justice Scrutton in an *Address delivered to the University of Cambridge Law Society* on 18th November 1920.][17]

Men like Lord Scarman are rare on the English Bench. Even Lord Denning, a great judge, did, infrequently though, nod when the working class and the coloured groups and radical issues were the subject. Even so, it is undeniable that British judges are not impartial angels. They are good Tories, rarely restive radicals.

Judicial bias is almost a built-in trait, according to many commentators of a British Justice. David Pannick, in his marvellous and happily hilarious (but studded with erudite anecdotes) book *Judges*, has established his thesis that disinterestedness is a myth. Judicial appointments being what they are, their prejudices offer no surprise. Lord Chief Justice Hewart "displayed 'a tendency to take sides in cases that came before him. Lawyers......said it was to be expected in a first-class advocate and that the failing would pass'. It did not. 'Hewart had been all his life a partisan, in politics as well as in the Courts, and it was not easy for him to lose the habit of seeing one side of the picture more clearly than the other."[18]

17 1 *Cambridge Law Journal*, page 8.

18 David Pannick: *Judges*, 1988 Ed., page 51.

Described by some as "the worst Lord Chief Justice of England since the 17th century he excelled in arbitrary and unjudicial behaviour".

Heuston says: Another (critic) states more tersely that Halsbury was quite unscrupulous in his appointments.

It is interesting that Lord Hailsham sought to dispel the mystery and obscurity about judicial appointments by publishing in 1986 a guide to his policies and procedures in this behalf. It is of some relevance to us in India because selection of the higher echelons of the judiciary is a secretive operation in India. Lord Hailsham's guidelines are these:

> "The Lord Chancellor's policy is to appoint to every judicial post the candidate who appears to him to be the best qualified to fill it and to perform its duties......It outlines the process of gathering information and broadly based consultations which precede an appointment. Lord Hailsham had earlier described how the practice in all High Court appointments is to hold a meeting between the Lord Chancellor and the Heads of Division (the Lord Chief Justice, the Master of the Rolls, the President of the Family Division, and the Vice-Chancellor) at which a number of names is always discussed. There is never a vote, but a consensus is usually arrived at......I never remember a case in which the decision, when made, was not in fact a collective one."[19]

Nevertheless, it is true that patronage plays a part and no mechanism exists to ensure that decisions are made on adequate information and proper criteria or public scrutiny.

A glance at the past regarding judicial appointments in Britain fills one with horror. Says Pannick:

> "In 1684 Robert Wright was promoted to the Bench while in a destitute state. His patron, Chief Justice Jeffreys, suggested to him that as you seem to be unfit for the bar or any other honest calling, I see nothing for it but that you should become a judge yourself. Despite the opinion of Lord Chancellor Guildford that Wright was the most unfit person in England to be made a judge......a dunce, and no lawyer; who is not worth a groat, having spent his estate by debauched living; who is without honesty........., the King was persuaded by Jeffreys to appoint Wright to the Bench. Wright became so pronounced a favourite of James II that in 1687 he was promoted to Chief Justice, greatly accelerating and furthering the Revolution in 1688 by his decisions. In all his judicial functions he displayed himself by his ignorance, stupidity and immorality to be one of the most sordid wretches ever to sit on the Bench in England.
>
> "Lord Halsbury, who held office as Lord Chancellor at the turn of the last century, appointed many undistinguished men to the Bench because of their political services to the Conservative Party. As Lord Salisbury, the Prime Minister wrote to Halsbury in 1897, the judicial salad requires both legal oil and political vinegar; but disastrous effects will follow if due proportion is not observed."[20]

19 Lord Hailsham: *The Door Wherein I Went,* (1978), page 254.

20 *Ibid,* pages 65-66.

Although things have changed, judges are still chosen in England without public discussion of the merits and demerits of the candidates. There is a sense of secrecy that surrounds the riddle of the Lord Chancellor's choice.

It is important to consider whether we should have a public procedure in regard to the selection to the higher posts on the Bench. Of course, in the U.S.A. the President appoints with the Senate's consent. The Senate has declined to confirm 27 of the nearly 140 Supreme Court nominees placed before it since 1789. Even the other Federal Judges appointed by the President have to secure a vote of the Senate. The English practice is different.

> "In 1972 the Justice Sub-Committee which reported on the judiciary wisely recommended that the Lord Chancellor should be helped in his task by an appointments committee. This would allow for interested bodies to make recommendations, or for interested persons to apply......The appointments committee could comprise representatives of the Law Society, the Bar, academic lawyers, the judiciary, and perhaps some lay members, for example highly trained and experienced personnel officers skilled in selection procedures. The Committee would not fetter the decision of the Lord Chancellor on whom to appoint. Nor would it introduce party politics into the process. It would, however, add an element of professionalism into what is still an amateur exercise. When judges are appointed to the Court of Appeal or the House of Lords, the Committee could usefully publish a report on the qualifications of the nominee. In this and other ways (such as the publication of an annual report on judicial appointments) the Committee would introduce a much needed public eye into what has hitherto been a private appointment process."[1]

In many European countries, career judges are the rule, like civil servants in our country. It is a matter for serious consideration for the Indian Parliament whether we too should have a Judicial Appointment Committee or Commission in preference to the confidential negotiations between the Chief Justices and the Chief Executives. "Law is too serious a matter to be left exclusively to Judges".[2]

Why? I agree with David Pannick:

> "But because judges necessarily have an important role to play in making and applying the law, there is every reason for ensuring that their selection, training, and working practices facilitate rather than frustrate their ability to decide cases wisely on behalf of the community."[3]

More importantly, as Justice Burger put it:

> "A Court which is final and unreviewable needs more careful scrutiny than any other. Unreviewable power is the most likely to self-indulge itself and the least likely to engage in dispassionate self-analysis.......In a country like ours, no public institution, or the people who operate it, can be above public debate."

1 *Ibid*, pages 67-68.
2 *Miliangos* v *George Frank Textiles Ltd.* (1976) AC 443 (481): (1975)3 All ER 801 HL.
3 David Pannick: *Judges*, 1988 Ed., page 73.

None can disagree with Jerome Frank, a great American Judge whose work "*Courts on Trial*" is a classic:

> "I am unable to conceive......that, in a democracy, it can ever be unwise to acquaint the public with the truth about the workings of any branch of Government. It is wholly undemocratic to treat the public as children who are unable to accept the inescapable shortcomings of man-made institutions......The best way to bring about the elimination of those shortcomings of our judicial system which are capable of being eliminated is to have all our citizens informed as to how that system now functions. It is a mistake, therefore, to try to establish and maintain, through ignorance, public esteem for our courts."[4]

Speaking on the legal profession, not the judges, Sir Zelman Cowen observed what the judiciary may duly remember:

> "The processes of our society invite debate and reasoned argument, and while it is understandable that there should be occasional explosion, I am sure that the debate on the professions will continue, and the future health of the professions will depend upon a continuing readiness to engage in debate and self-examination. Times are such that criticism will not go away by such expressions of repudiation, impatience and rejection, we are well warned that while the claim to expertise carries weight, that claim seems to have less weight in a society where the political temper is less authoritarian and more egalitarian. Moreover, the fact is that the authority of every profession is increasingly called into question as individuals and groups assert their right to participate in decisions that affect their future.......That, whether we like it or not, is the world in which we live."[5]

Independent judges are not an end but a means. The end is independence of justice, not bonded to bias, and administered by a bench-bar duet, the performers being open-minded, free from outside or inside pressures and never under obligations to, or suffer blackmail from, the Executive or dominant classes, mafia groups which may mug or terrorist gangs which may shoot justices and justice.

Global norms and risks revisited

The global dimensions of the problem emerge from my earlier references to the theme. An excerpt from H.R.I. (Human Rights Internet Reporter) sets the tone for a discussion on the status of independence of *justice, justices and justicing in India.* So I quote:

> "In 1985, the Seventh United Nations Congress on Crime Prevention and Control unanimously adopted the Basic Principles on the Independence of the Judiciary. The twenty principles were subsequently welcomed by the UN General Assembly which invited Governments to respect them and to take them into account in their national legislation and practice. They set forth principles concerning the independence of the judiciary, and the freedom of

4 David Pannick: *Judges*, page 205.

5 *1981 Reform*, page 19.

expression and association of judges, as well as guidelines regarding the qualification, selection, training, conditions of service, tenure, immunity, discipline, suspension and removal of judges."

Among the important principles are the following:

> "Everyone shall have the right to be tried by ordinary courts or tribunals using established legal procedures. Tribunals that do not use the duly established procedures of the legal process shall not be created to displace the jurisdiction belonging to the ordinary courts or judicial tribunals."
>
> "Judges, whether appointed or elected, shall have guaranteed tenure until a mandatory retirement age or the expiry of their term of office, where such exists."
>
> "Judges shall be subject to suspension or removal only for reasons of incapacity or behaviour that renders them unfit to discharge their duties."

This backdrop serves as an introduction to a study of the pathological erosion of Bench-Bar independence in India. The judiciary, in the first phase of Freedom, had been conditioned by British erudition and tradition of colonial vintage. This heritage, with all its merits, was allergic to radical ideas and human rights with crimson colours. The liberal dimensions of liberties appealed to the British Indian and Free India's judges, but as seen from *A.K. Gopalan's*[6] case and rulings on private property, gender justice, obscenity, labour relations *et al*, they did not take kindly to *avant-garde* ideologies projecting into the new frontiers of human rights. Some thoughtful jurists even called the Court the Conscience-keeper of the *status quo*. The Establishment, when it violated human justice, was not challenged by the judges, and the pontiffs on the high bench did much to stall land reforms, educational justice, nationalisation and the like. Some High Courts like Bihar and Andhra Pradesh and Karnataka, did their judicial best to break the back of land reforms laws notwithstanding the Ninth Schedule and other constitutional bullet-proofs. *Kochunni* and *Keshavananda et al* inhibited land reform legislation deepening the frustration of the landless and convincing them of the need for jungle terrorism against legal terrorism. Laws are make-believes, they feel, because they are full of loopholes, lacunae and judge-made torpedoes.

Nor did they promote gender justice, prison justice or social justice for bonded labourer, slum-dweller or other have-not sector. The mafia was not unhappy with that brand of judicial independence, since the 'haves' had it good. Of course, some jurists described the Courts as the Conscience-keepers of the proprietariat. Prof. Baxi in biting diction had a hard word about the higher courts' performance in generalised assertion.

"The artist", said Piccaso, "must discover a way to convince the general public the truth of his lies." For much too long the law persons—judges, lawyers and jurists everywhere in the world have successfully managed to convince the people of the truth of their lies concerning the nature of

6 AIR 1950 SC 27.

the judicial process. I consciously join, with this book, the slender minority of people who believe with Thomas Huxley that the "foundation of morality is to have done, once and for all, with lying".[7]

When the American judges, whose 'independent' pronouncement in the *Dred Scott* case had to be undone by a civil war, whose threats to Roosevelt's New Deal in the dark days of the great depression, meant to salvage the poor and the vulnerable categories, drove the President to the extreme move of 'packing' the Court, to save the Constitution from the Court and the Court from itself, the Executive and the Legislature had *prima facie* case against the Right Wing incarnating as 'robed brethren'. In India, the very first constitutional amendment, bearing on agrarian reforms and backward classes, was necessitated by the judges 'voiding' the values of the Freedom Struggle with elite eloquence. As Pandit Nehru in Parliament asserted, in the mood and diction of F.D. Roosevelt, a sentiment best brought out by quotes from F.D.R. and Panditji: Roosevelt warned:

> "We have, therefore, reached the point as a Nation where we must take action to save the Constitution from the Court and the Court from itself. We must find a way to take an appeal from the Supreme Court to the Constitution itself. We want a Supreme Court which will do justice under the Constitution—not over it. In our Courts we want a Government of laws and not of men. I want—as all Americans want—an independent judiciary as proposed by the framers of the Constitution."

Nehru argued:

> "We will honour our pledges. ......Within limits no judge and no Supreme Court can make itself a third chamber. No Supreme Court and no judiciary can stand in judgment over the sovereign will of Parliament representing the will of the entire community."

When the second generation political Administration, under Indira Gandhi *of the first phase,* launched on Bank Nationalisation, abolition of Princely Privy Purses, Land Reforms, taking of land without avaricious compensation and so on, the "ayatollahs" of the judiciary, asserting conservative 'independence', upheld values incongruous with our socialistic Republic's founding creed. The crisis that followed led to flaks and confrontations. This, in turn, led to exercises in Executive 'packing' of judicial offices and even constitutional changes (like Schedule IX) to exclude judicial jurisdiction from certain areas. Schedule IX was brought in by 1951 Amendment–though it has now taken giant's shape over the years. These Executive-Legislative manoeuvres ostensibly sought to suppress judicial excesses but operated to clip the free wings of the Court, with undesirable consequences of undermining judicial independence. A crisis was brewing. A cold war between the Court and the House, where the Judges struck down legislations where the 'haves' were hurt, deepened the gap. This escalating estrangement climaxed later, with deleterious and

7 Prof. Upendra Baxi in the Introduction to the book *Indian Supreme Court and Politics.*

desperate stratagems like 'supersession' by the Executive, to handcuff Judicial Power. Thus began a chain-reaction rendering impotent the Court's power as the sentinel on the *qui vive* of people's liberties. A battle of the tenses, between heritage and heresy, a clash between 'hands off' and 'hand-cuff'.

Justice Desai's Law Commission, in its 121st Report, touches on these aspects in its search for an Indian method to free judicial selection from Executive control.

The Commission made a study of the modus of appointment of judges in many countries like the U.S., the U.K., the U.S.S.R., France, Australia and so on, with a view to derive from comparative glances some lessons for Indian application designed to liberate the system from Executive thraldom. A constitutional amendment, geared to setting up of a judicial commission, had been under way and the Desai recommendations may edify the Law Ministry and the House on the problems of judicial appointment. But the 'bibliographic foreign travels' of the Desai Report disclose no enchanting novelties from the perspective of immunity from the political Executive or elimination of those inhibitions, allergies or affections of judges themselves. The expanding claims of human rights and the living hope of social justice are the driving force of the struggle of *independence of justice.*

An aside

The issues just discussed are of contemporary relevance to India and are being debated at various levels. This is evident from a recent seminar on the independence of the judiciary organised by the Creative Lawyers' Club. A few excerpts from a newspaper report will suffice for the present, although a more detailed discussion will be undertaken at a later stage of this lecture:

> "The process of appointment of judges has to be changed if the independence of judiciary has to be safeguarded, argued the eminent lawyer and jurist, Mr. Ram Jethmalani here on Wednesday."
>
> *** *** ***
>
> "Mr. Jethmalani also put forward a strong case for consultation of the Bar in appointment of judges, pointing out that it was the Bar which knew best the calibre of the judges. He also argued that the consultation process during appointment of judges should be made known to the public.
>
> *** *** ***
>
> "The Chief Justice of India, Mr. R.N. Mishra, at a seminar a few years back, stressing the need for judges to keep their behaviour above board, mentioned instances where members of the judicial community tried to canvass for appointments. He said while an honest judge could always resist pressure to compromise his integrity, there were cases when members of the judicial community sought favours or expressed desire for particular postings, so much so that things became questionable.
>
> "Mr. Mishra also referred to the commercialisation of the legal profession, pointing out instances where advocates had turned down postings as High Court judges as 'pointless'. 'The lustre attached to the post has gone'," he said.

*** *** ***

"Stressing the importance of maintaining propriety, the eminent jurist and Vice-Chancellor of University of Delhi, Prof. Upendra Baxi said that independence of judiciary would be a thing of the past within 10 years, unless the judiciary and the Bar took care to keep themselves above board. It is the threat from within that poses the greatest danger," he said.

"Prof. Baxi spoke of lack of information about what went into the appointment of judges, taking a dig at the Chief Justice, Mr. R.N. Mishra, who had referred to a write-up on 'making a judge' in Britain. Prof. Baxi pointed out that it might tell one about what happens in that country, there was no source of information about what went into the making of a judge in India."

*** *** ***

Mr. Bhandare, M.P. said that there had been no talk of corruption in the judiciary earlier, but such allegations were reported now. He also stressed the need to guard against the evils of influence and bias for keeping the judiciary independent.

The former High Court Judge, Mr. M.L. Verma, spoke about the need for a self-cleansing mechanism in the judicial community to preserve the integrity and the independence of the institution. He also stressed upon the need for judiciary and Bar to maintain propriety.[8]

Back to the Desai Commission

Chairman Desai (of the previous Central Law Commission) has done service by taking a global look at the problem but the focus is limited to freedom from Executive or political or electoral dependencia. It should have been wider because what hurts human rights is also class bias, moral callousness, social vices and willing collaboration with injustice where one's own interests coalesce with the ideologies and practices objected to by currently alienated categories. The human stuff of the judiciary has many dimensions often slurred over in our hurry to remove Government influence.

The instructive analysis by the Law Commission only emphasises that in most countries, politics (of the class in power) is the major factor, whether through the President, Prime Minister, Party-dominated electorate or other variants. But vesting the power to choose in the Chief Justice is no solution since he/she may have prejudices or favourities or ignorance about most judges in many states and may for extraneous reasons, share the institutions of top noted Executive. Collective wisdom with under participation has no substitute where selections to the highest judicial officers are the issues. The mild participation of the Bench and the Bar is poor consolation because these entrenched institutions, in their collective character, are unlikely to show concern for causes going against the profession's social status or economic interests or religious mores of the upper sector of society. Even professional excellence may have a class or communal perception, excluding heresies, colour categories and unconventional humanism radicalising

8 *Indian Express*, Kochi, dated 13.9.1991.

professional hues. The Establishment, with its 'dominant class' politics and its unwitting ventriloquists choose the judges, in the last analysis. By this process, the battle for independence of the judiciary *vis-a-vis* the marginalised masses and deprived victims, hungry for human justice, is lost at birth. A few freak wonders, as in the United States and, less rarely, in the United Kingdom, break out of these limitations and blaze the trail. If India is a Socialist Secular Democratic Republic, the judicial engineers must be selected by very different processes from what now obtains, with more people-oriented, value-specific criteria rooted in the ethos of the Preamble, Parts III, IV and IV A. The poser is: Do we take our Constitution seriously? Do we agree that judges are *not* the janitors of business houses and feudal edifices, *not* sentinels of communal structures and political house-keepers of prejudice-laden but powerful segments? Judicial radicals who would accelerate the Constitutional revolution was the dream of the founding fathers—not 'robed authority' commanding a progressive society fighting corruption and regressive policies in locomotion to halt or you will be shot with the fire power of Court writ! This fundamental is deliberately blurred or buried when the issue is debated. A new wave of *glasnost* and *perestroika,* with constructive intent and fruitful projects *vis-a-vis* selection of judges is the call of the Constitution, so as to fulfill itself. This is the spirit to miss which is to institutionalise Justice made to order, whoever be in power, alienating those fugitives from orthodoxy and multitudes of marginalised destitutes for whom the bells of the Constitution toll. Without competent cadres committed to the vibrant values of humanist, socialist slant, how can a constitutional revolution be operated through the rule of law? The Constitution is the value watershed of our radical *daridranarayana-based* jurisprudence. Prospective candidates must share this creed.

After all, Anatole France hit the nail on the head when he said:

> "To disarm the strong and arm the weak would be to change the social order, which it's my job to preserve. Justice is the means by which established injustices are sanctioned."

It is useful to note, however, that other mechanisms have been experimented with in other jurisdictions Anglo-American, using the Bar as watchdog over proper appointments, weaning the politician in power from playing politics with judicial personnel. But the corporate complexion of lawyers as a class does not make one optimistic in this regard. Nor is the Chief Justice institutionally efficient or sufficient to produce judicial independence. Be that as it may, in the U.K., the Justice Sub-Committee on the Judiciary (1972), says the Desai Report:

> "Recommended that while the Lord Chancellor should retain control of the appointment machinery, he should be helped in his task by a small advisory Appointments Committee. The exact composition of the Committee is not set out in the report. On the all-important question of composition of the Committee the view was that *it should include representatives of the Law Society, the Bar, academic lawyers, the judiciary and perhaps some lay members as, for example, highly trained and experienced personnel officers*

skilled in selection procedures. Under the proposed scheme, interested bodies could make recommendations to the Appointments Committee and even persons seeking judicial appointment may submit their names to it. The Lord Chancellor would be free to reject or accept the recommendations of the Committee and even would be free to select anyone whose name is not found in the list recommended by the Committee. But in such a case he would be under an obligation to consider the recommendation of the Committee and to submit his own candidates to the Committee for their comments and would not be able to make appointments without consulting them or applying his mind to the views expressed by them. Even earlier, a committee, styled as the Machinery of Government Committee, in the year 1918 recommended in its report that the Home Office should become a Ministry of Justice and that *the Lord Chancellor should be required in recommending persons for judgeship to consult a Committee consisting of the Prime Minister, the Minister of Justice, ex Lord Chancellor and the Lord Chief Justice.* Therefore, the debate about setting up of a committee to assist the Lord Chancellor has been in the offing for more than half a century. It must be confessed that there is also a body of opinion that no change is necessary in the system of appointment to judicial offices as proposed by the Sub-Committee. However, following the introduction of the new scheme by the Courts Act, 1971, those knowledgeable are veering round to the view that the question of reform must be carefully considered and that some improvement in the existing system is necessary. The Committee has examined the question of appointment to superior courts, the circuit benches and even Courts below them. Those who advocate the change assert that the present procedure is too much embedded in secrecy and that the acceptance and rejection are unsupported by reasons. They say that the selection procedures should not only be painstaking and fair but seem to be so. There is too much subjectivism in this procedure as the whole thing depends upon the opinion of the Lord Chancellor. *With reference to the proposal for a committee, an apprehension was voiced that such a broad based decision making body may encourage lobbying and generate pressure groups. It was also feared that, as the opinion of the Members of the Committee may vary, the horse trading would become inevitable. Some doubt was voiced even with regard to the composition of the Committee.*[9]

The Commission continues:

"President of United States of America has established a circuit judges nominating Commission to recommend names of the best qualified persons for appointment to the United States Court of Appeal. Under the Presidential Order thirteen panels were to be set up. *Each panel will have not more than eleven members, including its Chairman and must include members of both sexes, members of minority groups, and approximately equal number of lawyers and non-lawyers.* The function of each panel and the standard for selection to be followed have been set out in the order itself. *Briefly the standards for selection are that the recommendee must have good standing, must possess and have good reputation for integrity and good character, must*

9 *121st Report of the Law Commission of India, 1987,* Chapter VI, pages 95-96.

> *be enjoying sound health and must have outstanding legal ability and commitment to equal justice under law.*
>
> "The Chief Justice of Australia, somewhere in July 1977, advocated that the time is now ripe for a Judicial Appointments Committee to be set up in Australia. This view was conversant in the backdrop of the feeling that the Australian system for selection and appointment of Judges provided an opportunity for political influence. With a view to eliminating the same, the appointment must be made by, or pursuant to, *a recommendation from Judicial Appointments Committee to be composed of Judges,* lawyers and some laymen.
>
> "Similarly, the Royal Commission on Courts, chaired by Justice Beattle, who later on became Governor-General of New Zealand, recommended that *a Judicial Commission should consider all judicial appointments, including appointment of High Court Judges.*"[10]

The thrust in all these proposals is to restrain the political executive. But if the censors themselves are not activists in the new frontiers jurisprudence and of Human Rights in their radical dimensions, the panel they propose may produce judges with genetic disinclination to accept the new thinking on, and the unconventional extensions of, Human Rights in a universe with Third World suppressions and Fourth World dehumanisations. Judicial independence must slough off the old notion of mere exclusion of executive control over the judiciary. More, much more is called for if Justice,—not only Judges—is to be independent.

10 *Ibid,* paras 6.17, 6.18 and 6.19.

12

Current Indian Realities vis-a-vis People's Human Rights

The human rights heritage of Bharat, in its modern verbal apparel, may be traced to the Constitution of India which marks the watershed in this sublime branch of jurisprudence. The Charter of the United Nations (1945) and the Universal Declaration of Human Rights (1948) influenced the founding fathers of our Constitution. Mahatma Gandhi and Jawaharlal Nehru and many other legendary leaders like Dr. Ambedkar had a vision of a free nation where the humblest had fundamental freedoms—social, economic and political—like the highest and the wealthiest. These rights and duties lie spread out, as of today, in Parts III, IV and IVA, and an imaginative student, be he lawyer, judge or academic, statesman or social activist, can read almost everything in the Universal Declaration and the two Covenants into the constellation of Constitutional articles. Indeed, what has been known as the Bangalore Principles, declared by a Resolution dated 26th February 1988 of the Judges of the Commonwealth countries, affirms the importance of importing, by interpretation, the values enwombed in the UN instruments on human rights into domestic laws, as far as possible. Moreover, the Universal Declaration, passed unanimously by the General Assembly, casts an obligation on member States to bring the *corpus juris* of the country into line with the norms laid down in that paradigmatic masterpiece. India has ratified both the consequential Covenants and is duty bound to take steps as aforesaid. The initial concern and euphoria slowly wore off and so, the two Covenants could be drawn up as UN instruments only in 1966; and the reluctance of the member States to bring the Covenants into force is apparent from the delay until 1966 to pass them and *another ten long years* to bring them into force with the requisite number (35) of ratifications. The U.S. has not, with all its boasts, even now signed the Covenant on Economic, Social and Cultural Rights. The Protocol to the ICCPR which gives teeth to the Covenant still remains unratified by most of the Powers, U.S., U.K. and India included. The Cold War dampened the human rights idealism of the member nations. Indeed, the tone of the rhetoric shifted from human harmony to containment of communism. In Vietnam and Korea, in the Middle East and South America, ruthless violation of human rights in the name of the free world and the cult of democracy, with cliques and claques controlling Power, was indulged in. The double-speak on civil and political rights put to shame the very concept of fundamental freedoms. India, as it stepped out of colonial clutches, struck a new path; and Nehru, true to the Bandung spirit, wanted *Panchasheel* or Five Principles of international relations to generate global camaraderie. The sovereignty of the people was strengthened by India playing a leading role in the Non-Aligned Movement (NAM). People's human rights needed freedom from Super-Power pressure and NAM made sense as a response to cold war politics. NAM was:

> "A movement of states which espoused the position of not taking sides in the major division within world politics between the USA and USSR. A number of recently de-colonized countries have favoured non-alignment as a mark of their independence. A formal Non-Aligned Movement, begun in 1961, holds regular conferences; there were 103 members in 1991, but the numbers fluctuate."

Although the Universal Charter was adopted without a single dissent and India played a decisive role in the liberation and democratisation of subject nations, the United Nations proved to be ineffective; and consequently the Third World and the vast human numbers inhabiting it suffered impoverishment and emasculation of human rights, individual and collective. Moreover, the two Covenants proved to be glorious futilities; and what with a divided world and absence of any monitoring mechanism, nothing much was done to make Sovereign States accountable to humanity. True, Art. 2 of the Covenant on Economic, Social and Cultural Rights charged each State Party with the obligation to take steps with a view to achieving progressively the full realisation of rights recognised. But the world body failed to infuse reality into the enchanting and flickering diction of the articles of the Covenants. Moreover, the U.S. was loud only about the Political Covenant as its main agenda while the USSR emphasised the Economic content of the other Covenant. This dichotomy, with the two *then* Super-Powers taking sides, dominated the discourse on human rights. The Cold War stymied the warmth of humanity in its faith about the global future of universal human rights.

Some countries, particularly of the ASEAN grouping, refuted the rigid universality of human rights and asserted that:

> "While human rights are universal in nature, they must be considered in the context of a dynamic and evolving process of international norm setting, bearing in mind the significance of national and regional particularities and various historical, cultural and religious backgrounds" (Darryl D'Monte, 1993). The West immediately retaliated by sermonising that "differences in cultures do not and cannot absolve any one of us from our obligation to comply with the Universal Declaration of Human Rights......Torture, rape, racism, anti-semitism, arbitrary detentions, ethnic cleansings and politically motivated disappearance—none of this is tolerated by any faith or culture that respects

humanity, nor can they be justified by the demands of economic development or political expediency.[1]

India has struck a middle path blending both viewpoints. The Fundamental Rights inscribed in Part III echo the values of one Covenant even as Part IV provisions, read in the light of the Preamble, are succulent with the economic and social concerns of the ECOSOC Covenant. Part IVA goes further into ecological and environmental justice, gender justice and jurisprudence of compassion and common brotherhood, making it a fundamental duty of every citizen 'to protect and improve the natural environment including forests, lakes, rivers and wild life and to have compassion for living creatures, [Art. 51A(*g*)]. Likewise, humanism and defending the dignity of women are the vigilant fundamental duty of every Indian citizen. Textually, we have a Constitution which is fragrant with humanism, socialism, democracy, people-oriented mandates with a benign slant towards the suppressed human sector and a developmental paradigm committed to abolition of poverty and promotion of have-nots to a status of equality. The highest Court in India has ruled that social justice and socialist pattern are paramount in the governance of the country. For a variety of reasons, the Indian State has committed itself to the essentials of the international bill of human rights. But the British Raj had for long conditioned the ruling classes differently and that die-hard disposition haunts the thoughtways of the politicians in power and the psyche of the business community. So much so, notwithstanding the clear constitutional mandate, the imperial texture of the bureaucracy and the corruption of the politicos distorted governmental processes and covertly continued the feudal, capitalist and corrupt ethos using newspeak and double-speak to hide their intents.

In all humility and with burning conviction, I hold the view that without violating the spirit and text of the Constitution no authority in India can or should dubiously circumvent or disingenuously interpret into impotence this socialistic imperative and be victim of the Circean spell of foreign dazzling developmental models contrary to the culture, values and traditions of India sanctified by the struggle for Independence and poignant sufferings of the masses. The oath of office taken under the Constitution by the elite who administer it cannot be dismissed on opportunist grounds or xenophilic fascination, since that will be a betrayal of the Preambular quintessentials and normative principles enshrined in it and may tend to be a contra-Constitutional coup contrary to the Summit Court's considered rulings. I emphasize this point having regard to the glib forgetfulness of the operators of the Constitution that it creates a Secular Socialist Democratic Republic– nothing less, nothing else. It follows that human rights–civil, political, social and economic–belong to Indians as a title derived from the cornucopian Constitution. When we expound a Constitution the lofty, oft-quoted words of Chief Justice Marshall of the US Supreme Court must

1 *Perspectives on Human Rights* edited by Vijay K. Gupta, Introduction pages 7-8.

inspire our perspective since a Founding Deed must endure for ages and serve generations yet to come.

I must dwell at some length on the Indian Fundamental Law to drive home my point that the expanding horizon of human rights is painted in pregnant prose in the Paramount Law and its Preamble. The provisions of the Constitution and the laws must bear the impress of the International Instruments when the Bench and the Bar interpret, with luminous semantics the words used. Judges and lawyers must update their jurisprudence in tune with the noble UN instruments. With this object, the human rights lawyer needs to be properly educated, equipped and exposed. To borrow the words of a great Nigerian Judge:

> "He needs to read widely in the humanities. So, he must have access to a good library. He must master the general principles of law. He must also master national and international human rights norms and principles of their interpretation. He must himself develop a human rights culture. It is important for him to realise that human rights norms are not isolationist in nature; rather they are international in the sense that, subject to express provisions of national constitutions and laws, the principle and content of international human rights norms are basically the same. So, the way they have been interpreted in one country can be a useful guide to their approach and interpretation in another."[2]

The International Congress of Jurists held in Rio de Janeiro, Brazil, in December 1992 stated that:

> "......if lawyers are to discharge their obligations under the rule of law they will need to exercise individual initiative and act through......a self-governing Lawyers' Association. Such an Association must be entirely free of interference and control by the Executive."[3]

The education and exposure of human rights lawyers in this field of specialisation is a challenge to the Bar. Only an activist bar can broaden the rule of *locus standi,* innovate social action litigation and use the Court to promote public interest *lis*, since the Judges are obligated to do justice. This can best be achieved by permitting any person to put the judicial machinery in motion, like the *actio popularis* of Roman Law.

In a learned colloquium, (26-2-1988) Commonwealth jurists collected what has been referred to as 'Bangalore Principles' which may well be reproduced here:

> "(1) Fundamental human rights and freedoms are inherent in all humankind and find expression in constitutions and legal systems throughout the world and in the international human rights instruments.
>
> (2) These international human rights instruments provide important guidance in cases concerning fundamental human rights and freedoms.

2 (1992)18 CLB, pages 737-738.

3 (1992)18 CLB, page 742.

(3) There is an impressive body of jurisprudence, both international and national, concerning the interpretation of particular human rights and freedoms and their application. The body of jurisprudence is of practical relevance and value to judges and lawyers generally.

(4) In most countries whose legal systems are based upon the common law, international convention are not directly enforceable in national courts unless their provisions have been incorporated by legislation into domestic law. However, there is a growing tendency for national courts to have regard to these international norms for the purpose of deciding cases where the domestic law—whether constitutional, statute or common law—is uncertain or incomplete.

(5) This tendency is entirely welcome because it respects the universality of fundamental human rights and freedoms and the vital role of an independent judiciary in reconciling the competing claims of individuals and groups of persons with the general interests of the community.

(6) While it is desirable for the norms contained in the international human rights instruments to be still more widely recognised and applied by national courts, this process must take fully into account local laws, traditions, circumstances and needs.

(7) It is with the proper nature of the judicial process and well-established judicial functions for national courts to have regard to international obligations which a country undertakes—whether or not they have been incorporated into domestic law—for the purpose of removing ambiguity or uncertainty from national constitutions, legislation or common law.

(8) However, where national law is clear and inconsistent with the international obligations of the State concerned, in common law countries the national court is obliged to give effect to national law. In such cases the court should draw such inconsistency to the attention of the appropriate authorities since the supremacy of national law in no way mitigates a breach of an international legal obligation which is undertaken by a country.

(9) It is essential to redress a situation where, by reason of traditional legal training which has tended to ignore the international dimension, judges and practising lawyers are often unaware of the remarkable and comprehensive developments of statements of international human rights norms. For the practical implementation of these views it is desirable to make provision for appropriate courses in universities and colleges, and for lawyers and law enforcement officials; provision in libraries of relevant materials; promotion of expert advisory bodies knowledgeable about developments in this field; better dissemination of information to judges, lawyers and law enforcement officials; and meetings for exchanges of relevant information and experience.

(10) These views are expressed in recognition of the fact that judges and lawyers have a special contribution to make in the administration of justice in fostering universal respect for fundamental human rights and freedoms."

These principles have been reaffirmed in the Harare Declaration (1989) and in the Banjul Affirmation (1990) as well as the Abuja Confirmation

(1991). All of them insist that international instruments emanating from the UN strengthening human rights must be telescoped into national legal systems to the maximum extent language permits.

Lawyers and Judges are the engineers of human rights jurisprudence. The Indian Constitution and the many legislations which flesh out the human rights principles need a measure of sensitivity so that the international bill of rights may be integrated into the national *corpus juris*. An illustration of this semantic process is found in *Jolly George Varghese* v *The Bank of Cochin*.[4] The Supreme Court there observed:

> "(6) Right at the beginning, we may take up the bearing of Article 11 on the law that is to be applied by an Indian Court when there is a specific provision in the Civil Procedure Code, authorising detention for non-payment of a decree debt. The Covenant bans imprisonment merely for not discharging a decree debt. Unless there be some other vice or *mens rea* apart from failure to foot the decree, international law frowns on holding the debtor's person in civil prison, as hostage by the Court. India is now a signatory to this Covenant and Article 51(c) of the Constitution obligates the State to "foster respect for international law and treaty obligations in the dealings of organised peoples with one another". Even so, until the municipal law is changed to accommodate the Covenant what binds the Court is the former, not the latter. A.H. Robertson in "Human Rights—in National and International Law" rightly points out that international conventional law must go through the process of *transformation* into the municipal law before the international treaty can become an internal law.
>
> *** *** ***
>
> "The march of civilization has been a story of progressive subordination of property rights to personal freedom; and a by-product of this subordination finds noble expression in the declaration that 'No one shall be imprisoned merely on the ground of inability to fulfil a contractual obligation.' This revolutionary change in the regard for the human person is spanned by the possible shock that a resuscitated Shylock would suffer if a modern Daniel were to come to judgment when the former asks the pound of flesh from Antonio's bosom according to the tenor of the bond, by flatly refusing the mayhem on the debtor, because the inability of an impecunious obligee shall not imperil his liberty or person under the new dispensation proclaimed by the Universal Declaration of Human Rights.
>
> *** *** ***
>
> "The remedy for breaches of International Law in general is not to be found in the law courts of the State because International Law *per se* or *proprio vigore* has not the force or authority of civil law, till under its inspirational impact actual legislation is undertaken. I agree that the Declaration of Human Rights merely sets a common standard of achievement for all peoples and all nations but cannot create a binding set of rules. Member States may seek, through appropriate agencies, to initiate action when these basic rights are violated,

4 AIR 1980 SC 470.

but individual citizens cannot complain about their breach in the municipal Courts even if the country concerned has adopted the covenants and ratified the operational protocol. The individual cannot come to Court but may complain to the Human Rights Committee, which, in turn, will set in motion other procedures. In short, the basic human rights enshrined in the International Covenants above referred to may at best inform judicial institutions and inspire legislative action within member-States."

*** *** ***

"Counsel for the respondent did argue that (the proposition that) International Law is the vanishing point of jurisprudence is itself vanishing in a world where humanity is moving steadily, though slowly, towards a world order, led by that intensely active, although yet ineffectual body, the United Nations Organisation. Its resolutions and covenants mirror the conscience of mankind and inseminate, within the member States, progressive legislation, but till this last step of actual enactment of law takes place, the citizen in a world of sovereign States, has only inchoate rights in the domestic Courts under these international covenants."

I must, however, note that the Indian Supreme Court has, in a number of recent decisions, unhesitatingly ruled that *even in the absence* of Parliamentary Legislations under Art. 253 implementing International Covenants to which India is party, the provisions of such covenants, as are "not inconsistent with the Fundamental Rights and in harmony with its spirit, *must be read* into those provisions to enlarge the meaning and content......" and that "the executive power of the Union" under Art. 73 is also "available till the Parliament enacts Legislations......" and reference in this connection may be made, among others, to the Constitution Bench decision in *Maganbhai Ishwarbhai Patel.*[4a] of 1969 and to a rather recent decision in *Vishaka*[4b] in 1997.

The jurisprudence woven around the Preamble to our Constitution has many dimensions, radical and crimson. The value revolution and humanist transformation the Constitution has inaugurated has yet to blossom fully to make the lives of the many millions of our countrymen pulsate with material, moral and spiritual joy. The great vision of our founding fathers was that a just social order should bloom into existence in the fullness of time where the feeblest of the Indian fraternity shall have fulfilment, not frustration, where the State shall strive to wipe every tear from every eye, where people's sovereignty and democracy shall prevail. That is the mission of the Indian Republic projected in the Fundamental Rights (Part III) as well as the next Parts (IV and IVA) dealing with the Directive Principles of State Policy and the Fundamental Duties of the Citizen.

The Constitution is more than a legal parchment. It is a fabian socio-economic instrument with a revolutionary thrust. Indeed, the high purpose and the wealth of human rights which inhere in the citizens of India by

4a AIR 1969 SC 733.

4b AIR 1997 SC 3011 at 3014.

virtue of the Constitution are condensed, with delicious brevity and precious dignity, in the Preambular passages. We can never forget that the people of India as a whole, not the elite nor the upper strata nor, indeed, the power-brokers and creamy layers but *all the people* are the title-holders under the Constitution. That is why Justice Vivian Bose once stated that the Constitution was meant for the butcher, the baker and candle-stick maker; may I add, also for the tortured prisoner, the bonded labourer the discriminated gender, the marginalised dissenter and the disabled, deprived human.

When the British withdrew and the Indian people became free, they adopted a structure for their Constitution which definitely included Justice—social, economic and political; Liberty and Equality, together guaranteeing the dignity of each individual and the unity of the nation. This large fraternity of Indian community has been constituted into a Republic with its attributes of ultimate sovereignty, socialist texture, secular character and democratic culture. Such is the substantive structure and constitutional jurisprudence of the Preamble.

The Preambular Jurisprudence is as noble as the Vienna Declaration recently made by 183 nations. The New World Human Order is based upon sacred principles which are also found in the Indian Preamble. The cornerstone of the Indian Constitutional Order is thus humanist, secular, socialist and an expression of people's power.

Unfortunately, illiteracy about the Constitutional fundamentals and basic features is popular among our politicians and even the bureaucrats and judges who miss the luminous absolutes shining in the voluminous Constitution. As a people, we must insist on the new value revolution being implemented so that the Constitution may become vibrant as a rule of life. Only then, human rights find a fail-safe harbour in the Fundamental Law.

Jurisprudence cannot go it alone. It is people's militancy without violence, literacy without arrogance, sense of accountability without authoritarianism that can make the Constitution the great guarantee and perennial locomotive of People's rights. The *creme de la creme* of the Constitution, in its political vision, economic mission and developmental action, is what the Preamble tersely spells out. The Preamble itself is a value-based jurisprudence in its abbreviated excellence.

In *D.S. Nakara,*[5] the Preamble was used to strengthen the conclusion that a *socialist goal* was included in the founding faith of the Constitution. Says Justice Desai, speaking for a unanimous Bench:

> "Recall at this stage the Preamble, the floodlight illuminating the path to be pursued by the State to set up a Sovereign Socialist Secular Democratic Republic.
>
> Expression 'Socialist' was intentionally introduced in the Preamble by the Constitution (Forty-second Amendment) Act, 1976. In the objects and Reasons for amendment amongst other things, ushering in of socio-economic revolution was promised. The clarion call may be extracted:

5 AIR 1983 SC 130.

"The question of amending the Constitution for removing the difficulties which have arisen in achieving the objective of socio-economic revolution, which would end poverty and ignorance and disease and inequality of opportunity, has been engaging the active attention of Government and the public for some time.........

"It is, therefore, proposed to amend the Constitution to spell out expressly the high ideals of socialism......to make the directive principles more comprehensive........." * * *

"The principal aim of a socialist State is to eliminate inequality in income and status and standards of life. The basic framework of socialism is to provide a decent standard of life to the working people and especially provide security from cradle to grave. This amongst others on economic side envisaged equality and equitable distribution of income. This is a blend of Marxism and Gandhism leaning heavily towards Gandhian socialism. During the formative years, socialism aims at providing all opportunities for pursuing the educational activity."[6]

The Court heavily relied upon Part IV of the Constitution and quoted Chinnappa Reddy, J. in *Randhir Singh*:[7]

"Now, thanks to the rising social and political consciousness and the expectations roused as a consequence and the forward looking posture of this Court, the under-privileged also are clamouring for their rights and are seeking the intervention of the Court with touching faith and confidence in the Court. The Judges of the Court have a duty to redeem their constitutional oath and do justice no less to the pavement-dweller than to the guest of the Five Star Hotel."

Human dignity is inviolable and anything done derogatory to the dignity of womanhood is denounced by the Constitution (Art. 51). It is the duty of the State to respect and protect the same. It is primarily the dissemination of culture that brings out the radiant faculties of a person. The framers of the Constitution were aware that more than seventy per cent of the people, for whom they were drawing up the Constitution of India, were then illiterate. An individual cannot be assured of human dignity unless his personality is developed and the only way to do that is to educate him. This is why the Universal Declaration of Human Rights, 1948, emphasizes: "Education shall be directed to the full development of the human personality......" Art. 41, in Part IV of the Constitution, recognises an individual's 'right to education'. It says that "the State shall, within the limits of its economic capacity and development, make effective provision for securing the right......to education......". Although the Directive Principles are not justiceable they are not mere pious declarations. We may quote the words of Dr. Ambedkar in that respect.

"In enacting this part of the Constitution, the Assembly is giving certain directions of the future legislature and the future executive to show in what

6 AIR 1983 SC 130 at 139.
7 AIR 1982 SC 879.

manner they are to exercise the legislative and the executive power they will have. Surely it is not the intention to introduce in this part these principles as mere pious declarations. It is the intention of the Assembly that in future both the legislature and the executive should not merely pay lip-service to these principles but that they should be made the basis of all legislative and executive action that they may be taking hereafter in the matter of the governance of the country."[8]

A few observations of the High Bench are apt:

"In *Francis Coralie Mullin v Administrator, Union Territory of Delhi* (1981)2 SCR 516: AIR 1981 SC 746, this Court elaborating the right guaranteed under Article 21 of the Constitution of India held as under (at p. 753 of AIR):

"But the question which arises is whether the right to life is limited only to protection of limb or faculty or does it go further and embrace something more. We think that the right to life includes the right to live with human dignity and all that goes along with it, namely the bare necessaries of life such an adequate nutrition, clothing and shelter and facilities for reading, writing and expressing oneself in diverse forms, freely moving about the mixing and commingling with fellow human beings. Of course, the magnitude and content of the components of this right would depend upon the extent of economic development of the country, but it must in any view of the matter, include the right to the basic necessities of life and also the right to carry on such functions and activities to constitute the bare minimum expression of the human-self."

In *Bandhua Mukti Morcha v Union of India* (1984)2 SCR 67: AIR 1984 SC 802, this Court held as under (at pp. 811-812 of AIR):

"This right to live with human dignity enshrined in Article 21 derives its life breath from the Directive Principles of State Policy and particularly clauses (e) and (*f*) of Article 39 and Articles 41 and 42 and at the least, therefore, it must include protection of the health and strength of workers men and women, and of the tender age of children against abuse, opportunities and facilities for children to develop in a healthy manner and in conditions of freedom and dignity, educational facilities, just and human conditions of work and maternity relief. These are the minimum requirements which must exist in order to enable a person to live with human dignity and no State—neither the Central Government nor any State Government—has the right to take any action which will deprive a person of the enjoyment of these basic essential.

"'Right to life' is the compendious expression for all these rights which the Courts must enforce because they are basic to the dignified enjoyment of life. It extends to the full range of conduct which the individual is free to pursue. The right to education flows directly from right to life. The right to life under Art. 21 and the dignity of an individual cannot be assured unless it is accompanied by the right to education. The State Government is under an obligation to make endeavour to provide educational facilities at all levels to its citizens.

8 *Constituent Assembly Debates*, vol. VII, page 476.

> " The Fundamental Rights guaranteed under Part III of the Constitution of India including the right to freedom of speech and expression and other rights under Art. 19 cannot be appreciated and fully enjoyed unless a citizen is educated and is conscious of his individualistic dignity."[9]

Part IV of the Constitution also highlights the socialistic sheen of the scheme. Dr. Ambedkar, referring to this part, observed in the Constituent Assembly:

> "In my judgment, the Directive Principles have a great value, for they lay down that our ideal is economic democracy. Because we did not want merely a parliamentary form of Government to be instituted through the various mechanisms provided in the Constitution, without any direction as to what our economic ideal, as to what our social order ought to be, we deliberately included the Directive Principles in our Constitution."

The Supreme Court has explained the concept of distributive justice as a means of removing economic inequalities and remedying the injustices resulting from social inequality writ large. In *Lingappa Pochanna*[10] the Court stressed this aspect and Prof. Tope has commented thereon:

> "Law should be used as an instrument of distributive justice to achieve a fair division of wealth among the members of society based upon the principle 'From each according to his capacity, to each according to his needs'. Distributive justice comprehends more than achieving lessening of inequalities by differential taxation, giving debt relief or distribution of property owned by one to many who have none by imposing ceiling on holding both agricultural and urban or by direct regulation of contractual transactions by forbidding certain transactions and perhaps by requiring others. It also means that those who have been deprived of their properties by unconscionable bargains should be restored their property. All such laws may take the form of forced distribution of wealth as a means of achieving a fair division of material resources among the members of society or there may be legislative control of unfair agreements."[11]

Even environmental protection and unemployment elimination are part of constitutional justice (vide Arts. 48A and 51A(*g*). The Supreme Court, in a case which came before it on a number of occasions, while upholding the fundamental duty about the protection of environment, laid down:

> "We are not oblivious to the fact that the natural resources have got to be tapped for the purpose of social development, but one cannot forget at the same time that tapping of resources have to be done with requisite attention and care so that ecology and environment may not be affected in a serious way. It has always to be remembered that these are not permanent assets of mankind.

9 *Mohini Jain* v *State of Karnataka* AIR 1992 SC 1858.

10 AIR 1985 SC 389.

11 T.K. Tope: *Constitutional Law of India*, 2nd Ed., page 337.

"A.P. High Court held that preservation and protection of natural gifts is a part of right under Article 21. When indiscriminate operation of mines prove to be hazardous to natural wealth and environment, Courts intervene and issue directions even as to closures of mines. Article 51A confers a right on citizens to move Courts for appropriate writs."[12]

Democracy, with equality, on *a level playing ground,* is never achieved where cases of elite upper classes are able to prosper in opulent oasis, leaving sandy deserts for destitutes and under-privileged in a state of despair. Therefore, dynamic intervention by the State in favour of the weaker sections from a developmental angle is necessarily instrumental in fulfilment of socio-economic justice. Equality before the law is not a mere negative concept, but includes a command to the State to eliminate inequalities by affirmative action. Formal equality before the law is often a sham, or razzamatazz. Likewise, unequals being treated as equals in the economic and social fields is but baloney *vis-a-vis* the humbler sector. A giant corporation with multinational prowess and small-scale or tiny sector enterprise can never be treated equally. Procrustean equality is inequality coupled with cruelty, which is anathema to the Constitution (Art. 14). Granville Austin has pertinently stated:

"The Fundamental Rights and Directives Principles had their roots deep in the struggle for independence. And they were included in the Constitution in the hope and expectation that one day the tree of true liberty would bloom in India. Rights and Principles thus connect India's future, present, and past, adding greatly to the significance of their inclusion in the Constitution and giving strength to the pursuit of the social revolution in India.......... In the Directive Principles, however, one finds even clearer statement of social revolution. They aim at making the Indian masses free in the positive sense, free from passivity endangered by the centuries of coercion by society and by nature, free from abject physical conditions that had prevented them from fulfilling their best selves."[13]

In my humble submission, we owe a great tribute to the Founding Fathers for having incorporated into the Constitution, in shining diction, great ideas which embrace the whole gamut of human rights. But the Bench and the Bar must, by stature and culture, semantic sensitivity and fraternal feeling, read into the language used thoughts and tears which express compassionate humanism beyond lexical constraints of grammatical construction. Only great judges can unlock the latent sublimity and expound the puissant jurisprudence of value-charged Constitutions designed to govern, with creative flexibility, current and succeeding generations. Likewise, the Executive, entrusted with the task of translating into action and practical application the benign creed of the Constitution for the relevant human sector, must consist of echelons of excellence inspired by

12 T.K. Tope: *Constitutional Law of India*, 2nd Ed., page 341.

13 Granville Austin: *Indian Constitution: The Corner-stone of a Nation* (1966 Ed.), pages 50-51.

the compassion and developmental concern of the Paramount Parchment meant to redeem the tryst with destiny made by the far-sighted humanists who wrote, with futuristic vision, vibrant words invigorated by every new challenge to people's right to unfold their personality and faculties. Such is the approach which India of Gandhi expects of its constitutional engineers. The universe of human rights jurisprudence can come to terms and happily co-exist, given higher capabilities in the interpretive and operative instrumentalities. The public law of human rights is way beyond pettifoggery and logomachy but views issues inspired by the high purpose of promoting fundamental human rights, dignity and worth of the human person and equal rights of men and women and better standards of life in larger freedom.

Constitutional interpretation summons the Judge's higher vision. Lord Denning puts the task of the judge on a lofty plane.

> "He must not be a mere mechanic......... . He must be an architect...... . It is on his work that civilised society depends." [14]

In *Northman* v *Barnet, London Borough Council*[15] Lord Denning defends his view by referring to the European Court's approach to International Conventions:

> "The European Courts fill in gaps quite unashamedly, without hesitation. They ask simply: what is the sensible way of dealing with the situation so as to give effect to the presumed purpose of the legislation? They lay down the law accordingly......To our eyes—shortened by tradition—it is legislation, pure and simple. But to their eyes, it is fulfilling the true role of the Courts. They are giving effect to what the legislature intended, or may be presumed to have intended."

The U.S. Supreme Court has struck a similar creative note:

> "Legislation, both statutory and constitutional is enacted, it is true, from an experience of evils, but its general language should not, therefore, be necessarily confined to the form that evil had, therefore, taken. Time works changes, brings into existence new conditions and purposes. Therefore, a principle, to be vital, must be capable of wider application than mischief which gave it birth. This is peculiarly true of constitutions. They are not ephemeral enactments designed to meet passing occasions. They are, to use the words of Chief Justice Marshall, 'designed to approach immortality as nearly as human institutions can approach it'. The future is their care, and provisions for events of good and bad tendencies of which no prophecy can be made. In the application of a constitution, therefore, our contemplation cannot be only of what has been, but of what may be. Under any other rule a constitution would indeed be as easy of application as it would be deficient in efficacy and power. Its general principles would have little value, and be converted by precedent into impotent and lifeless formulae. Rights declared in the words might be lost in

14 Foreword to Rajeev Dhavan's: *The Supreme Court of India* (1977 Ed.).
15 (1978)1 WLR 220.

reality. And this has been recognised. The meaning and vitality of the Constitution have developed against narrow and restrictive construction."[16]

The story of the three masons bears repetition. When asked what he was doing, the first mason said, he was cutting stones; the second that he was making a living; and the third that he was building a cathedral. Judges neither merely dispose of dockets nor merely make a living by the judicial calling. They share the Constitution's passion for people's justice and adjudicate on their indefeasible claim for inviolable human rights.

The Court can rise sublime provided it imbibes the spirit of the Constitution and integrates the progressive concepts and dynamic thoughts which find a place in the instruments proceeding from the United Nations from time to time. In the felicitous style of Cardozo, he relies on Wheeler, J.:

> In *Dwy* v *Connecticut Co.*,[17] as expressing the tone and temper in which problems should be met: "That Court best serves the law which recognizes that the rules of law which grew up in a remote generation may, in the fullness of experience, be found to serve another generation badly, and which discards the old rule when it finds that another rule of law represents what should be according to the established and settled judgment of society, and no considerable property rights have become vested in reliance upon the old rule. It is thus great writers upon the common law have discovered the source and method of its growth, and in its growth found its health and life. It is not and it should not be stationary. Change of this character should not be left to the legislature."[18]

The Indian Supreme Court, in earlier rulings, was dragging its feet, occasionally ascending to noble heights. New to the noetic beauty of human rights justice and conditioned for long by colonial jural orthodoxies, narrower perspectives, traditional thinking, borrowed legalistics and vintage precedents, the judges truncated the spacious meanings of words used in the Constitution. Indeed, painful it is to know that a legal scholar, presenting his thesis with supportive citations, asserted that the juvenile stages of the Apex Court, studded with gems of British legal lore, turned to be the conscience-keeper of the propertied classes, with shining exceptions though. The *Privy Purses* case, the *Bank Nationalisation* case, the *Land Reforms* cases *et al* prove the charge. So too the dangerous *A.D.M. Jubbalpore* case. The later trends and luminous humanism in the case-law of the late seventies, the eighties and nineties have redeemed the Court from its regressive past and blazed the trail in opening up new vistas of humanitarian justice, public interest litigation, inseminating human rights genes in the judicial D.N.A. One or two examples may suffice, although the judiciary is doing us proud by its progressive pronouncements. Let us deal with the right to life.

16 (1909)54 L Ed 793 at page 801.
17 89 Conn 74 at 99.
18 Cardozo: *The Nature of the Judicial Process*, (1995 Ed.), pages 151-152.

Life is dear, precious, sacred and pregnant with divine potential and so it is that a Hymn in the *Rig Veda* recites:

> *"Grant us a hundred autumns that we may see the manifold world.*
> *"May we attain the long lives which have been ordained as from yore."*

The plenitude of possibilities and the fullness of faculties, if life is enriched by propitious circumstances, persuaded our founding fathers and the United Nations to accord the highest priority to the right to life. Bhagwati, J., in *Francis Coralie Mullin* v *Union Territory of Delhi,*[19] observed that:

> "The fundamental right to life......is the most precious human right and......forms the arc of all other rights......
>
> For the same reason, a two-Judge Bench opined in *Paramanand Katara* v *Union of India* (AIR 1989 SC 2039), that preservation of human life is of paramount importance, because if one's life is lost, the *status quo ante* cannot be restored as resurrection is beyond the capacity of man. Being of this view, the Bench held that when an injured citizen is brought for medical treatment, the professional ethics would require that he should be instantaneously attended and procedural criminal law should be allowed to operate thereafter. The Court stated that there is no legal impediment for a doctor to attend to such cases immediately."[20]

Of course, the lovely connotation of the term 'life', which has often been quoted by Judges, was first given by Field, J., where he distinguished human life from animal existence and definitionally endowed the concept with all that body and mind and soul could promote happiness and fulfilment. Field, J., with luminescent radiance, said:

> "......By the term 'life',......something more is meant than mere animal existence. The inhibition against its deprivation extends to all those limbs and faculties by which life is enjoyed. The provision equally prohibits the mutilation of the body by the amputation of an arm or leg, or the cutting out of an eye, or the destruction of any other organ of the body through which the soul communicates with the outer world. The deprivation not only of life, but of whatever God has given to everyone with life, for its growth and enjoyment, is prohibited by the provision in question, if its efficacy be not frittered away by judicial decision."[1]

Thus, dignity, health, education, shelter and other facilities for development of body, mind and soul are implied in the cornucopian expression 'life'. Of course, Courts cannot fly in the sky but must respond to the realities of the earth, and, therefore, while reading meaning into right to life, a certain measure of material and moral limitations must also be borne in mind by the Judges. Human dignity is a contrast of animal drudgery.

19 AIR 1981 SC 746.

20 B.L. Hansaria: *Right to Life and Liberty under the Constitution,* (1993 Ed.), pages 24-25.

1 *Ibid,* at page 25.

It includes 'some of the finer graces of human civilization, which make life worth living'.[2]

Pathak, CJ., regaled us likewise in *Vikram Deo Singh* v *State of Bihar*.[3]

> "We live in an age when this Court has demonstrated, while interpreting Article 21 of the Constitution, that every person is entitled to a *quality of life consistent with his human personality*. The right to live with human dignity is the fundamental right of every Indian citizen, and so,.........the State recognises the need for maintaining establishments for the care of those unfortunates, both women and children, who are the castaways of an imperfect social order for whom, therefore of necessity, provision must be made for their protection and welfare."

Sabyasachi Mukherjee, J., as he then was, expressed himself thus in *Ramsharan* v *Union of India*.[4]

> "It is true that life in its expanded horizons today includes all that give meaning to a man's life including his tradition, culture and heritage, and protection of that heritage in its full measure would certainly come within the encompass of an expanded concept of Article 21 of the Constitution."

The importance of life and liberty was recognised in the following words by Pathak, CJ., in *Kehar Singh* v *Union of India*.[5]

> "To any civilised society, there can be no attributes more important than the life and personal liberty of its members. That is evident from the paramount position given by the Courts to Article 21 of the Constitution. These twin attributes enjoy a fundamental ascendancy over all other attributes of the political and social order, and consequently the Legislature, the Executive and the Judiciary are more sensitive to them than to the other attributes of daily existence."

Before these decisions had become part of our constitutional heritage, the Apex Court had spread the wings of 'life' far enough, as would, appear from *State of H.P.* v *Umed Ram*,[6] in which it was pointed out:

> ......that the right to life embraces not only physical existence but the quality of life as understood in its richness and fullness by the ambit of the Constitution; and for residents of hilly areas, access to road is access to life itself, and so, there should be road for communication in reasonable conditions in view of our constitutional imperatives. Article 19(1)(*d*) read along with Article 38(2) was regarded as the other 'constitutional imperative'.[7]

A striking illustration of creative interpretation imparting a dynamic dimension is furnished by Kuldip Singh, J., in *Mohini Jain's* case.[8] In this case, (*Capitation Fee* case) the learned Judge wrote:

2 *The Board of Trustees, Port of Bombay* v *Dilip Kumar* AIR 1983 SC 109.
3 AIR 1988 SC 1782.
4 AIR 1989 SC 549, para 13.
5 AIR 1989 SC 653, para 7.
6 AIR 1986 SC 847, para 11.
7 B.L. Hansaria: *Right to Life and Liberty under the Constitution*, pages 26-27.
8 (1992)3 SCC 666.

"Right to life is the compendious expression for all those rights which the Courts must enforce because they are basic to the dignified enjoyment of life. It extends to the full range of conduct which the individual is free to pursue. The right to education flows directly from the right to life. The right to life under Article 21 and the dignity of an individual cannot be assured unless it is accompanied by the right to education........."

The horizon of human rights expands when judicial illumination brightens. The right to shelter is part of the right to life.[9] When shelterless humans are sought to be thrown out, *Olga Tellis* will come to rescue.

In *Prabhakaran Nair's* case[10] Mukherjee, J., emphasised the need for a National Housing Policy and observed that "after all, *shelter is one of our fundamental* rights". Still later, in *Shantistar Builders'* case the Court observed:

"Basic needs of man have traditionally been accepted to be three—food, clothing and shelter. The right to life is guaranteed in any civilized society. That would take within its sweep the right to food, the right to clothing, the right to decent environment and a reasonable accommodation to live in. The difference between the need of an animal and a human being for shelter has to be kept in view. For the animal it is the bare protection of the body; For a human being it has to be a suitable accommodation which would allow him to grow in every aspect—physical, mental and intellectual......".[11]

We must remember that Art. 25(1) of the Universal Declaration of Human Rights, 1948, specifically mentions "Housing" as one of the rights relating to 'life'. So also Art. 11 of the International Covenant of Economic, Social and Cultural Rights, 1966, recognizes "Housing" as included in the right–adequate standard of living.

It is true that certain earlier rulings,[12] have not had the sympathetic imagination to include 'livelihood' as implicit in the right to life, but in *Olga Tellis* Chandrachud, CJ., did say: "Deprive a person of his right to livelihood and you shall have to deprive him of his life". Did not Shakespeare in *Merchant of Venice* poetized elegantly poignant jurisprudence: "You take my life when you take the means whereby I live."

Olga Tellis, again, gives a lively idea in lovely diction which is expressed here:

"The sweep of the right to life conferred by Article 21 is wide and far-reaching. It does not mean merely that life cannot be extinguished or taken away as, for example, by the imposition and execution of the death sentence, except according to procedure established by law. That is but one aspect of the right to life. An equally important facet of that right is the right to livelihood because, no person can live without the means of living, that is, the means of livelihood. If the right to livelihood is not treated as a part of the constitutional right to life,

9 *Olga Tellis* v *Bombay Municipal Corporation* AIR 1986 SC 180: (1985)3 SCC 545.
10 AIR 1987 SC 2117.
11 AIR 1990 SC 630.
12 *Sant Ram,* in re AIR 1960 SC 932.

> the easiest way of depriving a person of his right to life would be to deprive him of his means of livelihood to the point of abrogation. Such deprivation would not only denude the life of its effective content and meaningfulness but it would make life impossible to live. And yet, such deprivation would not have to be in accordance with the procedure established by law, if the right to livelihood is not regarded as a part of the right to life. That, which alone makes it possible to live, leave aside what makes life livable, must be deemed to be an integral component of the right to life."[13]

Certain other facets of the right to life has strengthened the scope of Art. 21 and thereby affirms the fundamental freedom of life and liberty. Justice Hansaria has briefly summed up some aspects of the right to life protected by Art. 21:

> "*In State of Maharashtra* v *Chandrabhan* AIR 1983 SC 803, payment of subsistence allowance at the rate of Re. 1 per month was held to be violative, *inter alia*, of Article 21, by observing that this amount can never sustain a civil servant for even a day, much less for a month. Suspension for long period without concluding the departmental proceedings within a reasonable period and with reasonable diligence was held to be violative of this article in *O.P. Gupta* v *Union of India* AIR 1987 SC 2257 by pointing out that the expression 'life' does not connote animal existence or a continued drudgery through life."[14]

The right to work is a matter of great moment in a country of poverty and unemployment. Otherwise starvation becomes the rule of life. So it is that Justice Sawant speaking for the Constitution Bench in *Delhi Transport Corporation's* case stated:

> "The right to life includes right to livelihood. The right to livelihood, therefore, cannot hang on to the fancies of individuals in authority. The employment is not a bounty from them, nor can its survival be at their mercy. Income is the foundation of many fundamental rights and when work is the sole source of income, the right to work becomes as much fundamental. Fundamental rights can ill-afford to be consigned to the limbo of undefined premises and uncertain applications. That will be mockery of them."[15]

May be the implementation of the right to work can be implemented on a phased basis and not all at once. However, the State cannot encourage investment by millionaires resulting in loss of employment and ignore the hunger of the millions. Life includes livelihood.[16] In any case, the State is mandated not to hamper facilities necessary for securing livelihood. Nor can it inflict unemployment on large numbers in the name of industrial progress. Profit and progress for whom? The penurious or prosperous? The realities of life and *economics where man matters* (in Schumacher's Small is Beautiful) are implicit in Part IV of the Constitution; and deprivation

13 *Olga Tellis* v *Bombay Municipal Corporation* AIR 1986 SC 180: (1985)3 SCC 545.
14 B.L. Hansaria: *Right to Life and Liberty under the Constitution*, page 30.
15 *Delhi Transport Corporation* v *D.T.C. Mazdoor Congress* AIR 1991 SC 101 at page 173.
16 *Olga Tellis* v *Bombay Municipal Corporation* AIR 1986 SC 180: (1985)3 SCC 545.

of livelihood by State action or permission is violation of Constitutional obligation. Even the U.S. Supreme Court through Douglas, J., in *Barsky* v *Board of Regents,*[17] stated:

> "The right to work, I had assumed, was the most precious liberty that man possesses. Man has, indeed, as much right to work as he has to live, to be free, to own property.........To work means, to eat. It also means to live. For many, it would be better to work in jail than to stay idle on the curves."

An activist Court may in given circumstances insist upon implementation of the right to work through projects which are just fair and reasonable and may interdict clamorous projects catering to the luxury of the rich and withdrawing the right to bread from numberless indigents.

Education after *Mohini Jain* and *Unni Krishna* can no longer be regarded as outside the purview of the right to life. Kuldip Singh, J., and Jeevan Reddy, J., have illumined this area of law. Mohan, J., had eloquently presented the view:

> "that education is a preparation for living and for life here and hereafter and that education is at once a social and political necessity, and that victories are gained, peace is preserved, progress is achieved, civilisation is built up and history is made, not in battlefields but in educational institutions which are seed-beds of culture, where children in whose hands quiver the destinies of the future, are trained. (See paragraph 148). It was then observed in paragraphs 175 and 176 that education is enlightenment; it is the one that lends dignity to a man and if right to live means right to live with dignity, the word 'life' has to take within its fold the right to education."[18]

Obviously health is both life and dignity. The International Covenant concerned has recognized the right to everyone to the right to work in healthy conditions.

Ramaswamy, J., in *Subhas Chandra*[19] has claimed:

> "that the aim of fundamental rights being to create an egalitarian society and to make liberty available to all, to the tillers of the soil, wage-earners, labourers, wood-cutters, rickshaw-pullers, scavengers and hut-dwellers, the civil and political right to physical and mental health is to be treated as an integral part of the right to life."[20]

Without health how can you work, without work how can you live in dignity or live at all? The right to health is inseparable from the right to life. And, therefore, public health is a charge on the State's resources as is evident from the rulings of the Summit Court in *Vincent* case.[1] The jurisprudence of human health and the Constitutional law of India take a holistic view and insist on ecological justice and environmental protection,

17 (1954)347 US 442.
18 B.L. Hansaria: *Right to Life and Liberty under the Constitution,* page 33.
19 (1992)1 SCC 441.
20 B.L. Hansaria: *Right to Life and Liberty under the Constitution,* page 34.
1 *Vincent* v *Union of India* AIR 1987 SC 990; AIR 1981 SC 298.

as a *sine qua non* of the human rights for survival. Therefore, the lethal impact of pollution and ecological damage come within the scope of Constitutional protection. Article 51A(*g*) is mandatory on the preservation of natural environment including forests, lakes, rivers and wild life and ecological sensitivity is patently writ in the obligation to show compassion for living creatures. Article 48A, is a command to the State in the same direction.

Necessarily, a harvest of Case Laws substantiates this fundamental that life's lethal enemy is pollution and only a biosphere of ecological balance can sustain our existence. The *Ratlam Municipality* case[2] marks the beginning of a series of rulings in the ecological domain. The Indian Court has broken new ground in many ways, transforming public law into a people's means to gain human rights justice. Basic issues like national progress and its human rights parameters are challengingly essayed by Judges.

Do we need industrial development? Yes, but at what price? Certainly not by risking the life of the people. For whom do the bells of the Constitution toll? Justice Hansaria in his book on *Right to Life and Liberty under the Constitution* refers to:

> "*Rural Litigation and Entitlement Kendra* v *State of U.P.* AIR 1987 SC 359, in which the Court was seized with ecology versus industrial development question. The Court recognised in paragraph 3 that that was the first case of its type with wide and serious ramifications, because of which great attention was bestowed by, *inter alia*, pointing out in paragraph 19 that consciousness for environmental protection was of recent origin and it was the United Nations' Conference on World Environment held in Stockholm in June 1972 and the follow-up actions thereafter which spread this awareness. The Court noted in that paragraph that over thousands of years, man has been exploiting the ecological system for his sustenance, but with the growth of population, the demand for land increased and forest growth had been and is being cut down and man has started encroaching upon nature and its assets. The consequences of the same on ecology and environment have come to be realised. The need for maintaining forest growth requiring afforestation was emphasised, observing at the same time that natural resources have got to be tapped for the purpose of social development, but one cannot forget at the same time that tapping of resources has to be done with requisite attention and care so that ecology and environment may not be affected in any serious way and there may not be any depletion of water resources. The need for a long-term planning to keep up the national wealth was emphasised by stating that it has to be remembered that natural resources are permanent assets of mankind and are not intended to be exhausted in one generation. This was said to be a social obligation of every citizen, who was reminded about this being his fundamental duty as enshrined in Article 51A(g) of the Constitution.
>
> "Being of this view, exploitation of limestone from the Himalayan ranges was prohibited by ordering closure of certain quarries, because it was found

2 *Ratlam Municipality* v *Vardhichand* AIR 1980 SC 1622.

> that the mining operation had led to cutting down of forest and the digging of limestone and allowing the waste to roll down or be carried down by rain-water had affected the villages as also the agricultural lands located below the hills. The naturally formed streams had been blocked and the blast had disturbed the natural quiet, had shaken the soil, loosened the rocky structures and disturbed the entire ecology of the area. This apart, for removing the limestone quarried from the mine, roads had been laid down and for that purpose, hills had been interfered with and traffic hazard for the local population had increased. The Government was required to take policy decision keeping in view that the stake involved was large and far reaching as the evil consequences would last long as, once the unwanted situation sets in, amends or repairs would not be possible and the greenery of India may perish as some people doubt and the Thar desert may expand its limits."[3]

When we envision the integrality of Nature and Man, we understand the way Creation has been woven into a lovely whole. If you wound Nature, your march 'one step forward' will end as 'two steps back'. Human survival, sans which human rights are *non est*, is a lost cause, what with all the technological boasts of the West, if we do not evolve a constructive *modus vivendi* where a harmonious, yet progressive, relationship comes to be established. The adivasis and aborigines, who live closest to Nature, love earthly environs and ecology and reverentially preserve their kinship with the art of living and science of being, are our teachers in this biospherical paradigm. Chinnappa Reddy, J., in *Satchidananda Pandey*[4] instructively electrifies our ecological consciousness by quoting an enchanting missive by 'a wise Indian Chief of Seattle' in 1854 to 'the great White Chief in Washington'. The case related to an objection against a Five Star Hotel invading, through proximity, the Zoological Garden, Calcutta. Excerpts from this epistle quote in the judgment deeply stirs our environmental awareness and the timeless value of the nexus between Life and Mother Nature which crazy industrialisation and intoxicated technology destroys unless humanist jurisprudence commands the observance of a creative compassion.

The reply by the Red Indian native to the white European invader "is profound. It is beautiful. It is timeless. It contains the wisdom of the ages. It is the first ever and the most understanding statement on environment."[5]

The Seattle Chief's reply, rich with remarkable ecological excellence, reads:

> "How can you buy or sell the sky, the warmth of the land? The idea is strange to us.
>
> "If we do not own the freshness of the air and the sparkle of the water, how can you buy them.
>
> "Every part of the earth is sacred to my people. Every shining pine needle, every sandy shore, every mist in the dark woods, every clearing and humming

3 B.L. Hansaria: *Right to Life and Liberty under the Constitution,* pages 36-37.

4 AIR 1987 SC 1109.

5 AIR 1987 SC 1109 at page 1112.

insect is holy in the memory and experience of my people. The sap which courses through the trees carries the memories of the red man.

"The white man's dead forget the country of their birth when they go to walk among the stars. Our dead never forget this beautiful earth, for it is the mother of the red man. We are part of the earth and it is part of us. The perfumed flowers are our sisters: the horse, the great eagle, these are our brothers. The rocky crests, the juices in the meadows, the body heat of the pony and man—all belong to the same family."

*** *** ***

"The rivers are our brothers, they quench our thirst. The rivers carry our canoes, and feed our children. If we sell you our land you must remember, and teach your children, that the rivers are our brothers, and yours and you must henceforth give the kindness you would give any brother.

"We know that the white man does not understand our ways. One portion of land is the same to him as the next, for he is a stranger who comes in the night and takes from the land whatever he needs. The earth is not his brother but his enemy, and when he has conquered it, he moves on. He leaves his father's graves behind and he does not care.

"He kidnaps the earth from his children. His father's grave and his children's birth-right are forgotton. He treats his mother, the earth, and his brother, the sky, as things to be bought, plundered, sold like sheep or bright beads. His appetite will devour the earth and leave behind only a desert.

*** *** ***

"The air is precious to the red man, for all things share the same breath—the beast, the tree, the man, they all share the same breath. The white man does not seem to notice the air he breathes. Like a man lying for many days, he is numb to the stench. But if we sell you our land, you must remember that the air is precious to us, that the air shares its spirit with all the life it supports. The wind that gave our grandfather his first breath also receives the last sigh. And if we sell you our land, you must keep it apart and sacred as a place where even the white man can go to taste the wind that is sweetened by the meadow's flowers."[6]

Indian adivasis face and faced the same exterminatory terrorism from aggressive and thoughtless, heartless, acquisitively hungry imported technology without tears by developmental, industrial invaders. A page from a Jharkhand adivasi's book strikes a painful note which reminds us of the great guilt of reckless, even dangerous, developmental policy operators and rouses lethargic jurisprudents into evolving new legal parameters to save life. Writes Victor Das of Jharkhand:

"They had their own system of conserving water, and their well-kept forests assured them of regular rain. But today, there are big dams which are of no use to them, and their forests are being callously destroyed by you ...... like

6 *Satchidananda Pandey*, in re AIR 1989 SC 1109 at pages 1112-1113.

plucking feathers from a chicken which is still alive. They have a certain time for cutting timber and only during that time they cut and take only just that amount of timber they actually need, and no more. They have a certain time for hunting too. Indiscriminate killing of wild-life is not their style. They choose certain days to eat flowers and fruits of trees to give time for the tree to have some for herself to be pollinated, to give time for the birds to have their share and for the bees to collect honey, to squirrel to store enough for the dry summer, and of what is left, they take and eat, dancing and singing happily during their festivals. They are not violent in nature and when an elephant attacks their fields, they pray with humility......'Marang Gomke (big man), take however much you like, but don't destroy......leave some for us to eat.' They work on this good earth and grow crops and when this good earth gets tired producing crops, they allow her to rest and shift to other patches. And the good earth, left to herself, grows a new and beautiful forest for them in her bosom to recompense them for being so considerate to her.

"And what has happened today? The forests have been shaven clean by your industrialists, mining companies and forest contractors, enabling them to amass so much of wealth that can take care of their children for hundreds of years. In lieu of their traditional trees, the forest department has planted exotic trees which are of no use to them. The elixirs and herbs, which used to keep them fit to fight against any disease, are no longer available. During March-May, 1989 over three hundred of their people, all living in remote forest villages, died of an unknown disease. Later, you learnedly ascertained that it was pyogenic meningitis. But why did they die? Why were all of them forest-dwellers only? Why was not a single urbanite victimised by the disease? Do you know what your doctors have said? Listen ... Everything needed for their well-being has been taken away from them. Their land, their forests, their culture, all. Now they do not have anything left with which they can defend themselves against any deadly disease."[7]

Likewise is a Nicaragua's poetic tears:

"One day, the fields will stay green
and the earth black, sweet and wet.
Our children will grow tall on that earth
and our children's children...........
And they will be free
as the mountain trees and birds.
They will wake each day, happy to be alive knowing
the land was conquered once more, for them.
One day..............
Now we plough dry fields
each furrow wet with blood."

— ZAMORA

7 Victor Das: *Jharkhand Castle Over the Graves:* (1992 Ed.), pages 12-13.

Poetry is jurisprudence since both serve life and promote the joy of existence.

> 'Industrialise or perish was a guiltless slogan within limits but when maddening destruction, noxious pollution and ecological inhumanity are inflicted for the gluttonesque factories to flourish or high dams to be built and make Mammonist bucks, 'there's the rub'. For then, 'to be or not to be, that is the question' for the adivasi humanity, displaced peasantry and women toilers in tears.

Humanity, in its priorities, must maintain clean air and potable water, non-noxious soil and non-poisoned agriculture. M.C. Mehta (an Advocate and environmentalist) has made himself a legendary litigant using the forensic process for Operation Anti-pollution, to catalyze constitutional provisions and activise legislative objectives. In *State of Bihar* v *Murad Ali Khan*:[8]

> "The Supreme Court was mainly seized with the importance of wild-life for human beings, but some general observations were made in paragraph 4 about preservation of fauna and flora and the harmful effects of depredations inflicted on nature requiring restoration of serious ecological imbalances. Reference has been made to a series of international conventions for the preservation and protection of the environment and what was stated in the resolution of the UN General Assembly adopted on 29-10-1982, which declares that:
>
> "(*a*) Mankind is a part of nature and life depends on the uninterrupted functioning of natural systems which ensure the supply of energy and nutrients.
>
> (*b*) Civilization is rooted in nature, which has shaped human culture and influenced all artistic and scientific achievements, and living in harmony with nature gives man the best opportunities for the development of his creativity, did for rest and recreation."[9]

Swami Agnivesh and M.C. Mehta have figured in Court to extinguish bonded labour and environmental pollution often enough. By way of aside, one may say that social justice needs, beyond the Bench and the Bar, great litigants who are humanist battlers selflessly willing to wage offensives for human rights. Litigation is sometimes spiritual forensics.

The Court in *M.C. Mehta* v *Union of India*[10] stopped hazardous stone crushing and quarrying near Delhi city and noted the World Health Organisation's study to conclude Delhi to be the world's third most grubbiest, polluted and unhealthy city. Deliverance from this urban injustice is distances away. The rising levels of noise pollution and water contamination in cities discloses the indifference of the Executive and industrial magnates to the several laws of conservation and improvement of the quality of environment.

8 AIR 1989 SC 1.

9 B.L. Hansaria: *Right to Life and Liberty under the Constitution*, page 38.

10 (1992)3 SCC 256.

A divagation

The right to life is sustainable only if potable water, that essential gift of nature is available freely. But unconscionable industries, mindless about purificatory processes as initial investments, consume, pollute and inflict culpable calamity to common people. Jurisprudence jettisons life if it does not arrest profit-manic appetite of industries for water. Just one study illustrates my point. Dr. Iqbal Malik, of Vatavaran, has done a study and reports the grim result:[11]

> "While India is moving towards a water stress situation, free or subsidised water to industries which use obsolete technology, is resulting in the wastage of a huge quantity of precious drinking water.......
>
> "Industries consume it, waste it and pollute it without worrying about its cost. ......
>
> "The water discharged by industries is 100 times more polluted than discharges of community waste by human settlements. Such discharged water contain effluents, acids and metal.
>
> "Factories using similar technologies and processes consume widely varying quantities of water. Steel plants use 12-21 cubic metre of water per tonne of steel. The range for fertiliser plants is nine to 40 cubic metres per tonne of urea and paper manufacturing units consume anything between 230-450 cubic metre of water per a tonne of paper.
>
> "The wide variations in specific consumption of water among the 19 paper plants and nine fertiliser plants studied by the NGO reflect differences in operational efficiency and use of outdated technologies.
>
> "Dr. Iqbal Malik says the water consumption figures of the plants in the country are far higher than the international level. Steel manufacturers in the U.S. and Europe require as little as ten per cent of the water consumed by an Indian plant of the same size.
>
> "She says in the last 25 years while developed nations have reduced by 50 per cent water consumption by industries in India has increased by 50 per cent.
>
> In 1970 the water demand by industries was six billion kilo litres. It shot up to 150 billion kilo litres in 1990.
>
> "A wide variety of water pollutants are produced by chemical plants manufacturing acids, bases, pesticides, detergents and many other compounds, organic and inorganic. Acid wastes result not only from acid manufacturing plants but also from almost all other chemical plants as well. ....
>
> "Biological treatment was found to be well suited for waste from dairy and food industries. While chemical treatment works well for waste which is released by the metal plating industry.
>
> "The water problem can be substantially simplified by re-use of waste water and recovering some of the products from effluents. ....

11 *The Indian Express,* dated 22nd July 1996.

"Gujarat and Tamil Nadu have introduced water levies with good results. It shows that industries are perfectly capable of using water efficiently provided laws are enforced. In absolute terms more Indians are deprived of safe drinking water than citizens of any other country. About 60,000 villages and 125,000 urban colonies do not have potable water." —(UNI)

All these are evidences of a chemical warfare by industries against the people. Laws of regulation are sick symbols rather than arms of governance. Why? Because corporate regulatees control the public regulators through the invisible art of slush. And M.N.Cs make no bones about use of slush fund. So too influential native corporations. As Ralph Nader observes:

"The modern corporation is the engine of the world's largest production machine. If it is to be more than a mindless, parochial juggernaut, the hands of diverse human values and trusteeships for future generations must be exerted on the steering wheel. There should no longer be victims without representation. In any just legal system a victim would have the right to decide with others the behaviour of the perpetrator and his recompense."[12]

Public law must insist on transparency and right to information and *actio popularis* by easier processes.

Nuclear menace to life

One of the major threats to life is the menacing presence and proliferation of nuclear power and tests and bombs. Technology comes closest to thanatology (science of death) when the nuclear Frankenstein's monster, be it a bomb or humbler reactor, goes out of control and kills all life, radio-actively destroys or damages generations and, indeed, as happened in Chernobyl, makes life out of bounds for territories intensively affected by atomic burst. But the atomic 'priesthood' has such a mystic hold on the chauvinist governors of countries that, despite high cost, potential for disaster and risk to humanity, we find the right to life in perpetual fear of another Chernobyl disaster or Hiroshima horror and yet the nuclear nonsense remains triumphant. Nuclear cultists conceal the leaks, the malignant potential of radiation, the high hazards of nuclear waste and other terrors to which society may be victimised. And the concentrated power generation is often for tycoons, not the common humans. Safeguards are bluff as scientists have confessed. Information, the currency of democracy, is kept back by Governments and illusions of atomic boons are spread. The nuclear 'priesthood' plays with the lives of millions, escaping culpability by enacting ignorant atomic energy laws. As early as September 1973 the Pugwash Conference alerted the world:

"The Pugwash Conference consists of a group of distinguished scientists concerned about nuclear weapons and nuclear power. In a report, the Pugwash Conference Working Group on Radioactive Pollution of the Environment concluded: 'Owing to the potentially grave and as yet unresolved problems related to waste management, diversion of fissionable material,

12 *America Inc.*, page 18.

and major radioactivity releases arising from accidents, natural disasters, sabotage, or acts of war, the wisdom of a commitment to nuclear fission as a principal energy source for mankind must be seriously questioned at the present time'."[13]

There are honest scientists who 'see severe shortcomings in the economics of atomic power which include a high-cost spiral and new unpredictabilities that undermine stable planning'.[14]

The Three Mile Island (TMI) nuclear power plant was a near-disaster as the *Menace of Atomic Energy* by Ralph Nader and John Abbotts reveals.

Waste disposal baffles solution and deleteriousness of radioactive waste is a horrendous fact. "Radioactive violence is silent and long range, and it transcends the usual physiological alerts that humans possess. The nature of radioactivity, then, makes atomic energy a profound challenge to the civic mind, since its silent violence circumvents the normal human senses of the exposed populace."[15]

Courts have often held against the use of 'inherently hazardous instrumentality' as it affects a wide array of human rights of the living and the unborn. And now that terrorism is ubiquitous, mafia global, and nuclear thefts and sabotage, nuclear wastes and negligence-caused calamities omnipresent, society is constantly vulnerable to this grave governmentally practised atomic danger in hiding. Asks Ralph Nader:

> "Why are plans to evacuate populations around atomic plants needed but neither publicized nor practised? What are the full facts about worker exposure to radioactivity from the mines to the reprocessing plants, about low plant capacity, about the costs of decommissioning the plants after they are worn out, and about the sweetheart standards, inspections and compliance routines? Is atomic energy necessary for the nation's electric needs given the massive and costly waste of electricity? Why has Government policy since World War II accorded low priority to more tolerant or self-renewing energy alternatives in its research, development and promotional efforts? What are the more vigorous roles required of Congress, state and local Governments and citizens to assure the setting of more humane priorities?[16]

Private American Corporations, like General Electric, Westinghouse and others preach the virtues of atom fission. Governments keep the whole business secret because nuclear bombs need plutonium and in the seemingly innocent plants you get the source material:

> In choosing between energy alternatives, citizens in a democratic society should know about the maximum that can go wrong with each choice, both in terms of immediate and long-range impacts. For atomic energy this could

13 Ralph Nadar and John Abbotts: *The Menace of Atomic Energy*, page 106.

14 Preface to the book *The Menace of Atomic Energy* by Ralph Nader and John Abbotts, page 10.

15 *Ibid*, pages 10-11.

16 *Ibid*, page 12.

mean the devastation of a major metropolitan area, the radioactive contamination of hundreds of square miles of land and water, and a legacy of cancers for future generations. The prevention of any such catastrophe from any cause in a country scheduled to have over five hundred large plants in operation by the year 2000 places an unprecedented strain even on a peaceful world. A society which insists on a technology that is so vulnerable in a society which invites a destructive few to have great sway over the peaceful many. For sabotage and terrorism are not remote phenomena."[17]

Moreover, plutonium and terrorism are amenable to sabotage and nuclear power installations themselves become national security problems. Truth must out, lives saved, bluff called and anti-nuclear activists must campaign, especially since non-conventional energy is available. *Vayu, Varuna, Samudra, Surya* offer us energy in abundance. Then why seek *Yama*, as nuclear projects are hidden thanatos!

Jimmy Carter, in an address at the UN on 13th May 1976, stated:

"All of us must recognize that the widespread use of nuclear power brings many risks. Power reactors may malfunction and cause widespread radiological damage, unless stringent safety requirements are met. Radioactive wastes may be a menace to future generations and civilizations, unless they are effectively isolated within the biosphere forever. And terrorists or other criminals may steal plutonium and make weapons to threaten society or its political leaders with nuclear violence, unless strict security measures are developed and implemented to prevent nuclear theft. Beyond these dangers, there is the fearsome prospect that the spread of nuclear reactors will mean the spread of nuclear weapons to may nations."

Indian ruling classes are drugged into acceptance of nuclear policy largely because Pakistan and China possess the atomic secret and are our neighbours. A nuclear bomb dropped on Pakistan (and *vice versa*) will radioactively affect India as well due to proximity. Atoms have no national bias. And human rights activists do not accept the idolatry of geography since Earth is our home. Moreover, nuclear power plants are not fail-safe in India as in Chernobyl, assertions to the contrary notwithstanding. A. Gopalakrishnan, a former Chairman of the Atomic Energy Regulatory Board of the Government of India, has exposed the flaws in the safeguards and security propaganda.

The safety of nuclear power and the strategy for the future is a matter of moment for mankind and so the International Atomic Energy Agency (IAEA) formulated a Convention in Vienna (1991) and India has joined it. The leader of the Indian delegation to the Convention (Gopalakrishnan) actively participated in the discussions resulting in the Convention of 1994 in Vienna. Article 6 of the Convention obligates the contracting parties to ensure safety of Nuclear installations to be scrutinised at the International Peer Review Meetings.

17 *Ibid*, page 13.

The Department of Atomic Energy (DAE) takes care of Nuclear Safety in the country. However, there is legally enforced secrecy in the matter of nuclear power with the result that despite a large number of complaints about nuclear leakages and scepticism about safety, neither Parliament nor the people have been able to penetrate the iron curtain. Only an Indian Chernobyl will open the eyes of Government. But it will be too late, as in the case of Union Carbide instance. Kindly remember that those who die are mostly the poor. Do remember also that solar powered pumps, wind mill farms, and many hydel projects can wipe out the energy shortage with smaller investments in shorter periods. But then there will be no cutbacks and in a country where corruption and politics in illicit liaison control power, innocent technologies with the badge of 'Small is Beautiful' (Gandhian) has not a dog's chance. So I insist that all human rights activists of India and the Third World make a law gradually reducing nuclear power plants (many of them are too old to survive) and give priority to human rights-friendly energy projects. Even if multinationals enter the scene, human rights conditions must be made an imperative obligation. Unfortunately, the bosses in State Power seats, dressed in brief democratic authority, are angry when mega projects are criticised. A code of ethics for M.N.Cs *vis-a-vis* environment and other human rights is a categorical imperative, learning from the Bhopal disaster—the worst industrial catastrophe in history. The criticism of Cogentrix by environmentalists is ignored suggesting perhaps a surrender of human rights at the altar of corporate power. The irony is (going by newspaper reports) that Cogentrix, an M.N.C. insists that in the event of any environmental mishap which adversely affects living organisms, including man, or brings about any change in the climatic systems, which results from the working of the plant, the Company would not be liable to damages, taxes, fines or reparations. Why wonder? Based on some mysterious jurisprudence too arcane to locate in precedents, the Supreme Court of India directed the dismissal of all criminal cases pending or to be filed against the Union Carbide. What 'a riddle wrapped in a mystery inside an enigma'! And the beneficiary is Union Carbide. At times one sees the realism of the observation that the Supreme Court is final not because it is infallible; it is infallible because it is final. Is it always infallible?

Law is for man and cannot blink at assertions from high echelons where life of the masses are in jeopardy. How safe are our N-Reactors? Dr. A. Gopalakrishnan, former Chairman of the Atomic Energy Regulatory Board, recently answered this question.

> "Many of our nuclear installations have aged with time and have serious problems. Our efforts to find indigenous solutions, despite our capabilities, are not well-organised or focussed" and accused the Department of Atomic Energy (DAE) of having "uniquely failed in bringing together these strengths and coordinating them for the benefit of the nuclear sector."
>
> "According to the ex-Chairman, the current safety status of the nuclear installations under the DAE 'is a matter of great concern', a concern which increased after the AERB 'studied and documented more than 130 safety issues in these installations which warrant urgent corrective action'.

> "What are the specific problems with our nuclear installations? The risk of a hydrogen explosion at Tarapur is high because the containments have been inerted, the emergency core cooling systems at Madras and Rajasthan plants are totally dated, the potential for radioactive leaks from these reactors at Trombay and Tarapur is high, and the seismicity of sites of old structures like Cirus at Trombay and Tarapur has gone up."[18]

I am not entangling the reader in the Nuclear imbroglio but do emphasise the need for a new Nuclear Jurisprudence which gives expression to the right of the citizens to know and defend the Indian's right to life. Risks in extraordinary and irreversible processes cannot be decided by experts with self-interest and play God with the people. Therefore, human rights must be given high priority in grave risk domains.

Mass disasters and jejune jurisprudence plus health justice

It is a disaster of our individualistic, adversarial jurisprudence that we do not have a mass disaster-handling processual system. With multinational corporations establishing their empires like octopuses, the health of the people, their very life, is in peril. The midnight of 2nd December 1984, when Bhopal City was asleep death, disability and distress, unprecedented in the world's industrial history, descended deceptively on Bhopal's desperate citizens harrowingly huddled together in the cold, dark slums and yawning suburbs around the Union Carbide's *yama* campus; the felonious fumes frighteningly leaked from the delinquent Union Carbide plant, 'gassassinated' the hapless innocents in thousands and reduced them to vegetable existence; countless miserables were left alive sans eyes, sans limbs, sans lungs, sans everything! This is not foul fate but grave crime, and so, demands: (*a*) militant measures against corporate stratagems and cunning culprits and, (*b*) dynamic strategies of habilitative and compensative justice, beyond competitive Indo-American legal battles. Is the Indian judicial process, with its deck-by-deck slow motion, as good as dead for the masses who seek justice in their lifetime?

Many such Bhoposhimas may still occur and the foreign corporations, with crimes against humanity, will vanish unless legislation provides for quick, effective and versatile justice, taking care of people's life and limb. Here is a vacuum in jurisprudence while the invitation to M.N.Cs is multiplying, aggravating danger to human rights on a colossal scale. We need a code comprehensively relief-oriented, humanistically compensative, relentlessly punitive and forensically streamlined for mass delivery of justice to eyeless, speechless, rightless, remedyless humans whose very numbers are still a moot matter of guestimates and whose lot is too low for urgent action? Are creative jurists an extinct species and bovine bureaucrats the bosses of the State? Why do we witness legislative pachydermy, judicial immobility and stultifying sleeping sickness in public interest litigators? Is this phenomenon neo-colonial fatalism or subtle surrender to M.N.C. lobby?

18 *The Outlook*, dated 10-7-1996, page 22.

Juridical radicalism, running a creative course, can provide fail-safe social justice, given the will and intelligence both of which India does possess! It is unfortunate that our law-makers have flopped.

I hope all legal activists, legislative patriots and administrative statesmen will agree that 'to wipe every tear from every eye', which is our nation's tryst with freedom, social justice is the first imperative. Bhopal is a sad event, but more, a sombre portent. Can we not make it the last? Industrial pollution shall be halted and its price made too dear even for the Union Carbide. The law must keep its promise to the people.

A few constitutional seeds. Art. 48A mandates the State to safeguard the environment and Art. 51A obligates every citizen, be he minister, officer legislator or citizen simpliciter, to protect the natural environment. Article 41 calls upon the State to make 'effective provision for securing public assistance in cases of......sickness and disablement and undeserved want'.

There is Art. 39A, one of the pivotal provisions ensuring equal remedial justice. The operation of the legal system, regrettably, promotes injustice and denies equal opportunity which is a tragic commentary on the judicial process in a country of indigents and illiterates, slum miserables and rural destitutes, with an administration of justice designed to price out the poor from its portals. However, the Constitution directs the State to transmute the legal system to produce social justice on a basis of equal opportunity and to provide free legal services so that none is denied opportunities of securing relief by reason merely of economic, social and other disabilities.

The above constellation of constitutional clauses is the foundation of a compassionate jurisprudence environmentally alert, sensitively adaptive, creatively radical and climatized for Indian conditions. The Bhopal holocaust is a challenge to our Court system, including the Bench and the Bar, and an exposure of its procedural failures. The judicial pyramid is untouchable and unapproachable for the common Indian; and when an economic giant inflicts on the masses mortal wounds, asking for legal justice is like asking for the moon. The dialectics of the justice system reveals a clash of two forces. We should have a design of a relief-oriented scheme of justice comprehensively covering all the aspects of compensation and habilitation, easy access to the small people in slums, simplified hearings, early finality, effective delivery of remedies and so on. In short, we need an appropriate judicial technology to meet the needs of the masses.

Health, it is obvious, is a human right and a fundamental covered by the breadth of 'right to life'. Health is a right, not a governmental grace or service to be purchased.

We must, therefore, revise our ideas about health justice as implicit in the foremost human right viz. the right to life. Nahid F. Toubia, in a paper presented at the First International Conference on Health and Human Rights at Harvard University, makes an insightful statement:

"Adoption of the human rights paradigm has the potential to revolutionize the health field. The human right principle that 'all human beings are born free and equal in dignity and rights' is a powerful concept in spite of its simplicity. By applying the principle of equality to health, we have no choice but to examine the relationship between the individual and all those who have power to affect his or her health.

"In general, the medical literature reports only on disease resulting from 'natural' causes, while physical and psychological ill-health resulting from violations by the state, society or the family are rarely cited. The spread of AIDS among customers of commercial sex workers is usually couched in epidemiological terms of vector and carrier, while those social and political conditions that force young girls into virtual slavery to become these vectors—and the ultimate victims of AIDS—are rarely acknowledged. Domestic violence, with its obvious effects on health, has only recently and in very few countries been considered a health issue. Female circumcision, or female genital mutilation (FGM), was once considered only a health hazard but is now discussed in terms of a girl's right to preserve her body and sexuality intact. Health policies targeting members of ethnic or racial minorities without appropriate consultation are often reported as genetic or biological comparative studies, and not as the violation of rights that they frequently are.

"In the field of preventive medicine, we are often faced with the difficult choice between fostering public good and sustaining individual choice. Subjects that come to mind include tobacco smoking, alcohol and drug abuse, and the effect of media images on women's psychological and physical health, among others. Of particular prominence in this area is the largest international preventive health effort: namely, family planning programs and their potential human rights violations. Forced abortions and sterilizations, abuse of injectables, implants and other provider controlled methods have all been reported.

"Two other areas of health rights issues are environmental damage and pollution, which have been shown to put community health at risk. While a degree of economic development is vital to improving health standards, there exists a potential conflict between economic development/prosperity and health rights.

"In curative health care, most doctors and other health professionals are trained to believe that they know what is best for their patients. Patients' rights to full information and decision-making power decrease in direct correlation with lowered social, economic or gender status. This is more dramatic in countries in which illiteracy is high, public health information is practically non-existent, and the legal system is too weak to be utilized favourably. Removal of diseased or non-diseased bodily organs without patient permission and use of experimental procedures without informed consent are not uncommon."[19]

19 *Health and Human Rights,* (A journal of the Harvard School of Public Health), vol. I, pages 136-137.

A host of legal issues lie latent in this new approach—individual versus community, State versus free choice of people, right to information, medical negligence and availability of medicines at moderate prices and *free* for the poor. The message, in short, is that health and human rights form an inseparable synergy.

The right to health conceptually gains meaning only if it includes a right to *health protection* which latter term takes in access to facilities, preventive measures and environmental support for healthy conditions and quality of life. Article 25 of the Universal Declaration of 1948 reads:

> "Everyone has the right to a standard of living adequate for the health and well-being of himself and his family, including food, clothing, housing and medical care and the right to security in the event of.........sickness, disability......"

The language of the WHO Constitution has inspired the provisions of several treaties:

WHO Constitution (Preamble)

The enjoyment of the highest attainable standard of health is one of the fundamental rights of every human being without distinction of race, religion, political belief, economic or social conditions.

> "*International Covenant on Economic, Social and Cultural Rights*:
>
> "*Article 12(1)*: The States Parties to the present Covenant recognize the right of everyone to the enjoyment of the highest attainable standard of physical and mental health."

Convention on the rights of the child

> "*Article 24(1)*: States Parties recognize the right of the child to the enjoyment of the highest attainable standard of health."

African charter on human and people's rights

> "*Article 16*: Every individual shall have the right to enjoy the best attainable state of physical and mental health."

The important WHO and UNICEF Declaration of Alma-Ata adopted at the International Conference on Primary Health Care in 1978, also used similar language:

> "The Conference strongly reaffirms that health, which is a state of complete physical, mental and social well-being, and not merely the absence of disease or infirmity, is a fundamental human right and that the attainment of the highest possible level of health is a most important world-wide social goal whose realization requires the action of many other social and economic sectors in addition to the health sector."

Emphasis on non-discrimination in relation to health is reiterated in the following Conventions.

Convention on the elimination of all forms of racial discrimination

> *Article 5(e)(iv)* provides that States Parties undertake to prohibit and eliminate racial discrimination in the enjoyment of "the right to public health, medical care, social security and social services."

Convention on the elimination of all forms of discrimination against women

> *Article 11(1)(f)* provides that States Parties shall take all appropriate measures to eliminate discrimination against women in the enjoyment of "the right to protection of health and to safety in working conditions, including the safeguarding of the function of reproduction."

Article 12 of the same convention provides that all appropriate measures should be taken by States Parties to eliminate discrimination against women "in the field of health care in order to ensure on a basis of equality of men and women, access to health care services, including those related to family planning."

The Additional Protocol of the American Convention on Human Rights in the Area of Economic, Social and Cultural Rights (Protocol of San Salvador) uses the precise language "right to health". Article 10, entitled "Right to Health", reads: "(1) Everyone shall have the right to health, understood to mean the enjoyment of the highest level of physical, mental and social well-being. (2) In order to ensure the exercise of the right to health, the States Parties agree to recognize health as a public good......... ."

The American Declaration of the Rights and Duties of Man contains the following similar language:

> "*Article XI*: Every person has the right to the preservation of his health through sanitary and social measures relating to food, clothing, housing and medical care, to the extent permitted by public and community resources." * * *
>
> Twenty of the Constitutions of the Civil and Socialist law countries of the Hemisphere do include a statement on the right to health and/or the duty of the State in regard to the health of the nation. A right to health is proclaimed in five constitutions; a right to health protection is found in eight others. All the socialist law countries proclaim both a right and duty; of the civil law countries, only Argentina, Colombia and Costa Rica do not have a direct reference to the duty of the State in regard to health."[20]

We see clearly that health issues and rights discourse merge at many points and social and social justice blends both:

> "The use of rights language *vis-a-vis* social goals confers a special status on those goals. As Ronald Dworkin puts it, categorizing something as a right means that the right 'trumps' many other claims or goods. A special importance, status, priority, is implied in categorizing something as a right. Therefore, the use of rights language in connection with health issues emphasizes the importance of health care and health status. To speak of a right to health does not mean that that right should always take priority over all other goods, claims or other rights, but it does emphasize that health issues are of special importance given the impact of health on the life and survival of individuals."[1]

20 *Ibid*, pages 32-34.
1 *Ibid*, page 36.

The foundation of basic health can be traced to human dignity indefeasibly inscribed in International Law.

> "The concept of rights grows out of a perception of the inherent dignity of every human being. Thus, use of rights language in connection with health emphasizes that the dignity of each person must be central in all aspects of health, including health care, medical experimentation, and limitations on freedom in the name of health. The focus must be on the dignity of the individual rather than the good of the collectivity. The utilitarian principle is rejected by a rights approach. The greater good to the greater number may not override individual dignity."[2]

The WHO Declaration of Alma-Ata on Primary Health Care states:

> "The existing gross inequality in the health status of the people particularly between developed and developing countries as well as within countries is politically, socially and economically unacceptable and is, therefore, of common concern to all countries."

It requires only cursory consideration to understand how frequently equality and prohibition of discrimination is violated in many aspects of health status. In most countries, the health status of racial or ethnic minorities is far worse than that of the majority population. Environmental racism (the dumping of environmental wastes or governmental ignoring of pollution in areas inhabited by the poor) has been documented. Extensive discrimination against women in health care and health status is only beginning to be noted. Women's health issues have been given less attention in medical research; women's health problems have attracted less interest than those from which men suffer; and many common cultural practices affect women more negatively than men. Dr. Jonathan Mann has pointed out that societal discrimination and lack of respect for fundamental human rights directly affect the health status of the population. He suggests that:

> ".........the thinking that led to the Universal Declaration of Human Rights and its list of fundamental and inalienable rights may provide a more useful entry point into a thorough consideration of the 'conditions in which people can be healthy' than the approaches traditionally used in medicine and public health."[3]
>
> WHO has recognized the importance of participation in health matters. The Declaration of Alma-Ata on Primary Health Care states, "The people have the right and duty to participate individually and collectively in the planning and implementation of their health care."[4]

When we postulate a *right*, entitlement follows:

> "The Final Act of the Conference on Security and Cooperation in Europe (better known as the Helsinki Accords) succinctly provides that individuals are entitled to "know and act on their rights." Judge Buergenthal has

2 *Ibid*, pages 36-37.
3 *Ibid*, pages 37-38.
4 *Ibid*, page 38.

> written that the "recognition of the right to health as an internationally guaranteed right...... gives legal and political legitimacy to the claims for its enjoyment."[5]

The rhetoric of health as a human right must be translated into specific measures in jural terms. Otherwise it will be but 'words, words, words'.

> "The hearing on the Right to Health organized by the United Nations' Committee on Economic, Social and Cultural Rights (henceforth "ESC Committee") on 6th December 1993, referred to earlier, is one of the rare (possibly unique) occasions on which this question has been considered by a UN organ. The ESC Committee, which monitors implementation of the Economic Covenant, invited interested organizations and individuals to present their views on the scope of, and obligations relating to, Article 12 of the Economic Covenant. This article provides that States Parties 'recognize the right of everyone to the enjoyment of the highest attainable standard of physical and mental health."[6]

Health for All by 2000 A.D. is the obligation, and yet, what with MNC Pharmaceuticals and privatised huge hospitals making disease a most lucrative industry, the economic South is leaving millions of people to their stars to survive, hospitals and doctors being 'untouchable' and 'unapproachable' for the average human.

Nuclear weapons, even reactors, are a challenge to the health of human beings.

> "In 1993 the World Health Assembly of the WHO requested an Advisory Opinion from the International Court of Justice on the legality of the use of nuclear weapons, given their health effects. The ICJ fixed 10th June 1994 as the time-limit for submission of written statements by WHO and its member states and subsequently extended the time-limit to September 1994. The specific question addressed to the Court for an Advisory Opinion was,
>
> "In view of the health and environmental effects, would the use of nuclear weapons by a State in war or other armed conflict be a breach of its obligations under International Law including the WHO Constitution?"

Although the question does not refer to specific provisions of the WHO Constitution, the provision that "enjoyment of the highest attainable standard of health is one of the fundamental rights of every human being," and the provision that "Governments have a responsibility for the health of their peoples which can be fulfilled only by the provision of adequate health and social measures," would seem relevant. If the Court renders an advisory opinion on this request we may have a major contribution to understanding some of the international legal obligations relating to health.

Another case drawing on application of the right to health occurred in 1985. That year, the Inter-American Commission on Human Rights found a violation by Brazil of the American Declaration of the Rights and Duties

5 *Ibid*, pages 38-39.
6 *Ibid*, page 40.

of Man's provision on the right to preservation of health. The Commission found that the Brazilian Government had failed to take timely and effective measures on behalf of the Yanomami Indians and had thereby violated, *inter alia*, Art. XI of the American Declaration of the Rights and Duties of Man providing that "every person has the right to preservation of his health through sanitary and social measures relating to.........medical care, to the extent permitted by public and community resources.

In another example, a recent decision of a national Supreme Court concerns the invocation of a constitutional provision on the right to health. In the 1993 case of *Minors Oposa* v *Secretary of Department of Environment and Natural Resources* (DENR), the Supreme Court of the Philippines reversed a Trial Court that had dismissed a claim based on alleged violation of the Philippine Constitutional provisions on health. The case involved an effort to have logging licenses revoked because of environmental damage they allegedly caused. The Court found that a *prima facie* case had been made for violation of the Constitutional provisions on health and the environment. The decision was particularly interesting because the Court found that a group of minors had standing to file a class suit of this nature on behalf of themselves and succeeding generations, on the basis of inter-generational responsibility. They also held that invocation of the constitutional provisions in the case did not constitute a political question."[7]

To conclude on this aspect, let me quote the World Bank Report:

> "The World Bank devoted its 1993 Report on World Development (Investing in Health) to the importance of health issues in economic development. The Report concluded that:
>
> > "Improved health contributes to economic growth in four ways: it reduces production losses caused by worker illness; it permits the use of natural resources that had been totally or nearly inaccessible because of disease; it increases the enrollment of children in school and makes them better able to learn; and it frees for alternative uses resources that would otherwise have to be spent on treating illness.
> >
> > Investing in health, therefore, is a means for a developing country to promote its economic growth, and justifies the priority given to it. Developing countries should therefore be concerned with placing importance on health issues because, *inter alia*, it makes sound economic sense."[8]

My submission is that good health is a *sine qua non* of good life and the State shall never fail in this basic obligation. The Indian Constitution, reading Art. 21 with Arts. 39, 41, 42, 47 and 51A, casts a high priority burden on the State to bestow dynamic concern for ensuring the health of all its citizens, especially women and children and weaker sections.

7 *Ibid*, pages 43-44.
8 *Ibid*, pages 46-47.

If the State sacrifices the human rights to health of its people who are poor in large numbers for pampering the rich or surrendering to pressure from Big Business or raising resources regardless of the well-being of the populace it commits venal violation of its primary duty. It is an unhappy truth that tobacco is a lethal leaf that, through versatile uses, takes the life of around a million Indians through cancer and lung diseases, apart from pauperising its users, if they are not affluent. And yet, the Indian Government promotes tobacco cultivation, exports this deadly product and takes credit in its budget for fiscal earnings and unconscionably avoids the ban on tobacco in any form. The pipe, the puff, the glittering advertisement with a guilty unnoticed note of its toxic effect, and little concern for a strong policy to save the generation from the tempting tobacco vice, convict the rulers of succumbing to the foreign and native lobby at the expense of the human frailty to smoke, snuff, chew or otherwise consume themselves into dreaded disease and death. The Indian State is culpable of omission and commission in relation to its tobacco policy.

Similar is the case of alcoholism and the State's dereliction of duty to protect the life of the people. While vast areas of rural and urban India are struggling to get drinking water the Finance Ministry and the liquor lobby are opening up the Indian alcoholic market to foreign whisky and other brands of killer drinks, Gandhiji notwithstanding. It is well known that the toll of alcoholic deaths, accidents, crimes, broken homes, bankrupt families and a host of sex-related other deleterious consequences can be brought down if the Constitution's mandate in Art. 47 to 'endeavour to bring about prohibition of the consumption of intoxicating drinks and of drugs which are injurious to health' is heeded. But power is itself a boozer and human rights of the masses suffer the amnesia syndrome when the top brass in Government are corrupted by other addictions. Even so, some State Governments have made a beginning despite the specious argument of loss of revenue. There are four stages when hot drinks go to the head of the victim. He/she first becomes jocose, then bellicose, next lachrymose and finally comatose. People's rights then cease to matter.

The right to life and health necessarily summons the policy of access to pharmaceutical facilities and hospital attention for the poor *who too are persons.* Life-saving drugs, nourishing food with nutrient supplements, immunisation for children and price control of medicines, policing of pharmaceutical safety and purity are among the many measures the State, in the Third World is bound to take if human health is on the agenda of action. But the world scene is dismal.

Food without which starvation and death will follow, must be the highest priority for any State sensitive to the survival of the masses. But when hunger becomes Big Business, food self-reliance becomes a casualty. The struggle then is against a system profiting on hunger. The real forces creating hunger span the Third World and even other parts of the world. Marginalisation of developing countries which are being forced into becoming food importing countries is a scenario of trade liberalisation in agriculture. The penalty of lifting price controls in such situations is dismantling of food security and denial of distributive justice in food. When agribusiness interests displace traditional community-based systems of food production, the calamity of food insecurity is inevitable. The externalisation of food production and dependence on imports is a dangerous game. The current reality is that fewer than 10 transnational food companies control virtually every aspect of the worldwide food chain. Fewer than five companies control 90 per cent of the export market for each of wheat, corn, coffee, tea, cotton, tobacco and forest products. The same companies that control trade in commodities also control storage, transport and food processing facilities. Cargill, for example, is not only the world's largest grain company, it is also ranked as the world's largest food products corporation. Thus globalised monopoly exploits the food needs of the people worldwide. The M.N.Cs have succeeded in turning trade negotiations into power plays against nations. They demand that they be free to invest anywhere in the world with no domestic conditions. There and other grim features were revealed at a recent International Conference on Globalisation, Food Security and Sustainable Agriculture held in Delhi. The unconcern for the underdog in the matter of basic need for food is criminal negligence on the part of the political controllerate of Third World countries. Here is a stern role for Third World jurisprudence in securing the essential necessaries of life.

Let us take the Constitution and the two International Covenants seriously. Viewed in this perspective, the right to life, in its positive projection and equalitarian dimension, casts a considerable responsibility on the Administration. It is in this dynamic semantics and meliorative dialectics that the Supreme Court construed the right to life as inclusive of the right to livelihood. By the same token it covers the right to health and freedom from disease, to the degree medicine can reasonably be delivered by the State. Law and Policy must be geared to the goal of making life-saving and essential pharmaceuticals accessible to the indigent and illiterate unfortunates. Disease deprives a person of his right to life, even liberty. Only medicines cure illnesses. So the State plays with life if by oblique policy it fails to make medicines available or permits marking up of market prices so as to put it beyond common people's means to buy. The State, with power to control prices and regulate supplies of drugs, may sacrifice the lives of the poor millions in favour of the profits-hungry giant corporations by legislative pharmaceutical liberalism or *laissez faire*! Then the *procedure* of price fixation of essential pharmaceuticals, without reasonable, fair or just consideration of the likelihood of the little Indian being priced out by the Corporate, especially the transnational, manufacturer deliberately manipulating the market, is an unconstitutional exercise. Public power obligates a duty to exercise it in favour of the public and inaction or misaction is constitutional culpable.

The fundamental right of *every person* to equal protection of the law (Art. 14) is a mandate to the Executive and Legislature to use their powers to protect the citizen's equal right to health, be he rich or poor, be he primitive tribal or city-dweller. Taking a pragmatic look at the health scene in our country of millions of people beyond and below medical reach, the obligation of the State, obviously inviolable, must be spelt out clearly. It causes constitutional consternation to observe pharmaceutical corporate power to pressure the Administration into surrender of its national drug policy to placate the drug multinationals. The Paris Convention, *vis-a-vis* our country, is a conspiracy to conquer the Indian pharmaceutical market and to defeat the competitive development of the Indian sector, public or private, by cornering patents for manufacture and building strategic legal devices so that the evil empire of medical monopoly held by M.N.Cs may not be indigenously challenged by creative rivalry. Consequently the common Indian's health may be held to ransom. This peril becomes real because the Central Government has been abandoning the weaker sections in the matter of price control and self-reliance policy. With alarming unconcern for its commitment of Health For All by 2001 A.D., it shows persistently haunting affection for the Paris Convention. These are harsh charges and must be made good with responsible argument and evidence. But the social cornerstone of the edifice of State Policy on Pharmaceuticals must first be strengthened by surer humanist jurisprudence.

What are the Indian socio-economic realities in relation to therapeutic facilities and prevalence of maladies? There are no constitutional absolutes, although there are broad binding obligations cast on the State. Relativity is the rule of life when application of imperatives is judged.

The parameters are that (*a*) equal opportunity to live a life of good health must be effectively made available to the humblest; (*b*) the law must be functional in such a manner that health literacy, doctor's services and essential life-saving medicines reach the penurious or primitive people perishing for want of remedies. In our times, allopathic treatment has so expanded its curative potential and credibility among the classes and the masses, thanks to many medical advances, that equal curative opportunity can be actualised only if the economically weakest sector can claim the blessings of pharmaceuticals, life-saving or essential through state action. Research and Development under *Indian auspices*, must be strengthened, only where necessary, by imported medical technology, provided they are eventually indigenised and priced down to be within the purchasing power of the common man. Likewise, a widening public sector, with a large manufacturing agenda in the field of essential and life-saving drugs, becomes a 'health for all' commitment of the State.

In this context the Alma-Ata *magna carta* of the peoples everywhere to the human right to health is a heartening event and hopeful portent. There, 134 nations, *including India*, pledged urgent action to protect and promote the health of the peoples of the earth, and the Resolution of the 38th World Health Assembly (1985), *sponsored by India* and other countries, gave this promise practical shape. The UNCTAD also formulated guidelines on technology issues in the pharmaceutical sector in the developing countries identifying essential drugs and frowning upon the confusing profusion of profit-making formulations and brand names with iatrogenic toxicity and price inflation. The Non-Aligned Movement also addressed itself, at its Fifth Summit (1979), to the question of establishment of a rational and self-reliant pharmaceutical order in the context of the health needs and resources of the peoples of the developing world. This concern for Third World production, procurement and distribution of pharmaceuticals was reiterated at the Sixth Summit of the Non-Aligned Heads of State in Havana in 1979. The WHO has also enumerated guidelines to establish programme for essential drugs for developing countries. These seminal international instruments mark the march of a maturing world health order and supportive global 'iatrical' jurisprudence. Law and Life must meet and mate to make Man healthy and happy.

Any Indian activist, sensitised by the Alma-Ata call of Health For All by 2000 A.D., must turn to our national document on the subject. In the early seventies, during the humanist phase of the Indira Gandhi Government, a Committee headed by the late Hathiji was appointed to make recommendations on a comprehensive national pharmaceutical policy. The fundamental recommendations in that Report remains a beacon light to this day:

(1) Nationalization of Multinational Drug Companies.

(2) Establishment of a National Drug Authority.

(3) Priority Production of 117 Essential Drugs.

(4) Abolition of Brand Names and Introduction of Generic Names.

(5) Revision and updating of the Indian National Formulary.

(6) Strengthening of Quality Control.

(7) Elimination of Irrational Drug Combinations.

(8) Updating of Indian National Formulary.

(9) Journals to keep the medical profession wellinformed about new drugs and to liberate them from the misinformation opium of multinational pharmaceuticals.

Where do we stand now? Over a decade has distressingly passed; Governments have come and gone; Hathiji is icily dead, since not a single proposal of the Hathi Committee has incarnated as pharmaceutical policy.

The North is better off in the matter of curative status *vis-a-vis* health. The sombre scenario of developing countries is luridly different. A dialectical approach to a plan of 'justice in health' desiderates a study of social realities. The WHO estimates that 80 per cent of illnesses are preventable. In India 1.5 million children die annually from diarrhoeal diseases because of polluted water.

"Do you know?

— Half of the world's T.B. patients live in India, but we produce only $^1/_3$ of our T.B. drugs requirement.

— More than 40,000 children in India become blind each year for want of Vitamin A; yet Vitamin A is in short supply.

— Over 60 million people in India suffer from endemic goitre only for want of iodized salt.

Yet UNIDO has certified that India's Pharmaceutical Industry has the technological capacity for self-reliance.

The National Drug Policy is formulated in such a way that it protects the financial interests of the Pharmaceutical Industry

Not

The interest of the people! ! !"[9]

Why? For the Drug Corporate Power, with its control board abroad, profits, not people, matter. And it often drugs the drug policy of India.

Forty-eight per cent of Indians being below the poverty line and low purchasing power, poorly developed health services and vulnerability to diseases are a pathological deficiency. It is estimated that only 20 per cent of the people have access to modern medicine and the *per capita* consumption of drug in India is one of the lowest in the world. Leprosy, curable at cheap cost, rages among tribals. And veneral diseases among poor girls in the flesh market are common. Many thousands of children die of diarrhoea although Oral Rehydration Therapy at little cost could have saved most of them. The Delhi diarrhoea disaster, with heavy tolls of infant lives, proves our primitive status in medical facilities, with all our boasts of five-star hospitals. In India 40,000 children or more become blind *each year* for want of adequate intake of Vitamin A. But who cares for the pariah sector which has no purse? More instances of massive afflictions of the penurious masses can be cited but the WHO estimates that 60 to 80 per cent of the people in the Third World have, for all practical purposes, no access to medical services. What aggravates the agonising situation is the absence of the right drugs at the right time at the right cost with the right information. A social audit will substantiate that the wastage of scarce resources on about 60,000 drug formulations, many of which are hazardous and irrational drugs, is colossal.

It is true that private hospitals charging astronomical sums for treatment have entered the scene, but for the middle and the lower classes their presence is irrelevant. The question then arises: *Who* is India? For *whom* is sophisticated medicine meant and for whom is life a brief candle? Who matters? India (Private) Limited or India's Poor Unlimited? 60 foreign Drug Companies control 28% of India's drug production, and so market their astronomically priced products and formulations with flavoured advertisements that, notwithstanding the watch-dogging of the Finance Ministry and Human Resources Ministry, India's major National Health adversary is pharmaceutical imperialism. Dr. Yudkin wrote in *The Lancet*, 15th April 1978:

9 *Towards a National Drug Policy*—published by All India Drug Action Network—20th March 1986.

"A large proportion of the drug budget of the developing countries is spent on expensive preparations draining resources from Health Care in rural areas."

Enough is enough. Indian prices of medicines and hospital charges were once low. But thanks to the entry of the foreign drug industry, our soft State is facing sky-high prices beyond the reach of the moderate income groups. Indeed, one of the clearest enemies of food security and pharmaceutical facility *vis-a-vis* the Third World populace is the Final Act of the GATT negotiations—a highly controversial treaty to which the Indian Government is a signatory in deference to the socialist commitment, swadeshi self-reliance, wisdom and economic recolonisation potential. Critics call this international treat, GATTAstrophe. Whether that criticism is right or wrong, its current impact is the sacrifice of the humble human and his basic needs in favour of corporate power and its insatiable greed.

13

LIBERTY—A NON-NEGOTIABLE VALUE

'GIVE ME LIBERTY, or give me death' demanded Patrick Henry. Ingersoll luminously claimed: what light is to the eyes—what air is to the lungs—what love is to the heart, liberty is to the soul of man. Jefferson linked life and liberty together. Franklin D. Roosevelt inspired the world by his address where he said we would rather die on our feet than live on our knees. And Mahatma Gandhi gave the call: 'Do or die': when he started his final struggle to overthrow the imperial yoke. But this supreme value of personal or people's liberty is not a free gift. Eternal vigilance is the price of liberty. The Universal Declaration in Art. 3 proclaims that everyone has the right to life, liberty and security of person. But between rhetoric and reality there is a gaping gap. Detention without trial has been a legal tragedy and the highest Court, with all its boasts and all its hopes, did uphold the constitutionality of preventive detention in *A.K. Gopalan* in 1950, and in *ADM Jabalpur* in 1976, obliterated, during Emergency declared by the Executive, the right to life and liberty even if done *mala fide*. And even in this decade, TADA, a terrible stab on personal liberty, got away with it when the Supreme Court upheld its constitutional validity. So it is that, not the paramountcy of the Court and the Constitution, but the people, ever vigilant, alone can be the defender of this great right—Personal Liberty.

True, within limits, judges of the highest Court have fought on the side of freedom. Largely, the powerful people's movement during and after the 1976 Emergency emboldened the judges to uphold Art. 21 in many dimensions and forced Parliament to put the right to life beyond constitutional black-out, thanks to the 44th Amendment, International Covenant (ICCPR) and the basic structure theory which is now settled law.

Judge-made law has civilised our prisons, banished bar fetters and handcuffs, eliminated solitary confinement and injected constitutional karuna into incarceratory territory. In *Charles Sobraj*[1] the Court observed:

1 *Charles Sobraj* v *Supdt. Central Jail* AIR 1978 SC 1514.

> ".........Every prison sentence is a conditional deprivation of life and liberty, with civilized norms built in and unlimited trauma interdicted. In this sense, judicial policing of prison practices is implied in the sentencing power......"

In *Sunil Batra*[2] prison reform was emphasised by me in my separate judgment:

> "......Prison laws, now in bad shape, need rehabilitation; prison staff, soaked in the Raj past, need reorientation; prison house and practices, a hangover of the die-hard retributive ethos, reconstruction; prisoners, those noiseless, voiceless human heaps, cry for therapeutic technology; and prison justice, after long jurisprudential gestation, must now be reborn through judicial midwifery, if need be. No longer can the Constitution be curtained off from the incarcerated community since pervasive social justice is a fighting faith with Indian humanity. I hopefully, alert the nation and, for the nonce, leave follow-up action to the Administration with the note that stone walls and iron bars do not ensure a people's progress and revolutionary history teaches that these Bastilles are brittle before human upsurges and many tenants of iron cells are sensitive harbingers of Tomorrow—many a Socrates, Sri Aurobindo, Tilak, Thoreau, Bhagat Singh, Gandhi: So it is that there is urgency for bridging the human gap between prison praxis and prison justice; in one sense, it is a battle of tenses and in another, an imperative of social justice."

Many other progressive changes including legal aid and easier bail to the prisoner and the arrester have been directed by the Court. How far these values have been actualised within the prison walls is beyond me to assert. Compensation for illegal custody is now ordered by the Court and speedy trial made a fundamental right. But many instances of long under-trial custody still abound. We have miles to go before we can feel happy about prison justice. A critical newspaper report is enough to give an insight into the lawlessness of personal liberty lost for years. I quote:

> "The dark days spent in a prison cell have been unrelieved by even a flicker of hope; the long years lived behind towering walls uninterrupted by even a glimpse of the outside world. For during the eight years that Mohammed Hanif Sheikh, 32, has been incarcerated in the Nasik Central Jail, circumstances and a callous prison system have conspired to reduce the hapless undertrial to a permanent and forgotten inhabitant of the dreadful barracks.
>
> For Sheikh is a man who has slipped through the cracks of a rickety judicial system. Over the years he has watched thousands of his fellow undertrials be taken to Court at regular intervals; hundreds of men who were arrested after him be granted acquittal. But because of a legal tangle which resulted in the "disappearance" of his documents, he himself has never been produced in Court even once; never known if his trial will even commence."[3]

The National Human Rights Commission, a new noisy entrant into the lawless scene, prestigious but powerless, by sheer pressure and publicity

2 *Sunil Batra* v *Delhi Administration* AIR 1978 SC 1675: (1978)4 SCC 494.

3 *Sunday Times of India*, dated 2nd June 1996.

and high rank of the commission, has done an excellent job far beyond its limited statutory capabilities. If more powers were given to bite, not merely to bark, the NHRC would be a boon to victims of violations which are on the increase. The position is the same regarding the National and State Commissions for Women. Sensitive but sapless, each commission is a beautiful and ineffectual angel, beating in the void its luminous wings in vain: To create Commissions with grand eloquent promises and leave them without infrastructure or punitive power is a fraud on the nation and on the Commission and an illusion for international consumption. We need an Ombudsman mellow and militant and transfer of power to defend human rights with authority and decentralised presence.

Human rights of prisoners and sentencing jurisprudence

Penal Institutions are nevertheless human campuses and so basic human rights can never be banished from behind the bars. This subject has been discussed in Courts and the United Nations Congress and the ECOSOC Council and has transformed incarceratory conditions in many countries. The fundamental principle is that fundamental freedoms do not bid farewell to prisoners merely because of a Court sentence. That is why the Standard Minimum Rules relating to prisoners prepared under the auspices of the UNITED NATIONS deal with prison ethos and physical psychological milieus. Accommodation, personal hygiene, correctional policies, decent clothing, exercise and sport, medical services, fairness in discipline and restraint in punishment are covered by the UN instrument. Contact with the outside world, books and instructional literature, facilities for self-improvement and special care in progressive reformation are also part of the jail regiment.

Work therapy, maintenance of social relations and after care special attention to the mentally abnormal prisoners and for civil prisoners are matters of serious consideration. The General Assembly in its Resolution 45/111 of 14th December 1990 has highlighted the key principle that 'all prisoners shall be treated with the respect due to their inherent dignity and value as human beings'. Justice to women in custody must be gender sensitive as has been explained in a report on women prisoners by a committee, of which I happened to be the Chairman.

Juvenile justice also requires institutional culture where for eradication of the cause of the crime, educative, corrective and reformative methods should be adopted. Children are our treasure and humanism is the best tool to make an offender a non-offender.

> "As an old and experienced prisoner, however, I believe that Government have to begin the reform......Humanitarians can but supplement Government efforts. As it is, the humanitarian, if he attempted anything will first have to undo the mischief done in prisons where the environment hardens the criminal tendency, and in the case of innocent prisoners, they learn how to commit crimes without being detected. I hold that humanitarian effort cannot cope with the evil wrought in the jails."
>
> —GANDHIJI

The Supreme Court expanded on this thought:

> "Every prison sentence is a conditioned deprivation of life and liberty, with civilized norms built in and unlimited trauma interdicted. In this sense, judicial policing of prison practices is implied in the sentencing power. The Criminal judiciary have thus a duty to guardian their sentencees and visit prisons where necessary. Many of them do not know or exercise this obligation........."[4]

If the word of Chief Justice Warren Burger will strengthen my submission, let me quote him:

> "Even in this day of necessary budget austerity, I hope that the President and the Congress, in whose hands such matters must rest, will be willing to consider these two modest, but important steps. No one can guarantee results, but if we accept the moral proposition that we are our brothers' keepers and that there is a divine spark in every human being—hard as that is to believe at times—we must try."

Women have a special claim to compassion, defence of dignity and human rights and protection of her sensitive needs and personal integrity. The State must secure for her this dimension of social justice while she is in peril or under the process of being custodialised in a manner detrimental to her womanliness.

A policy for custodial justice is a condition of civilised administration. Alas, the exhaustive report by the A.N. Mulla Committee on jail reforms as well as the report of the committee on women prisoners' slumber in the pigeon holes of the Secretariat. In this situation of apathy, I go back to what I had once written about the human rights flag atop prison towers.

The right to life is the foremost human right and procedure whereby life and liberty may be curbed *vis-a-vis* sentencees must be humane not harsh, reasonable not Draconian. This issue was pointedly raised before the Supreme Court in *Sunil Batra (II)*.[5]

> "Are prisoners persons? Yes, of course. To answer in the negative is to convict the nation and the Constitution of dehumanisation and to repudiate the world legal order, which now recognises rights of prisoners in the International Covenant on Prisoners' Rights to which our country has signed assent. In *Batra* case, this Court has rejected the hands-off doctrine and it has been ruled that fundamental rights do not flee the person as he enters the prison although they may suffer shrinkage necessitated by incarceration. Our constitutional culture has now crystallised in favour of prison justice and judicial jurisdiction:
>
> "The jurisdictional reach and range of this Court's writ to hold prison caprice and cruelty in constitutional leash is incontestable, but teasing intrusion into administrative discretion is legal anathema, absent breaches of constitutional rights or prescribed procedures."

But this penological progress has a history.

4 *Charles Sobraj* v *Supdt. Central Jail* AIR 1978 SC 1514.

5 *Sunil Batra* v *Delhi Administration* AIR 1980 SC 1579: (1980)3 SCC 488.

Way back in 1931, before Hitler imploded in Europe, the Assembly of the League of Nations stressed the aspect of readaptation of offenders 'as a means of reclamation'. Then the long night of gas chambers came. Since Hitler's fall the ideology of human rights within prison bars has risen high. The UN Charter has put human rights on a higher footing than ever before and has spawned new penological thinking on prisoner's personhood and consequential rights. The philosophy which has informed the judiciary in this jurisdiction is what the United Nations Agency in the Standard Minimum Rules has stated:

> "Imprisonment and other measures which result in cutting off an offender from the outside world are afflictive by the very fact of taking from the person the right of self-determination by depriving him of his liberty. Therefore, the prison system shall not except as incidental to justifiable segregation or the maintenance of discipline, aggravate the suffering inherent in such a situation.
>
> The purpose of justification of a sentence of imprisonment of a similar measure deprivative of liberty is ultimately to protect society against crime. This end can only be achieved if the period of imprisonment is used to ensure, so far as possible, that upon his return to society the offender is not only willing but able to lead a law-abiding and self-supporting life.
>
> To this end, the institution should utilise all the remedial, educational, moral, spiritual and other forces and forms of assistance which are appropriate and available, and should seek to apply them according to the individual treatment needs of the prisoners."
>
> "The Standard Minimum Rules for treatment of prisoners approved by the United Nations Congress on the treatment of offenders, held at Geneva in 1955 laid down that 'the basis of training must be to accord to the prisoners the respect due to their dignity as human beings and to establish in them a will to lead a good and useful life on discharge and to fit them to do so'. The Assembly of the United Nations on the 6th December 1966, in the International Government on Civil and Political rights adopted unanimously the following resolution regarding the rights of prisoners:
>
> *Article 10.* (1) All persons deprived of their liberty shall be treated with humanity and with respect for the inherent dignity of the human person.
>
> (2)(*a*) Accused persons shall, save in exceptional circumstances, be segregated from convicted persons and shall be subject to separate treatment appropriate to their status as unconvicted persons.
>
> (*b*) Accused juvenile persons shall be separated from adults and brought as speedily as possible for adjudication.
>
> (3) The penitentiary system shall comprise treatment of prisoners, the essential aim of which shall be their reformation and social rehabilitation. Juvenile offenders shall be segregated from adults and be accorded treatment appropriate to their age and legal status".

The late Mr. Justice Narasimhan, in his long ago report on Prison Reform to the Tamil Nadu Government, has tersely traced International Developments in this area thus:

> "In the successive International Congresses held once in every five years, a review of the progress made in implementing the earlier resolutions on the subject was made and helpful suggestions were given to the various Governments. In the Second Congress held in London in 1960, one of the important resolutions was 'the Prisoner must be prepared as a free man in the community during the entire period of his detention.' In the Congress of 1970, while reviewing the Criminal Policy in the World, it was observed 'Prevention of Crime and the Social rehabilitation of criminals can benefit from general and specific measures adopted in the field of social action outside the criminal law.' It was further emphasised by some speakers that 'Criminal Law and Criminal Justice system are not static because they answer social needs which change continuously from time to time."

In the Congress of 1975, held at Geneva, it was again reiterated:

> "Modern trend is to eradicate the causes of crime rather than the criminals by educative, and reformative methods."

In the Second Congress held in London in 1960, a delegate from Brazil stated that:

> "It was the custom for Prisoners to spend the last part of their sentence in the open agricultural Institution where their families may live with them."

In India also in many States, open-air prisons for prisoners with agricultural background have been organised with minimum security arrangements. In some of these, the prisoners are allowed to stay with their families.

It also appears that in the USSR the whole personality of the prisoners is prepared for their release. They could participate in lectures, conferences, discussions on various subjects, amateur theatrical broadcasts, etc., as general means of social orientation. India respects International Law and the various Articles of the Constitution, the most significant of which is Art. 21, have projected a dynamic perspective so far as prison justice is concerned. However, until *Sunil Batra's* case prison precincts were thought to be out of bounds for the Court. Fortunately, the position today is different. While interpreting Arts. 14, 19 and 21 *vis-a-vis* prisoners' rights, the Supreme Court has brought into play creative humanism and, to an extent, has been inspired by rulings of the American Courts which had, by and large, struck a progressive note. The core principle has been best expressed in *Wolff* v *Macdonnel*, 'there is no iron curtain drawn between the Constitution and the Prisons of the country'.

The high tide of human rights, as applied to prison inmates, is a phenomenon of the last few years of the Supreme Court of India. A rapid survey without a detailed essay may perhaps be made:

"In *D. Bhuvan Mohan Patnaik and others* v *State of Andhra Pradesh and others* (AIR 1974 SC 2092 at page 2094, para 6) great stress was laid on the following rights of prisoners 'convicts are not, by mere reason of the conviction, denuded of all the fundamental rights which they otherwise possess.'"

In *Mohammed Giasuddin* v *State of Andhra Pradesh,*[6] the Supreme Court dwelt at length on the mode of treatment of criminals in prisons, the principles of punishment and other allied matters. The following extracts may be quoted:

"progressive criminologists across the world will agree that.........The infliction of harsh and savage punishment is thus a relic of past and regressive time.........We therefore direct the Government to see that within the frame—work of the Jail Rules, the appellant is assigned work not of a monotonous mechanical degrading type, but of a mental, intellectual or like type mixed with a little manual labour. We have also made the suggestion that the appellant must be paid a reasonable fraction of remuneration by way of wages for the work done, since unpaid work is bonded labour and humiliating. We strongly feel that that the humanitarian winds blow into the prison barricades. More in this decade when jail reforms, from abolition of convicts costume and conscript labour to restoration of basic companionship and atmosphere of self-respect and fraternal touch, are on the urgent agenda of the Nation. Our prisons should be correctional houses, not cruel iron aching the soul."

In *Sunil Batra I*[7] and *Sunil Batra II*[8] the Court had occasion to discuss in depth and *in extenso* prisoners rights and their constitutional roots. Judicial blinkers had earlier kept prisoners out of their vision; and Art. 21, what with the new ferment of thought relating to human rights, became the spring-board for judicial activism. The Court, in this pathfinding holding, had to speak powerfully, profoundly, philosophically, and at the same time, concretely. The abuses which abounded in many Central Prisons in the country and the circumstance that the voices of the victims could not be heard outside made it essential for the Court to expound the new penology founded on the constitutional norms.

"When prison trauma prevails, prison justice must invigilate and hence we broaden our 'habeas' jurisdiction. Jurisprudence cannot slumber when the very campuses of punitive justice witness torture."[9]

American Constitutional Law also is in similar vein:

"Federal Courts have intensified their oversight of State penal facilities, reflecting a heightened concern with the extent to which the ills that plague so-called correctional institution-overcrowding, understaffing, unsanitary facilities, brutality, constant fear of violence, lack of adequate medical and mental health care, poor food service, intrusive correspondence restrictions, inhumane

6 AIR 1957 SC 246.
7 AIR 1978 SC 1675.
8 AIR 1980 SC 1579.
9 AIR 1980 SC 1579: (1980)3 SCC 488.

isolation, segregation, inadequate or non-existent rehabilitative and/or educational programs, deficient recreational opportunities—violate the Eighth amendment ban on 'cruel and unusual punishment.'"

The Court, in *Sunil Batra,* observed:

> "The essence of the matter is that in our era of human rights consciousness the habeas writ has function plurality and the constitutional regard for human decency and dignity is tested by this capability. We ideologically accept the words of Will Durant. (Will Durant's Article, *'What Life Has Taught Me*): "It is time for all good men to come to the aid of their party, whose name is civilization."

We must now accept the fact that "hands-off prisons" is no longer a jurisdictional limitation for the Court if prisoners' rights are breached. The Court, in *Sunil Batra II* observed what aptly applies:

> "Where injustice, verging on inhumanity emerges from hacking human rights guaranteed in Part III and the victim beseeches the Court to intervene and relieve, the Court will be a functional futility as a constitutional instrumentality if its guns do not go into action until the wrong is righted. The Court is not a distant abstraction omnipotent in the books but an activist institution which is the cynosure of public hope. We hold that the Court can issue writs to meet the new challenges. Lord Scarman's similar admonition, in his *English Law—The New Dimensions*, is an encouraging omen. The objection, if any, is obsolete because in a prison situation, a Constitution Bench of this Court (Batra and Sobraj) did imprison the powers of prison officials, to put an undertrial under iron fetters or confine in solitary cells convicts with death sentences under appeal."

Basic constitutional rights cannot be halted at the prison gates and can be enforced within the prison campus.

> "Convicts are not, by mere reason of the conviction, denuded by all the fundamental rights which they otherwise possess. A compulsion under the authority of law, following upon a conviction, to live in a prison-house entails by its own force the deprivation of fundamental freedoms like the right to move freely throughout the territory of India or the right to 'practice' a profession......But the Constitution guarantees other freedoms like the right to acquire, hold and dispose of property for the exercise of which incarceration can be no impediment. Likewise, even a convict is entitled to the precious right guarantee by Article 21 of the Constitution that he shall not be deprived of his life or personal liberty except according to procedure established by law."

I must hasten to mention that considerations of security and prevention of escape cannot be abandoned based on a romantic concept of prisoners' rights. A prisoner's liberty is circumscribed by the very fact of his confinement. The full panoply of fundamental rights cannot be enjoyed by him, but the physical restrictions imposed on him may not be more than reasonably necessary for security. Once we accept the need to respect the dignity, decency and justice belonging to the prisoner, all else follows from those fundamentals. In *Sunil Batra II*, the Court has outlined the substantive and procedural right which are the prisoner's entitlement:

> "Inflictions may take many protean forms apart from physical assaults. Pushing the prisoner into a solitary cell, denial of the necessary amenity, and more dreadful sometimes, transfer to a distant prison where visits or society of friends or relations may be snapped, allotment of degrading labour, assigning him to a desperate or tough gang and the like, may be punitive in effect. Every such affliction or abridgement is an infraction of liberty or life in its wider sense and cannot be sustained unless Article 21 is satisfied. There must be a corrective legal procedure, fair and reasonable and effective. Such infraction will be arbitrary, under Article 14 if it is dependent on unguided discretion, unreasonable, under Article 19, if it is irremediable and unappealable, and unfair under Article 21 if it violates natural justice. The string of guidelines in *Batra* set out in the first judgment, which we adopt, provides for a hearing at some stages, a review by a superior, and early judicial consideration so that the proceedings may not hop from Caesar to Caesar. We direct strict compliance with those norms and institutional provisions for the purpose."

It is heartening to note the statement in the American Federal Standards:

> "Increased assertion and recognition of the rights of persons under correctional control has been an important force the change and accountability in correctional systems and practices. This section includes fourteen standards which set forth basic rights of inmates consistent with fundamental legal principles, sound correctional practices, and humane treatment of offenders."

Alas, torture is a tradition in many penal systems. That is why as a matter of policy, Articles 8 and 9 of the Declaration of the Protection of All Persons from Torture and other Cruel, Inhuman or Degrading Treatment of Punishment adopted by UN General Assembly should be implemented through municipal legislations.

> "*Article 8*. Any person who alleges that he has been subjected to torture or other cruel, inhuman or degrading treatment or punishment by or at the instigation of a public official shall have the right to complain to and to have his case impartially examined by the competent authorities of the State concerned.
>
> *Article 9*. Wherever there is reasonable ground to believe, that an act of torture as defined in Article 1 has been committed, the competent authorities of the State concerned shall promptly proceed to an impartial investigation even if there has been no formal complaint."

Judicial Power, as sentinel of sentencee's human rights, and penal praxis, tuned to the personhood of convicts, are the evolving standards of the New World Legal Order. Before concluding on this sub-topic, I would like to draw attention to two factors namely, substantive rights of prisoners and procedural remedies which prisoners must enjoy. The substantive rights of prisoners include the fundamental rights under the Constitution of the country concerned which must be interpreted by the Court in the widest amplitude permissible, having regard to the ascending awareness of

International Law in this field. The American Courts have blazed the trail and upheld the basic freedom of prisoners circumscribed, of course, by the legal imperatives of incarceration. Cruel and unusual punishment is taboo in the United States although legal tender in the Middle East. Right to life and liberty which can be infringed upon only according to fair, reasonable and just procedure is guaranteed under the Indian Constitutional Law. In a series of new thrust decisions, like *Sunil Batra I* and *Sunil Batra II*, by the Summit Court, prisoners have been assured many substantive rights in the Indian jurisdiction, interpreting, with imaginative humanism, Article 14 (Equal Protection) Article 19 (Freedom of Expression and the like subject to reasonable restrictions) and Article 21 (Protection of Life and Personal Liberty). Reformation, as contrasted with retribution and draconian deterrence, has been the guiding principle in prison treatment. Solitary confinement and physical abuse are anathema and rehabilitative procedures are desiderated. Class actions on behalf of prisoners are permissible having regard to the handicaps of confinement. The right to psychiatric treatment is implicit in Article 21 of the Indian Constitution for mental patients involuntarily confined. Psychiatric treatment brings in medical collaboration. A humane psychiatrist and stress-free physical environment, qualified staff sufficient to administer adequate medical treatment and individualised attention in cases of breakdown are among the substantive rights of prisoners. The conflicting interests of prison security and prisoner autonomy must be balanced in a progressive manner as has been attempted by the Boston University Center for Criminal Justice in its Model Rules and Regulations on Prisoners' Rights and Responsibilities. The freedom of prison newspapers to express controversial views, the freedom to have cultural clubs for self-expression the freedom of religious beliefs and practices, the reasonable right to parole and visitation rights by family and friends, are some of the very wholesome implications of rehabilitative treatment. In many of these matters, doctors have rightful part to play, especially where conditions are such that despair, tension, resentment and violence necessarily erupt. An imaginative psychiatrist is an active component in the protective machinery for prisoners' rights.

The remedial rights of prisoners require deeper understanding. The problem is not with the principle, but with the implementation. A realistic access to Courts requires more than access to petitions or writ application forms. The judicial process is a confusing morass and reasonable access to the Courts, to be meaningful, often requires reasonable access to lawyers and doctors. A free atmosphere for communication and interaction, including freedom of legal correspondence and freedom from harassment in pursuing judicial avenues. There must also be organisations ready to champion the causes of deprived prisoners and procedural provisions for class actions, test litigations, public interest petitions and other *pro bono* proceedings. Courts must be clothed with the power to go beyond individual cases and issue affirmative directions of a wider nature. Judicial relief, requiring administrative policy reform, ordering improvements in institutions and institutional services, directing release from solitary confinement and fetters, awarding damages for defiant violations by prison officials, are some of the potential range of judicial remedies which must be available to prisoners. The Indian Supreme Court and the High Courts have been gradually exercising jurisdiction in assuring prison justice, including improving the quality of food and amenities, payment of wages and appropriate standards of medical care. The radical humanism of the robed brethren is the necessary concomitant of the rights explosion of prison inmates. Financial limitations, sometimes pleaded by the State, cannot be accepted gullibly by the Court lest constitutional rights should be deprived of meaningful remedies.

At this point, a reference to *Sunil Batra II* may be illustrative of the new horizons. A few passages from *Sunil Batra II* will bring home the rule that judicial remedies must reach and relieve prison maladies:[10]

(A) Constitution of India, Arts. 32, 226—Prison vices-Dynamic role of *Habeas Corpus* writ.

> "The dynamic role of judicial remedies, after *Batra's* case, imparts to the *habeas corpus* writ a versatile vitality and operational utility that makes the healing presence of the law live up to its reputation as bastion of liberty even within the secrecy of the hidden cell. Blackstone called it 'the great and efficacious writ in all manner of illegal confinement' and Lord Denman proclaimed in 1839 that it had been 'for ages effectual to an extent never known in any other country'. So long as *Batra* remains good law, judicial policing of Bastille practices will broaden to embrace the wider range of prison vices."
>
> "The essence of the matter is that, in our era of human rights consciousness, the habeas writ has functional plurality and the constitutional regard for human decency and dignity is tested by this capability."
>
> "Protection of the prisoner within his rights is part of the office of Art. 21.
>
> 'Prisons are built with stones of law' and so it behoves the Court to insist that, in the eye of law, prisoners are persons, not animals, and punish the deviant 'guardians' of the prison system where they go berserk and defile the dignity of the human inmate. Prison houses are part of Indian earth and the Indian Constitution cannot be held at bay by jail officials 'dressed in a little, brief authority' when Part III is invoked by a convict. For when a prisoner is traumatized, the constitution suffers a shock. And when the Court takes cognizance of such violence and violation, it does, like the hound of Heaven. 'But with unhurrying chase. And unperturbed pace. Deliberate speed and Majestic instancy' follow the official offender and frown down the outlaw adventure."
>
> "Where the rights of a prisoner either under the Constitution or under other law, are violated the writ power of the Court can and should run to his rescue. There is a warrant for this vigil. The Court process casts the convict

10 I confine myself to the Head Notes in the Reports.

into the prison system and the deprivation of his freedom is not a blind penitentiary affliction but a belighted institutionalisation geared to a social good. The Court has a continuing responsibility to ensure that the constitutional purpose of the deprivation is not defeated by the prison administration."

Whether inside prison or outside, a person shall not be deprived of his guaranteed freedom save by methods 'right, just and fair'.

A prisoner wears the armour of basic freedom even behind bars and that on breach thereof by lawless officials the law will respond to his distress signals through 'writ' aid. The Indian human has a constant companion–the Court armed with the weapon. The weapon is 'habeas' the power is Part III and the projectile is *Batra* (AIR 1978 SC 1675). It is, therefore, the Court's concern, implicit in the power to deprive the sentencee of his personal liberty, to ensure that no more and no less than is warranted by the sentence happens. If the prisoner breaks down because of mental torture, psychic pressure or physical infliction beyond the licit limits of lawful imprisonment the Prison Administration shall be liable for the excess. On the contrary, if an influential convict is able to buy advantages and liberties to avoid or water down the deprivation implied in the sentence the Prison Establishment will be called to order for such adulteration or dilution of Court sentences by executive palliation, if unwarranted by law.

> "The Court is always ready to correct injustice but it is no practical proposition to drive every victim to move the Court for a writ, knowing the actual hurdles and the prison realities. True, technicalities and legal niceties are no impediment to the Court entertaining even an informal communication as a proceeding for *habeas corpus* if the basic facts are found; still the awe and distance of Courts, the legalese and mystique, keep the institution unapproachable. More realistic is to devise a method of taking the healing law to the injured victim. That system is best where the remedy will rush to the injury on the slightest summons. So, within the existing, dated legislation, new meanings is the best solution, but when lawmakers take far too long for social patience to suffer, as in this very case of prison reform, Courts have to make-do with interpretation and carve on wood and sculpt on stone ready at eand and not wait for far away marble architecture. Counsel revetted their attention on this pragmatic engineering and the Prisons Act prescriptions. By this legal energetics they desired the Court to read into vintage provisions legal remedies."

While Courts, with missionary zeal, may aggressively defend prisoners' rights, there are obvious limitations to the range of action. Moreover, the judicial process is too cumbersome and slow, too ill-equipped to handle the multitude of prisoner complaints effectively and too inadequate to mandate compliance especially where affirmative administrative steps are needed. Finally, prisoners, *ex hypothesi*, live in a nether world and to ventilate their grievances is itself an hazardous task. The dynamics of judicial power involves extraordinary sensitivity and activism if access to Courts is not to be a mere myth or ineffectual ritual.

Sentencing pluralism, social realism and judicial wisdom

The penal system and the sentencing process must become versatile instruments for reform of the individual and social defence. Here again, pre-sentencing exercises become important if the twin goals are to be accomplished. To improve the present system of judicial sentencing, the pre-sentence report must inform the judge or the sentencing board with opinions of Probation Officers, Sociologists, Psychiatrists and other specialists. Medical knowledge, especially the study of the mind and the brain and the psycho-somatic train, has outdistanced traditional techniques and tariff methods of sentencing. This new investigation is very important in cases of juvenile offenders and 'mental' sentencees. Judicial training for improving sentencing is also an imperative. Winifred A. Elkin, in her book, to which I have already made reference, has made the following criticism:

> "So much is the passing of sentence regarded as a matter only of law that psychology has only recently been made an optional subject in the bar examinations, and it is still not thought necessary for barristers, who are the judges of the future, to study penology and obtain some knowledge of the working and effects of different penal methods."

Judicial conferences and sentencing workshops and institutional training for trial judges are directly necessary. Law Schools giving special law courses in sentencing and correctional processes, exposure of judges to advanced psychological and neurological and other medical theories and practices relevant to justicing, and creation of Sentencing Boards with medical and other components are some of experiments which hold out promise for the future. I plead for sentencing research so as to systematize the value and wisdom of the new methodology and personnel for better crucial performance and creative consequence. Judges must have sentencing options if they are to be functionally successful. Courts must have the power to order compensation and damages in appropriate cases, direct psychiatric or other treatment and investigation where necessary prescribing probation or conditional suspension of imprisonment coupled with the duty to report at meditational centres, healing clinics, training schools or community service stations (for alcoholic and drunk addicts and drivers with substandard skills, for instance). These are among the choices for the judges. They must have responsible freedom to innovate and invent. Traffic offences are never successfully punished by mere imprisonment. Driving Schools attached to the Courts may well be thought of. In the case of juvenile offenders, special assistance from medical personnel becomes valuable. Borstal Schools, Attendance Centres, domiciliary visits, non-institutional treatment and the like hold out remedial prospects. Probation Homes and hostels, detention centres with therapeutic orientation, Approved Schools with work therapy, especially when run by voluntary organisations with commitments, are 'fresh woods and pastures new' and hold out higher healing hope. Rescue Homes for women and other classified treatment possibilities, depending on their background and social environs, need bolder experiments so that the findings may be of benefit to the judiciary. Judges may insist, in their sentence directions, on prison education and special training of the prisoner as a member of the community. This latter is vital to any process of rehabilitation. Indeed, psychiatric treatment of prisoners may be individual therapy or group therapy, even sending them to special institutions, or back to the family with work obligations. If cranial problems account for the crime, neurologists may be put in charge. Every step which is necessitous to achieve socialisation, of the prisoner, including censure and surgery, must be available to the Court. We may even go to the extent of suggesting corrections within the community in lieu of, as part of, or after incarceration. Aftercare for prisoners, as for patients, is sensitively significant. Correction without conviction, probation and parole, obliteration of conviction upon release from prison are on the cards. The Australian Law Reform Commission, in its Discussion Paper No. 10 (June 1979) has dealt with custodial and non-custodial sentencing options, including community service orders. In short, the old theology in regard to penalties is wholly out-moded. To put all the sentencing eggs in the imprisonment basket is stupidity unlimited. The very compulsion of advanced knowledge and higher awareness of correctional potential makes for the need of Law and Medicine to work together, blend their skills and make the art and science of sentencing a social defence project.

Crimes, like wars, come from the minds of men, and so, meditational techniques or work therapies are being recommended by the Courts and Reform Committees. Some American Trial Courts have recommended Transcendental Meditation and even the Indian Supreme Court, in one or two cases, has approvingly referred to Transcendental Meditation. The Tamil Nadu prisons, the New Zealand and U.S. prisons et al have meditational courses (Transcendental Meditation, Vipasana, Yoga and so on) inside prisons. In fact, the Tamil Nadu Prison Reform Committee, headed by a retired Chief Justice, has actually recommended this experiment. Medical review is called for to evaluate the advantages.

While on the Bench, I myself had occasion, in *Hiralal Mallick's*[10a] case to observe:

> "The combined physiological, psychological, and sociological changes produce an overall effect of fullness of life. That the elimination of mental, physical and behavioural abnormalities through the release of deep stresses produces a sense of fulfilment has long been understood in terms of spiritual development. With the tools of modern science, we can now systematically evaluate the objective causes and expressions of this inner, personal development produced by Transcendental Meditation."

In that very case, Justice Goswami, made the following separate observations:

10a AIR 1977 SC 2236.

"So far as the post-sentencing aspects are concerned, my learned Brother has gone into depth on matters which he has studied extensively. These will appertain to law reforms as well as prison reforms which the legislature and the implementing executive can profitably undertake. I hope and trust that my learned Brother's earnest and anxious observations in this judgment will not be a cry in the wilderness."

Japan has a progressive Treatment System and use a parole for bettering the morale of the inmates. The Soviet System which sets the pace for the Socialist Countries has a prison praxis worth study. Let me give you a Western author's reason relied on by J.M.J. Sethna, (Advocate, LLM, Harvard):

"The basis of the Soviet Penal System, according to Lenka Von Koerber, who had personally visited the Prisons in Russia before writing her book: *Soviet Russia Fights Crime*, is the political dictatorship of the working class. The aim of the Soviet prison system is to reform every prisoner by education and to make him a useful worker. It is for this reason that the work done by prisoners at prisons is collective and productive. Unproductive work is not employed. A prison sentence is never for less than a year, for the reformation of prisoners training them to be useful workers does require time. A prisoner may so well work in prison and behave himself that the prison authorities can reduce the term of his imprisonment, and release him before the expiry of his sentence. Two good days' work is reckoned to be equivalent to three day's detention, in the R.S.F.S.R. and one good day's work is equivalent to three day's detention in the Ukraine and White Russia.

"One good feature of the Soviet Russian Prison System is that prisoners are allowed wages for the work done by them.

"It is when wages are paid that a prisoner may send something out for his wife and children or other dependents at home and save them the hardship of starvation. Besides the prisoner's sense of self-respect, which must be developed in prison, is given a good impetus by his being paid wages."

"In Russian prisons, the prisoner gets 20 to 50 per cent of the wages of a free worker and as a rule two-thirds of the same to be paid to him and one-third is credited to him to be paid to him when he is released. He can earn more by skilled work. According to the quality of his work the prisoner in Russia gets wages.

"Illiterate persons are taught reading and writing. There are educational courses in Russian prisons. According to the inmate's abilities and aptitude, instruction and work are provided for him. According to the People's Commissariat of Justice, some 77,000 prisoners in the R.S.F.S.R. were students in polytechnic classes. Of these some 6,500 completed their courses in six to eighteen months.

"With a view to creating the attitude of Co-operation, there is, in every prison, a Council of Culture elected by the prisoners themselves. And there is what is known as the 'Comrades' Court in the prison, where house offence are tried: the Court is constituted by the prisoners themselves. Prison officers interfere only in exceptional cases. Prisoners are given a certain amount of self-Government which is essential towards their reformation and for developing the spirit of self-respect and mutual regard.

"Prisoners wear their own dress. Free speech is allowed, and there is no such thing as an artificially severe prison discipline to crush the prisoner. Solitary confinement does not exist. The prisoner is allowed to be almost always with his comrades.

"Reformation is well brought about. One of the striking illustrations of that is given by Lenka Von Koerber, regarding one Anna Zamajatina, a woman prisoner at the prison for women in Perm. She, who had thieved like a jackdaw and had been a notorious bandit, gave up her bad ways and became a thoroughly reformed, well-behaved and honest worker, and was allowed 120 roubles a month at machine work in the prison shoe-factory.

"There are dramatic troupes in every prison colony in Russia. The theatre and the cinema are the favourite recreation. In the Ukraine, most prisoners are allowed to go out on holidays. Every prisoner whose behaviour has been found satisfactory is allowed leave-every second, or at least every third, free day. In addition he is allowed, each year, ten to twenty days leave.

"One of the most interesting and important features of the Soviet Prison system is the existence of agricultural colonies for prisoners, where hundreds of men and women work without attempting to escape. The prisoners do all the work there themselves. In the summer, they work for about ten hours on the farm and can also work two hours more (overtime) at treble rates of wages.

"A good point about the Soviet prison system is that no stigma is attached to prisoners after their release. Soviet life does not condemn them as ex-convicts, but offers them opportunities for rehabilitation."

The Soviet Union is no more on the map but its finer ideas are good to remember. Former Chief Justice Burger of the U.S., if I recollect aright, once remarked to me that he appreciated the Soviet Prison praxis.

It is interesting that in the United Kingdom, Court direction to convicts to do community service is on the increase. Suspended sentences, conditional sentences and probation orders are also popular alternatives to imprisonment. In New Zealand, 'Periodic detention,' which involves part-time imprisonment and work outside, has been given statutory status. The sentence of 'periodic detention' is a successful alternative and, if carefully used, the Court can blend part-time custody with occupational freedom. Studies of the periodic detention system in New Zealand are said to be impressive and have aroused considerable interest in Australia and the United Kingdom. Each penal administration must search out creative alternatives congenial to its conditions so that the incidence of imprisonment can be reduced to the greatest degree consistent with the maintenance of public safety. As a policy, we should introduce flexibility of movement of inmates between custodial and non-custodial sentences and of the means by which this may be achieved. Liberalised paroles to enable higher studies, seasonal agricultural work and even day-time wage-earning may well be permitted. Likewise, a flexible mix of custody with ties of family and work therapy.

As a policy we must consider new sanctions and dispositions available to the Courts in sentencing, from the point of view of deterrent, punitive, incapacitation, rehabilitation and cost-benefit points of view. One must also support appropriate programmes for offenders to be able to enter community organisations and try participation in constructive work on carefully laid-out criteria. Open prisons must be more popular but must not be enough. Appropriate prison training for prisoners in custody must be more popular but must not be enough. Appropriate prison training for prisoners in custody must be prescribed by the Court, For instance, addicts of drugs and drinks must be subjected to in-prison anti-alcoholic treatment, Sex perverts and randy criminals must be subjected to hormone or other treatment even as the over-aggressives must be classified and corrected in other treatment centres. May be, a better policy for the provision of work in prisons like remuneration for work done, creative freedom for artistic expression, with incentives for improvement and more enlightened objectives of a Prison Industry Scheme may be part of the New Policy. I was astonished, while visiting the Wellington Central Prison, New Zealand, to see a woodcraft marvel, worth several thousand dollars, handmade by a farmer sentenced for rape because, the prison gave him room to unfold the artist within.

The Courts, as has been pointed out in the *Sunil Batra* cases (supra) must have running control over the sentencee's incarceration without too fussy interference. Indeed, the Trial Courts must have power to call for information by way of social, medical and psychiatric reports, to enable them to issue meaningful directives so as to rehabilitate the prisoners.

The wealth of opportunity for the curative skills of medical specialists, given monitoring powers and management voice, is an invitation to the doctor to use his creative intelligence for human deliverance. Judicial accountability for sentencing power and responsibility—not through popular elections as in some States in the U.S.—but by other procedures, is necessary. This policy is a concomitant of judicial power, for authority without accountability is tyranny. To report to the community through guarded procedures, is part of forensic democracy.

Medical collaboration in the forensic process fertilises the judicial discovery of truth and the due dispensation of justice to the victim. Victimology, a vital human dimension of criminology, needs a sympathetic participation of the medical profession, not merely in total retrieval and quick presentation of injury evidence, but also for judicial prescription of reparation for the victim and decriminalisation of the offender. In a rape case, for instance, medical evidence collected and preserved promptly and meaningfully is of importance; so also is the rehabilitation of the rapee, including abortion and undoing of the effects of shock on her nervous system. Equally necessary is the need to try hormone, castration or psychic therapy on the oversexed rapist to salvage him from the stranglehold of over-powering instant lust. Manic-depressive criminals can never be reformed without doctors' involvement. Cases involving narcotics and alcoholic addiction need medicaid to the offender to redeem him. Juvenile delinquency, mental disorders degenerating into criminality and other special situations where craving and crime and other pathological conditions conspire to invade society, can be punitively cured only with medical monitoring.

This burgeoning branch of criminology, has not as yet sufficiently drawn legislative and judicial concern. 'To wipe every tear from every eye'—Mahatma Gandhi's compassionate ambition—implies that the victims of crime—sometimes even the dependents of the convict—must be consoled and restored and the wrong-doer made to bear the responsibility for the suffering he has inflicted. A prisoner being directed to work and earn and to make reparation for the crime, brings home his obligation to undo. But victimology never means retributed torture any more than healing the wounded is performed by fresh wounds on the offender. Therefore, the punitive technology of prison treatment must be judicially separated from the reparative objective of victimology.

The responsibility for the crime through re-education of the criminal and for that purpose, casting an obligation to make compensation to the victim may be worthwhile. My point is best made by Winifred A. Elkin:

> "To many people it has always seemed a matter of common sense that an offender should be expected to make good the loss or damage he has caused, as far as it lies within his power. This is a very different matter from imposing a fine though both involve a payment of a sum of money. A fine is simply a punishment and the money is handed over to that impersonal entity, the Court. Compensation, paid to the person who has suffered from the offence, may help the offender to realize the harm he has done and forces him to take some measure of responsibility for it. As a matter both of expediency and ethics, the principle of restitution should play an integral part in any system of re-education."

Here again, medico-legal collaboration is necessary for competent reparation of the victim of crime, especially because restoration of the victim may need immediate and continuing medical attention. A man with a brain injury derives no satisfaction from the offender being in long-term custody unless, simultaneously, the Court directs neurological therapy for the brain damage. A rape victim may need abortion under judicial orders. Here, the doctor enters the scene. Some women become hysterical when matrimonial crimes are committed against them. Imprisonment of the offender is not equal to comprehensive justice in such cases. Judges are indifferent because they are ignorant. Genetic damage to a child born in circumstances where the pregnant mother had suffered trauma from an offender may need more than mere law. I emphasise the intimate and integrated alliance between Law and Medicine at various stages of the forensic process. The new horizons of victim compassion are real challenges to the system. In this context, we can understand the fundamental significance of judicure and medicure working in symbiosis.

Likewise, judicare and medicare must go together. Judicare without medicare is inadequate. Judicure without medicure leaves the wound half-healed. Even at the stage of free legal aid, so necessary for equal justice, a doctor in attendance in the Legal Aid Clinic is of great assistance. If a rape victim seeks legal aid, she cannot process her complaint properly unless medical resources are also available for her. In matrimonial crimes, in decoding imaginatively post-mortem certificates and inquest reports and in a variety of other ways, the legal aid lawyer benefits by the broad spectrum assistance from medical specialists. There must be a running covenant for collaboration between Law and Medicine if the criminal justice system is to fulfil its tryst with human destiny.

The radical, humanist thoughtways and sentence styles I have suggested will be resisted. It is a battle of the tenses. The past cannot hold the future prisoner for long:

What is at stake is civilization itself. This point cannot be more eloquently presented than in the magic words of Sir Winston Churchill who, when he was Home Secretary, argued, in sublime diction, for revolutionary action for human restoration in delinquent situations:

> "The mood and temper of the public in regard to the treatment of crime and criminals is one of the most unfailing tests of the civilization of any country. A calm dispassionate recognition of the rights of the accused and even of the convicted criminal against the State; a constant heartsearching of all charged with the deed of punishment; tireless efforts towards the discovery of regenerative processes; unfailing faith that there is a treasure, if you can find it, in the heart of every man. These are the symbols which in the treatment of crime stored up criminal make and measure the stored up strength of a nation and are sign and proof of the living virtue in it."

Gerontic criminology will yell 'no' to Churchill's thesis. But, remember,

> *"After the final no, there comes a yes:*
> *And on that yes, the future of the world depends.*
>
> —WALLACE STEVENS

Death sentence on death sentence

The broad generosity of the universal right to life frowns upon death penalty. However, in our global penal pluralism, death sentence as a punishment dies hard. In India too, capital punishment is still extant. In *Jagmohon Singh* case[11] death sentence has survived constitutional challenge. I have taken the view, aware though I am of judicial disagreement with me, that life is too sublime to be guillotined by judicial verdict.

Safeguards do guarantee the minimal rights of those facing death penalty and these have been the subject of ECOSOC resolution, 1984/50 of 25th May 1984. It reads thus:

11 *Jagmohon Singh* v *State of U.P.* AIR 1973 SC 947: (1973)1 SCC 20.

(1) In countries which have not abolished the death penalty, capital punishment may be imposed only for the most serious crimes, it being understood that their scope should not go beyond intentional crimes with lethal or other extremely grave consequences.

(2) Capital punishment may be imposed only for a crime for which the death penalty is prescribed by law at the time of its commission, it being understood that if, subsequent to the commission of the crime, provision is made by law for the imposition of a lighter penalty, the offender shall benefit thereby.

(3) Persons below 18 years of age at the time of the commission of the crime shall not be sentenced to death, nor shall the death sentence be carried out on pregnant women, or on new mothers, or on persons who have become insane.

(4) Capital punishment may be imposed only when the guilt of the person charged is based upon clear and convincing evidence leaving no room for an alternative explanation of the facts.

(5) Capital punishment may only be carried out pursuant to a final judgment rendered by a competent Court after legal process which gives all possible safeguards to ensure a fair trial, at least equal to those contained in Article 14 of the International Covenant on Civil and Political Rights, including the right of anyone suspected of or charged with a crime for which capital punishment may be imposed to adequate legal assistance at all stages of the proceedings.

(6) Anyone sentenced to death shall have the right to appeal to a Court of higher jurisdiction; and steps should be taken to ensure that such appeals shall become mandatory.

(7) Anyone sentenced to death shall have the right to seek pardon, or commutation of sentence; pardon or commutation of sentence may be granted in all cases of capital punishment.

(8) Capital punishment shall not be carried out pending any appeal or other recourse procedure or other proceeding relating to pardon or commutation of the sentence.

(9) Where capital punishment occurs, it shall be carried out so as to inflict the minimum possible suffering.

There is a treasure in every human being and never give up hope of rehabilitating him into finer personhood through appropriate therapeutics. Even the worst criminal, once his soul is recovered from the garbage of gross greed, carnal tension and other criminal vices becomes a good member of society. Gandhiji, quoted by those in authority, stood four square between the sentencee and death penalty, every cell of his soul revolting against the terrorism of capital punishment.

The purpose of punishment is to extinguish criminal tendency, not the person who commits the crime. Indeed, it is necessary to be clear and sure of our fundamentals *vis-a-vis* the theory of punishment. I have, while on the Bench, before and after, held the view that the soul of the sentencing strategy in any civilised criminal justice system is to recover the soul of the sentencee and make him a useful member of society.

The traditional trinity of theories competing for acceptance among criminologists are retribution, deterrence and rehabilitation and sometimes a blended brew of all the three. Deterrence, says Salmond, is all important because the 'chief end of the law of crime is to make the evil-doer an example and warning to all that are like-minded with him.' Salmond continues:

> "Punishment is, in the second place, preventive or disabling. Its primary and general purpose being to deter by fear, its secondary and special purpose is, wherever possible and expedient, to prevent a repetition of wrong-doing by the disablement of the offender. We hang murderers, not merely that we may put into the hearts of others like them the fear of a like fate, but for the same reason for which we kill snakes, namely, because it is better for us that they should be out of the world than in it."
>
> *** *** ***
>
> "Punishment is in the third place reformative. Offences are committed through the influence of motives upon character, and may be prevented either by a change of motives or by a change of character. Punishment as deterrent acts in the former method; punishment as reformative in the latter. This curative or medicinal function is practically limited to two particular species of penalty, namely imprisonment (where it pertains to the ideal rather than to the actual) and probation. It would seem, however, that this aspect of the criminal law is destined to increasing prominence. The new science of criminal anthropology would go far towards identifying crime with disease, and would willingly deliver many classes of criminal out of the hands of the men of law into those of the men of medicine."[12]

The jurisprudence of yesteryears stress deterrence more than reformation. There is yet another kind of criminal justice—retributive punishment:

> "It gratifies the instinct of revenge or retaliation, which exists not merely in the individual wronged but also by way of sympathetic extension in the society at large."
>
> *** *** ***
>
> "The emotion of retributive indignation, both in its self-regarding and its sympathetic forms, is even yet the mainspring of the criminal law. It is to the fact that the punishment of the wrong-doer is at the same time the vengeance of the wronged, that the administration of justice owes a great part of its strength and effectiveness. Did we punish criminals merely from an intellectual appreciation of the expediency of so doing, and not because their crimes arouse in us the emotion of anger and the instinct of retribution, the criminal law would be but a feeble instrument. Indignation against injustice is, moreover, one of the chief constituents of the moral sense of the community,

12 Sir John Salmond: *Jurisprudence*, 10th Ed., pages 111-112.

> and positive morality is no less dependent on it than is the law itself. It is good, therefore, that such instincts and emotion should be encouraged and strengthened by their satisfaction."[13]

The vengeful retributive philosophy is what we find in action in the Middle East system of punitive brutality, although the rest of the world more or less have bid farewell to this blood-thirsty operation.

Lex talionis is obnoxious but is exalted theologically:

> "Thine eye shall not pity; but life shall go for life, eye for eye, tooth for tooth, hand for hand, foot for foot". No such principle, indeed, is capable of literal interpretation; but subject to metaphorical and symbolical applications it is in Kant's view the guiding rule of the ideal scheme of criminal justice."[14]

Jurisprudence often reflects the values of the age and people and so changes from time to time. Criminal Justice, likewise, responds to the ethos of a community although certain universal norms are being woven by the civilised march of mankind. Indeed, the modern trend of criminal justice is a blend with human rights, so much so no country, in its jurisprudence, is an island and the new world legal order directs the broad course of criminal law even in its penal dimension. The unconscious impact of the changes in the normative nuances in criminal sentences as reverence for human life and considerations of compassion and rehabilitation received larger liberalism is best witnessed in judicial attitudes. To cite but one example, let us regard the great Judge Lord Denning who once stood for public denunciation as a social imperative when a convict is facing his sentence. Lord Denning with delectable brevity writes:

> *"Is capital punishment right or wrong?*
>
> I suppose that I am one of the few judges left now who have passed sentence of death. I have on many occasions, using the formula: 'You shall be hanged by the neck until you are dead: and may the Lord have mercy on your soul'. The Chaplain says, 'Amen'. It is never done now.
>
> "Is capital punishment right or wrong? In giving evidence before the Royal Commission on Capital Punishment I was in favour of it—for murder most foul. That was many years ago now. Some years afterwards I changed my mind. It is not a legal question. It is a question of policy. It is an ethical question. Is it right that we, as a society, should do a thing—hang a man which none of us individually would be prepared to do, or even to witness? On such grounds I changed my mind. Parliament was right to abolish capital punishment. It was right to abolish flogging. Those days are past".[15]

Since candour is a basic component of objective participation in a highly charged controversy it is fair to disclose that I prefer the reformation–rehabilitation theory of punishment and vote against death sentence by the State through the judicial process or by the far more frequent ferocity of

13 Sir John Salmond: *Jurisprudence*, 10th Ed., pages 116-117.

14 *Ibid*, page 118.

15 Lord Denning: *The Family Story*, pages 164-165.

taking life without even a trial, a methodology which dominates today the unconscionable operations by the armed apparatus of the State dispensing with the ritualistic inconvenience of judicial proceedings and the panoply of forensic fury in the adversarial circus. I am an abolitionist in the divine company of Jesus Christ and the compassionate philosophy of Mahatma Gandhi.

My stand on criminal justice is not meek and weak but positive and powerful and my understanding of penal reforms is not retreat from the terrorism of criminal barbarity but conversion by appropriate humanising techniques, including meditation, of an offender into a non-offender and catalyse the nobler being unto its true manifestation of goodness rather than suppress the anti-social impulses only to burst out as human bombs later. My perspective is against punitive cruelty because oftentimes it is curative futility.

Therefore, a reformative philosophy, rehabilitative strategy, therapeutic prison treatment and enlivening of prisoner's personality through a technology of fostering the fullness of being–such a creative art of social defense and correctional process activising fundamental guarantees of prisoner's rights, is the hopeful note of national prison policy struck by the Constitution and the Court. This is my thesis but I must argue my case and establish the justice of this policy. Tersely put, the State must discover and engineer the highway to human rehabilitation and put it into practice in the prison system rejecting the traumata of body and mind and injecting the culture of finer consciousness.

The New Penology–Gandhiji stood for it–sets much store by rehabilitative philosophy. Its spiritual core is the acceptance of human divinity and its social fall-out of the regeneration of the convict's basic goodness and authentic stature. Every saint has a past and every sinner a future. And the technology of rehabilitation is the key to the manifestation of the divinity already in man. This profound shift in human values and healing hope about every person is in harmony with the religion of man, the Law of human values and the Charter and Covenants which are currently inspiring the international order and many constitutional manifestos. If the words of Chief Justice Warren Burger will strengthen my submission, let me quote him:

> "Even in this day of necessary budget austerity, I hope that the President and the Congress, in whose hands such matters must rest, will be willing to consider these two modest, but important steps. No one can guarantee results, but if we accept the moral proposition that we are our brothers' keepers and that there is a divine spark in every human being—hard as that is to believe at times—we must try."

The cultural roots of India, with Valmiki, the greatest poet with a robber past–and such instances of conversion from criminality to nobility are legion here and elsewhere–fully corroborate the correctional philosophy advocated by radical penologists.

Rehabilitation is practicable, if we have faith in man. A convicted matricide who was once a professional singer once told me, when I was a Home Minister, that he be allowed to sing on the Radio Station to make a living for his starving wife. I arranged for it and he performed and sustained his family. Long years later, I received a letter from this penitent, who had since been released, telling me that he daily prayed for me because I had humanized him. A worker, C. Balan, who had murdered the manager but, on commutation of his death sentence at State Government's instance, lived to earn literary fame and blemishless life. The Chambal Valley dacoits, who surrendered on Jaya Prakash Narayan's intervention with P.C. Sethi, the then Chief Minister of Madhya Pradesh, turned a new leaf, were even forgiven by the victim-villagers and had moving stories of resurrection as good men, although Government failed to resettle them all in the Valley as useful agriculturists. Believe me, the best penological investment is the pursuit of the Court dictum: "rehabilitation must be the overriding goal of our correctional institutions."[16]

Such being my criminological manifesto let us scan the penalty of death and its justification in the New World Human Order and our own Constitutional Parameters.

No one is born criminal, the offender being often the victim of uncontrolable stresses. Roger Lanphear in his illuminating book, *Freedom from Crime*, writes:

> "S.L. Halleck, a psychiatrist and a professor at the University of Wisconsin, proposes that stress is indeed the ultimate cause of criminal behaviour. He feels this type of behaviour is a poor adaptation to the stress we experience. He says: 'The stresses that lead to mental illness are often the same stresses that lead to crime. ......While both mental illness behaviours and criminal behaviours provide a certain degree of matery over stress, the adaptations themselves often lead to some difficulty with the environment. Mental illness always has maladaptive quality, and criminality usually has a maladaptive quality! You can certainly view criminal behaviour as an adaptation, as long as our basic concepts of how stress affects us is understood. Initially, in the stress-adaptation' cycle, there is a stressful situation. This causes injury to our bodies and nervous system which makes us try to adapt. It is very natural that we would not want further injury, or that we would want to escape from the stress inducing situation. Unfortunately, we do not adapt in our best interests. The stress or injury has altered our ability to perceive or to use our best judgment. So, too often we make a wrong choice in adapting which leads to more difficulty. Then more 'overload' or stress-incurring situations, more injury; and more poor adaptations resulting in criminal behaviour from this maladaptive quality.
>
> "The criminal behaviour, therefore, can result from any attempt to adapt to a stressful situation. A very recent report of the United States Senate House Joint Economic Committee said that rising unemployment leads to a rise in not only stress-related diseases, such as strokes, heart and kidney diseases, but it

16 *Taylor* v *Sterrett* 344 F Sopp 411 (A.D. Tex 1972).

also leads to increase in murders and imprisonments. For each 1.4% rise in the unemployment rate, there are 1,700 additional homicides. Obviously, unemployment is a stressful situation. It is 'over load.' Injury results that isn't healed by average sleep and rest. Then the prisoner tries to adapt to the plight. He could blame others for his joblessness and seek revenge or he could steal for needed income. He might just blow up at innocent friends or even strangers. These attempts to adjust are of course not the solution to his plight. In fact, he'll just get into deeper trouble resulting in more stress."

Indeed it may look odd, but I have heard it argued at a seminar in the U.S. that some victims of brain tumour turned violent and burst into crime. Aetilogically speaking, the cerebral tumour, not the sufferer, is responsible for the explosive behaviour, even if it be murder. In short, whatever the Court's conviction at the end of the trial, the sentence must take cognizance of the socio-medical circumstances and other factors, lest the punitive impost be unscientific. In the matter of death sentence, there is another grave factor. The error is irreversible, since the sentencee is despatched to that "undiscovered country from whose bourne no traveller returns". True, crime and punishment have a functional nexus with the society in question. In India, the subject of capital punishment has not been subjected to exhaustive sociological, statistical or other study yet. Of course, there has been a significant statutory modification in 1955. Before Act 26 of 1955, sentence of death was the rule and the lesser sentence of life imprisonment required the Court to give special reasons to be recorded in writing. By the Criminal Procedure Code, 1973, a striking change was made in section 354(3).

"354(3). When the conviction is for an offence punishable with death or, in the alternative, with imprisonment for life or imprisonment for a term of years, the judgment shall state the reasons for the sentence awarded, and, in the case of sentence of death, the special reasons for such sentence."

"The unmistakable shift in legislative emphasis is that life imprisonment for murder is the rule and capital sentence the exception to be resorted to for reasons to be stated. In this context it may not be out of place to indicate—not that it is conclusive since it is now tentative—that under the Indian Penal Code (Amendment) Bill, 1972, section 302 of the Penal Code has been substituted by a less harsh provision limiting death penalty to a few special cases (vide section 122 of the new bill)."[17]

The Supreme Court in *Ediga Annamma*[17] (supra) where I wrote the judgment for myself and Sarkaria J., did take note of the fact that in *Jagmohan Singh's* case[18] the constitutionality of capital punishment had been upheld. Even then the Court went on to observe:

"Even so, when a wise discretion vests in the Court, what are the guidelines in this life and death choice? The humanism of our Constitution, echoing the concern of the Universal Declaration of Human Rights, is deeply concerned

17 *Ediga Annamma,* in re AIR 1974 SC 799 at pages 804-805.
18 *Jagmohon Singh* v *State of U.P.* AIR 1973 SC 947: (1973)1 SCC 20.

about the worth of the human person. Ignoring the constitutional content of *Anderson*, 100 California Reporter 152 and *Furman*, (1972) 408 U.S. 238, the humanist thrust of the judicial vote against cruel or unusual punishment cannot be lost on the Indian judiciary. The deterrence strategists argue that social defence is served only by its retention—Thanks to the strong association between murder and capital punishment in the public imagination—while the correctional therapists urge the reform of even murderers and not to extinguish them by execution. History hopefully reflects the march of civilization from terrorism to humanism and the geography of death penalty depicts retreat from country after country. The U.K. and the U.S.A. are notable instances. Among the socialist nations it has been restricted to very aggravated forms of murder. The *lex talionis* principle of life for life survives in some States still, only to highlight that in punitive practice, as in other matters, we do not live in 'one world', but do move zigzag forward to the view that the uniquely deterrent effect of death penalty is, in part, challenged by jurists, commissions and statistics. But as a counter-weight we have what an outstanding Justice of the Ontario Appeal Court said some years ago:

> 'The irrevocable character of the death penalty is a reason why all possible measures should be taken against injustice—not for its abolition. Nowadays, with the advent of armed criminals and the substantial increase in armed robberies, criminals of long standing if arrested, must expect long sentences. However, if they run no risk of hanging, when found guilty of murder, they will kill policemen and witnesses with the prospect of a future no more unhappy, as one of them put it, than being fed, lodged, and clothed for the rest of their lives.'

"The final position, as we see it, is neither with the absolute abolitionist nor with the Moasic retributionist. It is relativist, and humanist, conditioned by the sense of justice and prevailing situation of the given society. In England, men once believed it to be just that a thief should lose, his life (as some Arab Chieftains do today) but the British have gone abolitionist now without regrets. In contemporary India, the via media of legal deprivation of life being the exception and long deprivation of liberty the rule fits the social mood and realities and the direction of the penal and processual laws.

While deterrence through threat of death may still be a promising strategy in some frightful areas of murderous crime, to espouse a monolithic theory of its deterrent efficacy is unscientific and so we think it right to shift the emphasis, to accept composite factors of penal strategy and not to put all the punitive eggs in the 'hanging' basket but hopefully to try the humane mix."[19]

We held in that case "against guillotine, gas chamber, electric chair, firing squad or hangman's rope. 'Thou shalt not kill' is a slow commandment in law as in life, addressed to citizens as well as to States, in peace as in war. We make this survey to justify our general preference where section 302 keeps two options and the question is of great moment."

19 *Ediga Annamma*, in re AIR 1974 SC 799 at 805.

"Let us crystallise the positive indicators against death sentence under Indian Law currently. Where the murderer is too young or too old, the clemency of penal justice helps him. Where the offender suffers from socio-economic, psychic or penal compulsions insufficient to attract a legal exception or to downgrade the crime into a lesser one, judicial commutation is permissible. Other general social pressures, warranting judicial notice, with an extenuating impact may, in special cases, induce the lesser penalty. Extraordinary features in the judicial process, such as that the death sentence has hung over the head of the culprit excruciatingly long, may persuade the Court to be compassionate. Likewise, if others involved in the crime and similarly situated have received the benefit of life imprisonment or if the offence is only constructive, being under section 302 read with section 149, or again the accused has acted suddenly under another's instigation, without premeditation, perhaps the Court may humanely opt for life, even like where a just cause or real suspicion of wifely infidelity pushed the criminal into the crime. On the other hand, the weapons used and the manner of their use, the horrendous features of the crime and hapless, helpless state of the victim, and the like, steel the heart of the law for a sterner sentence. We cannot obviously feed into a judicial computer all such situations since they are astrological imponderables in an imperfect and undulating society. A legal policy on life or death cannot be left for *ad hoc* mood or individual predilection and so we have sought to objectify to the extent possible, abandoning retributive ruthlessness, amending the deterrent creed and accepting the trend against the extreme and irrevocable penalty of putting out life."[20]

Eventually, taking the social and personal factors present in the case the Court awarded only life imprisonment although the gruesome murder was of a young women and her tender child by a jealous rival woman with a young child.

The next case of significance is *Rajendra Prasad*.[1] By a majority of two to one, the Court in that case laid down the law as leaning against death sentence and slanting towards life imprisonment, after making an exhaustive survey of the odyssey of criminal justice, adventuring against capital punishment. A brief summary of the holding as condensed in the head note runs thus:

"Per Krishna Iyer, J., (Desai, J., agreeing) (Sen, J., dissenting): The criminal law of the Raj vintage has lost some of its vitality, notwithstanding its formal persistence in print in the Penal Code so far as section 302, I.P.C. is concerned. In the post-Constitution period section 302, I.P.C. and section 354(3) of the Code of Criminal Procedure have to be read in the human light of Parts III and IV, further illumined by the Preamble to the Constitution.

The retributive theory has had its day and is no longer valid. Deterrence and reformation are the primary social goals which make deprivation of life and liberty reasonable as penal panacea.

20 *Ibid*, at page 806.

1 *Rajendra Prasad* v *State of U.P.* AIR 1979 SC 916: 1979 Cr LJ 792.

The current ethos, with its strong emphasis on human rights and against death penalty, together with the ancient strains of culture spanning the period from Buddha to Gandhi must ethically inform the concept of social justice which is a paramount principle and cultural paradigm of our Constitution.

The personal and social, the motivational and physical circumstances, of the criminal are relevant factors in adjudging the penalty as clearly provided for under the new Code of 1973. So also the intense suffering already endured by prison torture or agonising death penalty hanging overhead consequent on the legal process."[2]

The Court did not and could not impose a blanket ban on death sentence in *Rajendra Prasad.* On the contrary, having regard for the Constitutionality of capital punishment in *Jagmohan Singh,* the judges delineated the grounds for and against death penalty.

Rajendra Prasad, a landmark ruling, has had the warm approval of Lord Scarman who relied on it in a dissenting minority judgment in the Privy Council and followed it up with a letter to me expressing how impressed he was with the reasoning therein. It may be worthwhile using some juridical space here on the Court's approach to use of the extreme penalty. The jurisprudence of death sentence, in countries where the law has not abolished it and the precedents are *ad hoc* responses with improvised reasons coloured by colonial lethality, mindless of the new (and ancient) humanism of the international human rights instruments. While the majority in *Rajendra Prasad* virtually narrowed down severely the applicability of death penalty. Sen J., as a consistent and persistent minority, dissented.

The founding fathers may have left us texts which embody human values and spiritual norms in broad terms leaving it to the highest Court to read into the Articles new meanings which have evolved through the passage of time. The Magna Carta signed on the Meadows of Runnymede has received expansive humanistic semantics on account of progressive thinking evolved through the centuries. Likewise the Indian Court must interpret the Indian Penal Code sensitised by the sublime change in the world legal order wrought by the UN Instruments and human rights fulfilment:

Wrote Wheeler, J.:

"That Court best serves the law which recognises that the rules of law which grew up in a remote generation may, in the fullness of experience, be found to serve another generation badly, and which discards the old rule when it finds that another rule of law represents what should be according to the established and settled judgment of society. ...."[3]

2 AIR 1979 SC 916-917.

3 *Dwy* v *Conneticut* 89 Conn 74 at page 89 cited in *Rajendra Prasad* v *State of U.P.* AIR 1979 SC 916 at page 922.

Benjamin N. Cordozo said:

> "If judges have woefully misinterpreted the mores of their day, or if the mores of their day are no longer those of ours, they ought not to tie, in helpless submission, the hands of their successors."[4]

It is no heresy to use the social philosophy of the Constitution as animating the petrified words of the Penal Code, especially when what is at stake is the precious life of a human. *Rajendra Prasad* canalised judicial discretion in the matter of death sentence and gave s. 302, I.P.C. a human face.

> "When the legislative text is too bald to be self-acting or suffers zigzag distortion in action, the primary obligation is on Parliament to enact necessary clauses by appropriate amendments to s. 302, I.P.C. But if legislative undertaking is not in sight judges who have to implement the Code cannot fold up their professional hands but must make the provision viable by evolution of supplementary principles, even if it may appear to possess the flavour of law-making."[5]

Viewed from this higher perspective:

> "This Court's tryst with the Constitution obligates it to lay down general rules, not a complete directory, which will end predictability to the law *vis-a-vis* the community and guide the judiciary in such a grim verdict as choice between life and death. The right to life, in our constitutional order, is too sacred to be wished away without so much as Directive Principles for its deprivation, save sweeping judicial discretion and reference for confirmation or appellate review—the know-how for exercise of either being left to the assumed infallibility of the curial process in the face of the daily reality that there are extreme variations among judges themselves on 'when' and 'why' the extreme penalty shall not be inflicted.
>
> "Currently, the welter of British Indian and post-Independence decisions and the impact of laconic legislative changes in the Criminal Procedure Code the competition among the retributive, deterrent, the reformative and even the existentialist theories of punishment and of statistical studies and sociological and cultural winds settle the lethal fate of the living man in the cage.
>
> "Law must be honest to itself. Is it not true that some judges count the number of fatal wounds, some the nature of the weapons used, others count the corpses or the degree of horror and yet others look into the age or sex of the offender and even the lapse of time between the trial court's award of death sentence and the final disposal of the appeal. With some judges, motives, provocations, primary or constructive guilt, mental disturbance and old feuds, the savagery of the murderous moment or the plan which has preceded the killing, the social milieu, the sublimated class complex and other odd factors enter the sentencing calculus. Stranger still, a good sentence of death by the trial court is sometimes upset by the Supreme Court because of Law's delays.

4 *The Nature of the Judicial Process* at page 152 cited in *Rajendra Prasad* v *State of U.P.* AIR 1979 SC 916 at page 922.

5 *Rajendra Prasad* v *State of U.P.* AIR 1979 SC 916 at page 924.

Courts have even directed execution of murderers who are mental cases, who do not fall within the McNaghten rules, because of the insane fury of the slaughter. A big margin of subjectivism, a preference for old English precedents, theories of modern penology, behavioural emphasis or social antecedents, judicial hubris or human rights perspectives, criminological literacy or fanatical reverence for outworn social philosophers buried in the debris of time except as part of history—this plurality of forces plays a part in swinging the pendulum of sentencing justice erratically. Therefore, until Parliament speaks, the Court cannot be silent. (Hopefully, s. 302, I.P.C. is being amended, at long last, but it is only half-way through as the Rajya Sabha proceedings show. We will revert to it later)".[6]

Suffice it to say that world opinion is reflected in the second optional Protocol to the International Covenant on Civil and Political Rights aiming at the abolition of the Death Penalty and proclaiming that abolition of the death penalty contributes to enhancement of human dignity and progressive development of human rights. No one within the jurisdiction of a State Party shall be executed. Gandhi country betrays the creed of the Father of the Nation, if it fails to ratify this Protocol.

These zigzags in sentencing makes chaos in the cosmos making the life of the man in the dock the plaything of the judge with the robe. It is interesting that several attempts have been made in India to abolish death sentence through legislation:

"In 1931, an abolition bill was introduced in the Legislative Assembly by Gaya Prasad Singh; but a motion for circulation of the bill was defeated after it was opposed by the Government.

The pattern after independence has been much the same. In 1956, a bill introduced in the Lok Sabha by Mukund Lal Agarwal was rejected after Government opposition. In 1958, a Resolution for abolition, moved in the Rajya Sabha by Prithvi Raj Kapur, was withdrawn after debate. (Its purpose had been served, said Shri Kapur). 'The ripples are created and it is in the air": *Rajya Sabha Debates,* 25th April 1958 Cols. 444-528. In 1961 a further Resolution moved in the Rajya Sabha by Mrs. Savitry Devi Nigam was negatived after debate.

"In 1962, however, Resolution moved in the Lok Sabha by Raghunath Singh received more serious attention: *Lok Sabha Debates*, 21st April 1962, Cols. 307-365. The Resolution was withdrawn, but only after the Government had given an undertaking that a transcript of the debate would be forwarded to the Law Commission, for consideration in the context of its review of the Penal Code and the Criminal Procedure Code. The result was a separate Law Commission Report on Capital Punishment, submitted to the Government in September 1967."

"At pages 354-55, the Law Commission summarized its main conclusions as follows:

6 *Rajendra Prasad* v *State of U.P.* AIR 1979 SC 916 at pages 924-925.

'It is difficult to rule out the validity of or the strength behind many of the arguments for abolition. Nor does commission treat lightly the argument based on the irrevocability of the sentence of death, the need for a modern approach, the severity of capital punishment, and the strong feeling shown by certain sections of public opinion in stressing deeper questions of human values.

Having regard, however, to the conditions in India, to the variety in the social upbringing of its inhabitants, to the disparity in the level of morality and education in the country, to the vastness of its area, to the diversity of its population and to the paramount need for maintaining law and order in the country at the present juncture, India cannot risk the experiment of abolition of capital punishment.'[7]

In short Gandhiji, venerated as the Father of the Nation, has failed in Parliament to make his creed operation, although he wrote long ago:

"God Alone Can Take Life
Because He Alone Gives it".

I took the view in *Rajendra Prasad* and I stick to it even now that even a shocking crime, without a closer study of many imponderable factors inducing its commission, is insufficient to justify a lethal verdict:

"Most murders are horrifying, and an adjective adds but sentiment, not argument. The personal story of an actor in a shocking murder, if considered, may bring tears and soften the sentence. He might have been tortured child, an ill-treated orphan, a jobless starveling, a badgered brother, a wounded son, a tragic person hardened by societal cruelty or vengeful justice, even a Hamlet or Parasurama. He might have been angelic boy but thrown into mafia company or inducted into dopes and drugs by parental neglect or morally-mentally retarded or disordered. Imagine a harijan village hacked out of existence by the genocidal fury of a kulak group and one survivor, days later. cutting to pieces the villain of the earlier outrage. Is the Court in error in reckoning the prior provocative barbarity as a sentencing factor?"[8]

I am not yet a total abolitionist. In rare cases some chronic murderers may be candidates for the gallows, but they are rare, very rare cases where the person is incurably murderous. The formal presence of death sentence in the Penal Code comes into play in extraordinary situations.

"A paranoid preoccupation with the horror of the particular crime oblivious to other social and individual aspects is an error. The fact that a man has been guilty of barbaric killing hardly means that his head must roll in the absence of proof of his murderous recidivism, of incurable criminal violence, of a mafia holding society in ransom and of incompatibility of peaceful co-existence between the man who did the murder and society and its members."[9]

7 *Rajendra Prasad* v *State of U.P.* AIR 1979 SC 916 at page 927.
8 *Ibid*, at page 930.
9 *Ibid*, at page 933.

I conclude as I did it in *Rajendra Prasad* that I must bid farewell to *lex talionis* and go with Gandhiji a long way:

> "British Justice has abandoned death penalty for murder for two decades now (Homicide Act, 1957) without escalation of murderous crime. Attempts to get round the Murder (Abolition of Death Penalty) Act, 1965 have failed in Parliament and as Barbara Wooton says, 'Capital punishment thus appeared to be itself sentenced to death' for murder. To quote the Royal Commission's recommendation for retention after Parliament has abolished death penalty is only of historical interest: "After the Abolition Act had been in force for over seven years, the Criminal Law Revision Committee considered whether any further changes in the penalty for murder were desirable. Their conclusions were almost entirely negative.
>
> "This perspective justifies judicial evolution of humane penal doctrine because the legislative text is not static; and as Chief Justice Warren wrote in *Trop* v *Dullers* (1958-356 US 86) the Court 'must draw its meaning from the evolving standards of a maturing society'. The great answer to grave crime is culturing of higher consciousness, removing the pressure of a perverted social order, and nourishing the inner awareness of man's true nature. This is true penal reform, including jail reform."
>
> *** *** ***
>
> "Count Leo Tolstoy in his *Recollections and Essays* denounces death penalty even against revolutionaries by arguments too Gandhian to be dismissed by Indian judges in the sentencing sector of discretion. We do not dogmatise but suggest the trend. Law by itself is no answer to Justice as the sublime instances of Socrates, Jesus and martyrs galore in the long history of Man point."[10]

Experiments in India with abolition of death sentence, as for instance in Travancore for a time, have taught us that hanging is no deterrent and abolition is no invitation to recidivism. The world over, country after country, is going abolitionist. Even in the United States after *Furman*, death sentence has a holiday, although later *some* States have brought back the electric chair.

Indian law is still wayward, with chancy sentencees. Then came the Constitution Bench decision in *Bachan Singh* v *State of Punjab*[11] in which all the judges, except Bhagawati, J., whose dissenting judgment is at AIR 1982 SC 1325, held that death sentence was not violative of Art. 21; but then stated that it ought to be imposed in the "rarest of rare cases" (a euphemism for judicial gamble) which is demanded by a real and abiding concern for the dignity of human life postulating resistance to taking a life through law's instrumentality. Because of this, death sentence ought to be awarded when the alternative option is "unquestionably foreclosed".

10 *Rajendra Prasad* v *State of U.P.* AIR 1979 SC 916 at page 937.

11 AIR 1980 SC 898.

Penal law wobbles still. For instance, in *Amruta*[12] the Supreme Court observed:

> "......We do know that the accused nurtured and was labouring under a sense of grievance and was often dejected and moody presumably because of his suspicions. He was apparently inclined to brood over the wrong suspected by him to have been done to him. While no one can hold a brief for a modern Othello, we cannot also lose sight of the fact that sexual jealousy and injured vanity often combine together to furnish powerful motive for murder, particularly among rustic rural folk to which class the accused belongs. After considering all the circumstances, we do not think that there are sufficient grounds for departing from the rule of normal punishment and imposing the sentence of death. We, therefore, allow the appeal, set aside the sentence of death and substitute the sentence of imprisonment for life. The conviction for murder is confirmed."

Vacillation still haunts the penal sentencing process. I wonder why we should not learn from the British abolishanist experience. The time has come for inflicting death sentence on death sentence save in grave national emergencies. *The right to life must win.*

India has ratified the two Covenants; and so must respect Art. 4 and Art. 6 of the I.C.C.P.R. Art. 4 expressly makes *non-derogable* the provision in Art. 6 which declares that every human being has inherent right to life. So much so, even *in time of public emergency which threatens the life of the nation,* the right to life of the citizen shall not be suspended. The time is ripe for *ADM, Jabalpur*[13] to be overruled and constitutional humanism restored.

It is comforting that in Islamic Pakistan, the Benazir Bhutto Government has decided to abolish death penalty for women. Why not SAARC countries follow this lead as the beginning of gender justice in the terminal stage of life? Gandhi country, crowded with V.I.Ps protected by security guards, do wake up to the abolition of death penalty as a tribute to a half-century span of Independence!

12 AIR 1983 SC 629.

13 *ADM, Jabalpur* v *Shivakanta Shukla* AIR 1976 SC 1207: (1976)2 SCC 52.

14

LAST LECTURE
THE TALE OF TEN CITIES

HUMAN RIGHTS ARE as ancient as homo sapiens but their current incarnation is coterminous with the birth of the United Nations in 1945 in San Francisco. From then on, this global boon went into universal humane action and from stage to stage moved and met to promote human rights through a series of superlative instruments. These momentous achievements were collectively critiqued and dynamic directions imparted in the light of the dialectic of new challenges and changes. The meetings were historic and the march of human rights is best epitomised by the thinking together of leaders of nations and NGOs as miniaturised world assemblies. The names of Ten Cities broadly represent these progressive processes although in later years, especially when commercial appetites were hurt, regressive currents under various guises have weakened the locomotion of human justice, people's power of self-determination and developing nations' capability to use their sovereignty to implement Project Human Rights. The only Super Power and its allies in the North are using their economic clout to inflict the dependencia syndrome on the South.

The epic event of 1945 which midwifed the UN at San Francisco was of glorious moment and revolutionary portent as the Charter, in its grandeur of diction and sublimity of vision, established. Never in the story of man has such a multidimensional institution of far-reaching significance been beheld, although fifty years after, the dreams of San Francisco remain unfulfilled. However, with all its shocking shortfalls, shameful genuflections, pitiful paralyses when the world would have wished it to act decisively, impartially and in fulfilment of its global obligations, we cannot, without consternation and bitterness, conceive of our dear human planet without the peerless and powerful United Nations which still voices the urges and aspirations of humanity. Never shall San Francisco cease to be on the map of the universal jurisprudence of human rights, for here began the greatest adventure history has known of peoples worldwide come together to redeem their collective tryst with destiny as spelt out in the unique Charter which established the UN I have told the reader about this organisation as an instrument of human liberation.

The weary world meeting in Manhattan, in the wake of untold sufferings and intolerable inhumanities adopted the Universal Declaration of Human Rights as early as 1948 which formed the foundation of the edifice of human right jurisprudence. This *magna carta* became the lodestar to guide the march of humanity preserving and promoting dignity, equality and better standards of life in larger freedom. In the years that followed, many fruitful humanitarian conventions were successfully held relating to the amelioration of the condition of the wounded and sick in armed conflicts on land or at sea. Prisoners of war, protection of civilians in time of war, concern for refugees, and of the status of women engaged the attention of the UN Stateless persons and prisoners slaves and victims of forced labour fell for consideration and adoption of instruments by the UN. The Declaration of the Rights of the Child was an important step in redeeming the promise of the rising generation. A most momentous declaration which transformed human condition and redrew the world map, was adopted on 14th December 1960, regarding the granting of Independence to colonial countries and peoples. Freedom's flag flew over emancipated nations and a new world order burgeoned.

Another supremely significant resolution adopted in December 1962 related to 'Permanent Sovereignty over Natural Resources' Indeed colonial countries politically freed could not be truly sovereign until their natural resources were beyond the exploitative reach of quasi-imperial operators. A miscellany of other progressive measures also sprang from the noble U.N. edifice in Manhattan. We may perhaps call this period the Manhattan era of human rights contributions.

Proclamation of Teheran

The world will gratefully remember Teheran the capital of Iran where the first inter-allied conference of World War II, attended by Stalin, Roosevelt and Churchill, was held in 1943. But, from the human rights angle, the Proclamation of Teheran, 1968 is more memorable. Twenty years after the Universal Declaration the UN had a scan of the successes and failures and produced a Proclamation which was adopted by a United Nations Conference. Various resolutions on particular problems, including the development of comprehensive legal aid systems, were adopted. Worry was writ large on the Conference since the international community had not ended conflict and violence in many parts of the world and the full realisation of human rights and fundamental freedoms were still bafflingly eluding mankind. Moreover, the rival schools of thought (Washington versus Moscow) between the ideologies of the two Covenants divisively weakened the battle for total attainment of human rights in its plenary content and a holistic emphasis became necessary. The Teheran Proclamation achieved this object of recognising both the Covenants as having created standards and obligations to which States should conform. (It is regrettable that the USA has still not ratified the ECOSOC Covenant). Articles 5, 12 and 13 are explicit and imperative that 'the full realisation of civil and political rights *without* the enjoyment of economic, social and cultural rights, is *impossible.* Women and youth receive special attention in building the New World Order. Equally importantly, Art. 19 reads:

> "Disarmament would release immense human and material resources now devoted to military purposes. These resources should be used for the promotion of human rights and fundamental freedoms. General and complete disarmament is one of the highest aspirations of all peoples."

The Teheran principles of giving social rights, the same status as civil rights abolishing the ideological antithesis between the two Covenants is a remarkable success. In India, Part IV (Social Rights) has been read into Part III (Civil Rights) by the Supreme Court, since social and economic equalisation is a *sine qua non* for civil equality. Planning is integral to this blending and calls for agrarian and industrial reform, regulation of labour condition, supply of essential commodities and services, regulation of prices, supply of free education at least up to a certain level and other methods of distributive justice.

In this context, Art. 3 of the Italian Constitution makes sense:

> "All citizens have equal social rank and are equal before the law without distinction of sex, race, language, religion, political opinion or social and personal conditions.
>
> "It is the task of the Republic to remove obstacles of an economic or social nature which, by materially restricting the freedom and equality of citizens, impede the complete development of human personality and the effective participation of all workers in the political, economic, and social organisation of the country."

Article 9 of the Cyprus Constitution has a flavour of socio-economic right being made a charge on the State. Article 45 of the Constitution of Eire reminds us of the blended brew.

In sum, the goal of development of the human personality is declared to be freedom and dignity consonant with physical, mental, social and spiritual welfare.

This clarion call to all peoples and governments is a reaffirmation and rebuff to the economically and unilaterally stronger powers to remember their global commitment. This unifying command makes Teheran a city, not of Ayatollahs and oil but of imperativeness of human rights 'in widest commonalty spread and the summons to demilitarise and devote the resources so released for the promotion of the welfare of penurious humanity and its sweet solidarity.

The Hague: the humanitarian justice capital of the world

No outline of human history in our century can pass by The Hague without saluting it as a hallowed home of international justice and humanitarian jurisprudence. The Permanent Court of International Justice set up by the League of Nations was replaced by the International Court of Justice, brought into being by the Charter of the United Nations and by the Statute of the Court which was made an integral part of the Charter. Long ago a Convention of 1899 for the Pacific Settlement of International Disputes established a Permanent Court of Arbitration—the forerunner of the World Court. The International Court of Justice has had, during its fifty years of existence, fallow and fertile periods, glorious and inglorious days of binding verdicts and rejected judgments—a peculiar pathology of its consensual and advisory universal human rights jurisprudence. In a world of more co-operation among nations this judicial institution has vast potential for resolving conflicts peacefully and defending human rights meaningfully.

It is of some interest to know that way back in July 1899 The Hague was the venue of the Declaration concerning Expanding Bullets (Dum-Dum bullets). Likewise, a convention respecting the Laws and Customs of War on Land was made at The Hague. The Convention for the Protection of Cultural Property in the Event of Armed Conflict, May 1954 also was made at The Hague. How heart-warming to feel the geographical ethos of justice and compassion of The Hague consecrated by Conventions and institutions of humanitarianism.

The city that deserves profound veneration when we glance through generations of war and amelioration of the savagery of war is Geneva where the world wove humanitarian jurisprudence.

Humanitarian law appeared in Europe during *the Age of Enlightenment.* "They formulated a fundamentally humanitarian doctrine according to which war should be limited to combat between soldiers, without posing a threat either to the civilian population or non-military objects.

It was mostly in Geneva that humanitarian law was developed, eventually to spread over the western world and to acquire the name of the *Law of Geneva. The Red Cross* also owed its origin to Henry Dunant, a citizen of Geneva, who was so horrified by the bleeding scenes of wounded soldiers abandoned on battlefields, that he made it his mission to find ways and means, in law and practice, to protect the victims of war. At the instance of the International Standing Committee for Aid to Wounded Soldiers (The Committee of Five), the Swiss Government convened a conference in Geneva, which resulted in the signing, on 22nd August 1864, of the Convention for the Amelioration of the Condition of the Wounded in Armies in the Field.

> "To emphasize the Swiss origins of the movement, the decision was soon taken to adopt, as the distinctive sign of the protection granted to wounded soldiers, the inversed colours of the Swiss flag (a white cross on a red ground), that is to say, a red cross on a white ground. In 1880, the Committee of Five became the International Committee of the Red Cross (ICRC), a name it has kept to this day. One by one, numerous National Societies were created and they adopted the same emblem. At the request of certain Islamic countries, the red crescent was also admitted. The red lion and sun was used for a time by Iran, but was abandoned (in 1980) in favour of the red crescent."[1]

1 *International Review of the Red Cross*, July-August 1984.

International jurists have distinguished between *human rights law* and *humanitarian law,* but the current trend is to view both through a compassionate lens to find overlapping areas, without being allergic to compartmentalisation of the two branches of jurisprudence. One of the effective means by which humanitarian processes in situations of armed conflicts operates is the use of the sublime instrument of the ICRC (International Committee of the Red Cross). In our world of ubiquitous belligerences and butcheries verging on genocide, the perennial presence of the Red Cross and the Red Crescent is a source of comfort to the conscience of peaceful peoples everywhere. The ICRC teams, in spite of risks, do a great job in areas of conflict intra-national and international. Some of the less known activities of the ICRC deserve to be disseminated.

Conscience and compassion in legal locomotion, through sad scenes of horror and cries of wounded soldiers left in pitiless neglect, pressured the International Committee of the Red Cross to sponsor the Geneva Convention and the supplementary Conventions. These international agreements establish the principle of disinterested aid to *all victims of war without discrimination* since they, through wounds, capture or shipwreck, are no longer enemies or capable agents of hostilities but merely suffering and helpless humans.

Humanitarian law, with its humble origin in Geneva, has become now a bulwark against the harshness, hardship and horror of war. The Humanitarian Conventions have been tuned to the current needs of a warring world with no holds barred and adapted to defend bleeding mankind victimised by victory through massacre. In between the two World Wars, the ICRC had laid the foundation for the establishment of a number of new Conventions like the Convention on the Treatment of Prisoners of War. Indeed, this was signed in the summer of 1929 and has protected millions of captured soldiers. With the end of World War II, the need to develop the humanitarian dimensions of International Law gained momentum. Governments and National Red Cross Societies facilitated the progress of this process.

> "Three former Conventions had to be revised: the Geneva Convention of 1929 for the Relief of the Wounded and Sick in Armies in the Field, the Xth Hague Convention of 1907 for the adaptation to Maritime Warfare of the Principles of the Geneva Convention, and the 1929 Convention on the Treatment of Prisoners of War. Furthermore, there was urgent need for a Convention for the protection of civilians, the absence of which had, during the world conflict, led to such grievous consequences."[2]

After careful scrutiny of the Draft Conventions, the matter came before the Conference held in Stockholm in August 1948. Considerable thought was bestowed on the various drafts and then emerged the 1949 Geneva Conventions.

2 *The Geneva Convention* of 12th August 1949, *International Committee of the Red Cross,* at page 2.

The following four Conventions were the product of the fruitful debates:

I. Geneva Convention for the Amelioration of the Condition of the Wounded and Sick in Armed Forces in the Field of 12th August 1949.

II. Geneva Convention for the Amelioration of the Condition of Wounded, Sick and Shipwrecked Members of Armed Forces at Sea, of 12th August 1949.

III. Geneva Convention relative to the Treatment of Prisoners of War, of 12th August 1949.

IV. Geneva Convention relative to the Protection of Civilian Persons in Time of War, of 12th August, 1949.[3]

After further Committee discussions, the Final Act was signed by a large number of countries. The general provisions of the Final Act deal with international conflicts, enemy occupation and civil war. They were followed by other special provisions which Contracting Parties may conclude dealing with the inalienability of the right of protected person, the duties of Protecting Powers, the activities of the International Committee of the Red Cross, and Conciliation procedure between the contracting Parties. Further refinements were made to the texts, one of the important contributions being the attempt to define 'War Crimes' in International Law. However, the fact remains "War Crimes" eludes precise definition altho' its ghastliness does help identify, even without formal definition, that class of crimes.

The Geneva Conventions are now universally accepted, more or less. The first Geneva Convention deals with the *wounded and sick,* even as the second Geneva Convention (the Maritime Convention) is an extension of the first and applies *to maritime warfare.* The third Geneva Convention with its annexes deals with *prisoners of war* and vastly extend The Hague Convention on the same subject. Humane regulation of the conditions of those in captivity is an aspect of International Law. The prisoners of War Convention has helped numberless people involved in conflicts. Even so, it has been felt that Agencies appointed to look after prisoners' interests and ensure that regulations concerning them are applied in full, should be as *independent* as possible of the political relations between the belligerents. This subject has been dealt with at length in the current third Geneva Convention.

The Fourth Geneva Convention (Civilians) is a constructive contribution in the humanitarian dimension to International Law. This new Convention is an elaboration which runs into several articles and prohibits in particular:

"(*a*) Violence to life and person, in particular torture, mutilations and cruel treatment.

(*b*) The taking of hostages.

(*c*) Deportations.

3 *Ibid,* at page 4.

(*d*) Outrages upon personal dignity, in particular humiliating or degrading treatment, or adverse treatment founded on differences of race, colour, nationality, religion, beliefs, sex, birth or social status.

(*e*) The passing of sentences and the carrying out of executions without previous judgment pronounced by a regularly constituted court affording all the judicial guarantees recognized as indispensable by civilized peoples."[4]

There is no need in this essay to go into greater detail except to state that now we have a fairly comprehensive set of Geneva Conventions. Even so, to witness the brutal violations of the humanitarian spirit in the maddening passion of battles among brothers of yesteryears, with Big Power megalomania and even UN peace keeping forces, makes us realise 'the petty done and the undone vast' in the field of Humanitarian Jurisprudence. World War II was a macro-scale disaster with scenes of savagery no eye had seen before, no heart conceived ever, and no human tongue could describe the desperate theatres of terror. This global holocaust had a seminal impact of awakening humankind to the urgency and adequacy of forbidding and punitively dealing with belligerent barbarity in the name of human dignity and peaceful progress of all peoples.

The march of law after World War II

The League of Nations addressed but minimally the laws to humanize war, even as, prior to World War I, precious little was achieved by way of regulating the laws of war. The optimist view that the world would disarm itself after the holocaust proved illusory. And the irony of it is that the Conference convened in Geneva in 1925 to end the arms trade produced a treaty on supervision but never entered into force due to lack of ratifications. The use of poison had been frowned upon by The Hague Regulations of 1899 and the Conference of 1925 strengthened it through the Protocol for the prohibition of the use of war of asphyxiating, poisonous and other gases and of bacteriological methods of warfare. The ban of 1925 has not won its humanitarian objective as is seen from the contemporary world struggling to extinguish sources of chemical warfare.

After the 2nd World War, the United Nations showed the same indifference as the League of Nations *vis-a-vis* armed conflicts and the Law of The Hague. However, the principal progressive step taken was the adoption, through an International Conference held in 1954 at The Hague under the auspices of the UNESCO, of The Hague Convention for the Protection of Cultural Property in the Event of Armed Conflicts. Cultural property of perpetual value is a global asset which shall not be a prey to the ravages of war. The International Military Tribunal at Nuremberg was also a great step to validate and integrate the punitive jurisprudence against war criminals.

4 *Ibid*, at page 19.

Geneva may well be described by humanity as its headquarters of the cosmic heart. War victims will ever remember Geneva, since guarantee for humane treatment of victims of armed conflicts emanate from instruments inscribed and brought into force from that city which has been neutral amidst the clash of arms.

Rio de Janeiro and its divine message

The city that has drawn humanity's nature-friendly sensitivity is Rio de Janeiro where a World Summit on Environment met to find solutions for problems which threaten the earth and its inhabitants.

The dialectics of technological progress and a world divided as North and South, developed and developing, generated demands for a creative approach to environment and ecology, sustainable development and a new philosophy of universal justice *vis-a-vis* dangerous levels of exploitation of Nature and of the Third World. The contradiction between pleasure plus profit at any cost and the terrible backlash of spiritual, moral and, most importantly, material degradation with death sentence on human civilisation, could not be resolved except through a fresh and dynamic vision of the World Order. The locomotive of such a transformation must come from the troika of science, statesmanship and a Nature-friendly New Humanism.

Mikhail Gorbachev once wrote what is pregnant with meaning to the International Life Institute:

> "Present day science and technology offer an opportunity to beautify, in the full sense of the word, life on Earth, to create conditions for the all-round development of every individual. But it is the very creations of the human mind and human hands that threaten the very existence of the human race. What a crying contradiction: We want science to cease to be the servant of two masters—life and death. We want it to serve life only. He emphasised the overriding importance of establishing sound, reasonable inter-state relations for cooperation and in search for ways to save life and in solving all the global problems on which the quality of life depends. Mankind can and must live in harmony with itself."[5]

We live in an indivisible world where the spiritual unity of creation is manifested in the material integrity of planet Earth and its inhabitants. Alvin Toffler has told us:

> "As the effects of irresponsibly applied technology become more grimly evident, a political backlash mounts. An offshore drilling accident that pollutes 800 square miles of the pacific triggers a shock wave of indignation all over the United States. A multi-millionaire industrialist in Nevada, Howard Hughes, prepares a lawsuit to prevent the Atomic Energy Commission from continuing its underground nuclear tests. In Seattle, the Boeing Company fights growing public clamor against its plans to build a supersonic jet transport. In Washington, public sentiment forces a reassessment of missile policy. At MIT, Wisconsin, Cornell, and other universities, scientists lay down test tubes and slide rules

5 Frolov: *The Ethics of Service: Jesus and Controversies,* pages 185-186.

during a "research moratorium" called to discuss the social implications of their work. Students organize "environmental teachings" and the President lectures the nation about the ecological menace. Additional evidences of deep concern over our technological course are turning up in Britain, France and other nations."[6]

As Toffler puts it:

"We have taught ourselves to create and combine the most powerful of technologies. We have not taken pains to learn about their consequences. Today these consequences threaten to destroy us. We must learn, and learn fast."[7]

"Modern industrial development has brought to India also the dangers from hazardous chemicals, and harmful micro-organisms, particularly those evolved through genetic engineering. While these have their uses, there is a need for great care in handling them in view of their potential for damaging the environment. The disastrous accident at Bhopal in 1984 has demonstrated the need for a carefully designed system for prevention, control and management of accidents while handling hazardous chemicals. In addition, a number of industries and processes generate hazardous wastes which need proper disposal. Indiscriminate import of such waste from developed countries, which are anxious to dispose them off, without having the capacity to deal with the wastes in an environmentally appropriate manner needs to be curbed."[8]

Dr. M.S. Swaminathan had entered a caveat as far back as 1968:

"Intensive cultivation of land without conservation of soil fertility and soil structure would lead ultimately to the springing up of deserts. Irrigation without arrangements for drainage would result in soils getting alkaline or saline. Indiscriminate use of pesticides, fungicides and herbicides could cause adverse changes in biological balance as well as lead to an increase in the incidence of cancer and other diseases, through the toxic residues being present in the grains or other edible parts. Unscientific tapping of underground water would lead to the rapid exhaustion of this wonderful capital resource left to us through ages of natural farming. The rapid replacement of numerous locally adapted varieties with one or two high yielding strains in large contiguous areas would result in the spread of serious diseases capable of wiping out entire crops."[9]

Today our dependence on foreign fertilisers, pesticides and even seeds has riddled agriculture with many new problems:

"The first UN Conference on the Human Environment held at Stockholm, Sweden, in 1972 aroused global consciousness on the need for subjecting all developmental activities to well defined ecological ground rules. It also

6 Alvin Toffler: *Future Shock,* page 430.

7 *Ibid,* page 440.

8 Ministry of Environment and Forest: *Environment and Development—India's Approach,* 1992, page 13.

9 Address at the Indian Service Congress 1968.

brought home the point that so long as widespread poverty persists there will be no hope for achieving harmony between humankind and nature. Twenty years later, in June 1992, a UN Conference on Environment and Development was held at Rio in Brazil to adopt an Earth Charter, an agenda for action in the 21st century and probably, global conventions on climate, biological diversity and forests."[10]

The late Rajiv Gandhi had pleaded at the Belgrade Summit of the Non-Aligned Movement for a Planet Protection Fund designed to make all countries, save the least developed, bear equitable financial burden for accessing environment friendly technology. It is an imperative need of our globe to discover innocent technologies eschewing destructive ones.

The Rio Declaration is mankind's last chance to save itself. Here are the essentials of Rio's soul:

"*Principle 1*: Human beings are at the centre of concerns for sustainable development. They are entitled to a healthy and productive life in harmony with nature.

"*Principle 3*: The right to development must be fulfilled so as to equitably meet the developmental and environmental needs of present and future generations.

"*Principle 4*: In order to achieve sustainable development, environmental protection shall constitute an integral part of the development process and cannot be considered in isolation from it.

"*Principle 7*: States shall cooperate in a spirit of global partnership to conserve, protect and restore the health and integrity of the earth's ecosystems. In view of the different contributions to global environmental degradation, states have common but differentiated responsibilities. The developed countries acknowledge the responsibility that they bear in the international pursuit of sustainable development in view of the pressures their societies place on the global environment and of the technologies and financial resources they command.

"*Principle 14*: The State should effectively cooperate to discourage or prevent the relocation and transfer to other states of any activities and substances that cause severe environmental degradation or are found to be harmful to human health.

"*Principle 16*: National authorities should endeavour to promote the internationalisation of environmental costs and the use of economic instruments, taking into account the approach that the polluter should, in principle, bear the cost of pollution, with due regard to the public interest and without distorting international trade and investment.

"*Principle 22*: Indigenous people and their communities, and other local communities, have a vital role in environmental management and development because of their knowledge and traditional practices. States should recognise and duly support their identity, culture and interests and enable their effective participation in the achievement of sustainable development."

10 *Monograph No. 4*—M.S. Swaminathan Foundations, Madras 1991.

Stockholm awakened a gluttonous globe to the dangers of reckless violence on Nature. Rio took stock of the perils and prescribed obligations through an Earth Charter. But the developed nations and the imitative developing countries are corruptly unconscionable in robbing and raping Nature. Humanity's hopes are down and despair is deepening. A comprehensive and far-reaching programme for sustainable development is Agenda 21 which constitutes humanity's creative hunger for survival.

Says Winston Churchill somewhere:

> "The dark ages may return—the stone age may return on the gleaming wings of science; and what might now shower immeasurable material blessings upon mankind may even bring about its total destruction. Beware I say! Time may be short."

Vienna: the well-spring of a new hope

When Napoleon was defeated a European Assembly was convened at Vienna by the victorious Powers (1814-15) to redraw the territorial map of Europe. Lovely and internationally fascinating city, Vienna was the venue of the World Conference on Human Rights in June 1993. A grandiloquent Preamble affirmed the dignity and worth inherent in the human person, expressed deep concern about die-hard discriminations and violent violations of human rights and solemnly committed the international community to promote human rights in larger measure and indulged in razzmatazz by 'invoking the spirit of our age and the realities of our time' to rededicate themselves to the global task of promoting and protecting human rights and fundamental freedoms the world over. Glorious clauses followed and a programme of action was chalked out. Magnificent to read but terrible doublespeak and newspeak more deceptive than George Orwell would have ever meant. Article 5, for instance, warns: All human rights are universal, indivisible and interdependent and interrelated. The international community must treat human right globally in a fair and equal manner, on the same footing and with the same emphasis.

This platitudinous assertion has lost its seriousness by frequency of repetition and infrequency of action. A clever computer may well have told us what the surrogates of Governments who met at Vienna would have orated to their Declaration. The right to development, the deleteriousness of dumping of toxic and dangerous products, the need to pare down the external debt burden of developing countries and several other such truisms have been emphatically verbalised. The human rights of women and of girl-child have been highlighted; the full and equal participation of women in political, civil, economic, social and cultural life, at the national, regional and international levels and the eradication of all forms of discrimination on grounds of sex are priority objectives of the international community.

Heavy accent on the inherent dignity and the unique contribution of indigenous people to the development and plurality of society and consequent obligation to raise their economic, social and cultural well-being is a welcome feature. Likewise the full and free participation of indigenous people in all aspects of society has also been accepted as a radical proposition. The child has also been the focus of attention reinforcing the plan of action adopted by the World Summit for Children. Article 27, turns attention on human rights justice in a beautiful condensation. Article 27 reads:

> "27. Every State should provide an effective framework of remedies to redress human rights grievances or violations. The administration of justice, including law enforcement and prosecutorial agencies and, especially, an independent judiciary and legal profession in full conformity with applicable standards contained in international human rights instruments, are essential to the full and non-discriminatory realization of human rights and indispensable to the processes of democracy and sustainable development. In this context, institutions concerned with the administration of justice should be properly funded, and an increased level of both technical and financial assistance should be provided by the international community. It is incumbent upon the United Nations to make use of special programmes of advisory services on a priority basis for the achievement of a strong and independent administration of justice."

There is a guilty reference to genocide, ethnic cleansing and systematic rape of women in War situations creating mass exodus. The breach of the Geneva Conventions of 1949 and the general violations of human rights including torture find a place in the Vienna document. Indeed in the implementation part there are some concrete proposals for increasing resources for the human rights programme, especially for the Centre for human rights. The focal role of the Centre is also stressed. More importantly the question of the establishment of a United Nations High Commissioner for Human Rights has been dealt with. Many other golden statements of implementation and monitoring methods are incorporated in the Declaration. A follow up to the World Conference. Special attention towards the goal of Universal ratification of International Human Rights Treaties and Protocols adopted within the framework of UN System was directed in the Vienna appeal.

These remarkable statements, partly appeals for action, partly confessions of guilt and partly inflated illusions about the future of human rights through a Commissioner sum up what a cynic may call the Vienna Stunt. The world is none the wiser, very much the sadder, Vienna notwithstanding.

Let us continue our global journey and halt for a while *at Cairo* to look at our over-crowded planet sinking in poverty, crying in hunger and disease and waiting for a message to make human worth and human resource the real wealth of the Earth. The International Conference on Population and Development met at Cairo and adopted on 13th September 1994 (later endorsed by the UN) the Programme of Action (POA). A voluminous 116 page Report exhaustively covers the issues of population explosion and developmental compulsion. Profoundly influenced by non-governmental organisations, women's groups and networks across the globe, this document faced squarely the huge escalation of human numbers already 5.6 billion strong and rising rapidly to over 7 billion people in 20 years.

Harrowing conditions of life in developing countries and the affluent creamy layer lapping up the food and other resources, abetted by multinational big business, create colossal misery and other woes incompatible with life in dignity and decency. Indian, why Asian poverty, aggravated by five-star affluence for a fraction and ill-starred millions drowned in privation, creates an unjust world system which will be blown up by revolutions.

Social justice, sans which human rights are writ in water, involves realistic policies of population regulation, remembering that every human being is the source of wealth if health and happiness is assured by distributive justice for the humblest and more mouths to eat with less food per capita does not breed more penurious pariahs. Maternal mortality and infant mortality are a curse which call for courageous and creative action by society. Certain principles were accepted at Cairo a few of which deserve recapitulation.

Principle 2 states:

> "Human beings are at the centre of concerns for sustainable development. People are the most important and valuable resource of any nation. All individuals have the right to an adequate standard of living for themselves and their families, including adequate food, clothing, housing, water and sanitation."

Principle 3 reads:

> "The right to development is a universal and inalienable right and an integral part of fundamental human rights. The human person is the central subject of development. The right to development must be fulfilled so as to equitably meet the population, development and environment needs of present and future generations.

Principle 4 is very important if women have title to personhood:

> "The advancement of gender equality and equity, the empowerment of women, the elimination of all kinds of violence against women, and the promotion of women's control over their own fertility, are cornerstones of population and development-related programmes. The human rights of women and the girl child are an inalienable, integral and indivisible part of universal human rights. The full and equal partnership of women in civil, cultural, economic, political and social life, at the national, regional and international levels, and the eradication of all forms of discrimination on grounds of sex, are priority objectives of the international community."

Principle 10 also bears on the dignity of personhood:

> "Everyone has the right to education, which must be directed to the full development of human resources, and human dignity and potential with particular attention to women and the girl child."

The girl child is a case for special concern:

> "Practices like female infanticide and the misuse of technologies to determine foetal sex and selectively abort female foetuses, and realities such as higher mortality rates among small girls and lower rates of school enrolment and retention for girls of all ages, violate the basic human rights of female children."

Family planning jurisprudence is a neglected branch of injustice and calls for creative restructuring of man-woman relationship in a fairer socio-economic milieu if gender justice and quality of life are to be a civilised value. A new universe of gender glory where sterile equality as a formal legality, is transcended to reach heights of gender empowerment, covering the entire gamut of foetus to funeral is the Cairo vision. But the sinister culture of male domination and genetic herrenvolk masquilinism fight back in all walks of life from home and temple to the farewell to life and all in between. The Cairo conspectus of values is a bold, frank version of humanity's sense of frank version of humanity's sense of realism and vision of the brave new world struggling to be born.

The mother is more than a parent and girl more than a child with an unwanted sex. Never will the world be great until a generation of free women does flourish. In all our debates on S.T.D., H.I.V., A.I.D.S. and property relations the cruel distortion against women ruins remedial justice. The over-emphasis of family as an unbreakable unit with religious reinforcement is sometimes a guise to warp the assertive equality of womanhood. Power everywhere is in the hands of man as a species and never does power part with its privilege and pleasure. Curative recommendations on a spectrum of gender justice are included in the Cairo Manifesto of 1994. Women of the world, never surrender. Your physical, moral, spiritual integrity is at stake. You will win if you educate, agitate and unite under the 'equal gender' banner. Not words but deeds are the need of the hour. India of today is guilty of outrages from foeticide and infanticide to saticide and dowrycide.

Social justice takes us on its wings to the beautiful city of Copenhagen in Denmark, cold outside but warm at heart, hospitably hosted the World Summit for Social Development in March 1995. A Declaration and Programme of Action, with the customary noises of conferences and instrument of eloquence, emerged from here. But the world's people, as distinguished from heads of Governments, insisted more and more that their voices be heard so that participatory discussions may take place and global society may not be *ex parte*. The pinnacle of peroration from the very start of the Declaration is worth listening to—

> "For the first time in history, at the invitation of the United Nations, we gather as Heads of State and Government to recognize the significance of social development and human well-being for all and to give to these goals the highest priority both now and into the twenty-first century.
>
> "We acknowledge that the people of the world have shown in different ways an urgent need to address profound social problems, especially poverty, unemployment and social exclusion, that affect every country. It is our task to address both their underlying and structural causes and their distressing consequence in order to reduce uncertainty and insecurity in the life of people.
>
> "We acknowledge that our societies must respond more effectively to the material and spiritual needs of individuals, their families and the communities in which they live throughout our diverse countries and regions. We must do

so as a matter of urgency, but also as a matter of sustained and unshakable commitment through the years ahead.

"We are convinced that democracy and transparent and accountable governance and administration in all sectors of society are indispensable foundations for the realization of social and people-centered sustainable development."

When confessionals are forthcoming from member nations there is surest satisfaction for victims everywhere. So the Copenhagen Declaration proves the guilt of gross neglect by the richer Powers. But crime confessed, how to punish by correctional therapeutics when Might in the dock enjoys the valiant verbosity of the verdict and ignores Right with none to challenge by contempt proceedings the unsocial villainy of violating fundamental undertakings of 1948 vintage!

Kindly read, with IMF controlled structural mutations inflicted on the South and Marakkesh GATT treaties in mind, the unrepentant nations' candid statement setting out the Current Social situation:

"We are witnessing in countries throughout the world the expansion of prosperity for some, unfortunately accompanied by an expansion of unspeakable poverty for others. This glaring contradiction is unacceptable and needs to be corrected through urgent actions.

"Globalization, which is a consequence of increased human mobility, enhanced communications, greatly increased trade and capital flows and technological developments, opens new opportunities for sustained economic growth and development of the world economy, particularly in developing countries. Globalization also permits countries to share experiences, to learn from one another's achievements and difficulties as well as a cross-fertilization of ideals, cultural values and aspirations. At the same time, the rapid processes of change and adjustment have been accompanied by intensified poverty, unemployment and social disintegration. Threats to human well-being, such as environmental risks, have also been globalized. Furthermore, the global transformations of the world economy are profoundly changing the parameters of social development in all countries. The challenge is how to manage these processes and threats so as to enhance their benefits and mitigate their negative effects upon people.

"More than one billion people in the world live in abject poverty, most of them go hungry every day. A large proportion, the majority of whom are women have very limited access to income, resources, education, health care or nutrition, particularly in Africa and the least developed countries.

"The major cause of the continued deterioration of the global environment is the unsustainable pattern of consumption and production, particularly in industrialised countries, which is a matter of grave concern, aggravating poverty and imbalances.

"One of the world's largest minorities, more than 1 in 10, are people with disabilities, who are too often forced into poverty, unemployment and social isolation. In addition, in all countries, older persons may be particularly vulnerable to social exclusion, poverty and marginalization."

The lot of Refugees and indigenous communities is lamented and excessive military expenditure condemned. Amen to this litany of culpable woes! But how do we go to redeem this distress syndrome? A pious promise is all that we get:

> "We, Heads of State and Government, are committed to a political, economic, ethical and spiritual vision for social development based on human dignity, human rights, equality, respect, peace, democracy, mutual responsibility and cooperation, and full respect for the various religious and ethical values and cultural backgrounds of people. Accordingly, we will give the highest priority in national, regional and international policies and actions to the promotion of social progress, justice and the betterment of the human condition, based on full participation by all."

A global commitment for social development is registered, but on paper. More commitments, restating the Family as the basic unit (with its patriarchal implications), have been added in this voluminous but no luminous ritual.

An alternative Copenhagen Declaration (on the assumption that the official verbal output is counterfeit Copenhagen coin) by N.G.Os. highly critical and making proposal has also been published. This polemic apart, we find in all these World Summits dissenting N.G.O. voices, reminding us of J.K. Stephen's lines on Wordsworth:

> *"Two voices are there: one is of the deep;*
> *It learns the storm-cloud's thunderous melody,*
> *Now roars, now murmurs with the changing sea,*
> *Now bird-like pipes, now closes soft in sleep:*
> *And one is of an old half-witted sheep*
> *Which bleats articulate monotony,*
> *And indicates that two and one are three,*
> *That grass is green, lakes damp, and mountains steep*
> *And, Wordsworth, both are thine."*

The most successfully participated and expectantly anticipated Summit Meet where the world's women fought for their rights and proclaimed an alternative Declaration is our last city in the global journey—*Beijing*. That crimson capital of China, the world's most populous nation with socialist terrain marred here and there by market-friendly temptations, was the venue of the largest summit gathering of Governments and voluntary bodies with focus on womanhood in its militant march towards a gender-just destination.

Without expending much space or expanding on the customary clauses, we may gain an insight into the responses and urges voiced in the Conference by looking at the preambular portion of the N.G.O. Beijing Declaration:

> "We, the N.G.O. women of the world, rich in our diversity, appreciate this opportunity to meet along with Governments in the largest global conference

ever to address women's issues and the existing barriers to our achieving equality, development and peace. We believe these goals cannot be realised without ending the oppression of women and girls and transforming the social, economic and political structures which underlie and perpetuate poverty, inequality, injustice, violence and war.

"While we acknowledge the progress made at this Fourth World Conference on Women, we are gravely concerned that important matters are not being addressed. A decade after the Nairobi Conference, the Forward Looking Strategies have not been fully implemented by any Government. We live in a world marked by growing poverty, inequality, injustice, environmentally destructive economic growth, war, sexism, racism, xenophobia, homophobia and other forms of discrimination and violence against women. Supported by the wisdom of our elders, inspired by indigenous peoples, energised by youth, and sustained by our sisterhood, we call for an end to these conditions and refuse to accept them as inevitable for the future of humanity.

"Resources are being squandered on the military with no gain in peace and common security. The dominant development model generates great material wealth for a few, while impoverishing many. The current global market economy creates both poverty and environmental degradation. It encourages over consumption and arms proliferation, depletes our natural resources and forests, and pollutes our air, water and soil. It fails to meet the fundamental material and spiritual needs of the peoples of the world. The unremunerated labour of women is presently estimated at eleven trillion dollars annually. Women do two-thirds of the world's work yet earn only 5% of its income and own less than 1% of its assets. Women are major contributors to every economy but much of our labour is neither recognised nor valued, and serves as an invisible subsidy."

Our planet will live in peace and well-being only when our mothers, sisters and daughters achieve full and real participation in all the affairs of the world. Summits, worldwide and regional, add to human rights literature. The Declarations are often repetitions. What about the platform of action, periodic social audit, pressure to perform and people's sanctions on breach? There's the rub.

Two more cities have gained global notice although the winds that blow from there are fraught with disastrous portents to the human rights of the vast masses spread over the South and sprinkled over the North. When World War II smashed the economies of nations and burnt into the consciousness of people the vital necessity of rebuilding the social security and developmental potential of victim countries, monetary reconstruction became a high priority item on the agenda of post-War habilitation. So, forty-four nations met in July 1944 at Bretton Woods, U.S.A., to achieve cooperation on money matters, stable exchanges and expansion of international trade. This was imperative if human life was to be bearable and human rights viable. The recommendations included the setting up of an International Monetary Fund (IMF) and an International Bank to assist reconstruction, especially in countries devastated by war. 'The only hope of effectively dealing with the world's major problems in the interest of all humankind is through the progressive development of a working world community'. Development needs money and so on 15th November 1947 the Bank and the Fund became specialized agencies of the United Nations. They are both by far the most controversial multilateral organizations *vis-a-vis* their injurious impact on developing countries. Bank-financed projects and IMF structural adjustment conditionalities adversely affected the borrowers, not so much because they were responsible to the UN as because it is not. The basic UN Principles included membership for peace-loving states and governance by one member one vote. The Bank, on the other hand, restricts membership to financial subscription and assent of powers. Weighted voting according to member's shares is wealth. The Bank and the Fund resisted control by the UN and so their savage pro-U.S. praxis went on unchecked. When the UN tried to set up its own Bank the idea was opposed by industrial powers and the SUNFED died. Many of the Bank-supported projects were failures and afflicted the human rights of people. The financial imperialism of the Bank has been criticised by informed social activists. Defiant of UN principles, the IMF has, through macro-economic conditionalities, debunked and debilitated developing nations' policies of self-reliance and social justice and by imposing conditionalities broken the back of their national commitments. The Bank-Fund betrayal of UN purposes, according to knowledgeable economists with human rights concerns, operates functionally to finish off the social, economic and cultural rights under the ECOSOC Covenant. In Indian vocabulary, swadeshi and self-reliance, poverty eradication and social justice are on the cross. A scholar, fearless and free, who writes on the desperate economies and political collapse will locate the assassination of Gandhian economic creed and Nehruvian socialist vision somewhere in the luxurious offices of Bank-Fund in Washington D.C. Walden Bello in his book *Dark Victory* shatters the myth of the IMF salvationary role. In Africa, South America, Asia, the IMF has, by its loan conditionalities, carried on a successful war against the poor with the complicity of Southern elites who 'lie back and enjoy roll back because they, too, profit hugely from it'. Many nations have suffered and India is facing its fatal turn, going by the spiralling living cost, rising unemployment, displacement of starvelings and indigenous people and dazzling affluent micro-sector and large-scale anti-social corruption. On India, Bello says Rollback has succeeded:

> "The surrender of leading countries like India to structural adjustment translated in the global arena into a deep erosion of the power and prestige of those institutions that had served as agents of Southern interests: the Non-Aligned Movement, UNCTAD, the Group of 77. The decomposition of the Third World was felt at the United Nations, where the United States was emboldened once again to use that body to front Northern interests, including providing legitimacy for the U.S.-led invasion of Iraq in 1991."[11]

The trick is that technocrats with U.S. training and empathy operate in the South for easy access and lethal grip for the IMF.

11 Walden Bello: *Dark Victory* at page 71.

In the very incisive and original work, *Food First*, the authors analyse the Bank-Fund stratagems, its standard killer-conditionalities, the dismantling of native progressive policies and the softening of resistance to market occupation by U.S. corporate powers. The U.S. has decisive voting power and loans are geared to subvert local development and support foreign import. Human Rights of the people of loanee nations versus Bank-Fund strategies is the tragic tale of the great cultures after the *Bretton Woods* offspring began to interfere in the internal economies of States and the economic rights of the poor.

The last city visited in this long journey is Marrakesh in Morocco. It is well-known that the GATT negotiations took a sudden turn opening wide the jaws of market-hungry G-7 Powers who could gulp down with ease the G-77 developing countries, rob their resources and win the world through market imperialism. The Punta del Este declaration (Uruguay) started the Round which resulted in the Dunkel Draft Text. Trade Related Intellectual Property Rights (TRIPS), Trade-Related Investment Measures (TRIMS) and Trade in Services (TRIS) expanded the scope of the negotiations and U.S. mounted pressure:

> "It being the principal beneficiary and was going through a grave trade recession, and the opposition by weaker countries began to crumble. Removal of farm subsidies, reduction of non-tariff barriers to trade and minimising restrictions on foreign investments (part of the Dunkel proposal) were meant to prise open Third World economies.
>
> "The marathon Uruguay Final Act was endorsed by the Ministerial meeting held in Marrakesh on 15th April 1994 in the face of sharp popular opposition inside India (and agitation in several other countries) about signing the GATT Final Act. Yet India (Government) assented."
>
> "The broad structural projection of GATT 1994 and its transformation to the WTO (the key, all-powerful multilateral institution of the future) is given as an introduction to the awesome halls of this new Treaty edifice. Marrakesh was witness to the World Trade Ministers' (including the Indian Commerce Minister) signatures approving over 20,000 pages of texts and tariff schedules. These plural plenty of signatures laid the groundwork for the creation of a new international organisation, the World Trade Organisation (WTO) which on 1.1.1995 took over all the business from the then existed GATT Secretariat.
>
> "The crux of the treaty endorsed by representatives from about 120 countries and covering everything from apples to zinc, is the understanding on market access by which countries will cut tariffs on industrial and farm goods by about 37 per cent. Services such as banking, insurance, travel and movement of labour, constituting annual trade worth four billion dollars, will in the future be governed by the WTO. Countries with closed farm markets will have to import at least three per cent of the domestic consumption of the product concerned, going up to five per cent over six years.
>
> "It also cuts trade-distorting subsidies for farmers. Poor nations (least developed countries) are, however, exempt from the agricultural reforms, introduced into the agreement for the first time.

> "While import quotas on textiles and clothing will be phased out over 10 years, anti-dumping rules by which imports are priced below their value in the domestic market have been clarified. Intellectual property rights guaranteeing greater protection for patents, copyright, rights of performers and producer-members have been endorsed."[12]

The constitutionality of the Indian Government's signature without parliamentary approval and violating the basics of the Socialist Republic's Part III & IV commitments is also reflected in the disastrous impact on people's rights. Poverty, disease, squalor, infant and maternal mortality and the shake-up of every aspect of the right to life, health and happiness follow upon the Marrakesh signatures on the marathon Uruguay Final Act.

A closer study by jurists will reveal how human rights of the countries of the South will terribly suffer if the Marrakesh treaties begin to hurt grievously the people whose hopes of a New World Order will vanish in despair.

Thus the World Summits and great promises will be put to sleep and requiem sung by Bretton Woods and Marrakesh on the Universal Declaration of Human Rights 1948, at least in India, in particular, because a Government, defeated shortly after, has put its signature to the Final Act. This brings to mind the sardonic lines of Woodie Gutterie (USA):

> *"Now as through this world I ramble,*
> *I have seen lots of funny men,*
> *Some will rob you with a six-gun*
> *And some with a fountain pen."*

The dialectic of contradiction between righteous human solidarity and forces of economic recolonisation must end in a dynamic victory for people's rights in a new synthesis of vigilant freedom never to be surrendered so long as the gladsome light of jurisprudence shines. Justice demands the price of determined struggle. Freedoms ask for more. In the emphatic words of Winston Churchill when Hitler invaded his island, we must resist the new economic militarist occupation forces with the vigour of Winston's eloquence:

> "We shall go on to the end, we shall fight in France, we shall fight on the seas and oceans, we shall fight with growing confidence and growing strength in the air, we shall defend our island, whatever the cost may be, we shall fight on the beaches, we shall fight on the landing grounds, we shall fight in the fields and in the streets, we shall fight in the hills; we shall never surrender."

Let us to the task.

Two things more and I am done. Is the GATT Final Act binding on India, constitutionally speaking? Arguments of learned length and arcane erudition will, with forensic persistence, be urged about the treaty-making power. I

12 Report by *Peoples' Commission on GATT, Front Line* dated 6th May 1994, pages 12-13.

cannot predict the imponderable end of these riddles wrapped in mysteries inside enigmas. Earlier I have expressed a view which, in all common sense, I still regard as sound.

Read literally, under Art. 253:

> "The treaty making power is wide in its amplitude and appears free from any express conditionalities that govern its exercise. But such a reading of the power is inevitably misleading. Suppose, the treaty making power results in a surrender of India's sovereignty, would not such an exercise of executive power (of which the treaty making power is a part) be regarded as unconstitutional. No doubt, a treaty—by itself—would not be enforceable in Indian Courts. Its provisions would not be the law of the land unless they were specifically enacted as part of Indian law by Parliament.[12a] But, that would not conclude constitutional misgivings about the treaty which may set up a powerful external enforcement of the treaty (as has been done in the case of the Uruguay Round) so that India and its people would feel the effect of non-compliance with the terms of the treaty. The treaty-making power must be deemed to be subject to certain express and implied limitations.
>
> The limitations on the exercise of the Treaty making power flow from certain principles which are fundamental to constitutional governance in India. The first is the general principle of accountability which requires Government to account to the people for every exercise of power through the aegis of institutions set up by and under the Constitution. Such accountability may be through the law which lays down norms which discipline and govern the exercise of the power. Where no such law exists—and none exists to discipline the exercise of the treaty making power—the Government is not free to do what it likes. Where the Government chooses to proceed without serious recourse to any form of accountability, other institutions of governance cannot stand idly by. Where Parliament is rendered powerless, other institutions must secure this accountability to such measure as may be deemed necessary. Where something is done in secret, simply breaking the veil of secrecy may be enough. It all depends on the facts and circumstances. The second principle which is fundamental to the rule of law is that no person's rights can be altered without reference to 'law'. If the executive simply interfere with the exercise of rights or alter them in any way other than *de minimus* infringement, this would be constitutionally improper and call for the interdiction of judicial processes. The third set of constraints flow from the basic structure of the Constitution. Although the basic structure doctrine was first enunciated to contain an over-extensive use of the power to amend the Constitution, the principles underlying the basic structure are also crucial aids to interpretation

12a For a different view, reference may be made to the decisions of the Supreme Court in *Maganbhai Iswarbhai Patel* AIR 1969 SC 783; *Gramophone Company* AIR 1984 SC 667; *Visakha* AIR 1997 SC 3011 *et al*, holding that the provisions of all International Convention, Covenants, Treaties etc., to which India is a party, become parts of our National Law, even without any Legislation under Article 253 of the Constitution and thus legally enforceable, save to the extent those are inconsistent with the provisions of our Constitution and the Laws.

and factors to be borne in mind when considering the exercise of executive power.

The Constitution makers intended the Government to be possessed of an executive power which is wider than the narrower duty to give effect to legislation.[13] But, in the exercise of this wider power, the rights of citizens cannot be taken away without specific legislative sanction and authority.[14] This rule is fundamental and a necessary adjunct to the recognition of a wide executive power. Equally, in normal circumstances, it is somewhat sanguinely assumed that all exercises of executive power would be consistent in a manner consistent with the principles of the basic structure of the Constitution. But, normal times tread unwarily into abnormality. That is why the touchstone of the basic structure has been inducted to discipline the exercise of even those special exercises of sovereign power such as the imposition of President's Rule and the like.[15] The older view that exercises of executive power are immune from judicial review has now correctly been abandoned.[16] While it is true that a word of caution has been sounded on the judiciary viewing questions of foreign policy,[17] this word of caution cannot be treated as an *ex cathedra* prohibition. There are situations where the rights of the citizens may be affected or where the very basic principles of constitutional governance are put in jeopardy. In such situations, judicial review will lie for it is the judiciary alone which can interpret the limits on the constitutional exercise of power by other constitutional functionaries within the limits of forbearance demanded by constitutional comity amongst institutions."[18]

Remember, Presidents and Ministers, a few lines from Dylan Thomas:

"The hand that signed the treaty bred a fever,
And famine grew, and locusts came;
Great is the hand that holds dominion over
Man by a scribbled name."

Human rights jurisprudence is diamond-hard and diamond-bright and will not, in the hands of great judges, fail the people for whom the bells of Constitutions loudly toll.

A note of hope, as I look around the regions of the world with longing eyes for experiments in defence of human rights. How inspiring to observe the European experiment setting incredible institutions in a continent of bleeding history! Churchill, De Gaul, Hitler and Mussolini and Quislings sleep where the luminous jurisprudence of the European Convention on

13 *Ram Jawayya Kapur* v *Union of India* AIR 1955 SC 549.

14 *Bijoe Emmanuel* v *State of Kerala* AIR 1987 SC 748.

15 *S.R. Bommai* v *Union of India* (1994)3 SCC 1; *M. Ishmail Faruqui* v *Union of India* AIR 1995 SC 605: (1994)6 SCC 360.

16 *Council for Civil Service Unions* v *Minister for Civil Service* (1984)3 All ER 935.

17 *Council for Civil Service Unions* v *Minister for Civil Service* (1984)3 All ER 935 approved in *S.R. Bommai* v *Union of India* (supra) at page 373.

18 *Report of the Peoples' Commission on GATT.*

Human Rights shines with unique lustre. This noble instrument was the essay in giving specific legal content to human rights, combining it with the establishment of machinery for supervision and enforcement. A beacon light from lands which once held the world in thralldom! The European Commission of Human Rights and the European Court of Human Rights are a paradigm for other parts of the world. The European Social Charter also arrests our attention.

The American Convention of Human Rights, adopted by the Organization of American States in San Jose, Costa Rica (1969), reaffirmed "their intention to consolidate in this hemisphere, within the framework of democratic institutions, a system of personal liberty and social justice based on the respect for the essential rights of man", which are 'based upon attributes of the human personality'. The right to life is protected 'from the moment of conception'. The other great rights find a place there. Even in time of war or emergency the 'right to judicial personality', the right to life and other very fundamental freedoms cannot be suspended. Competent organs (Commission and Court on Human Rights) are provided for. Any person or group has *locus standi* to move in the matter of violations. The juridical progressiveness of this Convention is fascinating. The Pact of San Jose, Costa Rica, is a step forward.

There is one special mention when Latin America is considered:

> "Latin America provides a store of contradictions in the field of human rights. Legal and political sophistication belongs to some of the Latin American socially elite groups, and the outcome of this sophistication is a desire to adopt legal instruments such as the American Convention of Human Rights which is broadly similar to the European Convention. At the same time social conditions in nearly all of Latin America entail inequalities and deprivation on such a scale that recourse absence of general social and economic development, the position relating to civil and political rights is itself precarious."[19]

Ten years later, the Organisation of African Unity drafted the African Charter on Human and People's Rights. (People's Rights is a good contribution).

19 Ian Brownlie: *Basic Documents on Human Rights*.

15

A Sombre Supplement

The Tagore Law Lectures were delivered by me many months ago. Between then and now, when the publisher has taken over the manuscript from the University, disturbing developments and changes and challenges have shaken the World Social Order which seek supplementary expression. With each passing day, age claims its price from me and my tireless toils for the causes of the forsaken humans rob all my spare hours. The abbreviation of life and the twilight of hope tinge with a browner shade my pensive perspective about the future of human rights. Even so, I felt that the gap between the delivery of the Lectures and the publication of the book might as well be partially bridged by putting in print some fresh reflections and later trends indicative of advance or retreat *vis-a-vis* the great cause of humanity. Whither goes the world? Endlessly craving for depravity, spinelessly surrendering human dignity and carnally sacrificing spiritual sublimity to the demands of worldliness, succumbing to materialist pleasures? In the process creeps in malefic corruption of the soul, maniac abuse of power and maddening arms race gambling with global peace and risking regional good neighbourliness. Consequence? Aggravation of tension, callous butchery on a macro-scale and total disregard for human life and rights, turning the good earth into a gory animal farm. Armaments are the worst homicidal sinners against human rights. And the *tamasic* (degradingly unholy) monopoly of the mind, as a savage engineer of human activities and appetites is equally hostile to human rights. And what a shame that slaves, serfs and commoditised people abound in our era of human-rights noises! Unless we deepen our feelings to reach the soul, open our hearts to embrace all, and enhance our value-set to a universal wholeness, we cannot humanize our world. Here comes the contradiction which a dialectical student perceives.

Vulgar violence and human-rights violations are an intrinsic part of the prevailing economic paradigm in which the unrestricted workings of the market and the unchecked and uncontrolled growth of competition–the new sacred cows–are seen as a natural and therefore inevitable process which, in the end, will automatically produce prosperity and well-being for humankind. In this paradigm, disequilibria and imbalances which occur are perceived and treated as incidental occurrences and exclusion, eviction, marginalization, misery and poverty as passing phenomena.

An Unhappy Addendum: United Nations, Human Rights and the Global Market Syndrome:

This dominant Western thought of boosting GNP growth as superseding all other goals and worshipping Mammonesque gods where Dives, with riches, and Lazarus, with his beggarly lot, will *together* be counted for reaching the *gross* national product, is in most cases, a goofy arithmetical illusion. The GNP cult was exposed by Mahbub Ul Haq who denigrated the 'developmental' fiction of GNP. A realisation came to me sharply after Haq wrote his Human Development in South Asia 1997 leading to a re-evaluation of 'progress'. He says in his Foreword to the book:

> "There is widespread consensus today that the purpose of development is not just to enlarge incomes, but to enlarge people's choices, and that these choices extend to a decent education, good health, political freedom, cultural identity, personal security, community participation, environmental security, and many other areas of human well being. Development must deal with the entire society, not just with the economy, and people must be put at the centre of the stage. As such, the quality and distribution of GNP growth become as important as the quantum of growth.
>
> Experience in many countries has also taught us that economic growth does not automatically translate into human development: a link between growth and human lives must be created through conscious national policies. My own rude awakening came quite early after a decade's experience with Pakistan's development planning."

While total national income in mathematical terms swelled, human lives of the lowly millions shrivelled. All the wealth added by 'progress' was hijacked by powerful grabbers. What is a hard reality is that human rights are unsafe at any speed, if GNP growth sans people-centred distributive justice is the scale of mensuration adopted. This agonising awakening is more distressing in the Indian subcontinent viewing the appalling scenario through the Haq lens.

> "In fact, the South Asia region has been sinking fast into a quagmire of human deprivation and despair, emerging as the most deprived region in the world. This reality is still not adequately recognized by national planners or international policy-makers."[1]

What a shock and shame that our *Socialist* Republic (so says the Constitution) has leaderships in all parties which covertly or overtly capitulate to xeno-capitalist carnivorousness and call it 'irreversible reform'. While a creamy layer in India consumes luxuries and is soaked in affluence, a staggering number—a quarter of our population (which is near-billion!) is

1 Mahbub Ul Haq in his Foreword to the book *Human Development in South Asia*, 1997.

bonded labour, a cousin of slave labour. Does larger GNP make sense to human rights sensitives as they behold this 'irreversible reform' syndrome? It is estimated that the total number of bonded labourers in our country (Bharat) is not less than 25 crores (250 millions) of which child labourers may be about 6 crores (60 millions).[2]

South Asia, says Haq, is the poorest and most deprived region in the world. The ghastly reality of over 500 million people surviving below the *absolute* poverty line—the most illiterate, the most malnourished, the least gender-sensitive and yet making comfortable investments in arms far more than in education and health—is utterly incompatible with the outrageous boast of 'irreversible reform' and advances in market availability and consumer-crazy, corrupt categories. All this is burningly relevant to the human rights haplessness of the large chunk of the populace, notwithstanding the harum-scarum assertions of *sarcari* economists.

To redress the desperate imbalance an ambitious human investment plan, earmarking, as Haq proposes, an additional 1.6 per cent of its GDP, is the desideratum, *not* the grand show of Western model goods and services and five-star fashions. A new vision and new sense of the masses 'hunger is the mandatory direction of the real irreversible reform if the salvage of the human rights of the humblest is the thrust of the historic mid-night tryst of August 1947. If we fail here, all talk of a new Social Order is a wily verbiage and a cute conspiracy against the huge human numbers in destitution and indignity. The barometer of human happiness is not the GNP, but the HDM (Human Deprivation Measure) of the people.

A tragic paradox is emerging. South Asia, failing to face the additional cost of essential human investment, is competing in the escalation of military expenditure. The arms race between India and Pakistan is the major contributor to the alarming level of military expenditure in the region (93% of the total expenditure). India is ranked by the World Bank as 142 (or 143?) in terms of per capita income and yet this Gandhian country ranks *highest in the world* in total arms imports. What a public crime! India spends two-third as much resources as it does on combined spending on education and health. It is clear that the right to life is losing its battle against the right to kill if these figures are to make sense.

What is important is the security of the people, with emphasis on income of the masses, environmental security and the like, not armaments escalation as the paramount factor of national security. Thus, if human rights are to be taken seriously in the 90s, there must be a reappraisal of the human cost of arms purchase as against human happiness in the true sense of enrichment of human personality. The Standing Armies in South Asia employ more than *two million soldiers*. Corruption in arms procurement is enormous; and while there are checks and balances that exist for the accountability of civilian projects and development programmes, there is none regarding spending for defence projects, for alleged reasons of sensitivity and secrecy. A spirit of commiseration and fraternity has to be

2 *The Review—Contemporary News and Views*, p. 9, vol, II No. 5th May 1997.

cultured in South Asia before the century leaves us, lest we should be sunk in slaughter and destitution. In Mother Teresa's words 'we ourselves feel that what we are doing is just a drop in the ocean but the ocean would be less because of that missing drop.'

> "However, human rights organizations cannot limit themselves to be reactive and only question and denounce economic structures and political patterns which tend to generate conflict and violence. They need also to reflect on and be pro-active in the creation of a new culture which is inspired by a new paradigm on social relations and relations with nature. The call for a focus on consciousness and cultural processes which underlie, structure, generate, maintain and reproduce conflicts and violence is rooted in the assumption that in the end economic, social and political processes are cultural phenomena which have their genesis in perceptions, valuations, attitudes and motivations which sustain and legitimize the institutional patterns in which culture is expressed.
>
> In this connection, it is proposed that it is not only imperative to analyse and understand the nature of the global culture of the North and/or West which underlies and shapes the dynamics of the global world economy as a process, but at the same time to critically examine in which way violence and conflict have been and are constitutive of the cultures of Asia."[3]

This spiritual root, if cut off for material conquests, the social order becomes a robber's paradise. So a serious dialogue between spiritual-religious thinkers and human rights activists is 'a consummation devoutly to be wished'. Silence is guilt when there is a duty to speak. We must debate with those who think that zonal peace and human rights need a balance of terror and readiness for war.

Are carcases the deterrents that save life and is the world cultural order to be held hostage to bombs and missiles?

The political zoo-keepers, however, may want more sales of missiles and lives lost if the market can flourish and profits peak! Exhortations of UN peace processes are placebos since humanity is but commodity for merchants of death. We have to fight *commoditisation* of human souls—the most corrupt disruption of the *divine* in us all.

Let us widen our view beyond South Asia and look at the world 'red in tooth and claw'. No man nor nation is an island, entire of itself. The global whole is our soul.

If build-up of armaments by rival nations continues, wars will break out, as two World Wars and many mini-wars have barbarously brought home to the peoples of the earth. The fury of armed conflict is the finis of human rights as the Preamble to the UN Charter poignantly proclaims. And yet, as the Churchillian zoological metaphor quoted later shows, disarmament conferences are guided by self-interest, gilded by glowing platitudes and

3 *Human Rights & Spirituality—Dialogue of Religions on Human Rights—The Final Document*—published by Asian Human Rights Commission, Hong Kong, at p. 114.

end in heated squabbles with periodic return to seeming normalcy and, again, revival of arms sales in peace for use in the next provocative, belligerent span. The UN has failed to end the scourge of war and the Security Council has often started, sometimes hesitantly supported and intervened in regional menagerie-like savageries, largely according to the business interests of the Sole Super-Power giving the impression that the UN is the alter ego of the U.S. And the veto power, when abused, as often it is, is also a veto on human rights.

The sombre contradiction between armaments deals and burst of bombs in belligerent breakouts and the peace so necessary for human survival and advance is best brought out by that great General and former U.S. President Dwight Eisenhower:

> "Every gun that is made, every warship launched, every rocket fired signifies, in the final sense, a theft from those who hunger and are not fed, those who are cold and are not clothed. This world in arms is not spending money alone. It is spending the sweat of its laborers, the genius of its scientists, the hopes of its children.............."

What is apt in this context is the allegoric picture presented by Winston Churchill talking about disarmament among nations, way back in 1928:

> "Once upon a time, all the animals in the zoo decided that they would disarm and arranged to have a conference to sort out the matter. So the rhinoceros while opening the proceedings said that the use of teeth was barbarous and horrible and ought to be strictly prohibited, by general consent. Horns, which were mainly defensive weapons, would of course, have to be allowed.
>
> "The buffalo, the stag, the porcupine and even the little hedgehog, all said they would vote with the rhino. But the lion and the tiger took a different view. They defended their teeth and claws, and described them as honourable weapons of immortal antiquity. The panther, the leopard, the puma and the whole tribe of small cats supported the lion and the tiger.
>
> "Then the bear spoke. He proposed that both teeth and horns should be banned and never used again for fighting by any animal. It would be quite enough if animals were allowed to give each other a good hug when they quarreled. No one could object to that. It was so fraternal and would be a great step forward towards peace. However, all the other animals were offended with the bear, and the turkey almost panicked.
>
> "The discussion got very hot and angry. All the animals began arguing so much about horns and hugging that they totally forgot about the peaceful intentions that had brought them together in the first place, and they began to exchange angry glances.
>
> "Luckily, the zoo-keepers pacified them and persuaded them to go back to their cages, after which the animals began to feel quite friendly with one another again."[4]

4 Bimal Chakraborty: *The United Nations and The Third World—Shifting Paradigms* at pages 144-145.

> "This is not a way of life at all in any true sense. Under the cloud of threatening war, it is humanity hanging from a cross of iron."[5]

Armaments escalation annihilates developmental resources and the World Military Order is a planetary peril; and human rights perish where the top brass takes over power.

> "The combination of nuclear weapons with intercontinental means of delivery have made any point on earth open to devastating attack in addition to posing a continuing threat to the world security. * * *
>
> "Armaments constituted a heavy burden that wasted away immense human efforts and scarce economic resources. Incidentally, the resources can be used only once, either for military or civilian purposes."[6]
>
> "The world urgently needs adequate production and equitable distribution of food. It needs vast production of medicines and vaccines, and redistribution of medical expertise and medical supplies to the millions of suffering people in the Third World. Adequate distribution of birth-control techniques is required to prevent an increase in global population growth 4.5 billion now to 6 billion in 2000. Reforestation of many areas of the world is a mandatory priority, since trees currently are used to provide fuel for the poor countries, and trees recycle carbon dioxide to produce oxygen. The riches of the sea must be equitably distributed among all nations on earth and must not be mined only by those few Western nations that currently possess the technology and expertise to do so. All the world's natural resources must be shared and used for the benefit of the family of man and not hoarded and wasted on production of weapons. Millions of the world's people must be delivered from their situation of illiteracy and poverty—a vicious cycle that perpetuates endemic overpopulation and hunger.
>
> "The air and the water of America and large ports of the world are fast becoming irretrievably polluted with carcinogenic and mutagenic poisons produced by industry to make profits. There are 4.5 million known toxic chemicals, and 375,000 new ones are produced annually. Most have never been adequately tested for carcinogenicity, and most are released to the environment, often illegally. Many of these chemicals are by-products of industries that produce plastic throwaway materials we don't need."[7]

George Kennan has articulated the dilemma eloquently:

> "We have gone piling weapon upon weapon, missile upon missile, new levels of destructiveness upon old ones. We have done this helplessly, almost involuntarily, like the victims of some sort of hypnotism, like men in a dream, like lemmings heading for the sea, like the children of Hamelin marching blinding behind their Pied Piper, and the result is that today we have achieved,

5 The Honorable Dwight D. Eisenhower 1890-1969, 34th President of the United States Supreme Commander, Integrated European Defence Forces.

6 Bimal Chakraborty: *The United Nations and The Third World–Shifting Paradigms* at page 145.

7 Dr. Helen Caldicott: *Missile Envy* at pages 306-307.

we and the Russians together, in the number of these devices, in their means of delivery, and above all in their destructiveness, levels of redundancy of such grotesque dimensions as to defy rational understanding. ...."[8]

This sorry view of humanity's new peril is the beginning of a necessary world-vision.

The UN saga of post-World War Disarmament is as rhetorically inspiring as the arms sales and their sanguinary uses are depressing. The first Disarmament Resolution was passed by the General Assembly in its first session in January 1946. In 1959 the Assembly unanimously affirmed that the issue of general and complete *disarmament was the most* important. The 18-Nation Disarmament Committee (1961), the Nuclear Test Ban Treaty (1963) (to which the U.K., the U.S. and the U.S.S.R. were signatories) prohibiting nuclear explosions in the atmosphere, outer space and under water registered remarkable progress in *parchment.* Of course, the latest plea of India for a comprehensive, phased elimination of nuclear weapons failed miserably because the U.S. dominated the universe and frowned on that move. In 1973, an effort was made by the Assembly for reduction of military budgets by 10% and utilization of part of the funds thus saved to provide developing countries with assistance. Widespread support in words, but non-implementation in deeds! The dialectic of verbal approval of disarmament and actual aggravation of the arms race is the dreaded reality of the era after the Soviet collapse.

Spending on arms proceeds unabated and the arms budgets are bulging. High military expenditure, far from providing employment, substantially cuts it down:

> "According to one U.S. Government estimate, a billion dollars of military expenditure created 76,000 jobs. But if the same amount was spent for civilian programs of the federal Government, it would have created an average of 1,00,000 jobs, and many more if channelled into activities particularly labour-intensive. If the same one billion dollars were released for private consumption by means of tax cuts, it would have created 112,000 new jobs."[9]

A 1971 study on the socio-economic consequences of the arms race, and military expenditure concluded:

> "Military expenditure contributes to acute imbalances in the international payment. Enormous social problems lie ahead for all countries. Public services, health, education, housing and now the protection of the environment.........all need the resources which the arms race consumes. Incidentally, the NIEO which was designed to change the ground rules for the lopsided world economy did not incorporate this aspect of the "disarmament dividend"—the resources released as a result of disarmament and diverted to the well-being of the poor."[10]

8 *Ibid,* at page 309.

9 Bimal Chakraborty: *The United Nations and The Third World—Shifting Paradigms* at page 148.

10 *Ibid,* at page 149.

How painful that the Security Council has utterly failed to fulfill its Charter obligation to prevent the creating and expanding of weapon-markets which will necessarily murder the masses and extinguish their human rights. The war business, expanding diabolically, has created a vested interest in more arms manufacture and trade.

> "During the 1980s, the U.S. sold $ 134 billion-worth of weapons and military services to 160 states and political movements. Under President Bush, U.S. arms sales doubled after the end of the cold war, from $ 7.8 billion in 1989 to $ 18.5 billion in 1990. Sales leapt to $ 31 billion in 1993 as President Clinton continued the high-pressure sales drive in desperation for jobs and economic growth. Britain is second in the international arms bazaar, with sales of $ 7.8 billion (£ 5.2 billion) in 1993, rising to $ 9 billion in 1994, over a fifth of world arms exports, sustaining over 100,000 jobs."

* * *

> "Military spending creates a pernicious web of 'pork barrel' politics which severely inhibits any U.S. Government from reducing arms spending. Similar influences pervade all major weapons producers, including the post-apartheid Government of South Africa."[11]

Awesome terrorism is not, therefore, the violence of extremist groups and insurgents but the callous business deals of powerful nations selling weapons, thus aiding and abetting mass homicide and farewell to human rights. Let us look back with lurid eyes:

> "During the 1930s, the inability of the League of Nations to cope with conflicts in Spain and the Balkans and with great power aggression plunged the world into war. Today the world is even more unstable, better armed and less capable of maintaining peace than ever. Global peace and security make it essential to strengthen the capacity of the Security Council to mediate between warring factions, regardless of state boundaries, and to intervene on the basis of international law if necessary. In 1992, the Secretary-General put forward an Agenda for Peace, an integrated programme for early-warning, preventive diplomacy and deployment of UN forces to deter hostilities. It recommended a wide range of peace-building activities to repatriate refugees, restore essential infrastructure, monitor elections, rebuild institutions and advance human rights. But the West did little. It dithered over the escalating crisis in Yugoslavia. It pulled troops out of Rwanda as genocide was executed before their eyes and silent guns. It allowed UNITA to defy UN-supervised elections in Angola. It permitted the Khmer Rouge to regroup in Cambodia, and stood aside from continuing conflicts in Afghanistan, Sudan, the crumbling Soviet empire and elsewhere.
>
> Peace, like policing, is too important to leave to factions in global politics. Responsibility for global security must be shared, with the Majority World taking a more proactive role within the framework of international law. The task of the UN has never been more urgent nor daunting and will grow sharply

11 Titus Alexander: *Unravelling Global Apartheid*, page 220.

> in the coming century. But peace-keeping and humanitarian relief can only be effective if the world community tackles the causes of conflict, where the UN is even weaker."[12]

The UN is now a paper Parliament making 'sound and fury signifying nothing' where the peace process is the dire desideratum.

> "All 183 member states of the UN have an equal vote in the General Assembly, but it is a powerless Parliament. It can initiate or endorse international legislation, like the Law of the Sea, and it has a limited role in relation to UN agencies. A majority vote can have moral authority as well as practical effect, which Western Governments actively thwart except on rare occasions when they want to be seen as acting in the interests of the world. The General Assembly can make recommendations to member states or the Security Council (Article 11), although it cannot make recommendations on any matters considered by the Security Council unless asked. Under the 'Uniting for Peace' resolution of 1950, it may act if the permanent members of the Security Council do not, but it lacks forces and resources to act independently.
>
> The West frequently ignores or plays down majority votes in the General Assembly. In 1971, the U.S. Congress voted to import chrome from the illegal white minority regime in Rhodesia, in violation of UN sanctions. In 1967 the General Assembly passed Resolution 242, calling on Israel to withdraw from the occupied territories of Egypt, Jordan and Syria, yet the illegal occupation continued for decades with U.S. assistance—in striking contrast to the swift expulsion of Iraq from Kuwait in 1991.
>
> On the economic front, the World Bank asserted its independence from the UN as early as 1947 when it granted a substantial loan to the Netherlands as it launched a full-scale colonial war against Indonesian nationalists."[13]

The democratisation of the Security Council alone can leash the dogs of war.

Nobel Prize winner Noel Baker in his acceptance speech quoted passages of pregnant meaning:

> "The problem of how to get rid of war, if we do not end it altogether, if we do not reduce and limit armaments, then we may be sure that in the future, as in the past, armaments will breed counter armaments; they will breed alliance and counter alliances, suspicions and distrust, they will produce internal crisis; they will lead at first perhaps to small local wars but in the long run and inevitably, to a great world war like that we have seen in our day and generation."[14]

Indeed, the world is on the verge of becoming a cannibal bedlam. Third World countries are victims of the arms trade syndrome. The Big Powers are merchants of death and spread the baloney that balance of terror

12 *Ibid*, page 160.

13 *Ibid*, page 161.

14 Bimal Chakraborty: *The United Nations and The Third World–Shifting Paradigms*, at page 149.

promotes peace. Thus the fatal arms arsenals scenario generates profits for arms manufacturers in the U.S. and other big powers. Thus selling arms is better than building dams is the superstition that developing countries digest. The interests of the Third World stand to gain if the diversion of resources from arms production to economic development takes place. It is a tragic fact that an alarming number of Third World countries are rivalling one another in establishing aggressive defence industries. It is painful to note that between 1945 and 1975, 119 wars took place and most of them were fought in the Third World, with weapons supplied by developed countries. Thus there was no nexus between the Disarmament Decade and the second UN Development Decade. So armaments arsenals were full and social deficits of hungry nations deepened. Human rights, inevitably, became a casualty globally. The current global gory scenario is still in embers and plenty of hostilities ready to stoke the fires of war. Are ashes and ghosts the Fifth Act of the twentieth-twenty-first century humanity's Shakespearean tragedy?

A paltry 17.5 billion dollars would have made possible the minimum needs to save life an accomplished fact. The figures worked out in 1977 in the *World Military and Social Expenditures* are tellingly informative.

"(*i*) A vaccination program to give protection against infectious diseases to all the world's children—$ 600 million.

(*ii*) A programme to extend literacy to all the adults in the world by the end of the century—$ 1.2 billion.

(*iii*) A preventive and community-oriented training program for a sharp increase in the numbers of medical auxiliaries—$ 250 million.

(*iv*) Increased development aid to improve the capacity of the third world to grow its own food and prevent malnutrition—$ 3.0 billion.

(*v*) An expanded minimum shelter program, incorporating self-help construction for the urban poor—$ 750 million.

(*vi*) Supplementary feeding to ensure full development for 200 million malnourished children—$ 4 million.

(*vii*) Supplementary feeding for 60 million malnourished pregnant and lactating women to protect their health and reduce infant mortality—$ 1.5 billion.

(*viii*) A major increase in the number of primary schools, with the addition of 100 million new places—$ 3.2 billion.

(*ix*) A hygienic water supply system, towards the goal of clean water for all humanity by 1990—$ 3.0 billion."[15]

It is ironic that the U.S. which talks much about human rights today was the first to commit macro-massacre by dropping atomic bombs on Hiroshima and Nagasaki in August 1945; and that was *after* the signing of

15 Bimal Chakraborty: *The United Nations and The Third World—Shifting Paradigms* at page 153.

the Charter on 26th June 1945. This sounded the tocsin of Globoshima or global extinction of the human species, unless the menace of the atom was manacled. An Atomic Energy Commission was brought into being; but decades after the nuclear threat to mankind the situation is still grim. So long as the potential for '*globoshima*' continues there is no sanctuary for human life or human rights. India took a firm and fair stance in this regard and offered many measures, stage by stage, to achieve atomic disarmament. The ecological repercussions of the radio-active fallout of nuclear explosions are terrible, creating holes in the Ozone layer and inviting the ultraviolet rays of the sun to penetrate the Earth's atmosphere with lethal effect. Environment and Ecology are allergy to the moneyocracy worldwide. The survival of homo sapiens depends on a firm stance on nuclear and other pollutive sources.

India voiced the gut Third World concern about the arms race—(*a la* the CTBT signature crisis), when it demanded ending of the arms race which would make it possible to double the income of 1.2 billion people below the destitution line and to provide shelter to 240 million homeless families. But the intoxicated nuclear Super-Power develops deafness when human rights of the humble billions of the earth's children claim economic justice. Humanist concerns and moral values do not bother the international corporate giants, who zero-in on markets and maximum profits as their sole objective. Where is the new thinking so urgently needed in our nuclear world to promote a New International Economic Order. Einstein has asserted the importance of awakening to the alarming danger way back in 1948. He said:

> "The 'cliches' of yesterday will no longer do today, and will, no doubt, be hopelessly out of date tomorrow. To bring this home to men all over the world is the most important and most fateful social task intellectuals have ever had to shoulder". In 1950, the same scientist warned, "the belief that it is possible to achieve security through armaments on a national scale, in the present state of military technology, is a disastrous illusion".[16]

It is a pathetic pity that the Third World is still oblivious to the need to unite and fight the lethal nuclear club (global bullies) and those countries that drain away the world's resources for killer preparations. On the contrary, the Third World countries ask for reducing their public expenditure by spending more on arms than on education and health. A new spirit of creative cooperation and trimmed military budgets are a condition precedent for a better life for the half-fed humankind, a *sine qua non* for survival.

It is the essence of human logic that political and military tensions must abate if human rights are to flourish in the Indian subcontinent. There is a spring of hope that Indo-Pakistan relations may improve and Bangladesh and Nepal also will have better ties with India. It is important that every human rights activist must pressurise the Governments to pursue policies

16 Bimal Chakraborty: *The United Nations and The Third World—Shifting Paradigms* at page 163.

of *modus vivendi* which will cost less in weapons and more diversion for health, education and social benefit. The "blue" rights (contained in the first Covenant) and the "red" rights (included in the second Covenant) are really indivisible and so the executive, legislative and adjudicative instrumentalities under the Constitution, Indian, Pakistani and Bangladeshi, must so interpret these rights as to make each Covenant complementary to the other and as paramount in their importance. However, even the famous four-fold President Roosevelt propositions include *freedom from want*; and at the time of the Charter in San Francisco, Article 68 required the ECOSOC to function, more or less, as a Commission of Human Rights. One might well conclude on a hopeful note that the Indian human rights future, in the background of a new awakening for formulating an Asian Human Rights Charter, will have a brighter prospect. But the pessimism, which is considerable, springs from the global tornado of Trans-National Corporations blowing hard on Third World countries to commoditise these countries to expropriate their resources. This means the sunset of human rights; and, therefore, a united counter-attack is necessary if socio-economic and cultural human rights are to be operational. The battle is hard because the new *mantras* of market-friendliness, liberalisation and globalisation are Trojan horses for the foreign corporate powers to land in India and destroy swaraj itself.

What then is the therapeutic ministration?

Spiritual realisation of material opportunities of 'Paradise Regained' is the hope. Dr. Helen Caldicott, in her *Missile Envy* addresses Americans and the world:

> "It is time for people to rise to their full moral and spiritual height, to take the world on their shoulders like Atlas, forgetting all other priorities in their lives, and to say, "I will save the earth". Each person can be as powerful as the most powerful person who ever lived. I have achieved a lot in a foreign country. I am an Australian and a woman, but neither of these factors has been an impediment. Think how much Americans could achieve by using and working through the democracy they have inherited from their forebears. All it takes is willpower and determination.
>
> "This quest is a spiritual adventure. It is time for mankind to achieve spiritual fulfillment. Each person has much to offer. However, it is imperative that the ego be controlled. Ego needs are enormous and can be extremely destructive when working with others. I have learned in this work that if my ego becomes dominant and I engage in negative thoughts, things always go wrong. If I meditate or pray and decide simply to do what is right—not because it feels right but because it is right—and I drop my own egocentric needs, things always fall into place in the most amazing way. Such action is enormously rewarding. As we work with others, we must remember only one thing, and that is our final common goal: elimination of nuclear weapons. We don't need our egos fulfilled; we need only to fulfill our destiny on the planet in the twentieth century: to save the world. We must learn to reinforce and support one another. True happiness lies in helping one another. We are all sons and daughters of God, and under the universal horror of the nuclear

Sword of Damocles, we will be united to work together in mutual respect and peace.

No other generation has inherited this enormous responsibility. We have been given the privilege of saving all past and all future generations, all animals, all plants. Think of the enormous variety of delicate butterflies; think of the gorgeous birds of the earth, of the endless designs of fish in the sea; think of the beautiful and exotic flowers with their gorgeous and seductive perfumes; think of the proud lions and tigers and of the wondrous prehistoric elephants and hippopotamuses; think of what we are about to destroy.

Rapid nuclear disarmament is the ultimate issue of preventive medicine.

It is the ultimate parenting issue.

It is the ultimate Republican and the ultimate Democratic issue.

It is the ultimate patriotic issue.

Above all, it is the ultimate religious issue.

We are the curators of life on earth; we hold it in the palms of our hands. Can we evolve spiritually and emotionally in time to control the overwhelming evil that our advanced and rational intellect has created? We will know the answer to this question in our lifetime. This generation will die having discovered the answer."[17]

It is not my intent to tell the reader that none among the Asia-Pacific people is disturbed over these distressing developments advancing towards Annihilation with relentless irreversibility. Is the 'White World' or the God's Seven (G-7) sure to shoot down the nations or force them to submit to a new colonisation process deprivatory of people's human rights? No. The South will awake and resist the North, unite with the humane souls, sensitive consciences and influential thinkers everywhere and strive to conspire to change this sorry scheme of things entire and remould it nearer to our heart's desire. A Human Manifesto, cognisant of the world's sorrow, is being written is Asia and elsewhere even as we worry that our planetary habitat is writing its obituary. The dark victory of the carnivorous G-7 Corporate Power will yield to a new Dawn of crimson hues. The Cassandra's curse of universal economic occupation of our resources will be belied:

"All are but parts of one stupendous whole,
Whose body Nature is, and God the soul."

The global village with East and West as one Whole is unfolding.

There is a light year's gap between the miserable life of the Third World masses and the glow of life of the growing glitterati and the richer elite addicted to First World luxuries. Rightly, therefore, there is a 'grand canyon', bitter and destitute, within the Third World which we may call the Fourth World within the Third World. This is an explosive alienation which threatens the stability of the global order because there can never be peace between

17 Dr. Helen Caldicott: *Missile Envy,* at pages 312-313.

the 'stone-age' masses and the nuclear age classes cornering and conquering wealth by threat and stealth.

> "It may be relevant to notice that the 1976 World Employment Conference sponsored by ILO defined Basic Needs (BN) as (*i*) adequate food, clothing and shelter, (*ii*) education and health, (*iii*) basic human rights, (*iv*) employment as a means and an end, and (*v*) improved quality of employment. It advocated their usefulness as a strategy of development. A discernible shift from raw GNP to 'qualitative growth' came to the surface ('actual physical survival at preferred qualitative levels of living'). The 1991 UNDP's Human Development Report relates quality of life to political freedom, human rights and individual self-respect. The Human development index combines purchasing power, life expectancy and literacy."[18]

The GATT and the WTO, the gory philosophy of more markets globally expanded and the resurrection of the old colonial paradigm of exploitation by monopoly capital clearly point to an inflammable contradiction which may win back the right to life in dignity and decency for the millions of humans gradually driven to despair.

Asian human rights: some efforts

The omens are good when compulsions are acute. Today the disaster of human rights looms before the South and so, for sheer survival, mankind has to fight back with an Asian Human Rights Charter. It is a good sign that there are active Asian Human Rights Organizations and I am associated with at least two of them, apart from national human rights defence bodies, official and non-official. People's rights, though crushed, have wider support now in the Asian continent. 'JUST', based in Malaysia, is campaigning for human rights and against the hypocrisy of inhumanity.

The Asian Human Rights Commission based in Hong Kong is working hard to produce an acceptable draft of an Asian Human Rights Charter. While accepting the universality and indivisibility of human rights, the Commission rightly goes beyond treating these rights as mere abstractions to Asian conditions. Culture and ethos may vary and we cannot have a rigid Procrustean type of human rights package. While the Declaration of Human Rights is valid world-wide there are variations which deserve to be taken note of regarding priorities and cultural identities. Several rights like Right to Development have special significance for Asian nations and have all been included in the Draft charter of the Asian Human Rights Commission. We have thus an excellent beginning projecting a comprehensive *magna carta* for Asia.

The Draft I have noted is in embryonic shape but it is a happy note that independently of Western models. Asian thought on human rights is taking shape consistently with the Universal Declaration of Human Rights.

18 Bimal Chakraborty: *The United Nations and The Third World—Shifting Paradigms* at page 93.

Another super-efficient and instructive Asian Human Rights Organisations called 'JUST' has been educating Asian and other readers about the threat to human rights through various means, one of them being Western weaponry creating an arms market by taking advantage of conflicts in the non-Western world. The focus of a researcher, if it turns on the current scenario, will reveal the capacity of Western weapons to slaughter entire armies and civilian communities. The technological terrorism of Western armies is tested out on the peoples of the non-Western world. There is an element of racism and cannibalism blended in the dreadful weapons of the West being made available for the Third World countries.

Everyone knows that on 6th August 1945 a uranium bomb was dropped on Hiroshima and three days later a plutonium bomb killed chunks of Nagasaki humanity. Not merely deaths but burns on Japanese bodies, disfigurements and cancers were part of the catastrophe. This was at a time when Japan was almost seeking surrender. Not Germany but Japan to be atom-bombed—that is the racist element. Prime Minister Mackenzie King of Canada mentioned about the event that it was 'fortunate that the use of the bomb should have been upon the *Japanese* rather than upon the *White races of Europe.*

The Vietnam war provided the U.S. with a testing ground for improved weapons and techniques which could inflict heavy human casualty. The napalm bomb and its effects are testified even today by the living Vietnamese victims whose bodies were burnt. Carpet bombs were also tried in Vietnam. Agent Orange and other chemical defoliants were indiscriminately used. Countless Vietnamese women even today give birth to children without eyes and brains. A whole nation has been poisoned by a nation which, in Super-Power rhetoric, speaks of human rights.

Look at the unbridled war against Iraq where armies were mowed down, and F 117 Stealth bombers entered the war in the Gulf. Indeed, the story is endless. Human Rights are a hostage to God's Seven's (G-7) hunger for profits. Many new types of killer weapons are ready for use in the name of preserving human rights by the self-appointed White House Policeman. The most inhuman weapons are ready to be used against the poorest of the poor in the Third World. A leading American psychologist, Scott Peck, asserts that the "use of technology in the war had served to deaden our sensitivity. Several years of placing all our gadgetry between us and our victims has had the effect of insulting our sciences." (and consciences).

Thus we are passing through the most frightening era where double-speak and double-think combine most horrendous weapons with most eloquent preachment of human rights. I would like to draw your attention to the Message of Rabindra Nath Tagore delivered by him with the vision of a seer a few months before his death—

> *Today* I live in the hope that the Saviour is coming—that he will be born in our midst in this poverty-shamed hovel *which is India*. I shall wait to hear the divine message of civilization which he will bring with him, the supreme word of

> promise that he will speak unto man from *this very eastern horizon* to give faith and strength to all who hear.
>
> As I look around I see the crumbling ruins of a proud civilization strewn like a vast heap of futility. *And yet I shall* not commit the grievous sin of losing faith in Man. I would rather look forward to the opening of a new chapter in his history after the *cataclysm* is over and the atmosphere rendered clean with the spirit of service and sacrifice. *Perhaps that dawn* will come from *this horizon*, from the East *where the sun rises*. A *day will come when unvanquished Man* will retrace his path of conquest, *despite all barriers*, to win back his lost *human heritage*.

The time has come for Asia, particularly South Asia, to rise and unite to defend human rights everywhere and to prevent Super-Power perceptions and military manoeuvres being used for political and Big Business Operations. Where do we go from here? Go back to the beginning by 'a voyage of the mind's return'. We may pump in more spiritual sanity and global rationality into the Great Instrument and Institution–the United Nations Organisation.

The saga of human rights in India is the theme of my lectures, less luminous than voluminous. All patriotic jurists, committed to the concerns of our common humanity and betterment of all people everywhere, must strive for a "U-turn" in the menacing stranglehold of Multi-Nationals Inc. over human destiny. This summons is the noblest call of planetary patriotism to every soul to do his high duty to the perennial process towards Destination Divinity–Divinity in every person.

The battle for human rights, already facing decline and fall, needs a contemporaneous struggle for vitalising the United Nations and, vicariously, its auxiliary institutions. The UN will be toothless, however numerous and politically pluralist, unless the Security Council, the global gendarme with power to strike, is more democratic, less oligarchic, universally representative, not cornered by Big Powers with Big Business interests. To reform and restructure the UN System, now an anaemic, impotent, bankrupt, polyglottic debating club, is the first task of human rights activists. Campaigns for UN Reform are invigorating new thinking and, if it fails, human rights will be but myth.

Specific proposals for democratisation of the Security Council, expanding its number of permanent members and reducing its Veto powers are on the agenda of international discussion today. The veto power has been applied in situations not contemplated by the UN founders but because a Super-Power insisted on blocking constructive action. There should be no veto power on enforcement of decisions of the World Court or on the admission of new members to the UN and on allied issues best decided by the World Court.

There should be Annual Statement of the World Reports by the Secretary General over television and radio networks, a UN Electronic Forum of Nations Programme. The world will then be able to mobilise its views on the action and inaction of the United Nations.

There is need for a change in another area. The global arms race, which costs colossal sums per year must be brought under control. An International Body is needed to oversee and enforce Arms control and disarmament treaties. Such a body is necessary to eliminate suspicion and achieve reduction in weapons. An International Disarmament Organisation, unhampered by any veto, must become a part of the UN System with power to monitor the arms race and to promote disarmament treaties, on-site inspections and other types of arms limitation processes, if farewell to arms on a global scale is to be a reality. The World Court must have power to interpret treaties and understandings and violations where new weapons are brought into the arsenal.

The dispute settlement process of the UN (Art. 33) has been ineffective. We need therefore a well-trained UN Conciliation and Mediation service, panels of Arbitrators, procedures for binding arbitration in the event of threat to world peace. A Charter amendment allowing parties to compel submission of disputes to the International Court of Justice is necessary if the current judicial futility of the World Court is to be eliminated.

The financial position of the UN is highly precarious. This shall not be. The World Court must be able to enforce payments of dues by nations. Indeed, the I.C.J. has been crippled by the Big Powers. In 1985 the U.S. withdrew completely its acceptance of general compulsory jurisdiction. There have been occasions when nations have not appeared or have walked out or have ignored the Court's rulings. To strengthen the World Court and to set up an International Criminal Court to try hijackers and terrorists is currently a MUST. To strengthen the UN's human rights machinery is also a necessity since at present there is much rhetoric but poor achievement. A UN High Commissioner for Human Rights with regional staffs, a Court of Human Rights, modelled after the European Court of Human Rights, ratifications by Governments of all existing Human Rights Conventions are some of the urgent imperatives.

The UN agencies must have power to intervene where GATT or WTO injuriously inflict economic wounds on nations. Bretton Woods bullies cannot subordinate the role of the UN. There are more creative suggestions once the subject is thrown open for world-wide discussion. One thing is certain, sans a radical change with a social justice fervour, the United Nations, already ebbing away, will die an unnatural death with no obituary except the intimidatory brutality of Might masquerading as Right and the U.S. making the UN a proxy of the U.S. when its interests are at stake.

If humankind, in macabre despair, finds no signs of sanity in the world's affairs, Walt Whitman's lines will inspire us to build a brave new world:

> "Where the populace rise at once against the never-ending audacity of elected persons."

Let us to the task of building a humane universe.

"Where women walk in public processions in the streets the same as the men,
Where they enter the public assembly and take places the same as the men,
Where the city of the faithfullest friends stands,
Where the city of the cleanliness of the sexes stands,
Where the city of the healthiest fathers stands,
Where the city of the best-bodied mothers stands,
There the great city stands."

INDEX